PERSPECTIVES ON ANTON BRUCKNER

Perspectives on Anton Bruckner

Edited by

Crawford Howie, Paul Hawkshaw
and Timothy Jackson

Ashgate

Aldershot • Burlington USA • Singapore • Sydney

Published by
Ashgate Publishing Limited
Gower House
Croft Road
Aldershot
Hants GU11 3HR
England

Ashgate Publishing Company
131 Main Street
Burlington, Vermont 05401-5600 USA

Ashgate website: http://www.ashgate.com

British Library Cataloguing-in-Publication data

Perspectives on Anton Bruckner
    1. Bruckner, Anton, 1824–1896 – Criticism and interpretation
    I. Howie, Crawford   II. Hawkshaw, Paul   III. Jackson, Timothy L.
    780.9'2

Library of Congress Cataloging-in-Publication data

Perspectives on Anton Bruckner / edited by Crawford Howie, Paul Hawkshaw, and Timothy Jackson.
    p. cm.
    Includes index.
    1. Bruckner, Anton, 1824–1896 – Criticism and interpretation. I. Howie, Crawford,
    II. Hawkshaw, Paul   III. Jackson, Timothy L.
    ML410.B88 P45 2000
    780'.92–dc21

00-029309

Printed on acid-free paper

ISBN 0 7546 0110 2

Typeset in Sabon by Express Typesetters, Farnham, Surrey
Printed and bound in Great Britain by MPG Books Ltd, Bodmin, Cornwall

Contents

List of plates

(between pages 68 and 69)

Acknowledgements

The original versions of many of the chapters in this book were presented at the second international conference *Perspectives on Anton Bruckner: Composer, Theorist, Teacher, Performer* (1–4 April 1996) at The University of Manchester, Great Britain, organized by Crawford Howie and Timothy L. Jackson. The editors wish to express their gratitude to the faculty, staff, and students at the University of Manchester and Connecticut College, USA, especially: John Casken (Professor of Music, University of Manchester); Keith Elcombe (Head of Music Department, University of Manchester); Professor Katharine Perera (Pro-Vice-Chancellor, University of Manchester); the members of the Artemis String Quartet (University of Manchester and Royal Northern College of Music, Manchester); Claire Gaudiani (President of Connecticut College); Lucas Held (Director of College Relations, Connecticut College); Roxanne Althouse (Adjunct Professor of Voice, Connecticut College); Patricia Harper (Adjunct Professor of Flute, Connecticut College); Kecia Ashford (Assistant Professor of Voice, Hardin Simmons University, formerly Connecticut College); and Paul L. Althouse (Professor of Musicology, Connecticut College), without whose help and encouragement the conference could never have taken place. Hofrat Dr Günter Brosche of the Music Collection of the Austrian National Library, Vienna, granted permission for the facsimiles, and the score of *Erinnerung* is reproduced by authority of the Musikwissenschaftlicher Verlag, Vienna. Richard Schauer, the London representative of N. Simrock, granted permission to reproduce excerpts from Wetz's First Symphony (Berlin, 1924).

Abbreviations

Kr   Kremsmünster: Benedictine Monastery, Music Archive
Wn   Vienna: Austrian National Library, Music Collection
Wst   Vienna: City and State Library, Music Collection

Auer, *Bruckner Gesammelte Briefe*   Auer, Max, ed. *Anton Bruckner. Gesammelte Briefe. Neue Folge.* (Regensburg: Gustav Bosse, 1924)

Bruckner Sämtliche Werke A   Haas, Robert and Orel, Alfred, eds, *Anton Bruckner Sämtliche Werke, Kritische Gesamtausgabe*, im Auftrage der Generaldirektion der Österreichischen Nationalbibliothek und der Internationalen Bruckner-Gesellschaft. Various publishers, 1930–53

Bruckner Sämtliche Werke B   Nowak, Leopold, ed., *Anton Bruckner Sämtliche Werke, Kritische Gesamtausgabe*, herausgeben von der Generaldirektion der Österreichischen Nationalbibliothek und der Internationalen Bruckner-Gesellschaft. (Vienna: Musikwissenschaftlicher Verlag der Internationalen Bruckner-Gesellschaft, 1951–)

Göllerich-Auer   Göllerich, August and Auer, Max, *Anton Bruckner, ein Lebens- und Schaffensbild*, 4 vols. in 9. Regensburg: Gustav Bosse, 1922–37

Harrandt-Schneider, *Bruckner Briefe I*   Harrandt, Andrea and Schneider, Otto eds., *Briefe: Band I 1852–1886, Anton Bruckner Sämtliche Werke*, 24/1. (Vienna: Musikwissenschaftlicher Verlag, 1998)

WAB   Grasberger, Renate, *Werkverzeichnis Anton Bruckner* (Tutzing: Hans Schneider, 1977)

Notes on contributors

Christa Brüstle has worked as a researcher and teacher at the Free University of Berlin since 1992. Her PhD thesis, completed in 1996, was concerned with the reception history of Anton Bruckner, particularly during the period of National Socialism in Germany, and formed the basis of a book, *Anton Bruckner und die Nachwelt*, which was published in 1998. Current research projects include the reception of Bach during the National-Socialist period and performance issues in modern music.

William Carragan is a contributing editor of the *Anton Bruckner Collected Edition*, Vienna, for which he has prepared new editions of the versions of the Second Symphony. He is currently continuing his research into the history of Bruckner performances. To date he has given four papers on various symphonies at international conferences, and served as consultant for several performances and recordings. He is a professor emeritus of physics at Hudson Valley Community College, Troy, New York, USA.

Constantin Floros was Professor of Musicology at the University of Hamburg from 1972 to 1995, and has been Professor Emeritus from 1995. His main research areas are in the music of the Middle Ages and the eighteenth, nineteenth and twentieth centuries. He has written about 150 articles and 20 books, the most recent being *Der Mensch, die Liebe und die Musik*, Zurich-Hamburg: Arche-Verlag, 2000.

Andrea Harrandt is on the staff of the Commission of Music Research at the Austrian Academy of Sciences. She is a leading figure in the Anton Bruckner Institut Linz and a contributor to the *Bruckner Gesamtausgabe* for which she has edited the first volume of letters (*Briefe* 1852–1886) and is currently working on the second volume. She has recently collaborated with E.W. Partsch on *Vergessene Komponisten des Biedermeier*, Tutzing: 2000.

Robert S. Hatten is Professor of Music Theory at Indiana University and author of *Musical Meaning in Beethoven: Markedness, Correlation, and Interpretation*, Indiana University Press, 1994. His other research interests include semiotic theories of musical meaning, musical gesture, Beethoven, Schubert, and twentieth-century opera. Eight lectures entitled 'Musical Gesture' may be found on the web as part of the Cybersemiotic Institute series (http:/www.chass.utoronto.ca/epc/srb/cyber/hatout.html).

Paul Hawkshaw is a member of the Faculty at the Yale University School of Music. He co-edited with Timothy L. Jackson a collection of essays, *Bruckner Studies*, Cambridge University Press, 1997, and edited the Psalms volumes for the *Bruckner Gesamtausgabe*. His critical report for the Mass in F minor has just been completed and he is currently working on a biography of the composer for Yale University Press.

Crawford Howie is a lecturer in music at the University of Manchester where he obtained his PhD in 1969. His teaching and research interests are in the 19th century in general, with particular emphasis on the sacred music of Schubert and Bruckner. He has written several articles in learned journals, and a major documentary biography of Bruckner is nearing completion.

Timothy L. Jackson is Associate Professor of Music Theory in the College of Music at the University of North Texas, where he also directs the new Center for Schenkerian Studies. He is the author of *Tchaikovsky: Symphony No. 6 (Pathétique)*, 1999, in the series Cambridge Music Handbooks, and co-editor of *Richard Strauss Studies* (forthcoming), *Sibelius Studies,* 2001, and *Bruckner Studies,* 1997, in the Cambridge Studies series. With Paul Hawkshaw, he co-authored the new Bruckner entry for *The New Grove Dictionary of Music and Musicians* (2nd edition).

Benjamin M. Korstvedt is Assistant Professor of Music at the University of St. Thomas in St. Paul, Minnesota. He has published widely on Bruckner and related topics, including *Anton Bruckner: Symphony no. 8,* Cambridge: CUP, 2000. Currently he is preparing a critical edition of the 1888 version of Bruckner's Fourth Symphony for the *Bruckner Gesamtausgabe*, and is at work on a book that explores music, criticism, and the cultural politics around Bruckner (and Brahms and Wagner) in Vienna in the 1880s and 1890s.

Joseph C. Kraus is Professor of Music Theory at the University of Nebraska-Lincoln. He has published numerous articles on the music of Tchaikovsky, Bruckner, Sibelius and Mozart. He continues to work on the relation between music and meaning in the late nineteenth century.

Edward Laufer is a Professor of Music at the University of Toronto. He studied composition at the University of Toronto, the Juilliard School and Princeton University, and Schenker's approach with Ernst Oster (the translator of *Der freie Satz*). He has read papers on various aspects of his main interest, classical music; and he has also published articles on Bruckner and Sibelius.

Thomas Leibnitz is a graduate of the University of Vienna where he studied musicology, German philology and studied and practised the violin and the piano. He gained his PhD in 1980. Since 1986 he has worked at the Musiksammlung der Österreichischen Nationalbibliothek. His research interests cover Brahms and Bruckner and particularly the Schalk Archive in the Musiksammlung.

Erik Levi read music at the Universities of Cambridge and York and the Berlin Staatliche Hochschule für Musik and is currently Senior Lecturer in Music, Royal Holloway University of London. His publications include *Music in the Third Reich*, Macmillan, 1994, and chapters and articles on various aspects of musical life in Germany during the 1920s, numerous entries for *The New Grove Dictionary of Opera* and *The New Grove Dictionary of Music and Musicians*, and reviews for *BBC Music Magazine*, *Tempo* and the *International Piano Quarterly*.

Peter Palmer is the music critic for the *Nottingham Evening Post*, a contributor to *Tempo* and *Organists' Review*, and the founding editor of *The Bruckner Journal*. He has written an article on the Swiss composer, Fritz Brun, for *The New Grove Dictionary of Music and Musicians* and made various translations on musical subjects. His interests include German Symbolist art and music.

John A. Phillips is a contributing editor of the *Bruckner Gesamtausgabe*, with six volumes published or in preparation, including the reconstruction of the Finale of the Ninth Symphony from the surviving sources, Vienna: MWV, 1994, 1999. He is also editor and co-author of the *Performing Edition* of the same movement, Samale-Phillips-Mazzuca-Cohrs, Adelaide-Bremen, 1991, 1992. He runs a small business in Adelaide, South Australia specializing in music typography.

Graham H. Phipps is Director of Graduate Studies and Professor of Music Theory at the University of North Texas. He has published articles in *The Musical Quarterly*, *The Journal of Musicology*, *19th-Century Music* and *Music Analysis* on the music of Chopin, Richard Strauss, Schoenberg, and Webern – the latter an essay on Cantata I, op. 29 which received the Elisabeth Lutyens Essay Prize offered by *Music Analysis* in 1984. His essay on Webern's Variations for Orchestra, op. 30, appears in *Music Theory and the Exploration of the Past*, University of Chicago Press, 1993; and his essay on Webern's influence upon the musical style of Luigi Dallapiccola appears in *Dallapiccola: Letture e prospettive*, Ricordi, 1997.

Thomas Röder studied music at the Konservatorium Nuremberg (1973–7) and, from 1977 on, musicology at the University of Erlangen, where he received the doctorate in 1984. He teaches music theory and musicology at the Erlangen

University. Among his main fields of research are the music of Anton Bruckner, music printing in the sixteenth century, and the music history of Nuremberg. Recent publications include 'Neues zur Fassungsfrage bei Anton Bruckner', in *Neues Musikwissenschaftliches Jahrbuch* 8, 1999.

Introduction

Anton Bruckner was an accomplished performer and teacher in addition to being a great composer. Few people in the history of western music can boast his level of achievement in all of these areas combined. Yet, a century after his death, Bruckner the man and the musician remain very much an enigma. A leading avant-garde figure of his generation, revered by many, censured by even more, he was one of the most complex creative personalities of the nineteenth century. His legacy has been rendered even more mysterious by two subsequent generations of admirers and detractors who have sought to invoke his name or use his music in the service of various personal, political and aesthetic agendas.

In the present collection of essays, an international group of scholars offers diverse theoretical and musicological perspectives on Bruckner the composer-teacher-performer. The chapters are divided into three parts. The first explores facets of Bruckner's formidable theoretical training and his application of it as part of the compositional process; the second brings a variety of analytical methodologies to bear on the heart of the composer's mature repertoire – the Second through to the Ninth Symphonies; and the third considers aspects of his career as a teacher and performer, his complex personality, his influence, and the dissemination of his music.

Bruckner came to Vienna from Linz in September 1868 not so much as an organist or composer as on the merits of his theoretical and contrapuntal prowess. In large part as a result of the ministrations of his principal Viennese advocate, Hofkapellmeister Johann Herbeck (1831–77), he was appointed Professor of Harmony and Counterpoint at the Conservatory of the *Gesellschaft der Musikfreunde*. To be sure, Herbeck had enhanced the Viennese offer by adding organ teaching to the Conservatory responsibilities and arranging for Bruckner to enter the Court Chapel as an unpaid organist. Bruckner had first attracted the attention of the Kapellmeister seven years earlier, on 21 November 1861, at the now famous examination in the *Piaristenkirche*. Bruckner was asked to improvise a fugue, after which Herbeck, who was on the jury, remarked that 'He should have examined us!' The death of the renowned theorist and long-time Conservatory teacher, Simon Sechter, on 10 September 1867, provided Herbeck an appropriate opportunity to bring his protegé to the imperial city.

Bruckner's status as heir-apparent to Sechter was hard-earned and well-deserved. He studied with the theorist, largely by correspondence, for five years between 1856 and 1861. The lessons began with elementary harmony and proceeded through four-part counterpoint to complex canon and fugue. Thousands of pages of exercises survive, testifying to the diligence with which Bruckner pursued his studies. In a letter of 13 January 1860 Sechter felt compelled to comment that he had never had such an industrious pupil and cautioned him against working too hard. On 26 March 1861, Sechter signed a certificate declaring that Bruckner's instruction in harmony and counterpoint had been completed.

Bruckner assumed his duties at the Conservatory in October 1868 at a starting annual salary of 800 Gulden and remained on the faculty until retiring in 1891. August Dürrnberger's *Elementar-Lehrbuch der Harmonie- und Generalbaßlehre*, Sechter's *Grundsätze der Musikalische Komposition*, Marpurg's *Abhandlung der Fuge* and Ernst Friedrich Richter's *Lehre von der Fuge* served as his texts, and Sechter's Fundamental Bass Theory provided the substance for his lectures. Bruckner was responsible for communicating Sechter's principles to a generation of Viennese students including Heinrich Schenker, the brothers Franz and Josef Schalk, Felix Mottl and a host of others. Student reminiscences report that the subjects of Bruckner's classes, both at the Conservatory and the University (where he also taught from 1876 to 1894), were always text-book harmony and counterpoint, not musical composition. Numerous anecdotes testify to his conscious separation of theory and practice in his lectures.

Paul Hawkshaw's chapter concerns Bruckner's investigation of traditional form and orchestration, the results of which are evident in the composer's manuscripts from throughout the Vienna years. A few months after completing his lessons with Sechter (at the latest by December 1861), the composer had again immersed himself in study – this time with Otto Kitzler (1834–1915), a cellist and conductor at the theatre in Linz. To this point in Bruckner's career, his knowledge of nineteenth-century music was limited. He had carefully studied and performed certain works by Schubert, Mendelssohn and Weber, but the repertoire to which he had been primarily exposed was relatively conservative – mostly eighteenth-century Austrian church music. This conservatism is reflected in his own early works: until 1856, he included figured bass parts (the *Ave Maria* a4 was the last score to do so), often with baroque-like arias and recitatives, and his orchestral scores employed an antiquated (essentially eighteenth-century) layout with the brass parts notated on the top staves. Credit must go to Kitzler for familiarizing Bruckner with nineteenth-century music and introducing him to the operas of Wagner, specifically *Tannhäuser* which Kitzler conducted in Linz on 13 February 1863. Prior to his studies with Kitzler, so far as is known, Bruckner had not attended the theatre.

The lessons with Kitzler continued without interruption until July 1863. The techniques and analytical vocabulary which Bruckner developed in these years became integral parts of his compositional process. Structural concepts such as *Erweiterung* (expansion), *Steigerung* (build-up), *Wiederholung* (return), *Repetierung* (repeat), *Periode* (period), *Glied* (phrase), *regelmässig und unregelmässig* (regular and irregular) – terms which are found over and over again in Bruckner's Vienna manuscripts – were the focus of the Kitzler exercises. Here Bruckner experimented for the first time with, and learned the terminology for, the Sonata and Rondo structures which he expanded throughout his career as a symphonic composer. In the course of his studies with Kitzler, Bruckner also began to analyse music from metrical, and in today's parlance, 'hypermetrical' perspectives. At this time, Bruckner first used the 'metrical grid', later employed extensively to analyse his own music and that of Mozart, Cherubini and Beethoven.

The completion of the Fifth Symphony in 1875 has been cited, with good reason, as the culmination of a major chapter in Bruckner's compositional history. In 1876 begins a period of intense self-criticism leading to the revision of many of the most important works composed to date. During this first 'revision period' (c. 1876–9), the Masses in D minor and F minor are subjected to a process of subtle 'fine tuning', with adjustments in voice leading and hypermetrical structure. These revisions are informed by Bruckner's careful analysis of Beethoven's symphonies and the music of Mozart – specifically of the Requiem – undertaken at the same time. The First Symphony underwent a similar 'rhythmic adjustment' in 1877, and Symphonies Nos 2–4 experienced more sweeping changes, some of which are discussed in this book. Voice-leading and large-scale metrical grids are concerns during Bruckner's later revision periods as well. Timothy L. Jackson's chapter examines the composer's motivations and objectives in analysing his own voice-leading.

Jackson argues that the issue of avoiding consecutives profoundly influenced Bruckner's orchestration and other aspects of his compositional process from c. 1890. Bruckner's initial, systematic studies of momentary doubling in 1877 were associated with his crusade to make music theory a subject accepted at the Vienna University (over Hanslick's objections). Furthermore, Bruckner's effort to ensure that his orchestrations contained 'correct' doublings was intimately connected with the revision of the orchestration of the Mass in F minor, and the First, Third, Fourth and Eighth Symphonies, and composition of the Ninth Symphony (1887–96). This concern with 'correct' doublings, which avoid 'infelicitous' two-note 'consecutives', helps to explain why Bruckner so extensively 'corrected' his disciples' re-orchestrations of the final versions of the Third and Fourth Symphonies (1887–8). The fact that such major 'corrections' proved necessary convinced the composer that it was better for him to re-orchestrate himself, which is why he revised the First Symphony (1890) without their assistance. In other words, because the disciples did not share his theoretical concern with the issue of momentary consecutives in an orchestral context, Bruckner no longer wanted them to re-orchestrate his music. Once his theoretical concern with momentary doublings is explained, it is obvious that his students' published re-orchestrations of the Fifth, Sixth, Eighth and Ninth Symphonies – undertaken without Bruckner's involvement – cannot be considered superior to Bruckner's.

In a conversation between Gustav Mahler and his brother Otto concerning the relative merits of Bruckner and Brahms, dating from the summer of 1893, Mahler is reported by Natalie Bauer-Lechner to have argued in favour of Brahms, observing that:

> In order to judge a work, you have to look at it as a whole. And in this respect, Brahms is indisputably the greater of the two, with his extraordinarily compact compositions which aren't at all obvious, but reveal greater depth and richness of content the more you enter into them ... With Bruckner, certainly, you are carried away by the magnificence and wealth of his inventiveness, but at the same time you are repeatedly disturbed by its fragmentary character, which breaks the spell.

Essentially the same criticism was voiced by Bruckner's erstwhile student Heinrich Schenker ('the often really considerable beauty of individual moments does not compensate for the lack of the organic...' etc.). Neither critique can be said to be original: indeed both Mahler and Schenker were essentially re-formulating – perhaps more precisely than Brahms, Hanslick and Kalbeck – critiques that had been current in 'sophisticated' Viennese musical circles since the 1870s, if not earlier. Brahms, in particular, criticized Bruckner's symphonies as too long – as an infelicitous concatenation of heterogeneous and disconnected materials. Bruckner's sensitivity to such criticism, especially in his later years, is mentioned by many commentators, including his student Carl Hruby:

> At first he had not taken much notice of critical attacks, but as he grew older the continual hostility of the press made him more and more sensitive. By the second year of our acquaintance, he had already changed markedly. We entered the classroom; Bruckner was sitting at the piano, lost in thought, and barely responded to our greeting. Suddenly he blurted out these curious words: 'Those people ... (by which he meant a certain species of critic) ... say that my ideas aren't consistent ...'

It is significant that the only symphony to be rejected from the canon by its creator, the 'Nullte' or 'Nullified' Symphony in D minor (1869), was the first to be composed after the move to Vienna in 1868. The reason for the 'annulment' remains mysterious, but perhaps Bruckner doubted the quality of his first essay in the symphonic genre in the 'challenging' and 'sophisticated' environment of 'the musical capital of the world'. In any event, as William Carragan observes in his study of the genesis of the Second Symphony (1871), this symphony was a 'pivotal creation' marking a turning point in Bruckner's approach to the genre, successfully launching the series of 'Vienna' Symphonies 2–9.

The issue of 'consistency' encompasses 'continuity' as well as intrinsic 'quality' of ideas. Bruckner's revisions of his symphonies seek to maximize 'consistency' by increasing 'compactness', 'continuity' and underlying 'organic' unity. His deference to Brahms suggests that, as a technician, Bruckner admired Brahms greatly. The chapters by Edward Laufer and Timothy L. Jackson demonstrate typically 'Brahmsian' features of 'subsurface continuity' and complex formal-harmonic counterpoint (also probably derived from Bruckner's careful study of Schubert and late Beethoven). This sophistication may reflect his espousal of 'Brahmsian' aesthetics (post-1876), not necessarily as articulated by apologists like Hanslick, but as realized in the technical aspects of Brahms's music. It is noteworthy that in his later works and revisions of his earlier symphonies Bruckner strove to achieve typically 'Brahmsian continuity' while remaining true to his own style; as Jackson observes, 'in Bruckner's post-1876 compositions and revisions, we find a newly "Brahmsian" aesthetic of motivic concision, concentration and linkage. In tonal concept, Bruckner's later versions grow away from Wagner's free-floating structures and closer to Brahms's firmly anchored armatures.'

In the post-1876 revisions of the Third and Fourth Symphonies, the emphasis on maximizing continuity is immediately apparent. Compare, for example, the 1874 and 1878 versions of the first movement of the Fourth Symphony, specifically the juncture between the first and second groups in the exposition. While, in the first version, the two groups are simply placed in apposition and segregated by a rest, the second version binds these sections together through the sustained F in the horns (cf. the 1874 version, Nowak, 1975, mm. 69–71 and the 1878 version, Nowak, 1953, mm. 73–5). But the revision also increases continuity at much deeper technical and semantic levels. Edward Laufer and Robert Hatten demonstrate from different but complementary perspectives that the 1878–80 revision of the Fourth Symphony forms an ingeniously continuous whole; from a more strictly technical perspective (Laufer) and in terms of semantics and semiotics (Hatten), both scholars confute the 'common wisdom' regarding the putative 'discontinuities' in Bruckner, showing these to be apparent rather than substantive.

Laufer's chapter is not merely a demonstration of continuity in a particular symphonic movement by Bruckner; rather, it is a broader inquiry into the very nature of musical continuity *per se*. Laufer's five paradigms of continuity, which shed light on Bruckner's ability to create the impression of unity in spite of heterogeneous materials, can be generalized. Although Bruckner juxtaposes stylistic topics such as the pastoral, the tragic and the heroic – and the heterogeneity of the collage can be so extreme that the composer was accused of incoherence – Hatten demonstrates that these stylistic shifts and juxtapositions are essential to Bruckner's larger discourse of pilgrim's progress, mystical illumination, and redemption. Indeed, as Hatten's semantic analysis reveals, these sudden shifts and unusual combinations of 'stylistic registers' – that is, of 'high' (heroic) and 'low' (pastoral) styles – participate in over-arching narratives.

In the course of making his sonata forms more 'compact' – again, reflecting 'sophisticated' Viennese influences – Bruckner simultaneously achieved a more complicated interaction of form and structure. In the first versions of the symphonies up to and including the Fifth (1876), the symphonic outer movements conform to the sonata paradigm rather strictly, with regular recapitulations; but beginning in approximately 1876, Bruckner began to handle sonata form in innovative ways, upsetting the traditional paradigm. More specifically, the definitive tonic return and reprise of the opening theme are held in abeyance until the end of the Finale (and thus the work as a whole) in the reversed recapitulations of the Finales of the Quintet and Seventh Symphony and the truncated reprises in the final revisions of the Third and Fourth Symphonies. If the definitive return is to be 'saved' – strategically reserved – then it may be 'anticipated' in various ways earlier in the sonata form. Studies of the Finale of the Third Symphony in the last version (1887–8) by Thomas Röder and the initial movements of the Sixth Symphony (1879–81) by Benjamin Korstvedt and Jackson suggest that Bruckner's larger strategy is to 'anticipate' but delay the definitive coincidence of tonic harmony and reprise of the opening thematic materials.

Several generations of Bruckner scholars have asserted that the major cuts in the Finales of the Third and Fourth Symphonies were 'forced upon' the composer by his disciples in the late 1880s. Through a careful reappraisal of the sources for the Third Symphony, Röder has shown this was not the case; rather, the abridgements were requested by the composer himself in 1879 (the same year in which he began working on the Sixth Symphony). At this time, Bruckner eliminated the first group (mm. 379–432), the second part of the second group and the first part of the third group (mm. 465–514). These cuts suggest that, as early as 1879, he had decided to postpone tonal and formal reprise and closure until the final measures of the symphony.

Bruckner would pursue a similar strategy in the outer movements of the contemporaneous Sixth Symphony. In the first movement, Korstvedt argues that the definitive thematic and tonic resolution are delayed until the coda (mm. 407–16). Taking as his point of departure contemporary critical observations concerning the tonal instability of the symphony's opening, Korstvedt identifies a crucial aspect of the work's harmonic-formal organization, specifically those features that make the tonic A sound like an unstable dominant of the subdominant D; this 'dominantization' of the putative tonic then becomes an essential compositional idea. Locating the onset of the recapitulation is problematic: is it initiated in E flat major at m. 195 with the thematic return, or in A major at m. 209 with the harmonic return? Beginning the design recapitulation in E flat major certainly weakens the tonal arrival on A major and, as Korstvedt observes, the cadence on A 'executes the tricky manoeuvre of restoring the tonal centricity of A while preserving its contextual harmonic ambiguity'. Thus, the reprise in m. 209 'anticipates' but does not fully achieve the definitive arrival on A, which is saved for the coda. In his study of the Sixth Symphony's slow movement, Jackson identifies an analogous but different 'anticipatory' strategy: in this sonata form, the tonic recapitulation in m. 93 is 'anticipated' within the development at m. 77. Although uncommon, Jackson argues that this type of 'anticipatory tonic recapitulation' in the development was explored by Brahms and Dvořák at approximately the same time, this 'advanced' treatment of sonata form being 'in the air' in Vienna and Prague.

It has been said that there is a disconnection between Bruckner's Sechterian theory and his own compositional practice. But was this in fact the case? Friedrich Eckstein, a long-time Bruckner pupil, maintains that fundamental bass theory played a significant part in Bruckner's compositional practice, reporting that, as Bruckner composed, he kept track of the fundamental bass progression along with the metrical structure. Indeed, in the surviving manuscripts, Bruckner does take note of the fundamental bass either with note-heads or, much more frequently, with pitch names followed by the annotation '*Fund[ament]*'. Yet, surprisingly, despite student reports and the annotations in the manuscripts (not to mention Bruckner's six years of arduous study with Sechter), virtually nothing has appeared linking Sechterian theory with Brucknerian practice. Thus Graham Phipps's systematic correlation of Bruckner's theoretical and compositional practices in the first movement of the Seventh Symphony constitutes a pioneering effort. He compellingly demonstrates ways in which Sechterian theory, to some extent enriched by Arnold Schoenberg, can account for Bruckner's tonally allusive harmonic language. Employing 'neo-Sechterian' analytical tools, Phipps not only provides a detailed account of Bruckner's complex harmonic syntax, but shows how this can relate to the larger tonal, rhythmic, architectonic, and even narrative strategies in the movement and symphony as a whole.

Of the common complaints about Bruckner, one of the most frequently encountered is that his symphonies last too long, a criticism that may be traced back to contemporary Viennese circles: Brahms, for instance, was reputed to have disparaged the Bruckner symphonies as 'giant symphonic snakes' ('*symphonische Riesenschlänge*'). While the Bruckner symphonies even in their final (abridged) versions are relatively 'long' in terms of their absolute 'clock' time (longer than the Brahms symphonies, for example), they also 'sound' long in terms of 'musical' time ('musical' time being differentiated from 'clock' time as the listener's subjective perception of duration). Taking the second, 1890 version of the Eighth Symphony as his point of departure, Joseph Kraus investigates those features of Bruckner's musical language that contribute to the listener's impression of great length and 'monumentality'. Building on a hypothesis of multiple 'tonal streams' (first proposed by Christopher Lewis), Kraus suggests that the second subject in the first movement (mm. 53–72) embodies three distinct planes of tonal action and narrative, i.e. 'tonal streams'. (Perhaps it was precisely this kind of 'shifting' that prompted Brahms to complain of 'dizziness' while listening to Bruckner!) The subjective impression of 'great length' is created because structural superposition implies the unfolding – albeit simultaneously – of several durational envelopes; this is 'multiply-directed time', as defined by Jonathan Kramer. Kraus posits that an analogous superposition of thematic elements from all movements in the coda to the Finale, combined with tonal-harmonic stasis, creates the impression of Kramer's 'vertical time' ('in which the linear interrelationships between past, present and future are suspended') – in other words, 'endless duration' or 'eternity'.

The impression of the 'great length' is intimately connected with the concept of 'monumentality' in the Vienna symphonies as reflecting the imperial grandeur of Vienna as the centre of the Habsburg empire. In so far as each of the analytical studies of other aspects of the symphonies discloses Bruckner's revisions in dialogue with Viennese musical aesthetics, each posits Bruckner's relationship to his Viennese heritage. To be sure, Bruckner 'protests' against Beethoven – in the positive sense as defined by Wittgenstein (see Peter Palmer's chapter) – but his music stands in a dialogical relationship, not only with Beethoven, but the whole Viennese tradition. It may be argued that Bruckner's original and frequently repeated intention to allow the *Te Deum* to serve as a Finale to his Ninth, should he not live to complete a purely instrumental fourth movement, somewhat weakens the element of 'protest' against Beethoven; but with the *Te Deum* as Finale, the symphony articulates a protest of a different kind, a humanistic manifesto being replaced by a Christian declaration. John Phillips examines the considerable amount of instrumental sketches and the manuscript evidence in light of biographical information to suggest that Bruckner may even have contemplated the possibility of a transition to the *Te Deum* from one or more points in the evolving Finale. Furthermore, based on reminiscences and contemporary reports in the mass media, he argues that the practice of performing the Ninth as a torso of three movements 'violates' Bruckner's final conception of the work. With the *Te Deum* as Finale, the symphony remains true to its dedication to the 'dear Lord'. Thus, the Ninth Symphony becomes Bruckner's musical equivalent to the Vienna cathedral – a structure that fascinated him throughout his Vienna years. The connection between the sacred and the secular in Bruckner's symphonic output is at its strongest in the Ninth; but it cannot be denied that all of Bruckner's later symphonies are intimately connected with his residence in Vienna. Indeed, they are, in the most profound sense of the epithet, 'Vienna Symphonies'.

There are two diametrically opposed views about Bruckner's creative instinct. The first is the essentially Romantic perception of an intimate connection between a composer's personality and his work, and the second, of more recent provenance, denies linkage between the life and the creative output. Constantin Floros argues that psychologist Erwin Ringel's hypothesis – namely, that Bruckner lacked a sense of self-worth – is uncorroborated by anecdotal evidence of friends and pupils. On the contrary, these reports disclose that Bruckner possessed a clear sense of direction and great determination as a composer. His comparative lack of interest in certain philosophical trends is not to be regarded as a lack of intelligence. The extent of Bruckner's participation in the cultural life of Vienna is uncertain. Most of his time seems to have been spent teaching and composing, and he used his vacations to visit Bayreuth, Steyr, St Florian and Vöcklabruck, where his sister Rosalie lived with her husband and two sons. It is true that he was an occasional opera-goer and even entertained the possibility of writing an opera himself in the 1890s. In September 1893 H. Bollé-Hellmund (a pseudonym for Fraulein Elisabeth Bollé) wrote to Bruckner, offering to provide him with an opera libretto of a religious nature which, she was sure, would be suitable. In his reply, Bruckner said that the libretto should be '*a la Lohengrin*, Romantic, religious, mysterious and, above all, free from all impurities'. Increasing ill-health, however, meant that Bruckner was unable to give serious consideration to what would have been an intriguing opera project. There is no record of his showing any particular interest in dramatic productions at either the *Burgtheater* or the *Volkstheater* or of his being aware of the major developments in painting and sculpture which led to the formation of the Vienna Secession in the late 1890s.

Some of the 'alien' aspects of Bruckner's character, his devout Catholicism in particular, were misinterpreted a hundred years ago and are perhaps even more misunderstood in our increasingly materialistic and secular times. Bruckner was single-minded in his pursuit of excellence, regarding his creativity as a God-given gift to be used wisely. The devotional, confessional aspects of Bruckner's music are unmistakeable. For Floros, the thematic connections between the sacred and secular compositions and the use of religious topoi in the symphonies are of particular importance.

Much has been made of Bruckner's lack of social graces; but it would appear that, generally speaking, his occasionally anti-social behaviour did not preclude acceptance as an outstanding musician. Bruckner enjoyed influential patronage from court circles even after Ludwig Herbeck's untimely death in 1877. The Lord Chamberlain, Prince Constantin zu Hohenlohe-Schillingsfürst, to whom he dedicated his Symphony no. 4, was a keen music-lover and well-disposed towards Bruckner, although his wife, Princess Marie zu Sayn-Wittgenstein-Berleburg detected a 'certain amount of calculated, self-satisfied clumsiness' in his court etiquette. He seems to have possessed a sufficient amount of 'peasant cunning' to survive the difficult transition between life as a church musician in a provincial town like Linz and life as a teacher, composer and organist in the Austrian capital.

Improvisational skills have always been an essential part of a performer's technical equipment. As a composer-performer, Bruckner followed in the footsteps of many of his Austrian and German predecessors who belonged to the Viennese tradition. Improvisation contests between Mozart and Clementi and Beethoven and Steibelt were important and highly impressive events in Viennese musical life. Beethoven made his mark in Vienna in the 1790s primarily as a virtuoso pianist performing at private concerts and musical soirées given by members of the aristocracy and the 'upwardly mobile' bourgeoisie. Bruckner's exploits as an improviser were largely confined to his duties as an organist at St Florian abbey, Linz Cathedral (he gained the post after proving to be the outstanding player in two preliminary 'contests') and the *Hofkapelle* in Vienna, and 'travelling virtuoso' is not a description one would readily associate with the composer. His 'travelling' was not nearly as extensive as that of Paganini and Liszt, but he did undertake two foreign journeys – to France and England in 1869 and 1871 respectively – as a 'musical ambassador' for Austria.

At the peak of his powers as an organ executant, Bruckner made a great impression on audiences at the churches of St Epvre in Nancy and Notre Dame in Paris, and at the Albert Hall and Crystal Palace in London. His repertoire was typical of the organ recitalist at that time – a mixture of original organ pieces (by Bach, Handel and Mendelssohn) and free improvisations on well-known melodies. Drawing on contemporary accounts of Bruckner's playing in London, Crawford Howie reveals that critical reception was mixed but his improvisational skills were acknowledged as outstanding. The constraints of a life divided between teaching and composing effectively ruled out the development of a career as a concert organist. Nevertheless, he took the opportunity of playing the organs in towns and cities in Austria and Germany which he visited to attend performances of his works in the 1880s. Although his technique was now less secure, his contrapuntal inventiveness still astounded his listeners.

Bruckner's connection with England was renewed in May 1887 when Hans Richter conducted the first British performance of his Seventh Symphony. Most of the audience on that occasion and the majority of the readers of the 'Bruckner' obituary notice in the *Musical Times* in November 1896 would probably not have recalled the composer's visit as an organ virtuoso in 1871. Provisional plans for a concert tour of England in 1872 did not come to fruition, and hardly any of his fairly insignificant output of organ music was published during his lifetime. It was well into the 1960s before his choral and orchestral music made a 'breakthrough' in Great Britain; but it is interesting to contemplate that the first seeds of his subsequent popularity were first sown almost a hundred years earlier in 1871.

Bruckner's friends, pupils and later admirers all contributed to the rich tapestry of Bruckner reception. Even during the composer's lifetime, however, reception of his music was clouded by political considerations which assumed an insidious character in Vienna in the nineteenth century, and in Germany and Austria during the 1930s and early 1940s. In the last decade of the century, Vienna, formerly a stronghold of Liberalism, was, in the words of Carl Schorske (*Fin-de-Siècle Vienna*), 'engulfed in a Christian-Social tidal wave'. Although Emperor Franz Joseph was able to stem the tide for a short time and initially refused to sanction the election of the anti-Semitic Karl Lueger as mayor of the city, he was eventually forced by the electorate to concede. And so the 'Christian-Social demagogues began a decade of rule in Vienna which combined all that was anathema to classical liberalism, anti-Semitism, clericalism, and municipal socialism'. The 'profound psychological repercussions' of this change were felt principally in Vienna but were by no means confined to the Austrian capital.

The *Wiener Akademische Wagner-Verein*, founded in 1872, and, to a lesser extent, the *Neuer Richard Wagner-Verein*, an ultra-nationalist splinter group formed in 1890, were largely responsible for either sponsoring performances of Bruckner's works in their original form or providing a platform for performances of his symphonies in arrangements for one or two pianos at weekly private or semi-private gatherings – so-called 'internen Abenden'. Many of Bruckner's friends and pupils, including Joseph Schalk and Ferdinand Löwe, were members of the Academic Wagner Sociey and availed themselves of the opportunity to promote his works. Andrea Harrandt identifies this as an important, albeit neglected, area of Bruckner reception. Recent performances and recordings of some of these arrangements confirm that they were often skilfully conceived and more than simply appetizers for the 'real thing'.

Joseph Schalk played a major role in establishing Bruckner as a specifically German nationalist composer. At issue here is not so much Schalk the musician and his promotion of Bruckner's symphonies in piano arrangements or his controversial involvement with the revision of Bruckner's works, but rather Schalk the writer and his contribution of various articles on the composer and his music to various journals, including the *Bayreuther Blätter*, published by Wagner and his disciples. Schalk often chose to be economical with the truth, exaggerating Bruckner's relationship with Wagner, presenting him as a true representative of a sublime and distinctively German music far removed from the trivialities of 'un-German' salon music which was all the rage in Vienna, and deliberately painting a German-nationalist portrait of the composer with clear anti-Semitic overtones – a portrait that was avidly seized upon by the National Socialist party in the 1930s and early 1940s. In the years immediately following the 1939–45 war, there was an understandable desire to break with the past and to present Bruckner in a different light. But can one totally dissociate Bruckner from his 'Germanness'? While Bruckner associated with some ultra-nationalists – and was promoted by them – there is no unequivocal evidence that Bruckner himself subscribed to extreme nationalist views. In fact, he may have been unaware of the more aggressively polemical aspects of German nationalism. Yet, while he cannot be held responsible for either the posthumous metaphysical elevation of his works or their appropriation as propaganda tools, there are particular qualities inherent in his music which attracted such interpretations and manipulations. As Thomas Leibnitz observes, it is important to address these difficult issues and 'deal honestly with the darker aspects of his music in a complex reception history'.

The association of Bruckner's music with the National Socialist movement in Germany during the 1930s and 1940s is, of course, one of the darkest and most unsavoury aspects of the history of Bruckner reception. Bruckner was one of Hitler's favourite composers. Correspondences between the careers of the two native sons of Upper Austria, who had triumphed over bourgeois Jewish Viennese Liberalism, were obvious. Bruckner's well-documented admiration for Wagner and his personal relationships with ultra-nationalist predecessors to the Nazi party certainly contributed to his value for the cultural propaganda of the Third Reich. Benjamin Korstvedt has pointed out that many published endorsements of the first Collected Works Edition of Bruckner's manuscript versions, for example, were replete with the terminology of National Socialism; the publications of the symphonies in use to that point had been 'contaminated' by 'foreign' influences which had to be 'purged' in a 'purifying' process to reveal the true German genius which was Bruckner. Christa Brüstle discusses the importance of Sigmund Hausegger in the movement to publish Bruckner's manuscript versions. It is intriguing that Hausegger, while caught up in the politics of his time and a supporter of the *Gesamtausgabe* from an ideological point of view, nevertheless continued to follow certain aspects of the earlier printed editions in practice.

Bruckner's visit to London in 1871 was a short, albeit highly significant, chapter in his career. Another eminent Austrian, who not only visited but eventually settled in Britain, was the philosopher Ludwig Wittgenstein. Wittgenstein belonged to one of the most distinguished families in *fin de siècle* Vienna. His father Karl was a wealthy industrialist and leading patron of the arts, and his brother Paul was a pianist of international stature; his sister Margarethe was immortalized in a portrait painted by Gustav Klimt, one of the leading Secessionists. Ludwig, a good amateur musician, had fairly conservative musical tastes; nevertheless, Bruckner was one of the composers he admired. During his first stay in England (1908–13) he studied mechanical engineering at Manchester University and mathematical logic with Bertrand Russell at Cambridge. He probably attended concerts given by Hans Richter and the Hallé orchestra and may have heard the occasional performance of a Bruckner symphony or the *Te Deum*. At Cambridge he became interested in the psychology of music and contributed to a paper on the subject of rhythm. Wittgenstein returned to England in 1929, became a naturalized British subject in 1938, and was professor of philosophy at Cambridge from 1939 to 1947. Peter Palmer discusses Wittgenstein's posthumously published *Vermischte Bemerkungen*, which contain remarks on a wide range of subjects including music. There are references to Brahms and Bruckner and their music, the most interesting of which is the suggestion that Bruckner's Ninth Symphony is 'a protest against' Beethoven's Ninth and that its relationship to the latter is akin to that between Lenau's Catholic Faust and Goethe's Enlightenment Faust. And yet, just as Lenau himself dismissed the notion that his *Faust* drama presented any kind of challenge to Goethe's, so Bruckner never had any intention of either protesting against or imitating Beethoven's work. His reasons were more practical and pragmatic – he particularly liked the key of D minor and it seemed to be the most suitable tonality for his principal theme. Even if one does not accept Wittgenstein's main thesis, there are certainly one or two important connecting threads between Lenau and Bruckner, in particular the 'vividly demonic component' in Lenau's poetry which Palmer compares with the 'high dissonance level' in Bruckner's Ninth. In general Wittgenstein's musical perceptions, albeit fleeting, are more positive than many of his philosophical arguments – summarized in another posthumously published work *Philosophical Investigations* – and provide a penetrating insight into the psyche of arguably the most important Viennese émigré to make his home in Britain in the twentieth century.

The small number of late nineteenth- and early twentieth-century symphonists who were influenced by Bruckner, taking him as a point of departure or as a model, includes Mahler, Sibelius (who was present at the first performance of Bruckner's revised Third Symphony in Vienna in December 1890), Franz Schmidt, Wilhelm Furtwängler, whose greatness as a conductor has always been recognized but whose reputation as a composer has increased significantly in the last decade, and Richard Wetz. Wetz, whose admiration and enthusiasm for Bruckner began in 1903 after a performance of the Seventh Symphony conducted by Artur Nikisch in Leipzig, deserves greater recognition. In his study of Wetz's three symphonies, Erik Levi reveals certain striking connections – orchestral, structural, melodic and harmonic – with Bruckner's symphonies. But Wetz was more than a Bruckner epigone; he had absorbed many stylistic features of the nineteenth-century symphony and, indeed, there is a strong original voice at times. Other compositions, noticeably his chamber music, show far less Brucknerian influence. Nevertheless, the First and Third Symphonies in particular provide sufficient proof that Wetz deserves to be called a 'Brucknerian composer', one of the very few who can lay claim to such a title.

Part One
Theoretical Perspective and Compositional Practice

1 A composer learns his craft: lessons in form and orchestration, 1861–3*

Paul Hawkshaw

For Anton Bruckner, completion of his counterpoint studies with Simon Sechter in March 1861 signalled the end of an extended compositional hiatus. A fruitful though brief creative period followed, which saw the completion of two great motets – *Ave Maria* (WAB 6) and *Afferentur Regi* (WAB 1), the *Festkantate* (WAB 16) for the new Linz Cathedral and a handful of smaller works.[1] By 25 April 1862, when Bruckner completed the cantata, he had already immersed himself again in study, this time investigating form and orchestration with the conductor/cellist, Otto Kitzler.[2] Most of the surviving exercises which Bruckner wrote for Kitzler are preserved in one volume – the so-called *Kitzler Studienbuch*.[3] Its 326 pages are full of autograph sketches, annotations, and exercises, as well as complete and incomplete compositions which testify to an extremely rigorous and extensive training in both form and orchestration. The *Kitzler Studienbuch* is fascinating for its insights into the history of musical pedagogy in the nineteenth century as well as for the historical and theoretical implications of the terminology and format of its exercises. As a document of musical analysis in the middle of the nineteenth century it is invaluable.

Due to its inaccessibility the *Studienbuch* has achieved little notoriety in the musical world. Leopold Nowak drew attention to its existence when he published the C minor String Quartet (WAB 111), one of the exercises in the miscellany. He later transcribed the F minor 'Student' Symphony (WAB 99) sketches located in the final pages of the miscellany.[4] Otherwise, with the

*A version of this chapter was read at the Second International Conference *Perspectives on Anton Bruckner* at The University of Manchester, Great Britain, 1–4 April 1996. The author is extremely grateful to the organizers of the conference, Dr. Crawford Howie and Professor Timothy L. Jackson, for their most helpful and encouraging comments and suggestions. The article first appeared in the *Musical Quarterly* LXXXII:2 (Summer 1998), pp. 336–61. The updated version is printed here with permission of Oxford University Press.

exception of the *March* in D Minor (WAB 96), *Three Orchestral Pieces* (WAB 97), and a Piano Sonata movement in G Minor, none of the exercises has been published.[5] After a brief overview of the contents of the miscellany, this chapter will illustrate some of the structural issues of concern to Bruckner and apply his analytical terminology to examples from the Sonata movement, String Quartet, F minor Symphony and another Kitzler composition, the Overture in G Minor (WAB 98). Possible contemporary theoretical sources for the exercises and formal concepts they represent will be identified. I will conclude with a few thoughts on the significance of the miscellany in the context of the composer's biography and our understanding of his music and working procedures. There is a wealth of knowledge to be obtained from the *Kitzler Studienbuch*.

* * *

The miscellany consists of 163 folios in various sizes in oblong format. They contain numerous autograph dates between Christmas 1861 and 10 July 1863 and are arranged in chronological order. Bruckner was responsible for the order because he numbered the pages himself and included occasional cross-references. Table 1.1 contains a list of the contents. The first column indicates the foliation; the second lists the autograph dates; the third identifies the object of study; and the fourth provides a brief description of the material on the pages in question. Throughout the miscellany, the exercises are in a wide variety of keys and metres and employ numerous textures from chorales through different broken-chord and arpeggiated figurations. The vast majority are in two-stave keyboard or four-stave string quartet score. Many are melody/bass skeletons with occasional chords and contrapuntal voices filled in or indicated by figured bass. Bruckner sometimes omitted accidentals and committed textbook errors in voice-leading – parallel fifths, for example – which would make an elementary harmony teacher cringe. These are probably a consequence of the speed with which he proceeded (as evidenced by the dates throughout) as well as an indication that both teacher and pupil were preoccupied with formal issues, not with details of counterpoint and voice-leading which the composer had already more than mastered with Simon Sechter.

The studies began with cadences and modulations to nearly-related keys (*verwandte Tonarten*). At first Bruckner was concerned with cadences and modulations within a single period (*Periode*). Here the standard format was to write out an eight-measure period followed by three or four alternative cadences or modulations for that period (Ex. 1.1).[6] On fol. 8r. he began to experiment with writing consecutive periods using the same material with different cadences and/or modulatory structures. In Ex. 1.2 he wrote his opening period cadencing in the dominant and followed it with a second eight-measure period. The term *Periode* refers to the groups of eight measures; his term for each four-measure subdivision is *Glied* which will be translated for the remainder of this article as 'phrase'. In his terminology the last four measures of the second period in Ex.

Table 1.1   Contents of the *Kitzler Studienbuch*

Foliation	Autograph dates	Subject of the exercise	Description
1r.–8r., l. 8		Cadences and Modulations within one 8-measure period	Piano and string quartet scores (Ex. 1.1)
8r., l. 9– 9v., l. 4		within two 8-measure periods	(Ex. 1.2)
9v., l. 5– 15v., l. 6	Christmas 1861 [10r.] 1 Jan. 1862 [13r.] 2 Jan. 1862 [13v.]	2- and 3-section Song Forms regular periods	Song and piano scores Waltz, Polka, Galop, Mazurka, Minuet 8- and 16-measure periods (Ex. 1.3)
15v., l. 7– 21v.	6 Jan. 1862 [16r.]	irregular periods trio forms	Piano scores Minuet and Trio, March and Trio Periods of 8–6–8, 6–4–6, 12–8–12 etc. measures Song in trio form 16 measure periods (Ex. 1.4)
22r.–29r.		expanded periods	Song and piano scores (Ex. 1.5)
29v.–39r., l. 4		Scherzo and Trio	Strinq quartet scores
38r.–40v.		Etude	Piano scores
41r.–52v.		Variations	Piano and string quartet scores
53r.–68v.		Rondo	Piano scores
69r.–70r.	6 Jun. 1862 Fri. before Pentecost [70r.]	Sonata form 9 thematic sketches	Piano scores (Ex. 1.6)
70v.–72v.		5 first groups with bridge sections	Piano sonatas
73r.–75r.		5 second groups [with closing sections]	for each of the previous 5 first groups with bridge sections
75v.–78v.		2 developments with recapitulations	for two of the previous expositions
79r.–82v.	29 Jun. 1862 [79r.]	Sonata Movement in G minor	complete movement
83r.–89r.		String Quartet in C Minor (WAB 111) 1st movement	Autograph score Sonata form
89v.–92v.	28 Jul. 1862 9:00pm [92v.]	Andante	Small Rondo form
93r.–93v.		Scherzo	Two-section song form
94r.		Trio	Two-section song form
94v.–98v.	Linz 7 Aug. 1862 [98v.]	Rondo	Middle Rondo form
99r.–103v.	15 Aug. 1862 7:30pm [103v.]	Rondo [alternate]	Large Rondo form
104r.–107r., l. 3	22 Aug. 1862 Kirnberger Wald [107r.]	'Der Trompeter an der Katzbach'	Song for bass and piano

107r., l. 4– 109v., l. 4	25 Aug. 1862 5:00pm [109v.]	Fantasies in small forms	Four piano pieces successive periods
109v., l. 5– 114v.	26 Aug. 1862 [109v.] 26 Aug. 1862 8:00pm [112r.]	Instrumentation Woodwinds, Contrabass, Piano	Arrangements of the fourth Fantasy
113r.–114r.	2 Sept. 1862 [113v.]	Five pieces	Piano pieces to be orchestrated two- and three-section song form
115r.–117r.		Brass	Chorales and fanfares
117v.–125v.		Orchestration of Beethoven's *Pathétique* Sonata	Orchestral score (exposition only)
126r.–133r.	Linz 12 Oct. 1862 [132r.]	Orchestral Compositions March in D minor (WAB 96)	Orchestral score and sketches March in three-section song form; Trio in two-section song form
133v.–143v.	10 Nov. 1862 [139r.] Linz 16 Nov. 1862 after 6:00pm [143v.]	Three Pieces (WAB 97)	Orchestral score and sketches – three-section song form
144r.–151r.	18 Nov. 1862 [144r.] 27 Nov. 1862 after 9:00pm [147r.] 1st Sunday of Advent 1862 [147v.] 5 Dec. 1862 [150v.]	Overture in G minor (WAB 98)	Sketches
152r.–153v.	7 Jan. 1863 [152r.]	Symphony in F Minor (WAB 99) 1st movement	Sketches
156r.–158r., l. 10			
154r.–154v.	13 Mar. 1863 14 Mar. [154r.]	Andante	
158r., l. 11– 160v.	10 Apr. 1863 [160r.]	Scherzo	
163r.	10 Apr. from 10:00am to noon 4:00–5:00pm 13 Apr. 1863		
161r.–162v.	[161r.]	Finale	
163r.	10 Jul. 1863	'Overture, Symphony, and Psalm completed'	

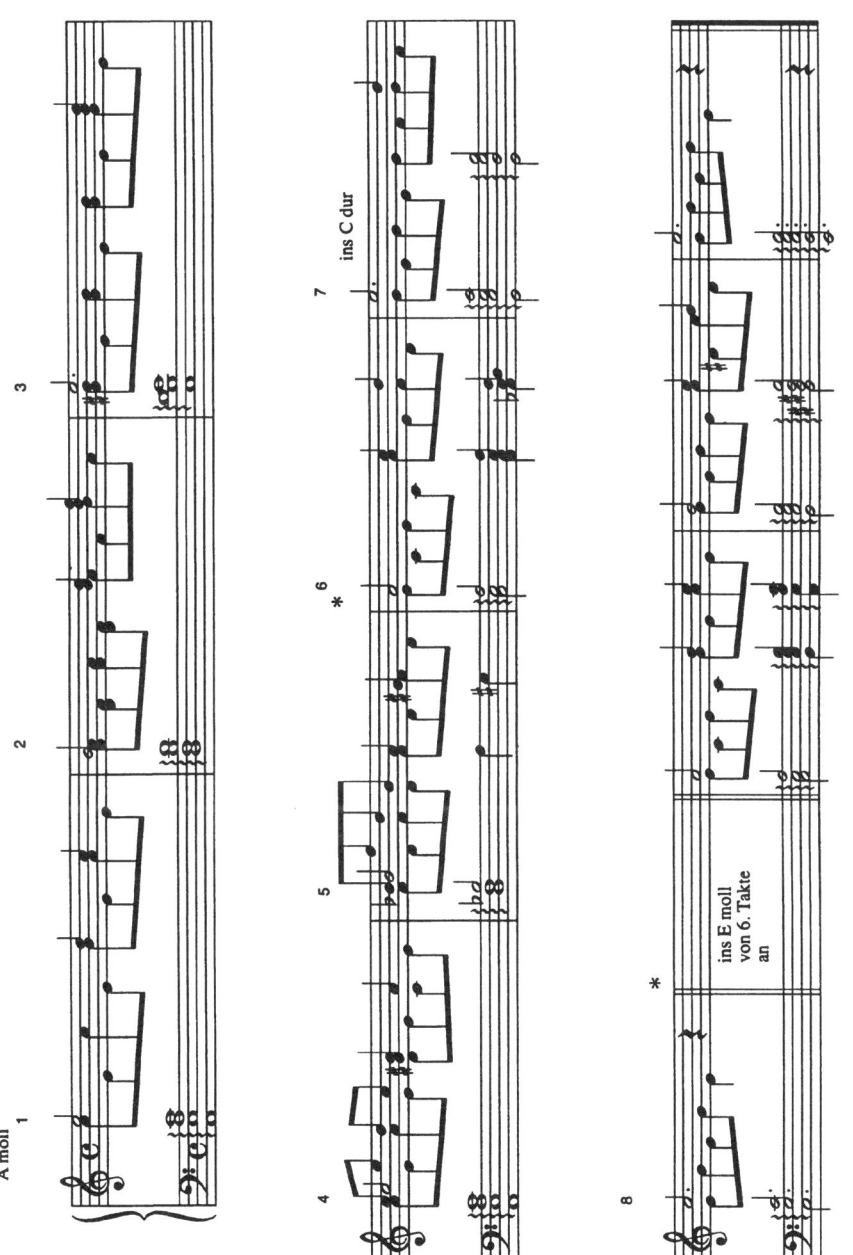

Ex. 1.1   *Kitzler Studienbuch*, fol. 7r, ll. 1–4

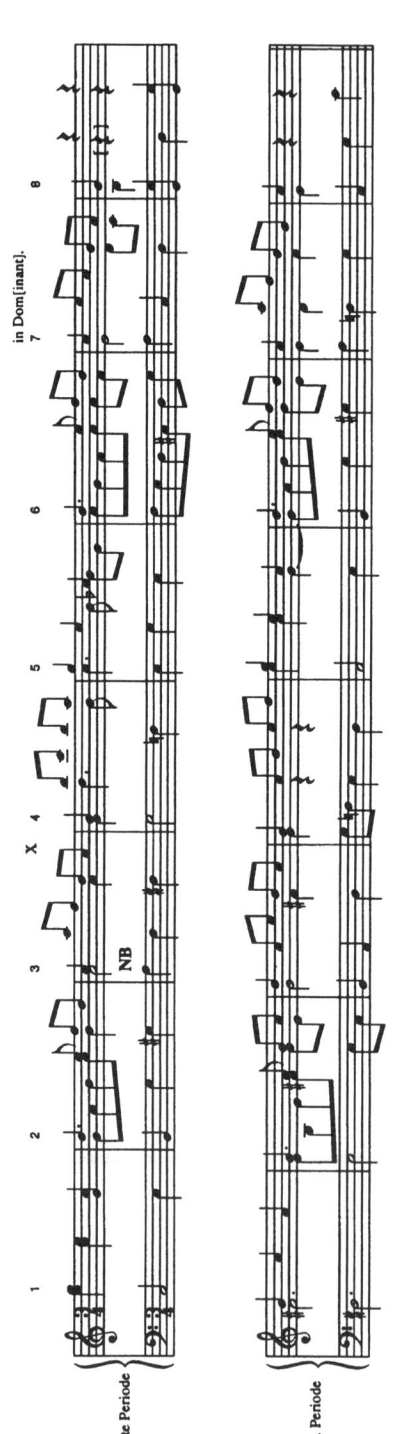

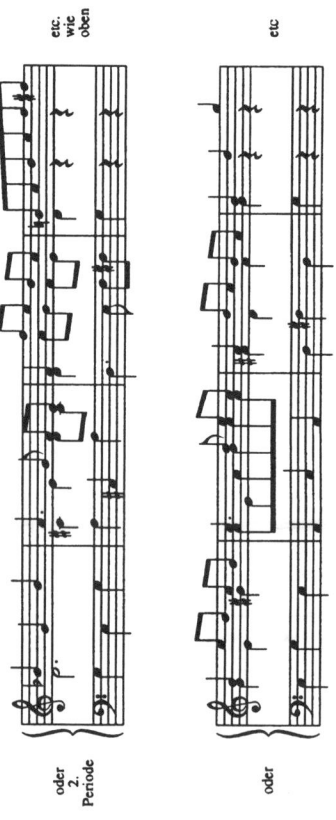

Ex. 1.2 *Kitzler Studienbuch*, fol. 8v, ll. 5–12

1.2 repeat (*Repetieren*) their counterparts in the first period with a different cadence, this one in the tonic. He then wrote two alternative openings for his second period, each of which is designed to connect with the final four measures of the original.[7] In these exercises Bruckner ended the first period in a variety of nearly related keys. Ex. 1.2, for instance, is preceded by a similar exercise using the same opening period cadencing in the tonic and followed by one in which the same period cadences in the relative minor.

At Christmas 1861 Bruckner began his investigation of two-section and three-section song form (*zweitheilige* and *dreitheilige Liedform*) which are the basis for many of the compositions in the remainder of the volume. At the outset, the former is defined as '2 periods of 8 measures where each one is an entity without repetition', and the latter as 'first period one entity; second period new; third period repeats the first one'.[8] The exercises in this part of the miscellany fall roughly into three categories which overlap in both their definition and chronology of study:[9]

1. those with periods of equal length (*regelmässige Perioden*) (fol. 9v.–15r.)
2. those with periods of different length (*unregelmässige Perioden*) (fol. 15v.–21v.)
3. those with expanded periods (*erweiterte Perioden*) (fol. 22r.–29r.).

The principal concern in the first two groups is the length of the periods rather than motivic relationships between periods. Exercises in the first group are in both two- and three-section song form. Most utilize eight-measure periods as in the song in Ex. 1.3. Instrumental compositions here include the Waltz, Polka, Galop, Mazurka, and Minuet; some have sixteen-measure periods. The exercises in group 2, periods of unequal lengths, are in three-section song form of 12–10–12 measures, 16–14–16, 8–10–8, etc.[10] Included among the exercises in irregular periods is Bruckner's copy of the vocal parts from the *Kyrie* of Haydn's *Nicolaimesse* in G major which he describes as being in three-section song form with periods of 6–8–6 measures.[11] The exercises with irregular periods are interrupted by Minuets and Marches with Trios where the Minuet or March is in two-section song form with repeated eight-measure periods. The Trios are either a single eight-measure period repeated, or a second Song Form with repeated eight-measure periods. This part of the miscellany concludes with a March/Trio combination of three- (March) and two-section (Trio) song form, all eight-measure periods, as well as a song in Trio form, where both the A and B sections are in two-section song form with unrepeated eight-measure periods. The orchestral March in D minor published by Jancik has the same form as this March.[12] The song is transcribed in Ex. 1.4; the poet of the text has yet to be identified.

To this point, with few exceptions, creating melodic relationships between periods has not been an object of the exercises. Beginning on fol. 22r. the focus of study becomes the expansion (*Erweiterung*) of a period through repetition of

Ex. 1.3 *Kitzler Studienbuch*, fol. 11r, ll. 1–9: two-section song form

10

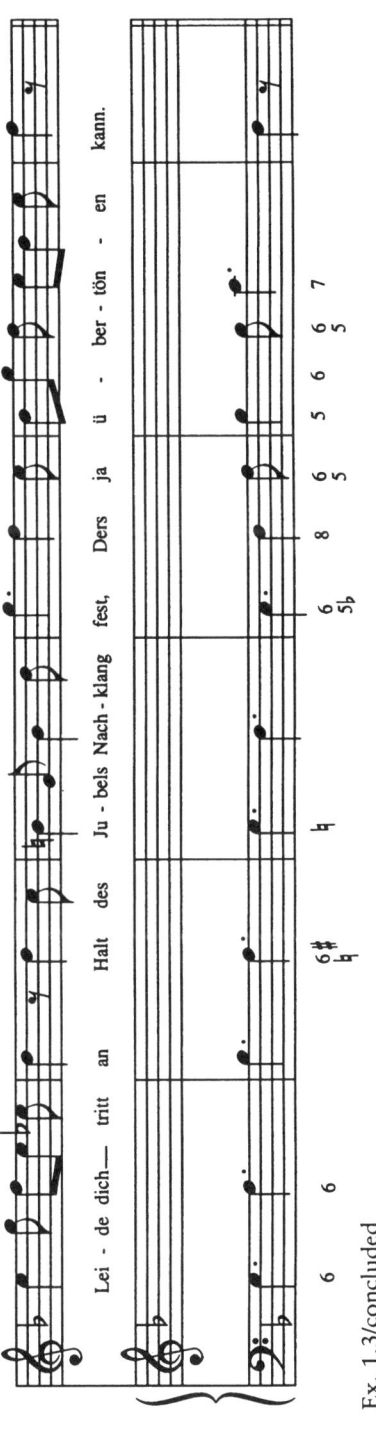

Ex. 1.3/concluded

11

Lied mit Trioform

12

Ex. 1.4 *Kitzler Studienbuch*, fol. 21v.: Song in trio form (text punctuation and orthography as in original)

Ex. 1.4/concluded

13

Ex. 1.5   *Kitzler Studienbach*, fol. 25v., ll. 3–8

all or part of it. Bruckner writes that a period, a phrase, or part of a phrase can be 'simply repeated, or raised (*gesteigert*) or lowered (*tiefer*) with different harmonization and modulation'.[13] Ex. 1.5 contains the first part, itself in two-section song form, of a larger Andante in Trio Form. In Bruckner's terminology the second section of the transcription (mm. 9ff.) is a period which has been expanded (*erweitert*) through simple repetition (*einfache Repetition*) in measures 17–20.[14]

Plate 1 contains a reproduction of the autograph manuscript of the little Piano Piece in E flat major (WAB 119) illustrating a number of features which Bruckner worked on at this point with Kitzler.[15] It is in two-section song form with irregular periods of eight and ten measures. The first period contains two phrases, the second of which is an expansion through repetition (*Erweiterung durch Wiederholung*) of the first. The second section contains two four-measure phrases with a two-measure extension (*Verlängerung*) at the *morendo*. On a smaller scale, measures 3 and 4 as well as 5 and 6 of the second section are actually expansions (*Erweiterungen*) of the first two. To judge by the fingerings in the manuscript, Bruckner probably took time away from his Kitzler studies to try out his new-found knowledge on a little piece for one of his piano students.

Beginning on fol. 29v. Bruckner began to apply his studies in phrase structure to larger forms – the Scherzo and Piano Etude – which are exercises in expansion through repetition of an entire period (*Erweiterung durch eine ganze Periode*).[16] The Etudes are followed by twenty-four pages of Themes and Variations, and thirty-two pages of Rondo exercises. The latter, like the Scherzo and Trio exercises, are described in terms of expansion of two- and three-section song form and will be illustrated in the discussion of the String Quartet movements below.

On 6 June 1862, on fol. 69r., Bruckner began his investigation of Sonata Form with nine thematic sketches entitled '*Sonatform. I. Satz. Bildung v[on] Themagruppe*'. The longest of these is twelve measures. They are in piano score as illustrated in Ex. 1.6, which contains the first of the nine and is the only one where the composer has identified individual motives. He (or perhaps Kitzler) obviously felt that this one was more suited to a String Quartet and contained too many motives as indicated by the autograph annotations at the beginning and end. He arrived at the latter conclusion despite his observation '(*eig[en]tl[ich]. II.*)' in m. 4 that his fourth motive was the same as the second one. Beethoven served as a point of reference for some of the Rondos because his name appears at the bottom of fol. 66v.

Next came five first groups complete with bridge sections described as '*Thema- und Übergangsgruppe*'. Five corresponding *Gesangsgruppe* or *Gesangsperiode* with short closing sections followed. He used the term *Schlussperiode* in two of the five to refer to the closing sections. Bruckner then proceeded to write development and recapitulation sections under the heading '*Mittelsatz-Gruppe. 2. Theil Sonatform I. Satz.*' for two of the five expositions he had already completed. The process of studying the individual components of

Ex. 1.6   *Kitzler Studienbuch*, fol. 69r, ll. 1–6: study for sonata form

16

sonata form took less than a month. On 29 June he began the complete Sonata Movement in G minor which Walburga Litschauer has included in her edition of the piano works.[17]

Having completed his investigation of all the necessary forms, the composer devoted most of the summer to the String Quartet, completed with alternative Rondo Finales on 15 August.[18] The *Studienbuch* then contains a large song *Der Trompeter an der Katzbach* and four piano Fantasies in three-section song form with what Bruckner describes as successive (*anreihenden*) periods.[19] The music of Mendelssohn was on his (and perhaps Kitzler's) mind with the piano pieces as indicated by his annotation:

> Do the Songs Without Words, for example by Mendelssohn, usually have two- or three-section song forms with an additional section (*Anhang*)? NB Sometimes both a closing period and an additional section.[21]

Annotations in the *Studienbuch* often follow this format: first he wrote a question and then, presumably as a result of a lesson with Kitzler or further personal investigation, answered himself.

Finally after nine months of instruction in forms for piano and string quartet, Kitzler began to introduce his pupil to orchestral composition. The exercises in instrumentation are interrupted by a bifolio (fol. 113–14) of five new compositions in piano score, presumably intended to be orchestrated. Only the fourth one returns on fol. 114v. in an arrangement for two clarinets and two bassoons. The instrumentation exercises also include an orchestration of the exposition of the opening movement of Beethoven's *Pathétique* Sonata. This and the Haydn *Kyrie* copied among the three-section song forms are the only music by other composers I have been able to identify in the entire miscellany.[21] Next he composed the March in D minor and Three Orchestral Pieces, orchestral experiments in two- and three-section song form. He sketched the Overture in G minor and Symphony in F minor in the *Studienbuch* and orchestrated them in separate manuscripts, both of which are now in the monastery library in Kremsmünster.[22] The last piece he wrote for Kitzler was Psalm 112 for double chorus, orchestra, and soloists, which occupied the month of June, and to which he refers on the last page of the miscellany: 'Overture, then Symphony, and Psalm completed 10 July 1863'.[23]

*   *   *

Because they have been published and are therefore easily accessible, the G minor Piano Sonata movement, the String Quartet, the Overture in G minor, and the F minor 'Student' Symphony – all Kitzler pieces – will serve as illustrations of some of the formal issues which Bruckner investigated. Of specific concern throughout much of the *Studienbuch* were the expansion of song forms into larger structures such as the Scherzo and Rondo, and the construction of sonata movements. Bruckner observed, for example, on fol. 93r., that the Scherzo portion of the third movement of the quartet is in two-section song form. The opening section has two periods of nine and ten measures respectively.[24] The second section of the Scherzo begins with an eleven measure period (mm. 20–30) followed by an expansion through repetition (*Erweiterung durch Wiederholung*) of the entire first section; the second period has an added measure and ends in the tonic.[25] The Trio is also in two-section song form with periods of eight and ten measures.

On fol. 88v. Bruckner describes the second movement of the quartet as 'Rondo Form: three-section song form with Trio, then repetition with variants'.[26] On fol. 94v. he provides a generic text-book definition of the same form:

> Small Rondo form is in three-section song form in the Theme Group and includes a Trio in two- or three-section song form; then repetition usually in variation with an additional section.[27]

In this movement the opening three-section song form has irregular periods of eleven, fifteen, and eleven measures respectively. The Trio (beginning at letter C) is also in three-section song form of eight, five, and seven measure periods. The return of the opening (mm. 58ff.) is, as the composer describes it, 'with variants' in periods of eleven, fourteen, and thirteen bars. The movement concludes with an eight-measure *Anhang* (m. 96ff.).

The first Rondo Finale, published by Nowak along with the other three movements in his 1955 edition, is described by Bruckner on fol. 94v. as being in 'Middle Rondo Form':

> Theme group in one or two periods etc., then a bridge group (or only a period), [then] a second period or group in the dominant
> Repetition of the theme group in the tonic, bridge[:] *only a connecting period* because now the second group stays in the tonic
> Theme group for the third time abbreviated with additional section[28]

When Bruckner first wrote out this definition, he described the *Themagruppe* as in two- or three-section song form. He crossed out 'in 2- or 3-section Song Form' and replaced it with 'in 1 or 2 periods etc.' probably to correspond to the compact circumstances of this particular movement. The theme group has only one period of eight measures, and the bridge to E Flat major ends in measure 21. The second theme, in the relative major, uses the opening phrase from the first group in augmentation, as Bruckner observes in the manuscript with the phrase *Vergrößerung des Thema[s]*.[29] A nine-measure passage returning to the tonic for the repeat of the opening theme begins at m. 44. The brevity of this passage was also noted by the composer on fol. 95r.: 'Here I was only able to make a short transition. Could this group be longer?'[30] He didn't answer his question. Since he made no alterations we can assume that he and his teacher were satisfied with his initial effort. Next follows a section of the movement omitted in Bruckner's description of the form: a repeat of the opening theme in the tonic (mm. 53–63) and a development (mm. 64–93).[31] As he prescribed, another repetition of the theme begins at m. 94; his *Zwischengruppe* occupies a mere seven measures before the return of the second theme in C major (m. 109). The *Anhang* beginning at letter H (m. 137) consists of a variation of the first development in the tonic, a final partial return of the opening theme (m. 166), and a brief coda (mm. 170–end).

The second Finale is in Large Rondo Form described on fol. 99r. as follows (corresponding measure numbers have been added in square brackets):

I. Theme group two- or three-section song form [1–18]
Bridge [19–32]
Second group (additional section?) [33–48]
Closing group [49–69]
First repetition of the theme group [70–87]
New middle group with developments and variations of the new motives [88–104]
Development Group, here of the principal motives [105–140]
Second repetition of the theme group, bridge, second group, closing group [141–206]
Third repetition of the theme group [207–214]
Additional section [215–233][32]

In this movement both the first and second groups are in two-section song form; the principal theme has periods of eight and ten measures and the second group in the relative major has two periods of eight measures (mm. 33–40 and 41–8). On fol. 99v. Bruckner asked himself whether the second group could have been in A flat or B flat major or F or G minor.[33] The A flat, F and G options are crossed out, presumably leaving B flat as an acceptable alternative. The second section of the development is distinguished from the first by an annotation above the staff over mm. 104 and 105: '*Motive Theile*'. Beginning at m. 141 the return of the two groups of thematic material proceeds exactly as Bruckner's formal description prescribes. This movement has a complete *Übergangsgruppe* between them (mm. 159–72) as opposed to the short 'connecting period' of the other Rondo. Under measure 197, towards the end of the return of the closing section, Bruckner observed that he could have copied mm. 57–69 verbatim on his way to the final return of the opening theme in C minor (m. 207); in the interests of variety he opted not to.[34] As was the case in the other Finale, the *Anhang* begins with a partial repetition of the opening theme group in the tonic.

The *Studienbuch* exercises in the individual sections of sonata form (fol. 69r.–78v.) illustrate that Bruckner studied a two-part classical Sonata structure: exposition (repeated) – development/recapitulation. It should come as no surprise that his earliest exercises in the form contain no evidence of the extended three-group Sonata movements characteristic of the later symphonies. His early attempts at expositions have two clear thematic groups (*Themagruppe* and *Gesangsgruppe* or *Gesangsperiode*) separated by a bridge group (*Übergangsgruppe*). A concise closing section or *Schlußgruppe* was composed at the same time as the *Gesangsthema*. The longest of these combination *Gesangs-Schlußgruppen* is thirty-three measures. When he set about to write an entire movement – i.e. not in instalments – he began to experiment with extending the closing section. In the G minor Sonata (fol. 79r.–82v.) edited by Walburga Litschauer in volume 12/3 of the Collected Works, the first group in three-section song form has fourteen measures (phrases of four, six, and four bars) and the second is an eight-measure period in F major (two phrases of four bars, mm. 29–36). Both groups are consistent in length and structure with the preceding exercises. Beginning at m. 37 there is a thirty-two-bar *Schlußgruppe* which begins in F major and moves to the dominant, D, introducing a new melodic idea in the left hand at m. 62. This is by far the longest section of the exposition and is extended when it returns in the tonic in the recapitulation, m. 148–83.

In his next sonata movement, the *Allegro moderato* of the String Quartet, the exposition again begins with a *Themagruppe* in three-section song form, an *Übergangsgruppe*, and a *Gesangsthema* consisting of a single period with two phrases. The first and second groups are again compact – sixteen (phrases of six–four–six) and twelve (phrases of six–six) measures respectively. The closing section, beginning at letter C (m. 41), is longer – twenty-five measures. Like its counterpart in the Piano Sonata movement, it features a new melodic idea with a brief reference to G minor at m. 44; in contrast to the sonata movement there is a return of the second group at m. 60. In the recapitulation this closing section is shortened to twenty-two measures, and the figure which had been introduced at m. 44 has less presence. Both the G-minor Sonata and the quartet movements have brief codas beginning at m. 184 and m. 174 respectively.

In the Overture in G minor, completed a few months later, Bruckner counted the number of measures in each section at the end of the sketch: fourteen for the first group (mm. 23–36), twenty-seven for the bridge (mm. 37–63), twenty-seven for the second group (mm. 64–90) and forty-four for the closing section (mm. 91–135), etc.[35] The *Schlußgruppe* is again the longest section of the exposition; here it is set apart by a double barline and a return to *Tempo Imo* (m. 91). Its motivic connection with preceding material is made explicit in its first two measures with their *fortissimo* chords and sixteenth-note string runs – a clear reference to the bridge which opened in a similar fashion at m. 37. The composer points out, in the sketch, that the subsequent melodic material (mm. 96ff.) is an 'augmentation of the opening motive [of the composition] enharmonically in E major'.[36]

In the first reading of the Overture, which Bruckner completed on 4 January 1863, the *Schlußgruppe* was abbreviated in the recapitulation to twenty measures, though it retained most of the augmentation of the opening theme (mm. 238ff.). In this reading the work ended with a forty-six measure coda.[37] On 6 January Bruckner added the slow introduction, which was not in the sketch, and on 22 January he completed a new ending to the piece.[38] He restored and augmented the *Schlußgruppe* to forty-eight measures and reduced the coda (mm. 281–end) to thirteen including the final return of the opening theme (m. 281) which was part of the original coda. The result is a balance in the movement similar to that of the G minor Piano Sonata. In the new reading of the Overture the *Schlußgruppe* is varied to the point that the augmentation of the opening motive, so obvious in the exposition, is eliminated.

The sonata movements in the F minor 'Student' Symphony, completed on 26 May, are far more extensive and harmonically adventuresome than anything Bruckner had yet done for Kitzler.[39] In the exposition of the opening movement, the *Schlußgruppe* (mm. 146–208) is similar in proportion and function to its counterpart in the String Quartet. In the symphony its connection to preceding material is made explicit with the melodic reference (first in inversion) in A flat major to the opening theme (mm. 180ff.). The structure of the Finale is closer to that of the final reading of the Overture in that both the exposition and recapitulation sections have proportionally long *Schlußgruppen* – approximately one-third of the exposition – set apart from the *Gesangsgruppe* by a *ritenuto* and return to *Tempo Imo* (mm. 92 and 297).[40] Specific reference to the first theme is reserved in the closing section of the exposition until the very end (mm. 137ff.). In the recapitulation the first theme is heard immediately in augmentation in the winds (mm. 299ff.).

* * *

Although it is tempting (especially in the context of his expansion of the closing group in the expositions of these pieces) to look for precursors of Bruckner's future structural innovations in the exercises, there is no evidence in either the *Kitzler Studienbuch* or the Kremsmünster manuscripts, that he saw them as anything other than applications of the prescriptions of standard nineteenth-century *Formenlehre* manuals. In fact, the contents of the *Studienbuch* demonstrate that, under Kitzler, Bruckner obtained a systematic and thorough grounding in both *Formenlehre* and orchestration. For the early 1860s, it was already a conservative training, a fact of which both Kitzler and his pupil were aware. Describing the studies much later in his memoirs Kitzler wrote:

> Before the orchestration exercises, I instructed Bruckner in the structure of musical composition with the help of a now out-of-print *Formenlehre* by Richter; I took him from eight-measure periods through all the necessary studies to the Sonata. ... In orchestration we used Marx whose examples, however, don't go further than Meyerbeer.[41]

Kitzler also says that, in conjunction with their studies, they investigated the Beethoven piano sonatas, and that Bruckner became more *au courant* by studying *Tannhäuser* which Kitzler conducted in Linz in February 1863.[42]

As far as specific text books are concerned, the Richter to which Kitzler refers is Ernst Friedrich Richter's *Grundzüge der musikalischen Form und ihre Analyse* (Leipzig: Georg Wigand, 1852), and the Marx is Adolph Bernhard Marx, *Die Lehre von musikalischen Komposition, praktisch theoretisch*, in four volumes (Leipzig: Breitkopf und Härtel) which went through a number of editions beginning in 1837. In a letter of 8 October 1863 Bruckner told his friend, Rudolf Weinwurm, that he [Bruckner] didn't own Marx, but Kitzler did.[43] Bruckner went on to say that he himself owned two volumes – a *Formenlehre* and an orchestration text – which he describes as 'quite dense' (*ziemlich gedrängt*) of Johann Christian Lobe's *Lehrbuch der musikalischen Komposition* published in four volumes (Leipzig: Breitkopf und Härtel) beginning in 1850.[44]

So far as can be ascertained at present, neither the formal definitions nor the exercises in the *Kitzler Studienbuch* can be traced to a specific text. Kitzler and his pupil did not follow the prescribed order of study of any of the three treatises in question; they apparently culled and collated from a variety of sources. Richter's little book provided the *modus operandi* as described in his Preface:

> The author recently prepared the following text for his composition students, and it is being published with them in mind. It is not my intention to treat this important aspect of composition [i.e. Form] in as detailed and extensive a manner as modern composition treatises. Rather, because his experience has been that only the practical road can achieve the objective, [the author] has tried to include the most general and important principles as well as the shortest and clearest possible directions.[45]

Richter advises students to proceed as follows:

> If much can be translated into musical sense, into a feeling for rhythm and symmetry, or antecedent and consequent phrases, the beginner must be prepared, before he proceeds to complete compositions, to investigate details in a variety of experiments. These should include, for example, the structure of basic periods, with antecedent and consequent, and the various cadences described herein; then the combination of such periods into whole pieces with specific modulations.[46]

Richter does not include harmony and counterpoint in his treatise. In comparison to Marx and Lobe, his fifty-two pages are remarkably succinct. This approach, of course, is exactly what Bruckner needed in 1861 after his Sechter studies in fundamental bass and counterpoint, and credit must go to Kitzler for matching his pupil with the appropriate text. Throughout, the contents of the *Studienbuch* have the appearance of exercises in composition, rather than studies in theory and analysis. In this sense they reflect a greater philosophical affinity with Richter's little composition treatise, than with Lobe's and Marx's more comprehensive theoretical, one might even say pedantic treatments.

At the outset Kitzler and Bruckner followed Richter exactly until fol. 9v. At that point they must have turned to another text – probably with input from Lobe. Richter does not discuss two- and three-section song form, and treats the subsequent forms found in the *Studienbuch* before the Sonata in a cursory manner. The order of study – two- and three-section song form, instrumental forms with Trios, Etude, Theme and Variations, and Rondo – follows the applicable chapters in the second and third volumes of Marx.[47] The reliance on two- and three-section song form as a basic building block for larger structures is consistent with him. Lobe is cited on fol. 41v. in the variation exercises for subdividing phrases into two-measure *Abschnitten*, possibly a reference to the variation section of his treatise.[48]

The nomenclature for the individual sections of the rondo and sonata movements – *Themagruppe, Übergangsgruppe, Gesangsgruppe, Schlußgruppe, Mittelsatzgruppe, Anhang* – is Lobe's.[49] Neither Lobe nor Marx discusses Rondo specifically in terms of Small, Middle and Large Forms, although Marx groups his Rondo types into small (*kleinen*) and large (*grössern*). Bruckner's (Kitzler's?) Small Rondo Form corresponds to the second of Marx's five Rondo types.[50] The Middle and Large Rondo forms in the *Studienbuch* are syntheses of Lobe's generic description of the form of a string quartet Finale and Richter's analysis of Rondo form.[51] Lobe prescribes beginning the development (which he refers to as *Mittelsatzgruppe*) of a Rondo with a repeat of the opening theme in the tonic as Bruckner does with his Middle Rondo of the Quartet mm. 53ff. Bruckner's formal description of the Large Rondo resembles Lobe's analysis of the Finale of Beethoven's String Quartet in F major, Op. 18, no. 1, with the exception that neither Lobe nor Beethoven subdivided the development into two sections, the first one based on new material.[52] Richter suggested beginning the development with 'new Motives'.[53] Lobe does point out that the *Anhang* of a Rondo can include an abbreviated repetition of the opening theme, a practice which Bruckner follows in both quartet Finales. During the studies in sonata form, as has already been mentioned, Bruckner consulted Lobe; his text is mentioned at this point in the *Studienbuch*.[54] For orchestration, as Kitzler observed in his memoirs, they returned to Marx who is often cited in these pages.[55]

Considerable credit is due Kitzler. Apart from identifying appropriate texts and synthesizing material, he must have been able to interact with Bruckner who was, after all, something of an unusual pupil: a world-class organist with an exceptional grasp of counterpoint and superb improvisational skills, yet with a professional musical experience confined primarily to churches in the rural reaches of Upper Austria. Kitzler had to bring Bruckner up to date with contemporary practice (i.e. with Wagner), introduce him to much of the standard non-liturgical repertoire (to Beethoven's music in particular), and instruct him in the fundamentals of form and orchestration.[56] These objectives were accomplished to the satisfaction of both teacher and pupil in less than two years. Kitzler reported in his memoirs that:

> one day he [Bruckner] asked me when he would be set free. When I replied that it could happen any day because he had already overtaken his teacher who had nothing more to offer him, he didn't want to let it happen so easily. He invited myself and my wife for a ride in the country and afterwards brought us to the Jägerhaus in the Kirnberger forest where the official liberation took place at a festive meal.[57]

Perhaps the most telling evidence of Kitzler's impact is that Bruckner's lifelong devotion to the music of Wagner stems from this period.

As far as the studies in form and orchestration are concerned, it is impossible to know precisely what passed between teacher and pupil. Kitzler was almost certainly responsible for the order of study and interpretation of the texts. The orchestral scores from the end of the study period – the Overture, F minor Symphony, and Psalm 112 – have dynamics, phrase markings, and string bowings giving the manuscripts the appearance of having been corrected or proof-read. Some of these are in a foreign hand which, in the absence of a positive identification, one assumes is Kitzler's.[58] It is logical to expect that he, with his experience as both cellist and conductor, would have advised Bruckner the organist about these matters. There is little evidence in the *Studienbuch* itself of a foreign hand, and no evidence that Kitzler corrected any of the exercises extensively. He appears to have followed Richter's advice and encouraged his pupil to experiment with a free hand, restricting his own role to that of sounding board and synthesizer of information.

*   *   *

The preceding remarks have only scratched the surface in terms of what can be learned from the *Kitzler Studienbuch*. When the manuscript is more accessible, it will no doubt reward investigators with a plethora of information, not only about Bruckner, but also about nineteenth-century theory, analysis, and pedagogy. For now it is appropriate to conclude this overview with a few observations about the significance of the miscellany in the larger context of Bruckner's career. With the possible exception of the March in D Minor, the Three Orchestra Pieces, the Overture, and the F Minor Symphony, the Kitzler exercises were never intended for public scrutiny.[59] A few, such as the String Quartet, are finished to a point that they can be performed; most are drafts in more preliminary states of completion. As such they are invaluable documents for the study of Bruckner's working methods and, in fact, many of the procedures in evidence in them are found throughout his Linz scores.[60]

One aspect of the Kitzler studies deserves further comment because of the notoriety it has obtained in the literature about Bruckner's later working procedures: the so-called metrical numbers which he wrote under his scores in the process of counting measures within periods. There is no question that this phenomenon began with Kitzler; the earliest surviving Bruckner manuscript with these numbers is the composition score of *Du Bist Wie Eine Blume*, which dates from early December 1861 – precisely the beginning of the Kitzler study period.[61] Exx. 1.1 through 1.4 above are typical of Bruckner's use of the numbers as an analytical tool in the *Studienbuch*. They are usually confined to passages where he was specifically concerned with the issue of phrase or period length (Exx. 1.1–1.3) or to passages where he struggled with the material as evidenced by deletions of various kinds (Ex. 1.4).[62] In the manuscript, mm. 28–30 of the song in the fourth example contain a series of erasures and corrections which are not evident in the transcription. They are the only measures in the composition with metrical numbers (4, 1, 2).

As the 1860s progressed, Bruckner used these metrical numbers less and less frequently to the point where they all but disappeared. None of the three great Mass scores – in D, E, and F minor – or the 'Nullte' Symphony score (1869), for example, had such numbers when they were first completed. Measure counting by periods began to appear as a regular feature in Bruckner's manuscripts again in the early 1870s with the B flat Symphony sketch and Second Symphony sources.[63] He inserted the numbers into the scores of the three Linz Masses and the First Symphony during his first revision period of 1876–7.[64] At that time the numbers were an analytical tool which he applied as a result of studies of the music of Mozart and Beethoven.[65] It is worthy of observation that, during this period of intense self-analysis, he returned to his musical roots – the Viennese classicists. In the process he systematically applied an analytical tool which he had learned fifteen years earlier from the teacher who introduced him to the fundamentals of classical form in the first place.

Bruckner received an extremely thorough and systematic, albeit conservative, grounding in both form and orchestration under Otto Kitzler. For the remainder of his life he regarded his 'liberation' from Kitzler as the beginning of his career as a professional composer. It would be interesting to know if either of them speculated, as they celebrated that July afternoon in 1863 in the Kirnberger forest, about what a career it would become.

Notes

1. Fugue in D minor (WAB 25), *Du bist wie eine Blume* (WAB 64), and *Der Abendhimmel* (WAB 55). WAB numbers refer to Renate Grasberger, *Werkverzeichnis Anton Bruckner* (Tutzing: Hans Schneider, 1977).
2. Autograph date on fol. 1r. of the autograph score of the cantata in the archive of the Maria-Empfängnis Dom, Linz. Otto Kitzler was born in Dresden, 16 March 1834, and died in Graz, 6 September 1915. For more on his relationship with Bruckner see Otto Kitzler, *Musikalische Erinnerungen mit Briefen von Wagner, Brahms, Bruckner, und Richard Pohl* (Brünn: Karl Winiker, 1904), pp. 29ff.
3. The miscellany is one of the few major Bruckner manuscripts remaining in private possession. I am very grateful to the owner, who wishes to remain anonymous, for allowing access to the miscellany and granting permission to reproduce and report on its contents.
4. Leopold Nowak, ed. *Bruckner Sämtliche Werke*, 13/1: *Streich-Quartett in C Moll*; and 10a: *Symphonie in F Moll, Kritische Bericht*, pp. 65ff. Bruckner composed both pieces as exercises for Kitzler.
5. Hans Jancik, ed., *Bruckner Sämtliche Werke*, 12/4, *Vier Orchesterstücke*; and 12/3, Walburga Litschauer, ed., *Werke für Klavier zu zwei Händen*, pp. 29ff.
6. The musical examples were prepared by Mr Jack Vees at the Yale Center for Studies in Music Technology. The original exercises often include very little alteration and reworking of material. These transcriptions contain the final reading of any erasures and corrections.
7. Above the exercise in Ex. 1.2 he wrote an alternate cadence – this one an incomplete (*unvollkommene*) cadence on the tonic – for the end of the first phrase (at the NB and X, m. 4). He observed in the right-hand margin at the end of lines 5 and 6 that the new cadence was preferable to the one on V in the example.

8. Fol. 11r.: '2[-]theilige Liedform, 2 Perioden, jede zu acht Tacten, woran jede aus einem einzigen Ganzen ohne Wiederholung besteht'.
    Fol. 12r.:
    'Dreitheilige Liedform.
    1.   Periode für sich ein Ganzes
    2.   „   neu
    3.   „   Wiederholung der 1ten Periode'.
9. The types of exercises overlap throughout the miscellany. Bruckner sometimes anticipated issues which later became specific subjects of investigation and often returned to structural types from early investigations in subsequent studies. In the first group of exercises here, for example, the *Lied* in three-section song form on fol. 12r. has periods of different lengths (ten and eight measures), and fol. 13r. contains a Waltz with a repeat (a type of expansion) within the second period. These are structural issues which are the focus of exercises in groups two and three.
10. This does not imply that three-section song forms throughout the miscellany have irregular phrases.
11. Fol. 17v. Bruckner had been acquainted with this Mass since his days in St Florian when he copied part of it, possibly in 1846 (St Florian Stiftsbibliothek 20/17).
12. *Bruckner Sämtliche Werke*, 12/4.
13. Fol. 26v.:
    'Wiederholt kann:
    a[.]   eine ganze Periode durch einf[ache]. Repe[tition] oder gesteigert oder tiefer verschie[det] in Harmonisierung u[nd] Modulationen
    b.   ein ganzes Glied
    c.   ein Theil eines Gliedes.'
14. This exercise is one of the more complete (in the sense that the inner voices are filled in) compositions in this part of the miscellany.
15. It has been dated anywhere from 1856 to 1868. Renate Grasberger, WAB, p. 135, for example, assigns the piece to St Florian or Linz around 1856. It belongs chronologically and stylistically with the exercises in the *Kitzler Studienbuch* and should be dated 1862 or 1863. The piece is written on very large (255 × 330mm.) 12-line, grey-staff, oblong format paper which Bruckner used in the *Studienbuch* between the spring of 1862 and April 1863. This paper is found in none of his other Linz sources. Paul Hawkshaw, The Manuscript Sources for Anton Bruckner's Linz Works: A Study of His Working Methods from 1856-1868, Ph.D. diss., Columbia University, 1984, pp. 18 and 74. The piece will serve as an illustration here because it is easier to reproduce in facsimile than the other exercises as a result of its location in the Music Collection of the Austrian National Library (Wn).
16. Fol. 39r. An illustration of this type of expansion will be provided with the discussion of the string quartet.
17. See note 5.
18. Leopold Nowak, ed. *Bruckner Sämtliche Werke*, 12. *Rondo C – Moll für Streichquartett* contains the second Rondo.
19. To the best of my knowledge, neither the song nor the piano pieces have yet been published.
20. Fol. 107v.:
    '?Die Lieder ohne Worte z[um] B[eispiel] v[on]. Mendelssohn haben meistens Liedform 2[–] o[der] 3[–]theilig mit Anhang? NB Zuweilen auch Schlußperiode u[nd] Anhang.'
21. Fol. 7v., ll. 10–14, contains an exercise labelled 'Männerchor / Adagio' with an annotation '?drüben v[on]. Messe As'. I have not been able to identify the Mass.
22. Kr C56.5 and C56.7.
23. 'Ouverture – dann Symphonie u[nd] Psalm beschlossen / 10. Juli 1863'. Otherwise

the Psalm is nowhere in evidence in the *Studienbuch*. Its autograph score is now preserved as Wn Mus. Hs. 3156.

24. The first of these has two phrases (*Glieder*) of four and five measures; the second has two phrases of four measures and a two measure extension (*Verlängerung*) (mm. 18–19). Bruckner did not number the measures here as he did in some places in the *Studienbuch* nor did he analyse the movement beyond pointing out the two-section song form.

25. A note in Bruckner's hand at the bottom of fol. 93r. observes that the Scherzo portion of the movement is in two- as opposed to three-section song form because the entire second section (mm. 20–end) is repeated. Without the second set of repeat dots the form would be AABA or *3-theilige Liedform*. See the discussion of the opening section of the Andante below. The extremely irregular period lengths of this movement and, in fact, of much of the quartet are not characteristic of the Kitzler exercises. Perhaps he felt freer to experiment in complete pieces.

26. '*Andante in Rondoform u[nd] zwar 3-theil[i]ge Liedform mit Trio, dann Repetition mit Variand[e].*'

27. '*Die kleine Rondoform ist 3[-]theilige Liedform in Themagruppe, der sich ein Trio in 2[-] o[der] 3[-]theil[i]ge[r] Liedform anschließt; dann Repetition meist in Variande mit Anhang.*'

28. '*Mittlere Rondoform mit Themagruppe in 1 o[der] 2 Perioden etc. dann Übergangsgruppe (o[der] nur Periode), Gesangsperiode- o[der] auch Gruppe in Dom[inante] Repetition der Themagruppe in Ton[ica,] Übergangsgruppe eig[en]tl[ich] n[ur] Zwischen-Periode weil in Tonica jetzt d[ie] Gesangsgruppe bleibt Themagruppe zum 3ten Mal verkürzt mit Anhang.*'

29. Fol. 95r.

30. '*Ich durfte hier nur einen kurzen Übergang machen. Dürfte dieß auch eine lange Gruppe werden?*'

31. As will be illustrated below, this section of the movement was part of the form described in the text books Bruckner was using. Why he omitted it in his description here is not clear; he (or perhaps Kitzler?) may have perceived the development as an optional addition to a prescribed form. Earlier in the miscellany (fol. 67r.–68v.) he wrote development sections (without the repeat of the opening theme in the tonic) for Rondos as additions to previously completed compositions, almost as though they could be inserted *ad libitum*.

32. '*Rondo in größeren Form.*
    I. Themagruppe 2[-] o[der] 3-theilige Liedform, Übergangsgruppe, Gesangsgruppe (Anhang?) Schlußgruppe[.] I. Repetition der Themagruppe Neue Mittelsatzgruppe, wobei Durchführungen u[nd] Varianden der neuen Motive hier kommen, Durchführungsgruppe, hier von den Hauptmotiven
    II. Repetition der Themagruppe, Übergangsgruppe, Gesangsgruppe, Schlußgruppe,
    III. Repetition der Themagruppe, Anhang.'

33. Fol. 99v.: '*?Gesangsgruppe auch Asdur, Bdur, o[der] Fmoll (Fmoll, Gmoll)?*'

34. Fol. 102v.: '*NB Von [m. 197] hätte es Note für Note vom 1. Theile abgeschrieben werden können. Nur der Mannigfaltigkeit wegen verändert.*'

35. Fol. 150r. The closing section has forty-five measures in the completed score. The slow introduction was not part of the sketch.

36. Fol. 145v. The sketch is a two-line treble/bass continuity draft. He wrote '*Verlängerung I. Motiv*' above the staff and '*oder enharmonisch Edur.*' under the bass.

37. The piece was conceived in this manner in the sketch for Kitzler; as Bruckner indicated on fol. 150r., the coda was originally to have forty-two measures. The 4 January date is at the end of the first reading in the autograph score, Kr C56.5, fol.

20v. Arthur D. Walker included the first reading of the score at the end of his edition of the piece: Anton Bruckner, *Overture G Minor* (London and New York: Ernst Eulenburg, 1971), pp. 62–74.

38.   The dates appear in Kr C56.5, fols. 2v. and 24r. respectively. He wrote out the new ending on two bifolios preserved at the end of the autograph score.

39.   The date is in Kr C56.7[a]., fol. 1r.

40.   The autograph manuscript of the Overture has a double bar line at the return to *Tempo Imo* in both the exposition and recapitulation. The symphony autograph does not.

41.   Kitzler, *Erinnerungen*, p. 29.

42.   In addition to the orchestration of the *Pathétique* Sonata, Bruckner refers to Beethoven on two other occasions in the Kitzler miscellany: fol. 43r. (variation exercises) and fol. 66v. (Rondos). No pieces are specified.

43.   Andrea Harrandt, ed., *Brückner Sämtliche Werke*, 24/1, *Briefe 1852–1886*, p. 37.

44.   Bruckner owned volumes 1 and 2 first published in 1850 and 1855 respectively.

45.   Richter, *Grundzüge*, foreword.

46.   Ibid., 52.

47.   Volume 2 first appeared in 1847 and volume 3 in 1857. The sections which correspond approximately to these pages of the *Kitzler Studienbuch* are vol. 2, pp. 69-95, and vol. 3, pp. 26–137.

48.   Lobe, *Lehrbuch*, 1, p. 171ff.

49.   Lobe, *Lehrbuch*, 1, pp. 315-16 (Sonata) and 331 (Rondo). In sonata form Lobe reserves the term *Mittelsatz* for the development, referring to the recapitulation as the *Repetition*. For Lobe the combination *Mittelsatzgruppe* with *Repetition* is the second part (*zweiter Theil*) of the sonata form, which is Bruckner's conception of the form as applied in the *Kitzler Studienbuch*. The composer does not employ the term Repetition with reference to the sonata.

50.   Marx, *Kompositionslehre* 3, pp. 123ff.

51.   Lobe, *Lehrbuch*, 1, pp. 331-3 and Richter, *Grundzüge*, pp. 38-9.

52.   Lobe, *Lehrbuch*, 1, p. 332.

53.   Richter, *Grundzüge*, p. 38.

54.   *The Kitzler Studienbuch*, fol. 69r., refers to Lobe, *Lehrbuch* 1:294–5. The subject is the construction of themes for sonata movements.

55.   *Kitzler Studienbuch*, fol. 125v. (Marx, *Kompositionslehre* 4:70); 130r. (ibid. 4:107 and 92); and fol. 144v. (ibid. 4[?]:189).

56.   In St Florian, which had an active musical establishment, Bruckner had encountered an extensive, albeit conservative, repertoire of Austrian church music including many works by Michael and Josef Haydn as well as Mozart. Schubert's secular music, as well as both the secular and sacred music of Mendelssohn was also cultivated at the monastery. His lifelong devotion to both composers stems from the St Florian years. Beethoven's music did not become a regular feature on the monastery programs until after the middle of the century. Walter Schulten, 'Anton Bruckners künstlerische Entwicklung in der St. Florianer Zeit, 1845–1855'. Ph.D. diss., Mainz, 1957.

57.   Kitzler, *Erinnerungen*, pp. 30f.

58.   Paul Hawkshaw, ed. *Bruckner Sämtliche Werke*, 20/5 (Psalm 112), Foreword.

59.   There is evidence that he tried to have some of the Kitzler pieces performed. On 8 October 1863 he wrote to Rudolf Weinwurm that he had shown some works (including the F minor Symphony) to the conductor Franz Lachner with no success. Harrandt, op. cit., p. 37. Manuscripts of the Overture (Music Collection of the Wiener Stadt- und Landesbibliothek (Wst) 3793/c), March in D minor and *Three Orchestra Pieces* (Wst 3794/c), and the Symphony (Wst 3795/c and Kremsmünster Benediktinerstift C56.7(b)) were prepared by an anonymous professional copyist.

Hawkshaw. Manuscript Sources, pp. 319–20. It is not likely that Bruckner would have absorbed the copying expense if he considered these pieces merely as exercises for Kitzler.

60. Ibid., pp. 107ff. and Paul Hawkshaw ed. *Bruckner Sämtliche Werke 20*, Critical Report.

61. Wn Mus. Hs. 3166.

62. In the Overture sketch on fol. 150r. he counted the measures in individual sections – first group, bridge, second group, closing section – of the piece and then added the totals for each of the two principal parts of the form (exposition – development/recapitulation). Here the concern seems to have been balance between sections and the overall length of the movement. Curious is that the total number of measures in the sketch (270) remained constant whatever adjustments Bruckner made to the individual sections. Eventually the slow introduction was added, and the sonata portion of the movement ended up with 271 measures. I believe this type of counting reflects a different, though related, analytical concern from the metrical numbers. Counting of measures in entire movements and large sections of movements was an old habit of Bruckner's from the St Florian days and stayed with him at least as late as the Mass in F Minor. Its implications in terms of Bruckner's long-range structural planning have yet to be investigated. Paul Hawkshaw. 'Weiteres über die Arbeitsweise Bruckners während seiner Linzer Jahre: Der Inhalt von Kremsmünster C56.2.' in *Bruckner Symposion Bericht*, 1992, p. 146.

63. Wn Mus. Hs. 6018 contains the B flat Symphony Sketch. I am grateful to William Carragan who drew my attention to the presence of the numbers in this source. Precisely what caused Bruckner to return to this practice is not clear. These numbers certainly had nothing to do with his illness of 1867 or number mania as has often been speculated. See for example Derek Watson, *Bruckner* (London: J. M. Dent & Sons, 1975), pp. 22–3 and 54.

64. Because he never revised the 'Nullte' Symphony, its score has no numbers.

65. For more on the composer's use of the numbers for analytical purposes see Timothy L. Jackson 'Bruckner's Metrical Numbers', in *Nineteenth Century Music* (Spring 1990), 101–31; and Paul Hawkshaw. 'An Anatomy of Change: Anton Bruckner's Revisions to the Mass in F Minor', in *Bruckner Studies* (Cambridge University Press, 1997), p. 17.

2 Bruckner's *Oktaven*: the problem of consecutives, doubling, and orchestral voice-leading*

Timothy L. Jackson

> 17 Think not that I am come to destroy the law, or the
> prophets: I am not come to destroy, but to fulfil.
> 18 For verily I say unto you, Till heaven and earth
> pass, one jot or one tittle shall in no wise pass from
> the law, till all be fulfilled.
>
> *Matthew*, 5, 17–18

In honour of the 100th anniversary of Bruckner's death (1896–1996)

It has long been an article of faith in Bruckner scholarship that the final revisions of the First, Third, Fourth, and Eighth Symphonies in the late 1880s and early 1890s were prompted by the conductor Herman Levi's 'rejection' of the Eighth Symphony in October 1887. Although Levi's opinion that the instrumentation of the Eighth Symphony was 'impossible' must have played a role in Bruckner's decision to revise it, Levi had little impact on the specifics of the revision. Furthermore, it is clear that Bruckner had already decided to revise the Fourth Symphony – employing his former students and disciples the Schalk brothers and Ferdinand Löwe as assistants – *before* Levi's 'rejection'.[1] In the present chapter, I shall propose that Bruckner's revisions to his disciples' re-orchestrations of the Third and Fourth Symphonies, and his re-orchestrations of the First and Eighth Symphonies were prompted by a consideration totally unrelated to Levi's

*An earlier, abbreviated version of this chapter was published in *Music and Letters*, 78 (1997), 391–408 and read at the National AMS Meeting in Pittsburgh in November 1992. The author gratefully acknowledges support from a NEH Grant to College Teachers in 1997–8 and a Senior Fulbright Teaching and Research Grant, which facilitated revision of the article and additional research in Austria in 1994–5.

practical concerns, namely the theoretical problem of consecutive octaves in an orchestral context. As a consequence of hearing orchestral performances of his symphonies, Bruckner became concerned that momentary doublings were creating the effect of parallel octaves thus resulting in 'bad' orchestral voice leading.

The true importance of Bruckner's analysis of 'octaves' for all aspects of future Bruckner research cannot be understated.[2] It provides a rationale for many of the composer's post-1888 revisions; it also sheds light on the true nature of his alleged 'collaboration' with his disciples, as well as his reasons for wishing to terminate that 'collaboration' c. 1890. For reasons to be presented below, I believe the word 'collaboration' – with its suggestion that the disciples enjoyed a certain autonomy with the composer's blessing – to be inaccurate: I dispute the designation of the Schalks and Löwe as 'collaborators'; as long as they enjoyed Bruckner's blessing, they were, at most, assistants. On the other hand, as soon as they began to revise and publish his music without his permission (c. 1890), they became neither assistants nor collaborators.

Bruckner was prepared to go to great lengths in the pursuit of 'correct' voice leading; indeed, after c. 1888, in order to ensure that his orchestrations met his stringent test for 'correctness', he was willing to delay still all-too-rare orchestral performances and pay out of his own pocket for expensive recopying of parts. After the first performance of the new arrangement of the Fourth Symphony on 22 January 1888 under Richter, I hypothesize that it was Bruckner's dissatisfaction with the effect of unwanted consecutives that prompted him to immediately (in February) undertake extensive revisions of the orchestration. As the orchestral voice leading was 'regulated' and the unwanted consecutives were eliminated, Bruckner carefully kept track of the revisions in his pocket calendar.[3] So concerned was he about this issue that for the next performance under Levi he footed the bill for re-copying the parts himself. Two years later, for the same reason, Bruckner 'took away' the score of his First Symphony from Richter and the Vienna Philharmonic and delayed its revival for a year in order to 'correct' the voice leading. Again, Bruckner 'regulated' the voice leading with the utmost care and thoroughness.

Some scholars have believed that Bruckner employed the Schalks and Löwe to help him re-orchestrate the Third and Fourth Symphonies because he thought that they possessed the practical, orchestral experience that he himself lacked. Without denigrating the disciples' musicianship, I do not believe that Bruckner ever considered them to be his superiors in the art of orchestration; on the contrary, in seeking their help with the revision of the Third and Fourth Symphonies, he gave them instructions, allowed them to assist him with score preparation, and then 'corrected' what they had done in light of his own ideas on orchestration and orchestral voice leading. Only once Bruckner's theoretical concern with the issue of octaves is understood will it be possible to explain the rationale for his revisions to their re-orchestrations, and also his dissatisfaction with their work to the point that he deliberately sought to exclude them from his revisional process. Furthermore, a full understanding of the significance of the 'octaves' issue will illuminate its impact on Bruckner's late orchestral style and his extensive use of voice leading diagrams in his post-1890 scores.

*   *   *

'I was officially assigned the job of tonal-modal janitor, mopping up parallel fifths all day, each year ...'.[4] With these words, the American composer Donald Martino condemned the 'traditional' teaching of harmony and counterpoint, with its oppressive focus on eliminating consecutives. While many professional theorists and composers spend much of their working lives engaged in this kind of 'janitorial' labour, remarkably little attention has been paid to the complex issues surrounding consecutives. All too frequently, in harmony and counterpoint classes, consecutive octaves and unisons are unequivocally disallowed. But the *practice* of the great composers speaks against such simplistic and one-dimensional rejection; *all* consecutives were neither considered 'bad' nor forbidden. The comments in Brahms's well-known compendium of *Oktaven und Quinten* reveal that, for him – and for the many composers he cites – not all consecutives are intrinsically 'evil' – indeed, some are even 'good' and 'beautiful'.[5] But if Brahms's collection now has achieved more general currency through Schenker's edition and commentary, his perception that not all octaves and fifths are 'bad' has not. Bruckner's study of *Oktaven* in Mozart's *Requiem*, Beethoven's Third and Ninth Symphonies, and in his own music remains, of course, much less well known.

As we shall see, Bruckner was concerned with a very specific compositional problem: in free composition, when does intermittent doubling become 'bad' consecutives, and when is it a 'desired' form of highlighting? Bruckner recognized that such intermittent doubling, generally of two notes, far from being 'forbidden' might be 'desirable' in certain contexts in order to bring out or highlight particular voice leading strands. His preoccupation with this question had practical ramifications for his own compositional process; keeping track of momentary consecutives was intimately connected with the final revisions of the F minor Mass, and the First, Third, Fourth, and Eighth Symphonies. Additionally, by c. 1889, analytical diagrams showing 'permitted' or 'desired' momentary doublings had become an integral part of Bruckner's compositional process. This procedure of identifying momentary doublings influenced the late revisions of the First, Third, Fourth, and Eighth Symphonies, and the compositional genesis of the Ninth Symphony and other last works.

Bruckner's investigation of 'permitted' or 'desired' doubling concerned the relationship between voices and figurative instrumental accompaniment and momentary doubling between conceptually independent orchestral 'voices' – a 'voice' being defined as either an instrument or consistently doubling group of instruments. Thus, for example, in an orchestral context, if the first horn momentarily doubled the violins, Bruckner wanted to 'keep track' and 'approve' of this doubling. But if he did not 'like' a particular doubling, he would revise the voice leading to eliminate it. In the present study, we shall reconstruct Bruckner's studies of such momentary doublings in the Mozart *Requiem* and Beethoven *Eroica* (c. 1876–7) and trace the ramifications of these studies upon his own revisional and compositional processes.

Recently, the controversy concerning the 'authenticity' of the last versions of the Third and Fourth Symphonies has flared up again, re-igniting the *Bruckner Streit* of the 1930s. Because Franz and Josef Schalk and Ferdinand Löwe participated in the re-orchestration of these symphonies, the first editions were greeted with suspicion if not outright rejection. With regard to the third, published version of the Fourth Symphony (1889), Benjamin Korstvedt has countered that 'Bruckner himself never evinced any doubt about the authority of this text; to the contrary, he authorized its publication, took part in preparing the premiere, and attended at least two later performances'. Bruckner's letters seem to provide further evidence in support of Korstvedt's thesis that the composer was 'satisfied' with the third published versions of both the Third and Fourth Symphonies. For example, in a letter of 1 January 1891 to August Göllerich, the composer stated unequivocally that he had 'grown fond' of the new Third Symphony. Writing to the conductor Hermann Levi on 14 January 1893 with regard to a concert planned for February 3, Bruckner requested that Levi perform the new edition of the Third, asserting that 'with regard to the first version, I don't want to know anything more about it'.[6] Bruckner also expressed similar sentiments concerning the last version of the Fourth Symphony. When he sent Levi the score of the third version of the Fourth Symphony, he wrote that the symphony was 'newly orchestrated and condensed. The success in Vienna [of the concert under Richter in Vienna in January 1888] is unforgettable to me'.[7] However, it is important to point out that Bruckner was only 'satisfied' with the symphony when he had 'corrected' the orchestral voice leading.[8]

Heretofore, the importance of Bruckner's analysis and diagramming of orchestral voice leading for this debate has not been recognized. Nor has its theoretical underpinnings been elucidated. But I shall argue that a systematic investigation of Bruckner's own study of the octaves-versus-doubling question offers unequivocal evidence that by c. 1890 at the latest, the composer had become dissatisfied with the 'collaboration' of his disciples. But only if we can elucidate Bruckner's investigation of the problem of octaves in an orchestral context – with all of its practical ramifications – will we understand why, in 1890, the composer recognized that he must revise the First Symphony's orchestration *himself*.

Understanding Bruckner's *rationale* for revisions to orchestration is fundamental. Korstvedt and others have maintained that the revisions were made primarily for practical reasons; furthermore, Korstvedt has proposed that '[changes to the orchestration] may have resulted more from a clearer understanding of how to orchestrate an imagined sonority than from a change in the imagined sonority itself. In other words, Bruckner did not change his mind about what he wanted to hear but rather about the way to get it, presumably after having heard the effect of his original scoring'.[9] In my view, Bruckner's motivation was fundamentally *theoretical*, not practical, in nature. As he heard more of his music in its orchestral guise, he became increasingly fastidious about consecutives in orchestral voice leading. His revisions to the orchestration of the First and Eighth Symphonies in 1890 provide the rosetta stone for understanding the way in which his theoretical consideration of consecutives in an orchestral context motivated his revision of the orchestration of his symphonies. But before we can understand his thinking on this issue, it is necessary to explore his investigation of the doubling-versus-consecutives problem beginning in 1877, and specifically his study of this problem in Mozart and Beethoven.

*   *   *

From 1860 until immediately before his death in 1896, Bruckner kept pocket diaries. Of these, 23 have survived complete or in fragments.[10] From 1879 on, after his appointment to the University of Vienna, the composer employed a diary specifically formatted for university and college professors – the *Akademischer Kalender der Österreichischen Hochschulen* – which arranges the year according to the academic calendar. The diaries contain annotations on a broad range of subjects: professional engagements, the weather, the current state of the composer's health, tests, honours received and rejection of works, travels abroad, pupils' debts, dancing partners at balls, names and addresses, household bills, and prayer annotations. Two diaries from 1876–7 contain extensive notes on Mozart's *Requiem* and Beethoven's Third and Ninth Symphonies.[11]

That Bruckner knew and studied some of the most famous pieces of Mozart, Beethoven, Cherubini, Schubert, Berlioz, Mendelssohn, Schumann, Liszt, Brahms, and Wagner is confirmed by contemporary reports, by his few surviving scores and diary notes, and by many quotations and allusions to these compositions – both obvious and subtle – worked into his own music.[12] Bruckner's student Friedrich Eckstein reports that the composer's apartment near the Schottenring in the Hessgasse was cluttered with mountains of books, scores, and music piled 'so high that only a Hercules could move them'.[13] Bruckner's attention was focused primarily on a few late Mozart works, especially the *Requiem* and the 'Jupiter' Symphony. In homage to Mozart, Bruckner quotes the famous four-note theme of the 'Jupiter' Finale (C–D–F–E) in the second group of the Finale of his own Eighth Symphony.[14] A further Mozartean aspect of the coda in the Finales of the later symphonies – the contrapuntal superposition of themes – is clearly modelled on the coda of the 'Jupiter' Finale. Eckstein reports in the foreword to his Bruckner-inspired reissue of Simon Sechter's commentary on the 'Jupiter' Finale that 'he [Bruckner] never tired of urging its careful study'.[15]

Bruckner's diary annotations concerning the Mozart *Requiem* consist of a series of observations concerning consecutive octaves keyed to page numbers in his score. A typical annotation reads as follows: 'Page 8 Moz[art] *Requiem*

Violin I [in octaves] with the Tenor and then the Alto. Page 12. I Violin [in octaves] with *Tenor* and then *Alto*. Page 12. I Violin in octaves with Alto. Similarly page 13'.[16] In Max Auer's completion of August Göllerich's biography of Bruckner, the diary entries concerning Mozart's *Requiem* are transcribed without any real commentary.[17] Since Auer fails to establish concordances between Bruckner's annotations and a particular score of the *Requiem*, his transcription is unreliable in a few places. A more accurate transcription, this time with commentary, is provided by Alfred Orel in an obscure publication from the Nazi period.[18] But Orel, like Auer before him, is unable to ascertain which edition of the Mozart *Requiem* Bruckner used:

> It is not always easy to ascertain to which places Bruckner is referring. While he provides many of the page numbers from the score, it nevertheless remains unknown which edition he was using. From the printed scores available to me none of them could have served as Bruckner's reference; perhaps he used a [manuscript] copy of the score.[19]

Because he is unable find a precise concordance, Orel was obliged to guess the points in the *Requiem* score corresponding to Bruckner's page references. As a consequence, his cross references to the edition by Brahms of the *Requiem* in *W. A. Mozarts Werke*, xxiv/1 (Leipzig, 1877) are both speculative and incomplete. In 1991, the present writer identified the edition Bruckner used, established concordances between page references in the notes and measures in the score, and thereby determined precisely which octaves attracted analytical comment. With Paul Hawkshaw's assistance, it was also possible to decipher previously unintelligible annotations in Bruckner's composing manuscript of the F minor Mass (Wn Mus. Hs. 2106) and to explain them as page references to the 1877 diary notes on the *Requiem*.[20]

As for identifying Bruckner's edition of Mozart's *Requiem*, the annotations include a reference to page 130, so his edition must have contained at least that number; assuming a date of 1877 for the notes, the score must have been published before then; and from Bruckner's detailed discussion of Mozart's instrumentation, it is also obvious that he was working with a full score, not a piano reduction. At least three different editions of the full score were published prior to 1877, but only one – the first, issued by Breitkopf und Härtel in 1800 – contains at least 130 pages (178, in fact). This must be the edition that Bruckner owned.

But what encouraged Bruckner to study Mozart in this way? Although the literature has focused almost exclusively on his intense religiosity and mysticism, there is evidence that he was also profoundly interested in the sciences. For many years, Bruckner was friendly with a medical man, a certain Dr Alexander Fränkel, who reported his aptitude 'in all realms of science'. Thus, we should not be astonished that a late diary entry dating from 1893–94 quotes the anatomist Josef Hyrtl's book *Die materialistische Weltanschauung unserer Zeit* published in 1865. Bruckner's systematic studies of octaves and metrical structure are related both to his scientific interests and his efforts to legitimize music as a 'science' in a university setting. The phraseology of Bruckner's inaugural lecture at the University of Vienna (drafted 25 November 1875) betrays his respect for the sciences and scientific method:

> Just as each branch of science must order and sift its materials by framing laws and rules, likewise musical science – if I may use this attribute – has dissected musical structure as far as (its) atoms and then resynthesized the elements according to specific principles, thereby arriving at a doctrine [*Lehre*], which could also be called musical architecture.[22]

In another diary entry, Bruckner proudly noted '30 April 1st time counterpoint at the University 1877. A[nton] Br[uckner] *m[anu] p[ropria]*'. He had finally succeeded in his crusade to make the authorities recognize practical music theory as a 'scientific' subject worthy of study at the university level.

From 1875 on – that is, from the time he initiated his campaign to make music theory a university subject – Bruckner became increasingly concerned with demonstrating the 'scientific' aspects of harmony, voice-leading, and meter, and testing the 'correctness' of his own and other composers' music from a musical-theoretical perspective.[22] Surely, it is no coincidence that the detailed voice-leading studies of the *Requiem* and the *Eroica* coincide temporally with his early career as a university professor.[23] By identifying passages where Mozart and Beethoven allowed momentary doubling or parallels between conceptually independent voices, Bruckner attempted to distinguish 'permitted' doubling from 'forbidden' consecutives and thereby establish 'specific [scientific] principles' governing consecutives in free composition.

The annotations concerning the *Requiem* are found on pages 10, 15, 19, and 21 of Bruckner's diary for the year 1877. Notes are found on page 19 just below the reminder of a test scheduled for 5 June 1877. They continue on page 10 below an annotation that it was 26 degrees at three o'clock in the afternoon on 24 July 1877. Although one cannot discount the possibility that Bruckner entered his remarks on the *Requiem* on half-empty diary pages at a later date, it seems reasonable to assume that they date from the summer of 1877.[24] Furthermore, the F minor Mass was performed on 17 June 1877 in the *Hofkapelle*. In my view, it was as a consequence of this particular performance that Bruckner became concerned about the 'correctness' of octaves in the *Gloria* and sought justification for his own practice in the Mozart *Requiem*. A further concordance between the *Requiem* notes and a dated 1877 revision to the violin parts in the *Credo* (Ex. 2.5 to be discussed below) also indicates that the diary notes are contemporaneous with the 1877 revision of the Mass.

*   *   *

After years of study with Simon Sechter, widely regarded as Austria's greatest counterpoint teacher, Bruckner had become one of his generation's most experienced and revered contrapuntists. The notes reveal Bruckner engaged with the problem of consecutive octaves and unisons in contrapuntal contexts in free composition. Under what circumstances are momentary consecutive octaves or unisons permitted between ostensibly independent voices, that is, between non-doubling yet contrapuntally related string parts and vocal lines? What precedents does Mozart have to offer? Specifically, in the *Requiem*, does he allow forbidden, potentially 'bad' consecutive octaves or unisons between contrapuntally related vocal lines and string parts? Bruckner's notes on the *Requiem* and a series of revisions to his own F minor Mass extending from 1877 to 1894 suggest that he came to the following conclusions: first, the rule concerning consecutives may be broken because momentary doublings do not necessarily constitute forbidden parallels; but second, inconsistent doublings do indeed invoke consecutives; and third, breaking a consistent doubling in inner voices helps reduce the effect of parallels.

Bruckner must have known that the *Requiem* was left unfinished at the time of Mozart's death and that it had been 'completed' by his pupil Franz Xaver Süssmayr. In 1877, he may have been acquainted with the account of the *Requiem*'s genesis in the first (1856–9) or second (1867) edition of Jahn's biography and with the first edition of Köchel's Catalogue (1862). But in all likelihood, he was unaware of the full extent of Süssmayr's contribution, since this was not generally known until after Brahms published his edition in 1877 and his *Revisionsbericht* in 1886, which distinguished Mozart's from Süssmayr's contributions. Therefore, if Bruckner were interested in learning Mozart's true practice with regard to consecutives, he could not have chosen his model more unwisely: the string parts are mostly by Süssmayr, who was much less fastidious than Mozart in his treatment of consecutives, as recent commentators have shown.[25] However, there is no evidence that studying the *Requiem* caused Bruckner to sanction a significantly freer attitude towards consecutives than Mozart. On the contrary, by carefully taking note of consecutives in his score – some of the same consecutives that have provoked so negative a reaction from Süssmayr's more recent critics – Bruckner appears to be both thorough and acute, querying each set of consecutives. In this respect, Bruckner's analysis of the *Requiem* is an enterprise related in spirit to Brahms's study of octaves and fifths. Like Brahms, Bruckner 'tests' the consecutives in the music of his predecessors to see if they are 'good' or 'bad', 'strong' or 'weak'. Although Brahms was also aware of and questioned the consecutives in the *Requiem*, he refrained from openly condemning Süssmayr. In a laconic editorial comment, he observed that 'he [Süssmayr] carefully copied Mozart's preliminary work and completed it with as great diligence as piety'.[26] Unlike Süssmayr's modern critics, Brahms preferred not to 'correct' Süssmayr; rather than trying to fix Süssmayr's completion, he published it with the caveat that '*everything questionable and doubtful* [my emphasis] in this score may be found in the manuscripts'. Incidentally, Schenker, in his personal copy of the Brahms edition of the *Requiem*, does not identify the parallels in Süssmayr's completion; if Schenker believed Süssmayr to be grossly incompetent (as some modern scholars have suggested), he left no indication to that effect.[27]

*   *   *

Bruckner notes during his analysis that Mozart's three upper voices are usually doubled by the three upper strings: 'The fundamental principle in the *Requiem* is strings with the voices either without figuration at the unison or with figuration at the octave, the first violin with soprano, the second violin with alto, the viola with tenor'.[28] This usual, regular doubling of corresponding voices may be schematized as shown in Fig. 2.1a. But Bruckner's primary concern was with

Figure 2.1   Instrumental doublings of voices in Mozart's *Requiem* as observed by Bruckner

(a) Doubling at the unison

(B) Doubling with figuration at the octave

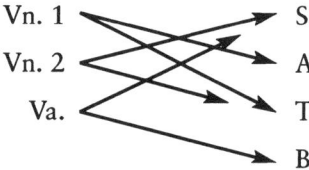

the way in which contrapuntal figuration in the string parts might create momentary doubling an octave higher or lower with non-corresponding vocal parts, in other words, consecutive octaves between conceptually independent voices. He observes that the first violin part generally forms such parallels with the alto or tenor, the second violin part with soprano or tenor, and the viola part with bass or soprano (Fig. 2.1b).[29] With these principles established, Bruckner put himself on the alert for consecutive octaves or unisons. It is worth beginning with a notorious example from the *Recordare*, mm. 21–3 (Ex. 2.1). Here the strings are conceived as independent parts, and momentary octaves and unisons strongly suggest forbidden consecutives. These measures have attracted the ire of Süssmayr's modern critics, who have condemned Süssmayr's completion as 'an unrelieved display of technical incompetence'.[30] Bruckner takes note of this passage (on page 61 of his score) with the following remark: 'As the viola proceeds in thirds with the bass [there are] bare octaves first with the soprano

Ex. 2.1   Mozart, Requiem, *Recordare*, mm. 20–23

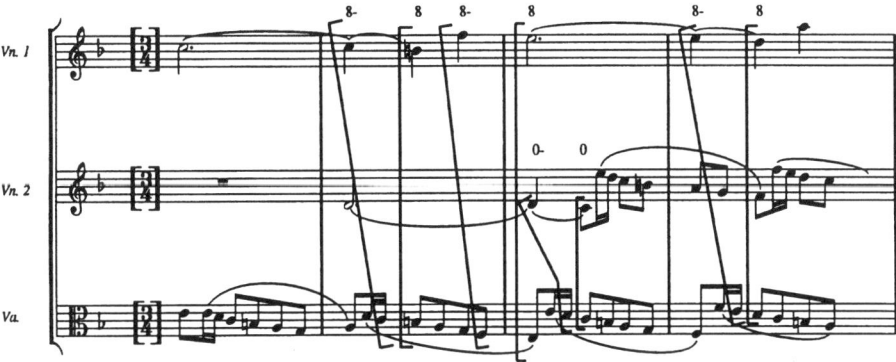

and bare unisons with the tenor in the course of this counterpoint'.[31] Since he was probably unaware that these octaves and unisons were written by Süssmayr – not Mozart – he may have interpreted them too generously as 'licences' rather than as outright 'mistakes'. To take another case, Bruckner's annotation of octave doublings between the first violin and alto in mm. 30–2 of the *Introit* (quoted above, Ex. 2.2) implies that the figuration in the first violin in these measures does not mediate the consecutive octaves.[32] Perhaps he was irritated by the octave doubling of the leading tone to tonic or by the abrupt leap to the leading tone in the violin; unfortunately his notes do not provide further commentary. Assuming that Mozart was able to complete the *Introit*, these octaves are, in fact, genuine.

Ex. 2.2   Mozart, Requiem, Introit, mm. 30–32

I now turn to the effect of Bruckner's study of consecutive octaves on his own music. The question whether such momentary doubling constitutes undesireable consecutives would concern Bruckner from 1877 to the end of his composing career. One of the most striking annotations on folio 36v. of the composing manuscript of the F minor Mass is displayed in Plate 2. Bruckner writes cryptically '*Moz*[art] *Req*[uiem] [*Seite*] *30 41 127 130* I. [Violin] *mit Tenor*'. The significance of Bruckner's annotation in his composing score now becomes clear. It is placed directly above mm. 248–9 in the *Gloria* fugue, and he was apparently concerned about the momentary consecutive octaves between the ostensibly

Ex. 2.3a   Bruckner, Mass in F minor, Gloria, mm. 247–9

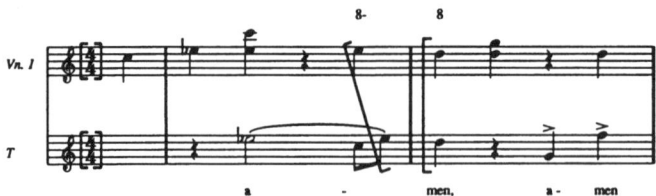

Ex. 2.3b   mm. 251–3

Ex. 2.3c   mm. 255–7

independent first violin line and the tenor '*I.* [Violin] *mit Tenor*', Ex. 2.3a). These octaves are formed between the violin figuration and the second counter-subject in the vocal line. Therefore, these consecutives replicate when the first violin line is transposed down a fourth with second counter-subject in the bass in mm. 252–53 (Ex. 2.3b), and likewise against the soprano in mm. 256–7 (Ex. 2.3c). Bruckner was sufficiently anxious about these octaves to seek a precedent – and presumably a justification – in Mozart's *Requiem*.

The annotation refers to m. 8 and mm. 60–1 of Mozart's *Dies irae*, where the tenor moves in direct octaves with the first violin part (Ex. 2.4a, b, see p. 41).[33] The other two references are to the *Offertorium*, m. 69, and to the *Sanctus*, m. 7, where direct octaves occur between the putatively independent first violin and tenor (Ex. 2.4c, d, see p. 42).[34] According to both Brahms's and Leopold Nowak's reconstructions of Mozart's autograph, the first violin lines in m. 10 of the *Dies Irae* and in m. 69 of the *Offertorium* are indeed by Mozart.[35] Thus in these two cases, at least, Bruckner could legitimately point to an authentic precedent in the *Requiem* to justify the 'licence' in his own F minor Mass. Emboldened by the Mozart examples, Bruckner approved the parallels in his own fugue in the Gloria.

According to Hawkshaw's reconstruction of Bruckner's revisions to the F minor Mass, most of the 1877 revisions concern the addition or subtraction of

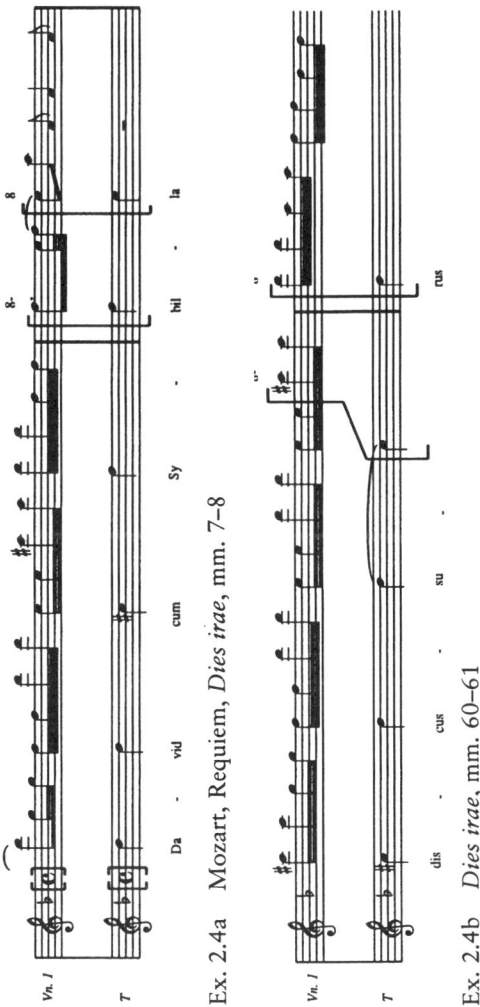

Ex. 2.4a   Mozart, Requiem, *Dies irae*, mm. 7–8

Ex. 2.4b   *Dies irae*, mm. 60–61

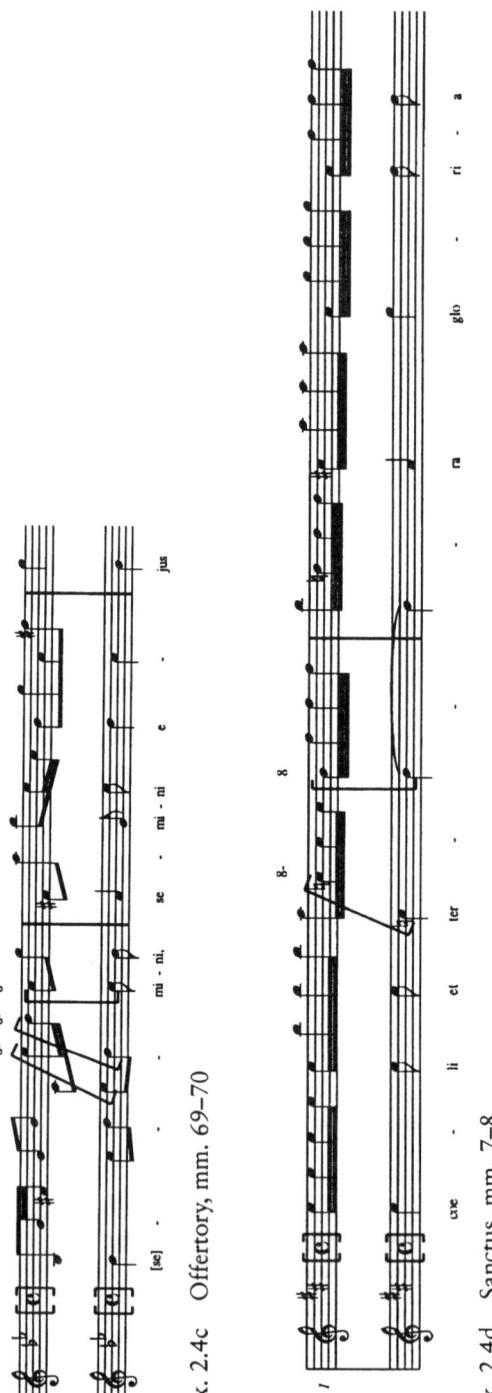

Ex. 2.4c   Offertory, mm. 69–70

Ex. 2.4d   Sanctus, mm. 7–8

42

measures in accordance with Bruckner's alterations to metrical structure, or else concern notation.[36] There is only one significant voice-leading revision, which occurs in the upper strings in the *Credo*, mm. 63–4 (Ex. 2.5, see p. 44). The new version is written into the composing autograph, fol. 53r., with the designation '1877 *Streicher neu*'. The original reading of the passage, as preserved in the presentation copy (Wn Mus. Hs. 31.246), is given in Ex. 2.5a and the 1877 revision inserted in the composing autograph in Ex. 2.5b. In the mm. 61–2 of the original version, the peak tones of the first violin figuration initially double the soprano at the octave. But in mm. 63–4, the first violin line breaks away, rejoining the soprano only in mm. 65–8. In 1877, Bruckner became dissatisfied with this *inconsistent* doubling. He modified the first violin part so that the violin's peak tones consistently double the soprano at the octave. This revision is probably related to Bruckner's observation concerning the *Requiem* that, when figuration is involved, the first violin generally doubles the soprano an octave higher. This lends further support to my hypothesis that the notes in the 1877 diary and the 1877 revision date from June–July of that year.

Bruckner's preoccupation with the question of when doubling constitutes consecutives is reflected in two late revisions to the *Et incarnatus est* and *Crucifixus* of the F minor Mass. In 1893–4, Bruckner revised the first violin line in mm. 169–73 of the *Crucifixus* to eliminate consecutive octaves (see Ex. 2.6, see p. 45). The modifications to the violin line eliminate or mitigate intermittent parallels with the alto (m. 169), tenor (m. 171), and soprano (m. 173). In the first version of m. 169, the effect of consecutive octaves between the first violin and the alto is not eliminated by the syncopation. In the final reading of the violin line, however, the registral shift of e♭² down an octave mitigates the consecutives (now by contrary motion) by suggesting that b♭¹ is prolonged (see the dotted slur in Ex. 2.6b). In m. 171 of the final version, Bruckner inserts b♭¹ into the first violin's descending line (see the first bracket in Ex. 2.6b). This interpolation retards the first violin's descent and thereby prevents consecutive octaves with the tenor. In m. 173 of the final version, Bruckner rejects the first violin's linear descent; disjunct motion in the new first violin line prevents octaves with the soprano.

After the appearance of the first edition of the F minor Mass 'edited' by Max von Oberleithner and Josef Schalk (c. 1893–4), Bruckner returned to a revision he had made in the early 1890s in the *Et incarnatus est* (*Credo*, mm. 138–9) and, on fol. 77r. of his own copy score (Wn Mus. Hs. 6015), he noted 'a g Schalk 1. Ob. 2. Clar' (the passages are compared in Ex. 2.7, see p. 46).[37] The print preserves the octave doubling between the first oboe and second clarinet, which Bruckner now wanted to break. The striking tritonal harmonic shift between the seventh chords of A major to E flat major (mm. 138–9), coupled with the sudden dynamic drop from *f* to *pp*, marks an important juncture between the end of one phrase and the beginning of the next. At this crucial point, Bruckner clearly wishes to avoid the consecutives in the inner voices; therefore, he eliminates the consecutive octaves between the first oboe and second clarinet in mm. 138–9 by

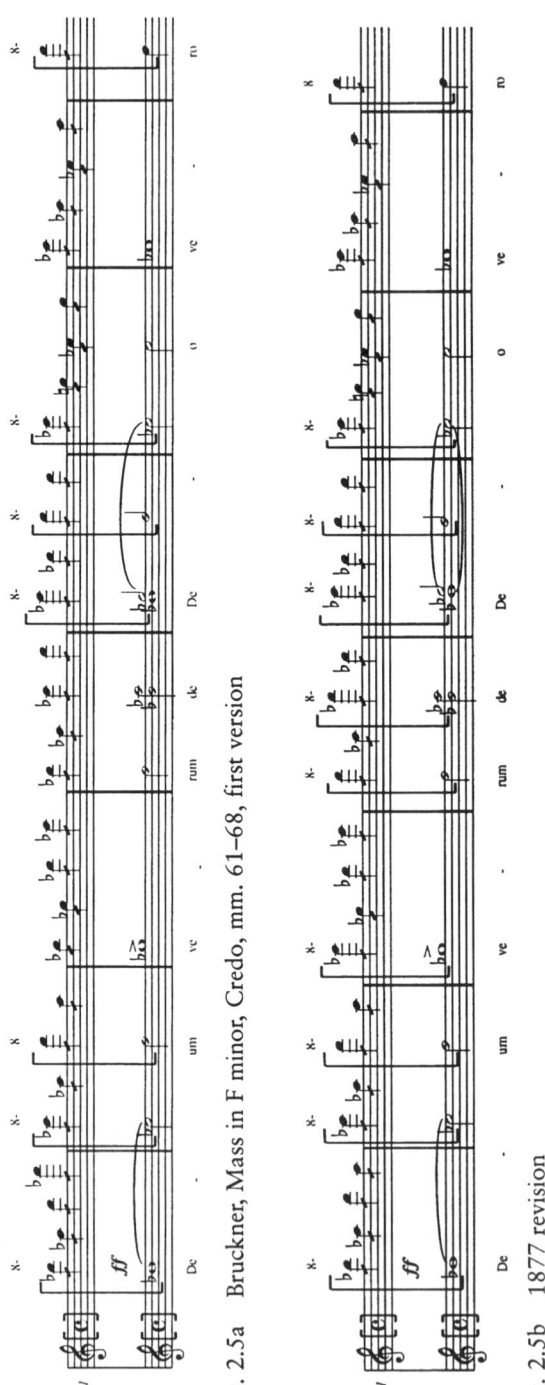

Ex. 2.5a   Bruckner, Mass in F minor, Credo, mm. 61–68, first version

Ex. 2.5b   1877 revision

Ex. 2.6a   Bruckner, Mass in F minor, *Crucifixus*, mm. 169–73, first version

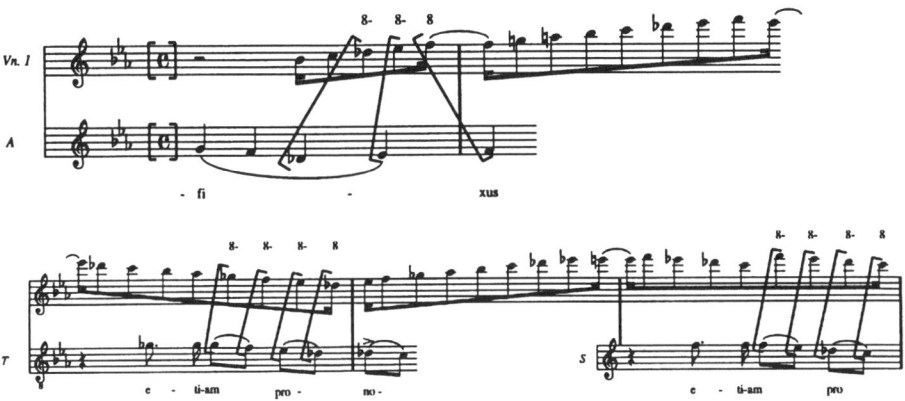

Ex. 2.6b   Bruckner's revisions, early 1890s, probably 1893–4

inserting the eighth note figure in the second clarinet (see bracket in Ex. 2.7b). While his early 1890s revision of m. 138 of the *Credo* is the converse of his '1877 *Streicher neu*' revision, the purpose remains the same, to avoid creating the impression of consecutives. In the earlier passage (*Credo*, mm. 63–64), Bruckner transforms intermittent doubling which suggests consecutives into consistent octave doubling. Here (m. 138), he eliminates the consecutives in the inner voices by the opposite procedure, i.e. by breaking a consistent octave doubling.

*   *   *

In his last years, c.1888, Bruckner exhibited renewed interest in the problem of momentary doubling in an orchestral context. In my view, this interest and concern stems from his hearing performances and being dissatisfied with momentary doublings. As in the case of the Mass in F minor, where a

Ex. 2.7a Bruckner, Mass in F minor, Credo, mm. 133–9, wind parts, ed. Oberleithner and Schalk, c. 1893–4

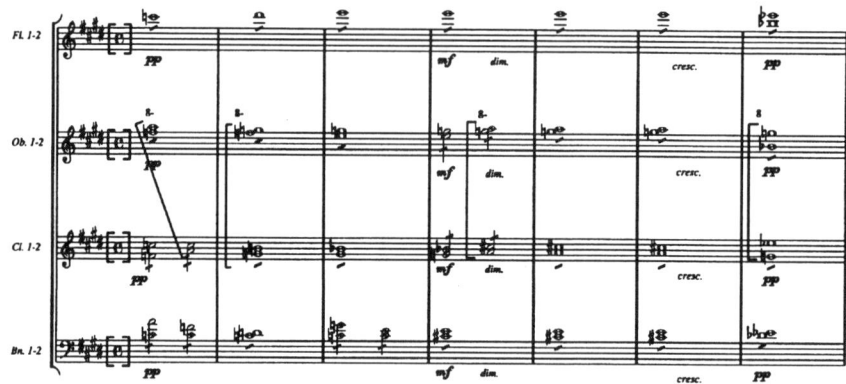

Ex. 2.7b Bruckner's revisions, early 1890s, probably 1893–4

performance in 1877 had sparked an investigation of momentary doubling in Mozart's *Requiem* and his own Mass, hearing performances of the First, Third, Fourth, Seventh, and Eighth Symphonies heightened his interest in this aspect of voice leading in orchestral music.

It is important to bear in mind that success and recognition came late in Bruckner's life and career. Until the late 1880s, Bruckner was largely a symphonic composer *on paper*, i.e. unheard in the concert hall. His symphonies were barely played and, for the most part, languished unpublished until the late 1880s and early 1890s.[38] The break-through came with the second performance of the Seventh Symphony in Munich on 10 March 1885 under Hermann Levi; this was one of Bruckner's first truly major triumphs and important for the wider dissemination of his music. The third version of the Fourth Symphony was first performed on 22 January 1888 (in Vienna under Richter); based on his experience of this performance, in February Bruckner made extensive revisions to the Franz Schalk/Ferdinand Löwe re-orchestration in the *Stichvorlage*. It is interesting that shortly thereafter, on 5 March 1888, Bruckner also began revising the *Stichvorlage* of Schalk's arrangement of the Finale of the Third Symphony. A larger picture emerges: in 1888, Bruckner was intimately involved in 'correcting' the disciples' arrangements of the Third and Fourth Symphonies.

As a consequence of hearing the arrangement of the Fourth Symphony, then, Bruckner returned to the issue of momentary doubling in an orchestral context, which he had considered in 1877 in the *Eroica*. In that 1877 study, he had concluded that essentially independent orchestral voices may double one another momentarily to create the effect of consecutive octaves or unisons, the purpose of these short, two-note doublings being to highlight a given dyad. For example, in mm. 23–9 of the first movement of the *Eroica*, the first clarinet and the second violin have independent parts. Nevertheless, as Bruckner noted in his score of the *Eroica*, in mm. 26–8, the first clarinet line and the lower voice within the polyphonic second violin line produce consecutive octaves on E♭-D before resuming their different courses (Ex. 2.8a). Bruckner also took note of another, more striking instance of this kind of momentary doubling, which occurs later in the first movement (Ex. 2.8b). In mm. 468–73, the florid first violin and third

Ex. 2.8a Beethoven, Symphony No. 3 (*Eroica*), first movement, mm. 23–9

Ex. 2.8b mm. 468–72

horn parts are clearly independent; however, in mm. 469–70 there are momentary consecutive octaves (in the margin, Bruckner remarks '*Corne + Viole in Octaven*'). Here the point of the momentary doubling was to highlight the A♭-G descending semitone. In each case, Bruckner called attention to the consecutives as licence forbidden in strict counterpoint but allowed in free composition.

Beginning c.1888 (i.e. approximately a decade after the study of voice leading in the *Eroica*), Bruckner began to diagram two-chord progressions to monitor the progression of each of the orchestral parts and thereby identify doublings of dyads between ostensibly independent voices. From approximately 1888 until the end of the composer's life, the voice-leading diagrams appear in the manuscripts in two main circumstances: firstly, when the composer is revising his own orchestration or the re-orchestrations of his students (for example, in the last revisions of the First, Third, Fourth, and Eighth Symphonies); secondly, when he is tracking the voice leading across page breaks in his manuscripts. Bruckner's disciples associated this diagramming procedure with a quest to expunge *all* consecutives, as is revealed by a letter from 6 October 1888, where Josef Schalk complains:

> Now he [Bruckner] is plagued with the severity of a delusion by an obsession with cleaning the composition of octave progressions. With this, he is wasting much time, tries awfully hard, but is unsusceptible to each objection made by Löwe or me. It is quite sad to see how he extinguishes everything at the expense of a natural voice leading and how he changes for the sake of this *idée fixe.*

Although Josef Schalk – and others – firmly believed that Bruckner's sole purpose in making the diagrams was to *eliminate* consecutives, I shall argue that Bruckner did not wish to eliminate *all* momentary doublings *per se.* This is borne out by one important fact, namely that Bruckner does not invariably eliminate consecutives even when he has the opportunity to do so. Indeed, Bruckner's intent was not to 'clean the composition of octave progressions' but to hear 'in the mind's ear' all of the details of the orchestral voice leading and to 'regulate' (Bruckner's own term) (i.e. to 'test and take account of') and 'approve' certain consecutives as 'permitted' momentary doublings and 'desired' reinforcements, and 'disapprove' and 'eliminate' others as undesired. However, from 1888 on, Bruckner's attitude towards momentary doublings does appear to have become stricter. To demonstrate this increasing stringency, I have arranged my examples in chronological order.

Let us begin with Bruckner's February 1888 revision of the Schalk–Löwe re-orchestration of the Finale of the Fourth Symphony, specifically with a passage at the end of the recapitulation. Ex. 2.9a (p. 49) shows the final published version (mm. 427ff.), which, for present purposes, can be taken as 'authentic', Ex. 2.9b (p. 50) shows the original (1880) version (mm. 461ff.). This passage embodies a reminiscence of the end of the descending-sixth theme presented towards the end of the second group (mm. 105 ff., a transformation of the second theme in the first movement). Comparing the 1880 and 1888 versions of this passage, the tonal substance remains essentially the same, but one is struck by the differences in orchestration and dynamics. Whereas in the 1880 version mm. 461–4 build dynamically from *f* to *ff* before suddenly collapsing to *pp* for the transition to the coda (which begins *pp* in m. 477 ff.), in the 1888 version the same reminiscence participates in a large, gradual diminuendo from *p* (m. 427) to the *pp* of the coda (m. 443 ff.). Bruckner's 1880 orchestration reinforces the *f* dynamic by the agitated six-against-four rhythmic patterns in the lower strings and winds. To achieve the *p* dynamic in the final version, the six-against-four conflict is excised as the figuration is eliminated from all instruments but the violins. The photograph of the *Stichvorlage* of this passage shows Bruckner's extensive revision; with a razor blade, he erased much of the Schalk–Löwe arrangement as he revised the orchestration.

Ex. 2.9a   Bruckner, Fourth Symphony, third version (1888), Finale, mm. 427–30

Ex. 2.9b   Fourth Symphony, second version, Finale (1880), mm. 461–4

Of especial significance for the present study is Bruckner's note – probably in pencil – below these measures (in the *Stichvorlage*): '*Tromp[ete] u[nd] Hörner im Einkl[ang] [mit] Violine / Fag[otte] = Pausanen u[nd] Viola*'. The first part of this note calls attention to the doubling unison of the first horns (in F) with the trumpets (in F) of the line a♭¹-b♭¹, and the unison of the second horns (in F) and the second violins of the line d♭¹-d¹, while its second part calls attention to the doubling at the unison of the bassoons, trombones, and violas. It is clear, both from the annotation and the orchestration itself, that Bruckner wanted to highlight by means of unison doublings the lines a♭¹-b♭¹ and d♭¹-d¹ in the trumpets, horns, and violin figuration as the bassoons, trumpets, and violas filled in the harmony. As the note and the orchestration make clear, these particular unisons appear to have been 'permitted', not 'forbidden'!

In the course of his revision of Franz Schalk's re-orchestration of the Finale of the Third Symphony, Bruckner studied and revised the doublings in the resolution of the diminished third chord on F sharp to the G chord in mm. 322–3 (Ex. 2.10, p. 52). It is noteworthy that the harmonic progression involves a so-called 'leading-tone chord', in this case, a diminished third chord; as we shall see shortly, in the 1890 revision of the Eighth Symphony, Bruckner carefully 'regulated' other leading-tone chord progressions (see Ex. 2.11). It would seem that Bruckner had become especially sensitive to unwanted consecutives in such leading-tone chord progressions.

This progression in the Third Symphony was 'checked' or 'regulated' on 18 August 1888 ('*18 Aug[ust] reg[uliert]*') – approximately six months after the previously discussed example. Bruckner's attitude to momentary doublings has now become very strict: the only momentary doublings between conceptually independent voices that he is prepared to allow are 'octaves by contrary motion'. A complete transcription of the voice leading diagrams is difficult, especially because Bruckner simultaneously revised the voice leading in the music and the diagrams (e.g. top of column three). However, it is possible to reconstruct Bruckner's thought process: to ensure that momentary octaves occur between conceptually independent voices only by contrary motion, Bruckner systematically checked the voice leading into each pitch class of the resolution chord, first B, then D, and then G.[39] In Column 1, he checked the doublings of voices moving to the pitch class B:

[Column 1]

Es / h [flutes 1-2]
Es / h [oboes 1-2]
Es / h [clarinets 1-2]
Es / h [violin 2]
C \ h [horn 2]
Es \ h [trombone 2]
As / h [cello 1]

Ex. 2.10   Bruckner, Third Symphony, third version (1889), Finale, mm. 322–3

The 'permitted' momentary doubling is between the upper winds and the second trombone, but notice that the octaves are by contrary motion. In the second column, Bruckner 'regulated' all of the voices moving to the pitch class D:

[Column 2]

Fis / d [horn 1]
Es / d [cancelled]
Fis / d [cancelled]
Fis \ d [cello]
As \ **d** [trombone 1]
C \ **d** [viola]
Es \ d [viola]

Notice that two doublings of F♯–D and E♭–D were cancelled, although the F♯–D doubling was 'permitted' between the first horn and the cello, again by contrary motion. The third column combines the results of Columns 1–2. Now there are no undesired doublings moving to the pitch classes D and B:

[Column 3]

[?]

C \ **d** [viola, from Column 2]
Fis / d [horn 1, from Column 2]
Fis \ d [cello, from Column 2]
C / **h** [horn 2, from Column 1]
As \ **d** [trombone 1, Column 2]
C \ **d** [viola, Column 2]
Es \ **h** [trombone 2, Column 1]

Column 4 combines the already checked motions into the pitch classes D and B with 'new' motions into the pitch class G, to complete the G major triad.

[Column 4]

[?]

Es \ d [viola, Column 2]
C \ d [viola, Column 2]

[?]

Fis / d [horn 1, Column 2]
C / h [horn 2, Column 1]
Es / g [trumpets 1-2]
Es \ g [trumpet 3]

As \ d [trombone 1, Column 2]
Es \ h [trombone 2, Column 1]
C \ **g** [bass trombone]
Es \ d [viola, repeats above]
C \ d [viola, repeats above]

In the above-quoted letter from October 1888, written approximately two months after this 'regulation' was made, Josef Schalk complains that Bruckner 'extinguishes everything at the expense of a natural voice leading'. By 'natural' voice leading, Schalk is probably referring to the so-called 'law of the shortest path'; that is, the idea that the parts should either be sustained or, whenever possible, move by step. Schalk is correct that Bruckner avoids the 'shortest' path in the brass parts to avoid momentary consecutives between non-doubling voices; to achieve this, the composer has assigned leaps – some quite large – to some of the brass instruments, which are difficult to execute, especially at the fast tempo. But the effect is precisely what Bruckner wanted: the only instruments which create momentary consecutive octaves do so by contrary motion.

Let us consider the progression shown in Ex. 2.11a (p. 55), which is taken from mm. 68–9 of the first movement of the Eighth Symphony (Wn. Ms. Hs. 19.480); Ex. 2.11b (p. 56) will facilitate comparison with the 1887 reading of this passage. Although the voice-leading annotations occur in the right margin of the manuscript page, they do not (in this case) simply indicate the voice leading across a page break; instead they refer to a measure in the middle of the page. The intent here is to 'regulate' or 'test' the orchestral voice leading from the last eighth-note of m. 68 to the downbeat of m. 69. As in the Finale of the Third Symphony, the progression being 'regulated' involves an augmented sixth chord – the so-called 'German' augmented sixth chord B♭–D–F–G♯ – moving to its resolution on A. In 1890, Bruckner revised his own revision of this passage, changing the orchestral voice leading.

The annotations call attention to and implicitly 'approve' of the fact that there are momentary doublings of essentially independent orchestral voices. Specifically, as revealed by the composer's annotations, Bruckner 'approves' of the fact that the G♯–A in the winds and violins, which together present a conceptually independent line, momentarily doubles another independent line in horns 1 and 2 (in F). Also 'approved' is the fact that the D–E in trumpet 1 (in F), which presents an independent line, momentarily doubles horn 3 (in B♭) and the viola part's top line. Again, the point is that, although trumpet 1 on the one hand, and horn 3 and the violas on the other articulate mutually independent lines, they are 'permitted' to momentarily double the D–E and then proceed on their separate ways. By contrast, the D–C♯ doubling in the fourth horn and violas was unproblematic since it was simply part of a single, consistently doubled line.

Examining this passage in the 1890 manuscript more closely, we notice that Bruckner pasted over the trumpet parts. In the original 1887 version of this

Ex. 2.11a   Bruckner, Eighth Symphony, second version (1890), first movement, mm. 68–70

Ex. 2.11b   Eighth Symphony, first version (1887), first movement, mm. 68–70

harmonic progression, the trumpets were silent on the last quarter of m. 68 (Ex. 2.11b). It seems probable that, in the course of revising the passage, Bruckner had written a different syncopated upbeat in the three trumpets, but had become dissatisfied with this initial revision (of the 1887 version); he therefore 'revised the revision', rewriting the trumpet parts on the paste-in. The voice-leading annotations were probably contemporaneous with this second (final) revision, 'regulating' and 'approving' the fact that the newly revised first trumpet part momentarily doubles the line D–E in the third horn and the violas. Through the voice-leading annotations, Bruckner 'tests' and 'approves' D–E as a 'permitted' doubling rather than 'forbidden' consecutives – a doubling that was not present in the 1887 version.

On 12 March 1890, the composer embarked on an extensive overhaul of his First Symphony, which delayed its performance for a year, and also held up work on the Ninth Symphony. As part of this 1890 revision, he went through the 1865–6 composing manuscript of this symphony making numerous annotations in pencil relevant to the revision. As I argued in my 1991 study of 'Bruckner's Metrical Numbers', many of the annotations in the composing manuscript post-date composition of the symphony. Bruckner created and revised the composing manuscript's metrical grid in 1877, and again in 1890. Additionally, he made a number of annotations concerning the voice leading, all of which I believe date from 1890. For example, across mm. 10–11 in the Trio of the Scherzo, he entered 'h/c' in pencil in the margin next to the bassoon and the first violin parts. To facilitate discussion, the two versions (i.e. the 1866 Linz and 1891 Vienna versions) of these measures are compared in Ex. 2.12a, b (see pp. 58–59). These annotations do not simply 'clarify' the voice leading across the page break; rather, Bruckner is unhappy with the momentary octaves between the first bassoon and the first violins because they are exposed in the thin, 'chamber-like' texture of the single string line against the winds. Bruckner's dissatisfaction with these consecutives is confirmed by his revision of the first violin line, which eliminates the octaves by beginning m. 10 on $a^{\flat 2}$ instead of c^2.

A number of voice leading annotations found in the highly contrapuntal third (closing) group of the First Symphony's Finale (m. 58ff.) will be discussed. Above mm. 60–1 in the Linz version, Bruckner wrote '*Fl.* = *Ob.* = *C[orni]* = *Fag[otte]/ Fl.* = *II. Violine*' (Plate 3, p. iv). The first reference is to the $E^{\flat}$–D momentary doubling in the first flute, second oboe, and third and fourth horns, all of which are otherwise independent lines (Ex. 2.13a, p. 60). The second refers to the C–B octaves between the second flute and second violins, again putatively independent parts. If we compare the Linz and Vienna versions (Linz, mm. 60–1 = Vienna, mm. 61–2, Ex. 2.13b, p. 61), we observe that Bruckner has preserved the doubling of the flutes and and third and fourth horns on $E^{\flat}$–D, but by isolating this doubling in the flute parts, he has made it clear that the flute lines are simply doubling the horns; in other words, the flute lines no longer create the impression of independent parts which unfelicitously create parallel octaves through momentary doubling. Bruckner was clearly unhappy with the C–B octaves between the second flute and second violins, since he eliminated these 'consecutives' in the Vienna version. The facsimile of m. 62 in the Linz version shows another (more familiar) way of indicating consecutives: by placing parallel lines above the 'offending' parts. In this way, Bruckner noted that the first trombone's E♭–C (third and fourth quarters) essentially forms consecutives with the e♭²–(d²–) c² sixteenths in the second violins ('accented' octaves). These consecutives were eliminated in the Vienna version (m. 63). If we look at the right hand margin of Plate 4, we notice that Bruckner has tracked the voice leading across the page break. But, in this case, the issue was not simply to follow

Ex. 2.12a   Bruckner, First Symphony, first version (1866), Trio of the Scherzo, mm. 9–10

Ex. 2.12b   First Symphony, second version (1891), Trio of the Scherzo, mm. 9–10

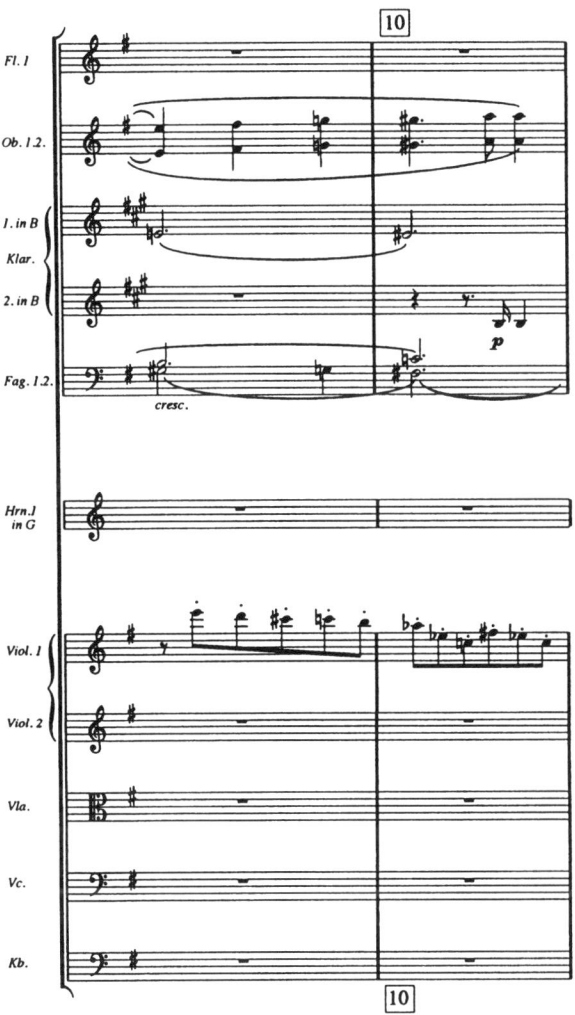

the voices across a page break; rather, Bruckner was no longer prepared to tolerate the momentary (two-note) doublings of the strings in the wind and brass parts. Therefore, these 'consecutives' were eliminated in the Vienna version (compare Linz, mm. 63–4, with Vienna, mm. 64–5).

Momentary, two-note doublings are like the highlights in a painting: such reinforcements have the effect of calling the ear's attention to particular voice leading strands. Bringing out certain dyads through doubling can reinforce motivic connections at all structural levels. For this reason, Bruckner recognized that momentary doublings must be handled in a sensitive and sophisticated way. From 1887 onward (i.e. from the period in which his disciples began to

Ex. 2.13a   Bruckner, First Symphony, first version (1866), Finale, mm. 60–61

Ex. 2.13b First Symphony, second version (1891), Finale, mm. 60–61

re-orchestrate his music and he heard increasing numbers of orchestral performances of his symphonies rather than piano arrangements), Bruckner became concerned that the momentary doublings in his scores were unwanted consecutives. His revision of the orchestral voice leading in the First Symphony reveals that, by the last years of his career in Vienna, Bruckner had became considerably more fastidious and 'conservative' regarding consecutives than he had been in Linz. Furthermore, whenever given the opportunity, Bruckner intervened in his student's re-orchestrations to ensure that momentary reinforcements through doubling occurred precisely in the way he wanted them. In my view, Bruckner's note regarding the Schalk print of the Mass in F minor indicates his *dissatisfaction* with its reading of this passage, specifically with the manner in which Schalk has allowed a doubling, which he himself no longer wanted.[40]

As I have demonstrated, Bruckner revised the orchestration in the First and Eighth Symphonies in accordance with his own ideas on 'good' orchestral voice leading. As Paul Hawkshaw has argued, through his will and other actions, Bruckner intended that the autograph manuscript versions of the First, Fifth, Sixth, Seventh, Eighth, and Ninth Symphonies be published. Bruckner believed that his own orchestration in these manuscripts met his test of 'good' voice leading. Additionally, he stood by the disciples' re-orchestrations of the Third and Fourth Symphonies for two fundamental reasons: firstly, he himself had requested and sanctioned the cuts in both Finales, and secondly, he had made extensive corrections to the disciples' re-orchestrations to bring them into line with his own ideas regarding consecutives. But after employing his disciples' services in re-orchestrating the Third and Fourth Symphonies, Bruckner realized that involving them in this process was a mistake because they were unsympathetic to his theoretical concerns. Even in the case of the Third and Fourth Symphony revisions, to the extent that the Schalks and Löwe could not follow – or agree with – Bruckner's theoretical basis for revising orchestration, they did not act, in fact, as 'collaborators' but rather simply as assistants whose work was then 'regulated' by the Master.

Not only were the disciples 'unsympathetic' to the composer's theoretical concerns, they revised Bruckner's own orchestral voice leading without allowing him to 'test' their revisions – and then performed and published their revisions rather than his version. A clear example is provided by the publication and performance of the Eighth Symphony. Josef Schalk wrote to Oberleithner on 5 August, 1891 instructing him to by-pass Bruckner, giving the 'corrections' directly to the engraver. Furthermore, Schalk wanted to make sure that Bruckner did not have a manuscript score at the rehearsal of the new edition or 'all our good work will come to naught'. Evidently, Schalk hoped that Bruckner would not hear the changes to the orchestration, and more specifically that he would not take note of any unapproved 'consecutives' created by the revisions. Hawkshaw – and Haas before him – have drawn all of the necessary conclusions from this attempt at deception.

But I have an even broader point to make. In a recent study, Edward Laufer recalls Schenker derisively quoting Bruckner's *bon mot*, 'That is the rule, gentlemen. Of course, *I* don't compose that way'. While Schenker was 'appalled' by his teacher's seemingly flippant dismissal of 'the rules', Laufer proposes that Bruckner did not, in fact, 'disregard and scorn ... musical laws which were taught for good reason; rather, he was intuitively obeying others which took precedence; ... [these] he could not have conceptualized, and hence he was unable and even unconcerned to explain them; but he followed them nonetheless'.[41] Like Brahms, Bruckner recognized that not *all* consecutives are 'bad', since they appear in the masterworks of the greatest composers. As we have seen, Bruckner even cited consecutives in Mozart's *Requiem* to justify analogous parallels in the *Gloria* of his own F minor Mass. At the same time, he was clearly dissatisfied with some of the consecutives he found in the *Requiem* (some of which may be ascribed to Süssmayr), and in Schalk's printed edition and earlier versions of his own Mass. Furthermore, perhaps he was disappointed that his studies of octaves failed to disclose general, 'scientific' laws regarding consecutives; rather, Bruckner's comment regarding 'the rules' suggests an unbridgeable gap between theory and practice. Since neither Bruckner nor Brahms could explain consecutives on the musical 'surface' by way of a relationship between structural levels (as Schenker would do later), they tend to regard consecutives as an apparent flouting of the rule. Whether such parallels are 'beautiful', 'permissible', 'questionable', or just plain 'bad', remained for them a matter of compositional 'taste', 'judgement', and ultimately – as Laufer says – 'intuition'. As creative artists, both Bruckner and Brahms were interested in how the letter, but not the spirit, of the Law might be broken.

Notes

1. Benjamin M. Korstvedt, 'The First Published Edition of Anton Bruckner's Fourth Symphony: Collaboration and Authenticity', in *Nineteenth-Century Music*, 20 (1996), pp. 3–26. An unpublished letter from Levi suggests that the conductor was very diplomatic in his 'rejection' of the Eighth Symphony's first version. Whether Levi's reaction had the slightest impact on the substance of Bruckner's revisions seems doubtful.
2. Perhaps I should add a note on my use of the term 'analysis' in the following remarks. Although Bruckner is dealing primarily, though not exclusively, with the problem of consecutive octaves versus doubling, his mode of thinking is certainly more 'analytical' than those of many nineteenth-century writers on music, who generally deal with such practical, technical problems rather superficially, if at all. 'Analysis' as we know it in our post-Schenker age is certainly more 'analytical' than in Bruckner's time, but I would give Bruckner credit for being very analytical by contemporary standards. Surely, it is significant that he was Schenker's teacher. Would Schenker have been so exercised by the problem of consecutives etc. if Bruckner and Brahms had not first raised the issue in so evocative a way?
3. Korstvedt, 'The First Published Edition', p. 15.
4. James Boros, 'A Conversation with Donald Martino', in *Perspectives of New Music*, 29 (1991), p. 215.

5.   Johannes Brahms, *Oktaven und Quinten u. a.*, facsimile edition with commentary by Heinrich Schenker, Vienna, 1933; Paul Mast, 'Brahms's Study, *Octaven u. Quinten u. A.*, with Schenker's Commentary Translated', in *Music Forum*, 5 (1980), pp. 1–196; Robert T. Laudon, 'The Debate about Consecutive Fifths: A Context for Brahms's Manuscript "Oktaven und Quinten"', in *Music and Letters*, 73 (1992), pp. 48–61.

6.   See below, Thomas Röder, 'Master and Disciple United: The 1889 Finale of the Third Symphony', p. 93ff.

7.   Korstvedt, 'The First Published Edition', p. 14.

8.   The letter continues: 'Since then [the January performance] I have, at my own initiative, made changes …'

9.   Korstvedt, 'The First Published Edition', p. 23.

10. For a detailed discussion of the diaries, see Elisabeth Maier, 'Access to an "Inner Biography" of Anton Bruckner', in *Bruckner Studies*, eds. Paul Hawkshaw and Timothy L. Jackson (Cambridge: Cambridge University Press, 1997), pp. 32–53. Maier is currently preparing a scholarly inventory and edition of the diaries, most of which are preserved in the Austrian National Library's Music Collection.

11. The notes on metrical structure in Beethoven's Third and Ninth Symphonies are found in the *Österreichischen Volks- und Wirtschafts-Kalender für das Schaltjahr 1876*, while the study of octaves are in the *Neuer Krakauer Schreib-Kalender für das Jahr 1877*, Wn Mus. Hs. 3182–1.

12. For more on Bruckner's extensive citations and allusions to the music of other composers see, Leopold Nowak, 'Mendelssohns *Paulus* und Anton Bruckner', *Über Anton Bruckner. Gesammelte Aufsätze*, (Vienna, 1985), pp. 191–4; Constantin Floros, 'Zur Deutung der Symphonik Bruckners – Das Adagio der Neunten Symphonie', in *Bruckner-Jahrbuch 1981*, (Linz, 1982), pp. 89–96; 'Die Zitate in Bruckner's Symphonik', in *Bruckner-Jahrbuch 1982/83*, (Linz, 1984), pp. 7–16; Timothy L. Jackson, '"Schubert as John the Baptist to Wagner-Jesus" – Large-scale Enharmonicism in Bruckner and his Models', in *Bruckner-Jahrbuch 1991–93*, (Linz, 1995), pp. 61–108; 'The Finale of Bruckner's Seventh Symphony and Tragic Reversed Sonata Form', in *Bruckner Studies*, pp. 140–208.

13. Friedrich Eckstein, *Erinnerungen an Anton Bruckner*, (Vienna, 1923), p. 7.

14. Wilhelm Glöde, 'Eine Hommage Anton Bruckners an Mozart?', in *Bruckner Jahrbuch 1984/85/86*, (Linz, 1988), pp. 7–14.

15. Simon Sechter, *Das Finale der Jupiter-Symphonie (C Dur) von W. A. Mozart*, ed. Friedrich Eckstein, (Vienna, 1923), p. 9.

16. 'Seite 8 Moz. *Requiem* Violin I mit Tenor dann Alt. Seite 12. I Violin Octav mit Alt. Seite 12. Ebenso Seite 13'. The interested reader may consult facsimiles of these diary pages in the earlier version of this study published in *Music and Letters*.

17. Göllerich-Auer, *Anton Bruckner*, IV/1, pp. 443–4.

18. Alfred Orel, 'Eine Mozartstudie Anton Bruckners', in *Mozart-Almanach für das Jahr 1941*, (Vienna, 1941), pp. 105–11.

19. Orel, 'Eine Mozartstudie', p. 107.

20. Paul Hawkshaw's findings are reported in 'An Anatomy of Change: Anton Bruckner's Revisions to the Mass in F Minor', in *Bruckner Studies*, pp. 1–30.

21. The complete text is published in *Bruckner, Vorlesungen über Harmonielehre und Kontrapunkt an der Universität Wien*, ed. Ernst Schwanzara, (Vienna, 1950), p. 53.

22. Timothy L. Jackson, 'Bruckner's Metrical Numbers', in *Nineteenth Century Music*, 14 (1990), pp. 101–31.

23. The metrical aspect of Bruckner's Beethoven studies is discussed by Leopold Nowak in 'Metrische Studien von Anton Bruckner an Beethovens III. und IX. Symphonie', and 'Anton Bruckners *Eroica*-Studien', in *Über Anton Bruckner. Gesammlte Aufsätze*, (Vienna, 1985), pp. 105–15, and 257–65. Bruckner's annotated scores of

Beethoven's Third and Ninth Symphonies are preserved in the Gesellschaft der Musikfreunde. I am grateful to Otto Biba for allowing me to consult them.

24. While one cannot discount the possibility that Bruckner could have entered the *Requiem* notes on still empty diary pages at a later date, it is probable that the *Requiem* analysis does indeed date from the summer of 1877.

25. Ernst Hess, 'Zur Ergänzung des Requiems von Mozart durch F. X. Süssmayr', in *Mozart-Jahrbuch*, 1959, pp. 99–108; Franz Beyer, *Wolfgang Amadeus Mozart. Requiem*, Munich, 1979, pp. 5–33; Richard Maunder, *Mozart's Requiem – On Preparing a New Edition* (Oxford: Oxford University Press, 1988). See also Walter Wlcek, *Franz Xaver Süssmayr als Kirchenkomponist* (Tutzing: Hanschneider, 1978).

26. George Henschel reports: 'Then we went together through the full score of Mozart's Requiem, which he [Brahms] had undertaken to prepare for a new edition of that master's works. I admired the great trouble he had taken in the revision of the score. Every note of Süssmayr's was most carefully distinguished from Mozart's own' (*Personal Recollections of Johannes Brahms*, (Boston, 1907), p. 34, quoted from Imogen Fellinger, 'Brahms's View of Mozart', in *Brahms. Biographical, Documentary, and Analytical Studies* (Cambridge: Cambridge University Press, 1983), pp. 48–49.

27. Schenker's score of the Mozart *Requiem* is preserved in the Oswald Jonas Memorial Collection at the University of California, Riverside.

28. 'Hauptgrundzug im *Requiem* ist: Streicher mit Gesang –; entweder ohne Variande im Einklang; oder mit Variande in der Oktave, I. mit Sopran. II. mit Alt. Viola mit Ten[or]'.

29. 'Im Mozartschen *Requiem* geht übrigens bei der Variande auch I. Violin in Oktav höher mit Alt oder Tenor. Viola auch mit Baß oder mit Sopran (Gesang) auch Contra[punkt]'.

30. Maunder, *Mozart's Requiem*, p. 57.

31. Page 61 of Bruckner's score: '*Seite 61. Viola als Terzen zum Baß macht mit Gesang (Canon)[.] offene Oktaven, off[ene] Einklänge, bald mit Sopran bald mit Tenor im Laufe des Contrap[unkts]*'.

32. Page 13 of Bruckner's score: '*Seite 12. I. Violin Oktav mit Alt. ebenso Seite 13*'.

33. Pages 30 and 41 of Bruckner's score.

34. Pages 127 and 130 of Bruckner's score.

35. Leopold Nowak, *Enstehungs- und Überlieferungsgeschichte des Requiem-Fragments*, Neue Mozart Ausgabe, I: 1/2/i, 1965.

36. See Hawkshaw, 'An Anatomy of Change'.

37. See Hawkshaw, 'An Anatomy of Change'.

38. The extent to which the Bruckner symphonies remained unknown in the nineteenth century is revealed by the lack of performances, especially of the first versions: the 'Nullte' Symphony, the first versions of the Second, Third, and Fourth Symphonies, and the second and third versions of the Fourth Symphony, the Sixth Symphony (in its entirety), the first version of the Eighth Symphony, and the Ninth Symphony were never played during the composer's lifetime. Additionally, Bruckner did not hear the Fifth Symphony, except as performed on two pianos.

39. I employ the term 'pitch class' rather than 'pitch' since I do not wish to specify register.

40. Some of the changes that Bruckner made to the F minor Mass in the early 1890s were incorporated in the printed edition, other revisions were modified yet again (presumably by Oberleithner and/or Schalk), while further revisions – such as those concerning the consecutive octaves in the Credo – were completely ignored. This annotation suggests Bruckner's irritation specifically with Schalk, but probably with Oberleithner as well; it is one of several indicators of Bruckner's concern in his last

years that he had lost control of the collaboration with disciples in the publication of his works.
41.   Edward Laufer, 'Aspects of Prolongation Procedures in Bruckner's Ninth Symphony *Adagio*', in *Bruckner Studies*, p. 209.

Part Two
Symphonist: Analytical Considerations

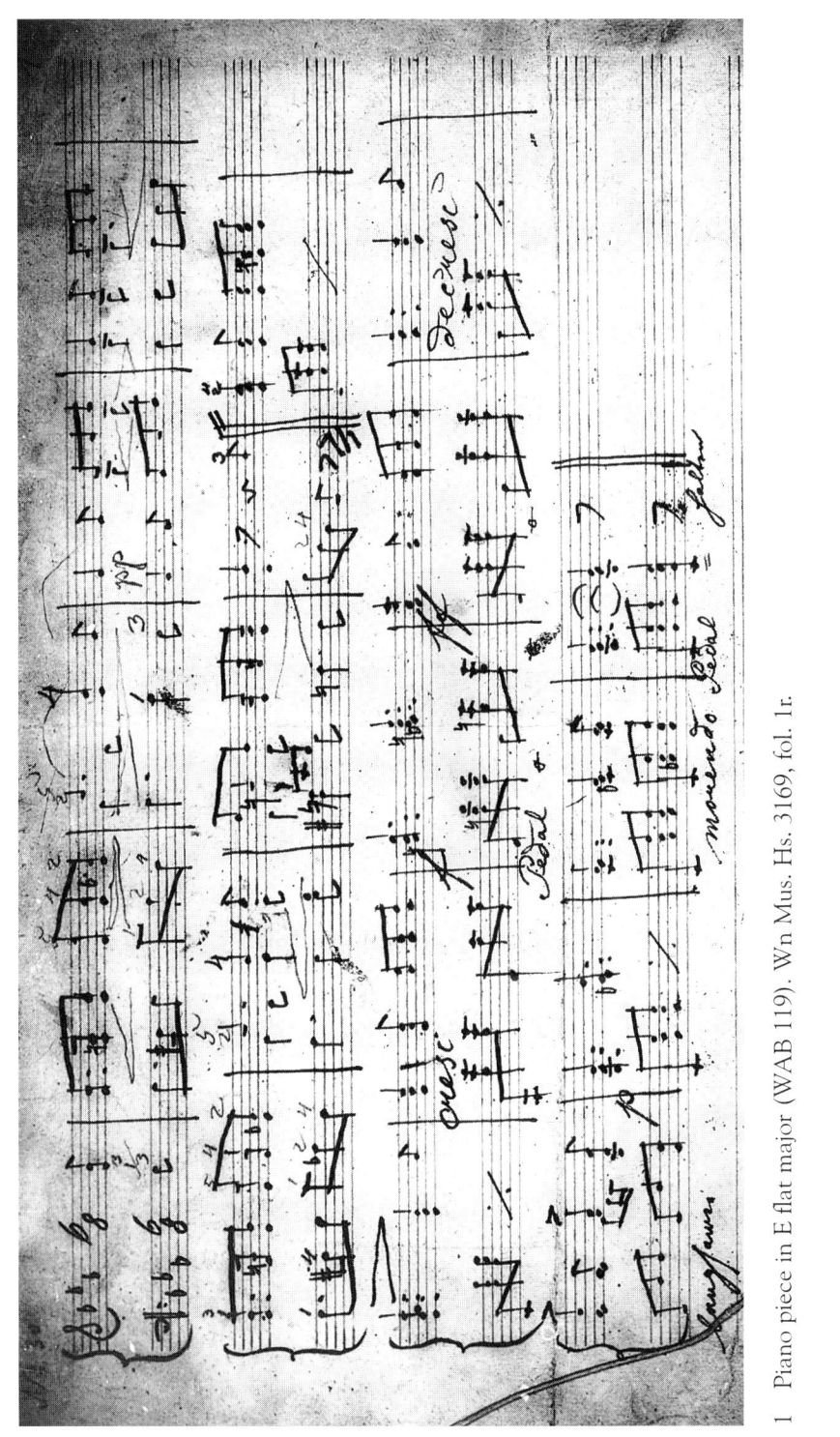

1 Piano piece in E flat major (WAB 119). Wn Mus. Hs. 3169, fol. 1r.

2   Mass in F minor, *Gloria*, autograph score. Wn Mus. Hs. 2106, fol. 36v

2   (concluded)

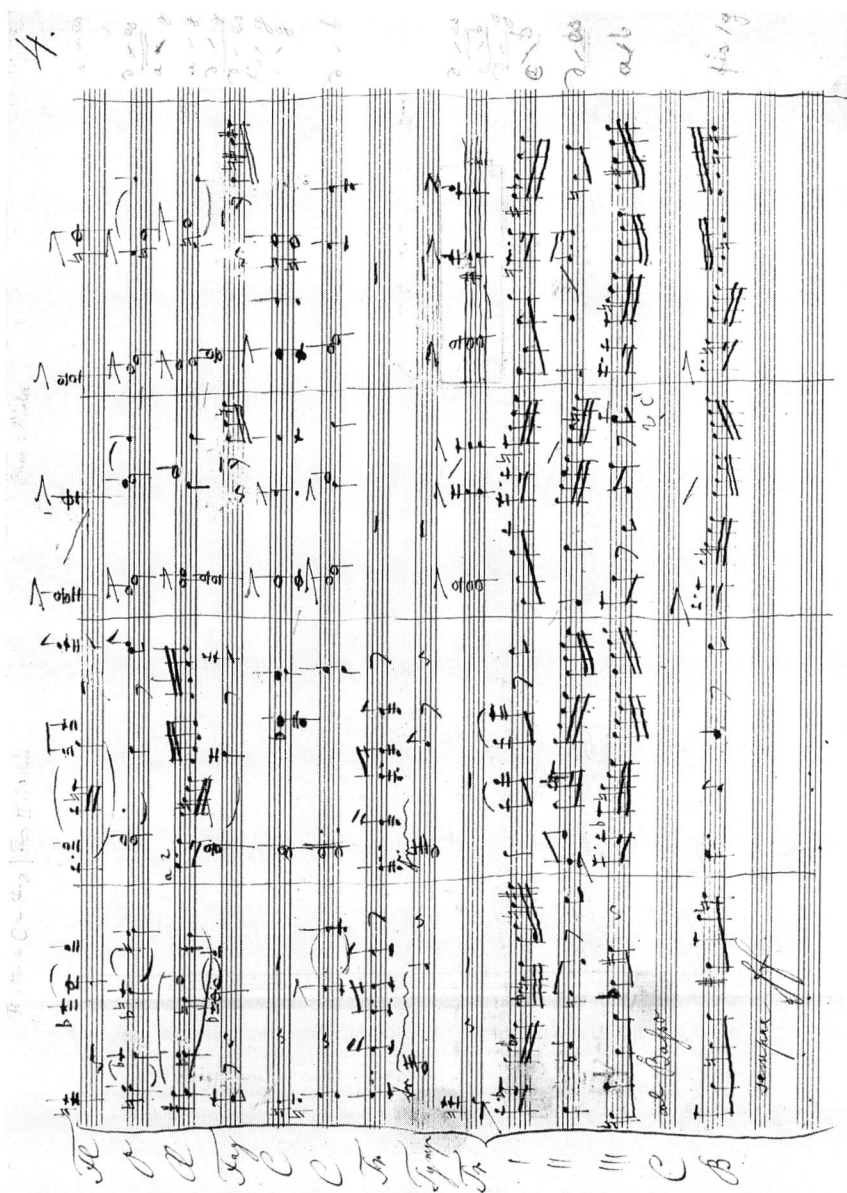

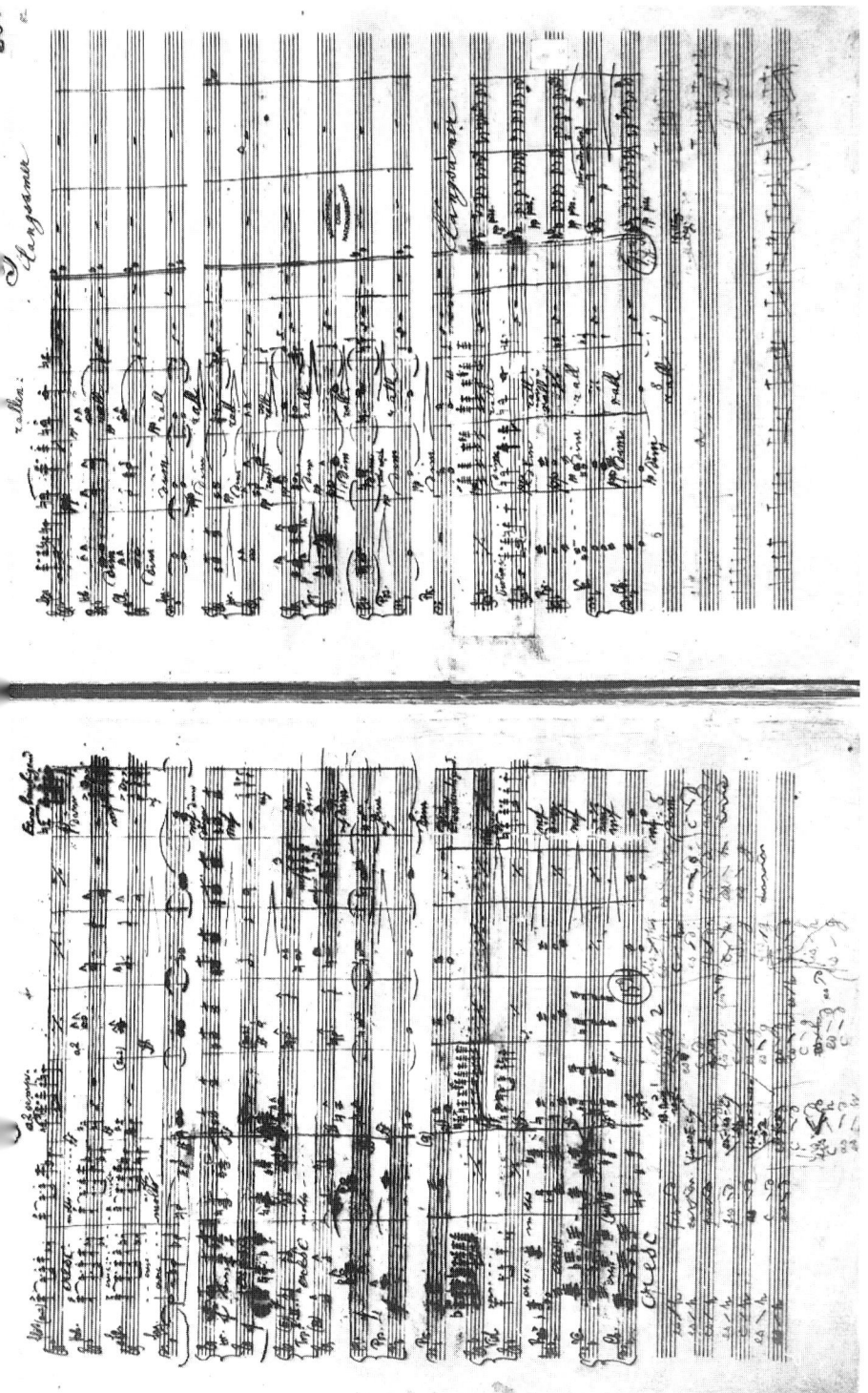

4   Autograph corrections to Symphony No. 3. Wn Mus. Hs. 6081, fols. 81v–82r

5 Revision of Symphony No. 3, part autograph. Wn Mus. Hs. 6081, fol. 72v

6   Copy of the score of Symphony No. 3. Wn Mus. Hs. 6029, fol. 16v

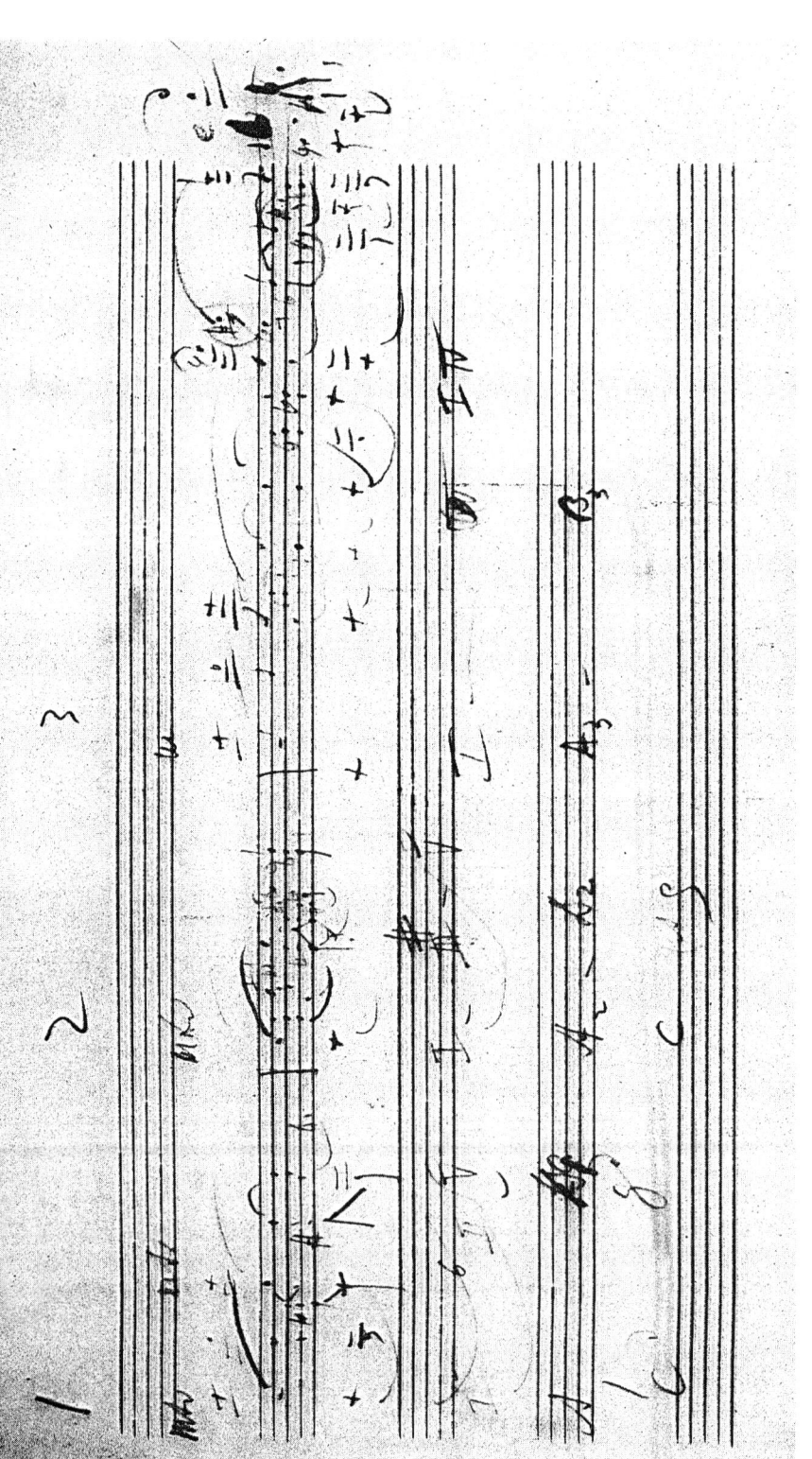

7 Schenker's first sketch of Brahms's Fourth Symphony, third movement. New York Public Library, Ernst Oster Collection, file 34, fol. 289v.

3 The early version of the Second Symphony

William Carragan

'Only in one point can we find the ideal equilibrium, in which the greatest
strength and lucidity is combined with the greatest splendour.'

George Santayana, *The Sense of Beauty*

The Second Symphony is a pivotal creation in Bruckner's work. In it, the concept
of the symphony that he would use for the rest of his life first came into being.
That concept included the two-part structure of the Allegro movements with a
three-theme exposition and reprise, and the five-part Rondo with coda that he
used for all of his subsequent symphonic Adagios but one. He also continued to
develop the use of orchestral texture as a thematic element, which he had already
employed in the D minor symphony composed in 1869, now called the 'Nullte'.
The Second initiated a monumental tetralogy of symphonies, concluding with
the Fifth, created without a break during the period 1871–76. This tetralogy can
be appreciated fully as such only if the early versions of the symphonies are
considered, since only they are truly contemporaneous with the continuous
development of the composer's style. The early versions of the Third and Fourth
have been published by the International Bruckner Society under Leopold
Nowak's editorship, and are being performed and recorded with increasing
frequency. The availability of these early versions is bringing about a major
reassessment of the quality and scope of Bruckner's accomplishments - and the
reassessment is entirely to the composer's credit. They have a structural integrity
and monumentality of form and texture that the more familiar later versions,
despite their wide appreciation, simply do not match.

As for the Second, it is the only Bruckner symphony yet to be published in its
early form. The first published score, printed in 1892 by Doblinger,[1] reproduces
the version of 1877 with some corrections and revisions. The well-known score
prepared by Robert Haas in 1938[2] is a combination of two versions made by
Bruckner in 1872 and 1877, and, though much closer to the version of 1877, is
actually neither. Leopold Nowak's edition of 1965[3] was a reissue of Haas's mixed
score, with several features introduced which bring the printed text closer to the
literal text of the composer. At present a new publication, instigated and

authorized by Leopold Nowak, is in preparation under the editorship of the present author as part of the Collected Works. It will include both scores, 1872 and 1877, together with a detailed critical report and will enable students and listeners to understand and appreciate more fully the part which the Second played in the development of Bruckner's art.[4]

The early version of the symphony has three variants: the first conceived in 1872, and the others performed in 1873 and 1876.[5] All include extended passages of bold and inventive music which have not been heard since the time of their composition. Precise dating of the changes is made possible by the existence of the composition score, three copy scores, and a nearly complete set of performing parts which were only used in performance under Bruckner's direction. The handwriting styles of the copyists who prepared and altered these sources are sufficiently distinguishable to make them extremely useful in identifying the symphony's chronological layers.

The manuscript sources for the Second Symphony are listed in Table 3.1.

Table 3.1   Sources for the Second Symphony

Music Collection of the Austrian National Library, Vienna (Wn)

Mus. Hs. 19.474	Composition score with changes dating from 1872 and1873. (Haas's source A)
Mus. Hs. 6035	Copy score, begun by Tenschert, completed by Carda. In its original form, it was dated 1872 by Carda; it was revised in 1872, 1873, and 1877, and probably also in 1876. In its altered form, it served as the printer's copy (*Stichvorlage*) for the first publication of 1892. (Haas's source D)
Mus. Hs. 6034	Copy score, prepared entirely by Carda, also originally dated by him 1872; revised in 1873 and 1877, and probably in 1876. (Haas's source B)
Mus. Hs. 6061	Orchestral part consisting of a brief passage for solo violin in Carda's hand. This solo was added to the Adagio in late 1872 or 1873. (Haas's source M)
Mus. Hs. 6060	Pages removed from Mus. Hs. 6035 in the course of revision. (Haas's source I.B)
Mus. Hs. 6059	Pages removed from Mus. Hs. 6034 in the course of revision. (Haas's source I.A)
Mus. Hs. 6095	Piano reduction by August Stradal of the material in Mus. Hs. 6059. (Haas's source O)
Mus. Hs. 6023	Holograph pages containing the 1877 changes to the Adagio. (Haas's source E)
Mus. Hs. 39.744	Holograph pages supporting the 1877 changes to the first movement and the development and recapitulated third theme group of the Finale. These were in private possession

Table 3.1 continued

in Haas's day and were unavailable to Nowak when he reissued Haas's score with corrections in 1965. (Haas's source F)

City and Provincial Library, Vienna (Wst)

M.H. 6781	Copy score prepared at the end of the 1877 revisions, bearing a dedication page to Franz Liszt. (Haas's source G)

Stift Kremsmünster, in Upper Austria (Kr)

Regenterei 56,8	More pages removed from Mus. Hs. 6034 and Mus. Hs. 6035 in the course of revision. Both Mus. Hs. 6034 and Mus. Hs. 6035 were also originally at Kremsmünster, and when they were moved to Vienna, these pages seem to have been inadvertently left behind. (Haas's source K)

Stift St. Florian (Sf)

Archiv 19/13	Orchestral parts prepared in 1872 by Carda with the help of several other copyists and subsequently revised in 1872, 1873, 1876, and 1877. (Haas's source C)

Whereabouts Unknown

Haas's source L	Pages removed from Mus. Hs. 6035, some of which had been inserts themselves. According to Haas, there are many annotations by Bruckner.
Source 'X'	At least thirty more pages removed from Mus. Hs. 6035, neither seen nor suspected by Haas.

Early Publications

Full score	Published in 1892 by Doblinger. The conductor's score follows the markings in Mus. Hs. 6035. (Haas's source H)
Piano reduction	For two hands, by August Stradal. (Haas's source N)

The dates of composition of the Second Symphony in its original form are the following, as given by Bruckner in Wn Mus. Hs. 19.474:

First movement	Begun 11 October 1871, [completed] 8 July 1872 in Vienna
Scherzo	[No dates given, but necessarily within the period 8-16 July 1872]
Trio	Sketched 16 July 1872 p.m., completed 18 July 1872 a.m.

Table 3.1   concluded

Adagio	Begun 18 July 1872, sketched 19 July 1872, 9:30 a.m. in Vienna, completed 25 July 1872 in Vienna
Finale	Sketches 28 July 1872 in Vienna, sketches 4 August 1872 in Vienna, begun on 10 August 1872 in Linz, completed on 11 September 1872 at St Florian

The symphony was created within a very short period, almost entirely during the summer of 1872. There are no surviving preliminary sketches, except for a very short fragment written on the back of the 1869 short-score sketch for a symphony in B flat which the composer abandoned (Wn Mus. Hs. 6018). The Second Symphony sketch is dated 1870. In fact, there is evidence in Bruckner's working score, Mus. Hs. 19.474, that it is here and there a filled-out orchestral sketch.[6] The first three movements, in the order first movement–Scherzo–Adagio, were completed in Vienna, and the Finale was sketched there as well. Then, sometime between August 4 and August 10, Bruckner went to Upper Austria, taking the manuscript with him, and there completed the Finale.

The folded sheets of the working score were not the only things he took with him. He also took a partially finished copy score, which had been prepared by the Viennese copyist Tenschert, and with it a sufficient supply of the hand-ruled manuscript paper that Tenschert had been using for the score to be completed. Tenschert had copied the opening movement and Scherzo, and the Adagio as far as measure 149, and perhaps straight through to the end of the movement. However, we do not now have the concluding pages of any form of the Adagio in Tenschert's hand, if indeed they ever existed. His name is known in the Second Symphony only through his signature at the end of the Scherzo, 'Tenschert Copist'. But he is also known to have copied two of the orchestral parts of the Mass in F Minor, in association with Franz Hlawaczek.[7]

The manuscript as we now know it was completed by a different copyist, Carda (apparently pronounced 'Tscharda'), who placed his signature at the end of the score, 'Linz 1872 Carda'. Most of this copy score, begun by Tenschert and completed by Carda, is preserved as Wn Mus. Hs. 6035. But some of its pages became separated from it during revision and are now in another bundle in Wn Mus. Hs. 6060; still more are at Kremsmünster Abbey in Upper Austria. Yet thirty-five more separated leaves were in private possession in 1938. Haas examined these leaves carefully and described them rather fully in the critical report to his edition, but he did not indicate where they were, and their present location is unknown. Furthermore, there were at least thirty more pages that had already disappeared by Haas's time. Perhaps Haas did not suspect the loss because he had not systematically reconstructed the original state of the first copy score in his 1938 study of the symphony.

Carda was also the chief copyist for the parts, and it seems that their preparation was the next phase of the project. Carda almost certainly stayed in

Linz as long as Bruckner was there, and four other copyists helped him with the string parts. This was in preparation for a rehearsal of the symphony by the Vienna Philharmonic under Otto Dessoff. The rehearsal did not lead to a performance, however, owing to the hostility of Dessoff, who thought the work 'nonsense' ('Unsinn') and impossible to perform, as well as opposition from a sufficient number of players.[8] A year later, on 26 October 1873, a performance by that orchestra did occur, under Bruckner's direction rather than Dessoff's, and it is pleasant to report that the whole orchestra had by that time become quite enthusiastic about the symphony. Even the reviews were by and large favourable, particularly mentioning Bruckner as a good conductor.[9]

Carda seems on manuscript evidence to have been working closely with Bruckner, entering various changes into the parts to make them ready for the performance. A second performance was arranged for 20 February 1876, and on that occasion another copyist entered additional changes. Finally, in 1876 or in 1877, both copy scores and the parts were extensively revised by two more copyists in preparation for a third performance to be under the direction of Johann Herbeck. That performance did not take place, and the manuscript parts were never used again.

It is interesting to note that several of the wind parts are labeled 'Symphony no. 3 in C minor'. This shows that at least for a while Bruckner contemplated admitting the 'Nullte' Symphony to the numbered canon as his second.[10] The string parts, which seem to have been made a little later than the wind parts, bear no number at all, and in several of the wind parts where 'no. 3' was indicated, a correction to 'no. 2' was made in pencil, possibly as late as the premiere in October 1873. Perhaps Bruckner felt that the new symphony was so much larger and grander in scope than its predecessor, that it would be better to regard the D minor symphony as a sort of second Study Symphony, and not give it a regular number.

The parts that have survived are one first violin, four second violins, four violas, five cellos, and four basses, all the woodwind and all the brass; the timpani is missing. Except in one case, the extant parts were the work of Carda at least up through measure 149 of the Adagio, very clearly in the order first movement–Scherzo–Adagio. There is abundant evidence in the first three movements that the copy score of Tenschert, not the holograph, was used as the basis for the parts.[11]

Sometime in the late summer or early fall of 1872, a very peculiar thing happened: every one of the parts was cut apart and rearranged in the order first movement–Adagio–Scherzo. The evidence from the parts that this was done before the Finale was copied into them is absolutely conclusive.[12] These events took place over a short period of time – from 11 September to sometime in October when the symphony was rehearsed by the Vienna Philharmonic under Otto Dessoff – and the indication that the symphony was never played with the Scherzo preceding the Adagio is compelling (always assuming that the whole symphony was ready to be played at the rehearsal). Nonetheless, the fact that the

Scherzo was composed before the Adagio, and further, that in that order, the last note of each movement is the first important note in the next, plead strongly for the earlier order. All through the months of composition, Bruckner conceived of the Scherzo as preceding the Adagio; only in that sequence can we be reasonably sure that we are hearing Bruckner's own conception without any influence from other people such as Herbeck. Accordingly, the first-concept version, designated the 'version of 1872', will be published with the inner movements in the earlier order, Scherzo-Adagio, with the statement that the 'variant of 1873', altered for the première, requires the middle movements to be played in the order Adagio–Scherzo. One may conjecture that Bruckner changed the effective and logical order of 1872 in order to avoid the accusation of copying the movement order of Beethoven's Ninth. Indeed, several of the 1873 reviewers mentioned the similarity of the two symphonies, and they had heard Bruckner's symphony only in the altered order, with the Scherzo third![13]

The parts were completed with the movements reordered. Carda finished all the winds and some of the strings, but for the other string parts assistant copyists were employed. They took up their work at measure 150 of the Adagio, appending their personal flourishes at the ends of the movements; one helper, Cervenka, also signed his work. Carda's own signature appears, under his graceful and distinctive flourish, only at the ends of three of the parts, but the same flourish without his name occurs very frequently throughout the parts that he copied.

Finally, Carda made another complete copy score, most of which now comprises Wn Mus. Hs. 6034, with separated pages preserved in Wn Mus. Hs. 6059 and at Stift Kremsmünster (Kr. Regenterei 56,8). This copy is written on different paper with smaller staves, and Carda's handwriting looks a little different, which may account for the fact that Haas did not realize that Carda copied the Finale in both manuscripts. The final page, now separated from the main manuscript and preserved in Wn Mus. Hs. 6059, bears merely the inscription 'Linz 1872'; but the identification of the copyist as Carda, considering the other signed score and the parts, can be considered absolute. Yet a third copy score, now in the City and Provincial Library of Vienna as Wst M.H. 6781, derives from Mus. Hs. 6035 in its final revision. It was probably copied in 1877, certainly by 1884, and bears a dedication page to Franz Liszt.

Early Changes to the Symphony

In working out the sequence of the various alterations Bruckner made to the symphony, the present editor expected that the parts would reveal that sequence more clearly than the scores, because the scores could be changed at any time Bruckner felt the need to do so, while the parts would only be changed when it became necessary to use them. Hence a principle can be enunciated: *an event in the parts is an event in history*. There are five events in the parts:

1. completion of the four movements, one by one
2. alterations contemporaneous with the completion of the symphony
3. changes resulting from the first rehearsal (October 1872), or in preparation for the first performance (26 October 1873)
4. changes made for the second performance (20 February 1876) or shortly thereafter
5. the comprehensive reworking of 1877

These layers can be identified on the basis of colours of pencils and inks, handwriting, degrees of consistency in the entering of alterations, and accidental features, such as physical indentation of datable inserts by the revision copyist's pencil while he was making other nearby changes.

Three alterations made at about the time of completion of the symphony can be clearly identified. One of these concerns several places in the first movement where the woodwinds play a distinctive five-note dotted rhythm which, by virtue of its recurrence in the Finale, may be considered the motto rhythm of the symphony. In the original version of a typical measure, the pitch of all five notes is the same; at an early stage, in four places, Bruckner altered the pitch of the short notes to a third or more below that of the longer notes. These measures can be seen in their earlier form in Wn Mus. Hs. 19.474. The earliest reading was also written into the copy score, Wn Mus. Hs. 6035, and the parts. These had to be altered in both Wn Mus. Hs. 6035 and the parts by painstakingly scratching off the notes affected and neatly inking in new pitches. In the other copy score, Wn Mus. Hs. 6034, one finds only the revised form of these passages. This alone proves that Wn Mus. Hs. 6035 is the earlier of the two copy scores, contrary to Haas's statement in his critical report. Furthermore, the fact that Wn Mus. Hs. 6034, the later score, is still dated 1872, shows that the change was an early one. It is curious that these laborious alterations are almost entirely inaudible in performance, serving only to thicken the texture slightly (Ex. 3.1).

The other two changes are of far greater importance. One of them, the reversal in order of the movements, has been discussed above. The other relates to the Adagio. Bruckner originally conceived this movement as a four-section A–B–A–B form with coda. However, toward the end of the compositional process, Bruckner decided that an elaborate fifth part would enhance the movement. The new form, A–B–A–B–A with coda, is the same as that of the Adagio of Beethoven's Ninth Symphony which, as we have seen, seems to have been the model for this symphony in other ways as well. The insertion of the fifth section can be explicitly seen in 19.474. Although it is not clear exactly when in 1872 it was brought in, the extension of the movement had to have been done by some time in September when the movements were reordered in the parts and copying was resumed. A feature of this fifth section, which Bruckner employed in every subsequent use of the form, was delicate, improvisatory, filigree-like passagework for the first violins. At first, this music, along with a short similar passage for the violas, was in groups of six or nine equal sixteenth-notes (Ex.

First Concept (1872)

Fig. 3.1e. First movement: dotted chords, first concept (1872)

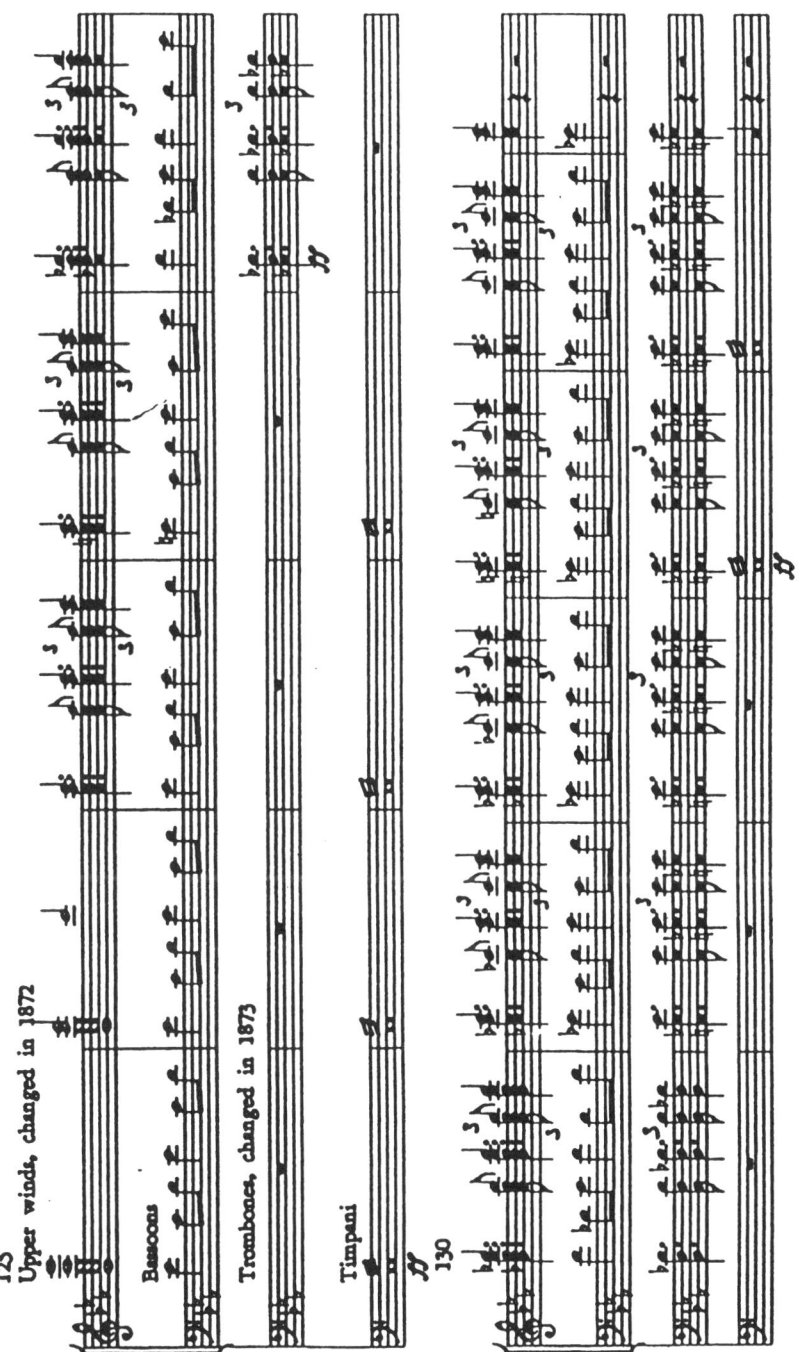

Ex. 3.1b   First movement: alterations in dotted chords (1872 and 1873)

Ex. 3.2a   Adagio: beginning of fifth part (1872)

3.2), producing a purling, 'watery' sound, reminiscent of the prologue to *Das Rheingold*. Soon afterward, though, Bruckner altered the groups of six notes to groups of five, and the groups of nine to irregular groups of eight and seven. This was done very artificially in Wn Mus. Hs. 19474 by scratching out one or two notes in each group; there was no rewriting of the figuration as there was later to be in 1877. This change was carried out before that section of the Adagio was copied into the parts because, although the early music in the first violin was detached and discarded in the revision of 1877, the area of the viola part containing the figuration remains and that figuration is in quintuplets, with no sign of having once been sextuplets.

Changes for the 1873 Performance

It is probable (but not certain) that the text which Bruckner brought to Otto

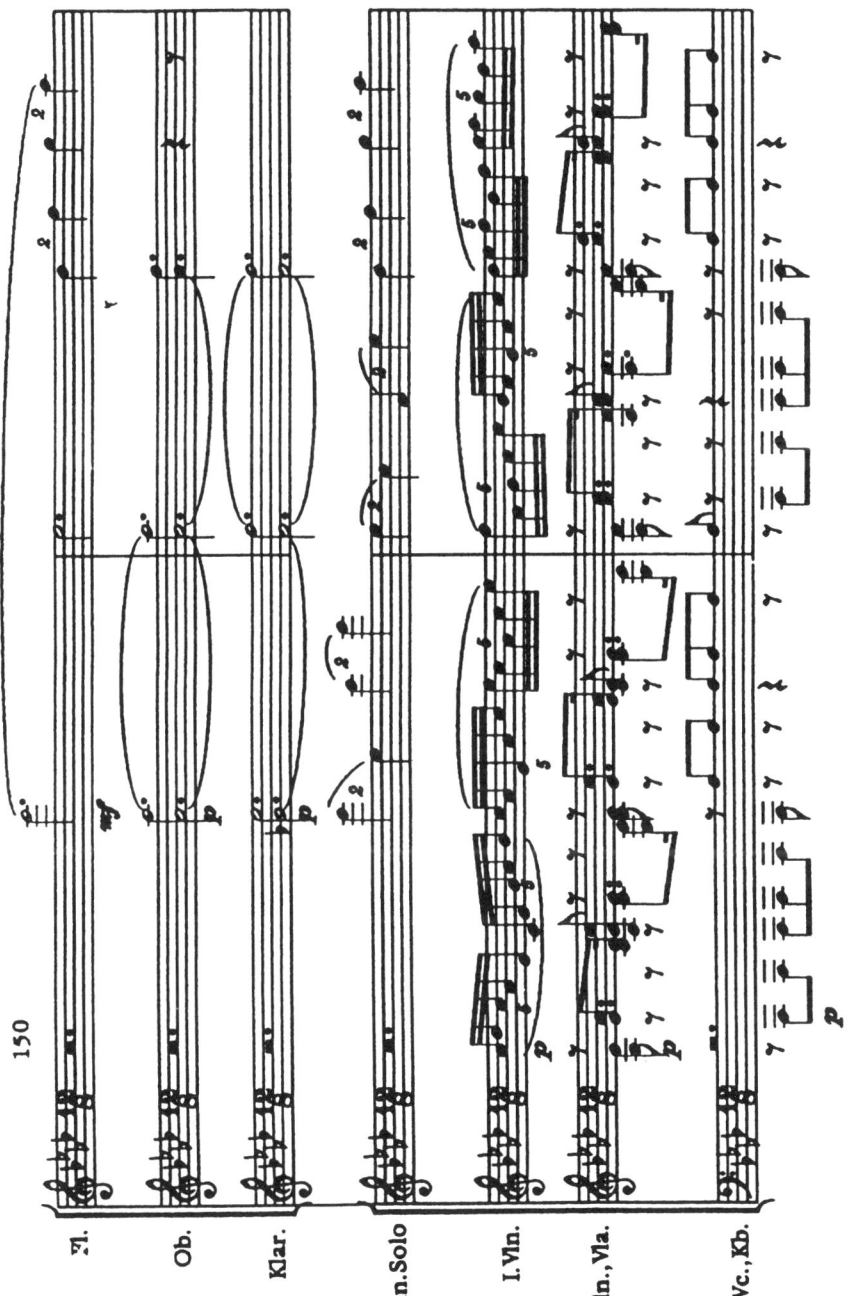

Example 3.2b   Adagio: beginning of fifth part (1873)

79

Example 3.2c   Adagio: beginning of fifth part (1877)

Dessoff and the Vienna Philharmonic at the rehearsal in October 1872 was the Tenschert-Carda copy score and the parts prepared by Carda and his helpers, incorporating all of the above-described revisions. The rehearsal may have led to two major adjustments to the Adagio. The first was apparently caused by the solo horn player's unstable upper register. Bruckner had originally concluded the Adagio with a lovely but treacherous horn solo; however, the parts (and Wn Mus. Hs. 19474) show this solo deleted and the music transferred to the first clarinet and the viola section. Nobody who has ever heard this symphony can doubt that the change was made for practicality only, but the removal of the horn solo became permanent at this very early stage of the symphony's existence. This means that in every subsequent performance and recording wherein the horn has been used, it has, strictly speaking, been incorrect. The change was entered into the parts by Carda, with the extra notes for the violas written on small pieces of music paper painstakingly inserted as hinged flaps.

The other 1872 Adagio change has long been thought to have been made at the instigation of Johann Herbeck, then the director of the Court Opera. He had been instrumental in convincing Bruckner to move to Vienna, and Bruckner had therefore placed considerable trust in his judgement. It seems to have been at this rehearsal, or shortly thereafter, that Herbeck suggested a violin solo for the fifth section of the Adagio. This solo, together with alterations to the bassoons, the upper pair of horns, and the alto and tenor trombones, was inked and pencilled directly into Bruckner's composition score, Wn Mus. Hs. 19.474, by Carda, who also prepared a special page for the solo violinist, now separated from the other parts and kept in Vienna (Wn Mus. Hs. 6061). The violin solo is in duple crotchets and duple quavers; although it is mainly confined to outlining the melody, together with the rhythmic complexities already caused by the shift from sextuplets to quintuplets in the first violins it must have created an amazingly detailed sound – not to say an impenetrable musical fog. At this time Carda also put the changes into the bassoon, horn, and trombone parts. These new texts were used in making the second copy score, now distributed among Wn Mus. Hs. 6034, 6059, and Kremsmünster. Ex. 3.2 shows the beginning of the fifth part of the Adagio in short score, in the readings of 1872, 1873, and 1877.

New trombone rhythms at two of the motto passages in the first movement (mm. 129-35 and 446–52) have also long been associated with Herbeck; they are entered directly into Wn Mus. Hs. 19.474 in pencil. This happened after Wn Mus. Hs. 6034 was copied, for the change is explicitly visible there as well as in 19.474 and 6035. Thus the change could be either from late 1872 or from 1873. In the new version, the trombones play in the motto rhythm instead of using the former half notes. The trombone passages were also extended slightly; and the kettledrum was introduced at m. 450 (Haas/Nowak 438), probably to correct an oversight. A change of the first and second horn from sounding G to C in m. 367 (Haas/Nowak 355) of the first movement, entered into 19.474 in rose-madder ink and showing as a change in Wn Mus. Hs. 6035 and 6034, is also from 1872 or 1873. The new first horn note is the same note that seems to have given problems in the Adagio, but here it is loud (*ff*) and therefore much easier to play.

It was almost certainly for the 1873 performance that the repeats of the Scherzo and Trio were cancelled. The repeats were scribbled out in the parts in a wide variety of methods, suggesting that the individual players were instructed to do it from the podium. The dating is ascertainable from the method of cancellation in one of the bass parts: the player used blue pencil for his notations, including the cancellation of the repeats. Another of his blue-pencil notations, the reinforcement of a rest, occurs at m. 516 (Haas/Nowak 504) in the first movement, in the first crescendo of the coda which was removed in 1876. So it may be concluded that the repeats were cancelled at an earlier time, which must be 1873.

Surely the most significant change made at this time was the deletion of Finale mm. 305–60 (following Haas/Nowak m. 289) and the substitution of twenty-four newly composed bars. Bruckner's manuscript of this alteration is now bound into Wn Mus. Hs. 19.474; it is written on the same kind of horizontal-format paper as the rest of that score and is entitled in rose-madder ink '*Neuer Satz (kürzer)*', i.e., 'new passage (shorter)'. A copy of that passage was also made on upright paper for use with the first copy score. Unfortunately it was in the 'private-possession' bundle that Haas saw in 1938, which has since vanished. Haas states that the pages were fastened together ('*zusammengeheftet*'), but also describes them as poorly preserved. Perhaps they were never protected by being bound into the copy score, and thus became damaged during use in 1873 and 1876. It is significant that Wn Mus. Hs. 6035 now shows the sort of damage along its lower and outer margins that vigorous use on a music rack might be expected to inflict, while the binding of Wn Mus. Hs. 6034 is faded but unworn.[14] For this and many other reasons, it is certain that 6035 in its varying states was the conductor's score. Since the insert pages with the *Neuer Satz* are lost, it cannot now be determined whether Carda copied them. But it is likely that he did, because it was certainly he who put the *Neuer Satz* into the parts. This was done by gluing in new paper with the new music on it, usually in such a way that the old music could still be seen. The indications in the parts guiding the eye to the inserted *Neuer Satz* were done neatly, with as little invasion of the original text as possible, so we may conjecture that the use of the *Neuer Satz* was not to be considered permanent. From today's perspective, the *Neuer Satz* is very charming, but the original material is far more bold and adventurous, and includes at one point a striking alternation of short viola notes with pizzicato chords in the rest of the strings. Perhaps it was this difficult, imaginative music which so offended Dessoff. (In 1877 Bruckner did eventually drop the *Neuer Satz*, but instead of restoring the 1872 music, he substituted new material which was only 18 measures long, viz. Haas/Nowak mm. 290–307.)

The date of 1873 for these changes, all entered by Carda, is consistent with the fact that Carda also made the two copy scores of the first version of the Third Symphony, one now at Bayreuth and one at Vienna (Wn Mus. Hs. 6033). These copies could not have been made until the end of 1873, when the Third

Symphony was finished. Although 6033 bears no signature, location, or date, it suggests that Carda was living in Vienna by then. Perhaps he had always lived there and only happened to be in Linz in the late summer and early fall of 1872 in order to be with Bruckner.

Yet another change to the Second Symphony's Finale at this time (1873) is the removal of the second crescendo in the coda, mm. 761–84 (Nowak mm. 656–79). The effect of this cut is to have the C major peroration at m. 785 (Nowak m. 680) burst in on the quiet quotation of earlier themes, without preparation, just as is done in the first movement. At the same time Bruckner seems to have been disturbed by the apparent weakness of the bass line in the finale peroration and added a fourth (!) trombone to double the contrabass part. It was written into the conductor's score in octave transposition rather roughly, the first page of the peroration now being preserved in Wn Mus. Hs. 6060, the rest in the lost bundle described by Haas. It was also written into the other copy score, neatly, by Carda, with '8va bassa' showing its proper sounding pitch; this music is now in Wn Mus. Hs. 6059. This trombone part descends to C (the organist's 'great C'), and is the only instance of Bruckner calling for such an extreme register for that instrument. He seems to have had the organ in mind when composing this passage, almost as if he were seated at the console, playing joyful chords in the motto rhythm on the manuals, with the melody as a pedal solo.[15] Adding the fourth trombone reminds one of an organist's reinforcement of pedal diapasons with a thirty-two-foot contra-bombarde, although it is not nearly as effective as that would be; only a tuba could produce enough sound to make the bass line really solid, and of course the tuba did not enter Bruckner's music until the composition of the stately chords of the introduction of the Fifth.

Changes for the 1876 Performance

These are much less complicated than the alterations for 1873, but they affect the sound of the symphony at highly critical points. First: the coda of the first movement was shortened by omitting the first crescendo. The cut, like all the revisions of 1876 indicated in the parts by a copyist using green pencil, created an awkwardness in the first violin line which was somewhat ameliorated in 1877.[16] The inner movements were not altered for the performance of 1876; the violin solo in the Adagio was kept; and the internal Scherzo repeats remained cancelled. However, in the Finale, some important changes were made. In the development, the fantasy on the second theme following the *Neuer Satz* was made more concise. In 1872, the contrast between the treatment of the wild and disruptive first theme and the noble, soaring, other-worldly second theme could hardly have been stronger. In both cases the themes show much more of their inner character here in the development than at any other place in the movement. However, the use of the *Neuer Satz* in 1873 threw the proportions off, and in 1876 the second theme material was cut and parity between the two sections restored.[17] The coda was abbreviated too, perhaps so that it would have a length similar to that of the first movement; although the second crescendo which had been removed in 1873 was restored, a much larger shortening was made by cutting the first crescendo and the quotations of earlier themes following it. Lastly, in the peroration Bruckner recognized the impossibility of getting a strong sound in the bass with the Finale's orchestra at the Finale's tempo, and rewrote the strings in unison, cancelling the impractical fourth trombone.

Another change, considerably more mysterious, must also have been carried out in 1876. This was a further rescoring and thickening of the melodic fragments in the fifth part of the Adagio. These changes seem to have been an afterthought since they were not entered into the parts. Perhaps Bruckner wanted to hear the tunes more clearly and quickly carried out appropriate revisions shortly after the performance, but by the time of the reworking of 1877, decided to go much further. Unfortunately the pages with these alterations are in source L and the editor has had to rely solely on Haas's description and printing of the passage in his *Vorlagenbericht;* if source L ever becomes available again, further evidence of the significance of this music (and the rest of the music included in it) may emerge.

The sequence of changes, revealed so clearly by the parts, should also be visible in the two early copy scores, Wn Mus. Hs. 6035 and 6034. It is, although it is not always easy to see. For example, the passage in the Finale from mm. 305 to 402 was disturbed several times, leaving in the scores an almost impenetrable tangle of stub ends, incomplete and shifted pages, paste overs sometimes concealing stub ends, strengthening strips of various widths and colours, and relocated sewing. In the first alteration to this music, done in 1873, mm. 305–60 were cut and the *Neuer Satz* added. Then in 1876 mm. 383–402 were cut, and a new tempo designation placed at m. 381. Eventually, in 1877, still different music was substituted for the *Neuer Satz,* and slightly but perceptibly later, the passage from mm. 374–82 was rewritten, shortened by two measures and reharmonized. Although the introduction of this new music and the reworking of mm. 374–82 occurred at different times, they were probably both done in 1877, quite likely only a few days apart, because both of the 1877 revision copyists were on hand both times. These changes, so easy to see in part after part, are obscured in the copy scores by a constant reshuffling of inserts and discarding and subsequent loss of important pages.

Supplementary Tempo Markings

A number of clarifications and additions were made in tempo indications. Some of these were entered into the parts by Carda in 1872 or 1873, as shown by occasional crowding in his writing; one of these was the change from *Allegro* to *Moderato* in the tempo of the first movement. Others seem to have been added by the players on instruction from the podium, as they are in a wide variety of hands. An interesting feature of these indications is the absence of any direction to play the second theme more slowly in the exposition and reprise, even in the printing of 1892. (However, such a relationship is essential for the later symphonies, and is made metronomically specific by Löwe in his 1888 edition of the Fourth.) Not until the first movement codetta, with its lovely woodwind solos, is there an indication to take a slower tempo.

Just as remarkable is the indication *Etwas langsamer* at measure 300 (Haas/Nowak m. 290) of the first movement and measure 403 (Haas/Nowak m. 328) of the Finale. In each case the music is a treatment of the second theme (*Gesangsthema*). Now these are examples of a structural element which occurs in most of Bruckner's outer movements near the end of the development (*Durchführung*), and always with an earnest solemnity. Although in the Second Symphony a slower tempo at this point has never been indicated in previous editions, which were based solely on the scores, for structural reasons it seems necessary; so it is gratifying to see the above-mentioned indication systematically entered into the parts in Carda's writing.[18] It turns out from indications in the parts that all the music beginning at m. 601 (Haas/Nowak m. 521), including the pre-coda climax, the second citation of the Kyrie of the Mass in F Minor, and the eerie pizzicato march, must be played at a slower and more flexible tempo, the basic tempo of the movement not being re-established until the beginning of the coda, at bar 695 (Haas/Nowak m. 590). This tempo structure would stand in all versions, even in the 1877 version, where the passage following bar 601 is completely rewritten and the citation of the Kyrie is removed. Its role in establishing the shape of the movement for the listener cannot be over-emphasized.

Comments on the Revision of 1877 and Haas's Edition

The many changes of 1877 include refinements of the shortenings of 1873 and 1876, as well as further abbreviations, rescorings, and the removal of some of the notorious general rest measures. It seems that Bruckner felt that the occasionally hurried revisions of 1873 and 1876 needed some detailed rethinking, not to mention the patching-up of problems caused by some of the deletions. Therefore, although at a cursory examination the version of 1877 seems quite close to the performing variant of 1876, it represents a great deal of thought on Bruckner's part and thus constitutes a new version while the 1876 music does not.

One of Bruckner's major concerns throughout his work was the appropriate manipulations of large blocks of music. Sometimes it was possible for him to appeal to guiding principles, as could be done in expositions and reprises, while in developments and codas, he was much more on his own, almost as Liszt was in composing his tone poems. Occasionally we can get an idea of what went through Bruckner's head by looking at his method of revision. For example, when he took out the first crescendo in the first movement coda in 1876, he also removed the corresponding first crescendo in the last movement coda to balance it. Many listeners have in the past been grateful to Haas for including both crescendos in the codas, because they produce a thrilling effect. However, as can now be seen, performing them in conjunction with music from 1877 is anachronistic and ultimately unethical, as the 1877 version has its own logic which stems from the composer, not from an editor. In his symphonies Bruckner seems to want the listener to experience the coda of the Finale in contrast or complement to that of the first movement; these changes maintain the symmetry of the two codas and a global logic for the symphony, despite the shortening.

A very curious feature of the 1877 version is that all four movements were slightly lengthened near their conclusions. In the first movement, Haas-Nowak m. 567 was added; except for the *fff* timpani, this is a rest measure.[19] In the slow movement, the clarinet ending was extended by the repetition of certain measures.[20] In the Scherzo, the upward scale at the end of the coda continues one octave higher through the interpolation of a measure. And in the Finale, an irregular three-measure phrase which creates a sense of excitement is made regular by the addition of Nowak m. 688.

An 1877 change which was made in only a few of the parts, sometimes in lead pencil and sometimes in ink, but which certainly belongs to the final conception of the symphony, is the alteration in tempo of the slow movement from *Adagio* to *Andante*. The interesting suggestion has been made that, with the slow movement now in second position rather than third, Bruckner took advantage of the major conceptual difference between the two tempos to reduce the contrast with the flanking movements.[21] If so, this change would be a refinement of a previously-made modification - the sort of thing we know Bruckner to have been doing at this time elsewhere.

Another area where major changes were made is the development of the Finale. This portion of the movement comprises: introduction, mm. 237–78; fantasy on the first theme, mm. 279–60; fantasy on the second theme, mm. 361–422; and transition to the reprise, mm. 423–62. The four sections have respectively 42, 82, 62, and 40 measures, and comprise a symmetrical structure enclosing the contrasting fantasy-treatments of the first and second themes. In the course of time both of these fantasy sections were shortened, the first theme in 1873 and later in 1877 (respectively the *Neuer Satz* and the 1877 material discussed above) and the second theme in 1876 and further in 1877. When the dust cleared and all revisions had been completed, the measure counts were (as given in the Nowak score): introduction, mm. 232–63; first theme, mm. 264–307; second theme, mm. 308–47, retransition, mm. 348–87, with respectively 32, 48, 40, and 40 measures. The retransition is uncuttable, but the other sections were reduced proportionally, by factors of 76, 59 (66 in 1873), and 65 per cent. This makes the fantasy sections less important, and perhaps they do not tell their story as eloquently in 1877 as they did in 1872, but the essential parity between them necessary for an effective antinomy is well maintained.

One further revision must be discussed here: that of the huge and multifarious third theme group in the reprise of the Finale. In 1872 this vast element stretched from m. 573 through m. 694, with subsections consisting of mm. 573–600 (outburst), 601–41 (crescendo, climax, and silence), 642–66 (codetta, quoting the Kyrie of the F Minor Mass), and 667–94 (pizzicato march). Three of the four subsections remained in 1877: the first, mm. 493–520 in the Nowak score and essentially unchanged; the second, drastically condensed, Nowak's mm. 521–39; *the third section or codetta removed*; and the almost unchanged last section, Nowak's mm. 563–89, with only a rest measure cut at the end. Perhaps Bruckner felt that the shortening of the development and the coda meant that this heavily-developed material should be cut also. (It is true that in Bruckner's later symphonies codettas tend to be omitted in recapitulations, and indeed the 1880 Finale of the Fourth has hardly any recapitulatory third theme group at all.) But what is important for us to realize is that, although Haas decided completely on his own to keep the 1872 codetta in his mixed version, he also wished to use the 1877 version of the music preceding it, which had been meant to lead directly into the pizzicato march, and not into the by-then-excised *Kyrie* citation. Thus in order to achieve musical continuity between the two incompatible passages, *Haas himself ventured to compose the first violin part in his measures 541 and 543* (These correspond to measures 643 and 645 in the 1872 score.) While this music sounds logical, and might even be what Bruckner would have done if he had made the other choices that Haas made, it is still true that Bruckner did not write it, nor did he ever employ Haas's structure in any of his versions. It is to Haas's credit that he put a vi-de over the second *Kyrie* citation, and over the many other passages from the 1872 version which he brought into the 1877 score, but from the present-day standpoint, it would have been closer to Bruckner's intentions if he had prepared a pure version, one of the five (1872, 1873, 1876, 1877, 1892) that are possible. So to mix the versions gives an improper impression of Bruckner's method of handling large forms, and misleads scholars and listeners alike. If we want to hear these features – the double crescendos, the long fantasies, and the two *Kyrie* citations, and for that matter the horn ending of the Adagio – we should listen to them in their proper context, which is the 1872 version.

There were even further changes (and some important corrections) made in 1892 for the first publication, which was overseen by Cyrill Hynais.[22] Whatever Hynais's role may have been, there is no reason to doubt that the changes and corrections were due to Bruckner himself. Discussion of these interesting matters must be deferred until the publication of the critical report to the Second Symphony, which will come out at the same time as the two new scores.

Conclusion

Work on the new edition of the Second Symphony was begun with a firm determination on the part of the editor to avoid all subjective judgements and judgements based on the sound of the symphony as one might like to hear it. The original intention was to determine the nature of the text handed to the first copyist on 11 September 1872, and call that the *Ur-Fassung* (original version). But the present study has shown such a simplistic approach to be inappropriate. The copy score, and probably the parts, of the first three movements were made before the composition of the Finale had been brought to conclusion, and the early changes to them must have been made soon afterward. Accordingly, the final decision has been to present each movement in the score as it was first conceived, and then to tabulate the subsequent changes in the critical report with as clear a dating as possible. This means that conductors will have quite an array of choices available to them, and editors can only hope devoutly that they will not mix the versions and create an even greater chaos than has obtained up to now. One could perhaps avoid some of the problems by presenting a presumed first-rehearsal version as the *Ur-Fassung*. But, aside from the ambiguity in the nature of that text caused by Carda's work both before and after the rehearsal, such a decision would mean the loss of the beautiful clarity of the sextuplets in the Adagio and the bold and melodically-integrated placing of the Scherzo before the Adagio. The editor is not willing to make that sacrifice, even at the risk of allowing a certain amount of subjectivity to creep into the edition. Besides, the critical report will give all of the revised material. In Leopold Nowak's words, these variants 'are all original versions'.[23] Indeed they are all beautiful music and the public has a right to hear them.

The quotation from George Santayana, a remark made by him in the midst of a discussion of architecture, may also be applied in many ways to the problem of the versions of Bruckner's symphonies.[24] To the present editor, concerning the Second Symphony, the 'one point' to which Santayana refers will always be the earliest 1872 version. In that version, the composer creates the finest balance between his vast and monumental forms, and the decoration and ornament which give the forms life and beauty. Other listeners might not agree with that choice, and the critical report to the new 1872 and 1877 editions will give them the other options which Bruckner employed. The only warning one must heed, is that straying from Bruckner's own versions as Haas did, and proponents of 'ideal' mixed versions continue to attempt, is also dangerously to stray from any possibility of finding Santayana's point of equilibrium in Bruckner's own thought.

Acknowledgements

The author acknowledges with enthusiasm the wholehearted cooperation, help, and encouragement of many gracious people. Among these are: in Austria, from the Collected Edition, Musicological Press of the International Bruckner Society, Prof. Dr Herbert Vogg and Dr Walburga Litschauer; from the Austrian National Library, Music Collection: Hofrat Dr Günter Brosche (director), Dr Ingeborg Pechotsch-Feichtinger, Dr Joseph Gmeiner, Mag. Sabine Kurth; at Stift St. Florian, o. DDr Karl Rehberger (archivist) and Dr Friedrich Buchmayr (librarian); at Stift Kremsmünster, P. Dr Alfons Mandorfer (choirmaster); and at the Anton Bruckner Institute Linz, Dr Elisabeth Maier (director) and Dr Andrea Harrandt. Also, in the United States, David Aldeborgh (Bruckner Archive, Poughkeepsie, New York), Paul Nudelman, Dr Paul Hawkshaw (Yale University), Dr Timothy Jackson (University of North Texas), the late Julia Carragan, Frederick Eaton, Laura Morgan, and Aaron Snyder. The author owes a particular debt of gratitude to the late Prof. Dr Leopold Nowak for selecting him to prepare the new edition of Bruckner's Second Symphony in the Collected Edition.

Notes

1. Anton Bruckner. *Symphonie no. 2 C-moll.* (Vienna: Ludwig Doblinger, 1892).
2. *Bruckner Sämtliche Werke A*, 2. Band: *II. Symphonie C-Moll*, ed. Robert Haas (Leipzig: Musikwissenschaftlicher Verlag GmbH., 1938). This publication includes Haas's *Vorlagenbericht* (critical apparatus).
3. *Bruckner Sämtliche Werke B*, 2. Band: *II. Symphonie C-Moll, Fassung von 1877, 2., revidierte Ausgabe*, ed. Leopold Nowak (Vienna: Musikwissenschaftlicher Verlag der Internationalen Bruckner-Gesellschaft Wien, 1965).
4. *Bruckner Sämtliche Werke B*, Band II/1: *II. Symphonie C-Moll, Fassung von 1872*, ed. William Carragan. Band II/2: *II. Symphonie C-Moll, Fassung von 1877, 3., revidierte Ausgabe*, ed. Leopold Nowak and William Carragan. *II. Symphonie C-Moll, Revisionsbericht*, ed. William Carragan (Vienna: Musikwissenschaftlicher Verlag der Internationalen Bruckner-Gesellschaft Wien) [forthcoming].
5. The late version likewise has a variant, that of the first printing of 1892. As with the variants of the early version, all details will be supplied in the new *Revisionsbericht*. The 1892 variant has to my knowledge never been recorded, and it would be most interesting to hear it.
6. Bruckner's technique involved writing out two lines for many measures in advance, then filling in the other lines until the desired texture was achieved. An illustration can be seen on a bifolio of a First Symphony source, Wn Mus. Hs. 6012, reproduced in facsimile in Göllerich-Auer, III/2, pp. 234–7.
7. This was first pointed out to me in 1990 by Paul Hawkshaw, with whom I have had many fruitful discussions, particularly about copyists.
8. As the rehearsal progressed, many of the players became enthusiastic and applauded, among them the cellist David Popper. Other people were also present, including Franz Liszt, who was completely charmed ('ganz entzückt') by the symphony. But Dessoff remained entrenched in his opposition. The goings-on at the rehearsal in October 1872 are described in Göllerich-Auer, IV/1, pp. 224–5.
9. One example: *"... eine Symphonie in C-moll von Bruckner, ein in der größter Dimensionen ausgeführter Tonwerk, welchem ein sehr ernster, pathetischer Charakter ebensowenig abzusprechen ist, als zahlreiche schöne, bedeutende Einzelheiten. Obwohl der Totaleindruck durch eine unersättliche Rhetorik und allzu breite, mitunter haltlos zerfallende motivische Form beeinträchtigt wird, war doch die Wirkung auf das Publicum eine günstige und die Aufnahme der Symphonie eine geradezu enthusiastische."* ("... a symphony in C minor by Bruckner, a composition carried out in the largest dimensions, of which a solemn, heartfelt character is no more to be denied than the many beautiful, significant passages. Although the overall impression was damaged by an insistent rhetoric and a too broad, occasionally insecurely disintegrating motivic form, the effect on the public was favourable and the performance of the symphony frankly enthusiastic.") *Neue Freie Presse*, no. 5298 (28 October 1873), p.6. From another review: *"Und trotzdem*

schulden wir dem Componisten das Geständniß, daß wir seit Jahren keine Composition eines zeitgenossischen Symphonikers kennen gelernt haben, welche uns in dem Zeitraum einer Stunde so viel Details voll Interesse, Bedeutsamkeit und künstlerischen Adel vorgeführt hätte. Bruckners Motive sind einfach, mitunter sogar populär und jugendlich frisch, die harmonische Wendung oft von bedeutsamer Originalität, die Mischung der Klangfarben meisterhaft." ("Nevertheless we owe the composer the admission that for years we have not known of a composition by a contemporary symphonist which offered in the period of an hour so many details full of interest, eloquence, and artistic nobility. Bruckner's themes are simple, occasionally even popular and youthfully fresh, the harmonic changes often of significant originality, the blending of tone colours masterly.") *Wiener Sonn- und Montags-Zeitung. Beilage zu Nr. 89* (2 November 1873), p.5. All reviews will be printed together with English translations in the forthcoming *Revisionsbericht*. I am grateful to Dr. Elisabeth Maier of the Anton Bruckner Institut Linz for collecting them for me.

10. Bruckner scholars are now in general agreement with Hawkshaw's finding that the "Nullte" Symphony was written in 1869, and not at all in 1863 (as had long been presumed). So the order and dates of composition of his first four completed symphonies are:

    Study Symphony, F minor, 1862/63
    First Symphony, C minor, 1866
    'Nullte' Symphony, D minor, 1869
    Second Symphony, C minor, 1871/72.

    The reference is: Paul Hawkshaw, 'The Date of Bruckner's "Nullified" Symphony in D Minor' in *Nineteenth Century Music* 6 (Spring 1983), pp. 252–63. Leopold Nowak told me that he had finally accepted Hawkshaw's conclusions, which indeed are inescapable.

11. Details will be included in the *Revisionsbericht*.
12. Tenschert's copy score was also rearranged at this time, but there is no evidence to indicate whether the Finale was already copied, since the Finale begins with a new signature of music paper.
13. Particularly noted was the fact that Bruckner recapitulated a theme from an earlier movement in the Finale. This is at m. 745 (Nowak measure 644), just following the first crescendo in the coda. Obviously the similarity is more apparent than real. One reviewer said that the Scherzo was a 'reine Beethoven-Copie' and again the Ninth must be meant.
14. Haas states in his *Vorlagenbericht* (page 2*) that the binding of Wn Mus. Hs. 6035 was 'erneuert' (restored?) in 1935.
15. Something like this is done by Bach in his Toccata in C major, S.564, which Bruckner played himself at the première of the Second Symphony. The review in the *Deutsche Zeitung*, no. 657 (28 October 1873), p.5, identifies what Bruckner played as the Toccata and Fugue in C Major, Peters Edition III, no. 8. The Schmieder catalogue notes that S. 564 is *Bach Organ Works* vol. III p. 72 in the Peters edition, which is the same; that edition is still in print! My thanks to the staff at the Joseph Patelson Music House in New York for helping me with this.
16. In 1872, the coda contained two crescendos, the first comprising mm. 500–31, the second mm. 532–67. (In the Haas and Nowak scores these are respectively mm. 488–519 and 520–53, the second crescendo being slightly abbreviated as it was in 1877.) Originally, in the first crescendo the first violin part began at m. 500 on c1 (middle C), while in the second crescendo it began on c2 (alto C), an octave higher. Now when the first crescendo was cut in 1876, as indicated in nearly all parts in

green pencil, Bruckner still wanted to begin the coda with the first violins on middle c. However, the higher tessitura had to be achieved somewhere in order for the violins to go on with the second-crescendo material, and in 1876 this was four measures later, at 1872 m. 536 (Haas/Nowak m. 524). In 1877, though, Bruckner wanted more material at the lower pitch, probably to approximate the air of great mystery created by the 1872 version. So he delayed the upward jump of the first violins for almost four more measures, only moving upward two eighth notes before the D flat of m. 540 (Haas/Nowak m. 528). A footnote on p. 46 of the Haas/Nowak score shows how, if the first crescendo is cut, the change in tessitura must be done according to the 1877 version. Of course it does not give the intermediate reading of 1876.

17. This abbreviation created parallel fifths between violas and cellos, which were only corrected, more or less, in 1877.

18. Professor Kurt Eichhorn, who conducted the Bruckner Orchestra of Linz in the première performance and recording of the new edition in 1991, was very interested in these features and felt that observing them added significantly to the performance. Other tempo clarifications can be detected by the listener in comparing Prof. Eichhorn's recording with ones already available. Prof. Eichhorn's recording was made in the Brucknerhaus at Linz, with Hiroshi Isaka as the engineer. It has been released by Camerata Records, Tokyo, as their CDs 30CM–195 and 30CM–196. The first CD is of the 1872 'first concept', and the second is of the 1873 first performance.

19. The addition of the measure near the end of the first movement is related to an amusing circumstance in editing history. In Mus. Hs. 19.474 the peroration, beginning on m. 568 (Haas/Nowak m. 554), includes twelve measures of rhythmical chords by the woodwinds and brasses. These conclude with an orchestral chord at m. 580 (Haas/Nowak m. 566), except for the two trumpets which by virtue of a repeat mark continue to play the rhythm through the measure until another orchestral chord at m. 581 (Haas 567). Now in 1877 the addition of the rest measure (Nowak 567) means that the trumpets no longer connect with an orchestral chord, and, as it were, fall off a cliff, since Nowak m. 567 contains only the timpani. All three copy scores, Wn Mus. Hs. 6035, 6034, and Wst Mus. Hs. 6781, agree on this point, and Nowak's score follows them, led by Haas's printing of the end of the movement on page 49* of his *Vorlagenbericht*. (It is not in the regular Haas score because at this point Haas is using the variant of 1873.) However, this reading is wrong. The evidence comes from two sources: the trumpet parts themselves (facsimile, Ex. 3.3), where the trumpets conclude the rhythm along with the rest of the orchestra, and also the 1892 first printing, where again the trumpets play only with the rest of the orchestra and there are effectively two full measures of timpani solo (Nowak's mm. 566, following the orchestral chord, and 567). The evidence from the parts is particularly significant because if the trumpets should have been playing through m. 566, Bruckner as conductor would have made sure they did. It is a great pleasure to know that the peculiar effect of the trumpeters falling off the cliff is not Bruckner's own. This circumstance underlines the fact that the changes of 1877 were not proofread until 1892. It is most regrettable that nearly all evidence of proofreading has vanished along with the galley proofs (with the conspicuous exception of an 1892 page glued into Mus. Hs. 6035 specifically at Bruckner's request to supply the missing Nowak measure 524), but there is every reason to believe that Bruckner carried out the proofreading himself. Only he would have known that the trumpet notes were in error in all three copy scores, and only he would have recognized the many other errors which had been made in haste by the revision copyists fifteen years before.

20. Certain aspects of this lengthening are discussed by Timothy Jackson in 'Bruckner's

Metrical Numbers' in *Nineteenth Century Music* 14 (Fall 1990), pp.101–31, where he seems to be correct about the relative significance of Herbeck and Bruckner himself in the revisions (p. 112). It is interesting that the addition of Nowak measure 688, which must have been done for the sake of metrical uniformity, is not supported by an explicit metrical grid; at this point near the end of the movement, Bruckner could simply apply the metrical thinking mentally. The *Revisionsbericht* will include both metrical grids (the composition grid of 1872 and the revision grid of 1877) in parallel tables for easy comparison. Jackson's powerful statements about the legitimacy of these grids, and their importance to both composer and analyst, are welcome and overdue in Bruckner studies.

21. Timothy Jackson, personal communication (1994).
22. Haas, *Vorlagenbericht*, page 8*.
23. Personal communication (1989).
24. George Santayana, *The Sense of Beauty, being the Outlines of Aesthetic Theory* (Cambridge, Massachusetts: MIT Press, 1988), p. 104.

Ex. 3.3   First movement, first trumpet part at end (facsimile)

4 Master and disciple united: the 1889 Finale of the Third Symphony

Thomas Röder

In 1950, Fritz Oeser published a new edition of the first print of Bruckner's Third Symphony which contained the second (1877) version.[1] According to Oeser, this version expressed the content of the 'Wagner' Symphony in the most satisfactory way.[2] Since Oeser had worked with Robert Haas from about 1940 until 1945, especially on the first publication of the earliest (1873) version of the symphony, this opinion was presumably that of the circle around Haas.[3] But, when the first version did not see the light of day at the end of the war, Oeser elected to edit the 1879 print instead.[4] If his aim was to influence modern programming, he was disappointed; the 1879 print did not become popular.

Oeser's edition was not incorporated into the collected works. Above all, it contradicted the editorial policy of the *Gesamtausgabe*, which is based almost exclusively on manuscript sources. Additionally, troublesome copyright issues had arisen after 1945. Oeser's edition was published by the West German successor of the Leipzig branch of the Musikwissenschaftlicher Verlag, the 'Brucknerverlag Wiesbaden'. However, Leopold Nowak, General Editor of the *Gesamtausgabe* since 1946, insisted that the 'real' complete edition of Bruckner's music was published in Vienna.[5] Some manuscript acquisitions also affected the editorial situation of the Third Symphony, whose striking feature until then had been its lack of first hand sources. In 1948, two years before Oeser's edition appeared, the autograph score of the 'Wagner' Symphony (which had been in the possession of Alma Mahler) was acquired by the Austrian National Library.[6] As a result it was now possible to publish the second score (1877-8) in a 'manuscript version', which appeared, albeit somewhat belatedly, in 1981.[7] At an undetermined point, presumably before the Second World War, the Austrian National Library obtained another source, the engraver's copy for the 1890 print.[8] This manuscript served as the basis for Leopold Nowak's publication of the third version of 1889.[9] With this edition, Leopold Nowak increased the number of published variants from two to three (piano scores not included).

Nowak did not use the subtitle '*Originalfassung*' for obvious reasons: in the case of the Third Symphony, there is no exclusive 'Original Version'.

In 1980 there was renewed interest in the specific problems posed by the last version of the Third Symphony. During the Linz *Bruckner Symposium* of that year, the long-standing doubts about its authenticity and 'Brucknerness' – particularly of its Finale – were expressed; the frequent changes of key-signature, the altered horn notation, the tenor clef for the bassoon, and the Wagnerian expression marks were all questioned.[10] It was no secret that Bruckner's former student and assistant, Franz Schalk, took part in preparing the engraver's copy of the 1889/90 print. Still, the extreme delay in preparing the critical commentary for Nowak's edition and the absence of at least some enlightening remarks on its editorial policy increased the suspicion which scholars and Bruckner lovers had of the new score.[11] The following remarks describe the genesis and some of the characteristics of the 1888/89 version of the Third Symphony. Of course, the last movement will receive the most attention since it was the starting point for the revision and is critical for the question of authenticity. I will begin with a reconstruction of the history of the 1888/89 version. It will, of necessity, be somewhat hypothetical given the incomplete and often contradictory evidence in the sources.

Reworking the Third Symphony: chronology, 1887–9

The success of the first performance of the Seventh Symphony at the end of 1884 sparked increasing interest in Bruckner's music. After this event, several conductors included the Third Symphony in their programmes.[12] It was the only Bruckner Symphony available in a printed score until 1889, when the Fourth was published by Gutmann. The response was not encouraging: critics and public compared the 'Wagner' Symphony unfavourably with the Seventh, and the dedication itself evoked expectations, prejudices, or emotions. The number of performances actually declined after 1885, although the general interest of the musical world in Bruckner's compositions continued to increase.

In the late 1880s, Bruckner was preoccupied with the management of his success as well as with the completion of his Eighth (until August 1887) and, immediately after, with the sketching of his Ninth Symphony.[13] At this time, Bruckner delegated preparatory work on his publications to former students, the Schalk brothers and Ferdinand Löwe. Franz Schalk prepared the engraver's copy of the *Te Deum* (1885, lost); Ferdinand Löwe worked on the Fourth Symphony in 1887; Josef Schalk and Löwe worked on the piano scores. In the process, the assistants created new orchestral clothes for two symphonies, and the composer hoped that these new versions would meet the public's expectations.

During 1887, as Löwe re-orchestrated the Fourth Symphony, Franz Schalk began similar work on the Third. In February 1888 when Bruckner recommended the revised Fourth Symphony to Hermann Levi, he characterised it as 'newly orchestrated and condensed'.[14] It must be said that the extent of Schalk's and Löwe's consultations with Bruckner is not known; the same is true of their own discussions. One assumes Schalk and Löwe communicated; in their revisions, both eliminated the recapitulation of the first theme of the Finale, for example. The similarities between these efforts could also be used as an argument for Bruckner's participation in the revisions. In the case of the Third, the composer had already identified this cut in the printed score of 1879.[15]

In the first half of October 1887, Hermann Levi rejected the newly-written Eighth Symphony. This meant that Bruckner had to continue working on this score.[16] Early in 1888, Bruckner corrected Löwe's revision of the Fourth three times, not only checking the alterations, but also his own contributions to this version.[17] He signed the score on 18 February 1888 and sent it to Levi nine days later.[18] At the same time he wrote to Levi that he had already made important changes in the text of the Eighth: 'It now looks quite different.'[19] In the meantime, sheets of the revised score of the Third were sent to Theodor Rättig, the publisher. Although Rättig still had almost a full stock of the first printed edition of 1879 on hand, he was persuaded by the composer or his young friends that another, improved version should be put on the market.[20]

Rättig reported that he received about fifty pages little by little and sent them to the engraver Brandstetter in Leipzig.[21] Either Bruckner checked each page before it was given to Rättig or he trusted Franz Schalk completely. The assumption that Schalk could have cooperated directly with Rättig during Bruckner's lifetime is somehow incredible, although it cannot be excluded. Rättig provides no information on this point. Schalk who began his *Kapellmeister* post at Reichenbach in the course of 1888, is supposed to have completed his work on the Third Symphony during the first months of that year. It is even plausible that large parts of the first three movements had already been engraved by the beginning of 1888. This may be the reason why Bruckner began to take a closer look at the Finale: Bruckner's earliest date in this movement was 5 March on the fringe of m. 313.[22] To the astonishment of his disciples and assistants, he dug deeper into the score and became engaged with Franz Schalk's suggestions.[23] It seems that Bruckner found more and more reasons for making these corrections. His dates proliferated; as Table 4.1 illustrates, Bruckner worked well over six months on this symphony, although not continuously.

In June or the first half of July, Gustav Mahler came to Vienna.[24] He had just given up his *Kapellmeister* post in Leipzig and finished his First Symphony. As soon as Mahler heard of the revision of the Third, he strongly recommended giving up the task altogether. As a result, Bruckner now found himself in a difficult situation. Regardless of the advice of his other young friends, Mahler was, without doubt, an authority for him, particularly regarding the Third. To question the first print of the Third was to question the collaboration between Bruckner and Mahler in 1878.[25] Bruckner took Mahler's advice in so far as he discarded the revision of the first three movements, despite the fact that about 50 plates already made had to be abandoned. But he did not follow Mahler when

Table 4.1   The dates in the 1888 Finale manuscript of Symphony No. 3

Thematic group	I	II	./.	III	I$^{Dev.}$	./.	II$^{Dev.}$	II	'III'	Coda
Letters:	A	B E/F	I	K N	O Q	R S	T	U V	W Y	Z
Date										
3–5					x					
3–12								x		
3–16			x							
3–19*									x	
5–12					x	x				
5–14						x				
5–22								x		
5–29										x
7–14		x								
7–19				x						
7–27		x						x		
7–29								x		
7–30		x								
7–31								x		
8–1		x						x		
8–2		x			x			x		
8–3		x								
8–4		x	x							
8–6			x		x					
8–7		x	x				x			
8–16				x						
8–17						x				
8–18						x				
8–19						x	(x)			
8–20									x	
8–21										x
8–23										x
8–24		x								
9–1		x	x				x	(x)		
9–4		x					x	(x)		
9–6		x								
9–9		x								
9–12		xx								
9–14		x								
9–15		x								
9–16		x								
9–17		x								
9–30			x							
	A	B E/F	I	K N	O Q	R S	T	U V	W Y	Z

[9–4: beginning of the revision of the first movement]

* Date not in the revision score but in a sketch bifolio.

he accepted and kept the new Finale, which he had mulled over for almost half a year. So, in fact, Schalk's manuscript became the starting point for his own new revision. After revising the Finale manuscript, the composer checked the other movements using the printed score. In taking the printed score as his point of departure, Bruckner accepted Mahler's advice to give up the revision and return to the print. Nevertheless, the result of checking the first three movements was a carefully 'updated' score, including some pages of new composition. Revising, improving, or polishing was obviously the composer's second nature. Bruckner was not deterred by a narrow-lined printed score that was difficult to work with; he made this revision even though it occupied about four additional months of an extremely busy period in his life.[26]

There are too many gaps and unreliable accounts to tell the story any more accurately. The only available documents are:

- the Bruckner-Schalk manuscript (Wn Mus. Hs. 6081) with all its dates
- letters by Bruckner and Josef Schalk
- reports by Rättig and Klose.[27]

Important documents which are lost include:

- the manuscript(s) from which Rättig engraved the new plates.[28]
- 52 engraved plates.[29]

The letters by Bruckner are rather insignificant or, at the very least, have to be interpreted. For instance, Bruckner wrote to Baron Wolzogen at the beginning of 1889 that he had been working on the Third since June 1888.[30] This is contradicted by the dates in the manuscript. If there is any accuracy to Bruckner's own report, it is probably in the context of Mahler's visit. Since Mahler encouraged Bruckner to leave the former version untouched, Bruckner may have felt that, from then on, the reworking was his own project.

Although there are many date entries in the manuscript, the chronology of the reworking is not at all clear. The composer was working continuously on the Eighth at the same time.[31] Indeed, working on several scores might be one of the reasons that so many date entries were necessary. Although there are obvious gaps in dating in the Finale, as well as in the other movements, it is evident from the manuscript that Bruckner scrutinized the undated passages as intensively as the dated ones. Table 4.1 illustrates that Bruckner started dating the Finale in the second section of the development. In May, he still seems to have been checking the same section. In July, after Mahler's intervention, he increasingly turned his attention to the first appearance of the second theme, the 'Polka-Chorale', often comparing this section with its counterpart in the recapitulation. Bruckner was still busy with this thematic group during the first half of September when he had already begun to revise the first movement. After the revision of the remaining movements, in March 1889 Bruckner entered his last date in the manuscript of the Third and, after a long interruption, a new date in a manuscript of the Eighth.[32]

Abridgements and transitions: an old tale of woe

Franz Schalk's copy of the Finale must have been based on some primary source or at least required instructions from Bruckner. In matters of orchestration, he may have felt that he had a free hand, but as far as the task of abbreviating the form was concerned, the severe abridgements had already been authorized by Bruckner: two in the printed score of 1879 and one in Bruckner's hand in his personal copy of the print.[33] This last abridgement occurs in the development; here Schalk may even have used Bruckner's own score as the basis for his revised copy. The first two cuts cancel the recapitulations of the first theme and the third thematic group. The cut of the third thematic group had not been completely marked in the 1879 printed score by mistake; it is found in the piano score.[34] In his new revision, Bruckner only had to make sure that all these sections were eliminated. If Schalk made the cuts, he did so according to precedents established by Bruckner. The only other abridgement in Schalk's Finale affected four measures which Bruckner also eliminated himself.[35] In this context Josef Schalk's comment to his brother Franz in June, 'By the way, your abridgements and transitions are kept' is strange.[36] There was no abridgement by Schalk to be kept.

Bruckner must have given further directions to his helpful young friend: he asked Schalk to make transitions in the Finale where beforehand sharp breaks were to be found. In the exposition, Schalk linked the first and second thematic groups together (mm. 63–4). In the second part of the Finale, he created a transition, his own *Ersatzkomposition* (before the coda, mm. 391/92). Although Bruckner accepted both of these additions, he rejected others. The result of the above-mentioned cut between mm. 192–3, for example, was the cancellation of a transition Schalk had made. Schalk proposed another transition between the chorale section from the end of the development and the beginning of the recapitulation, which then starts with the chorale/polka combination (after m. 361). Schalk planned a continuously marching passage with the pizzicato viola; Bruckner replaced it with two measures containing a final rest (359–60). He must have wanted a break at this important structural pomt.

The strategy of making cuts and welding the remaining sections together has a history.[37] A musical text without obvious breaks is more difficult for conductors to abridge. In fact, the 'Wagner' Symphony had already been cut in obvious places for the 1877 performance.[38] Presumably, Bruckner had to follow instructions from Johann Herbeck, who was originally scheduled to conduct. Two independent reports confirm that the duration of that performance was forty-five minutes, about eight minutes less than a regular performance of the last version.[39] In preparing the 1877 score for printing, Bruckner had already tried to make abridging more difficult. He accepted some cuts made for the performance and welded together two sections of the main theme crescendo in the first movement exposition.[40] The abridgements marked in the first print are advisory; they mark the maximum cuts possible. The exception occurs in the

Finale where the '*vi-de*' suggestions allow for some variability of the text. In any case, with regard to the very first score of 1873, an 'intact' state of the work was definitely violated in 1877. Any restitution thereafter would already have been an illusion; the original balance of the 'Wagner' Symphony was never to be achieved again. This perhaps explains why Bruckner never made any reference to an 'original' version or to any damage the piece could suffer from cutting, as he did in the case of the 'Romantic' or the Eighth.

The alterations raise a number of critical issues. The assumption that there is a sonata form to be 'spoiled' takes for granted that Bruckner composed from an orthodox formal position. The *fausse reprise* in the first movement made a cut of the recapitulation of the main theme a relatively easy matter.[41] This was done for the 1877 performance. The case of the Finale is not so clear cut. Ernst Kurth, who analysed only the abbreviated printed score of 1890, assumed the recapitulation of the Finale theme was hidden in the development.[42] Kurth took the authoritative state of this version for granted, although he mentioned the first print in the preliminary notes of his analysis. Later commentators ran the risk of judging from a point of view that has nothing to do with the work finished by the composer in any state after 1873. Robert Simpson, one of the harshest critics of this Finale movement, describes the juxtaposition of the chorale with the chorale/polka as a 'crass tautology' or even a kind of 'incestuous union'.[43] He deliberately uses metaphorical expressions which assume knowledge of and therefore a desire to hear the omitted music. But in terms of metaphorical description other solutions than Simpson's are possible: for instance, consecutive confrontation of sorrow (the 'pure' choral) and joy (the polka), or antithesis of mood as contrast to the following apotheosis section. It should be considered that the reappearance of the main theme, of this rude stormy crescendo at that point, makes no other sense than the fulfilment of a textbook law; critics of the cuts usually prefer a rigorous formalistic concept of 'absolute' music.

A defence of the abridgements is not necessary. There is nothing to defend; Bruckner accepted all cuts; he did so with consideration, and no abridgement was really quite new to him. It is remarkable how loose the fabric of this Finale is; the degree of thematic saturation always allows for a meaningful interpretation of the form.[44] One could stress the point that the final apotheosis comes too easily, that the trumpet theme from the first movement at measure 451 comes without enough preceding resistance and is, therefore, hollow, just a 'superficial apotheosis' and not an 'organic closing'.[45] With such an interpretation, an almost moral content for the symphonic conclusion is demanded, but the premises for this are not clarified. How hard should it be to attain the conclusion in order to project a dignified 'per aspera ad astra' narrative? Only the exuberant very first version of 1873 provides thematic procedures which mediate and gradually prepare the glorious final appearance of the symphony's main theme. After the abbreviations in 1877, there was no chance to regain the old state. One cannot resolve this critical dilemma by defending one's favourite version with philological arguments.

The inspiring interaction between master and 'disciple'

For Bruckner the Finale was not a place for arbitrary cuts. This is revealed by his behaviour in respect to the last abridgement. Here, Franz Schalk first observed the cut in the 1879 piano score (i.e. omitting mm. 465–514 in the second version).[46] Then he modified the subsequent section (mm. 515ff. in the second version) by reviving a passage from the cut parts of the development (see Ex. 4.1: a, b). He continued by adding harmonic progressions from the cancelled last tutti before the coda (Ex. 4.1: c, d). In doing so he changed the periodicity: two-measure periods became one-measure periods. In addition, Schalk reduced the prominent main theme fragment of four measures into two measures without adjusting the proportions (Ex. 4.1b). He reduced the thematic material to the initial notes of the main theme, a triplet rhythm taken over from the first movement, the wave-like figure of the third thematic section of the Finale, and a few harmonic progressions. It is easy to imagine that Bruckner, when arriving at this point, had to shake his head. In fact, he tried to correct the awkward first sequential section.[47] Then he realized that only a new composition of his own could solve the problems Schalk had created. The first sketch preserved is dated 19 March, quite early in the revision process.[48] From that day on, Bruckner became increasingly wary of his student's efforts.

In his replacement composition, Bruckner reintroduced the downward scales and the seventh chord in third inversion, both to be found in the previous version. Initially, Bruckner tried to suggest C major/minor through a dominant-like G (mm. 395ff.).[49] Finally he led the harmony from C sharp downwards in major thirds, to the tone F (mm. 413–21). Both ways are harmonically more intricate than Schalk's row of diminished seventh chords. The six–four–two chord and the dominant tableau are obviously the essential components of the pre-coda part of the Finale; in the 1878 version the trumpet theme from the first movement appears once again at the four–two chord as a kind of preparation (mm. 519, 523 and 527).

What, then, was Franz Schalk's contribution? Besides adding the dynamic marks and the German terminology, what role did he play in the revision?[50] To answer this question thoroughly, it would be necessary to do some physical research on the manuscript: to remove the many papers which Bruckner pasted over the staves, and to examine intensively the erased spots. It is not certain that the labour would be rewarded by any striking result. Changes of orchestration which Schalk can be shown to have made fall into the following categories:

– abandoning the classical concept of stable brass and timpani tuning
– softening of brass or woodwind or changing the blend of these by replacing doublings with solo parts
– adding one or more wind instruments where there was none before, to double or colour the pre-existing text

While Bruckner tolerated Schalk's first two suggestions – flexible tuning of

Ex. 4.1a   Franz Schalk's 'transition'; originally mm. 393ff. of the Finale, transcribed after the '*Stichvorlage*' of 1888/89 (Vienna, Österreichische Nationalbibliothek, Musiksammlung Mus. Hs. 6081, fol. 89 and 90)

Ex. 4.1a (continued); 4.1b

Ex. 4.1b (continued); 4.1c

Ex. 4.1c (continued); 4.1d

Ex. 4.1d (concluded)

brass and timpani and softening of the winds – in most of the other cases, he did not hesitate to correct his student. By doing so he made Schalk's suggestions his own. Often he erased Schalk's text or pasted over it. One example will illustrate this delicate interplay between the disciple and his master; here the end-result did not return to an earlier stage (see Plates 4 and 5).

The emergence of the symphony's primary theme toward the end of the development is a prominent and crucial point within this Finale.[51] According to Fritz Oeser, this

> G major peak gained splendour with the placement of the principal theme in the trumpets. The original disposition actually made more sense in that here this theme is announced (and mirrored in a strongly polyphonic way) in the darker tenor register first, saving the glorious discant (trumpet unison) for the end of the movement.

Oeser continues: 'For several reasons, the authenticity of the orchestration and of the dynamics also has to be questioned'.[52] However, the manuscript shows that the composer went to endless trouble modifying Schalk's suggestion into a score he could live with. Ultimately, he accepted some of the modifications in Schalk's arrangement. Schalk tried to achieve a firm chordal foundation in the lower register; it was his idea to keep the trombone parts out of motivic presentation in favour of sustained sounds.[53] The final shape of the trumpet parts was largely written by Bruckner; the first four measures (mm. 323–6) and the overall disposition were most probably by Schalk. In Schalk's contribution, the goal of the upper trumpets is clearly discernible: the sustained high sixth.[54] Of Schalk's treatment, Bruckner left untouched the part of the two lower horns, which present the inverted motive (mm. 324–6) one bar after the trumpet entry. This imitative layer is reinforced by woodwinds; Schalk clarifies the situation by giving both clarinets the main motive. Bruckner then intensifies this suggestion by erasing Schalk's text in the oboes (probably the dotted rhythm of the former score) and doubling the clarinet part. The dotted rhythm, which oboes and first clarinet played previously, was given over to the flute by Bruckner after some erasing. Without studying Schalk's score, Bruckner would not have had the opportunity to insert his masterly figuration in the upper violins, by which the harmonic centre G is suspended until the last crotchet.[55] Whether Schalk's 'original' score was prepared exclusively by him, and not as a result of some discussion with the composer, seems to be something of a moot point, since Schalk's score became a source of inspiration for Bruckner.

For Oeser, the 'strong polyphonic mirroring' in the lower brass relates to the 'glorious' end, where the main motive is presented in the trumpets. Should the opportunity for a colourful metaphorical interpretation serve as a basis for a value judgement? Even in the new version the passage retains the character of a prophecy, a vision, a foreshadowing of the end. The main effect is created by the non-tonic key and the paradoxical dynamics. These are common and stable features of both versions. Oeser's judgement is philologically at most half-right, and demonstrates with regard to style and aesthetics, that even connoisseurs of Bruckner's oeuvre were not immune to prejudices.

On the same page pairs of pitch names are visible. These reflect another aspect of Bruckner's 'regulation', not only in the context of his 'Wagner' Symphony, but in the context of the working technique of his late period. These letters are found on numerous pages and illustrate that the composer checked the horizontal progression of each part. Timothy Jackson discussed these annotations in chapter 2. The popular explanation reported by Bruckner's friends is that his aim was to detect and eliminate forbidden parallel fifths or octaves.[56] But sometimes he kept parallel fifths in the new version (see Ex. 4.2a). A more likely explanation is that he wanted to analyse the complexity of the part writing and particularly control the doublings. In Ex. 4.2b, the revised version shows an increased number of voices involved, which are all to be understood as leading-note situations. All leading-note progressions except two are carefully avoided.[57] Perhaps in pivotal harmonic progressions he wished to avoid emphasis of specific voice-leading by doubling.

Ex. 4.2 Voice leading as controlled by Bruckner. Thick line: two or more parts in unison. Interrupted line: octave doubling (4', 2'): (a) Transition mm. 48–9 (Finale, both versions); (b) Transition mm. 340–1 (Finale, version 1878), 322–3 (Finale, version 1888/89)

(a)

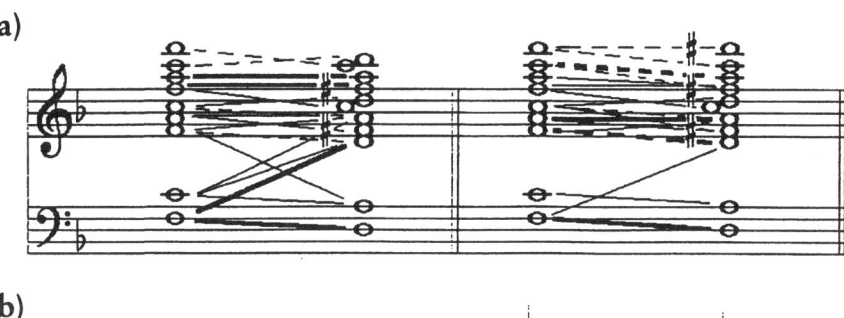

(b)

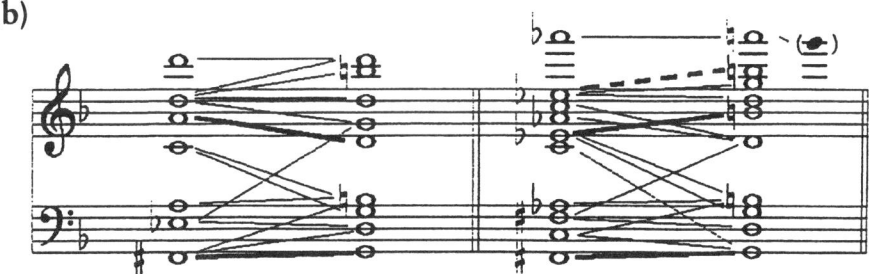

IV

Despite the division of labour involved in preparing this manuscript and despite assumptions that Bruckner's state of mind may not have been conducive to having good ideas, the authenticity of the Finale is not to be questioned. Aesthetic judgement is not the point here. Bruckner was decisive in his statements that the last version of his 'Wagner' Symphony is the valid one to be recommended to all interested conductors.[58] A manuscript copy of the whole score of this version is preserved in the Austrian National Library, its existence suggesting that Bruckner wanted to save the text.[59] The name of a young St Florian friend, Karl Aigner, appears in the Finale copy; it seems that Bruckner involved persons enjoying his confidence for this purpose.

The accurate but somehow amateurish copy contains not only the text of the revised score, but also many of its marginalia and, with the exception of the Finale, all metrical numbers.[60] If Bruckner wanted to save the correct text of this revision of the symphony, he did well to have it copied. It is common knowledge that there are several modifications in the printed edition.[61] As long as no evidence to the contrary surfaces, it must be assumed that these final modifications were made by Josef Schalk, who supervised the publication of the 'Wagner' Symphony in 1889/1890. Although these changes are non-essential, they are another indication of the untameable desire of the composer's disciples to unite with their adored master.

Notes

1. *Anton Bruckner, 3. Symphonie in d-Moll, 2. Fassung von 1878. Mit Einführung und den Hauptvarianten der Endfassung*, ed. Fritz Oeser (Wiesbaden: Brucknerverlag, 1950).
2. Ibid., p. III.
3. Proof sheets of this edition contain several handwritten marginalia by Oeser (Bruckner-Archiv in Wn).
4. Oeser was incorrect in assigning the first print to 1878. The publication of the score was announced in the first issue of the *Neue Wiener Zeitschrift für Musik* (1 October 1879), which reported that the symphony was to come out 'in several days' time': Gerold Wolfgang Gruber, 'Brahms und Bruckner in der zeitgenössischen Wiener Musikkritik', in *Bruckner Symposion 1983: Bericht* (Graz: Akademische Druck- und Verlagsanstalt, 1985), p. 202. The score was finally announced in the *Hofmeister-Monatsbericht* (March 1880), p. 74. A second announcement was made in the *Hofmeister-Monatsbericht* (February 1885), p. 26; piano score p. 34. Unfortunately the incorrect expression '1878-(print) version' is all too familiar to Bruckner scholars.
5. Leopold Nowak concedes that the Wiesbaden edition is a 'Zwischenedition', but acknowledges the existence of only one Complete Edition divided into two different strains by 'historical events'. Leopold Nowak, 'Die Bruckner-Gesamtausgabe: Ihre Geschichte und Schicksale', in *Bruckner-Jahrbuch 1982/83* (Linz, 1984), p. 45.
6. Leopold Nowak, 'Das Autograph von Anton Bruckners III. Symphonie', in *Phaidros 2*, 2nd ser. (1948), pp. 126 f.
7. *Bruckner Sämtliche Werke* B, III/2 (1981). This volume is incorrectly entitled '1877' version. Nowak actually edited the 1878 version which included two additional measures in the first movement, slight changes in the Scherzo, and a coda for the Scherzo. Cf. the author, 'Die Dritte Symphonie: unfaßbar', in *Bruckner Symposion: 1996 Bericht* (Linz, 1998), pp. 47–64.
8. Wn Mus. Hs. 6081 came from Franz Schalk's widow, Lili, at a date which is not clear. When Robert Haas wrote his Bruckner biography, the manuscript was still in her possession; cf. R. Haas, *Anton Bruckner* (Potsdam: Atheneum Verlag, 1934), p. 117. According to Fritz Oeser, the donation (or acquisition?) occurred before 1939; cf. Oeser, *3. Symphonie* (note 1), p. II. Leopold Nowak states that it was acquired in 1954; see Leopold Nowak, 'Das Bruckner-Erbe der österreichischen Nationalbibliothek', in *Österreichische Musikzeitschrift*, 21 (1966), pp. 526–31.
9. *Bruckner Sämtliche Werke* B, III/3 (1959).
10. Harry Halbreich, 'Bruckners Dritte Symphonie und ihre Fassungen', in *Bruckner Symposion 1980, Bericht* (Linz, 1981), pp. 75–83.
11. The present author completed the preparations of the critical commentary for all versions in the Collected Works Edition. Cf. Thomas Röder, ed., *Bruckner Sämtliche Werke B, Band 3: Revisionsbericht* (1997).
12. There were seven complete performances before 1890: (1885) 4 February: The Hague, Diligentia society (Johannes Verhulst); 15 October: Amsterdam, Apollo society (Daniel de Lange); 4 December: Frankfurt/Main, Museum Society (Karl Müller); 5 December: New York City, Symphony Society (Walter Damrosch); 11 December: Dresden, Königliche Kapelle (Ernst Schuch); (1886) 17 March: The

Hague, Diligentia (Richard Hol); 20 March: Utrecht, Stads-concert (R. Hol); 18 April (Scherzo only): Prague, Juristenconcert (Orchestra of the Landestheater, Gustav Mahler). Not all conductors were Wagnerians (Verhulst and Müller were known as rather conservative) and Verhulst usually delegated the performance of 'modern' music to his colleague Hol; it was probably Wilhelmus L. van Meurs, a Wagnerian who corresponded with Bruckner, who arranged the 1885 performance in The Hague. The composer, organist and conductor Daniel de Lange is known for his activity in the a cappella revival; as general secretary of the Amsterdam *Maatschappij tot Bevordering der Toonkunst*, de Lange informed Bruckner in 1887 that he had been granted honorary membership.

13. Bruckner finished the Eighth Symphony on 10 August and began to sketch the Ninth two days later: dates in the score of the Finale of Symphony no. 8 (Wn Mus. Hs. 19.480) and in the sketches for the Ninth in Kraków, Biblioteka Jagiellonska. Cf. Mariana E. Sonntag, 'A New Perspective on Anton Bruckner's Composition of the Ninth Symphony', in *Bruckner-Jahrbuch 1989/90* (Linz, 1992), p. 99.

14. Letter from 27 February 1888: '*Ich bin so frei hiemit die Partitur von der romantischen Sinfonie zu senden. Selbe ist neu instrumentiert und zusammengezogen*'. Franz Gräflinger, *Anton Bruckner: Leben und Schaffen (Umgearbeitete Bausteine)* (Berlin: Max Hesses Handbücher, No. 84, 1927), p. 340.

15. The cut is marked as a '*vi-de*' suggestion, mm. 379–433.

16. On 18 October 1887, Josef Schalk wrote to Levi that Bruckner was deeply hurt, but had nevertheless begun to revise the Eighth (cf. Robert Haas, ed., *Bruckner Sämtliche Werke* A, *IV: Vorlagenbericht*). (Vienna, Musikwissenschaftlicher Verlag, 1936, p. ii). Two days later Bruckner declared that he was now able to resume work (most presumably on the Eighth): '*Erst jetzt wird es mir gegönnt, Studien zu machen. Es wird das Möglichste geschehen ...*'. Letter to Levi, 20 October 1887, in Gräflinger (note 14), p. 339 f.

17. Bruckner's entry after m. 356 of the first movement: '*fertig z.[um] 3 Male. Feb 88*'. Benjamin Marcus Korstvedt, 'The First Published Edition of Anton Bruckner's Fourth Symphony: Collaboration and Authenticity', in *19th Century Music*, 20/1 (1996), p. 10.

18. Foreword in: *Bruckner Sämtliche Werke* B, VIII/2 (1955). The date is written at the end of the second movement (Korstvedt, ibid.).

19. '*Jetzt sieht sie schon anders aus.*' Gräflinger, *Bruckner* (note 14), p. 341.

20. In his report, Theodor Rättig lists 'Schalk, Schönaich, Eckstein, Paumgartner' and other friends, who persuaded the composer to tackle another reworking of the Third. Cf. Max Auer, 'Ein aufschlußreiches Dokument zur Frage der Fassungen bei Anton Bruckner,' in *Bruckner-Blätter*, 3/4 (1936), p. 2.

21. Ibid.

22. The Finale of the engraver's copy was, in its original state, completely hand written by Franz Schalk.

23. In June 1888, Josef Schalk reported to his brother that Bruckner 'unfortunately, is still sitting on the Finale of the Third', and that he 'has changed the composition of some passages' ('... *Bruckner, der leider noch immer über dem Finale der III. sitzt. Er hat einiges umkomponirt.*'). Thomas Leibnitz, *Die Brüder Schalk und Anton Bruckner: Dargestellt aus den Nachlaßbeständen der Musiksammlung der österreichischen Nationalbibliothek* (Tutzing: Hans Schneider, 1988), p. 134 (letter from 10 June 1888).

24. A letter of Joseph Schalk of 13 July 1888 provides the '*terminus ante quem*'; ibid., p.134.

25. Mahler had made the piano score of the symphony, possibly in conjunction with Rudolf Krzyzanowsky. He may also have made suggestions for the publication of the score including the elimination of two bars in the first movement (*Bruckner*

Sämtliche Werke B, III/2: mm. 67–8) and the removal of the Scherzo coda. Cf. Critical Report (Revisionsbericht, note 11), pp. 233 f. In this context, Mahler and the Schalk brothers were, to put it mildly, of opposing points of view. In 1899, Mahler reported that Bruckner once happily exclaimed to his student Behn: 'Now I'll have no further need of the Schalks'. This could have happened from late 1885 until spring 1886 when Behn probably studied with Bruckner. The reliability of this story is questionable, though it probably reflects the position of the Mahler circle. Cf. Henry Louis de la Grange, *Mahler*, vol. 1 (London: Gollancz 1974), pp. 46 f., notes on p. 845. I thank Professor Kurt Blaukopf, Vienna, for his comments.

26. The revision of the Third Symphony came to an end with the checking and work on the Scherzo on 3 and 4 March 1889. Bruckner added no remark, like *'fertig'* or *'ganz fertig'* – as he usually did – at this point.

27. For Rättig's report, see note 20. According to Friedrich Klose, Bruckner and Mahler met 'at another time' (*'ein anderes Mal'*) in the Vienna restaurant 'Roter Igel' to discuss the Third Symphony. Klose remembered only the word *'Klavierauszug'* from this talk. Since Klose began to take lessons in 1886, it is not really plausible that he overheard Bruckner and Mahler discussing a new piano arrangement. They must have been referring to their former collaboration and its role in the new reworking. Friedrich Klose, *Meine Lehrjahre bei Bruckner* (Regensburg: Gustav Bosse Verlag, 1927), p. 146.

28. It is strange that Rättig fails to name the person or persons who supplied 'about 50 sheets' – *'So erhielt ich mit der Zeit 50 Partitur-Seiten, die ich nun stechen ließ'.* Auer, *Dokument* (note 20), p. 2.

29. Rättig's remarks are written on the back of a letter that the Leipzig music engraver, Brandstetter, sent to him on 9 September 1890. The latter says that '52 plates for Bruckner's Symphony in D minor [...] have been melted down at your request'. (52 *'Platten zu Bruckner Symphonie d-moll sind infolge Ihres Auftrages [...] eingeschmolzen [...] worden'.*) Ibid., p. 1.

30. '[...] I'm healthy again and have been working since last June on the 3rd Symphony in D minor ... which I have improved thoroughly'. (*'[...] Ich bin wieder gesund, und arbeite seit verflossenem Juni an der 3. Sinfonie D-moll, [Wagner-Sinf.] welche ich gründlich verbessert habe. [...]'*). Letter from 1 January 1889. Auer, *Bruckner Gesammelte Briefe*, p. 223.

31. Documented by a letter to Levi 27 February 1888 (see note 14). In a letter from Joseph Schalk to Franz 26 November 1888: 'He [Bruckner] wants to present to you for your judgement each of the many changes which he is now making with extraordinary diligence to the Eighth or the Third'. (*'Jede der vielen Änderungen, die er jetzt mit außerordentlich angestrengtem Fleiß an der 8. od. 3. vornimmt, wünschte er vor allem dir und deinem Urtheil zu unterbreiten.'*) Leibnitz, *Brüder Schalk* note 23, p. 137.

32. Bruckner took up the revision of the Eighth on the same day: Bruckner, *Sämtliche Werke* B, VIII/2 (note 18), Foreword.

33. Two abridgements were indicated in the printed score with *'vi-de'* at mm. 379–432 and 465–514; Bruckner was responsible for them. The Finale fragment of the printed score (St Florian, XIX, 47), from Bruckner's estate, has autograph pencil additions *'vi-'* at m. 283, and *'-de'* after m. 296; for the 1890 version, these bars were omitted between 278/9 (at rehearsal letter P).

34. If the 1879 piano score of the Finale was made by Rudolf Krzyzanowsky, he may have been responsible for the cut of mm. 465–514. But even without documentary evidence it can be said that Bruckner knew of this cut before the piano arrangement came to print.

35. Between m. 192 and m. 193; a 'piano' bridge between the third thematic group and the end section. See below.

36. 'Hirsch and Löwe lassen dich herzlichst grüßen, auch Bruckner, der leider noch immer über dem Finale der III. sitzt. Er hat einiges umkomponirt. Deine Striche und Übergänge sind übrigens beibehalten worden.' 6 June 1888; cf. Leibnitz, *Brüder Schalk* (note 23), p. 134.

37. From the outset, length had been a problem for the Third Symphony. See, for instance, Bruckner's letter to the Vienna Philharmonic, 1 August 1875, where he agreed to divide the performance into two concerts: 'In closing, I would like to add that I will agree to a possible division of the symphony into two concerts.' ('Schließlich erlaube ich mir mitzutheilen, daß ich mich mit einer eventuellen Theilung der Sinfonie für zwei Conzerte einverstanden erkläre.') Harrandt-Schneider, *Bruckner Briefe I*, p. 157.

38. Thomas Röder: 'Die Orchesterstimmen der Dritten Symphonie von Anton Bruckner: welche Fassung wurde 1877 uraufgeführt?', in *Neues Musikwissen-schaftliches Jahrbuch*, V (1996), pp. 141–55.

39. On the last page of the first bassoon part there is a remark: '3/4 Stunde'. The Viennese critic, Josef Königstein (*Illustriertes Wiener Extrablatt*, 20 December 1877) reported: 'On Sunday at noon, the organist with the Napoleon-like head, Herr Anton Bruckner, put to flight the large audience at the second Society Concert within three quarters of an hour with his new Symphony in D minor' ('*Der Organist mit dem Napoleonskopfe, Herr Anton Bruckner, hat Sonntag Mittags innerhalb dreiviertel Stunden das zahlreich versammelte Publikum des zweiten Gesellschaftskonzertes mit seiner neuen Symphonie in D-moll total in die Flucht geschlagen*'). Fritz Oeser suggests in his edition a duration of 65 minutes; see Oeser (note 1), p. VIII.

40. Nowak did not adopt this 2-measure cut at m. 66/7 in *Bruckner Sämtliche Werke* B, vol. III/2. For the performance in 1877, the second appearance of the main theme crescendo was cancelled altogether.

41. August Halm, 'Über den Wert musikalischer Analysen II: Die Fausse Reprise im ersten Satz der Dritten Symphonie von Bruckner', in *Die Musik*, 21 (1929), pp. 591–5.

42. Ernst Kurth, *Bruckner*, vol. 2 (Berlin: Hesse, 1925), pp. 871 f.

43. Robert Simpson, *The Essence of Bruckner: An Essay Towards the Understanding of his Music* (London: Gollancz, 1977), p. 79. In a later article, Simpson compares the three versions of the Third Symphony thoroughly using similar arguments as in his book; for him, the quality of these versions declines in accordance with the reworkings. Cf. 'The 1873 Version of Bruckner's Third Symphony', in *Bruckner-Jahrbuch 1982/83* (Linz, 1984), pp. 27–32.

44. Thomas Röder, 'Das "verstümmelte" Finale. Zum vierten Satz von Anton Bruckners Dritter Symphonie', in *Mitteilungsblatt der Internationalen Anton-Bruckner-Gesellschaft*, 37 (1991), pp. 11–20.

45. Oeser, *3. Symphonie* (note 1), p. VII: '*Äußerliche Apotheose*', not '*organischer Abschluß*'.

46. The only critical examination of Franz Schalk's *Ersatzkomposition* is Bo Marschner, 'Die letzte (1889) Fassung von Anton Bruckners 3. Sinfonie. Ein Problemfall in der kritischen Gesamtausgabe', in *Neue Berlinische Musikzeitung*, 8 (1993, Beiheft zu Heft 3), pp. 22–32. The original Danish: 'Anton Bruckners 3. symphonie i dens seneste version [1889]', in *Otte ekkoer af musikforskning i Århus* (Århus, 1988), pp. 135–61; the article includes a facsimile of Schalk's composition, pp. 158–61.

47. The semitone shift of the initial note returns to the preceding note enharmonically (e♭–d♯) because of the deformation of the initial interval (octave instead of diminished tenth). Bruckner sketched an improvement of Schalk's composition, reviving its original disposition (mm. 283–86: sequence of initial diminished tenth with whole tone shift). Besides the crossings-out, this sketch is the only alteration

Bruckner made in Schalk's '*Ersatzkomposition*'.

48. This sketch bifolio is now to be found at the Biblioteka Jagiellonska Kraków. I'm indebted to Timothy Jackson who gave me the information about this source.

49. The stages of Bruckner's reworking are documented in detail in the *Revisionsbericht* (note 11), pp. 316–18. The dominant-like G appears after 24 measures (cf. p. 317).

50. As far as the score reveals at present, and there is not much genuine 'Schalk writing' left to see, he did not feel as free as Löwe in his treatment of the 'Romantic' Symphony.

51. III/2: mm. 341–50, III/3: mm. 323–32 (in both cases from letter 'S' to 'T').

52. '*Auch hat die G-Dur-Gipfelung durch die Verlagerung des Kopfthemas in die Trompeten zwar an Glanz gewonnen, doch ist die ursprüngliche Anlage insofern sinnvoller, als sie dieses Thema stark polyphon gespiegelt hier erst in der dunkleren Tenorlage vorankündigt und den strahlenden Diskant (Trompeten-Unisono) für den Satzschluß aufspart. Die Echtheit des Orchestersatzes wie der Dynamik ist aus verschiedenen Gründen anzuzweifeln.*' Oeser, *3. Symphonie* (note 1), p. VI.

53. At mm. 328–31, Bruckner found in the trombone parts some reason for heavy erasing and then prolonging the sustained chord. (Schalk's suggestion is not legible anymore, at least to the naked eye.)

54. Sixth g♯–e (in Nowak's score f♯–d), m. 329. The following measures (330, 331) again show working traces, most probably by Bruckner.

55. At m. 331; it is actually suspended by the ninth (A). Before this, the note G falls always on a transitory position (last quaver of the measure).

56. In the above quoted letter from 6 June 1888 (note 36), Joseph Schalk continues: 'Now he is plagued with a severe delusion, an obsession with ridding the composition of octave progressions. He is wasting much time and expending a terrible amount of energy in doing this, but is unsusceptible to each objection made by Löwe or me. It is quite sad to see how he extinguishes everything at the expense of a natural voice-leading and how he makes changes just for the sake of this idée fixe.' ('*Jetzt plagt ihn mit der Heftigkeit einer Wahnvorstellung die Sucht seinen Satz von Oktavenfortschreitungen zu reinigen. Dabei vertrödelt er viele Zeit, müht sich entsetzlich, ist aber gegen jeden Einwand Löwe's oder meinerseits unerschütterlich. Es ist recht traurig, wenn man sieht, wie er auf Kosten einer natürlichen Stimmführung alles ausrottet und ändert nur um dieser fixen Idee willen.*'). For a recent investigation into this issue, in particular Bruckner's analysis of octave doubling in Mozart's *Requiem*, Beethoven's Third Symphony and annotations in his own music, see Timothy Jackson, 'Bruckner's "Oktaven"', *Music and Letters*, 78 (1997), pp. 391–409.

57. For instance, a leap of an eleventh downwards (bass trombone, C–G), or a major seventh up (second horn), or a diminished fourth (alto and tenor trombone) were all acceptable, also octaves caused by contrary motion. (The A flat in the first chord might be a suggestion made by Schalk and accepted by Bruckner, cf. *Bruckner Sämtliche Werke* B, III/3, mm. 322/323).

58. Already in late 1889, Bruckner announces the 'new and improved edition' (the German '*Auflage*' also means 'printing'), which is to come out 'in a few months' time', to the Hamburg critic Josef Sittard. ('*In einigen Monaten kommt meine 3te Sinfonie [...] in neuer und verbesserter Auflage bei Rättig in Verlag.*') Undated letter, in *Drei Briefe von Anton Bruckner an Professor Josef Sittard. Im Besitz und im Faksimilie überreicht von Hans von Ohlendorff* (Hamburg, n. d.). In a letter to August Göllerich (1 January 1891), Bruckner declares that he has grown fond of the new Third Symphony. ('*Die neue D-moll Sinfonie ist mir jetzt ins Herz gewachsen.*') Cf. Auer, *Bruckner Gesammelte Briefe*, p. 236. In a letter to Herman Levi (14 January 1893), concerning a concert on 3 February, Bruckner asks for the new edition, 'which is incomparably better', and states that he is 'not interested in the

first edition anymore'. ('*Was Ihre Wahl für den 3. Febr. betrifft, ist sie ja herrlich und bitte ich ja selbst um die D-moll Sinfonie, die dem Meister gewidmet und bei Rättig in Wien verlegt ist. Nebenbei bitte aber um die neue Bearbeitung, [...] welche unvergleichlich besser ist (von der ersten Bearbeitung will ich nichts mehr wissen).*') Cf. Gräflinger (note 14), p. 354. On the same date as the first performance of the second print (Vienna, 21 December 1890), the Linz Musikverein gave a concert in which Adalbert Schreyer conducted the first printed version of 1879. In the newspaper report, there is a remark which says that Bruckner, in a letter, had attached importance to the performance of the 'new reading'. But obviously it was too late to change the scores: '*Bruckner hätte, wie wir einem uns zur Verfügung gestellten Schreiben desselben entnehmen, Wert darauf gelegt, daß die dritte Symphonie auch bei uns in der neuen Lesart aufgeführt werde; es erschien jedoch unmöglich, noch in letzter Stunde eine Änderung eintreten zu lassen, nachdem das Studium des Werkes nach der älteren Partitur bereits bis zum Abschlusse gediehen war.*' *Linzer Zeitung*, 23 December 1890.

59. Wn Mus. Hss. 6056, 6028, 6057, 6029 (in the sequence of the movements). This score was made by three copyists; according to a handwritten remark by Leopold Nowak, Wn Ms. Hss. 6056 and 6028 were copied by Leopold Hofmayr. The other copyists are unidentified.

60. Plates 5 and 6 illustrate an original and copied page of the Finale.

61. *Bruckner Sämtliche Werke* B, III/3 (note 9), Foreword.

5 Continuity in the Fourth Symphony (first movement)

Edward Laufer

For Arianna

It is generally held that despite the noble grandeur and magnificent sonorities of Bruckner's music, continuity, in a technical sense, is not a hallmark of his way of composing. Even the most considerable theorist of this century, Heinrich Schenker, Bruckner's erstwhile pupil, though he could find much to admire in Bruckner the artist and the symphonist, nonetheless throughout his life steadfastly denied Bruckner this compositional *sine qua non* – indeed any compositional technique at all.[1] The present consideration of the first movement of the Fourth Symphony will respond to this charge, and claim on the contrary that Bruckner's compositional technique does indeed encompass a logical and highly sophisticated way of composing, not only in proceeding from one point to the next, but also in binding together adjacent or non-adjacent sections by subtle associative means: in a word – continuity.

It was perhaps the composer's very real concern for tightness and continuity that prompted him to undertake the various revisions of his Fourth Symphony. It would make an interesting study to compare analytically the different versions from this technical standpoint, but this is not the time and place.[2] I have chosen, on advice from noted Bruckner scholars, the 1878 (Robert Haas) version as the basis for the ensuing study.[3]

The form of the movement may be outlined as follows:

Exposition

	(mm.)	
First subject	3–18	1st part, 1st period
	19–50	1st part, 2nd period (expanded restatement)
	51–74	2nd part
Second subject	75–86	a₁ (statement 75–82; restatement 83–86)
	87–97	b (transformation of 6th-figure)

114

	97–107	a$_2$
	107–118	codetta
Closing	119–131	1st part (cf. 1st subj., 2nd part, 51ff.)
	131–168	2nd part (cf. 1st subj., 2nd part, 51ff.)
	169–192	3rd part (cf. 2nd subj.), codetta
		(179–190, cf. 87ff.; 187–192, cf. 119)

Development

	193–216	Transitional episode (cf. 179ff.)
	217–252	1st part (cf. 1st subj., 1st and 2nd parts)
	253–287	2nd part (cf. 1st subj., 2nd part, 51ff.)
	287–333	3rd part (cf. 1st subj., 1st and 2nd parts, also
		2nd subj.'s 3rd-motive)
	334–364	Retransitional episode (cf. 2nd subj.'s 6th- and
		3rd-motives, 179ff.)

Recapitulation

First subject	365–380	1st part, 1st period
	381–412	1st part, 2nd period
	413–436	2nd part
Second subject	437–448	a$_1$ (statement 437–444; restatement 445–448)
	449–469	b (transformation of 6th-figure)
	459–469	a$_2$
	469–484	codetta (479–484 cf. also 245–252)
Closing	485–501	1st part (cf. 1st subj., 1st part; also 1st subj.,
		2nd part, 51ff.)
	517–532	extending episode
Coda	533–556	cf. 1st subj., 1st part
	557–573	(tonic peroration).

The term continuity can be understood in different senses. Beyond its usual meaning of merely designating smooth progression from one point to the next, continuity must inevitably be bound up with such procedures as modified restatement and transformation – whereby one motive is *varied* from point to point so as to become another.[4] A Schenkerian view, however, also includes various kinds of restatements: enlargements, contractions or summing-up, and more or less concealed middleground motives, which guarantee cohesion and continuity on a deeper level. For the present purposes, I set forth certain of the types of continuity to be discussed in this movement. But the distinctions between one type and another are not as clear-cut as the following designations might seem to suggest, since one type may coincide with another in certain respects. With this proviso, then, one might categorize different types of continuity as follows (with a few but not all instances noted). The analytical discussion to follow provides more detailed explanation and illustration.

- *modified restatement*: 'free' variation – perhaps an expanded restatement of a previously heard passage (as in Exx. 5.1, 5.34 [mm. 169–73, then 174–87], 5.70);
- *concealed association*: continuity is provided by the underlying presence of a middleground motive which can associate passages with distinctly different foreground features; moreover, even a single characteristic note may have special referential meaning (as in Exx. 5.2–4, 8 [the $g^{\flat 2}$–$a^{\flat 2}$], 5.18, 5.21–22, 5.23d, 5.31, 5.35, 5.40, 5.43, 5.46, 5.54, 5.57b, 5.58–59, 5.61–63, 5.67–68);[5]
- *linking technique*: the concluding notes of one phrase become the beginning of the next (as in Exx. 5.8, 5.9, 15.4, 15.48a, b);[6]
- *transformation*: one motive gives rise to another, such as through gradual modifications or step by step changes (as in Exx. 5.7, 5.10, 5.15, 5.18, 5.39, 5.48c, d, 5.50–1, 5.58);
- *progression to a goal*: continuity as a continuing process, whereby earlier implications or expectations are only subsequently realized, e.g. the motive of Ex. 5.21 culminating in Ex. 5.50, or the achieving of the primary tone g^3 ($\hat{3}$) only at the end of the movement (see also Exx. 5.23e, 5.49 [omission, then realization], 5.50–1, 65–6, and 69).

Exposition

Examples 5.1 and 5.2 show foreground and middleground reductions of the opening periods. Exx. 5.3 and 5.4 point up two main motive components, the neighbour-note figure, and the fifth-motive, paradoxically all the more significant and evocative for being so unassuming and simple: for it is not so much the motives themselves, but rather Bruckner's moulding and transforming them (thanks to their simplicity) into seemingly infinite guises throughout, which constitutes such a striking feature of Bruckner's way of composing. Exx. 5.1 and 5.2 indicate some of the ways in which these motives are worked in.

Although notated in Ex. 5.1 as a half-note, the initial $b^{\flat 1}$ is not yet the primary tone : the g^3 ($\hat{3}$) primary tone (but given as g^2 in the relevant sketches) will only appear at the end of the movement (mm. 557ff., Exx. 5.60, 5.65–66, and 5.69), its arrival being celebrated only there, in a glorious blaze of sound, the final peroration, the goal to which the top line has striven throughout![7] Technically, this magnificent delay is most unusual, for in a Schenkerian view of form and the fundamental line, by the time a coda is reached, the fundamental line will have attained the concluding $\hat{1}$, which the coda would then extend. One may therefore ascribe some programmatic meaning to Bruckner's arriving on the goal $\hat{3}$ only at the conclusion! In Ex. 5.1, the $b^{\flat 1}$ (m. 3) to $b^{\flat 2}$ (m. 19) establishes $b^{\flat 1}$, which initiates the long journey to the high g^3.[8]

Exx. 5.1,2,3,4

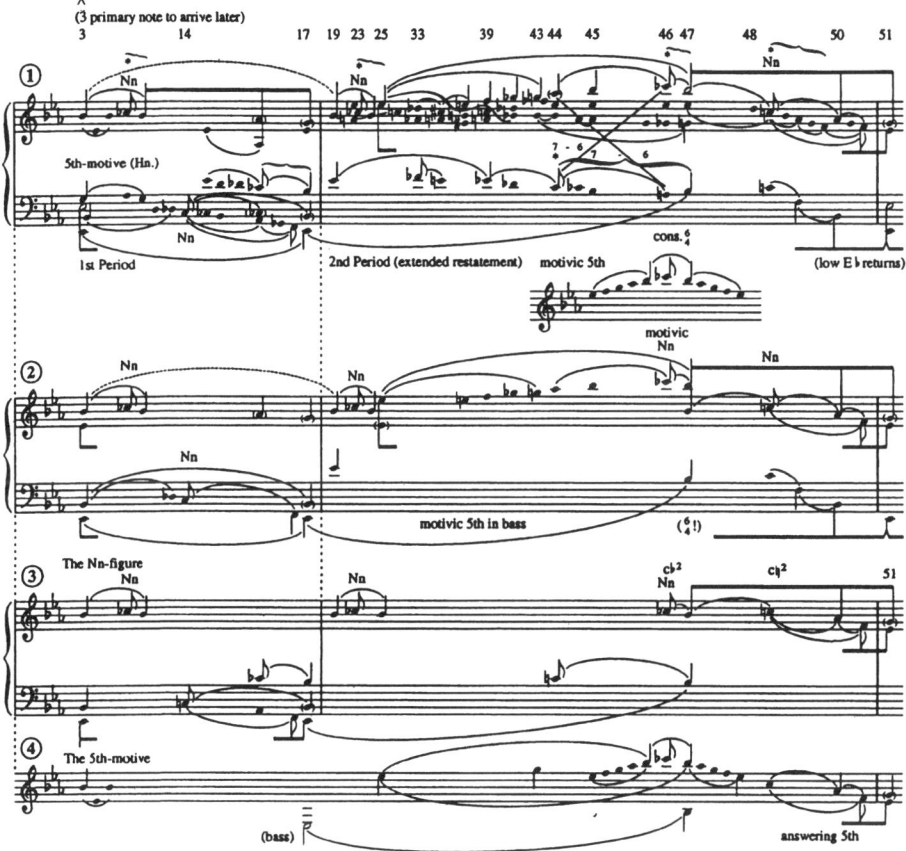

The idea behind the second period (mm. 19–51) concerns that aspect of continuity which consists in restating the first period, but in modified form (type 1, as noted above). As in Exx. 5.1–4, a remarkable expansion takes place: the b^{b1}-c^{b2}-b^{b1} neighbour-note figure is recomposed, the fifth-motive appears in enlargement in top and bass voices, and the descending third-figure b^{b1}-a^{b1}-g^1 (indicated by the beam) also recurs. The chromatic bass, filling in the descending fourth, mm. 39–47, harks back to its predecessor in mm. 12–16, and the bass fifth c^1-f, mm. 48–9, (which perhaps is associated with the fifth-motive) recomposes that fifth of mm. 14–16. Additionally, the first period's bass E^b-F-E^b is suggested in the inner voice e^{b2}-f^1-e^{b1}, mm. 28–50–51. (This is continuity as concealed association, type 2 as above.) The second period is clearly set off from the first, by register (the low E^b of m. 17 drops out, but is still to be understood as the bass note), colour, and orchestration; but this separation only enhances the effect of the motivic transformations. Such transformations guarantee cohesion by this type of continuity: the foreground of the music is thereby set free, so to speak, to search out ever new foreground aspects.

Reading the fifth $e^{\flat 2}$-$b^{\flat 2}$, mm. 23–46, as in Ex. 5.5 is plausible but not so good because 7–6 suspensions bind the notes $a^{\flat 2}$-$c^{\flat 3}$ together as a voice-exchange, as shown in Ex. 5.6. Exx. 5.4 and 5.7 indicate the rising fifth-motive $e^{\flat 1}$-$b^{\flat 1}$ being answered by a descending fifth c^2-f^1; and (Ex. 5.7) the rising fifth $e^{\flat 1}$-$b^{\flat 1}$ then going beyond itself to become an octave-figure $e^{\flat 1}$-$e^{\flat 2}$ (the point, $b^{\flat 1}$, at which the fifth is thus expanded is marked by the rhythmic subdivision into triplet quarter notes). One motive thus *becomes* another; here indeed is a very subtle form of continuity (continuity as transformation: type 4 above)!

Exx. 5.5,6,7

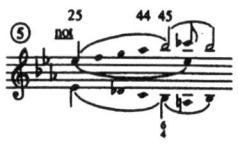

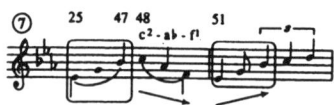

Exx. 5.8–12 show the second part of the first subject, mm. 51–74. In m. 59, the eventual primary tone g^3 is alluded to in the guise of $g^{\flat 2}$: as $^\flat\hat{3}$, $g^{\flat 2}$ is here the 'wrong' $\hat{3}$, as if conveying a programmatic meaning. One's perception of the 'wrong' verses the 'right' $\hat{3}$ is clarified only by taking the course of the movement as a whole into account (Ex. 5.69). In this sense, one can regard the quest for the 'right' $\hat{3}$ as a vast continuing process (continuity of type 5 above), completed only when that $\hat{3}$ is attained. The long delay in attaining the 'right' $\hat{3}$ expresses Bruckner's compositional idea of creating a sense of a magnificent span reaching across the entire movement; landing on the 'wrong' step, before finding the 'right' one, becomes a musical metaphor, emblematic of conflict eventually to be overcome: as an archetypal principle, it is a not infrequent programmatic notion in music, and as 'romantic' in spirit as Bruckner's fanciful program (of which more later).

Ex. 5.12 shows the basic progression underlying the movement up to m. 67. It may be noted (Ex. 5.13) that the bass composes the fifth-motive $E^\flat$-$B^\flat$, with the characteristic $c^\flat$ neighbour note (a subtle reference to the $c^{\flat 2}$ in m. 7); this

Exx. 5.8,9,10,11,12,13

neighbour note is decisively marked by dwelling on $c♭$ in mm. 59–61. The sense of leading on to the second subject is heightened by the contrast between the more stable harmonic foreground (mm. 51–8) characteristic of exposition of material and of less stable harmonic foreground (mm. 59–67) characteristic of the developmental aspect. This contrast is a signal that something new is in the offing. Of course, when the second subject appears (m. 75), it *is* a 'new' idea: 'something rich and strange', but at the same time the nature of its links to the preceding renders the contrast all the more remarkable. There is the reference to the first subject: Ex. 5.9 (the bracketed figure becoming the figure in broken brackets shown above in Ex. 5.8). The opening horn motive $b♭^1$-$e♭^1$-$b♭^1$, c^2 has become f^1-c^1-g^1 (mm. 67, Ex. 5.9); the fourth f^1-c^1 (m. 67, Ex. 5.8) becomes f^1-$b♭$ (m. 75, Ex. 5.8) – a beautiful instance of continuity and linking technique (type 3). The descending octave figure $e♭^2$-$e♭^1$ in m. 51, Ex. 5.15 (cf. also Ex. 5.7), gives rise to the descending line $g♭^2$-$a♮^1$, in mm. 59ff. This descending figure is indicated again in Ex. 5.10: by a miraculous concatenation of events, the third $g♭^2$-$e♭^2$ (mm. 59–61) is expanded to the seventh $g♭^2$-$a♮^1$, thereupon becoming the sixth f^2-$a♮^1$

(mm. 67ff.) which turns into the descending sixth f^2-a^{b1} of the second subject (mm. 75ff.). As if this remarkable continuity by transformation were not enough, Bruckner composes further subtle links: Ex. 5.8, mm. 65ff., the circled notes a^{b2}-g^{b2}-f^2 link to mm. 76–7 of the second subject; additionally, as shown in Ex. 5.14 (cf. Ex. 5.9), the fourth f^1-c^1 becomes the viola part in mm. 75–7, and the descending and ascending third-figure (broken brace in Ex. 5.14), which will assume greater significance later in the development section.

Ex. 5.14

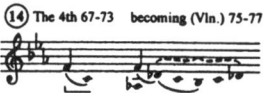

Ex. 5.15

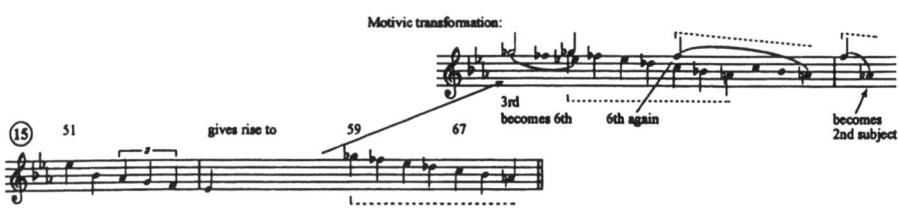

Ex. 5.16

Exx. 5.17–22 show the second subject. Exx. 5.17–19 illustrate motivic continuity through the descending sixth-figure (concealed association and transformation). As shown in Ex. 5.18a, the sixth-figure (referred to above; designated by the broken bracket) is not only the foreground motive in m. 75, but, in enlargement, the carrier of the top line mm. 79–82; similarly, its restatement at m. 83 gives rise to the enlargement at mm. 87ff. Ex. 5.19 suggests that the middleground top voice b^{b2}-a^{b2}-g^2 starts (but does not complete) yet another expansion of this sixth-figure. The bass in mm. 87–93, Ex. 5.17, g^b-B^{b}, picks up the line that had just been heard in the top voice in mm. 76–81, g^{b2}-b^{b1}. If this organic continuity is remarkable in itself, it is all the more so when one realizes that the sixth-motive, Ex. 5.18b, is itself a transformation of the first subject, and this association with the first subject becomes clearer in Ex. 5.18c when the first subject's neighbour-note figure reappears as well!

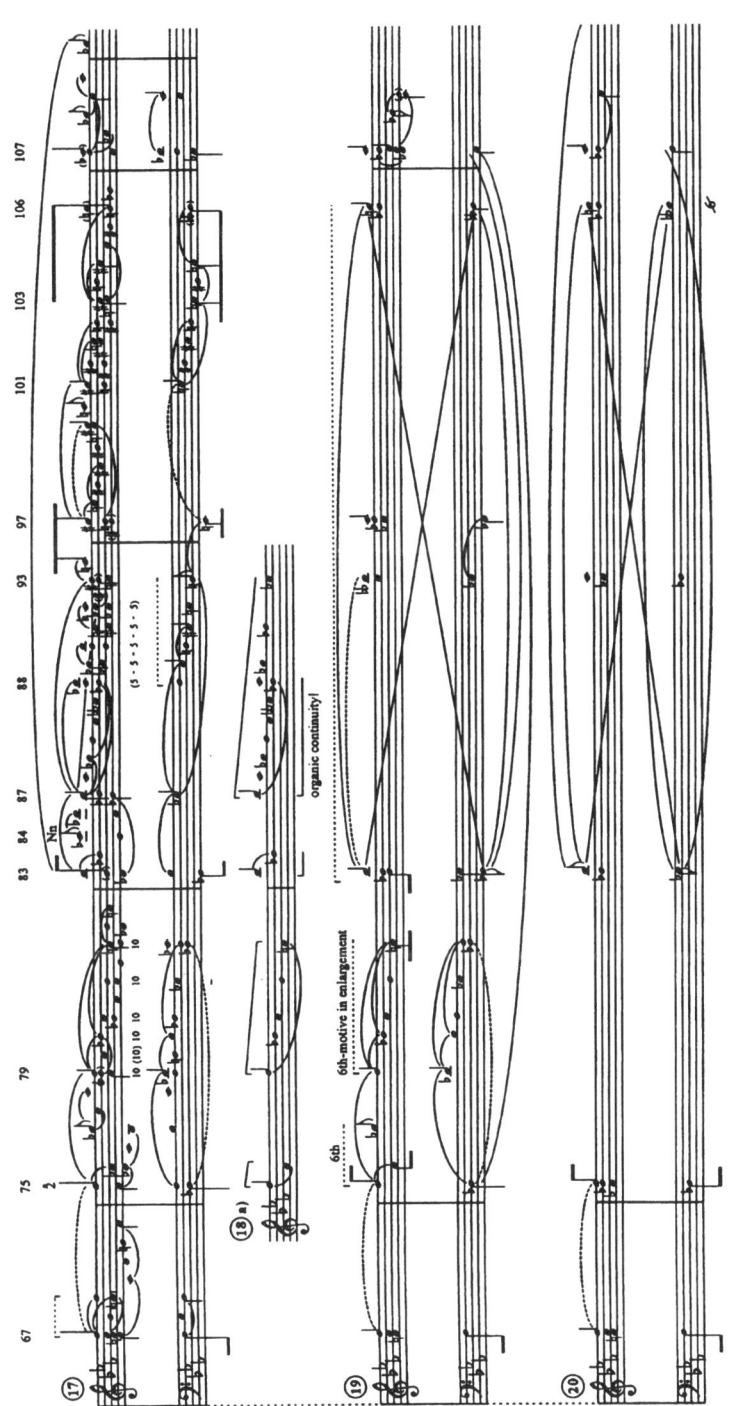

Exx. 5.17,18a,19,20

121

If the sixth-motive binds mm. 83–106 together as a motivic entity, the passage is an harmonic entity as well, with the augmented sixth chord in m. 106 marking the end at the voice exchange. The texture, too, marks this formal articulation: all instruments drop out, leaving only the cellos. The viola counterpoint from mm. 75–77 (Ex. 5.21) reappears just at this point, mm. 105–7, in the cellos, relating beginning and ending points of the entire second-subject area. As another subtle associative detail, Ex. 5.22, the rhythmic guise of m. 87 is a variant of the characteristic rhythmic figure from m. 43, the first subject.

The next analytical sketches (Exx. 5.23–27) broach a fascinating point: a dichotomy between continuity and apparent discontinuity (in a voice leading sense) in this movement. The matter turns on how one is to read the closing section, mm. 119–68. Perhaps the most obvious reading would be as given in Ex. 5.23a (the bass progression only is shown): the goal V arrives definitively in m. 119 and is extended by means of an auxiliary cadence, the bass d^b-f-B^b, mm. 141–73, expressing a modified restatement of mm. 75–119. It is true that the string figures of mm. 110–14 and the b^{b2}-f^2-b^{b1} figure of mm. 119–20 on the dominant associate with the similar figures in mm. 174ff. and the b^{b2}-f^2-b^{b1} figure of mm. 187–8; but otherwise the two B^b-points really have little to do with one another and are not motivically connected. On these counts, this reading would be open to question. Ex. 5.23b takes into account the return of the second subject's motives at m. 169, thus supporting reading the intervening B^b at m. 119 as filling in the fifth d^b-G^b (mm. 75–167). But the B^b section at m. 119 is too impetuously emphasized to be merely a 'filling' third between d^b and G^b. Ex. 5.23c revises Ex. 5.23b to give the B^b at m. 119 its due emphasis by taking the entire passage in mm. 119–68 as a parenthetical interpolation (see the reduction in Ex. 5.23d), and in this sense, as an aspect of *discontinuity*.

To consider this last reading further, a few additional points may be noted. Formally, mm. 119–31 pick up the motive of the first subject (second part), Ex. 5.15, in order to close off the exposition with this reminder of it, in the spirit of a codetta. Mm. 131–51 continue the same motive; mm. 151–65 act as a vast *unisono* upbeat to the brass outburst of mm. 165–68. The compositional reason for this build-up is revealed by the rhythmic and registral association of that outburst with mm. 114ff. (Ex. 5.23e): mm. 165–68 thereby frame and, in a sense, set the closing section apart as an episode unto itself. Immediately thereafter (m. 169), Bruckner picks up the second subject from where it had left off (in m. 118) and concludes it (see the asterisks, Ex. 5.24). In other words, *motivically* the closing section amounts to a parenthetical insertion: Bruckner could have gone directly from m. 114, or m. 118, to m. 169, and he could have placed the closing section *after* the 'completion' of the second subject. This 'discontinuity' provides a further sense of delay in arriving at the goal V – a delay which perhaps parallels and enhances the programmatic intent in withholding the $\hat{3}$-arrival at the end of the recapitulation!

Harmonically, a vast auxiliary cadence extends from the second subject (Ex.

Ex. 5.18b

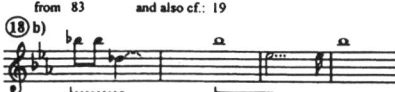

Ex. 5.18c

Ex. 5.21

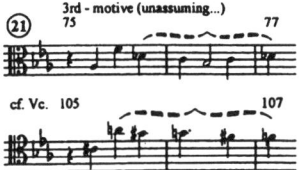

Ex. 5.22

5.23d, bass d♭ in m.75) all the way to the second subject's completion as the codetta (bass f in m. 169) and thence to the goal dominant B♭ (m. 173). These three points (d♭-f-B♭) are motivically connected. Thus, to the question – why not simply as Ex. 5.23a, one could indeed say that the motivic association of these points is such as to suggest strongly that they should be read together – that they belong together as one entity. If the closing section's B♭ (m. 119) in a *poetic* sense anticipates the goal dominant (m. 173), the former is not yet the *real* point of arrival – rather, a 'trying out' step, a foreshadowing, a harbinger. But even if Exx. 5.24–26 do present a convincing reading, perhaps there is nonetheless a measure of duality here, which – unlike the unequivocal directness of earlier classical masters – is intrinsic to Bruckner's multi-faceted compositional technique.

Ex. 5.23a,b,c,d,e

Moreover, only a composer to whom it was given to hear in such large-scale spans could conceive of an auxiliary cadence such as this. Ex. 5.24 shows the second subject and codetta, without the (interpolated) closing section; Ex. 5.25 the interpolation itself; Ex. 5.26 a reduction of both; and Ex. 5.27 another notation for the bass.

Certainly a curious passage is the unison crescendo from m. 153 leading to the brass outburst mm. 165–68, discussed above. Ex. 5.29 shows the harmonic basis: an extension (*not* composing-out) of a diminished seventh chord. Why should Bruckner draw out a diminished seventh? One can note the thinner unison texture leading to the richness of the arrival in m.165. There is the sense of the unstable seventh-sonority reaching for the goal (m. 169), the stable sonority. But perhaps a better answer is that this unstable sonority organically derives from the diminished-seventh motive of m. 145!

Exx. 5.28, 32, and 33 present the second subject and closing section in more detail. These analytical sketches reveal something of the quite striking compositional intent, whereby foreground motives move into the middleground to create underlying continuity (continuity by concealed association). Thus, Ex. 5.31 shows how the motive of m. 51 is very freely transformed as a *middleground* motive, upon which the foreground of mm. 110–65 is placed. In other words, *the motive of m. 51* in these four freely recomposed enlargements becomes the basis for the second subject's continuation (mm. 110–15) *and* the

Exx. 5.24,25,26,27

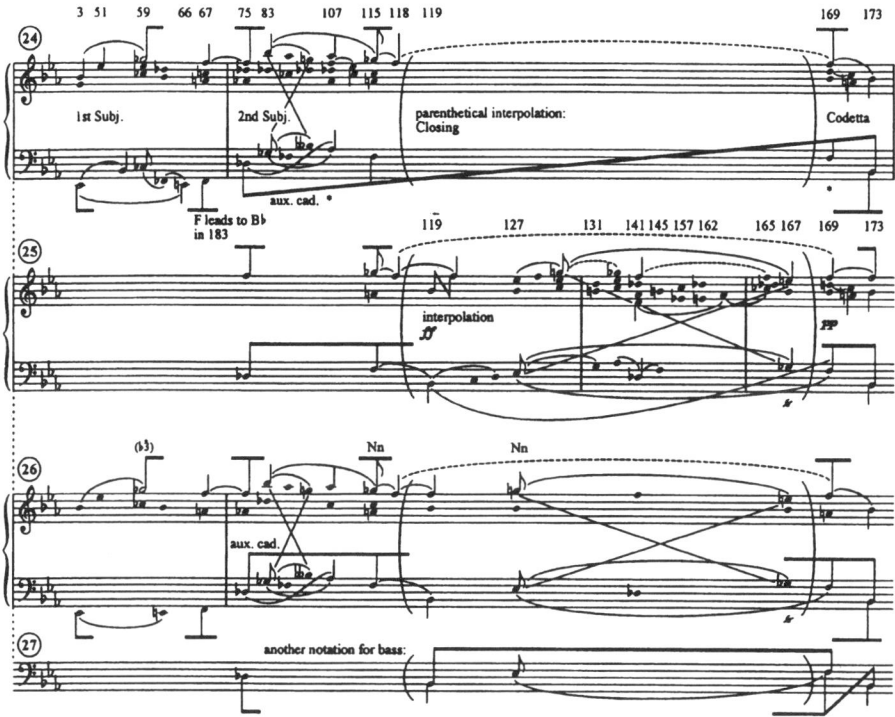

interpolated closing section (mm. 119–65)! This is an astonishing Brucknerian inspiration: in a real, technical sense, the hidden motivic *continuity* (the motive of m. 51 as middleground, upon which the successive enlargements are placed), paradoxically connects mm. 107–14, from the second subject area, to the *"discontinuity"* of the *parenthetical* closing section! Foreground expressions of this motive are shown in Ex. 5.30. After the rising contours of Ex. 5.31, an answering descending line is due; and mm. 169–73 provide this, to complete and close off the exposition.

Exx. 5.34–37 sketch the conclusion of the exposition. In mm. 169–73, beneath an understood f^2 ($\hat{2}$ of the fundamental line) there is a partial descent: the third d^2-c^2-$b^{\flat 1}$ only, not a fifth f^2-$b^{\flat 1}$. Almost invariably in a classical second subject area there is a descending fifth attached to the note of the fundamental line; so perhaps here too a fifth-descent would be 'expected', and indeed the fifth f^2-$b^\flat$ now provides this in mm. 174–87, even though this descent is not supported by an independent bass. But the fascinating point here is that these descents are *motivic*: in a beautifully concealed guise, they derive from the second subject's sixth-motive (see Ex. 5.35 ; also cf. mm. 87 and 115)! The $d^{\flat 3}$ of m.177 connects registrally to the c^3 in m. 186, marking the c^3-$b^{\flat 2}$ neighbour-note figure there : this figure (mm. 183–87) is also motivic, being a reference to the $c^{\flat 2}$-$b^{\flat 1}$

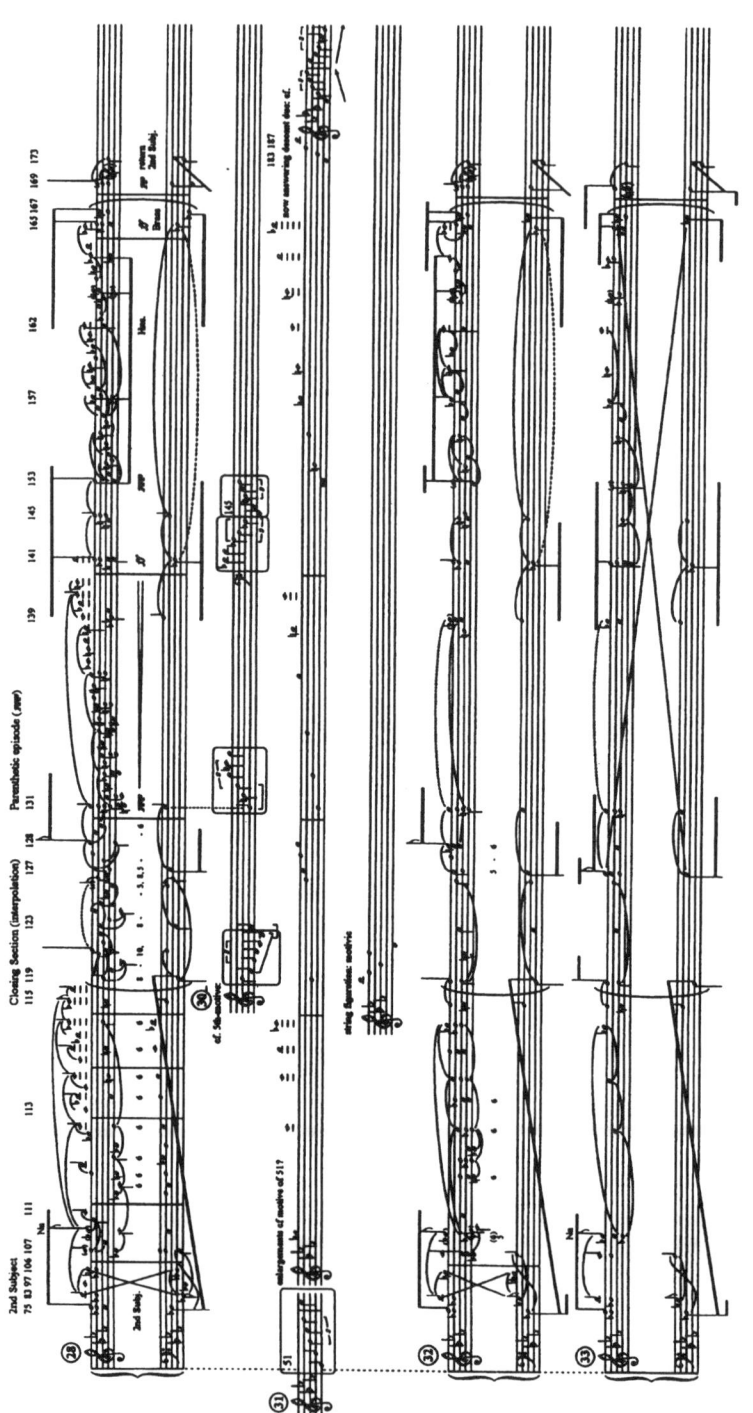

Exx. 5.28,30,31,32,33

126

Ex. 5.29

neighbour-note figure of the opening (Ex. 5.3)! The unfolding is shown in Ex. 5.37. The unassuming third-figure, m. 172 (broken brace), another reference to the second subject (m. 75, violas), will emerge in full splendour in the development section (mm. 305–60, Exx. 50–51). The $g^{\flat 2}$ (m. 179) is also rich in connotations, recalling the earlier $^{\flat}3$ (m. 59), the diminished-third chord which hailed the second subject (m. 66), and the second subject's neighbour note $g^{\flat 2}$ (m. 76). Bruckner celebrates the arrival on $b^{\flat 2}$ (m. 187) by a subtle reference to the motive of m. 119 (cf. m. 51). This wealth of motivic references and links indeed suggests the breadth and subtlety of Bruckner's multi-facetted compositional technique.

Development

The overall idea behind the formal design of the development section is to suggest a freely composed restatement of the formal design of the exposition – in a sense analogous to the repetition of the exposition in a classical symphony. One might therefore regard the development as a whole, in terms of our consideration of continuity types, as a modified restatement on a vast scale. First of all, the development continues without a break out of the exposition (continuity by linking technique). Thereafter, in a general way, continuity is assured by manifold expressions of transformations and by concealed associations (in which foreground motives occur in the middleground). The descending sixth-motive becomes the first subject's fifth-motive, which is, in turn, associated with the second subject's third-motive (Exx. 5.48c and 50–51). The second subject's third-motive exemplifies continuity as process, or realization of earlier implications; a possible programmatic meaning will be suggested later. Concealed associations prepare and lead back into the recapitulation; the way in which the fifth-motive at the beginning of the recapitulation is prepared by the same fifth in the middleground in the latter part of the development will be discussed below.

Exx. 5.38–43 sketch the beginning of the development section. The development's beginning so clearly joins motivically with the end of the exposition that the exposition passes seamlessly into the development. One can readily regard mm. 193–216 as a transitional episode to an ensuing 'first part' of the development section (mm. 217ff.). There are other aspects of continuity: mm.

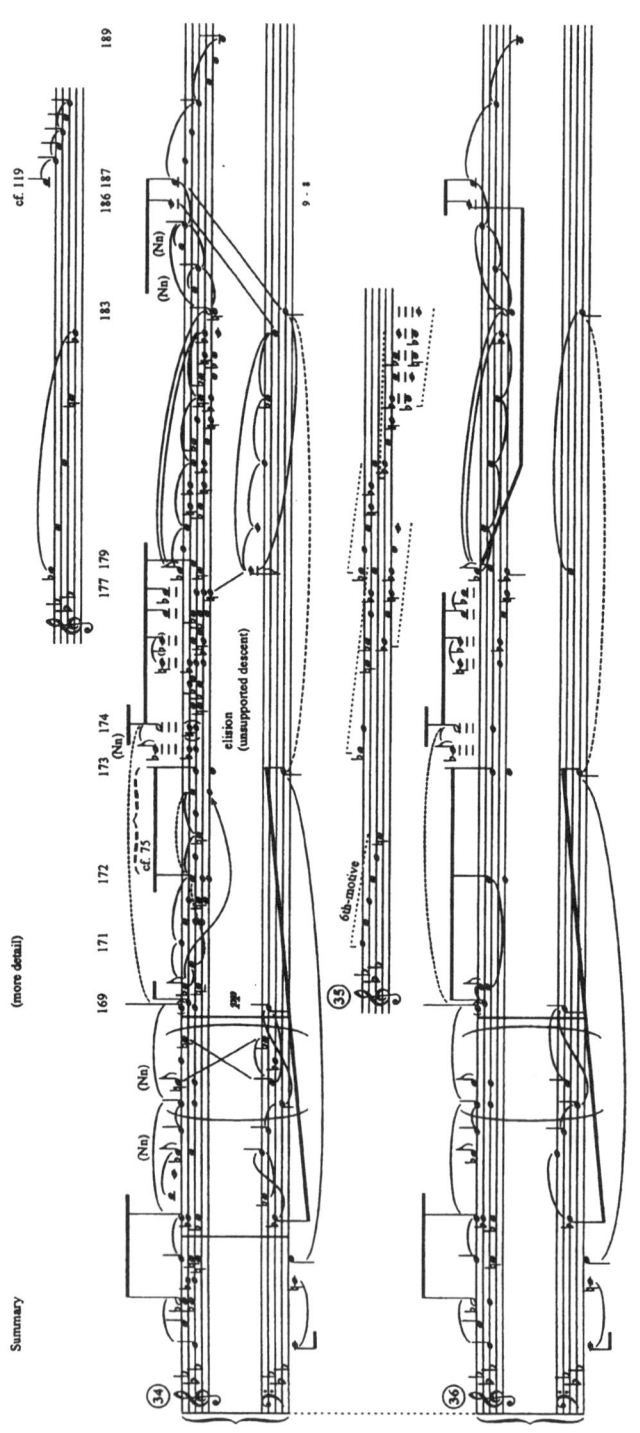

Exx. 5.34, 35, 36

128

Ex. 5.37

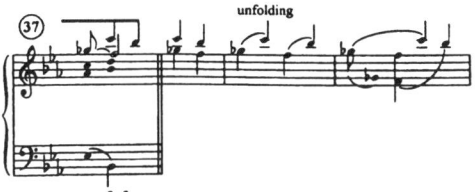

193–96 are a transformation of mm. 87, 119, and 188; mm. 201ff. pick up mm. 179ff. (continuity by linking technique); mm. 209–10 are a rhythmic diminution of mm. 193ff.; mm. 193–96 are also rhythmically akin to the outburst at mm. 165–68 (these are instances of continuity as transformation).

The scale-figures of mm. 193ff., mm. 201ff. and mm. 109ff. take on new meaning as one realizes they are by no means idle 'scale-figures' but expressions of the second subject's sixth-figure, transformed and filled in (Exx. 5.39 and 40). As in Ex. 5.38, this figure quite remarkably becomes the fifth-motive of the first subject and indeed also the motive of m. 223 (which was the motive in m. 51). Thus, the transition creates continuity by combining motivic elements of both first and second subjects. Ex. 5.43 suggests how the overall top line takes up the foreground motive of m. 51. Although mm. 193–216 constitute a striking contrast to mm. 217ff. (the 'first part' of the development section), beneath the surface there are very close motivic associations. How different is the *sound* from one section to another, and yet how remarkably are the sections bound together by concealed continuations!

As noted earlier, with the clear return of the first theme in m. 217, no doubt Bruckner's intent was to suggest that the whole exposition was somehow to be restated and recomposed, with mm. 253–87 freely corresponding to mm. 51–73, and mm. 297–333 to the exposition's second subject area (but also combining elements of both subjects). The compositional principle is similar to that noted at the outset, where the second period (mm. 19–51) had been an expanded, modified recomposition of the first.

Exx. 5.44–47 sketch the first two parts of the development section proper, Ex. 5.47 providing an overview. In the first part (mm. 183–252), the top voice 'tries out' the motivic fifth (Ex. 5.44, top system), first as f^2-$b^{\flat 2}$ then as f^3-$b^{\flat 2}$. The foreground, too, suggests 'trying out', as with the tentative, charming clashes between the horn and the strings (mm. 221, 222, 234 – not shown in the sketches). Then, in the development's second part, mm. 253ff., the motivic fifth appears boldly in the outer voices (brackets, Ex. 5.44, mm. 253–67) and, as in Ex. 5.46, the fifth is extended to an octave (continuity by transformation), as an enlargement of the motive of mm. 51 and 253 and corresponding to mm. 51ff. The diminished-third chord (m. 275) recalls that same sonority in m. 66, which had signalled the arrival of the second subject, and now yet again heralds the second subject, but in a transformed aspect (mm. 297ff.). (After m. 287 the

Exx. 5.38,39,40,41,42

130

Ex. 5.43

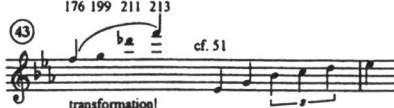

Exx. 5.44,45,46

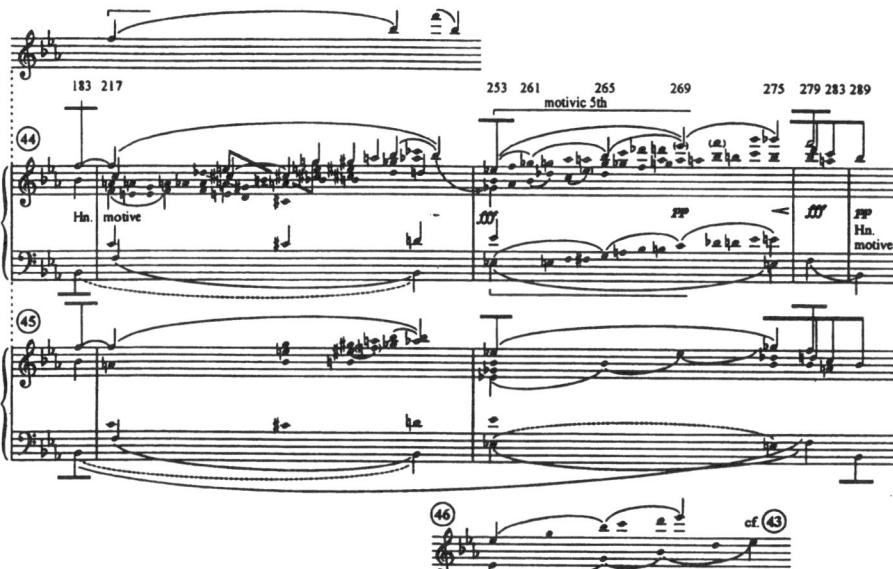

Ex. 5.47

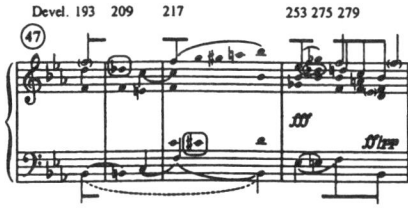

second subject area was due, since, as has been noted, the development follows the general order and outline of the exposition.) But why does the passage at mm. 289ff. seem to pick up from where m. 236 left off? If the second subject aspect is taken care of in the development by the viola line (mm. 297ff.) and the brass chorale (mm. 305ff.), then mm. 287–97 form a transition to these points, as if to clarify the motivic derivation of mm. 305ff.: indeed, mm. 289–304 (as transition) *combine* elements of both first and second subjects (see Ex. 5.48). Ex. 5.49 shows the neighbour-note and fifth-motives of the first subject; after an

Ex. 5.48

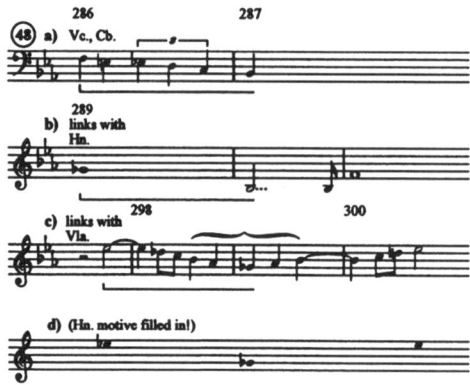

Ex. 5.49

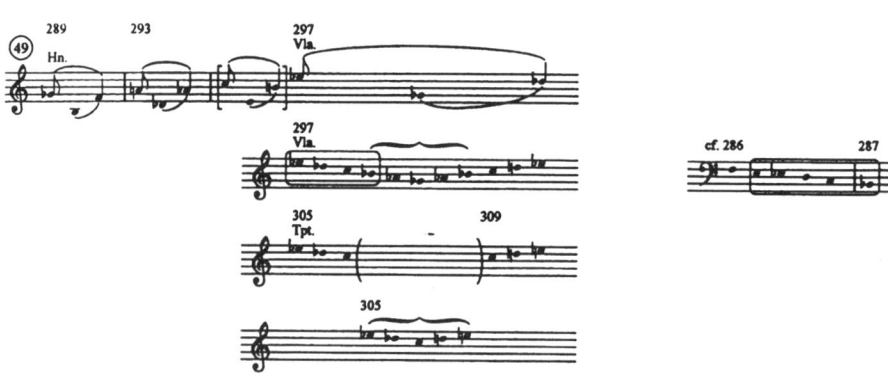

'omitted' step (shown in square brackets in Ex. 5.49), the due continuation appears (m. 297) in the violas (filled in); the relationship to the 'chorale' motive (trumpets, mm. 305ff.) is now also revealed! This chain of continuity (as shown in Exx. 5.48–49) is especially magical, for otherwise the whole chorale passage (mm. 305–33), except for its rhythmic association with the first subject, would appear extraneous: exactly the kind of *non sequitur* which would make the Bruckner critics frown. In fact, this third part of the development (mm. 287–359) is one of the glories of the movement! As in Ex. 5.50a, the rising thirds prepare the falling and rising thirds of Ex. 5.50b (marked with the braces). These falling and rising thirds most marvelously are *taken from the second subject*: Ex. 5.47c, Ex. 5.34 (m. 172), and Ex. 5.21 (m. 75)! This third-motive has emerged from its being an unassuming, inner-voice counterpoint in mm. 75–76 to a magnificent, sonorous proclamation – a programmatic meaning will be suggested later (here is continuity as realization of a process). Moreover, the rising line of Ex. 5.50b, the fifth $e^{\flat 2}$-f^2-g^2-$a^{\flat 1}$-$b^{\flat 1}$ turns out to be the motivic fifth of the returning first subject (m. 360, recapitulation), beautifully concealed!

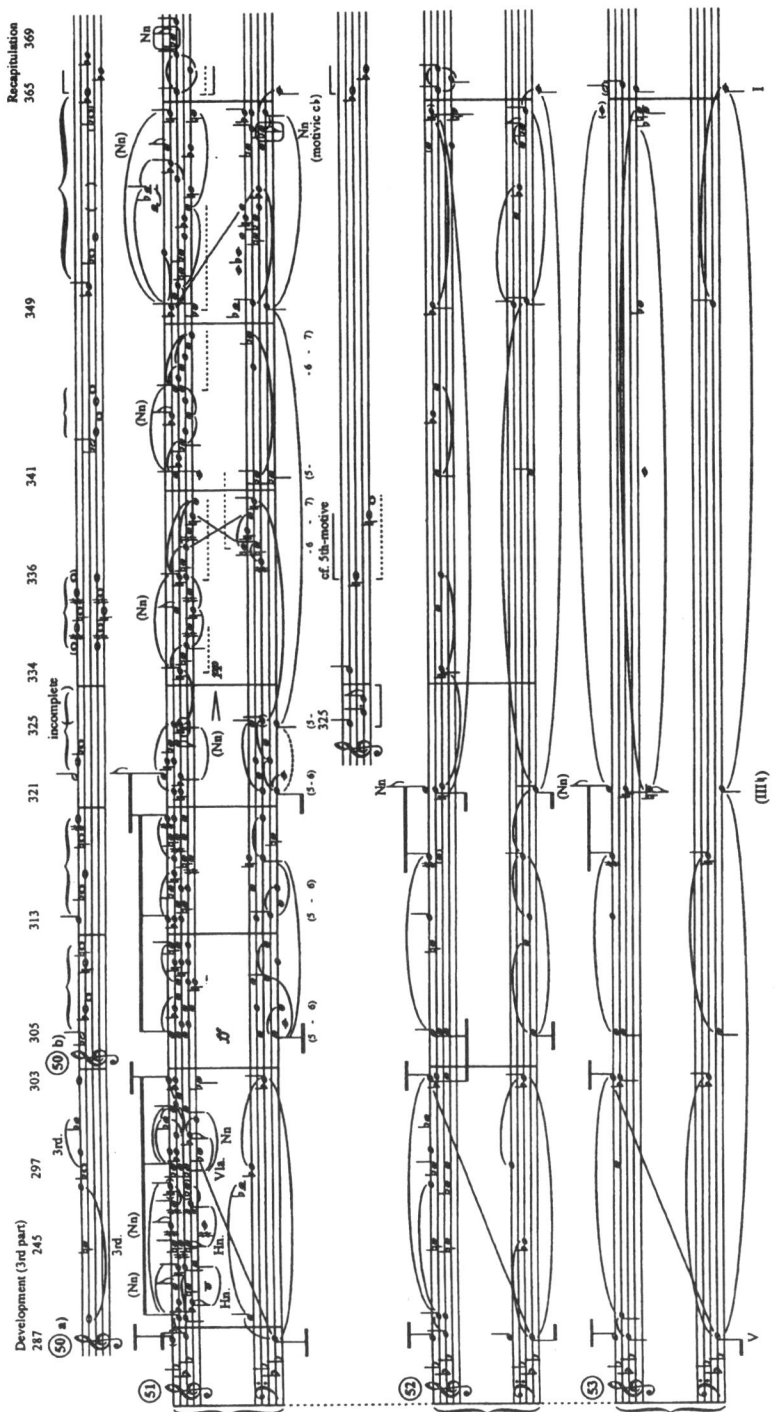

Exx. 5.50,51,52,53

Continuity is established between development and recapitulation by composing this motivic fifth $e\flat^2$-$b\flat^1$ in the middleground (mm. 305–49): this is continuity as concealed association – an indeed remarkable way of preparing the restatement of this motive in the foreground at the beginning of the recapitulation.

The neighbour note $c\flat^2$ of the first subject (m. 369) takes on new meaning by alluding to the $b\natural^1$ in the G-major chord of mm. 321–51 (circled, in Ex. 5.51). The latter point is an intermediate goal (Ex. 5.54) between the dominant and the tonic (m. 360, Exx. 5.51–53), whose *raison d'être* is possibly an enlargement of the rising-falling third-figure $B\flat$-$A\flat$-G-$A\flat$-$B\flat$ (Ex. 5.54), as well as the revaluing of the $b\natural^1$ as $c\flat^2$ in m. 369.[9] That G intermediate goal is also emphasized by the foreground appearance of the fifth-motive at m. 325 (Ex. 5.51). The g^2 at that point (m. 321) is not really the $\hat{3}$: it *alludes* to the $\hat{3}$, but is a neighbour note to the f^2 (mm. 193–303). The $f\sharp^2$ preceding the g^2 (m. 319) for its part alludes to the previous $g\flat^2$s. At m. 334 (Ex. 5.51) Bruckner works in the descending sixth-figure (broken brackets) from the second subject in a beautifully concealed transformation; this descending sixth in turn is subtly transformed to become the first subject (fifth-motive), as shown.

The foreground continuity, on the other hand, from the end of the development to the onset of the recapitulation, is quite straightforward – providing a sense of resolution and clarity after the preceding complexities. The timpani roll (mm. 351ff.) looks ahead to mm. 367ff., and the flute figure in mm. 353–54 connects with m. 365 (continuity by linking technique); this figure probably harks back to mm. 283–84 and mm. 297–98 (continuity as transformation).

Recapitulation

The point of a recapitulation is not merely to restate material for the sake of

Ex. 5.54

Ex. 5.55

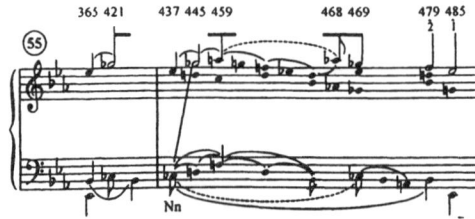

formal balance; more than that, musical material previously heard now appears in a new perspective, with fresh, different emphasis, with a sense of fulfilling and realizing earlier implications, or clarifying certain hidden associations. Bruckner recomposes the second subject area (Ex. 5.56); the $f\sharp^2$ (m. 445) ties in with the first subject's $g\flat^2$ (m. 421) creating a new tonal perspective. Ex. 5.57a reveals another relationship with the first subject area (Exx. 55.6–57): the first subject's middleground (mm. 365–421) becomes the middleground basis for the second subject (mm. 437–69). This corresponds to continuity by concealed association. The same type of continuity is shown in Exx. 5.58–59: the first subject's fifth motive appears in a new light, as a middleground feature in the second subject, and then in the closing section (Ex. 5.63). In the initial discussion of types of continuity, it was observed that even a single characteristic note could have special referential meaning (as an aspect of concealed association). How beautifully the $a\flat^2$ neighbour notes of the closing section (Exx. 5.65–66 and 69) associate, as reminders, with the subdominant sonority at the opening, mm. 15–16. Indeed, the 'plagal cadence' underlying the closing section (Exx. 5.60 and 65–66) refers to the subdominant sonority of mm. 15–16 – another expression of continuity by concealed association.

Ex. 5.55 provides an overview of the recapitulation to the closing section (mm. 48ff.); Exx. 5.56–57 show further detail. As in the exposition, Bruckner still withholds the primary tone g^3, reaching $g\flat^2$ instead in mm. 421 and 445 (the due g^3 will not be achieved until the coda). At m. 437 the second subject melody now appears in the cellos, as if it were an inner voice, in this way causing the $f\sharp^2$ ($=g\flat^2$) at m. 445 to be asserted as the top voice. The presentation of the second subject is different from what it had been in the exposition: at mm. 445ff. the descending sixth-figure ($f\sharp^2$-a^1) does *not* appear in enlargement, providing the kind of continuity as had been the case in the exposition (Ex. 5.18a: the descending sixth $b\flat^2$-$d\flat^2$ had appeared in enlargement). Instead, the motivic sixth d^3-f^2 (f^2 understood, cf. broken bracket in Ex. 5.56, mm. 449–59), not only expands the D major area, supporting the reading of $f\sharp^2$ (m. 445) as the top voice rather than the $e\flat^2$ (m. 437), but also (by this change with respect to the exposition) signals further changes to come. There is still continuity by concealed association, but now in two different guises: one concerned with the fifth-motive, the other with the neighbour-note figure. Ex. 5.58 shows the recomposition of the fifth-motive in enlargement in the middleground; this motivic coherence in the middleground helps to guarantee the cohesiveness and continuity in the foreground. In the upper voice, at first the line rises from $e\flat^2$ to $g\flat^2$ (Exx. 5.56–57, mm. 365–421; mm. 437–45) but then it proceeds to a 'false fifth': in other words, not to $b\flat^2$ but only to a^2 ($b\flat\flat^2$, m. 459), giving the sense that a 'correction' to $b\flat^2$ is due. (The neighbour-note figures, Ex. 5.58, include the missing semitones, which fill in the rising 'fifth' chromatically). The fifth-motive (plus neighbour note) appears in enlargement in the bass (Ex. 5.59), providing the harmonic *raison d'être* for the entire passage, and the fifth-motive is worked in also as in Ex. 5.57b (asterisks) – $a\flat^2$-d^2-$a\flat^2$.

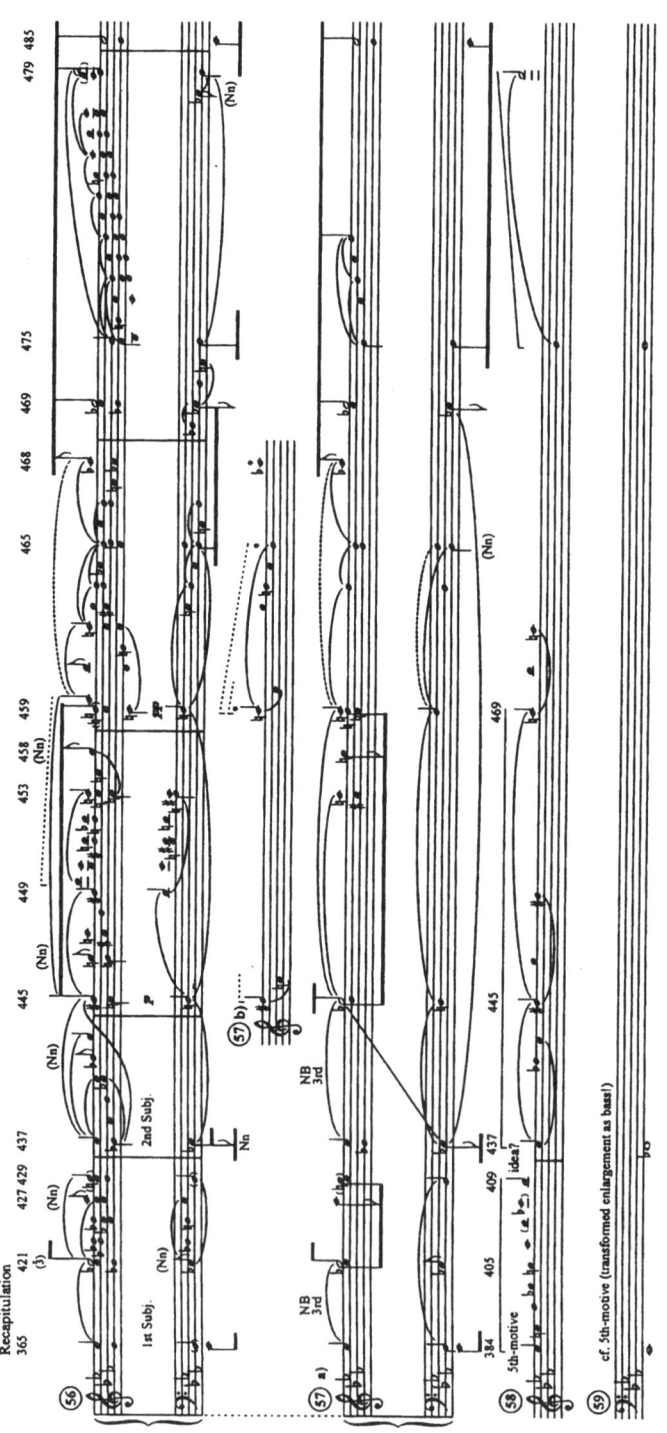

Exx. 5.56,57,57,58,59

The second aspect of continuity in the second subject area here (again, continuity as concealed association) is as shown in Ex. 5.57a. The neighbour-note figure (which derives from the $b^{\flat 1}$-$c^{\flat 2}$-$b^{\flat 1}$ neighbour-note figure from the first subject) is composed in various guises in the upper voice ($g^{\flat 2}$-$a^{\flat 2}$-$g^{\natural 2}$; $g^{\flat 2}$-$g^{\natural 2}$-f^2; $g^{\flat 2}$ m. 445 – $a^{\flat 2}$ m. 468 – $g^{\flat 2}$ m. 469) and in the bass in enlargement $B^{\flat}$-$c^{\flat}$-$B^{\flat}$ (mm. 365–421–429); this figure is recomposed as $c^{\flat}$-$B^{\flat}$-$c^{\flat}$ (mm. 437–465–469). The $B^{\flat}$ at m. 465 supports an *illusory* V, functioning as a neighbour note between the two $c^{\flat}$s! (One must read the $B^{\flat}$ this way, since the second-subject motive at m. 437 returns at mm. 469ff., connecting the $c^{\flat}$ points.) Here is indeed a subtle way of making the foreground $c^{\flat 2}$ of the opening motive organic in a deeper, middleground sense (Ex. 5.59).

Ex. 5.60 provides a synopsis of the closing section and coda, from the simplest underlying progression (Ex. 5.60a) to more elaborated versions (Exx. 5.61b and c). As in Ex. 5.61 (cf. also Ex. 5.57), the $g^{\flat 2}$s (mm. 421 and 445) are coda-like reminders of the previous $g^{\flat 2}$s and the earlier $^{\flat}\hat{3}$. (The references to $g^{\flat 2}$ in its different contexts would belong to the type of continuity as concealed association, in which a single characteristic note has referential significance). It is as if Bruckner were trying again and again to attain the g^2 ($\hat{3}$); the 'false' $g^{\flat 2}$ is finally, conclusively, set aside and replaced by the g^3 at m. 557, as if thereby symbolically overcoming the past struggles and dark forces in a blaze of triumphant glory and confirmation of the true goal.

For the close of the movement, Bruckner sums up in the coda – and to some extent in the closing section as well – certain salient features from earlier on. The emphasized $a^{\flat 2}$ neighbour note in m. 519 is a reference, on a very grand scale, to the opening's *subdominant* inflections (see the asterisks, Ex. 5.62). In this way,

Ex. 5.60

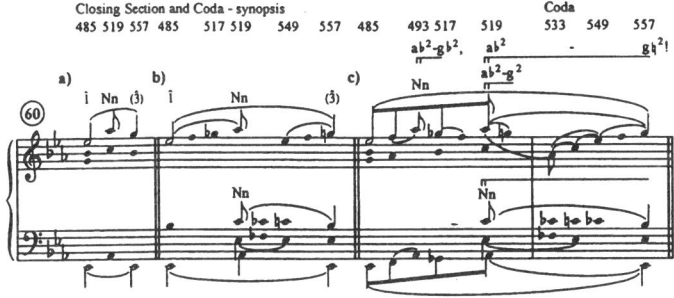

Ex. 5.61

the c-c♭-B♭ (neighbour-note feature) of the opening is subtly recomposed at the coda; as in Ex. 5.60c, the c♭ is made more independent by the F♭ (E major) harmony in mm. 533ff. The opening casts its harmonic shadow over the movement and by this striking summing-up, over the coda too, in beautifully organic fashion – organic, in the sense of continuity by concealed association! Moreover (Ex. 5.61), by overshooting the mark, the neighbour note a♭² enhances the climactic arrival on the final g². Foreground and middleground sketches (Exx. 5.65–66) provide further detail. In remarkable manner, Bruckner brings back and summarizes certain main motivic aspects in the final glorious peroration. In more or less concealed guise, the fifth-motive is worked in (Ex. 5.63): at the coda (mm. 533ff.), the fifth-motive goes beyond its bounds, so to speak, to culminate in a rise to the $\hat{3}$, g² (m. 557), once again, continuity by concealed association. The fifth-motive (Ex. 5.63, mm. 523ff.) leading up to the g² suggests what was termed continuity as process. As in Ex. 5.64, the neighbour-note figure from the first subject is recomposed, rising stepwise from m. 517 (g♭²-a♭²-b♭♭¹-c²). There, m. 517, the tutti unison outburst marks g♭² – again the 'wrong' note, which refers to the earlier motions to g♭².[10]

Ex. 5.62

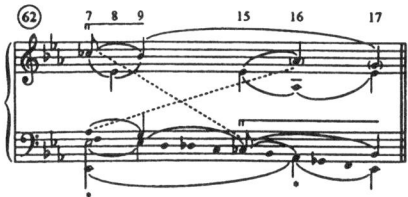

Moreover (Exx. 5.65–66), the a♭² neighbour note in mm. 519–22 harks back to the a♭² neighbour note at mm. 493ff., and ultimately to m. 16 (Exx. 5.1–2) with references as well to mm. 65–67 and 427–29. In mm. 523ff., the a♭ neighbour note recomposes mm. 15–18, as a further coda-like summing up, remarkably combined with an expression of the fifth-motive a♭¹-e♭², the latter taking a 'running start', then exceeding the fifth to ascend to the goal g². The manifold associations evoked by the a♭² exemplify that type of continuity (concealed association) in which a single characteristic note takes on special referential meaning. As shown in Ex. 5.67, the continuity from mm. 533ff. has to do with a middleground enlargement of the foreground motive of m. 51 (again, concealed association) – a beautiful way of tying together different motivic aspects.

As in Ex. 5.66, one could read parenthetical passages here (mm. 501–16, and 523–32) as in the closing section of the exposition (mm. 119–68). These extend the a♭² neighbour note, and thereby make the resolutions (to g♭² and finally to g²) the more climactic. That is, it is as if the a♭² at m. 493 were trying out the step to an understood g² (m. 501), only to get to the 'wrong' note g♭² (m. 517); on its last attempt, the a♭² (m. 519) finds the aimed for g² (m. 557)! The passages

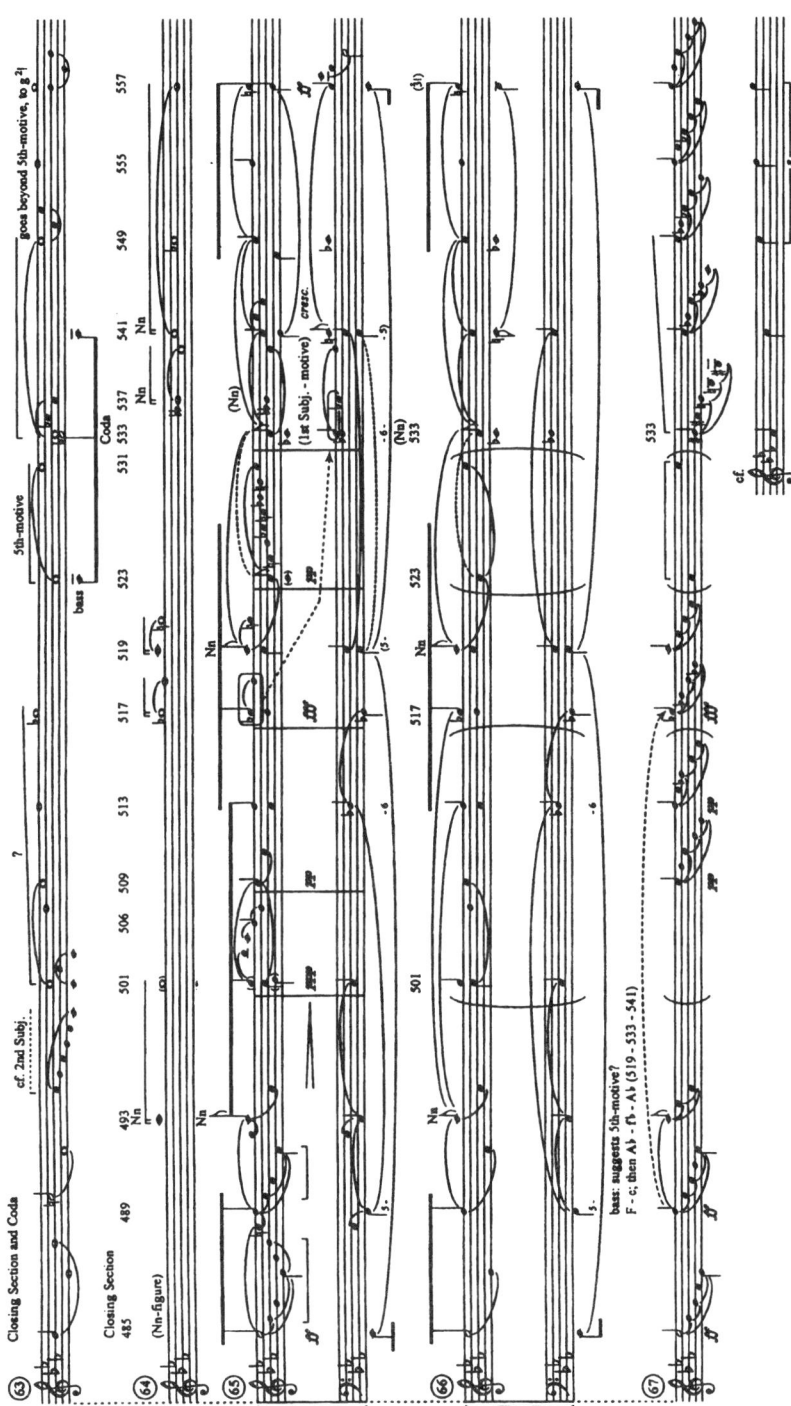

Exx. 5.63,64,65,66,67

Ex. 5.68

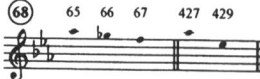

at mm. 501–16 and mm. 523–32 (Ex. 5.66) may be heard as 'parenthetical' in the sense that m. 494 associates motivically with m. 517 (the g^{b2}-f^2 half-step, m. 517, is picked up at m. 533). The passage at mm. 501ff. is set apart motivically and by dynamic contrast (*ppp*); mm. 523–32 also pause 'in the shadows', so to speak, as if the music could have proceeded directly from m. 524 to m. 533. These parenthetical passages (which belong together in that they are similar to one another in motivic figuration and rising contours) may be construed here, in the closing section of the recapitulation, as analogous to the parenthetical interpolations in the closing section of the exposition (Exx. 5.24–26, also Exx. 5.28 and 32–33). As in Exx. 5.25–26, the B♭ dominant in m. 119 had anticipated the closing B♭ dominant of m. 173; but, in the recapitulation, the E♭ tonic is definitively expressed already in m. 485, unlike the corresponding dominant in the exposition. That one must read the tonic here (and not only at m. 557, by analogy with the exposition) has to do with two points: the stability created by Bruckner's recomposing the closing section in this way suggests that the closing section has now achieved the sense of fulfilment and realization aimed for all along (continuity as process). Secondly, there is no dominant to lead to the tonic at m. 557 so mm. 485–557 constitute a vast plagal cadence extending the tonic from m. 485. The apparent discontinuity in the closing section of the exposition is surmounted here to mark the arrival on the tonic. In this new tonic context, the parenthetical passages (mm. 501–16, and mm. 523–32) appear to be only momentary digressions, which further enhance the final sense of arrival. Ex. 5.69 presents a quick overview of the whole movement.

The analytical sketches will have suggested that despite the often vaunted Brucknerian stops and starts – with attendant disruptions in continuity – there is at work in this movement a constant line of direction, both by point to point connections (whereby one motive *becomes* another), and by far-flung associations (where one motive recalls another). It is indeed astonishing, for example, how the fifth-motive (Ex. 5.4) becomes the octave-figure (Ex. 5.7); how it becomes the second subject motive (Ex. 5.18c); how the motive as transformed in Ex. 5.7 becomes the guiding line of Ex. 5.31; how the descending fifth (Ex. 5.4) inevitably becomes the sixth of Ex. 5.35 and the inner voice in Ex. 5.48 – just to review a few transformations already discussed. But the point is not just the motivic *interrelatedness*: it is also the apparent opposite – the motivic *variety* which emerges. That is, a motive such as the fifth-motive (Ex. 5.4) is only overtly characteristic and recognizable if restated fairly exactly. Just because this motive is so short and contains so few elements, it is on the one hand very malleable. On the other hand, if two or three elements are changed, the whole motive is

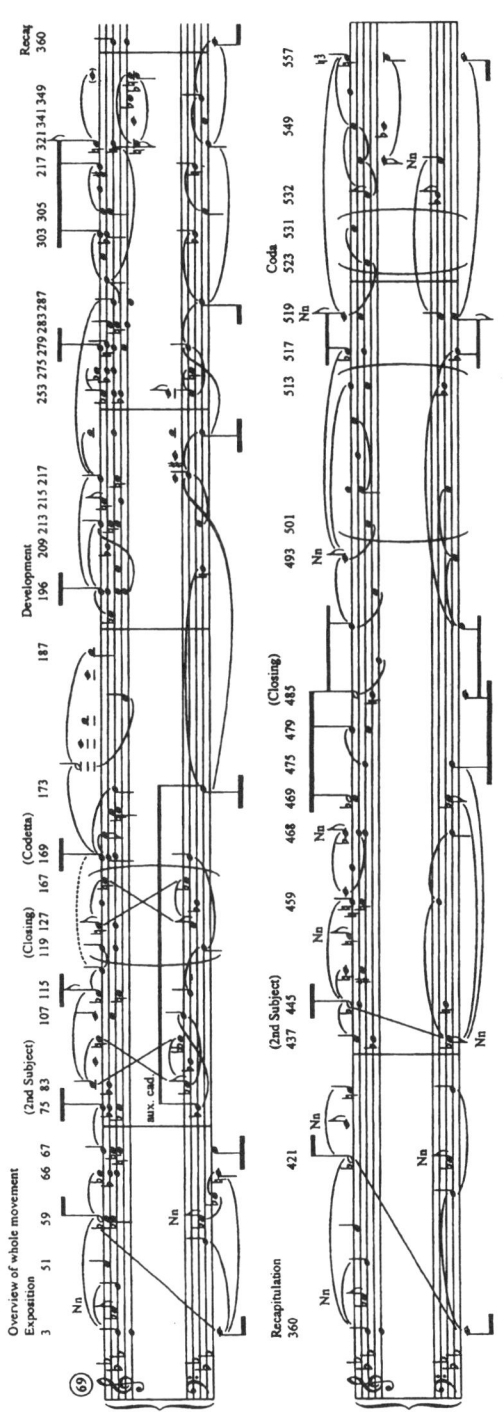

Ex. 5.69

141

altered to the point where it seems like a different motive altogether (thus the variant of m. 51 is in this sense a 'new' motive). Such transformations offer the music not only the inner continuity of relatedness, but also the infinite variety and freshness of a constantly evolving musical line. That the derivations and continuity may be subtly concealed only enhances the artistic result. Thus the very hidden transformation of the third-figure from the second subject (Ex. 5.21) into the 'chorale' episode of the development section (Ex. 5.50) is one of the marvels of the movement. One perceives relatedness and continuity even without being aware of the specific derivation.

In the rhythmic domain, the regularity of the four-bar groups could give rise to rigidity. But (to take only one example) in the *expanded restatement* noted in Exs. 5.1 and 2, the rhythmic *effect* is altered.[11] Thus in Ex. 5.70, the four-bar group mm. 11–14 becomes a seven-bar unit, mm. 39–45: the fifteen bars of the first period (mm. 3–18) become 33 in the second period (mm. 19–51)! Certainly, the dichotomy between the regular four-bar groupings on the one hand, and the irregular, changing, extended melodic designs applied to this four-bar basis on the other hand, brings forth renewed rhythmic vitality and breadth.

Ex. 5.70

The parenthetical passages noted in the closing sections of both exposition and recapitulation present a special challenge: the possibly problematic continuity–discontinuity dichotomy. Perhaps, too, a technical 'problem', if such it be, concerns the development section (Exx. 5.44–45 and 47): from about mm. 173 to 287, the main bass note is B♭ – for about 100 measures! Is this a weakness? Is this stability – being 'anchored' on B♭ – somehow at cross-purposes with the principle of developmental contrast, in that a development would aim at contrasting its harmonically less stable character with the more stable character of the preceding and ensuing expositional sections? Or perhaps the very solidity of the background bass enables the foreground to 'roam' all the more freely? But in fact, *in a background sense,* it is a characteristic of almost all development sections to *extend* or lead to the dominant in some way.

Programmatic Implications

To what extent can we take to heart Bruckner's own program, probably present right from the time he started composing the symphony? Göllerich reports that he [Bruckner] once explained the beginning of the first movement:

> a medieval town; from its towers there resounds the horn player's morning-call. By and by, the hustle and bustle of the town sets in'. According to Theodor Helm, he [Bruckner] explained the first movement thus: 'Medieval town; dawn; from the town's towers resound the morning wake-up calls; the gates open; on their proud steeds, the knights gallop forth into the open air; the magic of the woods surrounds them; the rustle of the woods, the birds' songs. And thus the romantic picture goes on and on.[12]

Bruckner's fanciful programme, in my view, is something more than a homage to Wagner – more than mere romantic scenes of yore.[13] The poetic or programmatic aspect of a musical work is bound up with its technical means: the image of knights setting forth in quest of noble *accomplishment* corresponds to the musical process whereby the initial b^{b1} of the horn's fifth-motive – the 'morning-call' – sets forth in quest of the triumphant high g^3, which will be *accomplished* at the end of the movement. This process of quest and fulfilment must also be regarded as continuity, for it is a process in which the middleground aspects (such as the final expansion of the fifth-motive a^{b1}–e^{b2} to a^{b1}–g^2, Ex. 5.63) are guided by and *continue* towards the final destination.

Furthermore, Bruckner referred to a 'contemplative mood of nature': specifically, the second subject's motive in the first violins (m. 75, Ex. 5.18) really is tone-painting. The descending sixth 'imitates the chirping of a forest bird [the titmouse]; the cantabile viola theme [mm. 75–6, Ex. 5.21] moreover expresses one's own feeling of happiness in being able to listen, in the woods, to such intimate sounds of nature'.[14] The descending sixth 'bird-motive' which pervades the second subject by the enlargements shown in Exx. 5.17–18 thus brings about continuity not only in a technical but in a programmatic sense. Likewise, inasmuch as reaching for a goal can contribute to a sense of continuity, Bruckner's 'inner happiness' motive (the falling and rising third-motive of mm. 75–6, Ex. 5.21), suggests *programmatic* arrival as well – a state of serene happiness – at its culmination in the 'chorale' section of the development (Exx. 5.5.50–53). And possibly, the final rising third e^{b2}-f^2-g^2 (mm. 549–57, Exx. 5.63, 65–66), as a last reminder of that motive, expresses the jubilant, splendid affirmation of that motive's connotation of 'inner happiness'. One can posit, as has been suggested, an underlying programmatic notion, a musical metaphor for the overcoming and triumphal resolution of difficulty, as represented by the top line's finally attaining the high g^3 (3̂). Once attained, the g^3 is not led down to close on the 1̂ but remains on high, as if going on, shining out into the hereafter. And this metaphor for continuous struggle culminating in victory may be associated with a sense of continuity, both of structure and programmatic discourse, throughout the movement.

Notes

1. For Schenker's comments, see Hellmut Federhofer, 'Heinrich Schenkers Bruckner

Verständnis', in *Archiv für Musikwissenschaft*, 34/3 (1982), pp. 198–217, and my own essay 'Some aspects of prolongation procedures in the Ninth Symphony', in *Bruckner Studies*, ed. Jackson and Hawkshaw (Cambridge University Press, 1997), pp. 209–55.

2. The history of the four versions of this symphony (1874, 1878, 1881, and 1888) is conveniently summarized in Hans F. Redlich's introductory remarks to the Eulenburg edition of the score (No. 462, London n.d.).

3. Anton Bruckner, *Sämtliche Werke. Kritische Gesamtausgabe, 4. Band*, Brucknerverlag, Wiesbaden (1936, new edition 1949).

4. This procedure of step by step variation and transformation of a motive may be compared to what Arnold Schoenberg termed 'variants': see his *Fundamentals of Musical Composition* (St Martin's Press, New York, 1967), pp. 8–15.

5. Charles Burkhart, 'Schenker's Motivic Parallelisms', in *Journal of Music Theory*, 22 (1978), p. 174 discusses Schenker's concept of 'hidden' repetition.

6. Oswald Jonas described linking technique in *Das Wesen des musikalischen Kunstwerks* (Vienna: Saturn-Verlag, 1934), pp. 12–20. Reprinted as *Einführung in die Lehre Heinrich Schenkers* (Vienna: Universal Edition, 1972). Trans. and ed. John Rothgeb, *Introduction to the Theory of Heinrich Schenker* (New York: Longman, 1982), pp. 3–10.

7. There are, of course, many instances of a long delay in reaching the primary tone, such as Bach, Prelude in E (WTC I); Beethoven, Piano Sonatas Op. 13 and Op. 27 No. 2; Schubert, *Mein!, Trock'ne Blumen, Des Baches Wiegenlied, Auf dem Flusse, Wasserflut*; Brahms, Intermezzo Op. 116 No. 6, and Ballade Op. 118 No. 3. But Bruckner's procedure is perhaps unique in that the primary tone arrives only in the *coda*. The eventual arrival of the $\hat{3}$ is shown in Exx. 5.60, 65–66, and 69.

8. But in a real sense, the first movement – as in Bruckner's symphonies generally – directs the sense of cumulation to the Finale: by withholding the primary tone until the *end* of the first movement, Bruckner enhances the feeling that the music must now proceed beyond that point.

9. While Bruckner's harmonic progression V–III–I may have come about for these reasons, it should be noted that this large-scale progression does occur in Classical development sections as well, for reasons associated with motivic features of the particular work, e.g. first movements of Mozart's Piano Sonatas K. 280, 332, and 333; his Symphony in E flat K. 543, and Trio in E flat K. 498; Beethoven's Violin Sonata Op. 24, and First and Sixth Symphonies. See my article 'Voice-leading Procedures in Development Sections', in *Studies in Music*, 13 (1991), pp. 69–120; also David Beach, 'A Recurring Pattern in Mozart's Music', in *Journal of Music Theory*, 27 (1983), pp. 1–29; 'The Initial Movement of Mozart's Piano Sonatas K. 280 and K. 332: Some Striking Similarities', in *Intégrale*, 8 (1994), pp. 125–46; 'Schubert's Experiments with Sonata Form: Formal-Tonal Design verses Underlying Structure', in *Music Theory Spectrum*, 15 (1993), pp. 1–18 and Channan Willner, 'Chromaticism and the Mediant in Four Late Haydn Works', in *Theory and Practice*, 13 (1988), pp. 79–114.

10. Cf. mm. 59, 66, 76, 108, 115, 167, 173, 179, 275, 320, 421, 445, 469.

11. For Bruckner's own notes on the rhythmic structure of the periods and the placement of cadences, see Göllerich-Auer, IV/1, 441–42.

12. Ibid., p. 518.

13. For the parallels between Bruckner's programme and Wagner's *Lohengrin* and *Siegfried*, see Constantin Floros, *Brahms und Bruckner* (Wiesbaden: Breitkopf und Härtel, 1980) pp. 175–76.

14. Ibid., pp. 161 and 171.

6 The expressive role of disjunction: a semiotic approach to form and meaning in the Fourth and Fifth Symphonies

Robert S. Hatten

Introduction

An inescapable critical problem is posed by the disjunctive aspect of Bruckner's symphonic forms. The fault lines are exposed early in the reception history of Bruckner's symphonies with Heinrich Schenker's deprecating analysis of his teacher's 'grandiose, isolated cells'.[1] Wilhelm Kienzl criticizes the Finale of the Fourth Symphony along similar lines, noting the lack of expressive coherence such isolated units create: '[their] unmediated juxtaposition and delightful individuality ... [do] not allow a unified feeling to arise in the listener'.[2] Thematic contrast, traditionally interpretable as dramatic conflict, does not in itself constitute an aesthetic problem. The juxtaposition of contrasting material is a hallmark of the Classical style and functions as a dramatic premise for many a movement by Beethoven. What Schenker and Kienzl criticize is not the juxtaposing of contrasting thematic blocks in themselves, but the apparently unmotivated nature of that juxtaposition. For Schenker, the grandiose or monumental character of a given thematic section was perhaps isolated not only by disjunctive contrast, but by the absence of voice-leading connections that could absorb that contrast into a coherent overall progression. Kienzl's perceived lack of a 'unified feeling' may be due to a thematic logic deemed inadequate in mediating the disorienting shift between affective planes – lacking the continuity of Brahms's developing variation, for example. If neither voice-leading logic nor thematic unfolding can accommodate these startling disjunctions in Bruckner's formal plotting, are we to conclude that Bruckner, despite the considerable skill with which he designs his 'cells', was ultimately inadequate as a composer of

145

symphonic forms? Or are we missing a crucial perspective on Bruckner's mastery of formal design? Might disjunction be understood as significant in ways that earlier analyses of voice-leading and thematic development are not fully suited to reveal? If so, might an approach that considers dramatic form and the varieties of expressive meaning provide convincing motivations for Bruckner's compositional choices?

The large- and small-scale disjunctions and juxtapositions found in the Fourth and the Fifth Symphonies will be examined here for their contribution to the coherent realization of a motivated dramatic scheme. Several analytical approaches developed in my work on Beethoven will help illuminate the productive role of Bruckner's discontinuities in light of his expressive goals.[3] The first of these approaches involves a theory of expressive genres which distinguishes typical dramatic trajectories in terms of their traversal from an initial state to a final goal. For example, a movement (or a complete symphonic cycle of movements) may begin tragically and end triumphantly (the victory symphony). Or, as is often the case in late Beethoven, the outcome of an initially tragic situation may be one of transcendence: the tragic is not defeated despite struggle, but through some form of transformation a positive state is achieved on a 'higher' plane than that of the tragic struggle. One form of transformation is that achieved by spiritual abnegation or positive resignation, in which acceptance neutralizes what might otherwise be perceived as negative, displacing or rising above it to a more positively experienced state. In sacred terms, the willed or willing surrender to faith and the transcendent outcome of personal sacrifice constitute familiar models for Bruckner. In secular terms, the concept of *Bildung* (as developed in Goethe's *Wilhelm Meisters Lehrjahre*) was another possibility in the German Romantic culture from which Bruckner drew.[4] Transformations may also be achieved through the action and/or recognition of an external force that redeems suffering or justifies extreme effort, perhaps leading to a final blaze of glory (in sacred terms, an epiphany or transfiguration; in secular terms, a psychologically integrative moment of insight or awareness). Still another possible dramatic trajectory might begin in a positive state (for example, from within the pastoral field), progressively introduce tragic threats to that serenity, and move ultimately to a transfigured form of the original state.

A theory of expressive genres, or dramatic trajectories, draws upon other theories of expressive meaning in music, an important one being Ratner's reconstruction of Classical topics (extended by the addition of Romantic ones, as noted below), and the expressive associations that topics bring to bear.[5] Certain topics may be conceived as larger *fields* or expressive stages in the dramatic course of an expressive genre. Three examples are the *heroic* (cued by such topics as fanfare and march, but also by dotted rhythms and strongly marked gestures), the *pastoral* (cued by such topics as the musette and the horn call or hunting topic, but also by simplicity as reflected in various musical dimensions), and the *tragic* (cued by minor mode and many of the Baroque-derived expressive devices, such as the sigh figure and the use of the diminished-seventh chord). The heroic may support the triumphant, or the pastoral the transcendent, as these topical fields are further interpreted within dramatic trajectories.

Another approach contributing to expressive interpretation involves the identification of agency in music. One needs to distinguish events that are caused, willed, or achieved by the agent (or persona, or character) in the expressive drama from those that happen to the agent as a result of action by an opposing agent – whether conceived as another character or as generalized Fate. Furthermore, one needs to distinguish levels of agency. A Romantic ironic shift between levels of discourse can suggest either a higher capacity on the part of the original agent (who can rise above the ongoing discourse, either to reflect upon it or to comment critically) or the imposition of another agency (perhaps attributable to the composer). The latter may suggest a composed-in narrative function, with the higher-level persona commenting on, or perhaps directing, the ongoing discourse. The celebrated Romantic ironic capability of literature may be emulated in music by a sudden shift in style, or what I call stylistic register, among high, middle and low styles.

A further interpretive approach involves what I call musical tropes. Simple irony (cueing a meaning opposed to that which is ostensibly expressed) is itself a primary trope, capable of operating upon an entire discourse as a figuration of its content. Friedrich Schlegel described irony as permanent parabasis,[6] and Paul De Man defines that parabasis as 'the interruption of a discourse by a shift in the rhetorical register'.[7] At a more local level, De Man considers this trope an anacoluthon, or 'a break in the syntactical expectations of the pattern [of a sentence]'.[8] Applications to music are conceivable for other tropes as well. I have construed metaphor in music as resulting from the fusion of contradictory meanings in a single functional location (the expressive meaning derived, for example, from a fusion of two topical associations). But irony typically works at a higher level, disrupting both stable meanings as well as the more unstable, creative tropes. It is difficult to pin down the meaning of an ironically inflected discourse, since the irony (Romantic or simple) promotes a condition of instability with respect to meaning. Fortunately, in the case of Bruckner we are not dealing with an irony as embedded as one might find in Shostakovich, for example, and the appropriate interpretation need not be as difficult.

In my work on Beethoven I have developed an approach to musical meaning based on stylistic oppositions, creating the more 'literal' associations of musical meaning that I call *correlations*. Occasionally I will refer to such familiar meanings that have become a part of the Viennese stylistic tradition from which Bruckner draws. In addition, Bruckner often alludes to his favourite composer next to Schubert, namely Wagner, and these allusions or near quotations are meant to convey a particular expressive meaning that has been established in advance by the context of the opera or music drama from which it is drawn. The term *intertextuality* has been borrowed from literary studies to capture the sharing of meanings drawn from such allusions to works or styles.

Erinnerung

To set up the compositional issues raised by Bruckner's use of disjunctive sections, I turn first to his striking use of self-contained, motto-like themes. The technique is already apparent in a fascinating character piece for piano which was written, according to Walburga Litschauer, around 1868 toward the end of Bruckner's residence in Linz.[9] This charming little piece, entitled *Erinnerung* (*Reminiscence*), aspires to an orchestral climax; thus, its use for comparison with the Fifth Symphony may not appear quite so unorthodox. My reason for introducing the piece, however, is that it illustrates a marked tendency in Bruckner's style: the use of short thematic ideas presented with *leitmotivic* concision and featuring a marked chromatic twist either melodically, tonally, or both.

As may be seen in Ex. 6.1, the first phrase modulates from A♭ to C minor by reinterpreting the subdominant chord D♭ as Neapolitan of C minor. The melody emphasizes the chromatic modulation by a double neighbour motion within the narrow ambit of a diminished third. As effective as this motto-like theme appears, with its expressively marked chromatic modulation (familiar to us from such examples as the Chopin Prelude in C minor), it offers little suggestion for continuation because of its self-enclosed character. Thus, Bruckner merely takes the model and sequences it, slightly varying it harmonically.

A contrasting phrase (bars 5–8) serves as consequent, with a mannerist use of echo-like imitation to enhance the texture, perhaps even to suggest a self-reflective reminiscence. The first eight-bar period ends on V of B♭ minor, with another mannerist melodic turn. The parallel period (bars 9–16) offers a surprise harmonic twist with a drop to *pianissimo* in bar 12, followed by an inversion of the consequent motive in more thoroughgoing imitation (bars 13–16). What had been a resignational, reminiscent drop of a sixth echoed by a seventh is now a purposeful ascent of a fourth, driving the music forward with fresh energy. Thus we see the expressive motivation for melodic inversion, which is not merely a formal developmental technique. Having injected new energy, this consequent phrase demands its own consequent, and the following phrase (bars 17–20) re-inverts the figure, with less systematic answering in the alto voice. As the music winds down, we find another mannerist feature of Bruckner's style, an over-extended liquidation (bars 21–28), perhaps resulting from the desire to preserve a four-bar hypermetric structure.

The *tempo primo* re-introduces the theme above continuous arpeggiation, and this third large period moves to two climaxes (not shown). The second climax is reached by means of a triadic sequence (bars 39–40) similar to the one Bruckner uses twice to build to a climax in the second movement of the Fifth Symphony, and also to create the transfigurational climax in the coda of the Fourth Symphony's Finale. The pattern is i–VII–III in minor and I–V/III♯ III♯ in major. This sequence breaks down as chromatic-third progressions highlight a monumental, triple-forte climax that is dynamically and expressively far out of

Ex. 6.1 *Erinnerung*, bars 1–30, character piece for piano from Bruckner's Linz period

proportion to the modest dimensions of the work. A quiet 8-bar coda closes the piece.

The characteristic thematic features of *Erinnerung* provide an instructive comparison with thematic construction in the Fifth Symphony. Ex. 6.2 shows the first appearance of the motto theme that becomes the subject for the fugue in the Finale. Note the Neapolitan-flavoured modulation by chromatic third from G♭ to B♭ at the end, and the diminished-third in the melody. Ex. 6.3 displays the Allegro first theme of the opening movement. Its prominent diminished third (G♭–F–E♮) and its self-sufficient motto character are achieved without modulation. The chorale-prelude-like second theme of this same movement is excerpted in Ex. 6.4. Its chromatic shifts create a marked interior modulation. In each case, I would argue, Bruckner creates a theme that functions like a *Leitmotiv* along the lines of Wagner's Fate motive. These themes, with their surprising harmonic twists, are obviously weighted with significance, but that significance may be interpreted as enigmatic, tragic, or mystical, depending on the context.

Two compositional problems emerge from such a thematic language. First, given the self-sufficient status of these motto-like themes, how can one convincingly create musical continuity? Second, how are the themes expressively motivated to function as part of a larger, dramatic scheme? To put these issues

Ex. 6.2   Fifth Symphony, brass chorale introduction of fugue subject from the Finale

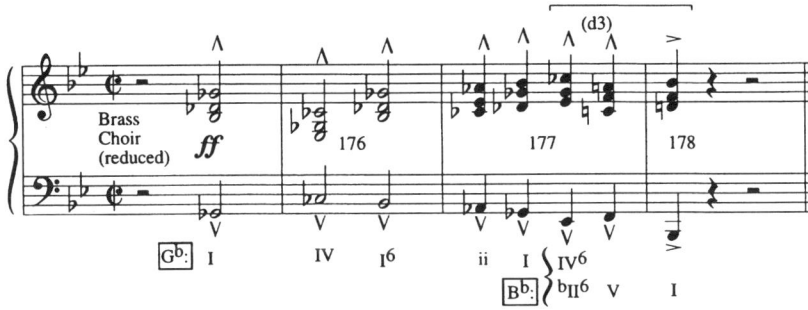

Ex. 6.3   Fifth Symphony, first theme (of the Allegro) from the first movement

Ex. 6.4   Fifth Symphony, second theme from the first movement

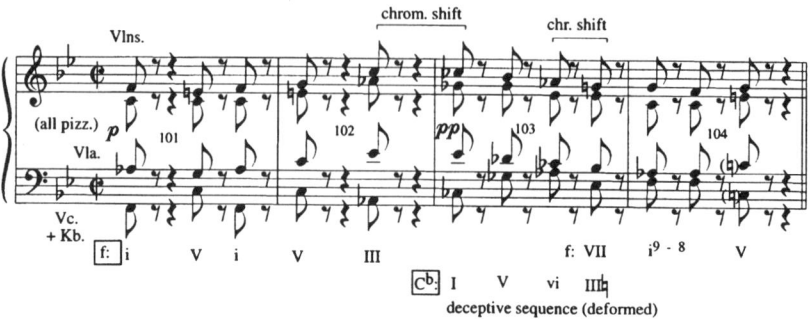

together, *does Bruckner satisfactorily resolve the problem of continuity, and how does a plausible dramatic trajectory contribute to that solution?* I will pursue these questions with regard to the Fourth Symphony as a whole, with special attention to expressive motivations for some of the extensive revisions in the Finale. I will begin, however, by examining the outer movements of the Fifth Symphony, which is not as problematic a score with respect to revisions. One might assume that Bruckner's formal and dramatic intentions were never subject to as much self-criticism in the Fifth Symphony, and perhaps something of what Bruckner learned from writing the Fifth influenced his revisions of the Fourth.

Fifth Symphony

In the Finale of the Fifth Symphony, by way of contrast with the first movement, there are two rather obvious and built-in guarantees of textural continuity. First, the fugue's continuous texture is a typical feature of the genre. Second, when the disjunct motto-subject (Ex. 6.2) becomes the first phrase of the climactic chorale prelude, there is an underlying continuity despite the disjunctive chorale phrases, since a continuous background texture binds them into a larger whole (a typical feature of this type of chorale-prelude). Fugue and chorale prelude are employed as topics in support of a basic dramatic scenario. The developmental fugue can be interpreted as a struggle between the chorale motto ('faith') and the ironically questioning motive in the clarinet ('doubt'). The apotheosis of the chorale prelude clearly indicates a triumphant affirmation of faith. This dramatic trajectory is a familiar one from the Fourth Symphony, as well; it is the generic redemption narrative that may be found throughout the nineteenth century and was most powerfully modelled for Bruckner in Wagner's operas and music dramas, from *Tannhäuser* to *Götterdämmerung* and *Parsifal*.

The compositional issues raised by Bruckner's use of motto-like themes are most acute in the first movement. Here, typical analyses of thematic integration or subtle motivic interrelationships are not in themselves adequate to account for coherence in the face of self-contained ideas and the disjunctive sections they spawn. I will argue that an expressive interpretation is crucial to our understanding of 'purely musical' design in this movement, and that the reconstruction of dramatic continuity will draw on expressive interpretation as an integral part of the analysis. I will also argue that an interpretation grounded in musical topics and the thematizing of tonal relationships may not only help justify unusual tonal and thematic disjunctions, but also help explain why other compositional choices might not be quite as successful.

Consider the three opening thematic and textural blocks of the introduction (Ex. 6.5). The movement begins with what might have been a lament bass, but the major mode and the reversal by means of an oppositional ascent help keep the introduction poised between two affects (mournful descent, hopeful ascent). The raised $\hat{4}$ serves as enigmatic trigger for that reversal, and the unsettled oscillation between poles of the tritone span may connote uncertainty. The spiritual context of that disquiet is cued by the overlaid sequence of suspensions, with their learned-style liturgical echoes. A combination of walking bass and chorale-like suspensions foreshadows the 'pilgrim's processional' topic of the second theme. That topic, as Constantin Floros has shown, appears for the first time in Bruckner's Fourth Symphony and has its topical origin in Berlioz's *Harold in Italy*.[10] While suggesting reverential awe mixed with mournful uncertainty, the opening theme soon tips the balance to lament as overlapping ascent gives way to sequential descent, and the darker sighs of lowered $\hat{6}$ to $\hat{5}$ express a more direct grief. The marked diminished third, G♭–F–E♮ (bars 9–10), is emblematic of the tragic (compare the E♭–D–C♯ diminished third in the opening theme of Beethoven's *Eroica* Symphony).

After winding down to a half cadence, the ensuing silence is brutally disrupted by a fanfare-like arpeggiation in dotted rhythm on G♭, the ♭VI. Then, after another silence, a sturdy brass chorale phrase enunciates the dominant of D. The fanfare returns on B♭, now heard as ♭VI of D. And the brass chorale returns, as well, this time on the dominant of A. In his analysis of the movement, Robert Simpson construes these discontinuous opening blocks in terms of a tonal strategy for the movement, the 'search for a tonality'.[11] One can certainly interpret Bruckner's choices in this light, as the ensuing emphasis on V of A turns out to be a false dominant preparation for the Allegro, which slips back into B♭, now minor, for the first theme. Indeed, the D minor implied by mixture appears in a dramatic role at the undercut climax of the development, but as a key it does not outlast its motto theme. A problem with Simpson's tonal premise for the movement is that it is too accommodating; if any key is as plausible as another in avoiding B♭, why might these particular ones have been chosen?

Simpson also implies that Bruckner's primary motivation was large-scale tonal structure. I would like to take a different tack by considering the locally expressive value of those keys as unmitigated shifts in perspective, creating dramatically motivated disjunctions even when one may trace a traditional progression binding the sections. The G♭ fanfare, which suggests a traditional

Ex. 6.5   Fifth Symphony, introduction (opening excerpt) from the first movement

deceptive move to ♭VI of B♭ (foreshadowed by previous references to ♭6̂), has a much more disruptive effect when its sudden unison abrades smooth progressional voice-leading from the previous V by forcing a tritone leap in the upper voice. Note also the extreme conflict in styles, from the highly refined opening to the bald force of a near-*tutti* primitive unison. The next thematic block, also isolated by rests, is a brass chorale which does not so much respond to the fanfare, either in character or in key, but rather projects yet another perspective. With this highly disjunctive opening, we are challenged to construct a scenario that would provide dramatic continuity where textural, topical, tonal, and thematic continuities are tenuous, at best.

One difficulty in construing this section dramatically is that we have no clear clue as to the agency of these three perspectives, as opposed to the contextualized dramatic significance of Wagner's contrasting *Leitmotive*. After-the-fact tonal explanations inevitably stretch credulity, since Bruckner does not always satisfactorily resolve or fully account for the dissonances that his keys introduce, when considered from a Classical perspective.

If one were to assign roles to these themes, one might start by attempting to assess their degree of subjectivity or intimacy, hence their suitability as expressive of a persona or agency. In that case, all three are rather objective, if not monumental, in their effect. But clearly the first is pitched at a more intimate, human scale, and its increasingly personalized suspensions and sigh figures bespeak the expression of an individual agent. The fanfare might then be construed as a brutal intrusion of fate, along the Beethoven model. The ensuing brass chorale is interpretable oppositionally as an emblem of faith – powerful, but at this point objectified and remote.

After the second chorale statement, a flurry of excitement over an A pedal anticipates the Allegro tempo and leads to a third chorale block. This culminating statement appears to encompass something of the tragic premise of the symphony, with its grating neighbour chord that is nevertheless absorbed into the brilliance of triumphant, diatonic faith. Associatively, if the A major harmony suggests a world of faith, it cannot at this point be sustained, since the rhetoric of expressive genre demands heroic struggle and either triumphant victory or transcendent serenity if a positive outcome is to be satisfactorily achieved.

Note how Bruckner arrives at his tragically inflected key of B♭ minor for the Allegro proper: the extracted A from the introduction 'resolves' to D, but as $\hat{3}$ of B♭, and the main theme mutates $\hat{3}$ to minor. The local tonal symbolism is concise and effective: a potential tonic is three times demoted, from $\hat{1}$ to $\hat{3}$, then mutated to a minor ♭$\hat{3}$, and finally relegated to the fifth of a VI chord (see Ex. 6.3, bars 55–6). The shift of realms, from idealized faith to tragic reality, is made poignant by such expressively motivated modulatory transformation.

At this point, having interpreted the striking disjunctiveness of the introduction as setting up a series of dramatic oppositions, we might expect the movement to develop them without further loss of momentum. But the main theme is also motto-like, as noted earlier. Its diminished-third kernel, G♭–F–E♮ (Ex. 6.3, bars 56–7), is understood as derived from the end of the opening phrase, and our assumption of agency appears confirmed: the Allegro will treat the tragic issue embodied by that marked chromatic cell.

Though softly presented in the strings, the motto-like Allegro theme projects an element of the heroic, both tonally and rhythmically. The immediate resolution of G♭–F–E♮ to F and the dotted arpeggiation of the resulting half-cadence suggest the determined action and character of a motivated agent – the persona of the movement. But the continuation of such a self-contained motto theme can only be by sequence, if its *leitmotivic* significance is to be sustained. Thematic continuity is thus merely additive at first, with later intensification by the typical developmental techniques of fragmentation and sequencing of fragments. Since the expressive energy is in the motto itself, its sequential development cannot help but gradually expend that energy, until a premonitory rise to the *fortissimo* statement of the theme offers renewal. This time the motto-like character of the theme is sharply stamped with a full *tutti*. The expressive crux, however, is again focused in the motto-theme itself, despite a sequential continuation in two fragments. And like the first continuation, this one can only spin out the motto's energies. The dissolution to a quiet B♭ surrounded by C♭ and A as neighbours suggests a liquidation of the thematic diminished third. In a sense, the whole first theme group, despite its surface textural continuity, sounds somewhat introductory and self-enclosed: the theme, so complete in itself, can generate little of consequence; at this point it is still more of a premise than a generative idea.

The second theme group, which enters without any modulatory preparation when B♭ simply drops into F minor, further exemplifies the shifting, *perspectival* character of these thematic blocks. The chorale-prelude texture is a full realization of the pilgrim's processional topic. As may be seen in Ex. 6.4, each phrase of this chorale prelude has a chromatic tonal shift for what I have termed the 'deceptive sequence', I–V–vi–iii–IV–I (or i–v–VI–III–iv–i in minor). The first phrase, for example, slips into C♭ major and emerges on a half-cadence in F minor. The liturgical associations of the deceptive sequence are clear (as found in the 'threefold Amen'), but perhaps one can dig deeper. Bruckner uses the sequence in his *Te Deum*, written seven years later, at the words '*gloria Patris Judex crederis*' ('[in the] glory of the Father we believe [that Jesus will come to be our] Judge'). The character of the sequence easily supports the authoritative sense of this phrase, and in the *Te Deum* passage the sequence is not deformed. The Fifth Symphony's subtle twisting of the sequence provides a further shift in perspective, perhaps suggesting a deeper reflection upon, or questioning of, the diatonic assurances of faith.

Continuity is built into the second theme by the ongoing texture of the chorale prelude. At the same time, a very successful technique of expressive variation is employed by Bruckner. Each disjunct chorale phrase first fills in the minor third (tragically weighted in opposition to the major mode opening, but less marked than the chromatically-filled diminished third) and then refracts the pizzicato deceptive sequence with more humanly expressive sigh figures. Thus, there is a kind of dialogical tension between the intimate sustained expressions of the foregrounded persona and the mystical remove of the backgrounded pizzicato chorale.

A contrasting middle section in D♭ introduces the Romantic horn call as topic, here in the service of a resignational recall of the diminished third C♭–A–B♭ from the end of the first theme group. This section also foreshadows the key and lyric aspect of the third theme group, which arrives deceptively in D♭ as VI of F minor (Ex. 6.6). The theme features two contrasting ideas that are counterpointed in contrary motion. The four-bar breadth of the lyric idea in the woodwinds only

Ex. 6.6   Fifth Symphony, third theme from the first movement

briefly disguises the fact that it, too, will be treated as yet another discrete perspective. The cellos and basses counter with a self-contained ostinato on a descending, dotted-arpeggio figure Dᵇ–Aᵇ–F that chromatically fills the third from Aᵇ to F, perhaps as integrative reminder of the first theme. When the lyric idea is then fragmented in the consequent four-bar phrase, this ostinato figure comes to the fore. The further integrative character of the Dᵇ theme is enhanced by its emergent, chorale-based cadence punctuated by the brass. Note an echo of the deceptive cadence patterning supporting the authoritative close, dramatically twisting to Bᵇ (!). This chordal punctuation appears to overpower both the lyric and the heroic/tragic motives with which the phrase began. Motto-theme technique is here expanded, in that a complete expressive argument with significant tonal shift is packed into an eight-bar theme.

As a result, Bruckner has little choice but to sequence the entire complex. The resulting continuation is, in my view, less successful, as Bruckner grinds away with the dotted figure in incessant one-bar repetitions and four-bar hyper-measures. Here the motto character of the figure, though intervallically varied, cannot sustain interest. Even the liquidation seems overextended, not unlike the overdone liquidation in the piano piece, *Erinnerung*, noted earlier. Furthermore, the associative use of key leads to another surprising return of Bᵇ major, in a unison sequence to Gᵇ and F that recalls the opening. A surprise transformation underlaid by a pedal C–Dᵇ–C motion turns that F into a tonic to conclude the exposition in the grammatically proper key of the dominant. That this is only a last minute manoeuver illustrates the fundamentally un-Classical nature of Bruckner's appropriation of sonata form, and yet the vestigial key plan is evidence of the importance of sonata form for Bruckner, even when it only serves as a compositional framework. Nevertheless, his negotiation of compositional drama with an inherited form often generates its own energy.

The development section, for example, demonstrates the skill with which Bruckner exploits the dramatic consequences of his motto-driven thematic technique. As shown in Ex. 6.7, previously disjunct or distant ideas are

Ex. 6.7   Fifth Symphony, opening of the development from the first movement

juxtaposed without intervening silences, which creates the effect of sudden shifts of frame or perspective akin to the technique of montage in film. The device transforms discrete disjunction into a successive integration of ideas and, as in film, such close cutting accelerates tension. A related technique, simultaneous integration or stratification of topical strands (not simply the traditional counterpointing of thematic lines), is also in evidence, as the chorale opening is layered with the fragmented first theme (bars 247–8).

Traditional developmental techniques are also on display, though perhaps with a motto-inspired self-consciousness in their marked settings: note the stretto imitation of the four-bar first theme (bars 243–6), followed by a mirror-inversional treatment of its head. The second movement will end with just such a mirrored-motto summing up of the main theme, within a Picardy-third tonic (a late addition to the score). And the coda to the Finale of the Fourth Symphony (see below) also exploits the enigmatic effect of its three-note motto in emblematic mirror inversion.

Returning to the development, a rhetorically conventional struggle ensues, leading in continuous and climactic course to a mythic impasse: the fateful fanfare figure drives down onto a minor third, here B♭–G, repeated in furious frustration. As in the development of the first movement of Beethoven's *Eroica*, the model for such tragic impasses, the crisis is dramatically displaced by an unexpected solution (Ex. 6.8). Unlike Beethoven, Bruckner need not devise a new

Ex. 6.8   Fifth Symphony, dramatic crux in the development from the first movement

theme; he has plenty to choose from and, in fact, one is eminently suitable: the chorale-like second theme. Also unlike Beethoven, Bruckner does not first collapse onto a dominant to prepare his distant key; instead, in perhaps his most dramatic splicing yet, he simply undercuts the minor third ostinato before its resonance has a chance to die away, allowing the ear to discover four pianissimo horns sustaining the first chorale phrase from the second theme. This phrase is then expressively developed: it moves from D minor to an unexpected D♭ major, retaining its *leitmotivic* character while shedding the deceptive sequence and overlaid sighs. The modulatory twist preserves the mystical quality of the theme, while the simpler harmonization displaces the frustrated climax with a more serene and radiant transformation of the chorale prelude.

The disjunction at this point serves not only as the crux of the development, but also as the turning point in Bruckner's formally ingenious path to the recapitulation by way of the introduction. The chorale phrase undercuts a last, brief outburst, first with a staccato version in the woodwinds and then with a string pizzicato version that falters and breaks on a sigh. This weakening of the chorale-prelude idea provides an opening for the emblematic brass chorale of faith which, as in the introduction, is followed by a dominant-pedal passage leading directly, and more climactically, to the main theme in a *tutti* recapitulation.

The development section's montage and integration of themes provides further evidence that the initial disjunctions of the movement may best be understood in terms of their role in a perspectival conflict scheme. While the conflict scheme may not be original, the perspectival aspect gives the symphony its distinctive character, and points toward the twentieth century. But how do we attribute agency? Do we really understand the development section in terms of a personal struggle? Has the struggle between tragic despair and hopeful faith been projected onto a larger screen than can comfortably be associated with an individual persona? And what of the conflicting roles certain themes play? For example, the second theme, with its peculiar mix of mystical insight and personalized grief, must first serve to undercut the vicious struggle of the development by means of a vision of grace that transcends the tragic. Yet it fails in its pizzicato reincarnation and relinquishes its role to the emblematic brass chorale of objective faith that in turn displaces it. Is this completely satisfactory, or are there simply more themes than there are distinctive roles in this dramatic scenario?

In this regard, it is illuminating that Bruckner's attention during a Wagner opera performance was typically directed toward the orchestra, to the extent that he could lose track of the plot or dramatic scenario.[12] Bruckner may well have learned the techniques of montage and thematic integration from Wagner. The development section from the Prelude to *Die Meistersinger* is instructive. In the extended passage leading to the triumphant return in C major, music associated with Walther's and Eva's frustrated passion is spliced between statements of the Beckmesser version of the *Meistersinger* theme, creating a montage-like inten-sification. Wagner's masterstroke of dramatic integration occurs when the passionate music bursts into a climax undergirded by the magisterial version of the *Meistersinger* theme in the bass. As I interpret it, this successful dramatic integration foreshadows Hans Sachs's agency in channelling Walther's and Eva's love into the proprieties of Nüremberg society, resulting in a marriage rather than a tragic elopement. Sachs thereby orchestrates the equilibrium of a society that needs rules as much as it needs passion and artistic inspiration. Hence the ensuing and oft-cited contrapuntal *tour de force* of the quodlibet return section is perhaps not as dramatically significant as the prior integrative climax, but serves instead as a settled thematic reflection of the opera's eventual resolution of personal and artistic conflicts.

Bruckner's thematic integrations aspire to a similar dramatic significance, though they are at times less successful. Consider the coda's obsessively integrative use of the bass line from the opening chorale with the head motive of the first theme. Coming after a dissolution at the end of the recapitulation, the coda would appear to be reinstating the conflict as unresolved, a familiar strategy when the ultimate resolution is to be deferred to the Finale. The expressive identity of the two motives can be hard to fix since they have apparently evolved to serve more than one expressive function, and there is no clear dramatic programme, as in Wagner, to help guide the listener. Perhaps one would want to conceive of Bruckner's opening bass line as more fateful from the start, given its transformation to an obsessive ostinato in the coda. But there was a better candidate for a fate motive in the introduction, namely the fanfare figure, which is also integrated in a final, tragic, *tutti* statement of the main theme.

Furthermore, whereas thematic integration may serve the purposes of coherence and thematic closure by the device of 'summing up', integration is not always mediation or resolution of conflict, as implied by the *Meistersinger* prelude. The motto-climax of Bruckner's coda illustrates this nicely. The culminating *tutti* statement of the first theme in B♭ minor is answered, or refracted, by a loose mirror inversion of the theme in F♯/G♭ minor. Thus, if the tonal issue between B♭ and G♭ were conceived as emblematic, the tonally integrative mirror inversion makes it enigmatic as well. The subsequent resolution to B♭ major, however, can be understood as a Picardy third rather than as a definitive resolution in B♭ major, which is effectively deferred to the Finale.

The problem of disjunction in Bruckner's music is particularly challenging in the first movement of the Fifth Symphony, and merely analysing instances of thematic integration, or claiming a tonal strategy based on deferrals of B♭ major, while offering some insight, cannot fully satisfy our nagging sense that something remains to be explained. I have demonstrated that Bruckner's choice of thematic material – its motto-like or *leitmotivic* concision – is a fundamental premise for both the first and last movements, and that this thematic design, with its inherent problems for continuous development, is already stylistically foreshadowed by its use in the mannerist early piano work, '*Erinnerung*'. I have also suggested motivations for Bruckner's disjunctions, and at times critiqued his modes of continuity, from the perspectives of various approaches to musical meaning. These approaches include the identification of topics and the interpretation of their implied agency and function in an evolving dramatic scenario, the expressive role of thematized tonal relationships or associative keys, the montage-like development of multiply-perspectival material, and the dramatic role of juxtapositions, interruptions, and reversals. Taken together, they provide strong evidence for the expressive claims I have made.

The issue of disjunction is particularly acute and more of a thematic premise in the first movement of the Fifth Symphony than in the first movement of the Fourth. Nevertheless, it is safe to conclude at this point that Bruckner conceives sonata form as a flexible framework for a thematically-generated dramatic form in which the peculiarities of his themes (their tonal features, their expressive character, and their self-sufficiency, in this case) often motivate unusual formal and developmental choices – compositional strategies that can help justify surface discontinuities in terms of deeper-level dramatic continuities.

Fourth Symphony

Bruckner's expressive genre for the Fourth Symphony offers a dramatic trajectory that begins with the visionary, descends to the more realistic, is threatened by the tragic, and ultimately finds transfiguration in a blaze of affirmation. The personal agency of this dramatic journey is suggested by the allegorical connotation of the pilgrim's processional topic, namely, that of the individual who undergoes a 'pilgrim's progress' in terms of affective and spiritual states. The dramatic trajectory and its allegorical personification in turn guide a coherent and plausible interpretation of the expressive significance of the work. Indeed, that interpretation will help us understand Bruckner's deliberate use of disjunction as part of the drama, rather than as formal mannerism or compositional flaw.

The issue of disjunction is most acute in the Finale of 1880, which is problematic for many critics.[13] Robert Simpson finds its architecture less convincing than that of the previous three movements, Donald F. Tovey confuses its structure with that of the typical Brucknerian slow movement, and Ernst Kurth views it as a hybrid of rondo and sonata forms.[14] Are there telling clues in the changes Bruckner made in the course of rewriting and revising the Finale that would support expressive arguments for the significance of its disjunctions, and in turn suggest a more realistic analysis? A semiotic interpretation of disjunctions in the Finale requires us to examine their role in a larger expressive scheme. The initial stages of that strategy may be found in the first two movements.

First movement

The first major disjunction in the opening movement (which is much more continuous than the opening movement of the Fifth Symphony) occurs at the beginning of the second theme group (S, bar 75). In this oft-quoted passage (Ex. 6.9) Bruckner prepares the dominant key of B♭ by establishing its dominant in

Ex. 6.9   Fourth Symphony, chromatic-third shift to the second theme from the first movement

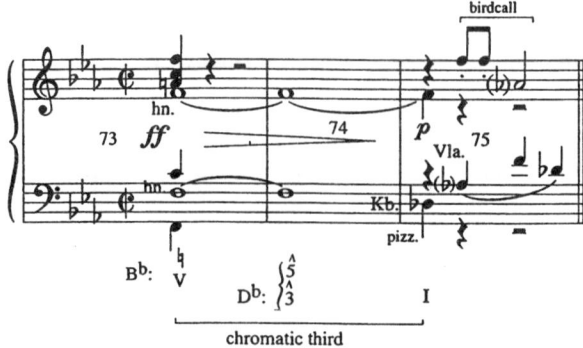

typical sonata fashion only to subvert tonal expectation by dropping a chromatic third from F to D♭ major. Coincident with the tonal shift is a topical one, from the heroic and triumphant blaze of the transition to the lower 'stylistic register' of the pastoral.[15] The disjunctive arrival of the second theme reinforces its oppositional role in the movement, although the undercutting of a triumphant moment by a pastoral one need not imply a negative or tragic connotation for the latter. If the opening theme group (P) offers a progression from metaphysical contemplation (as suggested by the profound horn motto, a familiar Romantic topic), through heroic topical elements to a kind of spiritual exaltation, then the second theme group may be understood as undercutting that triumphant exaltation by shifting to a simpler level of everyday reality (as suggested by a low-style rustic setting with characteristic bird call, and as supported by the tempo marking in the 1889 edition: *gemächlich*, or 'comfortable').

Further interpretation of this juxtaposition might begin with a construal along the lines of 'gentle chiding', in the sense of undercutting the pretensions of an early and, at this stage, unearned exaltation. A higher interpretive synthesis might treat the two contrasting topics as complementary perspectives on life, engendering a trope along the lines of an 'all-embracing' spiritual experience.[16] Evidence that an interpretation of troping is plausible comes from the Finale of the Third Symphony, the celebrated passage which combines a polka and a chorale to suggest, as Bruckner explained, 'the stark dualism of this world'.[17] The emergent meaning of such a trope need not require a formal integration of the two themes – and certainly not of their two topics, in this case – but may be supported by their discrete juxtaposition, or stratification, in the case of the polka/chorale.[18]

Still another expressive aspect of the sudden drop from exaltation to pastoral contentedness is that it marks a shift in the discourse level.[19] According to this interpretation, the movement traces the progression of spiritual or psychic states of a presumed agent or persona. Just as a single character (or narrator) in a novel may shift from one kind of discourse to another (with its attendant jargon, phraseology, fields of meaning, and social register), so may a musical agent or persona experience shifts in discourse that dramatically alter or interrupt the progress of psychological or spiritual states.[20] These shifts may be experienced in various ways: as moments of sudden insight (epiphanies), as disruptions that suggest an external agency thwarting the goals of the persona, or as reversals that may revise or reorient the direction of the persona's journey.

The shift to the second theme group would qualify as a moment of insight, as well as a deflection or deferral from the 'willed' outcome of the modulation to the dominant. My evidence is the use of a chromatic-third harmonic progression (between the F and D♭ triads), which by this time in the nineteenth century had become a Romantic style type with a correlation based on its aural effect in a major-key context: sudden transformation of tonal center to a distantly-related but also major key or chord, achieved consonantly by mediation of a common tone. The oppositions supporting the chromatic-third shift's stylistic correlation include direct tonal shift vs. gradual modulation, displacement vs. chromatically 'earned' direct modulation, and consonant shift vs dissonant wrenching (as in the case of more extreme chromatic modulations). A formal consequence of the chromatic-third shift may be displacement; hence, the progression supports the large-scale disjunction of topic and texture in this example.[21]

But Bruckner also earns his disjunction in a deeper, thematic sense. If we return to the opening of the movement, we find the first chromatic pitch is C♯, or ♭6̂ (bar 7 in the horn motto).[22] It is not long before that chromatic pitch generates a move to ♭VI (tonicized in bars 59–62 as one limb of a transitional sequence following the mutation to E♭ minor). The recapitulation then brings the second theme back in B major (enharmonically, C♭), and a chromatic-third drop from E♭. One could trace numerous other examples of ♭6̂ in its pathos-laden role as an element of modal mixture in this symphony. Its expressive correlation of pathos or poignancy was well-established in the Classical period.[23]

The chromatic-third relationship is also used structurally to close the tonal parenthesis of the second theme's disjunctive D♭ (Table 6.1). There are two striking tonal shifts, reduced as Ex. 6.10a,b. The first restores the bypassed key of B♭ but not yet with the second theme (Ex. 6.10a). It reverses the original shift (Ex. 6.9), since from a cadential or 'arrival' $^6_4$ in D♭ the bass drops by chromatic third to F, to restore B♭ by means of its dominant.[24] The next shift occurs after the music has lost its way, diminishing by bar 151 to an ambiguous unison F (Ex. 6.10b).[25] We are held in suspense by an extended chromatic scale in the strings and woodwinds, ascending to a brass cadence that at first suggests D♭ has triumphed (bars 165–6). But the shift this time is to the German augmented-sixth of B♭ (bars 167–8),[26] understood as such only when it resolves to an arrival/cadential $^6_4$ in B♭ (bars 169ff) with an extended pedal-point on the dominant. This more abrasive change of gears from D♭ to B♭ sums up the

Table 6.1   Diagram of the second theme group from the first movement of the Fourth Symphony.

bar:	75	87	107	119		169	
	S	*tutti*	S	<P2		S	+
K							
V/B♭	D♭	G♭, chrom. seq. to A [Interruption]	D♭	V^{m9}/B♭	B♭, seq. modul. D♭-B♭: Gr⁺⁶	**B♭**	
	stg.	*tutti*	stg+ww/tmb — tutti +cl/hn	[——————— Interruption]		<brass choir> stg	
	p	*f*	*pp*	*mf*————*ff*		*ppp*	

Ex. 9	Ex. 10a	Ex. 10b
(bars 73–75)	(bars 105-115)	(bars 165-169)

S = second theme proper, <P2 = derived from bars 57ff of the principal theme group, K = cadential or closural material.

Ex. 6.10   Fourth Symphony, second theme group from the first movement:
(a) return to B♭ after first interruption
(b) return to B♭ after second interruption

(a)

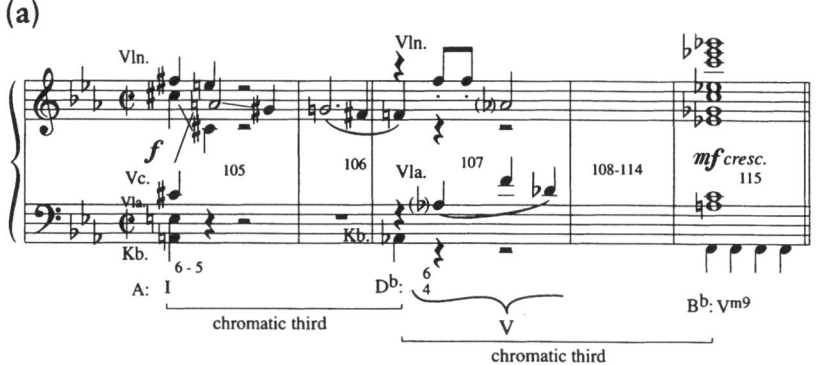

(b)

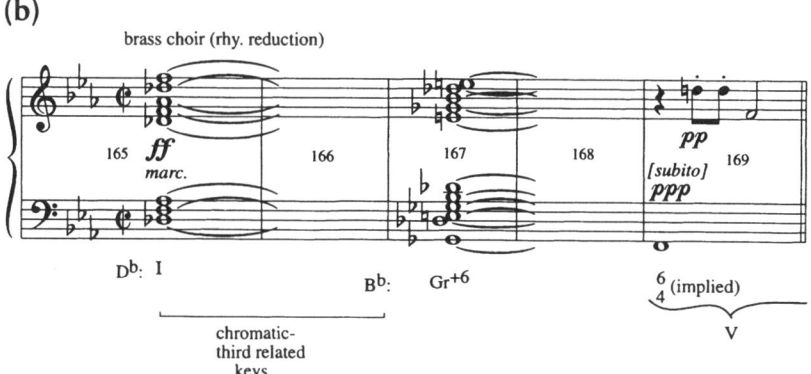

transformational aspect of previously abrupt tonal shifts in the movement, while the second theme finally appears in the 'proper' key of B♭ to close the exposition.

The development section sustains this interruptive strategy. A representative example, beginning in bar 287, involves a *subito piano* undercutting of the triumphant music drawn from the end of the first theme group. Here, the shift is to a translucent texture (high string tremolos) and a transformational development of the opening motto in the horns and woodwinds. The transcendent connotations of this texture are reminiscent of the opening of Wagner's Prelude to *Lohengrin*.[27] This allusion, which brings with it contextual associations of purity and innocence, may be cited as an example of intertextuality.[28]

A further intertextual link with Wagner appears in the coda to the Finale and constitutes a significant change that first appears in the 1880 version. From bar 507 a trumpet signal leads to a chord progression (bars 517ff) faintly reminiscent of the Valhalla motive from the *Ring* cycle (Ex. 6.11). The trumpet signal and sequential 'elevation' of the (different) chord progression are associated motivically and orchestrationally with the closing passage of *Götterdämmerung*

Ex. 6.11   Fourth Symphony, transfigurational sequence in the coda to the Finale

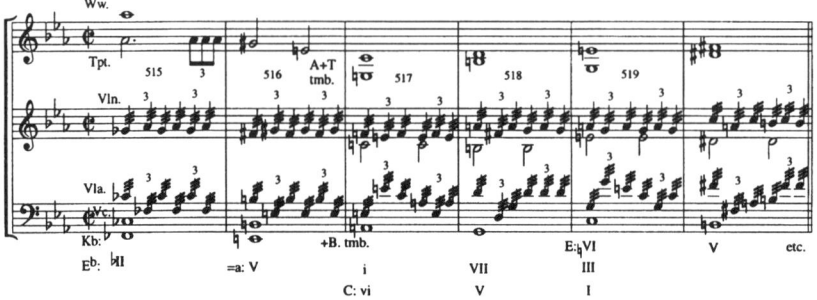

(act 3, scene 3, bars 562ff; the triplet-sixteenth signal appears in the trombones, and the Valhalla motive is sequenced up by step instead of third). The significance that Bruckner draws from the allusion is again related to transcendence; but given the context of simultaneous destruction and redemptive rebirth at the end of the *Ring* cycle, the allusion may carry the weight of tragic experience into a more profound transformation akin to transfiguration.[29]

Second movement

The second movement offers an allusion to a topic that emerges only in the Romantic era. The 'pilgrims' processional' is a type of music featured in second movements by Berlioz (*Harold in Italy*),[30] Mendelssohn ('Italian' Symphony), and less obviously, Brahms (Third Symphony). Operatically, the most famous example is Wagner's *Tannhäuser* (act 1, scene 3, bars 93–114). The characteristic ingredients are (1) a quiet Andante, (2) a correspondingly slower, march-like ostinato or walking-bass background (often alternating tonic and dominant pitches in quarter-notes or pizzicato eighths), and (3) a lyrical, often chorale-like foregrounded line. The return of the theme in measure 13 illustrates most of these features (Ex. 6.12). Spiritual connotations would arise merely from the allusion to chorale-prelude texture; but the interpretation of the topic in Bruckner moves toward the allegorical, suggesting a pilgrim's progress or spiritual journey undertaken by the compositional persona.[31] With its key (C minor) and ostinato, foreshadowed by the opening of the coda to the first movement (bar 501–end), the Andante begins solemnly with a sense of purposeful direction. When its yearning sighs are undercut by wrong notes (the Gᵇ's in bar 9 and bar 19), the second disruption provokes a swift series of modulations leading to Eᵇ minor in bar 24. The chorale (modal hymn) then begins with another shift, to VI (Cᵇ major) in bar 25. The expressive associations

Ex. 6.12   Fourth Symphony, main theme from the second movement, exemplifying the pilgrims' processional topic

of E♭ minor and C♮ major are clearly invoked from the first movement.

Alternation among themes is coupled with an increasingly transformational, not merely variational, treament of the opening theme; this leads to a stretto return with diminutional scales saturating the texture in bars 193ff. The return expands to a transfigurational moment at bar 201, but after barely more than three bars that goal is undercut by a sudden textural reduction and diminuendo. The device is Wagnerian, and the undercutting merely fuels a higher climax, achieved in bar 221 as an apotheosis with even denser textural diminutions. This climax lasts a little longer, some eight measures, before being undercut (bar 228) and fading into an enigmatic coda (bars 237–end). In the coda, unsettled chromatic questionings in the horn, viola, and clarinet are only slightly palliated by a Picardy-third cadence. Clearly, something of the transfigurational remains to be achieved.

Perhaps it was this concern that led Bruckner to incorporate the pilgrims' processional topic into the Finale of 1880, where it initiates the second theme group. Having left the allegorical spiritual journey unfulfilled in the Andante, Bruckner could then bring it to completion in the coda to the Finale with a powerful Wagnerian transfiguration (motivating the *Götterdämmerung* allusion discussed above).[32]

Third movement

The third movement is a topically 'characteristic' hunting scherzo with a *Ländler* trio. Bruckner ventured an interpretation of the Scherzo as a 'Hunting of the Hare' and the Trio as a 'Dance-melody during the Huntsmen's Repast'.[33] The self-enclosed, characteristic world of the movement, strikingly in the dominant key of B♭ (stylistically associated with hunting music), may excuse it from too significant a role in the expressive journey of the work as a whole; one might view it as a kind of relief from the more serious concerns of the other three movements. But the heroic vs. pastoral opposition and its resulting trope are also found in this movement. The Scherzo's fanfare-like opening is contrasted at bar 35 by a theme in the strings that opens with a chromatic-third chord progression, lightly dismissed by a jocular horn-fifth reply.[34] The Trio in G♭ also contrasts by chromatic third with the Scherzo's B♭. The pastoral pedal and musette-like texture of the Trio exhibit the more rustic side of the pastoral topical field, as did the second theme in the first movement.[35]

Overview of the Finale

A formal outline of the Finale (Table 6.2) reveals its unusual structure, including an interesting parallel with the first movement's exposition: the use of a *tutti* interruption in place of a third theme group. In the first movement, the interruptions occurred twice, in bars 87 and 119 (prepared by the tonal shift in bar 115), and they were parenthetically framed by the pastoral second theme in contrasting, typically chromatically third-related keys D♭ (twice) and B♭ (Table 6.1). In the Finale, a single interruption (bars 155–82) is delayed until near the end of the *Gesangsperiode* (S), a group that has its own internal shifts in key and theme/topic (to be discussed below). As in the first movement, a portentous or fateful idea from the first group is employed for the interruption; in the Finale, it is the fanfare that had responded to the initial *Hauptthema*. In turn, a significant theme from the second group (S2) penetrates the first group in the development (First Phase) and is notably absent from the second group (Second Phase).

The interruptive passage (P2) is subject to development as well; its corresponding section in the development (Disruption, bars 295–338) is treated more integratively, including both the first theme group's motives. This time it interrupts a truncated version of the second group and reaches a significant, if soon undercut, expressive climax. In the recapitulation's *Gesangsperiode* (S) the interruption idea is 'resolved' by integration of the fanfare motive (bars 457–64), in its own undercut transformation as pastoral 'yodel'.

Finally, the coda introduces two new ideas to accomplish a transfigurational close. The first may be understood as a poetic transformation-as-reminiscence of the pilgrim's processional motive, emerging from the solo horn (bars 489–504). The second, introduced by a solemn trumpet signal (bar 517), is an 'elevation sequence' (transfiguring the triumphant chorale tune that emerged from the climactic interruption in the development section, bars 322ff) and Phrygian descent. Together, these ideas mystically restore an E♭ major not heard since its brief, triumphant breakthrough at the end of the first theme group of the exposition. As glowing transformation of the omnipresent minor mode in this initially tragic movement, the close to an E♭ major triad accomplishes transcendence without denying the tragic reality (b6̂) that motivates the expressive pilgrimage.

Closer interpretation of the Finale

Bruckner begins the Finale on the dominant minor with an allusion to the ♭6̂ in the motto of the first movement, now transformed in its expressive purport from

Table 6.2   Outline of the Finale (1880 version) of the Fourth Symphony.

Exposition

    P: Two spans leading to climaxes:

            1. Introductory motto fragment, leading to definitive motto theme (*Hauptthema*)

                B♭ minor to E♭ minor with Phrygian inflection (bars 1–42, 43–50)

tonal shift   2. fanfare motives, leading to breakthrough climax and peroration in E♭ major

                G♭ pickup to ♭$\hat{6}$ (E♭♭ spelled as D, D minor implied) sequential ascent to E♭ major   (bars 51–92)

tonal shift

    S: Continuous juxtaposition, developing variation, and integration of themes:

            1. Pilgrim's processional (*Langsamer*)   (bars 93–104)

                C minor

mode/topic   2. 'Quintessential theme' (*a Tempo*)   (bars 105–108)
   shift   C major

            3. Rustic dance (pastoral simplicity)   (bars 109ff.)

                G major, minor, modulatory

            4. Integration of 2 & 3   (bars 125ff.)

                A♭ major, modulatory

            5. Quintessential theme   (bars 139–42)

                F major

            6. Rustic fragments   (bars 143–54)

                G♭ major

Interruption P2 (parenthetical; takes place of third theme group): P2 fanfare motives + fateful descending line (cf. Wotan's spear/contract motif)

                B♭ minor to D♭ major   (bars 155–82)

undercut by: 7. S(K): return, via yodel-transformation of arpeggiated fanfare motive, to rustic motive and key

                G♭ major to B♭ major   (bars 183–202)

Development

tonal shift   First Phase

            [P1] Inversion of introductory motto fragment, restores 'crisis' (bars 203ff)

                B♭ minor, ameliorating modulation toward:

            [S2] Transformation of quintessential theme (brass chorale, then string orchestra)

                G♭ major (spelled F♯), then (sequentially varied) to G♯ minor

                                      (bars 237ff)

            [S3] Liquidation via integration of fragments with rustic motive

                modulatory to V^6/F minor   (bars 248–68)

            Second Phase

            [S1] Pilgrim's processional (*Langsamer*)   (bars 269–94)

                F minor, D minor circle-of-fifths 'frustration,' static liquidation over descending bass

Disruption: (not parenthetical this time)   (bars 295–338)

            [P1 and P2] integration of fanfare crisis with *Hauptthema*, leading to chorale-like potentially positive climax, internally *undercut* by diminuendo and ritard; C minor, modulatory

            Third Phase   (bars 339–382)

Table 6.2 concluded

tonal and *modal shifts*	[P1]	Retransition, using inversion of Hauptthema in eerie harmonization (augmented triad), and 'last gasp' swell of emotion (arpeggiated sequence of *Hauptthema* fragment through diminished seventh) D major, minor, modulatory to vii°7 of E♭ minor

Recapitulation

P:	1.	*Hauptthema* without introductory lead-in; intervallic reversal in fifth bar leads to sequential modulation up to implied G♭ (bars 383–392) E♭ minor to G♭ (cf. G♭ at end of exposition)
tonal shift	2.	Fanfare to quasi-breakthrough climax (this time on a dominant, not tonic) G♭ to ♭2̂ (E♭♭ spelled as D natural) and stepwise sequential ascent to climax on V/F♯ minor [G♭ minor] (bars 392–411)
S: (continuous)	1.	Pilgrim's processional (*a Tempo, temporal integration*, with fragment of quintessential theme in the flute) (bars 413–30) F♯ minor [G♭ minor]
tonal shift	2.	Quintessential theme (bars 431–4) D [E♭♭] major
	3.	Rustic theme (bars 435ff) A [B♭♭] major, minor
[<tpt 336–7]	4.	New *countermelody* transforming quintessential theme (bars 449ff) E [F♭] major, modulatory leading to *integration* of yodel-transformation of P2 fanfare motive and climax; modulatory, ending in D♭ to B♭ chromatic third triadic shift (bars 457–64)
undercut by:	5.	Liquidation (subito pp) (bars 465–76) establishing V/E♭ minor

Coda

[P1]	1.	Motto fragment in mirror inversion (bars 477–88) E♭ minor, i–VI
[<S1]	2.	Emerging solo horn lament theme, broken off (~parenthetical) (bars 489–504)
	3.	Trumpet signal (mm. 507ff) with motto fragment return (bars 505–16) E♭ minor, i–VI
[<tpt 328-9]	4.	Transfigurational elevation-sequence (i VII III) (bars 517–end) *tonal shift* to A minor, modulatory sequence up by thirds, then bass descent through Phrygian E♭ (C♭–B♭–A♭–G♭–F♭–E♭) to brilliant E♭ major, with ♭6̂ neighbor; allusion to opening of first movement

Romantic longing to foreboding. The enigmatic three-note motive, which will develop into the head motive of the main theme in bar 43, begins here on ♭6̂ and resolves after a descending octave leap. The pulsing tonic-pedal ostinato adds to the sense of foreboding in this introductory passage.

Cyclic motivic integration, a subtle hint of Beethoven's strategy in the Finale of the Ninth, appears in the (associative) horns, with the rhythmic motive of the Scherzo as background pulsation in bars 29–42, and a motto fragment of the first movement's opening theme in bars 79–83. But Bruckner's expressive genre differs from Beethoven's; the pilgrims' processional topic and key (C minor) from the Andante is not rejected, since it will play a role in the working out of the tragic premise for the movement. It is re-engaged (appropriately, with the tempo indication *Langsamer*) to launch the second theme group at bar 93.[36]

Before the topical recall of the second movement, however, the introductory motto culminates in a definitive statement, expanded to what Bruckner labels as the *Hauptthema* for the movement, and played in unison and octaves by the full orchestra in E♭ minor (Ex. 6.13). It features the move to ♭6̂ (C♭) directly from 1̂, as well as a ♭2̂ (Phrygian) inflection prefigured in the plaintive horn solo at the

Ex. 6.13   Fourth Symphony, *Hauptthema* from the Finale

end of the second movement. The unison motto is answered by a fanfare whose upbeat accomplishes a shift to G♭, but whose downbeat, an open fifth on ♭6̂ (E♭♭ spelled enharmonically as D), shifts further to D minor and ultimately an oblique chromatic ascent (bars 55ff)[37] to another unison, on G♭. After a ♭6̂ to 5̂ establishment of the dominant of E♭ minor in the bass, the G♭ in the upper voice is pulled up to G natural as part of a neighbour figure around the fifth of the dominant-seventh chord (Ex. 6.14, m. 76). The breakthrough of G♭ to G♮ is heard as victorious, as though E♭ major were achieved through an enormous effort of the will, but the triumphant mood cannot be sustained.[38] As in the opening theme group of the first movement, exaltation is quickly undercut dynamically and texturally, leading to a sudden drop of a third for the second theme group. But whereas that exposition provided a transition to the dominant and then twice deferred its arrival, the Finale's exposition is itself a transition to the definitive theme and ultimately the definitive tonic key of E♭ major, thus making a further transition dramatically redundant. Fortunately, the shift to C minor for the second group requires no transition, having been thematically prepared by the comparable shift in the first movement, and associatively prepared by the use of C minor for the same topic in the second movement. Expressively, then, the sudden shift to C minor and the pilgrimage motif may be interpreted as re-engaging the spiritual journey left unfinished at the end of the Andante.

The initial imitative treatment of the second theme is reminiscent of Bruckner's similar ploy in bars 101 and 109 of the slow movement, where imitation in inversion and then in a tight stretto offered a developmental contribution (the 'learned' topic) to a thematic transformation.[39] After a mere twelve bars, however, the pilgrimage suddenly brightens (bars 105ff) with a

Ex. 6.14   Fourth Symphony, breakthrough of ♭3 to ♮3 near the end of the first theme group in the exposition of the Finale

theme that had *initiated* the second group in both 1874 and 1878 versions of the Finale (in each case, however, after a two-bar march-ostinato in pizzicato eighths). Only four bars long, the closed tonal and melodic structure of the theme projects a highly memorable line that has a clear expressive function (Ex. 6.15). I refer to such themes or motives as 'quintessential', since they encapsulate the essence of an expressive state.[40] This theme, however, has proven unbearably naive or saccharine to some English critics.[41] Its inherent quality, while an important aesthetic criterion, should not blind us to its role in the drama. The theme marks a critical turn in the pilgrimage by offering an almost beatific consolation (although still preserving the poignant ♭6̂) and by directing the discourse toward rustic simplicity in the pastoral dance which follows. In this section each topic proposes an expressive alternative, but the initially abrupt juxtapositions are ameliorated by a continuous texture and ongoing developing variation.

In Bruckner's larger formal design, the quintessential theme functions as a highly memorable expressive marker of a shift to a more positive state. The theme migrates to the first theme group in the development, where it is transformed into a brass chorale emblematic of the assurances of faith. In its first appearance, however, the quintessential theme is already somewhat transformational, as it recycles the descending sixth associated with the rustic second theme in the first movement (Ex. 6.9), and integrative, as it varies a turn

Ex. 6.15   Fourth Symphony, 'quintessential' theme from second theme group in the exposition of the Finale

figure from the processional theme launching this group. The rustic dance that follows also features a (partially filled-in) version of the pastoral sixth, and an integrative merging of both quintessential and rustic themes (bars 125–8) is featured before the quintessential theme returns in F major with a reaffirmation of its welling sentiment (bars 139–41).[42] Here, the second half of the quintessential theme injects greater concern, sequencing melodically so as to transform the F pedal into a dominant. When the rustic dance continues (bars 143ff), the shift to G♭ as a deceptive ♭VI combined with the reduction in dynamics and texture leads us to question the assurances of this theme. Indeed, ♭6̂ resolves to 5̂ of B♭ minor for an even softer, premonitory V^{m9} on which the one-bar motive is suspended in anticipatory repetitions (bars 147–50).

B♭ minor literally explodes in bar 155, with devastating effect for the attempted vision of grace. This interruption, which might fit a schematic analysis as the third theme group (functionally providing the dominant, though in the minor mode), is treated here as a parenthetical disruption rather than as a closing group. Hence, the absence of this section and the integration of the fanfare motive into the second theme group in the recapitulation is clearly motivated (cf. note 32). The stormy fanfare ends with a fateful scalar descent in brass and strings (bars 179–82).[43] The descent is interrupted (bars 183ff, Ex. 6.16) by a *subito pianissimo* return to the G♭ major of bars 143–6 (still interpreted as VI of Bb minor). Here, the disjunction is especially telling, since the fearsome character of the fanfare is undercut by a yodel-like transformation of its arpeggio motive. The sudden reversion to pastoral is so extreme as to suggest a touch of irony, as in Mahler.

The return to the pastoral world, although integrating the descending sixth of the quintessential theme, cannot be sustained. A chromatic-third sequence from G♭ through D to B♭ (bar 196) – the ultimate goal of the first movement's exposition, as well – sets up a return to the introduction's tragic foreboding in B♭ minor (bar 203). With an inversion of his introductory motto fragment, Bruckner initiates a weighty development section. At bar 229 the chromatically ascending ostinato repetitions in the bass are shifted to a higher register, *subito piano*. The winds continue a chain-suspension idea (begun in bar 225) that

Ex. 6.16   Fourth Symphony, undercutting of the interruption section and return to G♭ major for the close of the second theme group in the Finale

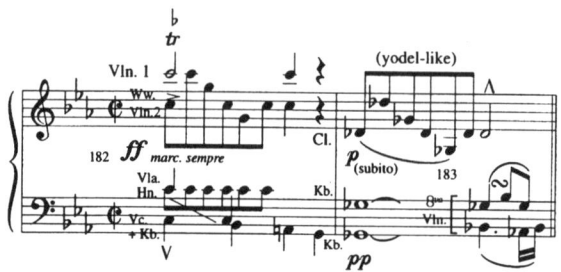

remarkably deflects the tragic introductory music into the spiritual realm of the pious processional. When the quintessential theme follows suit (bars 237ff), it is augmented and transformed into a near-liturgical brass chorale in F♯ major, the enharmonic equivalent of the previous positive realm of G♭ major.

An antiphonal response from the string choir intensifies by sequencing to G♯ minor (bar 245) as the quintessential theme once more appears to question its own assurances, moving from consolation to grim insistence and even pleading. Fragments of the quintessential theme merge with fragments from the rustic dance (beginning in bar 253) into a motivic mosaic that allows for textural enhancement through inversion (bar 257) and mirror inversion (bar 261). Familiar chromatic-third sequences lead to E♭ major, which mutates to minor with the familiar ♭6̂ to 5̂ sigh figures (C♭ to B♭ in the first violins, bars 261–4). At the end of the liquidation and dissolution of this section, the C♭ softly transforms to C♮ (bar 265), and with the bass simultaneously ascending from E♭ to E♮, Bruckner prepares a return of the pilgrims' processional music in F minor (Second Phase, bar 269).

Stretto imitation at the fifth serves as textural intensification, but the developmental climax this time is a circle-of-fifths root progression in D minor with sequential suspensions (bars 283–5). The use of an unmarked progression[44] – the stylistically common circle-of-fifths sequence – is appropriate as a less-than-transcendent expressive plaint that may express 'circular frustration' with a pilgrimage unable to achieve its goal of transcendence. Further evidence of frustration is found in the repetitive stasis of ii–V (bars 285–6), and the chromatic drift downward as the music subsides to a near-clockwork state of suspended animation (bars 291–4).

This stasis sets up a rude disruption (bar 295) by a fanfare texture analogous to the one in the exposition, integratively enhanced this time by the *Hauptthema* in mirror inversion and C minor. The bald sequencing to A♭, D♭, D, E♭, E, and back to C appears intentionally brutal, but a climactic brass chorale beginning in bar 322 manages to transform, if not fully transfigure, the negative energies of the tragic *Hauptthema*. The potential cadence in E♭ major (bars 335–6) is dissonantly undercut in a powerful expressive crux at bar 336, as chromatic wrenchings to an E major $^6_3$ destroy the trumpets' climactic G ($\hat{3}$ of E♭) in a tragically-motivated negation, and the triumphant near-deliverance collapses in disorientation. The music quickly subsides in bar 339 to a D major–D minor mutation in the horns, emblematic of this tragic reversal.[45]

In the ensuing retransition (Third Phase, bars 339–82) the shift to an enigmatic first-inversion C major triad (bars 343–50) is only weakly interpretable as V^6/III in D minor, and when a 6–5 motion transforms the chord to root position E minor, we are left unprepared for what follows: a chilling transformation of the motto, inverted in the winds and accompanied by the horns with a new and dissonant harmonization (Ex. 6.17; compare Ex. 6.13).

Ex. 6.17   Fourth Symphony, retransition to the recapitulation of the Finale – inverted motto fragment with eerie harmonization

The III$^+$ underlines by its instability the 'questioning' suggested by the motivic inversion; indeed, the effect is one of near irrational disorientation, as the very possibility of deliverance from the tragic appears to be in question. After a deceptive move to B♭ (VI in D minor), that pitch is reinterpreted as a pedal-dominant tremolo in the timpani, signalling impending recapitulation. The material used in this premonitory section, taken from the second large expressive gesture of the exposition (the breakthrough of G♭ to G♮), cannot muster the strength to emerge triumphantly. Instead, its pleading sequences subside to one last, forlorn, diminished-seventh drop to the leading tone as an anacrusis to the return.

By beginning the recapitulation with the tragic *Hauptthema* (and E♭ minor) stage of the exposition (bars 383ff), Bruckner saves his introductory music to launch the coda. As a result, the second theme is approached more quickly by means of a direct chromatic ascent to a V^{m9} of F♯/G♭ minor (bars 409–11). This climactic moment reflects the breakthrough of the analogous location in the exposition, although remaining on a dominant and frustrating its goal. This time, the resolution to F♯ minor bridges the earlier disjunction between first and second groups, and the pilgrims' processional returns to the unfinished 'progress' of an implied spiritual journey. The unusual key most likely alludes to the G♭ or F♯ major areas that were never satisfactorily sustained as pastoral (G♭) or hymnic (brass chorale in F♯) visions earlier in the exposition and the development, respectively. If so, the tonality is now brought into the realm of the purposeful pilgrims' progress with its realistic, melancholy environment.

As before, a modulatory drift sets in, dissolving in a despairing stepwise descent in bars 427–30 that prefigures the stepwise Phrygian descent from C♭ down to E♭ at the end of the movement. The oblique dissonance against the sustained E♭ in horns and upper strings is typical of Schubert.[46] The liquidation is clearly tragic in its purport, recalling the analogous winding down and static frustration of this theme in the development section. There, an interruption restored the tragic crisis; here, the shift is to the quintessential theme, missing from the second group in the development section and all the more miraculous in its enhanced role as a sudden, joyous epiphany (bars 431–4).

The choice of key, D major, continues the local half-step descent and the logical progression of keys from F♯ minor (moving to A major for the rustic dance, and E major for a version of the quintessential theme with a new countermelody). Although this attention to the sharp side might appear highly un-Classical for a recapitulation, the F♯ minor is to be understood as G♭ minor, placing the keys of the second group on the flat side and culminating in the Neapolitan E (= F♭, the Phrygian ♭$\hat{2}$ of E♭). This key (E or F♭ major) highlights another remarkable transformation, in that the new countermelody in the upper strings (bars 449ff) appears derived from the crux of the development – the undercut phrase in the trumpets from bars 335–7. If so, then there is further support for the exhilarating sense of fulfilment in this affirmative theme. Indeed, there may also be a sense of transformative resolution in the treatment of a descending line, especially in contrast to the fateful character of the brass descent in the first interruption section from the exposition.

Further modulatory development leads to an apotheosis of the quintessential theme (bars 461–4) in a texture that integrates the arpeggiated motive of the interruptive fanfare (compare bars 51ff). Perhaps the D♭ to D♮ breakthrough (suggested by the chromatic third sequence from D♭ to B♭ major) serves as a kind of expressive resolution of the B♭ minor from the exposition's third theme group. At any rate, transcendence still cannot be sustained; a *subito pianissimo* undercuts the apotheosis, and a lament-bass, descending in familiar oblique fashion under a sustained Eb, prepares the coda.

The coda resolves the introductory B♭ minor to E♭ minor and features a $\hat{1}$ to ♭$\hat{6}$ bass ostinato reminiscent of the *Hauptthema*'s motivic interval. The alternation every two bars in the bass may suggest the accompaniment of the pilgrims' processional topic, warped from its stable $\hat{1}$–$\hat{5}$. The three-note motto is presented in mirror inversion in a synthesis of the introductory texture and the *Hauptthema*'s interval structure. Transformation into a hymn topic (beginning in bar 489) with plagal harmonization might have sufficed for a typical closural coda. Bruckner even features a poignant, resignational horn solo echoing the pilgrim's processional melodic motive and emerging from the midst of the hymn-like texture (bars 491–504). But the solo is left hanging on a ii$^{\varnothing\frac{6}{5}}$, and a more extraordinary passage is ushered in to conclude the spiritual and tonal journey.

Triplets in the trumpets (bars 507ff) almost immediately herald the transfiguring allusion to the close of Wagner's *Götterdämmerung* that leads the expressive pilgrimage of Bruckner's symphony to a comparably high plane. The stepwise melodic ascent ($\hat{1}$–$\hat{2}$–$\hat{3}$ in each key, recalling the last three notes of Wagner's magisterial Valhalla motive) has been heard before – as part of the chorale tune introduced in the climactic interruption of the development (see the trumpets, bars 328–9). The frustrated chorale is here transfigured by means of a sequence that progressively elevates its core melodic ascent to a transcendent level.

Upon reaching C♭ and ♭VI of Eb in bar 525, Bruckner opens up a wedge, with upper voices continuing to ascend while a Phrygian descent from C♭ in the bass features F♭ to E♭ as an ultimate, grinding resolution against C♭–D♭–E♭ in the upper voices. The Picardy-third E♭ major triad with which the symphony ends is enhanced expressively by ♭$\hat{6}$ to $\hat{5}$ oscillations in the high register of the first violins and by the open-fifth portion of the first movement's motto in the horns (a subtle integrative touch, when compared with Bruckner's excessive quotation of the initial theme in earlier versions of the Finale).[47]

Conclusion

While there is clearly an integrative strategy at work in the Finale, themes (including those from earlier movements) are not simply restated. Rather, Bruckner incorporates their topical premises, or progressively transforms their expressive sense, in order to fulfil the premises of his allegorical journey. As a consequence, I would claim that our sense of a deeper cyclical integration in this symphony results from the dramatic evolution of a spiritual pilgrimage, not merely from a series of motivic or tonal associations. Bruckner often eschews the continuity of developmental struggle found in Beethoven's heroic style, relying instead on the montage of tonal or topical shifts, breakthroughs, interruptions, and disruptions to develop the drama. As a consequence the allegorical 'pilgrim's progress' is a more appropriate topical conceit for the oppositional stages of this drama. I do not mean to imply that we can simply affix labels to what Schenker criticized as Bruckner's 'isolated cells'. In fact, a highly sophisticated set of compositional strategies often justifies the disjunctions from both tonal and topical perspectives, as I have demonstrated. While clearly interpretable as dramatic stages in an ongoing pilgrim's progress toward transfiguration, the disjunctive theme groups and interruptive sections also undergo various forms of synthesis or integration, ranging from the trading of material between first and second groups, to the reconciliation of expressive extremes by means of thematic transformations. A network of associative tonalities (G♭ major/minor in the finale, or C minor in the slow movement and the *Gesangsperiode* of the Finale) and thematized harmonic progressions (e.g., the chromatic-third relationship), coordinate with topics to provide another level of coherence and to promote continuity across dramatic divides.

An overall expressive genre emerges from the especially well conceived first, second and fourth movement schemes. The opening theme of the first movement suggests a transcendent vision, and the sudden drop in stylistic register for the second theme is a way of marking the opening as both metaphysical beginning and potential goal. After the many struggles and digressions of the allegorized spiritual pilgrimage, and despite the brief triumphal breakthroughs in the Finale, the ultimate outcome is achieved not by wilful struggle but by spiritual transfiguration. The quintessential theme hints at such an insight, and its transformation to a brass chorale in the development section (suggesting an affirmation of faith) is in keeping with its epiphanic arrival in the recapitulation. The tragic-to-transcendent trajectory is familiar from Beethoven's late style; what is fascinating is the contextual emergence of the tragic in this symphony, since the first movement begins with just a hint of plaintiveness in its pastoral horn solo. Only in the development does the power of tragic minor really make itself felt. The mournful second movement provides unmistakable evidence for the allegorical treatment of a pilgrimage from suffering, past initial triumphs and despairs, to intuitions of spiritual joy – left painfully incomplete in the coda. But the ensuing Scherzo is hardly part of this progression, instead featuring characteristic hunting music. The Finale, then, bears the weight of making the expressive genre convincing. As with Beethoven, expressive outcomes are often mixed, and Bruckner's insistence on $\flat\hat{6}$ to $\hat{5}$ in the closing E$\flat$ triad of the Finale sustains an awareness of tragic reality that, as in Beethoven's late works, cannot be defeated by wilful struggle, but may be transcended by spiritual trans-figuration.

Understanding the coherence of Bruckner's formal strategies presupposes a knowledge of topics and their implied agencies, along with a range of subtle thematic derivations and integrations, that support a continuity of expressive and dramatic meaning. From this standpoint the most extreme disjunctions may be interpreted not as signs of compositional shortwindedness, but as breathtaking dramatic gambits which motivate (and are coordinated by) dramas of epic scale. Although the first and last movements of Bruckner's Fourth Symphony may differ in surprising ways from Classical sonata-form expectations, nevertheless it is spiritual *drama*, not liturgical *ritual*, that unfolds over such broad spans. Bruckner is not tedious when we adjust to his scale; nor are his extended periods conceived merely to suggest Gothic spaciousness, or to promote a kind of monumentalized contemplation. Rather, the impressive dimensions are dramatically motivated by topical and tonal disjunctions that defer closure, and formally motivated by the compensatory balance of weight and proportion accorded to such expanded sections.

Deryck Cooke maintains that one should approach Bruckner's symphonies not as 'dynamic phases of a drama but as so many different viewpoints from which to absorb the basic material', and that Bruckner's 'stance is not Romantic, but medieval' in its religious mentality.[48] Cooke also claims that 'the music has no need to go anywhere, no need to find a point of arrival, because it is already there'.[49] My interpretation of the Fourth Symphony suggests otherwise. I have argued that Bruckner's disjunctions serve a larger dramatic scheme which moves from the visionary opening, past early triumphs and pastoral insights, to a more sober spiritual pilgrimage. That pilgrimage overcomes tragic disruptions and premature frustration or static resignation to emerge transfigured at the end. As in Beethoven's 'characteristic' Sixth Symphony (*Pastoral*), Nature serves as backdrop for a journey of the spirit; but in Bruckner the pastoral is not the only background. The journey is also allegorized by a distinctively Romantic topic, the pilgrims' processional.

Despite his original treatment of topics and relationships, Bruckner draws from a common stylistic heritage, as well as an intertextual pool, that includes late Beethoven, Schubert, Berlioz, Liszt, and Wagner. Thus, there is ample evidence for the kinds of expressive interpretations I have offered, even if some of my claims may appear speculative. What I hope to have established, however, is the subtlety, flexibility, and sophistication with which Bruckner negotiates a balance between disjunction and continuity. His dramatic disruptions are absorbed or transcended – if not always Classically resolved – by subsequent integrations, transformations, and transfigurations. Shocking or enigmatic disjunctions are motivated by a dramatic scenario that demands a unique tonal-thematic form. Whereas the compositional struggle to encompass such extremes may have led Bruckner to epic length, the resulting drama endows his symphonies with mythic power.

Notes

1. Heinrich Schenker, 'Anton Bruckner', in *Die Zukunft*, 5 (Berlin, 1893), p. 137. Cited by Martin Eybl, 'Grandiose Isolierzellen und rasselnde Fugenmechanik – Zu Schenkers Kritik an seinem Lehrer Bruckner', in *Bruckner Symposion-Bericht 1988: Anton Bruckner als Schuler und Lehrer* (Wien: Musikwissenschaftlicher Verlag, 1992), pp 137–8.
2. Wilhelm Kienzl, *Im Konzert. Von Tonwerken und nachschaffenden Tonkünstlern empfangene Eindrücke* (Berlin, 1908), p. 34, cited by Eybl, 'Grandiose Isolierzellen', p. 138.
3. Robert S Hatten, *Musical Meaning in Beethoven: Markedness, Correlation, and Interpretation* (Bloomington and Indianapolis: Indiana University Press (*Advances in Semiotics*), 1994). For a more complete theoretical account of the approaches described here, see Chapters 1–4 and 7. The expressive genres I outline for Bruckner fall roughly into the 'redemption paradigm' described by Warren Darcy, 'Bruckner's Sonata Deformations', in *Bruckner Studies*, Timothy L Jackson and Paul Hawkshaw eds. (Cambridge: Cambridge University Press, 1997), p. 259.
4. Hatten, *Musical Meaning*, pp 281–6.
5. For an introduction to topics in Classical music, see Leonard Ratner, *Classic Music* (New York: Schirmer, 1980), pp 3–30. For a useful approach to topics and their interpretation in Bruckner, see Constantin Floros, *Brahms und Bruckner: Studien zur musikalischen Exegetik* (Wiesbaden: Breitkopf und Härtel, 1980) and idem., 'Weltliches und Religioses in Bruckners Symphonik', in *Bruckner Symposion-Bericht 1989: Orchestermusik im 19. Jahrhundert.* (Musikwissenschaftlicher Verlag, 1992), pp 179–88.

6. Friedrich Schlegel, 'Zur Philosophie' (1797), Fragment 668, in *Philosophische Lehrjahre I (1796–1806)*, Ernst Behler ed., in *K. A.* (Paderborn/Vienna/Munich: Verlag Ferdinand Schöningh, 1963), 18:85, cited by Paul De Man, 'The Concept of Irony' (1977), in *Aesthetic Ideology*, Andrzej Warminski ed. (Minneapolis/London: University of Minnesota Press, 1996), p. 179.

7. De Man, 'Concept of Irony', p. 178.

8. Ibid.

9. Walburga Litschauer, Vorwort, in *Bruckner Sämtliche Werke*, 11, XII.

10. Floros, *Brahms und Bruckner*, pp. 160–6.

11. Robert Simpson, *The Essence of Bruckner* (London: Victor Gollancz, 1967), p. 104.

12. Erwin Doernberg, *The Life and Symphonies of Anton Bruckner* (London: Barrie and Rockliff, 1960), pp. 21–2, 86.

13. The other distinct versions were composed in 1874 and 1878 (*'Volksfest'*). Besides the 1881 revision for a performance that December, a final cutting and editing in 1887–8 was published by Gutmann in 1889. I am indebted to Benjamin Korstvedt for factual information relating to Bruckner's 1881 and 1887–8 revisions of the 1880 Finale of the Fourth Symphony.

14. Simpson, *Essence of Bruckner*, p. 95; Donald F Tovey, 'Bruckner', in *Symphonies and Other Orchestral Works* (Oxford: Oxford University, 1989), p. 260; Ernst Kurth, *Bruckner*, vol. 2 (Hildesheim: Georg Olms, 1971 (1925)), pp 658–60. Kurth's analysis is understandable, given that the revision published in 1889, with its extensive cuts, was the only text he knew. See note 24 for more on these cuts.

15. This tonal and stylistic 'drop' is reminiscent of Beethoven's procedure in the Finale of the Ninth Symphony. The high style on 'vor Gott' is undercut by the shift to the low-style Turkish march. A chromatic third relationship is also involved as a hinge, but in the Beethoven example, the tonal shift precedes the stylistic shift.

16. I offer the 'all-embracing' trope as one interpretation of the Beethoven example described in the preceding note (Hatten, *Musical Meaning*, Chapter 7). Note that in the Bruckner movement, the pastoral as high style (metaphysical connotations of the horn call amid 'rustlings' of nature) has already been introduced at the beginning; thus, the bird-call element is crucial to our understanding the second theme's pastoral element as rustic, and hence suggestive of a lower style. One might also argue that the contrapuntal combination of motives in the second theme adds a hint of learned style, thereby raising its stylistic level or suggesting another trope, between learned style and pastoral simplicity. In this case I would interpret the learned as inflecting the pastoral with a connotation of the spiritual (hence, pantheistic) – clearly an appropriate inflection if one maintains that the exalted/ heroic and pastoral topics also complement each other tropologically.

17. Cited by Hans Redlich, *Bruckner and Mahler* (London: J. M. Dent and Sons, 1963), p. 60.

18. I would not, however, construe the troping as ironically undercutting the seriousness of the chorale by means of the polka (compare the more wrenching undercutting in the Finale, bar 183, discussed below). Bruckner strikes me as too sincere in his compositional intentions for such an interpretation, based on my reading of his personality. At best, one might consider a kind of cosmic irony to emerge at a much higher level, rather than the kind of sardonic irony that one might attribute to a Mahler or a Schoenberg. Bruckner records the juxtaposition of styles, and marvels at the 'stark duality' of their opposed connotations (according to Bruckner, humour and worldly joy vs. sadness and pain, based on his actual experience on the street of hearing a ball being celebrated next door to a wake).

19. See Hatten, *Musical Meaning*, Chapter 7, for more on this concept and its connection to Romantic irony.

20. For the concept of different kinds of discourse in the novel, see Mikhail Bakhtin,

Problems of Dostoevsky's Poetics, Caryl Emerson, ed. and trans. (Minneapolis: University of Minnesota Press, 1984) and *The Dialogic Imagination: Four Essays by M. M. Bakhtin*, Michael Holquist, ed., Caryl Emerson and Michael Holquist, trans. (Austin: The University of Texas Press, 1981).

21. Perhaps the most striking example of this kind of chromatic-third correlation is the last movement of Schumann's *Fantasy*, Op. 17. There, the chromatic-third progression is used (1) as a marked thematic progression without textural contrast (the opening motto progression in bars 1–3), (2) as a marked thematic shift of key and texture in a more exploratory theme (the 'second' theme beginning in A♭ at bar 34), and (3) as the basis for the large-scale tonal motion of the first half (bars 1–71, C–A♭–F). In the first two instances, we can hear a direct, chord-to-chord displacement, which I interpret as an awe-filled moment implying a kind of metaphysical insight. Other works whose overall tonal structure features major third-related keys (e.g., the first movement of Liszt's *Faust Symphony*) will generally exploit chromatic-third relationships at lower levels as well, where their chord-to-chord effect is most striking.

22. The three note motive C♭–E♭–B♭ is, perhaps not coincidentally, a transposition of the famous F–A–E motto, used in this shape by Dietrich and Schumann in their movements of the violin sonata dedicated to Joachim. Its letter symbolism, as an abbreviation of '*frei aber einsam*', is clearly a species of musical meaning not aurally accessible by the untutored listener. Note, however, that the motto's private symbolism is supported by more 'public' correlations in the style: the poignance of the lowered $\hat{6}$ to $\hat{5}$ and the starkness of the 'empty' open-fifth interval. (For further discussion of the open-fifth correlation in Beethoven, see Hatten, *Musical Meaning*, Chapter 2).

23. According to Deryck Cooke, the lowered $\hat{6}$ to $\hat{5}$ is 'the most widely used of all terms of musical language', almost invariably appearing whenever a composer wishes to express grief (*The Language of Music*, Oxford: Oxford University Press, 1959, p. 146). Used in a major-key context, however, the mixture suggests poignancy rather than outright grief.

24. The term 'arrival $^6_4$' is introduced in Hatten, *Musical Meaning*, p. 15, where it is used to describe the rhetorical effect of certain cadential $^6_4$'s in Beethoven that resolve tonal and/or thematic events, especially when their arrival sounds more resolutional than the ultimate cadence (which may be absent altogether).

25. The ambiguity involves three keys: since bars 131–8 tonicize C minor, the F could be $\hat{4}$ of C minor; but a deceptive move to VI in bar 139 was reinterpreted as V of D♭, thus the F could be $\hat{3}$ of D♭ major (until we realize that D♭ was merely a Neapolitan expansion); and since we expect by this time that B♭ will close the exposition, F is understood most logically as $\hat{5}$ of B♭.

26. Interestingly, in the 1874 version of the Finale the progression involves a chromatic-third root relationship between enharmonic spellings of ♭VI in D♭ and a German augmented-sixth in B♭ (bars 152–4).

27. Floros, *Brahms und Bruckner*, pp. 174–6, draws further comparisons between this movement and both *Lohengrin* (tower music from the third scene of the third act) and *Siegfried* (nature music in the second act).

28. In Hatten, 'The Place of Intertextuality in Music Studies', in *American Journal of Semiotics*, 3:4 (1985), pp. 69–82, I suggest constraints on this concept, which originates in literary theory. The use of common elements in the 'home' style need not be understood as intertextual, even though they are readily found in other works, since their imported meaning is general and gains specificity only within the context of the given work's appropriation of them. More distinctive borrowings or allusions from works in the same style (period), or allusions to previous styles and/or specific works in those styles, would be better considered as intertextual, in

my view, since these usages can potentially import rich networks of pre-established meaning that might not have been 'earned' by the prevailing musical discourse of the given work.

29.   Interestingly, this allusion appears for the first time in the 1880 version, and it represents a solution to the problem of providing a sufficiently transcendent ending to an increasingly integrative and cyclical expressive genre. Wagner's concept of transfiguration, drawn from Beethoven's late-style expressive genres that deliver a transcendent ending akin to an act of grace, became a familiar Romantic topic exploited by Strauss, Mahler, and Schoenberg. The key ingredient is a miraculous tonal shift, elevation, or transformation, that transcends the ever-present tragic, as opposed to a victory achieved through the will. (For more on this distinction, and the abnegational hinge found in Beethoven, see Hatten, *Musical Meaning*, Chapter 1).

30.   Constantin Floros was the first to observe a more extensive link between Bruckner's use of a pilgrim's march in this movement and the second movement of the Berlioz as model (*Brahms und Bruckner*, pp. 160–6, 178–9). Bruckner's earlier programmatic description of the movement as '*Lied, Gebeth, Ständchen*' suggests, if not an exact description, a direct inspiration from the Berlioz, which features a serenade as its third movement. Floros considers the opening theme of the Bruckner a funeral march with a song-like character (hence, *Lied*), the chorale at bar 25 as the prayer (*Gebeth*), and (although marked by Bruckner in a copy as '*Ständchen*') the theme at bar 51 as the actual pilgrims' march, based on its analogy to the Berlioz (pizzicato accompaniment, separated chorale phrases that modulate and cadence in a new key). He suggests that the serenade idea makes sense only in relation to a supposed verbal explanation Bruckner gave of the movement: 'in the second movement a love-smitten youth [serenader] wishes to enter [his beloved's room] at the window, but he will not be admitted', and the real structural and expressive parallels are with the second movement of the Berlioz, conceived as a *Nachtstück* ('*Marche de Pèlerins chantant la prière du soir*'). While this analysis certainly makes sense, my construal of the pilgrims' processional as a topic is somewhat broader, as indicated by my examples. I include the opening theme of the Andante (not solely the chorale with pizzicato accompaniment at bar 51) in this topic, since the character of the opening does not seem to be funereal, but rather indicative of a solemn, perhaps melancholy processional. Interestingly, the theme at bar 51 may be understood as integrating the topics, not the specfic motives, of the processional at the beginning and the chorale at bar 25. Topical integration is an area likely to be overlooked by analysts concerned with purely motivic integration.

31.   Another example of the pilgrims' processional as a topic with allegorical significance in Bruckner is found in the Finale of the Seventh Symphony (beginning at bar 35).

32.   The allusion, like the pilgrim's processional topic, also appears for the first time in the coda to the 1880 version, suggesting Bruckner's concern to achieve a fully integrated expressive genre. By contrast, the improvements in the 1878 version, as compared with the 1874 Finale, are primarily due to trimming excess fat, that is, cutting out overextended passages of motivic sequencing and development. Thus, the 1874 version is 616 bars long, whereas the 1878 version is reduced to 477 bars; the 1880 version is then enlarged with these additions to 541 bars. Ironically, Bruckner specified a drastic cut in the 1880 Finale for its performance in December 1881, documented in a letter to the conductor Felix Mottl dated 23 November 1881 (reprinted in Alfred Orel, *Bruckner-Brevier*, Vienna, 1943, pp. 216–7). The cut, from bars 350–431, wreaks havoc with the elements of sonata form by omitting the striking retransition to the recapitulation, the beginning of the recapitulation, and even the beginning of the second theme group. But it also damages the expressive

genre, since the omitted portion of the second theme group is the pilgrims' processional music (the second group would then begin as it did in previous versions, with what I call the 'quintessential theme', see below and note 40). I cannot understand this change, since the earlier revisions appear to be progressive improvements. Perhaps Bruckner felt that the recapitulation (though already shortened by reserving the introductory material for the coda and omitting the stormy disruption of the 'closing' theme from the exposition) would nevertheless allow the expressive drama to sag; or perhaps he merely felt that he had overused the interruptive strategy. Redlich suggests that some of the cuts were proposed by Herbeck and the conductor Richter (*Bruckner and Mahler*, p. 91).

In the revision of 1887–8 published in 1889, Bruckner excised only the first group of the recapitulation (bars 383–412, beginning with the *tutti Hauptthema*), with the result that the excision 'lends importance to the coda by making it a real culmination' (Benjamin Korstvedt, personal communication). I would add that this final revision preserves the pilgrims' processional (though shifted to D minor), but it tilts the delicate negotiation between expressive genre and sonata form too much in favour of the former to sustain the productive tension between the two.

33. Redlich, *Bruckner and Mahler*, p. 89.
34. The chromatic-third progression is similar in effect to that found in the opening theme of the String Quintet, composed in 1878–9. The jocular, horn-fifth dismissal of seriousness may be compared to a similar effect in the last movement of Beethoven's Piano Sonata in A Major, op. 101 (bars 55–8) where a pianissimo horn-fifth figure is mockingly rejected by a *forte* gesture that leads to a more energetic and rustic dance.
35. Philip Barford claims the trio is 'a *Ländler* of the kind always heard at a sentimental *Heimatabend* in Styria' (*Bruckner Symphonies*, Seattle: University of Washington, 1978, p. 40). Floros notes the barrel-organ effect of its texture (*Brahms und Bruckner*, p. 179) .
36. See note 32 for the compositional history of the pilgrim's processional topic in the finale.
37. The passage is reminiscent of the fateful *ombra* music in the Overture to *Don Giovanni*, specifically bars 23–6.
38. The breakthrough of G♭ to G♮ first appears in the 1880 version, although the 1878 version features the G♮ arrival without first establishing G♭ as a clear contrast. Recall, as well, that the second movement's progress in C minor was first deflected by the pitch G♭. As an aside, I would observe that G♮ achieves the expressive effect of a positive arrival even though harmonically it is an upper neighbour to the fifth of the dominant – or alternatively, the thirteenth of the dominant. The sudden *tutti* supports the positive arrival, and the significance of the ♭$\hat{3}$ to ♭$\hat{3}$'Picardy' move is independent of its reduced harmonic-functional status in this case.
39. My construal of 'learned' contrapuntal development as essentially topical is not far from claiming that such developmental techniques as imitation, mirror inversion, augmentation, and stretto effects – all of which can be found in this symphony – are being used somewhat manneristically as textural and topical enhancements (as well as for their expressive connotations) more than as essential syntactic components of the thematic discourse. By not essentially syntactic I mean that these techniques do not always carry the burden of progressive intensification the way they do in a Classical development.
40. See Hatten, *Musical Meaning*, Chapter 4. In Beethoven, an analogous 'quintessential' theme is found in the first two bars of the Piano Sonata in A major, Op. 101; its quotation as poetic reminiscence in the transition to the Finale is perhaps motivated as much by its prototypical exemplification of the pastoral topic as by its beauty.

41. See Tovey's reference to its critics ('Bruckner', p. 262) and Robert Simpson's judgement of its banality (*Essence of Bruckner*, p. 97).
42. Beethoven handled this expressive technique more subtly, as a vision of grace; compare, for example, the two-bar Neapolitan vision that floats above the depths of tragic F sharp minor in the first theme of the slow movement of the Piano Sonata in B♭ major, Op. 106 ('Hammerklavier'), analysed in Hatten, *Musical Meaning*, Chapter 1.
43. The accented scalar descent is reminiscent of the contract motive from Wagner's *Ring* cycle; in both cases the stylistic expressive correlation is one of implacable fatefulness.
44. For discussion of the strategic use of unmarked themes in Beethoven, see Hatten, *Musical Meaning*, Chapters 5 and 6.
45. Compare Mahler's marking of this progression (as A major to minor) in the first movement of the Sixth Symphony (with the celebrated motto rhythm, bars 57–60).
46. For an especially good example of obliquely-derived dissonance, see the first theme and transition section from the first movement of Schubert's Piano Sonata in A major, D 959.
47. Ernst Kurth (*Bruckner*, p. 658) suggests an image of the opening theme as undergoing an *Auflösung* ('dissolution' or 'dissolving') within the final, resolutional harmony.
48. Deryck Cooke, 'Anton Bruckner', in *The New Grove: Late Romantic Masters* (New York: Norton, 1985), p. 50.
49. Ibid, p. 50.

7 'Harmonic daring' and symphonic design in the Sixth Symphony: an essay in historical musical analysis

Benjamin M. Korstvedt

'*Die Sechste, die keckste*'
Anton Bruckner

Anton Bruckner once described his Sixth Symphony as 'the boldest', or as he put it 'die keckste', of his works in the genre, yet despite the composer's high estimation, this symphony has been consigned to the margins of the canon of his works.[1] It was not performed in its entirety during the composer's lifetime, and it remains the most rarely played of his mature symphonies.[2] Moreover, its critical reception has been ambivalent.[3] Ever since Robert Haas characterized the symphony as a 'step-child' in 1934, many if not most critics have felt compelled to adopt a similar tone of apologetic advocacy when discussing the work.[4] This soft pedalling has tended to deflect attention away from the qualities that prompted Bruckner to assert that the work was one of his most daring.

Unlike their modern counterparts, early commentators did not shy away from expressing surprise, and even confusion, about certain salient features of the symphony, notably the tonal complexity of both the opening theme of the first movement and the movement as a whole. As one critic wrote, the opening of the symphony, with its harmonic 'boldness', 'must astonish even those familiar with Bruckner's music'.[5] This earlier viewpoint can be a valuable analytic starting point; not only does it share Bruckner's own sense of the piece's daring, but, as will become clear, early reviews of the symphony point to certain overlooked musical features that prove crucial to understanding the structural design of the first movement. This paper, then, sets itself a dual task: it seeks to recover something of the boldness that Bruckner and other early listeners perceived in

185

the Sixth Symphony and it tries to fold this nineteenth-century perception into an analysis that accommodates modern concerns about symphonic form.

*   *   *

We begin with the critical reception of the first complete public performance of the symphony on 26 February 1899 under Gustav Mahler.[6] Both sympathetic and unsympathetic reviewers puzzled over the harmonic orientation of the exposition of the first movement. One critic wrote, 'the beginning of this alleged A major symphony is peculiar. For a long time, one hears the tonalities of D minor and F sharp minor, and later E minor and B major, but not the ostensible main tonality'.[7] Theodor Helm, a critic who had long supported Bruckner, also remarked on the tonality of the first movement. Helm declared the first movement to be one of Bruckner's 'clearest, most convincing and most fortunately disposed'.[8] He too placed particular emphasis on the odd harmonic twists of the 'lapidary' primary theme, and wrote that the opening phrase cast the pitch A more as the dominant of D minor than a tonic in its own right (see Ex. 7.1). This, wrote Helm, is 'real Brucknerian harmonic daring (echt Brucknersche harmonische Kühnheit)'.[9]

The opening of the symphony clearly impressed these critics with its dissonance and its tonal complexity, yet, in typical nineteenth-century fashion, they made no attempt to relate these features to larger formal issues. More surprisingly, although several modern scholars have commented on the harmonic and modal nature of the primary theme, none has seriously considered its tonal and formal implications.[10] Rather, latter-day observers have tended to explain the work's structure in terms of modern paradigms of sonata form, a strategy that is only partially satisfactory. Many of Bruckner's symphonic movements, including this one, do betray some rather obvious outward similarities to 'textbook sonata form', yet the probative value of these similarities is limited; indeed, blunt application of *Formenlehre* is apt to neglect or misconstrue animating musical processes that inhabit the outward form. To take the case at hand, the tonal plan of the first movement of the Sixth Symphony is, if judged by textbook standards, skewed: the movement does not open with a passage that unambiguously establishes a single stable tonic key, the recapitulation does not solidly reaffirm the tonic key, and the second theme group is recapitulated entirely in the submediant, not the tonic. If the argument is formulated in these terms, Bruckner is easily convicted on the old charge of 'formlessness'.

Yet if we resist the urge to draw convenient, if imperfect, parallels between the layout of this movement and schematic models of sonata form, we can begin to see the ways in which this movement does embody a basic principle of sonata form. As Edward Cone famously suggested, 'more important than [sonata] form as a pattern, is the unifying principle behind it'.[11] This so-called 'sonata principle' consists, as Charles Rosen wrote following Cone, of the establishment and resolution of the 'large-scale dissonance', which is typically created in the

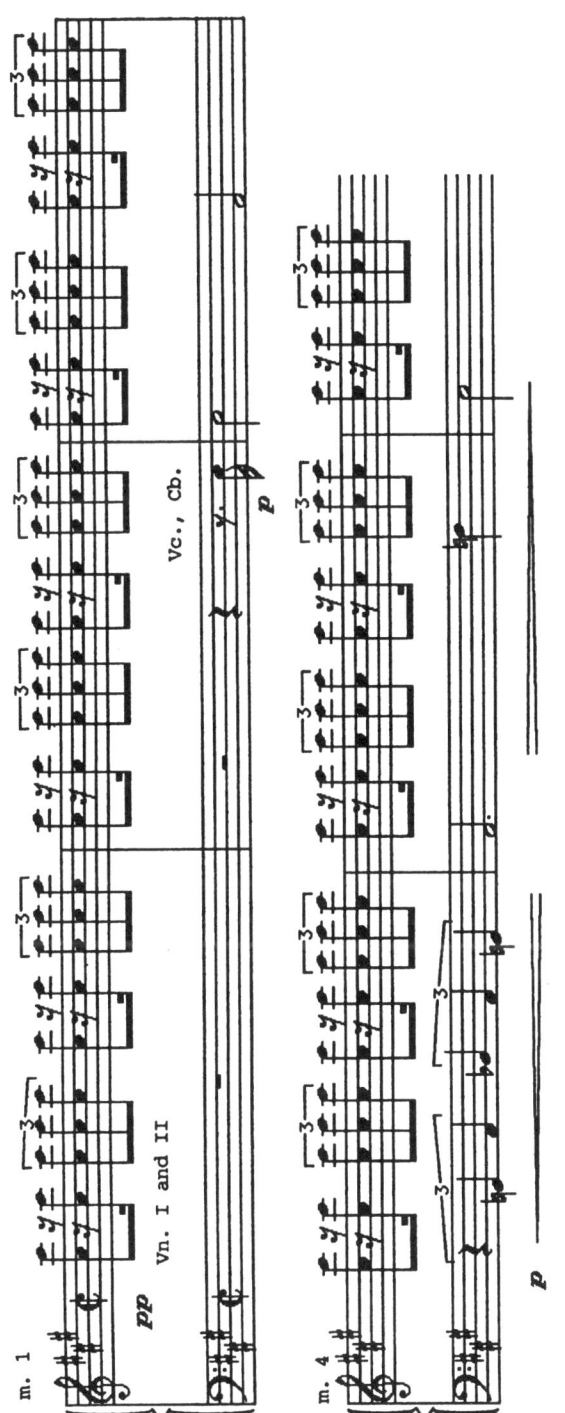

Ex. 7.1   Primary theme, mm. 1–6

187

exposition by 'the material played outside of the tonic (i.e., in the second group) [which] is dissonant with respect to the center of stability, or tonic'.[12] By recapitulating this dissonant material in the tonic key, the recapitulation 'resolves' the 'dissonance' created in the first half of the movement.[13] Sonata form is thus framed as a large harmonic progression from the dissonance of the exposition to the resolution of the recapitulation.

In the sonata forms of Beethoven and Mozart that are the models for the standard formulation, the process of large-scale dissonance and resolution is typically founded on a hierarchical pattern of key relationships, and especially, on the fundamental polarity of tonic and dominant. Bruckner's harmonic style, with its range of modulation, its complex sonorities, and its rich chromaticism, mitigates against the establishment and maintenance of two tonal poles. Thus, as his harmonic style evolved, Bruckner increasingly sought new ways to establish a coherent large-scale process of dissonance and resolution. The first movement of the Sixth Symphony essays a particularly fascinating approach to this problem. Here Bruckner created an underlying dynamic of dissonance and resolution based not so much on the classical scheme of key relations as on a unique fusion of thematic and tonal processes. In short, the first statement of the primary theme exposes not a stable tonic key area, but a dissonant tonal complex, and in the course of the movement this dissonance is incrementally resolved.

This process is set in motion at the very outset of the movement. Helm's claim that the pitch A is initially the dominant of D minor, and not a tonic in its own right, goes too far; but it is true that A first appears in a rather ambiguous harmonic context. The opening statement of the primary theme group (mm. 1–24) eschews any decisive sense of tonal stability; indeed, it subtly undercuts the stability of A by surrounding it with the pitches G natural and B♭ (see Ex. 7.1). These pitches do, *pace* Helm, momentarily hint at the dominant of D minor, but the gesture in mm. 5–6 quickly draws the music back toward A.[14] (See Ex. 7.2, which charts the harmonic progress of mm. 1–15.) The almost immediate repetition of the opening gesture a major third higher, on C♯ (mm. 9–12), intensifies the tonal energy of the music. In this statement, the dominant-seventh inflection of the primary theme is more clearly heard, partly because it has now moved away from the stabilizing force of the tonic triad and partly because the pointed voice-leading in the horn and second violin in mm. 7–8 quite clearly, if only momentarily, suggests the dominant of F♯ minor. Here the dotted figure that ends the gesture does not fall back to its starting point; rather it breaks out to a new harmony, V/V of A major, and thus draws the music back into the orbit of the tonic key. The turn back to A is continued by the second clause of the primary theme group (mm. 15–24), which effectively establishes the dominant of the home key.

The tonal energy of this passage is heightened by the insistent repetition of the pitch C♯, which is sounded continuously throughout the first ten measures of the piece. In one way, the logic of the choice of C♯ as the ground-tone for this passage

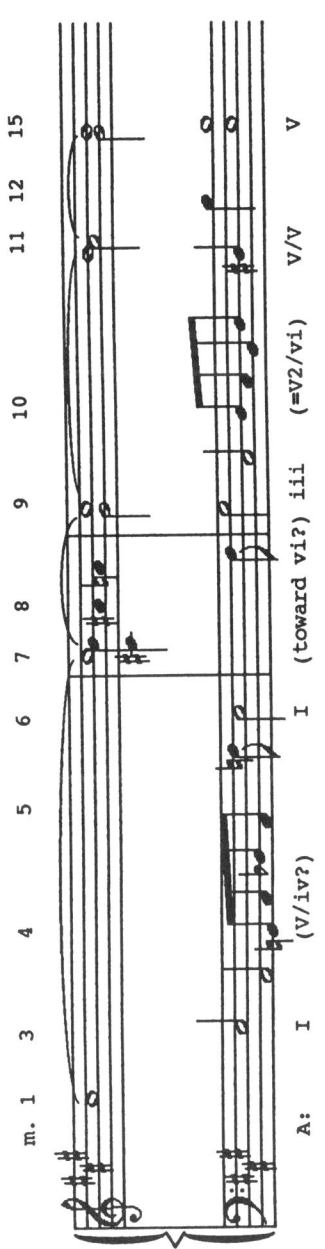

Ex. 7.2   mm. 1–15, harmonic framework

189

is manifest: it is the common tone of A major and C♯. The choice of C♯ serves another purpose as well. As a rule, Bruckner's symphonies begin with a tremolo or repeated notes in the strings. In all of the earlier symphonies the opening figure is based on a stable sonority, either the root of the tonic triad or the tonic triad itself.[15] The third is potentially the most active and intense chord-tone in a major triad, and here this latent energy is heightened by the friction of the G♮ in the bass in m. 4, against which the C♯ is a leading tone.[16]

Bruckner immediately restates the entire thematic complex very forcefully (mm. 25–48). While the initial statement was sparely orchestrated with the low strings and solo winds set against the light rhythmic ostinato of the upper strings, the restatement is massively scored. The background rhythm is transferred from violins to pounding double stops in the lower strings, the brass section enters *fortissimo*, and the tune is given to violins in octaves supported by horns, trumpets and massed woodwinds. Certain harmonic details are also rearranged (see Ex. 7.3). Most importantly, the pass through F♯ minor is intensified by means

Ex. 7.3   mm. 28–37, harmonic framework

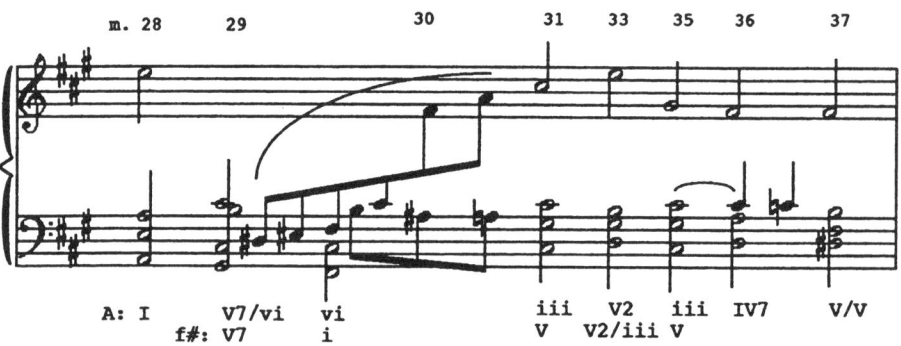

of an upward sweeping figure in the horns (mm. 29–31). And, since the counterstatement does not return to the tonal region of A but concludes by modulating in anticipation of the second theme group, the music is pulled back toward the home key differently (and less firmly) than in mm. 13–25 by a series of chords that assert the key of A major without sounding a tonic triad (A: V⁷–iii–IV⁷–V⁶/V).

So, Bruckner's bold opening does not unequivocally establish its tonic key, but instead inflects the tonic with a glint of dominant-seventh colour and thus creates a strategic sense of instability. While not strong enough to undermine the tonic key, this dominant-seventh implication does point beyond the initial tonality. As Robert Morgan once noted, thematic passages based on dominant-seventh harmonies rather than tonic harmonies point beyond themselves and suggest 'the presence of an implied tonic'.[17] Moreover, the sequential repetition of this gesture generates additional tonal impetus. It creates a sense of what Carl

Dahlhaus termed 'centripetal harmony': open-ended harmony that strives to reach an 'unheard' tonal centre, the absence of which constitutes a structural dissonance and is thus a source of continuity.[18] In the present instance, the 'unheard' tonal centre most strongly implied is F♯, which is invoked by the repeated appearance of its dominant (mm. 9–10 and 31–2).[19] As we shall see, this implication will be realized.

It is also important to note that the tonal energy of this opening derives from the intervallic content of the primary theme itself, especially the dissonant turn in its second bar. The theme is itself, in other words, inherently unstable and thus kinetic. This thematic basis of the movement's motivating tonal impetus is crucial; as we shall see, it allows Bruckner to fuse the movement's formative tonal process with the thematic framework of sonata form. At the main formal hinges of the movement, namely the beginning of the recapitulation and coda, both the primary theme and its associated tonal/harmonic dissonance return. This fusion of thematic and formal processes occurs most decisively at the beginning of the recapitulation: here A is recapitulated in a way that carefully preserves the tonal ambiguity it accrued in the exposition (see mm. 209–12), but the succeeding passage reasserts and then resolves the implication of C♯ as the dominant of F♯ (mm. 233–45). The coda is then left to resolve the dissonance of the primary theme onto a conclusive tonic triad. Both of these passages deserve a closer look.

The approach to the recapitulation beginning with its preparation in mm. 183–94 and continuing through the cadence on A in m. 209, as several other writers have noted, executes the tricky manoeuvre of restoring the tonal centricity of A while preserving its contextual harmonic ambiguity. Bruckner employs both tonal and thematic elements in establishing this delicate balance. The harmonic approach to the recapitulation is equivocal. A is arrived at enharmonically from a distant tonal region (E♭/A♭) and the mediating progression does little to clarify the connection between the two key areas: in m. 207 an A♭ in the bass, initially the root of a minor triad, becomes the leading tone of A with the aid of the timpani's entry on E (see Ex. 7.4). The thematic recapitulation is also equivocal. The reappearance of the primary theme (m. 195) does not coincide with the return of the tonic (m. 209). Moreover, the appearance of A major in m. 209 is proclaimed by an announcement of the primary theme with its G natural. Thus while the tonic is attained forcefully (the progression in mm. 208–9 resolves the tritone D/G♯ and the bass moves from dominant to tonic on a structural down beat) it is not securely established because its connection to the preceding tonal area is obscure and the following passage does not confirm the key of A. Rather, the continuation of the recapitulation of the primary theme group (mm. 233–45) amplifies and then resolves the implication of C♯ as the dominant of an unheard tonic F♯. In the exposition, Bruckner scrupulously avoided harmonizing C♯ with a third; without the leading-tone (and therefore without the tritone between the third and seventh of the chord) the dominant implication of the sonority was not fully present. With the inflection of E natural

Ex. 7.4   Approach to the recapitulation

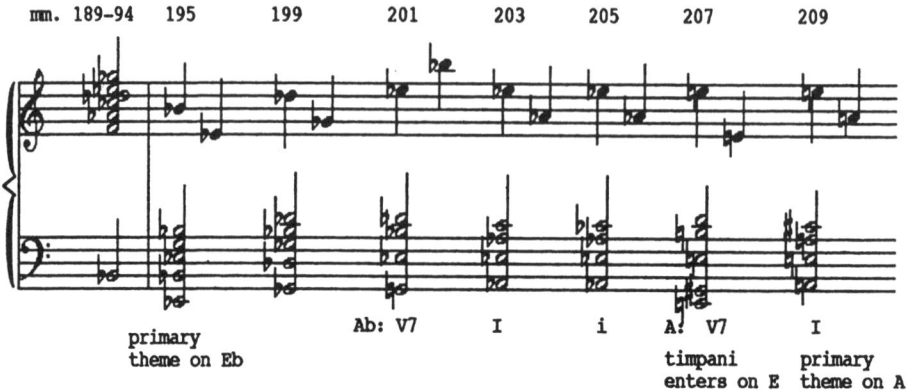

to E♯ in m. 239, C♯ is finally presented as the root of a full dominant harmony (note how the bass emphasizes the seventh in mm. 237–44). This leads directly to its resolution in m. 245 (see Ex. 7.5). Indeed, this progression from C♯ to F♯ is the most clearly articulated cadence in the entire movement: it outlines a clear IV–V–I progression, resolves the pertinent tritone (E♯/B closes onto F♯/A), occurs on a hypermetrical downbeat and, perhaps most importantly, is confirmed by the succeeding thematic passage in F♯. Thus the latent tonic status acquired by F♯ in the exposition, which was reinforced by the V7/F♯ heard in mm. 213–14, is here made real by the thematic passage in F♯ in mm. 237–45.

Ex. 7.5   mm. 233–45, harmonic framework

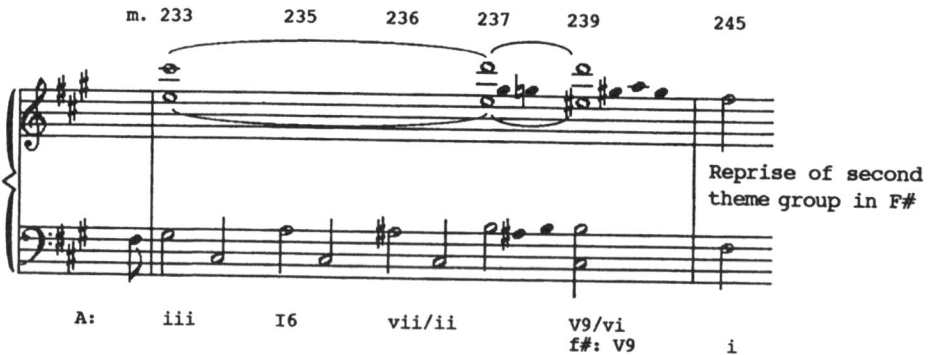

The coda brings the structural process of the movement to a conclusion by transforming the movement's opening theme from a source of dissonance, and thus musical impetus, into a source of musical stability. The coda begins in A major (m. 309). Although the cadence in A is somewhat indecisive locally (it succeeds a brief passage of stasis on an E major triad – not a dominant seventh

– with no sense of decisive closure), it is preceded by an extensive cadential preparation spelled out by the reprise of the closing theme group (mm. 285–308). This theme group, which had begun on C major in the exposition, is recapitulated beginning on D and, by means of a grand series of parallel sixth chords, lands on E in m. 305, thus articulating a big IV–V progression in the tonic key (see Ex. 7.6). With A major thus established the coda begins with the dissonant primary theme (or more precisely, its main motive) sounded simultaneously in its original guise and its inversion, again inflecting the tonic triad with dominant seventh colour (mm. 309–12). The main motive is immediately restated on the crucial degree of F♯, but here the motive is significantly altered: it is recast as a pure triad (see Ex. 7.7). Then, in m. 317, the music begins to swing broadly from the pivotal pitch of D♭ (= C♯) through a series of arcs, passing through A (m. 329–33) and B♭ (m. 337) before finally coming to rest on G♭ (=F♯) in m. 349. Suddenly a triple-forte tutti statement of a stabilizing, triadic variant of the primary theme rings out in D (Ex. 7.8).[20] (This forceful subdominant may be taken as a delayed response to the emphasis on the dominant of D in the opening thematic statement.) The final seventeen measures (mm. 353–69) at last tonicize A: a largely plagal cadence on A (IV–iv–vii$^{06}_{5}$–I) is followed by eight measures of the primary motive (mm. 361–8), now recast so as to gravitate toward A, above a tonic pedal (Ex. 7.9). After a sixteen-bar period in mm. 353–68, the music comes to a halt in m. 369; yet even here the resolution is not absolute: the coda has been dominated by plagal progressions, and even at the end a clinching authentic cadence on A is absent. Moreover, a confirming triadic version of the primary theme is not sounded on A, but only on F♯ (mm. 313–16) and, more powerfully, D (mm. 353–60). Thus ultimate thematic resolution is withheld until the final measures of the Finale, where the triadic version of the theme that opened the symphony finally resounds in the tonic (mm. 407–16 of the Finale).[21]

*   *   *

Over the course of the movement, the three appearances of the primary theme outline a large harmonic progression; the dissonant, centrifugal harmony is restated and partially resolved in the recapitulation and finally stabilized in the coda (see Ex. 7.10). This underlying framework bears some similarity to Ernst Kurth's notion of *Gerüstpfeiler* (framing pillars). In *Romantic Harmony and its Crisis in Wagner's 'Tristan'* Kurth showed that in certain densely chromatic and modulatory compositions (he used the prelude to the third act of *Tristan* as his prime example) the music creates 'widely spaced framing points' that scaffold it.[22] The contrasting episodes lying between these pillars may well be complex, yet in Kurth's model the harmonic progression outlined by the structural chords themselves is, as a rule, simple. As he put it, 'if we were to assemble these boundary chords into a progression, disregarding everything lying in between, it

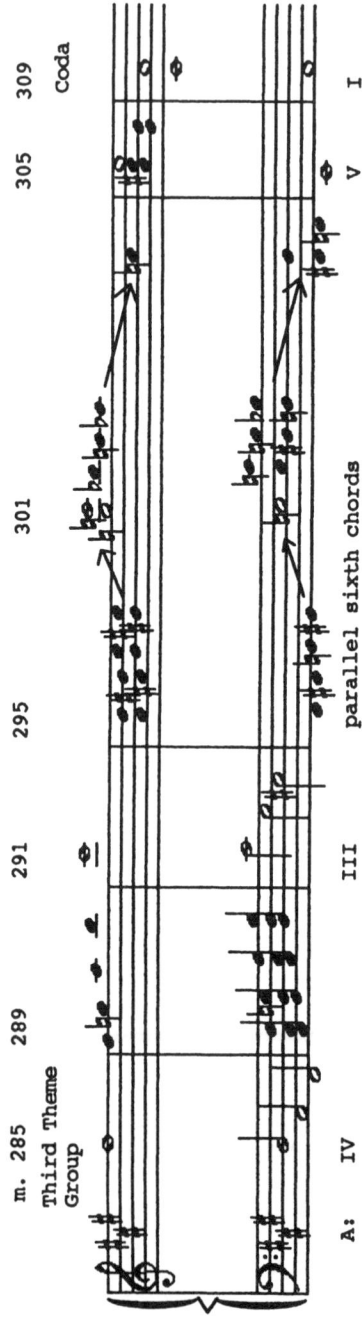

Ex. 7.6   Approach to the coda

194

Ex. 7.7   Variant of the primary theme, mm. 313–16

would be extremely simple'.[23] The large-scale progression spelled out in the opening movement of the Sixth Symphony is not particularly simple; in contrast to Kurth's example, it is based on dissonant sonorities and it focuses on secondary harmonic functions. (Its blending of tonic and submediant is of course typical of late nineteenth-century harmony.) Yet this tonal scaffolding does serve a function similar to that of Kurth's *Gerüstpfeiler*: it supports and helps articulate the span of the movement in a way that accommodates Bruckner's characteristic chromaticism, remote modulation, episodic formal approach, and expansive time scale.

Kurth's *Gerüstpfeiler* can help us to comprehend another aspect of the formal design of this movement. As Kurth suggested, such construction gives the composer considerable freedom to move in the areas 'lying in between' the framework of the pillars. Bruckner certainly took advantage of this opportunity; the movement encompasses great heterogeneity. The second theme group, for instance, does seem to stand in splendid isolation. The pulse of this section is markedly different than that of the preceding music; it is marked *Bedeutend langsamer* (significantly slower) and its rhythms are based on quarter-note triplets, not straight quarter notes.[24] The music of this section also displays a very different sort of thematic organization than does the primary theme. Not only is this theme group one of Bruckner's most lushly embroidered and thematically rich (it includes half a dozen distinct sections), but its various sections do not display the sharply defined melodic contrasts of the opening passage. Rather, they vary a stock of elements (notably intervallic patterns that mimic fourth-species counterpoint and various superimpositions and juxtapositions of hemiola patterns) in ways that create the effect not of clear development, but as Dahlhaus put it, of 'an analytically elusive but clearly perceivable similarity ... like a written-out memory image'.[25] Furthermore, in contrast with the primary theme, its harmonic manner is based less on functional progressions than on localized harmonies, and thus seems somewhat static. In this section, passages that imply relatively distant key areas are set against each other with little mediation; the key of E is pre-eminent not because of any definite cadential activity, but because of its strategic placement at the beginning of the passage, its repetition, the distinctive thematic material presented in this key, and the fact that E is presented as an actual tonic, rather than being implied by its dominant. Thus although this theme group wanders harmonically, it is anchored by the returns of the local tonic of E. Yet despite its relatively placid unfolding the second theme group does

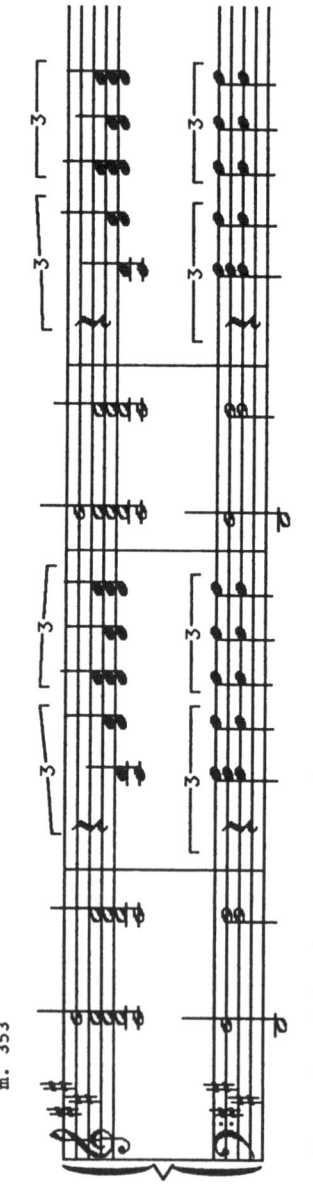

trumpet and trombone parts only

Ex. 7.8   Variant of primary theme, mm. 353–6

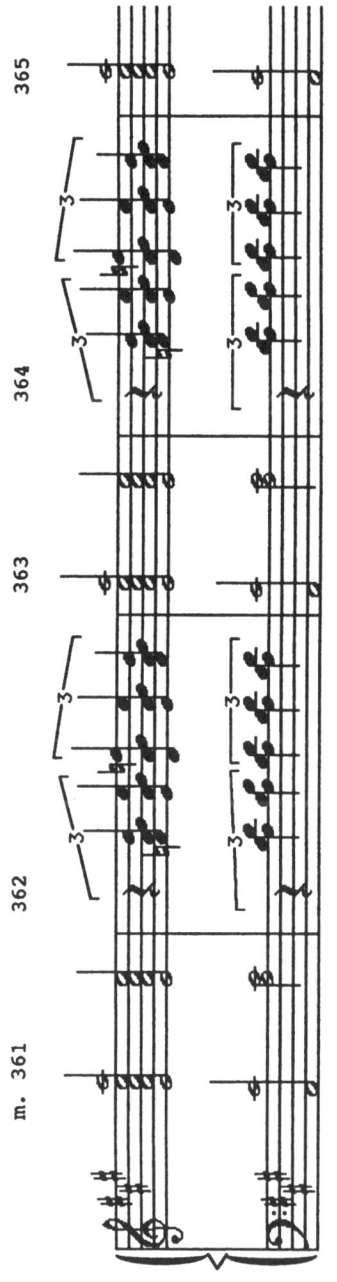

brass parts only

Ex. 7.9   Variant of primary theme, mm. 361–5

197

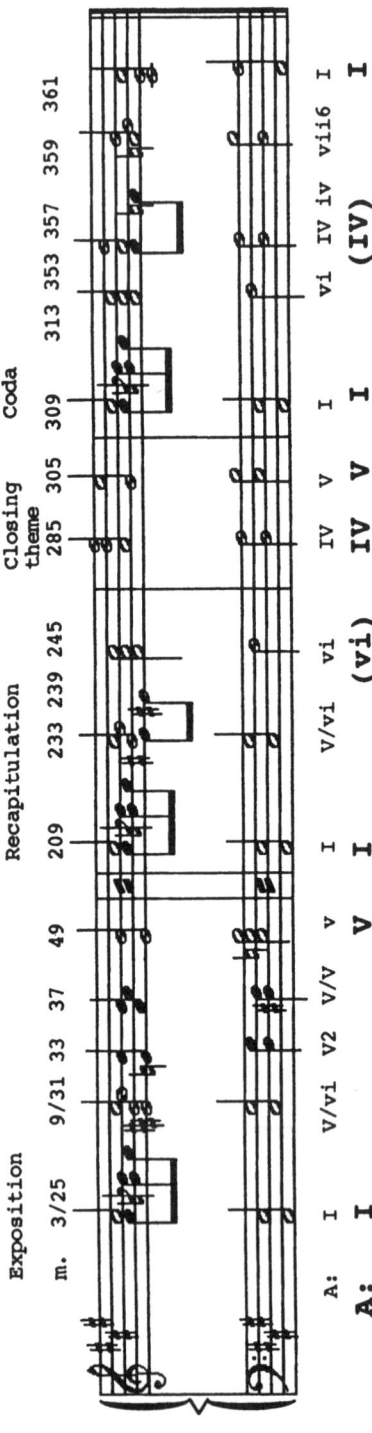

Ex. 7.10 First movement, harmonic 'pillars'

not lie inertly within the structural framework established by the primary theme. As we have seen, the tonic/dominant relationship established between the primary and secondary thematic passages in the exposition helps establish A as the tonal centre, and the recapitulation of the second theme group in F♯ helps to resolve the structural dissonance centered on C♯.

The development section also plays a finely judged part in the structural dynamic of the movement.[26] This section does not, as is usual, play with dissonance, fragmentation, and discontinuity. Instead it minimizes rather than maximizes the harmonic and gestural fissures of the thematic material and thus increases the forward motion of the music. Indeed the culminating passage of this section (mm. 159–82), which is based on the main motive of the primary theme, seems more accurately described by the German term *Durchführung* than it is by the English 'development section'.[27] The melodic material of this passage is clearly based on the primary motive of the first theme (the rhythm of this motive is preserved and its contour transformed yet recognizable) but here the music moves with a broader sweep than anywhere else in the movement. The falling fifth of the opening is expanded and inverted into a rising octave and the ending of the motive is altered such that the phrasing assumes an antecedent/consequent pattern: each phrase ends on an active tone that resolves into the beginning of the succeeding phrase. Thus unlike the exposition, the tonal motion in this passage is smoothly coherent. And in contrast to the halting six-bar patterns of the initial statement of the primary theme, here both the phrase structure and the harmonic rhythm enunciate a vigorously striding, four-bar swing and thus generate real forward momentum.

Again, Bruckner brings this episode to bear on his larger formal plan. In mm. 180–1, after twenty-four bars of gathering energy, the music deflects in mid-phrase away from C major to the dominant of D♭. Suddenly the music collapses into quiet stasis, and coils into a harmonic knot based on a six-pitch aggregate in Eb minor (mm. 183–94, the pitch collection can be seen in Ex. 7.4). As with the second theme group, what had been a local phenomenon is here drawn back to the larger structural process of the movement. Not only does the hypermetrical momentum of mm. 159–94 serve as the background against which the metrical rupture of the recapitulation plays out, but the dissonant brooding in E flat minor prepares the harmonic pivot of A♭/E♭ to A that initiates the recapitulation.

*   *   *

The task of making sense of Bruckner historically, stylistically and critically has long challenged critics. Estimating Bruckner's musical connection to Wagner and to the musical avant-garde of his time has proven particularly troublesome. In the nineteenth century both sympathetic and antagonistic critics generally agreed, despite their radically differing evaluations, that Bruckner's music was essentially similar to Wagner's. Eduard Hanslick expressed a commonly held view when he suggested that the nature of Bruckner's style was 'the application of Wagner's dramatic style to the symphony'.[28] In contrast, modern critics have tended to minimize Bruckner's indebtedness to Wagner, and for the past half century this view has shaped our understanding of Bruckner's music, prompting us, among other things, to approach Bruckner symphonies as 'absolute music' and to analyse them pre-eminently in terms of the traditional categories of sonata form. These approaches have not proven wholly adequate. While simplistic notions of Bruckner as 'Wagnerian symphonist' are not helpful, addressing his music with a cognizance of the aesthetic issues pertinent to nineteenth-century criticism can point us toward a more historically cogent and, I would argue, more analytically perceptive comprehension of his music.

A case in point: in the nineteenth century, one aspect of Bruckner's music that was commonly heard as modern – and thus by the standards of the time, Wagnerian – was its harmony; witness the several allusions to the harmonic 'boldness' and 'daring' (terms that often were applied to the music of Wagner and his followers) of the Sixth Symphony. This identification is understandable; the opening of the Sixth Symphony is based on a real (as opposed to tonal) chromatic sequence, a Wagnerian hallmark. But, as Dahlhaus among others has noted, this kind of musical construction is hard to reconcile with the syntactic demands of the symphony and seems more naturally suited to the genres of the music drama and the symphonic poem.[29] Indeed, Wagner himself drew a distinction between harmonic procedures appropriate for symphonic music and those appropriate for music drama; on one occasion, he wrote that a 'fundamental difference' exists between 'modulation in pure instrumental music and in drama', since 'swift and free transitions are in the latter often just as necessary as they are unjustified in the former, owing to a lack of motive'.[30] Similarly, in 'On the Application of Music to the Drama' ('Über die Anwendung der Musik auf das Drama'), Wagner was openly suspicious of attempts to import musical gestures, especially harmonic gestures, derived from dramatic music into the symphony.[31] Without any dramatic context, the use of such gestures in a symphony could only produce 'contrived effects (*gesuchter Effekte*)', not 'a well-motivated effect (*wohlmotivierte Wirkung*)'. Ultimately such stylistically mistaken appropriation would lead to the 'utter ruin (vollen Verderb)' of the symphonic genre.[32]

Thus, despite some similarities of harmonic style, Bruckner's compositional aims cannot easily be reconciled with Wagner's view that the symphony had been surpassed, if not wholly supplanted, by the *Gesamtkunstwerk*. By not only composing ostentatiously post-Beethovenian symphonies, but applying a chromatic, 'Wagnerian' tonal language to the paradigmatic genre of absolute music Bruckner set himself a task, as Klaus Kropfinger noted, that proved incompatible in important ways with Wagner's own position.[33] Bruckner certainly did not attempt to justify his characteristically progressive harmony dramatically; rather, as in the Sixth Symphony, he sought to bring 'harmonic daring' into the service of the formal and rhetorical demands of symphonic convention. Indeed, aspects of Bruckner's formal approach are frankly non-Wagnerian, notably their blithe recapitulations, which seem to proceed in inspired indifference to any scruples about the value of such formal conventions. Perhaps Bruckner's adaptation of symphonic traditions was more progressive than Wagner's rejection of them. As Thomas Grey has suggested, Wagner's late pronouncements on the symphony, which permit 'in the musical drama all that was denied to the symphony', contain an element of 'defensive repositioning' in light of the increasing prestige of the symphony in the late 1870s.[34] Bruckner, unconcerned with upholding the preserve of the music drama, was free to apply lessons learned from his great predecessor to very different symphonic projects.

Whatever his lack of accord with Wagner's conception of the symphonic, Bruckner did effectively appropriate characteristic elements of the main progressive orchestral genre of the mid-nineteenth century, the symphonic poem.[35] For example, Bruckner's tendency to characterize the various sections of his movements by tempo, instrumentation, and harmonic style as well as by thematic material and key may derive from the symphonic poem. More interesting is the way in which Bruckner adapts the technique of thematic transformation. The Sixth Symphony is a prime instance. The opening theme (Ex. 7.1) is particularly well-suited to this type of treatment; its distinctive falling fifth and especially its rhythmic profile, with striking triplet figures, ensure that the theme will retain its identity in a variety of guises.[36] Thus, the counterstatement of the opening theme (mm. 25–40) preserves the rhythmic, melodic and tonal substance of the opening gesture, but dramatically transforms its musical character from broodingly meditative to demonically energetic. Bruckner's use of thematic variation goes beyond such immediate, dramatic changes, however; as he did with chromatic sequential harmony, he takes over a device associated with a progressive, programmatic genre and adapts it to more traditionally symphonic purposes. Each appearance of a structural harmonic pillar is obviously associated with a return to the primary theme (mm. 1–48, 195–244, 309–69), but Bruckner does more, however, than simply identify the crucial harmonic pillars by tagging them thematically. He transforms the theme in ways that are essential to the overall structural process of the movement. For example, he uses a broadly striding version of the theme to generate momentum for the recapitulation and, once the reprise arrives, he deploys a grandiose variant of the theme to drive the music through the tonal knot preceding the arrival of A. Finally, in the coda dissonance is exchanged for consonance, and the primary motive is moulded into a major triad to become a source of stability (see Ex. 7.7, 7.8 and 7.9).

By expanding its depth of field to include late nineteenth-century aesthetic concerns and critical responses, musical analysis can further the ongoing critical re-evaluation of Bruckner. By elucidating the innovative and masterful ways in which he synthesized the harmonic vocabulary of the 'music of the future', the thematic logic of the symphonic poem, and the formal and rhetorical demands of large-scale symphonic form, analysis can allow us to get past the old, polemically inspired position that Bruckner was essentially a naive composer who crudely fitted gestures from the genres of music drama, symphonic poem, and mass into the empty formal shell of the symphony. On these terms, analysis can participate alongside historiography and textual criticism in the evolution of a new, more critically sound picture of Bruckner and his music.

Acknowledgements

A version of this paper was read at the annual meeting of Music Theory Midwest at Carleton College in May 1997. I owe particular thanks to James Buhler, William Carragan, Robert Hatten, Morten Solvik, Christopher Hasty and Thomas Christensen for their helpful and encouraging responses to this article.

Notes

1. See Hans-Hubert Schönzeler, *Bruckner* (New York: Grossman, 1970), p. 67.
2. For example the Concertgebouw Orchestra performed the Sixth Symphony a total of thirty-three times through the 1993–94 season. In comparison, the orchestra performed the Third through Fifth and the Seventh through Ninth Symphonies each at least twice as many times; see Nico P. H. Steffen, 'Die Bruckner-Tradition des Königlichen Concertgebouw-Orchester, Teil 6', in *Studien und Berichte* (Newsletter of the International Bruckner Gesellschaft), 45 (December 1995), pp. 5–17.
3. The two most influential English-speaking advocates of the work have been Donald Francis Tovey (*Essays in Musical Analysis*, 2, *Symphonies (II), Variations and Orchestral Polyphony*, (Oxford: Oxford University Press, 1935, pp. 79–84) and Robert Simpson (*The Essence of Bruckner*, rev. edn, London: Victor Gollancz, 1992, pp. 123–41).
4. Haas wrote, 'In practice, she is a stepchild among her sisters' ('Sie ist in der Praxis das Stiefkind unter ihren Schwestern'), *Anton Bruckner* (Potsdam: Athenaion, 1934), p. 137. Haas's label 'stepchild' was repeated literally by several later critics including Werner Wolff, *Anton Bruckner: Rustic Genius* (New York: Dutton, 1942), p. 218 and Hermann Odermatt, *Bruckner Symphonien* (Zurich: Apollo Verlag, 1949), p. 16. Moreover, a remarkable number of later writers have echoed Haas's term less literally; for example, Hans Redlich called the symphony a 'problem child', *Bruckner and Mahler* (London: Dent, 1955), p. 95.
5. 'Die Kühnheit der Harmonien muß selbst die Kenner der Bruckner'schen Musik noch staunen machen', 'Hagen', review of 'The Seventh Philharmonic Concert', *Ostdeutsche Rundschau*, 28 February 1899; rpt. in Robert Haas and Leopold Nowak, *Anton Bruckner Sämtliche Werke: VI. Symphonie A-Dur, Revisionsbericht* (Vienna: Musikwissenschaftlicher Verlag, 1986), p. 75.
6. Mahler's performance was the first to include all four movements of the symphony; in 1883 the Vienna Philharmonic under Otto Jahn had performed the two inner movements, but not the first movement and Finale. In his 1899 performance Mahler made some cuts (for example, mm. 275–84 in the first movement) and changes in orchestration (see Robert Helm, Review of Bruckner's Sixth Symphony, *Deutsche Zeitung*, 28 February 1899; rpt. in Haas and Nowak, *VI. Symphonie A-Dur, Revisionsbericht*, pp. 74–5). The first uncut performance was given by Karl Pohlig in Stuttgart on 15 March 1901.

7. 'Eigenartig ist der Anfang des ersten Satz dieser angeblichen A-dur Symphonie. Man hört nämlich die Tonarten D-moll und Fis-moll, weiterhin E-moll und H-Dur, aber lange nicht die aneblich dominirende Tonart', 's.k.', review of 'The Seventh Philharmonic Concert', *Neues Wiener Journal*, 2 March 1899; rpt. in Haas and Nowak, *VI. Symphonie A-Dur, Revisionsbericht*, p. 79.

8. 'den klarsten, überzeugendsten, glücklichst disponirt, welche Bruckner schrieb', Helm, review of Bruckner's Sixth Symphony, p. 72.

9. Helm, review, p. 73

10. For example, Ernst Kurth suggested, if only in passing, that the G natural, B flat and F natural of measures 4–5 foreshadow the many subdominant-related keys later in the symphony; see Kurth, *Bruckner* (Berlin: Max Hesses Verlag, 1925), vol. 1, pp. 545–6. Robert Simpson discussed the key scheme of the first movement of the symphony at some length, but did not, however, explore the role that the tonal disposition of the primary theme plays in this scheme; *Essence of Bruckner*, pp. 124–9.

11. Edward Cone, *Musical Form and Musical Performance* (New York: W.W. Norton, 1968), pp. 76–78.

12. Charles Rosen, *Sonata Forms*, rev. edn (New York: W.W. Norton, 1988), p. 229.

13. Rosen, *Sonata Forms*, pp. 284–5.

14. My analysis is based on *Anton Bruckner Sämtliche Werke, Band 6: VI. Symphonie A-Dur (Originalfassung)*, ed. Leopold Nowak (Vienna: Musikwissenschaftlicher Verlag, 1952).

15. The one exception to his rule is the Fifth Symphony, which starts with a slow introduction. For a tabulation of the opening sonorities of each of Bruckner's symphonies see Peter Benary, 'Zu Anton Bruckners Personalstil', in *Musiktheorie* 8 (1993), p. 128.

16. Ernst Kurth wrote that this C♯ is a 'highly agitated whirring in the sonic atmosphere (moreover, it is the intense major third of the tonic triad)'; see Kurth, *Bruckner*, vol. 1, p. 292; quoted and trans. in Lee Rothfarb, *Ernst Kurth: Selected Writings* (Cambridge: Cambridge University Press, 1991), p. 163.

17. 'Dissonant Prolongation: Theoretical and Compositional Precedents', in *Journal of Music Theory*, 20 (1976), p. 57. Arnold Whittall wrote similarly that 'at various times in *Parsifal* it is possible to feel that a tonality is present and identifiable through emphasis on its dominant note or chord, even when the tonic itself is absent'; 'The Music' in Lucy Beckett, *Richard Wagner: Parsifal* (Cambridge: Cambridge University Press, 1981), p. 65.

18. Dahlhaus contrasted the 'centripetal harmony' of the opening of Brahms's Piano Concerto in D minor, op. 15 with 'centrifugal harmony' as exemplified by Wagner's 'Prelude' to *Tristan und Isolde*. Dahlhaus argued that in the Brahms passage the 'sole ambition' of the music 'is to reach its center', while in the *Tristan* Prelude 'the movement is away from any center'; see 'Issues in Composition' in *Between Romanticism and Modernism: Four Studies in the Music of the Later Nineteenth Century*, trans. Mary Whittall (Berkeley and Los Angeles: University of California Press, 1980), p. 74.

19. Again one of the reviews of the première hinted at this tonal strategy ('s.k.', review). Ernst Kurth seems to have perceived something similar too. He sensed an 'intense double tendency (*intensive Doppelstrebung*)' in this movement: as Kurth heard it, the opening theme reaches out in broad tonal circles embracing both dominant (E major and C♯ minor) and subdominant (F Major and D minor) impulses; *Bruckner*, vol. 1, pp. 545–6, note 1.

20. The coda echoes two earlier passages. Harmonically it expands upon the progression at the close of the first half of the movement, mm. 129–44, which features root position triads progressing by minor thirds and perfect fourths

204 Perspectives on Anton Bruckner

downwards. Thematically and rhythmically, the coda recalls the periodic elaboration of the primary theme in the central section of the development section (mm. 159–82).

21. Bruckner's tendency to defer final resolution until the last possible moment was not, of course, an isolated one. Recently several scholars have observed the propensity of progressive late-ninteenth century composers to postpone full tonal resolution until well after the thematic recapitulation. Stephen Parkany argued that in the first movement of his First Symphony Bruckner 'withholds' full resolution of crucial thematic dissonance until 'the final, paramount wave of the movement'; see, 'The "Kecke Beserl" and Bruckner's Symphonic Tradition' in *Atti del XIV Congresso della Societa Internazionale di Musicologica Bologna, 1987*, ed. Angelo Pomilio, et al. (Turin: Edizioni di Torino, 1990), vol. 3, p. 813. Thomas Grey observed a similar phenomenon in Wagner's overtures of the 1840s. In these works, Grey wrote, Wagner experimented with the 'possible recapitulatory function of the coda' by shifting 'the emphasis of resolution closer to the end of the work'; see 'Wagner, the Overture and the Aesthetics of Musical Form', in *Nineteenth Century Music*, 12 (1988), p. 11.

22. Ernst Kurth, *Romantische Harmonie und ihre Krise in Wagners 'Tristan'*, 3rd. edn (Berlin: Max Hesses Verlag; 1923; rpt., Hildesheim: Georg Olms Verlag, 1968), p. 317; quoted and trans. in Lee Rothfarb, *Ernst Kurth: Selected Writings*, p. 144.

23. Kurth, *Romantische Harmonie*, 317; quoted and trans. Rothfarb, *Ernst Kurth*, p. 146

24. In practice this usually means that the tempo here drops by about a third (typically from ca. MM half-note = 60 to ca. MM half-note = 40); thus, the quarter note stays roughly the same, but since in the second theme group each measure has six quarter notes, not four, the music moves at a different, slower pace.

25. Carl Dahlhaus, *Nineteenth-Century Music*, trans. J. Bradford Robinson (Berkeley and Los Angeles: University of California Press, 1989), p. 273.

26. Bruckner did not use the term 'development section', or its German counterpart '*Durchführung*'. He modelled sonata form as a two-part, not a three-part, structure, and typically diagrammed symphonic movements in two parts (labelled *erste Teil* and *zweite Teil*), not the now customary tripartite scheme of exposition, development and recapitulation.

27. Think of Anton Webern's comment, '*Durchführen heisst: Durch weite Räume fuhren!*'; see *Die Weg zur Neue Musik* (Vienna: Universal Edition, 1960), p. 63.

28. Eduard Hanslick, review of Bruckner's Eighth Symphony, *Neue Freie Presse*, 23 December 1892; English translation in Hanslick, *Music Criticisms 1846–99*, ed. and trans. Henry Pleasants (Baltimore: Penguin Books, 1950), p. 288.

29. Carl Dahlhaus, 'Issues in Composition', pp. 45–52.

30. 'Über Modulation in der reinen Instrumentalmusik und im Drama. Grundverschiedenheit. Schnelle und freie Übergänge sind hier oft so nothwendig als dort unstatthaft, wegen der fehlenden Motive'. This fragment appears in Wagner's *Tristan* Sketchbook; quoted and trans. in Carolyn Abbate, 'Wagner, "On Modulation", and *Tristan*', in *Cambridge Opera Journal*, 1 (1989), p. 37.

31. 'Über die Anwendung der Musik auf das Drama', in *Bayreuther Blätter*, November 1879; rpt. in *Richard Wagners gesammelte Schriften*, ed. Julius Kapp (Leipzig: Hesse & Becker Verlag, n.d.), vol. 13, p. 284. The English translation is in *Richard Wagner's Prose Works*, ed. and trans. William Ashton-Ellis (London: Routledge and Kegan Paul, 1897), vol. 6, pp. 173–9.

32. Wagner, 'Über die Anwendung', p. 295.

33. Klaus Kropfinger, *Wagner and Beethoven: Richard Wagner's Reception of Beethoven*, trans. Peter Palmer (Cambridge: Cambridge University Press, 1991), p. 253.

34. Thomas Grey, *Wagner's Musical Prose* (Cambridge: Cambridge University Press, 1995), p. 313.
35. Bruckner not only knew Liszt personally (he very nearly dedicated his Second Symphony to Liszt), but studied several of Liszt's compositions, including the *Faust-Symphonie* and *Tasso*; see Constantin Floros, *Brahms und Bruckner: Studien zur musikalischen Exegetik* (Wiesbaden: Breitkopf und Härtel, 1980), pp. 158–60.
36. August Göllerich and Max Auer suggested that the primary theme may derive from the Austrian Army's bugle call for retreat, with which it bears some melodic similarity. In late summer 1879, shortly before he started sketching the Sixth Symphony, Bruckner improvised on the organ at St Florian before a gathering of military officers; Bruckner reported that he intended to use a 'militärisches Thema … "die Retraite"'; see Göllerich and Auer, *Anton Bruckner: eine Lebens- und Schaffens-Bild*, 4 vols. in 9 parts (Regensburg: Gustav Bosse Verlag, 1922–37) , vol. 2, part 1, p. 270 and vol. 4, part 1, pp. 674–5. Rudolf Stephan also discussed this possibility and published a facsimile of the pertinent bugle call; see 'In und Jenseits der Tradition: zur Sechsten Symphonie Anton Bruckners', in *Österreichische Musikzeitschrift*, 51 (1996), p. 28. Although it has not been widely remarked, the opening gesture of the Sixth Symphony is also akin to a theme that appears prominently in all four versions (1874, 1878, 1880 and 1888) of the Finale of the Fourth Symphony; see m. 105ff of the familiar 1880 version, for example.

8 The Adagio of the Sixth Symphony and the anticipatory tonic recapitulation in Bruckner, Brahms and Dvořák

Timothy L. Jackson

Carl Hruby reports Bruckner saying that 'What I mean is that Hanslick understands Brahms about as much as he understands Wagner, me or anyone else'.[1] This pointed remark is highly informative since it indicates that Bruckner was sufficiently knowledgeable regarding Brahms's music to recognize how little that critic – although putatively Brahms's apologist – understood Brahms's work on a technical level. Furthermore, one may extrapolate from Bruckner's observation that Hanslick's lack of grounding prevented him from recognizing those technical features which Brahms, Wagner, and Bruckner had mastered and held in common. Bruckner's deferential attitude towards Brahms suggests that, as a *technician*, there was much to be admired in Brahms. Furthermore, the fact that Brahms had edited the Mozart Requiem (1877) and the Schubert Symphonies (1884–5) for Breitkopf und Härtel – works which Bruckner revered – might also have raised him in Bruckner's esteem.

Hans Redlich has proposed that Brahms was inspired to compose his own first string Quintet in F major by Bruckner's Quintet in the same key. Whether or not this was the case, the analysis of the music of Bruckner and Brahms – especially of those works dating from the early 1880s – reveals striking technical similarities. For example, the Finale of Bruckner's Quintet (1878–9) is structured over a large-scale auxiliary cadence leading from C as dominant of F minor to F major; similarly, the Finale of Brahms's Third Symphony, completed in 1883, is a colossal auxiliary cadence in which C, as dominant of F minor, definitively resolves to F major only at the end of the movement.[2] Since it is unlikely that Brahms was familiar with the Bruckner Quintet before its publication in 1884, these – and other – remarkable correspondences probably result less from direct mutual influence than from shared circumstances; clearly, both composers were working within the Viennese tradition – and thinking along similar lines.

Hruby also preserves Bruckner's important comments regarding his own formal-harmonic innovations, and their relationship to that Viennese tradition. Following a performance of Beethoven's *Eroica*, a symphony which Bruckner revered and had studied closely (especially its metrical and orchestral voice leading aspects), Hruby recalls:

> After he had spent a while sunk in thought, his gaze as it were turned inwards, he suddenly broke the silence: 'I think, if Beethoven were still alive today, and I went to him, showed him my Seventh Symphony and said to him, "Don't you think, Herr von Beethoven, that the Seventh isn't as bad as certain people make it out to be – those people who make an example of it and portray me as an idiot" – then, maybe, Beethoven might take me by the hand and say, "My dear Bruckner, don't bother yourself about it. It was no better for me, and the same gentlemen who use me as a stick to beat you with still don't really understand my last quartets, however much they may pretend to."'[3]

After apologizing to Beethoven's shade for 'going beyond' him in terms of form, Bruckner asserts that 'I've always said that a true artist can work out his own form and then stick to it'. These comments document not only Bruckner's assimilation of the formal innovations of the late-Beethoven quartets, but reveal that he consciously 'went beyond' them. Here we may speculate that both Brahms's and Bruckner's more or less contemporary innovations in design-structural counterpoint were inspired by late Beethoven – and also by Schubert. In this study, I shall examine a particular type of sonata form in which a strongly emphasized tonic supports a recapitulation of the opening (i.e. first group) material at the beginning of the development; therefore this sonata form might be said to feature an 'anticipatory tonic recapitulation'. To my knowledge, this type of sonata first occurs in Brahms's chamber music in the 1860s, and was then employed by Brahms, Bruckner, and Dvořák in the 1880s in a symphonic context.

The Adagio of Bruckner's Sixth Symphony (1881), which is exceptional among Bruckner's slow movements for its use of sonata – rather than rondo – form, also features a clearly marked return to the tonic in the development (m. 77ff.).[4] Although this strongly emphasized tonic in the development supports a *transformation* of the opening theme rather than a literal restatement, I shall propose that it may be considered an 'anticipatory tonic recapitulation'. To contextualize Bruckner's use of this special variant of sonata form, I shall present additional examples of the anticipatory tonic recapitulation, all from the second half of the nineteenth century: the first movement of Brahms's Piano Quartet in G minor, Op. 25 (1861), the Finale of the Piano Quartet in A major, Op. 26 (1862), the *Allegro giocoso* of the Fourth Symphony (1885), and the first movement of Dvořák's Eighth Symphony, Op. 88 (1889). Additionally, I shall discuss the role of the 'anticipatory tonic' in the Sixth Symphony's outer movements.

As is well known, in the laconic section on sonata form in *Free Composition* Schenker does not present an exhaustive inventory of design-structure counterpoints in the sonata, a deficiency which Oster sought to address in his notes and addendum.[5] Recently, analysts have begun to augment Schenker's and Oster's published accounts of sonata form. While David Beach has studied subdominant recapitulations in Schubert, Carl Schachter's analysis of the ♭III recapitulation in the Finale of Schubert's Ninth Symphony sheds further light on the problem of Schubert's off-tonic recapitulations. More recently, this writer has investigated the structural and dramatic aspects of the 'reversed recapitulation' (whereby the second group is recapitulated before the first) and the 'partially reversed' recapitulation.[6]

In a valuable pair of articles, Jack Adrian elucidated various meanings of the tonic at the beginning of the development.[7] His study of 'The Function of the Apparent Tonic at the Beginning of Development Sections' demonstrated that this tonic may be 'apparent' rather than 'real' because it does not represent the tonic scale step or *Stufe*; while his article on 'The Ternary-Sonata Form' investigated the converse situation where this tonic is 'real'.[8] In the first case, the apparent tonic is absorbed into the larger harmonic progression in a number of ways: it may be reconstrued as an applied chord, or it may arise from III through a 5–6 exchange. In the second case, when the tonic initiating the development is real, Adrian identifies '*ternary* sonata form' because the structural tonic returns *three* times in the course of the sonata: at the opening, and the beginnings of the development and recapitulation. Therefore, Adrian's ternary sonata form contains *three*, rather than the customary two 'structural downbeats' as defined by Robert Morgan.[9] According to Adrian, the small repertoire of ternary sonatas includes the first movements of Brahms's Violin Sonata in G major Op. 78 (1878–79), Piano Trio in C major Op. 87 (1880), Fourth Symphony Op. 98 (1884–5), and Clarinet Sonata Op. 120, No. 2 (1894).[10]

At first blush, Adrian's description of ternary sonata form seems to suggest *two* interruptions in the background (Ex. 8.1a, p. 209), a structural bar form (AAB). But Adrian does not posit ternary structure at the deepest level; rather, he preserves binary structure in the background by assigning greater structural weight to the *second* interruption terminating the development (Ex. 8.1b). He observes that 'the mere presence of the development section leading to the articulation of a dominant followed by a recapitulation forces one to attribute greater structural importance to this dominant than to that of the second subject'.[11] Thus, in Adrian's model, the dominant supporting the second subject functions as a divider, caught within the prolongation of tonic harmony, which is continued by the tonic at the beginning of the development.

But what about the other interpretative possibility displayed in Ex. 8.1c? In this model, the first interruption supported by dominant harmony in the second group is fundamental. The initial dominant functions as a structural harmony at the most background level; this dominant is regained at the end of the development. The tonic return of the opening material at the outset of the

Ex. 8.1   (a) Background of ternary sonata form with two equally weighted interruptions;
(b) Background of ternary sonata form with the first interruption subordinate to the
second; (c) Background of ternary sonata form with the second interruption subordinate
to the first

(a)

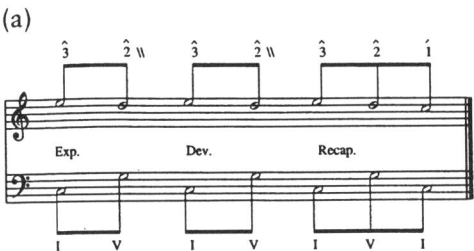

(b)

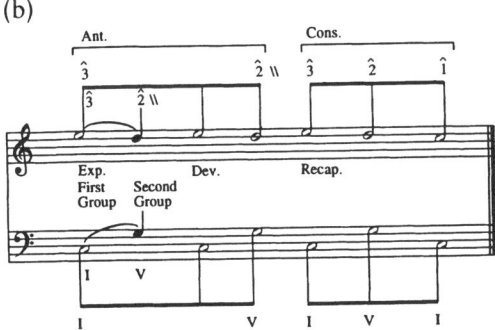

(c)

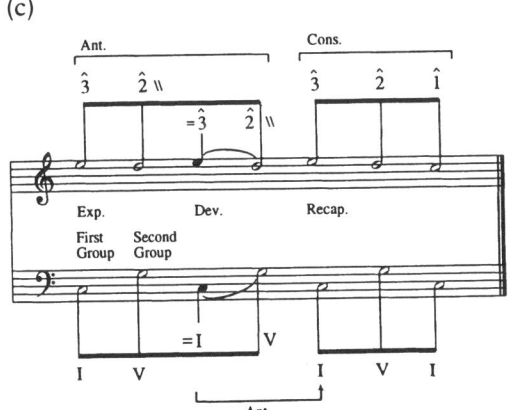

development is understood to *anticipate* the tonic reprise *without* prolonging the
background tonic. Neither fish nor fowl, this anticipatory tonic is not 'apparent'
because it is independent from a more background harmony; and it is also 'less-
than-real' since it does not continue the prolongation of the initial tonic, which
has been relinquished.

210 Perspectives on Anton Bruckner

In various analyses of pieces featuring two interruptions, Schenker did not subordinate one interruption to another. From his analysis of Brahms's Fourth Symphony, third movement, discussed below (Ex. 8.4b, p. 215), it would appear that he did not consider that possibility. But, in my view, Adrian convincingly posits the subordination of one interruption; perhaps the binary structure of interruption form is so deeply ingrained in our psyches that we naturally assimilate two interruptions within a single interrupted antecedent–consequent structure. In both possible interpretations (Exx. 8.1b, c), the exposition and development interruptions are subsumed within the antecedent, and the recapitulation within the consequent.

But assuming the subordination of one interruption by another, which is the 'most background' (i.e. the most fundamental)? Is it the first interruption (at the beginning of the second group, Ex. 8.1c) or the second (at the end of the development, Ex. 8.1b)? In the discussion of middleground interruption in *Free Composition*, Schenker asserts that 'the initial succession $\hat{3}$–$\hat{2}$ gives the impression that it is the first attempt at the complete fundamental line'.[12] On principle, then – had he considered this particular issue – Schenker might have been inclined to hear the first interruption as fundamental with all further interruptions subservient to the initial one. Of course, Schenker's assertion contradicts Adrian's perception of the first interruption as *less* significant than the second.

It is dangerous to determine structural priorities in the abstract; rather, the relative weight of the two interruptions depends upon the subtleties in the interaction of design and structure in a given piece. If the tonic recapitulation at the beginning of the development is perceived as 'anticipatory' in nature (as in the examples presented in this chapter), the initial interruption at the second group may be construed as fundamental; but if the tonic recapitulation at the outset of the development is heard as a 'real' return at the deepest structural level (as in Adrian's examples), then the background interruption may be postponed until the end of the development.

*   *   *

The distinction between 'design' and 'structure', first made by Felix Salzer, will be assumed throughout the present discussion.[13] Additionally, the terms 'exposition space', 'development space', and 'recapitulation space' will be used to refer to the three large durational units of sonata form.[14] All of the Brahms pieces to be discussed feature a 'double' exposition of the initial material or first subject, which is *restated* within the first group (Op. 25, I, m. 1 = m. 27; Op. 26, IV, m. 1 = m. 17; Op. 98, III, m. 1 = m. 35). In Op. 98, the outer voices are inverted so that the melody is shifted into the bass, but the principle of binary presentation of the material (i.e. of 'double exposition') still applies. This 'double exposition' aspect is then preserved in the course of the sonata by recapitulating the first statement at the beginning of the development space and the second at the outset of the recapitulation space. Thus, in these sonatas, the *design* recapitulation could be said to begin in development space and extend into recapitulation space.

In Brahms's G minor Piano Quartet, the development space comprises mm. 160–264, and recapitulation space mm. 265–363 (Ex. 8.2). Elements of the

Ex. 8.2   Brahms, Piano Quartet in G minor, Op. 25, first movement, middleground

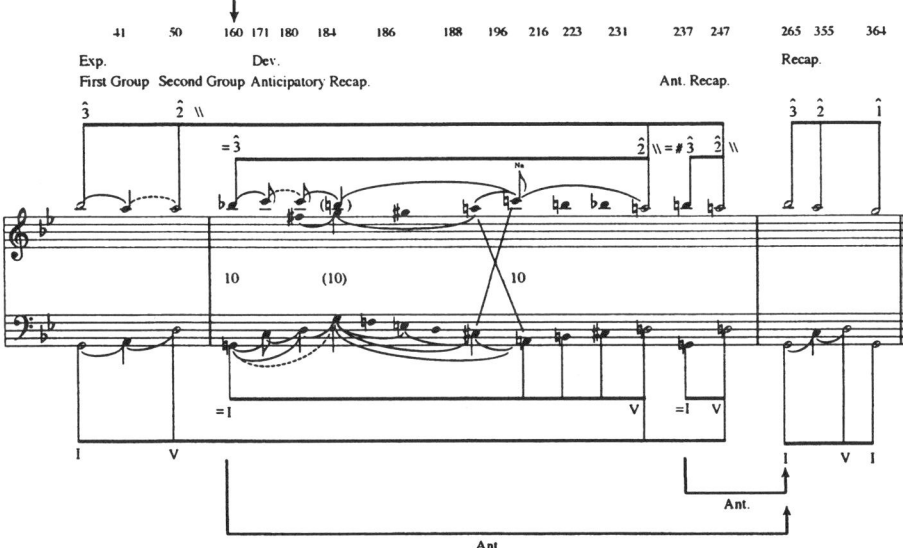

design recapitulation are stretched out across both the development and recapitulation spaces as follows: mm. 161–76 = 1–20, mm. 237–46 = 11–20, mm. 259–79 = 21–41, mm. 281–303 = 79–98, and mm. 316–42 = 113–40. Because of the exact replication of mm. 1–10 by mm. 161–69, Robert Pascall and David Nivans interpret m. 160 as the beginning of the recapitulation in a 'binary sonata form'.[15] Pascall identifies the form as 'a sonata with displaced development', whereby 'the development section has been moved into the recapitulation (or the recapitulation has been split into two unequal parts and the first of these has been displaced, if one so prefers)'. Most scholars regard the recapitulation as beginning in m. 237, while Edwin Evans and David Fenske locate it later in m. 265.[16] Pinpointing the definitive tonic return marking the beginning of the recapitulation is problematic because of the tonic returns of opening material in m. 160ff. and 237ff. Nivans interprets these tonics as structural (his Exx. 12, 18, and 19). Without committing himself with regard to m. 160, Webster reads the tonic major in m. 237 as structural (his Ex. 3); Rothstein, on the other hand, asserts that 'the real tonic is delayed until m. 265'.

In this sonata, the design and the tonal recapitulations are clearly distinct: the *design* recapitulation is initiated in m. 160, interrupted by the main body of the development, and then resumed in m. 237 (Pascall), while the *tonal* recapitulation, which supports a reprise of the second statement of the initial idea, is delayed until m. 265 (Rothstein). I explain the tonic return of the initial material in m. 160 as 'anticipatory' since it anticipates the 'real' tonic recapitulation in m. 265 (Ex. 8.2). Indeed, I posit that *both* the minor and major tonics in m. 160ff. and 237ff. are anticipatory in nature, adumbrating the definitive return of the structural tonic supporting the *Kopfton* in m. 265. According to my interpretation, mm. 237–64 recompose the 'I–V' structure of the main body of the development (mm. 161–236) in diminution and with mixture. As shown in Ex. 8.2, the bass in the development is concerned with filling in the ascending fifth G–D, as the top voice works out the upper neighbour C within the chromatic line B♭–B–C–B–B♭–A.

Brahms again employs the anticipatory tonic reprise at the beginning of the development space (m. 206ff., Ex. 8.3, p. 213) in the Finale of his A major Piano Quartet. Since the opening material is stated in the tonic at the outset of the development, the composer avoids the potential monotony of yet another, literal restatement at the beginning of the reprise by varying m. 17ff. in the tonic minor (m. 243ff.). Example 8.3 indicates that this A minor reprise is prepared by mixture in the exposition's inner voice interruption $\hat{5}$–$\hat{4}$–$♭\hat{3}$–$\hat{2}$ (E–D–C–B). Through the enharmonic association of C with B♯ (marked with asterisks in the example), $♭\hat{3}$ is reincarnated as $♯\hat{2}$ in the A major anticipatory reprise at the beginning of the development space (m. 205ff.).

My last example from Brahms, the *Allegro giocoso* of the Fourth Symphony, may be considered a sonata form with an anticipatory tonic recapitulation, as delineated in the following scheme:

> Exposition, mm. 1–88
>> First Group, mm. 1–50
>> Second Group, mm. 51–88
> Development, mm. 89–198
>> *Anticipatory tonic recapitulation, mm. 89–113 = mm. 1–10*
> Recapitulation, mm. 199–end
>> First Group, mm. 199–246 = mm. 10–50
>> Second Group, mm. 247–end

Notice that Schenker, in an unpublished, rather hastily notated graph of the *Allegro giocoso* of Brahms's Fourth Symphony preserved in the Oster Collection (Exx. 8.4b and e, Plate 7) does not weigh the tonic arrivals and interruptions relative to one another. In other words, Schenker does not consider how the apparently *tripartite* interruption structure ($\hat{3}$–$\hat{2}$, $\hat{3}$–$\hat{2}$, $\hat{3}$–[$\hat{4}$–$\hat{3}$–] $\hat{2}$–$\hat{1}$) might be absorbed within a binary interrupted background (the issue raised the discussion of Ex. 8.1). Perhaps this is because Schenker's analysis predates his own formal definition of 'interruption' in *Free Composition*, although the background graphs shown in Ex. 8.4b and e already suggest the technique.

As sometimes happens in the unpublished graphs, Schenker vacillates between two quite different interpretations of the development section. In Ex. 8.4b, the

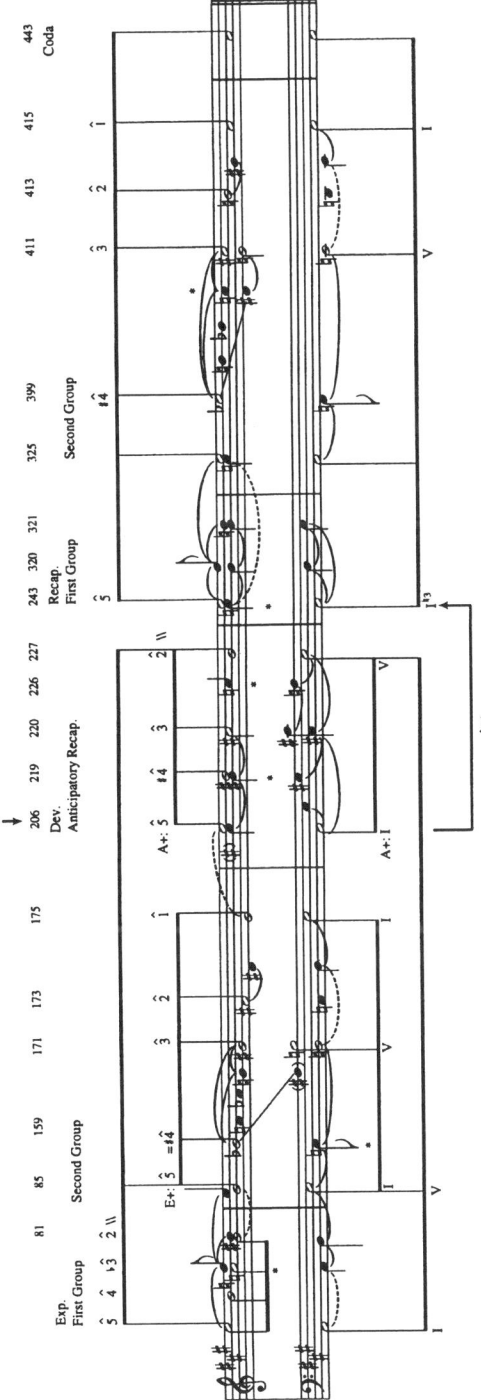

Ex. 8.3   Brahms, Piano Quartet in A major, Op. 26, Finale, middleground

fundamental harmonies or *Stufen* are clearly labelled I–III♯³–V (C–E–G), while in Ex. 8.4e, they are I–VI–II⁶–V (C–A–F–G) with E interpolated between F and G.[17] In my view, Schenker's second, possibly later reading is to be preferred because it accords the A greater structural weight than the E, which I believe is to be construed as the upper fifth of A rather than the upper third of C (in other words, the E functions as V/A rather than as III♯³/C).[18] Furthermore, the second reading reveals a magnificent enlargement in the bass of the opening melody over the course of the development and recapitulation (indicated with asterisks in Ex. 8.4a and c) – a motivic connection not pointed out by Schenker.

It is significant that, in this example, the role of the anticipatory tonic recapitulation is paradoxically dualistic: the tonic reprise at the beginning of the development is *both* 'anticipatory' *and* 'real'. In other words, the music suggests both of the scenarios shown in Ex. 8.1 (ex. 8.4c = Ex. 8.1c and Ex. 8.4d = 8.1b). How does Brahms create this remarkable paradox?

In the discussion of 'interruption' in *Free Composition*, one of Schenker's primary concerns is to distinguish an *interrupting* $\hat{2}$, supported by an interrupting dominant, from $\hat{2}$ as a *passing* tone placed over a dividing dominant. But, in the *Allegro giocoso*, Brahms deliberately obscures this fundamental distinction in the following way. By restating the Allegro's opening music (mm. 1–7) at the beginning of the development and rejoining its continuation (m. 10ff.) at the end of the development (m. 192ff.), the music suggests – paradoxically – that the *same* dominant chord (m. 10 = m. 192), which initially acts as a divider supporting a passing $\hat{2}$, is *both* a structural dominant supporting an interrupting $\hat{2}$ (Ex. 8.4c) *and* a dividing dominant supporting a large-scale passing $\hat{2}$. In other words, the foreground divider supporting the passing 2 in m. 10 is 'transferred' into the background in m. 192 (Ex. 8.4d). According to the first interpretation, then (Ex. 8.4c), the tonic return in m. 89 is 'anticipatory' in nature, anticipating the definitive tonic return in m. 224, while in the second interpretation the tonic return in m. 89 is 'real' with the entire development inserted into a massive expansion of the initial *Anstieg* (mm. 1–39 are enlarged in mm. 89–232). Although at odds with 'classical'

Ex. 8. 4   (a) Brahms, Fourth Symphony, third movement, first theme, mm. 1–4b; (b) Brahms, Fourth Symphony, third movement, transcription of Schenker's middleground sketch; (c) Brahms, Fourth Symphony, third movement, middleground with the second interruption subordinate to the first (compare with Ex. 8.1c); (d) Brahms, Fourth Symphony, third movement, second interruption eliminated; (e) Brahms, Fourth Symphony, third movement, transcription of Schenker's revised reading of the middleground

(a)

Ex. 8.4 continued

(b)

(c)

215

Ex. 8.4 continued

(d)

216

Ex. 8.4 concluded

(e)

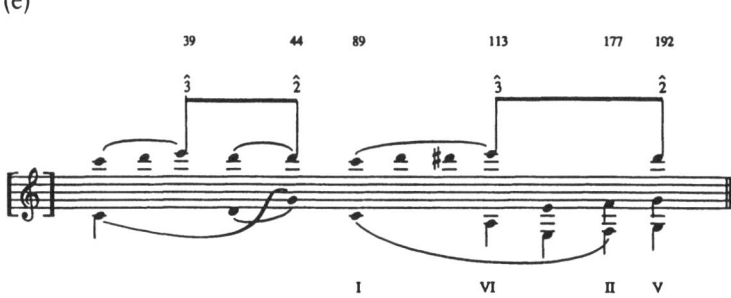

clarity, Brahms reveled in paradoxes of this nature; as I have suggested in my study of the Brahms Haydn Variations Op. 56a–b', he was fascinated by this kind of paradoxical dualism.[19]

In the first movement of Dvořák's Eighth Symphony, the initial sixteen-measure motto theme recurs twice (mm. 127–42 and 219–34), the tonic supporting the anticipatory recapitulation at the beginning of the development space (Ex. 8.5b, p. 218). While the first tonic return at the beginning of the development space (m. 127ff.) can be understood to anticipate the second in the reprise, the 'anticipation' is free rather than literal. Like Brahms (who probably served as a model), Dvořák wishes to avoid the monotony of three identical statements of the opening music in the tonic; therefore, the third presentation of the motto, i.e. the definitive design recapitulation, occurs within development space over the extended dominant pedal. Now design and structure are 'out of phase': while the second return in m. 219 initiates the *design* recapitulation at the end of development space, the *tonal* recapitulation is delayed until m. 235. In spite of its relative brevity, I construe the dominant at the end of the exposition (mm. 121–6) as a background interrupting dominant; perhaps the considerable extension of the dominant at the end of the development (mm. 219–34) compensates for this earlier dominant's brevity.

Example 8.5 proposes that the large-scale structure grows organically out of the triadic theme first presented by the flute in m. 16ff. (motive 'x' in Ex. 8.5a). Thus, through the course of the exposition, the bass presents a massive enlargement of 'x' (Ex. 8.5b); indeed, this motivic enlargement is responsible for the motion to III in the second group yielding G–(F♯–)B–D, an unusual procedure for a *major* mode sonata exposition. The graph suggests that Dvořák's anticipatory tonic recapitulation at the beginning of the development is connected with the composer's desire to project the same G–(F♯)–B–D motivic bass progression over the course of the development ('x' in Ex. 8.5b). Observe that even the neighbor note motive E–D of the flute theme (motive 'y' in Ex. 8.5a) is replicated in enlargement in the development ('y' in Ex. 8.5b)!

* * *

Ex. 8.5 (a) Dvořák, Eighth Symphony, first movement, triadic theme; (b) Dvořák, Eighth Symphony, first movement, triadic theme in the bass creates anticipatory tonic recapitulation

(a)

(b)

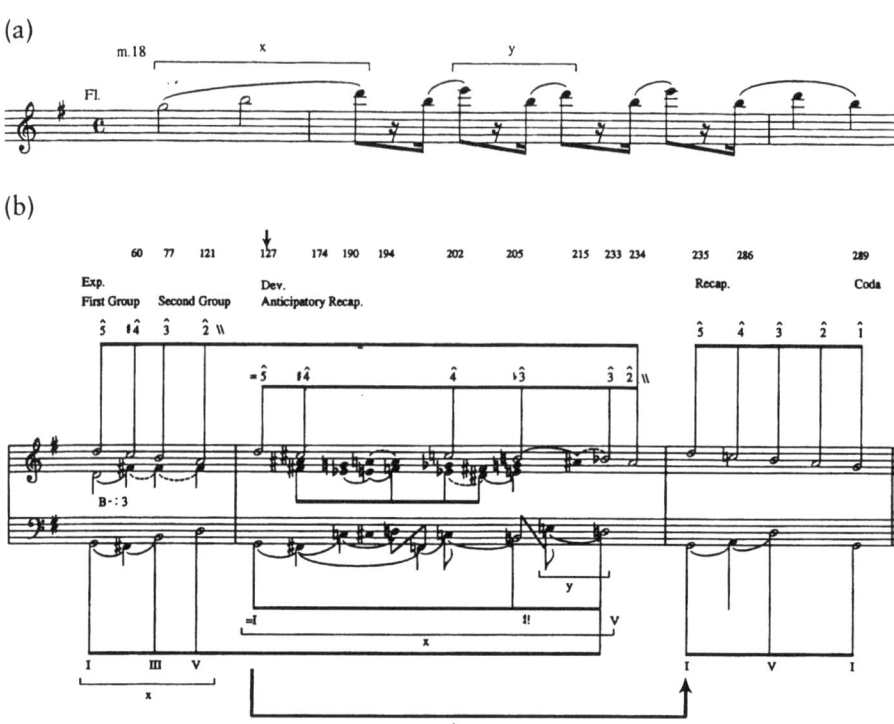

In the course of revising his sonata forms to make them more 'compact' – a strategy reflecting Bruckner's sensitivity to 'sophisticated' Viennese criticism and influences (especially Brahms's) – Bruckner simultaneously achieved a more complicated interaction of form and structure. In the first versions of the symphonies up to and including the Fifth (1876), the outer movements conform to the sonata paradigm rather strictly, featuring regular recapitulations, at least in terms of design; but beginning in approximately 1876, Bruckner began to handle sonata form in highly innovative ways, upsetting the traditional paradigm. In the reversed recapitulations of the Finales of the String Quintet and Seventh Symphony and the truncated reprises in the final revisions of the Third and Fourth Symphonies, the definitive tonic return and reprise of the opening theme are held in abeyance until the end of the Finale (and thus the work as a whole). However, if the *definitive* return is to be 'saved' – strategically reserved – then it may be 'anticipated' in various ways earlier in the sonata form.

'Tonic-anticipation' becomes a central compositional idea – one might say, 'narrative theme' – in Bruckner's Sixth Symphony. In the outer movements and in the Scherzo, Bruckner anticipates the tonic while deferring its definitive arrival until late in each of these movements.[20] To contextualize the anticipatory tonic in the Adagio within the symphony as a whole, let us first consider the 'narrative discourse' of 'tonic anticipation' in the other movements.

As in a number of Bruckner's symphonies, the first movement's large-scale harmonic structure becomes paradigmatic for the last movement, thereby relating the outer movements structurally as well as thematically: in both movements, the overall strategy is to revalue the putative tonic arrival at the beginning of the recapitulation.[21] As shown in Ex. 8.6a, p. 220, the descending fifth motto 'm' from the opening is restated sequentially as B♭–E♭ (mm. 189–195) and E♭–A♭ = G♯ (mm. 195–207) at the beginning of the recapitulation. It is noteworthy that the design recapitulation (i.e. the recapitulation of the first group's design) begins on E♭ in m. 195 *before* the tonal recapitulation is secured on A in m. 209 (thus, design can be said to 'outpace' or 'anticipate' structure). This premature design recapitulation both emphasizes the arrival on E♭ and undermines the sense of tonic arrival in m. 209; indeed, this putative tonic can be construed both as an 'anticipatory' tonic and dominant of the subdominant (m. 285). Recomposed as a V–III–I arpeggiation – in D rather than A – 'm' is then attenuated over the course of the recapitulation. If the tonic at the beginning of the coda (m. 309) is interpreted as both 'anticipatory' and the dominant of the subdominant, the coda essentially recomposes the recapitulation's A–F♯–D arpeggiation (i.e. 'm'). Thus, the 'tonics' in the recapitulation and coda (m. 209ff. and 309ff.) may be heard to 'anticipate' the definitive tonic epiphany at the end of the coda (m. 361ff., see the arrows in Ex. 8.6a).

This 'narrative discourse' of 'tonic-anticipation' is recomposed in the Finale. Here, the harmony moves from the dominant E at the end of the exposition through the raised mediant C♯ at the climax of the development (m. 233ff.) to the putative tonic A (m. 245ff.) at the beginning of the recapitulation (Ex. 8.6b, p. 221). But, in view of the manner in which the recapitulation ultimately cadences strongly on F major (the submediant rather than the tonic, m. 371), this A major can be retrospectively re-interpreted both as an 'anticipatory' tonic and the major mediant (III♯) of F.[22] In other words, the A chord as 'the-tonic-which-becomes-the-mediant' may be understood to 'anticipate' rather than realize the definitive tonic arrival (DTA, which is deferred to the end of the coda, see the arrow in Ex. 8.6b). Example 8.6c (p. 222) suggests that in the Scherzo, too, the putative arrival on the tonic A in m. 21 is 'anticipatory' in nature, the definitive tonic arrival being 'saved' until the Scherzo's conclusion (m. 101ff.).

The second, slow movement re-explores this compositionally thematicized idea of 'anticipation', but in a rather different way than the outer movements; in this Adagio in sonata form, Bruckner's intention is to anticipate the reprise's tonic harmony at the outset of the development (as in the previously cited examples from Brahms and Dvořák), rather than at the beginning of the reprise (as in the Sixth Symphony's flanking movements). Here, the potential redundancy of three tonic presentations of the opening material is avoided by transforming the initial theme in the development's 'anticipatory recapitulation' (mm. 77ff.).

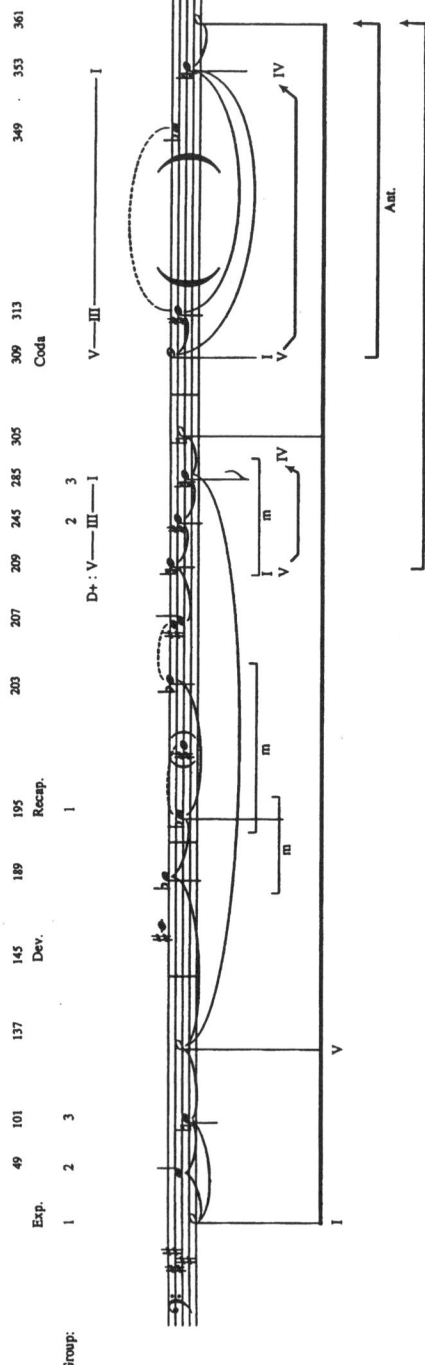

Ex. 8.6 (a) Bruckner, Sixth Symphony, first movement, anticipatory tonics in the recapitulation (m.209) and coda (m. 309); (b) Bruckner, Sixth Symphony, Finale, anticipatory tonics in the recapitulation (m. 245) and coda (m. 385); (c) Bruckner, Sixth Symphony, Scherzo, anticipatory tonic in the Scherzo (m. 21)

Ex. 8.6 continued

(b)

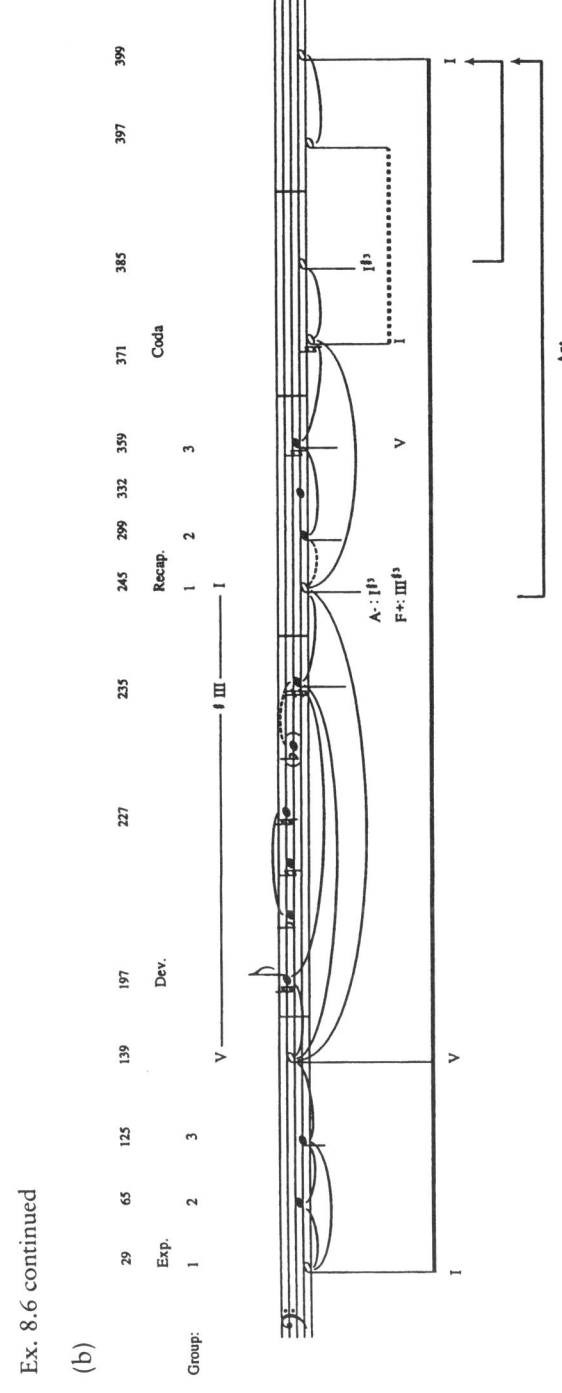

221

Ex. 8.6 concluded

(c)

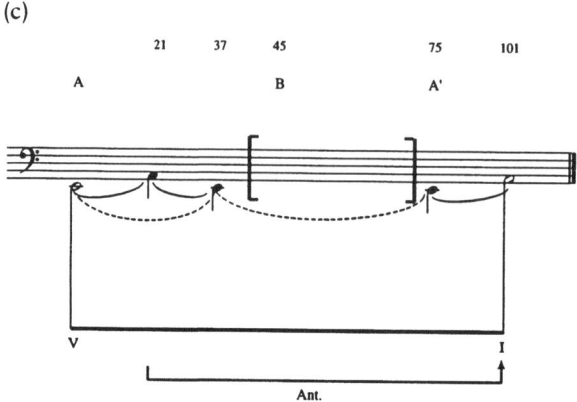

Let us clarify the Adagio's sonata form. In his expositions and recapitulations, Bruckner generally subdivides the exposition and recapitulation into *three* rather than two groups; the Adagio conforms to this basic formal pattern as follows:

> Exposition, mm. 1–68
>> First Group, mm. 1–24
>> Second Group, mm. 25–52
>> Third (Closing) Group, mm. 53–68 (funeral march)
>>> Transition, mm. 69–76
> Development, mm. 77–92
>> *Anticipatory Transformed Tonic Recapitulation, mm. 77–92* (allusion to *Liebestod*)
> Recapitulation, mm. 93–140
>> First Group, mm. 93–112
>> Second Group, mm. 113–32
>> Third (Closing) Group, mm. 133–40 (funeral march)
> Coda, mm. 141–end

If the slow movement of the Sixth Symphony is already exceptional in its use of sonata form, it displays additional striking features that have passed virtually without comment in the literature. These include: (1) the anticipatory tonic (F) major in the development; (2) the unusual appearance of the second subject in the exposition in the key of the leading tone, i.e. in E major, rather than in the customary dominant; (3) the funeral march character of the third group; and (4) the motivic reference to the *Liebestodmotiv* from *Tristan* in the development.[23]

While the anticipatory tonic in the development (m. 77ff.) supports a *transformation* rather than a literal return of the opening music (as was the case in some of the previously discussed examples), the principle of the anticipatory

Ex. 8.7   (a) Wagner, Tristan, *Liebestod*; (b) Bruckner, Sixth Symphony, Adagio, opening
theme, mm. 1–4; (c) Bruckner, Sixth Symphony, Adagio, mm. 77–80

(a)

(b)

(c)

tonic recapitulation remains the same. In the transformation, the violin part (Ex.
8.7c) extracts the *Liebestodmotiv* (Ex. 8.7a) from the opening theme (Ex. 8.7b),
preserving Wagner's original transposition of the motive up a minor third, while
the bass instruments present the opening theme's *Kopfmotiv* in inversion.

The *Anstieg* to the *Kopfton* a³ ($\hat{3}$, m. 39) is attenuated over the first and
second groups in the exposition.[24] Example 8.8a shows that A belongs with the
tonic F but is rhythmically shifted to occur later over the dominant C (Ex. 8.8b).
The ascending passing tone G is then chromatically displaced by G♯, which

Ex. 8.8   Bruckner, Sixth Symphony, Adagio, middleground parallelism of the first and
second group in the exposition and recapitulation

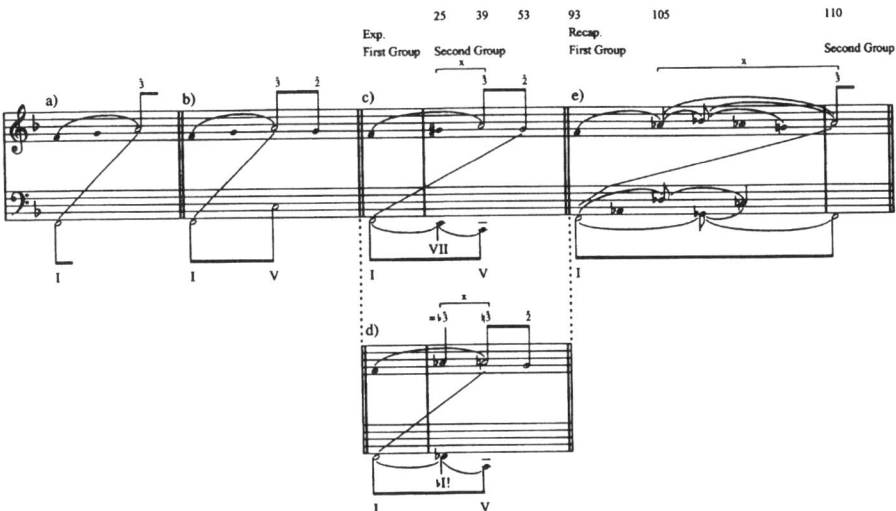

resolves as a leading tone to A. This chromatic leading tone motive G♯–A, labelled 'x' in Exx. 8.8–8.9, recurs throughout the Adagio in various guises. Supporting G♯ with an E major chord creates the unusual ♯VII (E+) prolongation in the second group. In the recapitulation, the first group suggests an *Anstieg* to a♭³ (♭3̂, m. 105, Ex. 8.8d), which initially 'eclipses' the true *Kopfton* a², but then ascends to it (♮3̂, m. 113) at the beginning of the second group, thereby presenting an enlargement of the initial *Anstieg* (compare Exx. 8.8c–d).

Example 8.9 displays the middleground voice-leading of the Adagio as a whole. In the course of the development, the bass articulates *two* ascents from C to F, the first arrival on the tonic F (m. 77) 'anticipating' the second (m. 93), as

Ex. 8.9   Bruckner, Sixth Symphony, Adagio, middleground

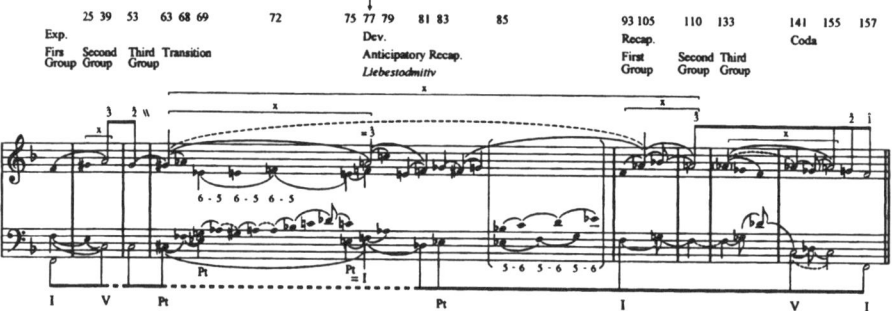

the upper voice works in nested enlargements of the chromatic motive 'x'. Placing the anticipatory tonic in the larger context reveals its deeper significance: supporting 3̂ in the development, this tonic anticipates the resolution of the second group's tonal displacement of ♭3̂ to 3̂ (see the brackets in Ex. 8.9). In other words, the larger tonal drama concerns the anticipation of the definitive 'return' of I supporting 3̂; this definitive 'return' – 'anticipated' in the development – is withheld until the recapitulation of the second group.

The anticipatory tonic supporting the *Kopfton*, in conjunction with the allusion to the *Liebestodmotiv*, might have deeper, programmatic significance. Renunciation – 'withdrawal' from the phenomenal world through death – is possibly represented by the *Kopfton's* 'eclipse' (i.e. the displacements of A by G♯/A♭).[25] Bruckner's subtle reference to the *Liebestodmotiv*, in conjunction with the anticipatory 'vision' of the *Kopfton*, might signify Isolde's redemptive perception of the noumenal; but witnessing the noumenal has mortal consequences, and perhaps the heroine's passing is mourned in the funereal third group.

Whatever the motivations – whether overtly programmatic or purely abstract in nature – Bruckner's use of the 'anticipatory tonic recapitulation' in the Sixth Symphony Adagio bespeaks a distinctly 1880s' Viennese sophistication in its special coordination of design and tonal structure. In light of the examples of the particular transformation of sonata form that I have identified in Bruckner,

Brahms, and Dvořák, it is clear that this technique was 'in the air' in Vienna and Prague. The similarly 'advanced' freedom in the treatment of the sonata paradigm in Brahms's Fourth Symphony would profoundly impress the young Richard Strauss, who assisted Hans von Bülow in preparing the Meiningen Orchestra for its 1885 première. In a enthusiastic report to his parents, Strauss praised the new symphony as 'a gigantic work, new and original in its greatness of conception and invention, [and] *its genius in the treatment of form …*' [my emphasis][26]. The remark is a harbinger of formal revolutions soon to come.

Notes

1. Quoted from *Bruckner Remembered*, ed. Stephen Johnson (London: Faber and Faber, 1998), p. 160.
2. For an analysis of these 'auxiliary cadence sonata forms', see Timothy L. Jackson, 'Observations on Crystallization and Entropy: Sexuality and Auxiliary Cadences in the Music of Jean Sibelius and Other Composers', in *Sibelius Studies*, ed. Timothy L. Jackson and Veijo Murtomäki (Cambridge: Cambridge University Press 2000), pp. 175–273.
3. *Bruckner Remembered*, p. 160.
4. The Adagio of the Sixth Symphony presents a striking exception to the rule; indeed, this Adagio is the only slow movement in Bruckner's entire symphonic output to exhibit sonata form. Beginning with the Second Symphony in C minor (1871), Bruckner generally adhered to five-part rondo form in his slow movements: $A^1B^1A^2B^2A^3$+Coda. The five-part $A^1B^1A^2B^2A^3$+Coda form is an extension of the three-part A^1BA^2+Coda *Lied* form realized in increasingly complex ways in Bruckner's Symphonies "00" (1863), I (1865–66), and "0" (1869). The composing manuscript of the Second Symphony's Andante (1870–1, Wn Mus. Hs. 19.474) reveals that it was initially conceived in A^1BA^2+Coda form and that the climactic third cycle was added later.
5. Heinrich Schenker, *Der freie Satz. Neue musikalische Theorien und Phantasien* (Vienna: Universal Edition, 1935). Trans. by Ernst Oster, *Free Composition* (New York: Longman 1979), pp. 133–40.
6. David Beach, 'Schubert's Experiments with Sonata Form: Formal-Tonal Design versus Underlying Structure', in *Music Theory Spectrum*, 15 (1993): 1–18. Carl Schachter, 'Mozart's Last and Beethoven's First: Echoes of K. 551 in the First Movement of Opus 21', in *Mozart Studies*, ed. Cliff Eisen (Oxford: Clarendon Press, 1991), pp. 227–51. Timothy L. Jackson, 'The Tragic Reversed Recapitulation in the German Classical Tradition', in *Journal of Music Theory*, 40 (1996), pp. 23–72; 'The Finale of Bruckner's Seventh Symphony and Tragic Reversed Sonata Form', in *Bruckner Studies*, eds. Timothy L. Jackson and Paul Hawkshaw (Cambridge: Cambridge University Press, 1996), pp. 140–208; *Tchaikovsky's Sixth Symphony* (Cambridge: Cambridge University Press, 1999).
7. Jack Adrian, 'The Function of the Apparent Tonic at the Beginning of Development Sections', in *Intégral*, 5 (1990), pp. 1–53; 'The Ternary-Sonata Form', in *Journal of Music Theory*, 34 (1990), pp. 57–80.
8. The distinction between 'real' and 'apparent' tonics – an analytical issue of central importance – has been discussed rather widely in the recent Schenkerian literature.
9. Robert Morgan, 'The Delayed Structural Downbeat and its Effect on the Tonal and Rhythmic Structure of Sonata Form' (Ph.D. diss., Princeton University, 1969).
10. The first movement of Brahms's Fourth Symphony articulates the final tonic at the

beginning of the coda rather than at the outset of the recapitulation (see Jackson, 'The Tragic Reversed Recapitulation', pp. 54–60).

11. 'The Ternary Sonata Form', pp. 76–7.
12. Schenker, *Free Composition*, p. 36.
13. For a recent discussion of 'design' and 'structure' see also Beach, 'Schubert's Experiments', pp. 1–18.
14. For this use of the term 'space', see James Hepokoski, *Sibelius: Symphony No. 5* (Cambridge: Cambridge University Press, 1993); 'Fiery-Pused Libertine or Domestic Hero? Strauss's *Don Juan* Revisited', in *Richard Strauss. New Perspectives on the Composer and His Work*, ed. Bryan Gilliam (Durham: Duke University Press), pp. 135–76.
15. Robert Pascall, 'Some Special Uses of Sonata Form by Brahms', in *Soundings, 4* (1974), p. 59. David B. Nivans, 'Brahms and the Binary Sonata: A Structuralist Interpretation' (Ph. D. diss., University of California, Los Angeles, 1992), p. 89.
16. Daniel Gregory Mason, *The Chamber Music of Brahms* (New York: AMS, 1933, repr. 1970), p. 26; Ivor Keys, *Brahms Chamber Music* (Seattle: University of Washington Press, 1974), p. 14; James Webster, 'Schubert's Sonata Form and Brahms's First Maturity', in *19th-Century Music*, 2 (1974), pp. 18–35, *19th-Century Music*, 3 (1975), pp. 52–71, here p. 63; Walter Frisch, *Brahms and the Principle of Developing Variation* (Berkeley: University of California Press, 1984), p. 71; Michael Musgrave, *The Music of Brahms* (London, Boston and Henley: Routledge and Kegan Paul, 1985), p. 99; William Rothstein, Review of Walter Frisch, *Brahms and the Principle of Developing Variation, Journal of Music Theory*, 30 (1986), p. 287; Edwin Evans, *Handbook to the Chamber and Orchestral Music of Johannes Brahms*. Vols. 2–3 (New York: Burt Franklin (1912–1938) 1970); David Edward Fenske, 'Texture in the Chamber Music of Johannes Brahms' (Ph.D. diss., University of Wisconsin, 1973), p. 266.
17. Schenker's unpublished graphs are preserved in the Ernst Oster Collection in the New York Public Library, File 34, pp. 288–90.
18. Surely, the E chord in m. 112 functions as an applied dominant to A in m. 113, and is not the main harmony (III♮³), as indicated in Schenker's graph, Ex. 8.4c. In the quick graph (Ex. 8.4e), Schenker seems to correct this basic mistake.
19. For a discussion of paradox in Brahms, see Timothy L. Jackson, 'Diachronic Transformation in a Schenkerian Context. A Study of the Brahms Haydn Variations Op. 56a–b', in *Schenker Studies 2*, eds. Hedi Siegel and Carl Schachter (Cambridge: Cambridge University Press, 1999), pp. 239–75.
20. In my more recent work, I refer to the concept of the 'definitive tonic arrival' by its abbreviation 'DTA' (see Jackson, 'Observations of Crystallization and Entropy', *Sibelius Studies*).
21. Structural parallelism between the outer movements creates the 'super-sonata' effect across the symphony whereby the first movement occupies exposition space, the Finale recapitulation space, and the inner movements development space (for a discussion of 'super-sonata form', see Timothy L. Jackson, *Tchaikovsky, Sixth Symphony (Pathétique)* (Cambridge: Cambridge University Press, 1999), especially Chapter 3, 'Form and Large-scale Harmony', pp. 22–35. Notice that, in the first movement of Bruckner's Sixth Symphony, the whole tone lower-neighbour motive G–A prominent in the opening theme is enlarged to become the lower neighbour D–E (mm. 285–305, Ex. 8.6a).
22. The tonic A of m. 245 can be understood as the initial term of an internal auxiliary cadence in the key of the submediant (F major: III♮³ – V – I). Bruckner's model may have been the Finale of Beethoven's Seventh Symphony, which similarly 'devalues' its tonic as III♮3 of ♭VI in A major (for a discussion of this type of internal auxiliary cadence in the Beethoven, see Jackson, 'Observations on Crystallization and

Entropy', in *Sibelius Studies*, pp. 200–4).

23.   Tovey (1989, 265) observes a motion to the 'remote' key of E major, without probing further. As Floros (1984) observes, Bruckner alludes to the *Liebestodmotiv* in the Finale, mm. 81–2; Floros does not, however, point out the motivic reference to this motive in the Adagio.

24.   Notice that in Exx. 8.8 and 8.9, the actual registers are reduced to a single octave.

25.   For a discussion of the tonal symbolism of the 'phenomenal' and 'noumenal' in Wagner and Bruckner, see Timothy L. Jackson, 'Die Wagner'sche "Umarmungs"-Metapher bei Bruckner und Wagner', in *Bruckner-Problem, Beiheft der Archiv für Musikwissenschaft*, ed. Albrecht Riethmüller (Stuttgart: Franz Steiner Verlag, 1999), pp. 134–52.

26.   R. Larry Todd, 'Strauss before Liszt and Wagner', in *New Perspectives on Richard Strauss*, ed. by Bryan Gilliam, Duke University Press, 1992, p. 4.

9 Bruckner's free application of strict Sechterian theory with stimulation from Wagnerian sources: an assessment of the first movement of the Seventh Symphony

Graham H. Phipps

Sources for Bruckner's Synthesis

> In one way or another all chords are naturally related to one another, as are all men. Whether they make up a family, a nation, or a race is certainly not without interest; but it is not an essential question if we place it beside the idea of species, which gives perspectives other than those admitted by the special relationships.[1]

With these words, Arnold Schoenberg summarizes the effect of the generations of music theorists from the mid-eighteenth to late-nineteenth century whose work, culminating in the pedagogy of Simon Sechter, characterized harmonic practice entirely in terms of diatonic chord roots.[2] Sechter's formulations, given in the context of strict voice-leading considerations, insisted that:

> All fundamentals remain diatonic and only their members – i.e., their respective thirds, fifths, sevenths and ninths – may bear changes, according to which they are connected to the scale of the principal key through the scales of secondarily related keys.[3]

In his unpublished treatise, *Vom Canon*, Sechter demonstrated how broadly his concept of diatonic relationships could be applied.[4] In one of the canons in Sechter's treatise (Ex. 9.1), a series of VI–IV–II–V motions are connected by semitone so that each concluding V is reinterpreted as VI in a new key. As a

Ex. 9.1 Simon Sechter, *Vom Canon*, illustration of secondarily related scales. (a) Bass line with Sechter's indication of fundamentals; (b) Sechter's realization

(a)

(b)

Realization in Canon

result, in this canon the concept of secondarily related keys ('*Nebentonleiter*') brings into direct relationship the full range of all minor keys. If the notation of sharps and flats is taken literally, the range of related keys extends from the minor key of six sharps to that of five flats; application of enharmonic spellings – as, indeed, Sechter provides in the example – allows for a direct connection between diatonic harmonies in all possible keys.[5] Furthermore, it should be noted that for him tonic harmony need not be present in any key in order to establish its identity.[6]

As is well known, Anton Bruckner devoted six years of his professional life to intensive private study with Sechter; during this period, the master required his student to abstain from any free composition so that he might acquire the tools of harmonic training based upon strict voice-leading principles. Bruckner's own comment from his later years as a teacher, 'Observe gentlemen, that's the rule; naturally I do not write that way' ('*Segn's mein Herrn, dass ist die Regl, i schreib natirli not a so*'), has often been cited as evidence that Bruckner did not apply this strict training to his own composition. In conformity with this point of view, Heinrich Schenker asserted:

> Despite his many years of teaching, Bruckner did not recognize how countless new [events] can arise from the meaning of a rule that rest upon its inner meaning, although they may appear unrelated to it.[7]

Such statements notwithstanding, there is ample evidence that Bruckner did, in fact, both as teacher and as pedagogue, rely upon the harmonic essence of Sechter's strict rules of counterpoint as a basis for free composition. In this connection, Bruckner's student Friedrich Eckstein commented:

> For simple musical examples [such as those given in his lessons] it is to be observed that, according to Bruckner's precedent, the fundamental notes were always provided in unstemmed black note-heads under the bass line. Bruckner adhered strictly to this type of notation, not only with his students, even those who were quite advanced in counterpoint, but I have also frequently seen that, in his own scores as he was working with them, he both numbered the measures of the periods and notated the fundamental notes, either with such black note-heads or with the help of letters.[8]

Eckstein has also provided examples of 'free' chord connections from his studies with Bruckner.[9]

Hitherto, in the literature of music analysis, Sechter's harmonic precepts have been assessed only in terms of literal application of strict voice leading; they have not been accorded application in free composition. Unfortunately, the published record of Sechter's students and disciples, while demonstrating how Wagner's music may be explained in terms of Sechterian harmonic concepts, has limited such explanation to applications involving strict voice-leading.[10]

To find support for a broader interpretation of Sechter's premises one must look to the writings of Arnold Schoenberg. The quotation cited at the beginning of this essay summarizes Schoenberg's adaptation of Sechter's theory to the chromatic harmonic vocabulary of *fin de siècle* Vienna. The immediate context for Schoenberg's remark is his statement of need for a systematic means to identify the most far-reaching aspects of harmonic connection between indirectly-related chords (*Verbindungen*).[11] In his *Harmonielehre*, Schoenberg offers a set of guidelines drawn directly from the three essential concepts of Sechterian theory: (1) all chords are based upon diatonic roots; (2) chords with chromatic pitches as their spelled roots represent diatonic notes; and (3) all chord progressions are based upon third or fifth motions.[12] The third of these concepts includes the corollary premise that stepwise root motions comprise two motions with a suppressed interdominant.[13]

Schoenberg's guidelines permit today's music analyst to make application of Sechterian harmonic theory to the chromatic music of the late nineteenth century that can extend the observations made by Sechter's students and disciples beyond the limitations of strict voice leading. With the support of Schoenberg's guidelines, I shall demonstrate in this essay how the first movement of Bruckner's Seventh Symphony illustrates an appropriation of Sechter's precepts, extending the strict contrapuntal explanations of their origins to embrace free applications of their harmonic essence.

Before examining the Seventh Symphony, it is useful to observe that the first movements of the Fifth and Sixth Symphonies illustrate free treatment of the notion of secondarily related key applied as a means for double referencing the principal key. Thus, as examples, the principal keys of B flat major in the first movement of the Fifth Symphony and A major in the first movement of the Sixth Symphony are presented at the beginnings of their expositions in the context of natural submediant and major dominant of D minor, respectively; it is only at a later point in the two movements that these initial impressions are replaced and the beginning harmonies actually become tonics.

In his Seventh Symphony, Bruckner extends this line of harmonic thinking to encompass traditionally accepted modal and tonal attributes of the key of E major as the basis for a special *Trauerode* in honour of the composer whom he most idolized, Richard Wagner. This synthesis of modal and tonal qualities was in many respects the result of Bruckner's diverse musical interests and activities during the early 1880s. While his work on the Seventh Symphony was in progress, Bruckner was revising his E minor Mass – a work from the late 1860s that integrated archaic features from Renaissance polyphony with mid-nineteenth-century chromatic harmony.[14] During the same period, he maintained an almost obsessive interest in the music of Richard Wagner, attending at least one and very likely two performances of *Parsifal* at the time of its première in July 1882 at Bayreuth and presenting organ recitals that featured improvisations on themes from Wagner.[15] Hence, the very nature of his own musical activities provided a contextual basis for a grand synthesis of widely divergent musical sources ranging from the conservative elements of Renaissance polyphony and strict harmonic Sechterian pedagogy to the most progressive aspects of chromatic practice derived from the music of Richard Wagner.

Three Subjects in the Exposition

The effects of this synthesis are evident in the initial presentation of the first subject in the first movement of Bruckner's Seventh Symphony. In this setting, the composer establishes a norm of the nine-measure phrase. In this essay, the conclusion of the basic phrase is defined by its arrival at a cadence. From this perspective, there are two basic phrase types, the freestanding phrase, and the elided phrase. In addition, two subtypes of elided phrases may be identified:

(1) in which the cadence chord is prolonged; and (2) in which the cadence chord forms a conjunction with the following phrase. Throughout the movement, elided phrases will be shown to conform with four- and eight-measure groupings; freestanding phrases, on the other hand, will break this metric regularity. Accordingly, it is significant that the first phrase in Bruckner's Seventh Symphony is a freestanding nine-measure phrase.[16]

The first period is organized as a double presentation of a two-phrase idea presenting two contrasting paths to the dominant. In the first phrase, (Ex. 9.2)

Ex. 9.2   First subject, first phrase, mm. 1–11

the path is by means of directly related harmonies with motions by fifth involving tonic, dominant, and supertonic harmony plus the suggestion of the submediant borrowed from the parallel minor key. In this setting, one may ask: (1) is the c–e–g of m. 7 to be understood as a fundamental chord or, rather, as the initial element of an augmented-sixth harmony that joins a♯ with these pitches and thereby introduces a F♯ root representative ('*Stellvertreter*')?[17] and, (2) is the final B major chord to be understood as tonic or dominant? That is: Has the phrase actually modulated to the dominant key?

In the second phrase, (Ex. 9.3) within the same nine-measure durational

Ex. 9.3   First subject, second phrase, mm. 12–20

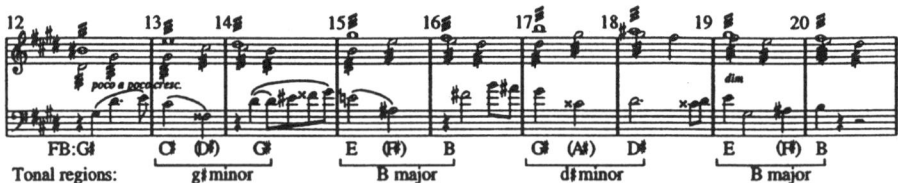

frame, the path to dominant harmony includes one indirectly related harmony introduced by means of a motive that sequences by upward thirds – from G♯ minor to B major to D♯ minor before the final descent to B major at m. 20.[18]

Since both phrases provide motion to the same tonal goal, they do not really constitute an antecedent/consequent pair. Yet, these two phrases provide a contrast of fifth motions (C, F♯ and B) with one of third motions (G♯–B–D♯) within identical durational spaces of nine measures.[19]

Bruckner's restatement of this phrase pair, mm. 25–51, is not a perfunctory one. Rather, it extends the tonal space of E major beyond its family of directly related keys. Whereas the melody of the first phrase is retained, its transfer in this setting to the soprano voice allows the new bass to clarify the ambiguities of the earlier presentation. The C major chord at m. 29 clearly achieves independent harmonic status;[20] the melodic a♯ (m. 30) is harmonized as a different type of F♯ *Stellvertreter*;[21] and the final cadence (m. 33) becomes V–I in the key of B major.

But it is the restated second phrase (mm. 34–51) (Ex. 9.4) that reveals the full

Ex. 9.4   First subject, fourth phrase with incise and first Wagner quotation, mm. 34–51

scope of the key of E in Bruckner's harmonic language. As in the restated first phrase (mm. 25–33), placement of the melody in the soprano allows more explicit resolution in the regions of G♯ minor and B major at mm. 36 and 38, respectively. The melodic adjustment in the soprano voice at m. 39 permits the implied leading-tone resolutions f*–(g♯) and a♯–(b) in mm. 35–38 to be transferred to explicit ones in the bass voice, b♯–c♯ and g♯–a. As a result the upward-third motion of tonal regions (G♯ minor to B major) is countered by a downward third motion (C♯ minor to A major). To this point, therefore, the harmonic regions in the phrase have all been directly related to E major – as iii to V countered by vi to IV. The A major harmony that temporarily completes this tonal motion appears in the eighth measure of the phrase (m. 40); it could easily pass through F♯ harmony – i.e., some form of ii, ii°, vii°[7]/V, or augmented-sixth chord – to B major to complete the phrase in its ninth measure. Indeed, the motion that concludes this phrase from the second half of m. 50 to m. 51 satisfies this expectation.

If one considers the nine-measure phrase as definitive for the first subject, then the intervening portion of the phrase between the first half of m. 41 and the second half of m. 50 may be understood as an incise.[22] Two features of these intervening measures enhance such a perception: first, the incise begins with a re-harmonization of the previous four notes in the bass line; second, and more importantly, Bruckner inserts a recognizable allusion to Wagner's *Parsifal* to highlight the beginning of the incise. This re-harmonization extends the downward-third tonal motions into the realm of indirectly related keys by changing the harmonic meaning of the four bass notes from a pair of $\#\hat{7}$–$\hat{1}$ motions in C♯ minor and A major (mm. 39–41) to a pair of 5–6 motions in F minor and C♯ minor (mm. 41–3). As a result, the D♭ major harmony (m. 42) is introduced not as the enharmonically spelled major submediant chord of E major; rather, it is derived as a natural submediant in the region of F minor. The allusion to *Parsifal* highlights this surprising extension of tonal regions into the realm of F minor as the minor Neapolitan of E. The *Abendmahlmotiv* does not occur in *Parsifal* in D♭ major until m. 323 of Act I, where Gurnemanz, describing Kundry's sense of guilt concerning her past life, sings: 'She lives here today, perhaps renewed, to cleanse her guilt from her earlier life' ('*Hier lebt sie heut', vielleicht erneut, zu büssen Schuld aus früh'rem Leben*').[23] Bruckner's means of reharmonizing his own bass line with this allusion and then concluding the phrase with his own material is, at the very least, suggestive. Could this be Bruckner's idiosyncratic way of using allusions to Wagner to justify his own free application of Sechter's harmonic theory?

But there is another critical aspect of the allusion to Wagner: it permits Bruckner to infuse his E major setting with the connotations of lament by introducing the primary characteristic of the Phrygian mode, its 'lowered second scale degree'. Here, as in the Sechter canon shown above in Ex. 9.1, a secondarily related key (*Nebentonleiter*), namely F minor, is established without actually stating its tonic function. This Phrygian characteristic, F minor, is significant for two reasons: it appears at the exact moment when the phrase might be expected to close; and its appearance as a minor chord permits a double reference for secondary keys. Thus, for example, the context for A♭ major here is the natural mediant – i.e., relative major – of the minor Neapolitan region, F minor; in other circumstances A♭ major might be thought of as an enharmonic major III in the home key of E major.[24]

Taken as a unit, the second subject may be seen as a complex digressive passage starting and ending in the key of B major/minor. This subject is constructed as a single musical phrase – i.e., lacking internal cadences – comprising three sets of paired entries, identified as *dux* and *comes*. Here, as in the first subject, the durational unit for each contrapuntal entry is nine measures.

In the first *dux* (Ex. 9.5), Bruckner extends the possibilities for double referencing of tonal regions by taking a circuitous route to connect the initial B major to its diatonic second scale degree C♯ minor. The initial *dux* comprises two

Ex. 9.5   Second subject, first *dux* statement, mm. 51–59

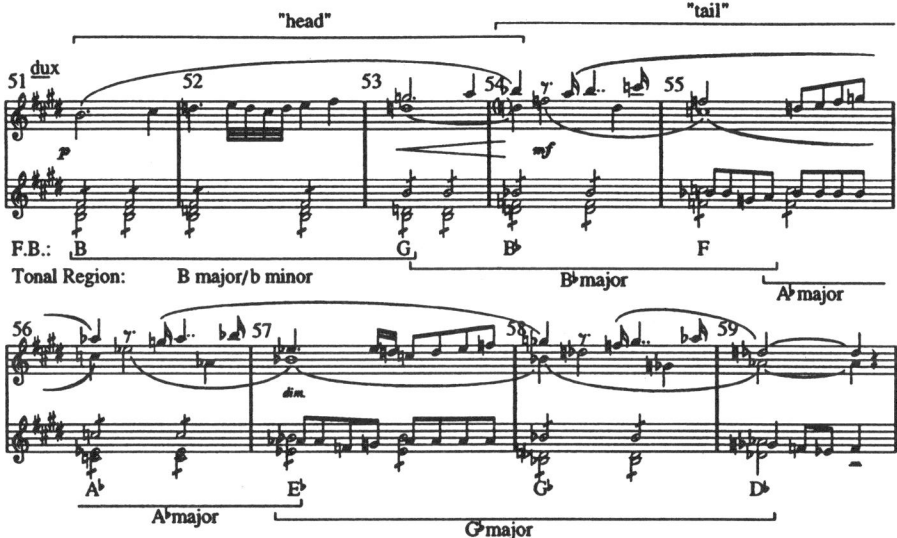

parts: a 'head' of four measures that outlines an ascending scale-like motion encompassing a diminished octave; and, by elision, a 'tail' of six measures set in downward step sequence. In contrast to the normative downward melodic step sequence from eighteenth- and nineteenth-century practice, however, this one is not supported by a downward circle-of-fifths. Rather, the sequential pattern alternates between upward fifth and upward third. The resultant harmonic path to the supertonic, C♯ (spelled enharmonically as D♭), presents the concluding harmony not as supertonic of B major, but rather as dominant of G♭/F♯ major.

The matching *comes* (Ex. 9.6) appears in the low strings at the level of C♯ with two alterations. (1) The final pitch of the 'head' in both mm. 62 and 64 is changed from an upper neighbour to a harmonic note. Thus, for example, exact transposition of m. 54 would have produced d natural as the final sixteenth note in m. 62; in this bassline setting, however, Bruckner substitutes an f♯[7] harmony for the expected D.[25] (2) The final pitch of the 'tail' is adjusted downward by step so that the *comes* returns to its starting point, c♯/d♭ (downbeat of m. 67). The concluding D♭ harmony is subsequently transformed from a V[7]/iv in D♭/C♯ minor to a supertonic function chord in B major, enharmonically notated as a G[7] chord, providing a smooth preparation for the following tonic six-four chord (m. 69) that harmonizes the beginning pitch for the second pair of entries.[26]

This *comes* becomes the occasion for Bruckner's second Wagnerian reference, this time from *Tannhäuser*, presented as a brief countermelody to the 'head' of

Ex. 9.6   Second subject, first *comes* statement, mm. 59–69

the c♯ *Cantus firmus*. While the earlier *Parsifal* reference may be only an allusion, this reference, I will argue, takes on the quality of a true quotation. It hearkens back to Bruckner's first experience of Wagner's music, a performance of *Tannhäuser* under the baton of his teacher Otto Kitzler.[27] Although the quotation consists of only three pitches, it is easily recalled as the 'head' of Wagner's *Reuemotiv*, memorable because of its abrupt harmonic and timbral contrast from what precedes it in Wagner's setting.[28]

Bruckner's engagement of this motive illustrates both his intimate knowledge of its use in *Tannhäuser* and his ability to assimilate the most chromatic aspects of Wagner's musical language with his own materials. Had Bruckner only experienced *Tannhäuser* as an auditor at the performance, the appropriation of details from the *Pilgerchor*, as given below, might be an unrealistic interpretation. Franz Scheder, however, provides an important clue. The following entry appears in his *Chronologie* for Friday, 13 February, 1863:

Otto Kitzler directs the Linz premiére of *Tannhäuser*. The 'Frohsinn' [chorus] rehearses the Pilgrim's Chorus under Bruckner's direction.
[*Otto Kitzler leitet die Linzer Erstaufführung des 'Tannhäuser.' Der 'Frohsinn' unter Brucknérs Einstudierung wirkte beim Pilgerchor mit.*][29]

According to this entry, Bruckner took an active role in this performance of *Tannhäuser*; as an assistant conductor he helped prepare the local male chorus, known as *Männergesangverein 'Frohsinn'*. Accordingly, we might expect that he would have known both the harmonic details and their association with specific texts in a manner that would have permitted the interpretation given below.[30]

Wagner uses the *Reuemotiv* three times in *Tannhäuser*. The first appearance, in the Overture (mm. 17–32), follows an E major setting of the *Gnadenheilmotiv* with motions connecting a series of dominant harmonies that resolve upward by third: B major to D major to F major before returning to the dominant of E major. In its second setting, in Act I, Scene 3 (mm. 53–69) the *Reuemotiv* appears at its original tonal level, but this time grafted to a G major beginning phrase, 'Toward Thee, my Jesus Christ, I wander'. (*'Zu dir wall ich, mein Jesus Christ'*.) The text of the *Reuemotiv* in this passage is: 'Ah, the burden of sin presses heavily upon me; I can no longer bear it! Therefore, I desire neither quiet nor rest, and happily choose toil and torment'. (*'Ach, schwer drückt mich der Sünden Last, kann länger sie nicht mehr ertragen! Drum will ich auch nicht Ruh' noch Rast, und wähle gern mir Müh' und Plagen'*.) The third appearance of the *Reuemotiv*, in Act III, Scene I (mm. 73–88) (Ex. 9.7), however, introduces the actual pitch level of Bruckner's quotation. The initial coupling of the *Gnadenheilmotiv* and the *Reuemotiv* is restored, but now at the tonal level of E♭ major. As a consequence of this transposition, the second sequential link in the motive connects D♭ major and F♭ major harmonies where the melody descends from d♭–c–c♭. The text for this passage is, 'Through atonement and penance have I been reconciled with the Lord' (*'Durch Sühn und Buß hab ich versöhnt den Herren'*). The words *'hab ich versöhnt'* set the pitches quoted by Bruckner. Returning to Ex. 9.6, a literal transposition of the *dux* in the bass line would have led to a conclusion on D♯ – identical with Wagner's tonal goal. Bruckner's tonal adjustment in m. 67 allows him to 'reconcile' a particular feature of Wagner's E♭/D♯ setting with his own tonal plan that requires a return to B major. Here, as in the earlier Wagner reference at m. 42, Bruckner uses his own material to adjust the tonal implications provided from Wagner's original contexts.

Bruckner's second set of paired entries (Ex. 9.8) is modified so as to produce a motion from B to C-natural (mm. 69–77). The second *dux*, now in the upper strings, comprises two successive statements of the 'head' connecting b to b♭ twice with some internal chromatic adjustment in the second statement. The fundamental bass for this entry combines upward step motions followed by downward fifth in the first presentation of the 'head' with upward step motion followed by downward third in the second presentation, illustrating a passage

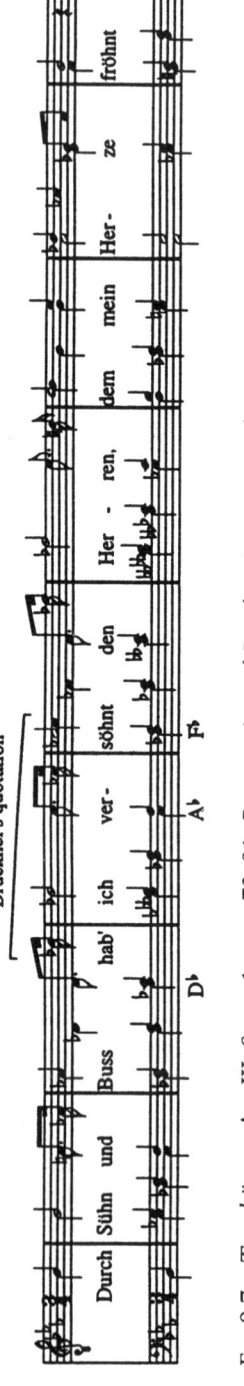

Ex. 9.7 *Tannhäuser*, Act III, Scene 1, mm. 73–81, *Reuemotiv*, and Bruckner's quotation from it

238

Ex. 9.8   Second subject, second paired entry with adjustments to the 'head', mm. 69–80

that contrasts fifth motions with third motions. In the paired *comes* (mm. 77–80), the clarinet and horn modify the 'head' 'correcting' the diminished octave motion to that of a unison to and from C natural, thereby permitting extension through directly related harmonies to the dominant of E (mm. 80–9).

In the third set of paired entries (Ex. 9.9), the *dux* restates the 'head' and adjusts the 'tail' to conclude on B. The fundamental bass pattern in the 'tail' of this entry alternates upward fifths with downward thirds as follows: B♭–F–D♭–A♭–E–B, thus allowing the 'tail' to return to the initial pitch level on B. The *comes* (mm. 103–23) inverts the 'head' and extends the 'tail' by means of internal repetitions over a dominant pedal, setting up one of the most dramatic cadences in the movement in the key of B major/minor at m. 123.

Bruckner's expositions typically contain three subjects, the first with full orchestra, the second employing chamber effects, and the third marked by a return of the *tutti*. His third subjects are driven by strong motivic rhythms and directed toward the tonal goal of the exposition, its true second key area. This

Ex. 9.9   Second subject, third dux statement with adjusted 'tail', mm. 89–98

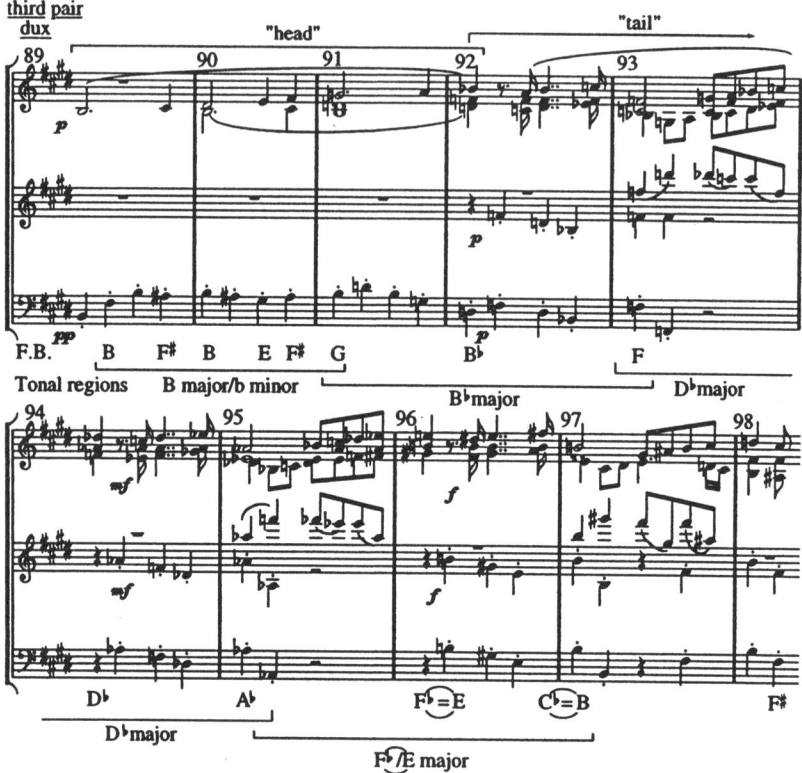

description applies in a specific sense to the first movement of the Seventh Symphony, where the third subject is presented in the form of a single phrase made of harmonic blocks, each of which contains repetitions of the sort of motivic rhythm described above. Unlike the first-movement expositions of the Fourth and Fifth Symphonies,[31] however, that of the Seventh Symphony dwells for a particularly long time in and around the key of B, the tonal goal of the exposition. Since all three paired entry units in the exposition of the second subject are initiated with a B major or B minor reference, the continued reference to B in the third subject seems disproportionately long.

The third subject, despite its contrasting rhythmic and motivic nature, recalls some of the tonal features of its predecessor. Its beginning with four-measure harmonic blocks of repeated motivic statements contrasts with the phrase paradigm of nine-measure units characterizing the first two subjects. The second of these harmonic blocks (mm. 127–30), however, seems incompatible with the notion of a concluding phrase confirming the sense of tonal arrival; the use of minor dominant harmony here, although easily explainable with reference to the temporary tonal center of B, weakens the sense of tonal definition by denying the leading tone a♮. Rather than viewing this phrase as one of regular four-measure units, I propose an alternative reading of mm. 123–53, one that finds the basic phrase to consist of the first four measures (mm. 123–26) as its 'head', and the final five measures (mm. 149–53) as its 'tail'.[32] Viewed from this perspective, a nine-measure basic phrase emerges. The 'head' in B minor is countered by a change of mode in the 'tail', and, indeed, it is not until m. 149 that the mode swing occurs from B minor to B major.

Taken as such, the intervening 22 measures (mm. 127–48) are explained as an incise. There is also a rationale for finding the nine-measure periodicity factor underlying this passage. The incise consists of three overlapping differentiated segments. The basic element for the first segment (mm. 127–35) is a single measure comprising a harmony that is sustained for three quarter notes and then followed on the fourth beat of the measure by its dominant. This measure is repeated in groups of four on F♯ minor and D major/minor harmonies, respectively. Since the measure-unit ends with dominant harmony, the resolution that completes this segment is carried over from the final quarter note of the eighth measure to the downbeat of the ninth measure (m. 135).

The basic element for the second segment (mm. 135–41) is a two-measure unit that outlines a pattern of descending thirds. The two-measure unit becomes the basis for a descending step sequence. If that sequence were maintained, (Ex. 9.10), a simple intervallic adjustment at the end of its eighth measure would lead to an arrival on F♯/G♭ in the ninth measure of the segment. In this instance, however, by making three chromatic alterations – g-natural in place of g♭ (m. 139), and c-natural and f-natural in place of c♭ and f♭, respectively (m. 140) – Bruckner omits one two-measure sequential link while still arriving on the F♯/G♭ (m. 141) that the sequence would have generated. As a result this segment, while based upon a nine-measure model, comprises only seven measures.

The third segment (mm. 141–49) comprises a nine-measure digression beginning and ending with F♯ harmony. The entire passage may be diagrammed as follows:

mm. 123–26, 127–35   135–41   141–49   149–53
      4 +   [4 + 4 + 1
                  2 + 2 + 2 + 1
                        2 + 2 + 2 + 2 + 1] + 5

In characterizing Bruckner's exposition in terms of its three subjects, I have provided an outline of its thematic materials. These three subjects correspond with the normative tonal plan for a sonata-form exposition as follows: The first subject acts as first key area concluding with a half cadence at m. 51. The second and third subjects comprise a second key area in B major with identifying theme and closing theme, respectively. There is no real transition; furthermore, the dominant key is ascendant for more than two-thirds of this exposition. Were the recapitulation to restate second-key material in exact transposition, as is usual, one can imagine that, despite the internal harmonic richness of each subject's

Ex. 9.10   Second segment of the incise, mm. 135–41; Bruckner's adjustment to an exact step sequence

respective presentation, the reprise would exhibit no large-scale tonal diversity. Therefore, one might expect Bruckner to provide for the recapitulation the transition that does not occur in the exposition.

Development: Contrapuntal Rigour and the Church Style

The development takes an orderly approach to the three subjects, subjecting each in succession to a regimen of 'learned' techniques. First, two entries of the inverted first subject form an antecedent/consequent phrase pair that modulates from B major to D minor. Parallel entries (mm. 165 and 173) lead to vastly different endings that represent the full range of Bruckner's tonal language. At m. 171 (Ex. 9.11), the antecedent phrase concludes with a half cadence in B minor that is reminiscent of Palestrinian features found in Bruckner's E-minor Mass. Identical harmonic resolution and treatment of outer voices (Ex. 9.12) is found in the cadence that closes the 'Kyrie' movement. In the choral setting, the inner voices are treated more strictly, forming a typical Renaissance *clausula*, the

Ex. 9.11   First subject treatment in the development; first phrase, mm. 165–71

Ex. 9.12   Final cadence in the Kyrie movement of the E minor Mass, mm. 110–17

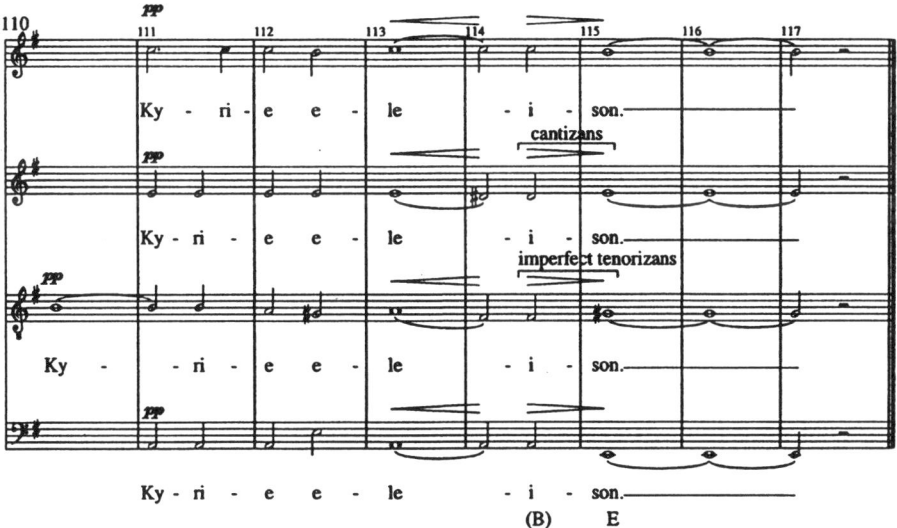

alto carrying the *cantizans* pattern taken from Renaissance practice and the tenor carrying an imperfect *tenorizans* pattern.[33] In comparison, the cadence at m. 171 in the first movement of the Seventh Symphony sacrifices both *cantizans* and *tenorizans* patterns through free voicing of the inner parts.

Whereas the antecedent phrase (mm. 165–73) begins in B major and ends on its dominant F♯, the consequent phrase (mm. 173–81) (Ex. 9.13) begins in B minor and ends on A, the dominant of D minor. In contrast to the Renaissance-like cadence of the antecedent, the consequent ends with a series of deceptive resolutions that employ some of the most advanced aspects of Bruckner's harmonic language. The series begins with a deceptive ascending step resolution of the B^9 chord to C^7 (mm. 176–7) comprising a V–to–VI motion in the region of the subdominant E minor; this harmony, in turn, is treated as a dominant and resolved deceptively by descending third to an $E\flat^4_2$ chord (m. 179) comprising a V–to–V/VI motion in the region of F minor (in turn the minor Neapolitan region of E minor); the goal of this phrase is then achieved at m. 181 when the E♭ chord is reinterpreted as an A harmony, the dominant of D minor, by changing the

Ex. 9.13   First subject treatment in the development; second phrase, mm. 173–81

quality of its fifth from diminished to perfect and replacing its ninth with its root, as diagrammed:

9th	b♭	
7th	g	g
5th	e♭	e
3rd	c♯	c♯
root		A

Prolonged A harmony (mm. 181–4) prepares the re-introduction of Bruckner's second subject (m. 185). The principal feature of the 'head' of this subject, melodic motion encompassing a diminished octave (as shown in Ex. 9.5 above), makes possible a modulating tonal plan. When Bruckner inverts this 'head'-motive (mm. 185–9 in the 'celli), he establishes a motion that permits f-natural, the initial third of D minor harmony, to connect to f♯, the fifth of dominant harmony in E minor. Through sequence procedure, the tonal motion is carried to F♯ minor (mm. 189–92 in the violins); and at this point (Ex. 9.14) the diminished octave of the 'head' is adjusted and extended to a richly elaborated cadential preparation in the key of E major. Cadential preparations occur in F♯ minor (mm. 194–5) and in G♯ minor (mm. 201–2) before this final E major preparation. All three preparations are resolved deceptively so that the A$^6_4$ harmony at m. 196 and the G$^6_5$ harmony at m. 211 are both V$^6_5$/VI harmonies in those respective regions – the harmonic motion being by downward third; and the E major harmony at m. 203 appears as VI in G♯ minor. From m. 211, the passage is extended by means of a chromatically ascending bassline through successive deceptive V-to–VI motions leading to vii°$^6_5$ of E minor at m. 218.

The third subject is re-introduced with a fourteen-measure passage (mm. 219–32) that modulates from E minor to C minor by means of reinterpreting D (natural VII of E minor) as d (ii from the region of C minor). As in the

Ex. 9.14   Second subject treatment in the development with deceptive resolutions, mm. 193–211

exposition, the third subject is based upon a single nine-measure phrase that has been interrupted with an incise. In this instance, the 'head' (mm. 219–22) comprises a four-measure harmonic block on E minor harmony. The 'middle' (mm. 223–24) initiates a circle-of-fifths motion from E to A – anticipating resolution to D. The following two measures, a harmonic block of D-major (mm. 225–26), serve as an incise – prolonging a harmony that is directly related to E minor. The 'tail' of the phrase (mm. 227–29) begins by changing the quality of D harmony from major to minor, producing a chord that is directly related to the new key of C minor.[34] The phrase concludes with a complete diatonic circle of fifths in C minor and a cadence on the dominant at m. 229 with prolongation of that harmony through m. 232.

One of the basic premises of Sechterian theory is that the large-scale tonal motions in a given composition are derived from and directly related to foreground harmonic motions, particularly those occurring in the work's expository phase. This premise is essential to Arnold Schoenberg's *Grundgestalt* theory; based upon his adaptation of Sechter's harmonic concepts in *Harmonielehre*,[35] Schoenberg offers the following summary:

> I myself consider the totality of a piece as the *idea*: the idea which its creator wanted to present. But because of the lack of better terms I am forced to define the term idea in the following manner:
> Every tone which is added to a beginning tone makes the meaning of that tone doubtful. If, for instance, G follows after C, the ear may not be sure whether this expresses C major or G major, or even F major or E minor; and the addition of other tones may or may not clarify this problem. In this manner there is produced a state of unrest, of imbalance which grows throughout most of the piece, and is enforced further by similar functions of the rhythm. The method by which balance is restored seems to me the real *idea* of the composition.[36]

In the first movement of Bruckner's Seventh Symphony, a 'state of unrest' is produced in the restatement of the consequent phrase of the first subject (mm. 34–41) where the succession of tonal regions has been altered from that of the initial statement of this phrase (mm. 12–20) to become G♯ minor, B major, C♯ minor, A major. This succession of tonal regions – upward minor third, upward major second, downward major third – that occurs within the 'head' of the restated consequent phrase, is transposed and becomes the tonal plan for the entire development section, outlining its principal sections: B major/minor as the announcement of the first subject (m. 165), D minor as the announcement of the second subject (m. 185), E minor as the announcement of the third subject (m. 219), and C minor as the tonal goal of the entire section (m. 233). This projection of lower-level tonal organization from the exposition of the first subject into the tonal plan for one of the principal sections of the movement illustrates Bruckner's free application of strict Sechterian harmonic principles.

Conflict between Tonal and Thematic Return

Nineteenth-century concepts of musical form are primarily based upon thematic materials. Thus, for example, A. B. Marx derives an explanation of *Sonatenform* from the Rondo and uses Beethoven as his exemplar.[37] The thematic explanation of sonata form and its ties to Beethoven are crucial to our understanding of the formal plan for the first movement of Bruckner's Seventh Symphony. The first movement of Beethoven's Eighth Symphony in F major, Op. 93, provides an excellent example of discrepancies that can occur between thematic and tonal arrivals within an exposition. Whereas Beethoven's second key area is clearly that of the dominant, C major at m. 46, the theme that is associated with this key has already been introduced at the level of D major in m. 38. Hence, thematic arrival precedes the tonal arrival for the second subject of the exposition. This idea is carried to larger proportions in several works by Schubert.[38]

In Bruckner's Seventh Symphony, tension between thematic and tonal arrivals is even more highly dramatized since this discrepancy is reserved for the recapitulation.[39] In the Seventh Symphony, the recapitulation is thematic, occurring at m. 249 in C minor, following a dramatic emphasis on this minor submediant of E major. This return is set up in two steps. First, C minor is established through its diatonic circle of fifths and dominant pedal point (mm. 226–32). Second, C minor is given thematic status by means of a restatement of the inverted first subject from the beginning of the Development, now played by full orchestra at *fortissimo* dynamic level. In this instance, however, phrase length is informative: this second step in the dramatization of C minor, despite its rhythmic and dynamic force, comprises 16 measures, not the nine-measure unit that Bruckner employed to introduce his first and second subjects in the exposition. The passage outlines a harmonic plan of downward third motions following the initial C minor harmony: D (mm. 237–40) to B♭ (mm. 241–42) to a G substitute (mm. 243–48).[40]

The actual recapitulation is identified by two features: return of the initial form of the first subject's head and re-establishment of the nine-measure phrase (mm. 249–57) (Ex. 9.15) ending with an arrival on dominant harmony in D minor. The return is masked, however, first, because it has already been

Ex. 9.15   Thematic recapitulation of the first subject, mm. 249–61

preempted at m. 233 by a much more dramatic tonal arrival in C minor; and second, because, when stated in the minor mode, the 'head' of the first subject is transformed into a likeness of the opening gesture of the *Trauermarsch* from *Götterdämmerung*.[41] Following the four-measure prolongation of the final harmony, a sequential restatement of the thematic entry occurs in m. 261 at the level of D minor. Exact restatement would take this passage to a first-inversion dominant harmony of E minor at m. 269. But such an arrival does not occur. In fact, despite the ensuing tonal return in E major at m. 281, there is no dominant harmony to prepare that return. The B^6 harmony that would have been produced at m. 269 by an exact sequence of the C minor to D minor phrase is replaced by an $E\flat^4_2$ harmony. While the thematic material of this passage is taken from the first subject, its tonal treatment is reminiscent of Bruckner's handling of the second subject in at least two respects: (1) in its sequential restatement, the phrase is adjusted so that it avoids two tonal motions by upward major second, just as in the first *comes* statement at m. 67; and (2) the chord of arrival, the $E\flat^4_2$ of m. 269, and its resolution to a C^7 chord are identical with the chord and resolution that adjusted the second *dux* at mm. 75–7 so that it could move to C major. That is to say: Bruckner employs the same harmonic procedure in the recapitulation to return to the tonic key *from* the region of C major/minor that he had used previously to move *to* that region in his exposition. The method of approach to his tonal arrival at m. 281, in contrast to the potential exact transposition by upward step of the phrase shown in Ex. 9.15, is through a series of deceptive resolutions that harmonize a stepwise ascending bassline, outlined as follows:

chords:	C^7	A^6_5	d	A^4_3	$B\flat^4_3$	$E\flat^6_5$	E^6
bassline:	c	c$\sharp$	d	e	f	g	g$\sharp$
functions:	F:V	V^6_5/vi	vi	V^4_3/vi			
				d:V^4_3	V^4_3/bII		
					E♭:V^4_3	V^6_5/IV	
						A♭:V^6_5	bVI^6
							F♭/E:I^6

At this point (m. 281), the first paired set of phrases from mm. 3–20 of the exposition are restated at their original tonal level. The extension is modified at m. 301 so that it suggests motion to the region of B major.

Given that Bruckner avoids dominant harmony in preparing for the tonal return at m. 281, it is surprising to find that he turns toward the dominant here and later in the recapitulation. In this first instance (m. 302), a weakly asserted dominant of B major is resolved deceptively to V^4_3/♭VI in that region. Again, a series of upward step deceptive harmonic motions re-establishes the principal key, E major (m. 319). Hence, for the time being at least, the dominant of B major has not been given dramatic emphasis.

The second subject treatment begins (m. 319) as a transposition from the exposition. Were this a literal transposition, both tonally and in terms of durational space (preserving the temporal dimensions of the second subject from the exposition), the third subject would enter also on E at m. 391. In fact, there is an important arrival on E at m. 391; that is to say, the predicted temporal space is maintained for a significant reassertion of the tonic pitch.[42] But, by the time this arrival on E has occurred, the third subject has already been introduced, not at the expected level of E minor, but rather at the level of G major. Accordingly, the third subject enters prematurely, at m. 363, as a deceptive resolution of a powerfully motivated dominant to its flat submediant in the key of B major.

But Bruckner never realizes his dominant key in the recapitulation; rather, he revises his third subject so that it can lead back to tonic harmony. Its arrival there, precisely when the third subject's tonic arrival might have been expected, motivates the close of the movement: at m. 391, as a continuation of the single phrase that embodied his third subject, he reintroduces the material from the second phrase of his original first subject transposed so as to begin at the level of E minor.[43] In this setting, the upward-third sequence of three members in the original phrase is extended to a series of five, passing through the following tonal regions: E minor (mm. 392–4), G major (mm. 394–96), B minor (mm. 396–98), D major (mm. 398–400), and F♯ minor (mm. 400–2), before returning to the tonic at m. 413.

The recapitulation comes to a close (Ex. 9.16) with a second reference to the

Ex. 9.16   Final cadence at end of recapitulation, mm. 409–13

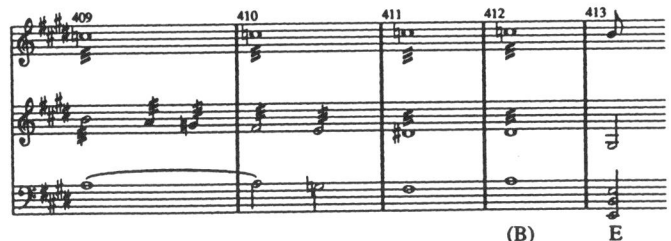

style of the E minor Mass. The cadence at m. 413 is a replica of that at m. 171, but one that serves a radically different musical and poetic function. Despite the identical resolutions of outer voices and of relative harmonic functions, the first of these cadences is on the dominant of the prevailing tonality at that point, whereas the final cadence is unequivocally on the tonic.[44]

Corresponding temporal units play an important role in the articulation of form in this movement. In addition to the importance of nine-measure units for identifying announcement phrases, there are two further significant temporal correspondences worthy of note.[45] First, Bruckner allocates the same durational space containing the same tonal relations between the beginning and end for the second subject of his exposition (mm. 51–123) as he does for the combination of second subject and third subject in the recapitulation (mm. 319–91). Second, if one compares exposition and recapitulation in thematic terms, they are almost identical in length, the recapitulation containing one extra measure.[46] Table 9.1 summarizes the various temporal correspondences between exposition and recapitulation.

Table 9.1:   Corresponding Phrases in Bruckner's Seventh Symphony, First movement

	Exposition 1–164		164 mm.	Recapitulation 249–413			165 mm.
1st subject:							
	1–51 (4 phrases)			249–319 (4 phrases)			
				i)	249–57	V/d	9
					(257–60)		3
				ii)	261–69	V$\frac{4}{2}$/A♭	9
					269–80		12
	1–2		2				
i)	3–11	V/E	9	iii)	281–89	V/E	9
ii)	12–20	V/E	9	iv)	290–98	V/E	9
	(21–24)	to E	4		(299–302)	to G	4
iii)	25–33	V/E	9				
					(303–10)		4+4
iv)	34–51	V/e	8 (+9) + 1		311–19		9
2nd subject:							
	51–123 (single phrase: 6 entries)			319–63 (single phrase: 4 entries)			
	51–59	on B	9		319–27	on E	9
	59–69	on C♯	9 + 2		327–35	on F♯	9
	69–77	on B	9		335–43	on E	9
	77–89	on C	8 (+4) + 1				
	89–103	on B	9 + 6				
	103–23	on B	8 (+12) + 1		343–63	on E	8 (+12) + 1
3rd subject:							
	123–64 (single phrase: in blocks)			363–413 (single phrase: in blocks)			
	b		4	G			4
	f♯		4	C/c/C			4
				E♭			2
				G♭ e♭ F d E♭ c D			2
	D/d/D		4	A/a/A			4
	bassline		6				12
	G♭6–b♭/a♯°7		4				
	B7–G$\frac{6}{5}$		4				
	F♯ pedal		4				
		(2nd sub.)		E pedal			22
	B		12	E			1

Table 9.1 concluded

Development: 165–249

        Part I: 165–232

                Event 1:   165–85   b to d   1st subject
                                     <u>7 + 1</u> + 7 + 6

                Event 2:   185–211   d–e–f♯–e   2nd subject
                                       4 + 4 + 18

                Event 2b: 211–18 stepwise ascending base

                Event 3:   219–32   e to c
                                       4 + 4 + 2 + 4

        Part II: 233–48   False recapitulation

                Event 4:   233–48
                                       4 + 4 + 8

Coda: 413–443   E major with pedal
                            31

Conclusions

Bruckner's recapitulation may be accounted for as follows: the tonal return of the first subject does not occur until m. 281 and is not preceded by dominant harmony. The double statement of paired phrases from the exposition is reduced to a single statement followed by a fragmentary passage lacking a convincing cadence but leading to arrival on the tonic for the second subject. Whereas the second subject is treated as an announcement of the second key in the exposition, it becomes a real transition in the recapitulation, providing the tonal motion from tonic to dominant that would be its customary role in an exposition. The third subject corrects this exposition-like feature by avoiding the arrival in the dominant key at the outset and by adjusting its own tonal plan to lead back from G major (as ♭VI of B major) to the original tonic. However, this tonic arrival, at m. 391, is not cadential. Rather, Bruckner returns to the incompletely stated first subject to complete the phrase initiated by his third subject. The cadence that he supplies, with its references to liturgical music and suggestions of Renaissance style, suggests the triumph of spiritual values over temporal ones.

    Emphatic assertion of B in the exposition and denial of it in the recapitulation of the first movement are significant for the symphony as a whole.[47] In the second and third movements, there is not so much as an extended passage or cadence in the key of B major or minor. In fact, the tonal plan for the middle two movements outlines a downward spiral of third motions from the E major of the first movement, to C♯ minor in the Adagio, to A minor in the Scherzo, to F major in the Trio.

While the final movement begins and ends clearly enough in E major, cadences in B and E are reserved until the end of the recapitulation. Once again, the nine-measure phrase defines the formal structure of this movement, announcing the first subject of the exposition with a pair of phrases that begin on tonic (mm. 1–9) and dominant (mm. 11–19), but modulate to the indirectly related keys A♭ major and B♭ major, respectively. The tonal plan of the exposition avoids the dominant key; its second subject enters in A♭ major (m. 35) – following a half cadence in F minor – and the third subject proceeds from an initial A minor (m. 93) to conclusion of the exposition in C major. Whereas the gesture of the B minor entry of the third subject at m. 191 matches that of the announcement of this subject at m. 93 in the exposition, neither is the entry approached by cadential preparation nor does it lead to any sort of definitive ending in the key of B. In fact, the only cadence in B in the entire movement occurs in the reorganized restatement of the first subject at m. 299 as an internal element preparing the final phrase. This final phrase of the recapitulation ends at m. 315 with the only cadence in E major of the entire movement. It is also important to observe that the restatement of the first subject at m. 275 is approached by the *Zwitterakkord* of E major, representing its supertonic scale degree; this important tonal return is prepared by the suppression of dominant harmony.[48] The resultant emphases on secondary keys of A, C, and F are characteristics of the Phrygian repertory on E and resemble the tonal plan of Bruckner's E minor Mass. Bruckner's special treatment of the dominant places into the macro-structure a projection of the most basic tenet of Sechterian harmonic theory: the understanding that harmonic motion by fifth is the essence of all harmony so that where harmonies appear to move by step, a suppressed dominant is understood. Hence, the avoidance of B as a tonal goal may be seen on the one hand as an attribute of the Phrygian character of Bruckner's E major in this work, and, on the other hand, as a large-scale architectural realization of the principle of the 'suppressed' interdominant.

While the first movement of the Seventh Symphony does not present the Phrygian characteristics of E major as primary tonal regions, it does, nonetheless, refer to them in significant ways. But Bruckner does not introduce these modal characteristics into his Seventh Symphony through specific references to liturgical music. Rather, it is his references to Wagner that introduce characteristics of the Phrygian mode: (1) F as the flatted-second scale degree *(Parsifal)*; (2) retrogressive upward-third motions, found commonly in e–to–g and a–to–c melodic motions *(Tannhäuser)*; and (3) C as the reciting tone *(Götterdämmerung)*. Bruckner brings order to this vast array of connotative materials by acquiring the modal characteristics directly from Wagner's contexts and retaining them while replacing Wagner's musical ideas with his own. This compositional strategy allows Bruckner to impart to his symphony not only the musical essence of Wagner's motives, but also their contextual poetic meanings. Thus it is that the themes of repentance (*büssen* from *Parsifal* and *reuen* from *Tannhäuser*) and of celebration in the honourable death of the proto-German hero Siegfried (*Trauermarsch* from *Götterdämmerung*) become the themes of Bruckner's Seventh Symphony and permit its author to extend an allegorical redemption to the Bayreuth master through free compositional mastery of the strict harmonic guidelines from Sechterian pedagogy.

Notes

1. Arnold Schoenberg, *Theory of Harmony*, trans. Roy E. Carter (Berkeley, 1978), p. 228. This essay was in many ways stimulated by insightful observations on form and harmonic language by members of my doctoral seminar on Bruckner at UNT during Spring 1999. In addition, I am indebted to Timothy Jackson for his careful reading of the text and his many excellent suggestions and to Paul Hawkshaw for providing information about Bruckner's use of metrical numbers in the Seventh Symphony.
2. In a short essay entitled '*Etwas über mich selbst*', quoted in full in Jordan Markus, *Simon Sechter: Biographisches Denkmal* (Vienna, 1888), pp. 57–58, Sechter acknowledged the following theorists whose works he had studied: Marpurg, Kirnberger, C.P.E. Bach, Albrechtsberger, Mattheson, Türk, Gottfried Weber, Reicha, A.B. Marx, and Riepel.
3. Simon Sechter, *Die Grundsätze der musikalischen Komposition* (Leipzig, 1853), I, p. 128.
    '*Alle Fundamente bleiben diatonisch und nur ihre Antheile, d.h. Terz, Quint, Sept und Non, eine Änderung erleiden, je nachdem sie auf eine mit der Haupttonleiter verwandte Nebentonleiter Bezug haben.*'
4. This treatise was most likely intended as part of a fourth volume for *Die Grundsätze*. Walter Zeleny, *Die historischen Grundlagen des Theoriesystems von Simon Sechter* (Tutzing, 1979), p. 286, quotes a letter, dated 22 June 1855, from Sechter to an unidentified prospective publisher, in which he described *Vom Canon* as a section of 'the fourth and final part of my treatise'. The manuscript is found in the Archive of the Library of the Gesellschaft der Musikfreunde in Vienna.
5. *Die Grundsätze*, I, p. 119, identifies related keys as follows:
    When C major is the tonic key, the related keys are G major, F major, A minor, E minor, D minor, G minor, C minor and F minor.
    ('*Wenn die Haupttonleiter C dur ist, so sind die verwandten Tonleitern G dur, F dur, A moll, E moll, D moll, G moll, C moll und F moll.*')
    Here and elsewhere in the treatise, the related keys ('*verwandten Tonleitern*') correspond to the major or minor diatonic chords in any given key plus the opposite mode of the tonic, dominant, and subdominant chords. For Sechter, each of these related keys becomes a secondarily related key ('*Nebentonleiter*') to the main tonic and, accordingly, has its own set of related keys. In this essay, the term 'directly related' will be used in reference to harmonies or keys that Sechter defines as related to the tonic key; and the term 'indirectly related' will be used in reference to harmonies or keys that he defines as related to a secondarily related key.
6. Tonal identity in passages that do not include the tonic is also discussed by Carl Schachter, 'Analysis by Key: Another Look at Modulation', in *Music Analysis*, 6 (1987), p. 296, especially in reference to a passage from the third movement of Schubert's Piano Sonata in A minor, D. 845.
7. '*Wie sich aus dem Sinn der Regel zahllos Neues ergeben kann, das, so frei es scheint, doch innerhalb der Regel ruht, hat Bruckner trotz seiner vielen Lehrjahre nicht erkannt.*'

For further discussion of Schenker's criticism of Bruckner, see Helmut Federhofer, 'Heinrich Schenkers Bruckner-Verständnis', in *Archiv für Musikwissenschaft*, 34 (1982), pp. 198–217; and Robert Wason, *Viennese Harmonic Theory from Albrechtsberger to Schenker and Schoenberg* (Ann Arbor, Michigan, 1985), pp. 84 and 119. Edward Laufer, 'Some Aspects of Prolongation Procedures in the Ninth Symphony (Scherzo and Adagio)', in *Bruckner Studies*, ed. Timothy L. Jackson and Paul Hawkshaw (Cambridge, 1997), pp. 222f., offers counter criticism of Schenker's assessment of Bruckner.

8. Friedrich Eckstein, *Erinnerungen an Anton Bruckner* (Vienna, 1923), p. 30:
   '*Zu diesen einfachen Notenspielen ist zu bemerken, daß in ihnen, nach Bruckners Vorgang, die Fundamentaltöne stets unter der Baßstimme in ungestielten schwarzen Notenköpfen angegeben sind. Bruckner hat nicht allein bei seinen Schülern, auch bei solchen, die im Kontrapunkt schon weit vorgeschritten waren, strenge auf diese Art der Notierung gehalten, ich habe sogar des öfteren gesehen, daß er selbst in seinen eigenen Partituren, während er an diesen arbeitete, nicht allein die Takte der Perioden numerierte, sondern mitunter auch die Fundamentaltöne, sei es in solchen schwarzen Notenköpfen, sei es mit Hilfe von Buchstaben, notierte.*'

9. Ibid., pp. 42–43.

10. Included in this category are Carl Mayrberger, *Die Harmonik Richard Wagner's an den Leitmotiven aus* 'Tristan und Isolde' (Chemnitz, 1882); Josef Schalk, 'Das Gesetz der Tonalität', in *Bayreuther Blätter*, 11 (1888), pp. 192–7 and 381–7, and 12 (1889), pp. 191–8; and Cyrill Hynais, 'Die Harmonik R. Wagner's in Bezug auf die Fundamentaltheorie Sechter's', in *Neue Musikalische Presse*, 10 (1901), pp. 50–2, 67–9, 81–3, and 97–100.

11. He offers the remark in criticism of the commonly used terms 'third relationship' and 'fifth relationship' that he finds to be insufficient in accounting for indirect relations, as, for example between C major and E♭ major chords, *Theory of Harmony*, ibid., especially Ex. 159.

12. Ibid., p. 123. It is important to observe also that the only positive reference that the author makes to any theorist of the past is to Sechter, p. 270.

13. Schoenberg, Ibid., p. 119, refers to stepwise harmonic motions with the terms 'superstrong' ('*überstark*') and 'overskipping' ('*überspringend*'). Sechter, *Die Grundsätze*, I, p. 35, introduces the term 'suppressed fundamental' ('*verschweigte Fundament*') to describe the missing chord; later, p. 143, he introduces the term 'interfundamental' ('*Zwischenfundament*') to identify this missing chord, which always has a dominant relationship to the second chord in a stepwise motion. Thus, for example, VI–V motions are understood as VI–II–V (with the II suppressed) and IV–V motions are understood as IV–II–V (with II suppressed).

14. For discussion of Palestrinian aspects in the E minor Mass, see A. C. Howie, 'Traditional and Novel Elements in Bruckner's Sacred Music', in *The Musical Quarterly*, 69 (1981), pp. 556–8.

15. Göllerich/Auer lists the following related entries: August 28, 1882, improvisation on theme from *Parsifal* at St Florian, II/1, p. 280; and during 1883 improvisations on two separate occasions at the newly built Votivkirche in Vienna – *Trauermarsch* from *Götterdämmerung* and *Verwandlungsmusik* from *Parsifal* – and on the Great Organ at Klosterneuburg – themes from Act I of *Siegfried*, IV/2, pp. 83–5.

16. At first glance, this lack of *Vierhebigkeit* may seem contrary to the pedagogies of both Bruckner and his teacher Sechter, both of whom appear to limit their ideas on phrase grouping to even-numbered measure units. In *Die Grundsätze*, III, p. 39, Sechter describes only eight-measure units. Timothy L. Jackson, 'Bruckner's Metrical Numbers', in *19th-Century Music*, 14 (1990–1), p. 104, provides documentation that although Bruckner recognized odd-numbered phrase lengths

occasionally in his own scores, he regarded only the even-numbered measure groupings as '*regelmäßig*'. Jackson advances the theory that Bruckner used numbers in his scores to aid his increasingly complex ideas about meter. Curiously, however, Bruckner did not include the cadence measure in the metrical groupings. Thus, for example, period 1 is grouped by Bruckner (Wn Mus.Hs.19.479) in the following way: 10 + 12 + 10 + 8 + 8, ending with m.50 that precedes the final cadence in this period. By contrast, I propose a reading of mm. 1–51 as follows: (2) + 9 + 9 + (4) + 9 + 8 + (9) + 1. My reading of this passage is consistent with that of Schoenberg, who also includes the cadence measure in his phrase groupings. See 'Brahms the Progressive', in *Style and Idea*, ed. Leonard Stein (New York, 1975), p. 425. Two examples from Beethoven might serve as precedents for Bruckner's use of odd-numbered phrase groups at the beginning of the exposition. The exposition in the first movement of Symphony No. 1 in C major, op. 21, begins with a 21-measure phrase; that of the first movement of Symphony No. 3 in E flat major, op. 55, pairs a 13-measure antecedent phrase with a 9-measure consequent.

17. Sechter's harmonic pedagogy understands the resultant German augmented-sixth chord (described by Sechter as a ninth chord on the second scale degree ('*Septnonaccord der 2ten Stufe*')) to be an incomplete supertonic ninth chord with major third, diminished fifth, minor seventh, minor ninth, and missing root. As such, this harmony is registered as a representative for F♯ harmony. See Sechter, *Die Grundsätze*, I, p. 147, where this chord is first mentioned; and a later reference, pp. 186–93, where the author applies the term '*Zwitterakkord*' – literally 'mongrel' or 'hybrid' chord.

18. Of these tonal regions, only D♯ minor lies outside the circle of regions directly related to the tonic key of E major; this region, however, is directly related to the secondarily related key ('*Nebentonleiter*') of B major that both precedes and follows it in this passage.

19. The first break in periodicity occurs at m. 20 where the melodic line is extended from b to f♯. The latter is initially presented in m. 23 as the dominant of B major; the subsequent lowering of its third (a♯ to a), however, alters its tonal meaning to that of supertonic function in E major, thereby permitting a smooth return to the tonic key.

20. In linear 5–6 motions of this type, Sechter consistently identifies both as independent harmonies.

21. As with the German augmented-sixth chord, Sechter explains the diminished-seventh chord as an incomplete ninth chord with the root missing. Accordingly, both are supertonic function chords; the only difference between the a♯ diminished-seventh chord of m. 30 and the augmented-sixth chord of m. 8 is the quality of the fifth above the fundamental bass. That is, the implicit c-natural as a chord member in the first instance contrasts with with explicit c-sharp in the second instance. See Sechter, *Die Grundsätze*, I, p. 152, where the author illustrates how diminished-seventh chords and augmented-sixth chords may be used interchangeably in a circle-of-fifths progression.

22. H. C. Koch, *Introductory Essay on Composition: The Mechanical Rules of Melody*, trans. Nancy Kovaleff Baker (New Haven, 1983), pp. 1–2, explains that musical periods are constructed of sections in which 'a certain proportion or relation can be found in the number of their measures once they are reduced to their essential components'. On p. 9 he defines the incise as 'an incomplete segment of a phrase that does not end a complete idea'. Finally, on p. 14, he explains how regular four-measure phrases may be made irregular through the insertion of an incise. Although it is not likely that Bruckner knew Koch's work, nonetheless, his knowledge of instrumental music from the classic repertory would provide easy access to examples of incises. Christopher Lewis, 'The Mind's Chronology: Narrative Times

and Harmonic Disruption in Postromantic Music', in *The Second Practice of Nineteenth-Century Tonality*, ed. William Kinderman and Harald Krebs (Lincoln, Nebraska, 1996), pp. 124–29, describes 'temporal disruptions and displacements' in the second movement of Bruckner's Seventh Symphony in terms of what he finds to be independently coherent harmonic progressions. In contrast to his approach, I consider in this essay that the nine-measure element of periodicity establishes the basis for the norm and that immediately adjacent harmonies, either within the basic phrase or in the incises and extensions that enlarge it, form the logical basis for determination of larger-scale harmonic motions. Hence, the incise supports the harmonic patterns of chords found in the basic phrase.

23. The initial statement of Wagner's *Abendmahlmotiv* that opens the Prelude to Act I of *Parsifal* appears in A♭ major.

24. This stylized Phrygian characteristic is also found in Bruckner's E minor Mass with its F minor passages in the *Crucifixus* section of the Credo.

25. Similarly, the $e°^7$ chord on the last sixteenth-note in m. 64 becomes a *Stellvertreter* for the c-natural that would have occurred with an exact transposition from m. 56.

26. Sechter, *Die Grundsätze*, I, p. 215, explains this particular use of enharmonic notation whereby $V^7/♭II$ may be re-interpreted as a German augmented-sixth chord, the roots of which are a tritone apart. Accordingly, the chord in m. 68, spelled as g–b–d–f, might be expected to function as V^7 of C (♭II of B minor); its enharmonic equivalent, however, Sechter regards as a ninth chord on the second scale degree with the root understood (C♯–[e♯–g–b–d]). See n. 17.

27. Although the sources differ as to the exact date, they reveal an amazing coincidence: Bruckner's first hearing of Wagner's music took place in Linz either on February 13, 1863 – twenty years to the date before Wagner's death in Venice, as given by Otto Kitzler, *Erinnerungen*, p. 28 – or on February 12 – the eve of his *Todestag*, as given by Göllerich/Auer III/1, p. 142. At some point, most likely when he was at work on the second movement, Bruckner surely must have realized this coincidence.

28. *Tannhäuser* begins with clarinets, horns, and bassoons providing a pair of eight-measure phrases both of which move from tonic to dominant in E major; immediately thereafter, the low strings present the *Reuemotiv* in the form of an upward third sequence connecting secondarily related minor mode regions in a spiral of ascending minor thirds. It should be noted that this pattern of tonal regions moving by ascending third matches that in the second phrase of Bruckner's first subject, mm. 12–20. As such, Wagner's example employs advanced harmonic language similar to that documented in Sechter's treatise *Vom Canon*.

29. Franz Scheder, *Anton Bruckner Chronologie* (Tutzing, 1996), Textband, p. 127.

30. For further discussion of Bruckner's involvement in the Linz première of *Tannhäuser*, see Göllerich-Auer, III/1, pp. 142–3.

31. In the Fourth Symphony, the second subject enters in D♭ major and, although the third subject enters in the goal key of B♭ major, it contains a significant reference back to the D♭ of the second subject. In the Fifth Symphony, the second subject enters in the goal key of F only to be contradicted by the D♭ entry of the third subject.

32. Measure 153 is both the concluding measure of the basic phrase initiated at m. 123 and, by elision, the beginning of a twelve-measure extension of tonic harmony (mm. 153–64).

33. The two-voice clausula is illustrated by Pietro Aaron in *Thoscanello de la Musica* (Venice, 1523), trans. Peter Bergquist (Colorado Springs, Colorado, 1970), II, p. 18. Aaron's example shows a combination of a $\hat{1}–\hat{7}–\hat{1}$ (*Cantizans*) pattern in the upper voice with a $\hat{2}–\hat{1}$ (*Tenorizans*) pattern in the lower voice. A common variant of the latter shows a $\hat{2}–\hat{3}$ motion, allowing inclusion of the major third in the final cadence pair. Gioseffe Zarlino, *The Art of Counterpoint: Part Three of 'Le Istitutioni*

Harmoniche', *1558*, trans. Guy A. Marco and Claude V. Palisca (New Haven, 1968), p. 151, refers to this variant as an imperfect cadence.

34. Sechter, *Die Grundsätze*, Vol. I, p. 57, states that, since the sixth scale degree is variable, both ii° and ii are considered diatonic chords in the minor mode.

35. See n. 12, above.

36. 'New Music, Outmoded Music, Style and Idea', *Style and Idea*, pp. 122–3.

37. A. B. Marx, *Die Lehre von der musikalischen Komposition* (Leipzig, 1837), III, pp. 201–300, derives sonata form from his descriptions of 'fourth-' and 'fifth-rondo form'. For discussion of Bruckner's derivations of sonata form, see Paul Hawkshaw, 'A Composer Learns His Craft: Anton Bruckner's Lessons in Form and Orchestration, 1861–63', in *The Musical Quarterly*, 82 (1998), pp. 336–61.

38. Thus, in the first movement of Schubert's Great C major Symphony, D. 944, the true second key of G major, established with the flute/clarinet melody at m. 174, has been preceded by the same theme given to oboe/bassoon in E minor at m. 134. It is important to observe that this false tonal entry at m. 134 does not lead to any authentic cadences in E minor. Rather, following two half cadences in that key (mm. 140 and 148, respectively), a transitional passage leads to the G major presentation of the theme. Another example of this phenomenon is found in the first movement of Schubert's Quintet for Strings in C major, D. 956.

39. The return that defines the beginning of a recapitulation can be either thematic or tonal. In the first movement of Schubert's Fifth Symphony in B♭ major, D. 485, the recapitulation is thematic but not tonal, occurring in the subdominant key at m. 167. In the first movement of Beethoven's Fourth Symphony in B♭ major, op. 60, by contrast, the recapitulation is tonal but not thematic occurring with the return of tonic harmony at m. 312, preceding the thematic return at m. 337. See Warren Darcy, 'Bruckner's Sonata Deformations', in *Bruckner Studies*, pp. 266–71, for description of discrepancies between tonal and thematic arrivals in Bruckner symphony movements for which he uses the term 'non-congruent'.

40. The actual harmonies here are d⁻⁴₂, b♭⁷ over a c pedal, and b°⁷ into a G.

41. Bruckner plays out this suggestion in his second movement, where the opening motive is an even closer reminiscence of the beginning of the *Trauermarsch*, presented in Bruckner's own key of C♯ minor, but ultimately brought to the famous climax (at rehearsal letter W, m. 177) in C major. See Stephen Parkany, 'Kurth's Bruckner and the Adagio of the Seventh Symphony', in *19th-Century Music*, 11 (1987), pp. 262–81, for further discussion of Wagnerian 'allusions' in this movement.

42. The second subject in the exposition comprises the 73-measure segment from mm. 51–123. Were the material transposed exactly in the recapitulation, it would proceed from its initiation at m. 319 to an arrival on E at m. 391.

43. It should be noted that in mid-nineteenth-century music literature it is common to find thematic entries appearing at the middle of a phrase. An example that might have been known to Bruckner is found in the F♯ major Romance, Op. 28, No. 2, by Robert Schumann, where the return of the initial theme occurs over a dominant pedal (m. 18).

44. Compare the cadence in Ex. 9.11 with that in Ex. 9.16.

45. The second movement also begins with a nine-measure phrase, as observed by Stephen Parkany, 'Kurth's Bruckner', pp. 269–70. In addition, observe that the antecedent/consequent phrase pair that open the final movement are also both nine measures in length.

46. For further discussion of Bruckner's use of proportional relationships, see Leopold Nowak, 'Anton Bruckners Formwille, dargestellt am Finale seiner V. Symphonie', and 'Studien zu den Formverhältnissen in der e-Moll-Messe von Anton Bruckner', in *Über Anton Bruckner* (Vienna, 1985), pp. 43–6, and 160–75; and Leopold

Brauneiss, 'Zahlen und Proportionen in Bruckners Siebenter Symphonie', in *Bruckner Jahrbuch* (1994–6), pp. 33–46.

47. In assessing the complex network of harmonic relationships in this movement, it might be well to consult the timpanist – one who usually participates actively in the tonal return of sonata-form movements by contributing the dominant pitch. In fact, Bruckner's Seventh Symphony is an isolated instance of a major-key symphony from the nineteenth-century repertory in which the timpanist never plays the dominant pitch. In the first movement, his only entrance comes at the aforementioned arrival on E at m. 391, from which point he prolongs the tonic pitch to the end of the movement – some 53 measures in all.

48. Karl Mayrberger, *Die Harmonik Richard Wagner*, p. 6, characterizes the 'suppressed' dominant in terms of the rhetorical term 'ellipsis', as follows:

> Just as ellipsis is a figure in rhetoric that makes it possible in conditions of agitated feeling or aroused passion, and occasionally even for the sake of brevity and elegance, to omit a word, or even several words; so is such a suppression of the resolution of dissonance nothing other than a harmonic ellipsis that the auditor can easily complete – although the composer has, as it were, taken it away from him.
>
> (*Wie in der Rhetorik die Ellipsis eine Figur ist, vermöge welcher in bewegten Gefühl oder in aufgeregter Leidenschaft, zuweilen auch der Kürze und Zierlichkeit halber, ein Wort oder auch mehrere ausgelassen werden können, so ist ein solches Verschweigen der Dissonanz-Auflösung, welche der Hörer leicht erganzen kann, obwohl sie ihm der Komponist quasi vorwegnimmt, nichts Anderes als eine harmonische Ellipsis.*)

10 Musical time in the Eighth Symphony

Joseph C. Kraus

> At this end of the twentieth century, generations and technological light years
> removed from the cultural milieu that produced them, Bruckner's symphonies may
> sound exotic or quaint, wondrous or naïve. Those epic essays may seem to unfold
> outside the boundaries of time; their clock speed, to borrow a term from digital
> parlance, may simply not compute in lives where cell phones accompany every step
> of the day and extended vacations are a forgotten concept.[1]

With these words, music critic Lawrence B. Johnson of the *New York Times*
continues a conversation about the Bruckner symphonies that has changed
remarkably little in the past 100 years. The great length and monumental
proportions of these pieces have led inevitably to their being labelled as 'long-
winded' or 'sluggish' in their pacing, and 'overblown' in their overall
conception.[2] Exactly how does time pass for the listener in a Bruckner
symphony? This article will explore a few possibilities, using ideas from
Jonathan Kramer's book *The Time of Music* as a point of departure.[3] Mr.
Kramer's interesting and implicative study dating from 1988 identifies two basic
classes of musical time: linear time and non-linear time. Linear time is goal-
directed and associated with left-brain activity, and can be linked to the
metaphorical state of 'becoming'. Non-linear time, on the other hand, is static
and associated with right-brain activity, and can be linked to the metaphorical
state of 'being'. In addition to goal-directed linear time, admittedly a
preoccupation of Western European culture, Kramer also recognizes several
other types of musical time which the listener may experience: (1) multiply-
directed time, where frequent discontinuities interrupt and re-order linear time;
(2) gestural time, when beginning, middle and ending gestures occupy
unconventional positions in a musical work; (3) moment time, marked by a
series of unconnected, static segments called moments; and (4) vertical time, an
unusual experience of stasis where one's very sense of the passage of time is
suspended. Although many of the pieces cited by Kramer in his study come from
the music of the twentieth century, he also discusses music of the previous
centuries to illustrate his new strategies for perceiving temporalities. My purpose
is to consider several passages from the Bruckner Eighth in light of these new

strategies, in order to investigate linear as well as non-linear aspects of the music.

Let us begin with an example of multiply-directed linear time in the first movement of the symphony. The pertinent music from the second area of the exposition is represented in Ex. 10.1. Note that this highly ambiguous passage presents three independent tonal streams, centering around the keys of G, G♭ and A respectively. By reading any of the systems from left to right, we may discover that each stream is continuous in itself, but interrupts the other competing streams in real time. Hence, a structural *discontinuity* is produced for the passage as a whole, which may be read in a strictly left-to-right fashion, skipping back and forth between the various streams.[4] This situation would seem to invoke Kramer's concept of multiply-directed linear time, where frequent discontinuities interrupt the *telos* so often that the linearity seems reordered. As a result, some passages 'can progress in more than one direction at once', and 'their continuations need not follow them directly'.[5] For example, in bars 52–4 (stream 1) we hear the beginning of a linear ascent, b^1–c^2 in the soprano. The goal of the ascent, d^3, is eventually reached in bar 68, and is then prolonged by a descending fourth progression to a^2 in bars 68–72, but only after many interruptions. The first of these in G♭ major at bar 55 shows another direction in which the music of bar 54 can progress. As shown, the $F\sharp^{\circ}_5^6$ from stream 1 may be enharmonically reinterpreted as a common tone $A^{\circ 7}$ in G♭; the diminished-seventh chord, therefore, is multiply-directed, with one resolution immediate, the other postponed for some 14 bars. The interruption of stream 2 at bar 58 follows a similar plan, with the resolution of the $vii^{\circ 7}$ of V delayed by its reinterpretation as a common tone diminished seventh in stream 3; the eventual resolution to V of G♭ in stream 2 takes place later at bar 64. The third stream twice initiates a linear descent from e^2, in bars 59 and 65. Instead of stopping again on b^1 the second time at bar 66, however, we may hear eventual closure on a^1 at bar 69, also the climactic point for stream 1, above.

The discontinuities encountered in this passage, though signalling multiply-directed time, do not destroy linearity, for each of the streams is, by itself, goal-directed. This situation also differs from the chromatic parentheses encountered in earlier nineteenth-century music, since the interrupting streams in G♭ and A produce their own, competing continuities. The challenge for the listener is to appreciate these continuities, as they exist in creative conflict with the sequence of interruptions. The late Christopher Lewis recognized similar discontinuities in the Adagio of Bruckner's Seventh Symphony, and related them to narrative discontinuities in a film by Maurizio Nichetti (*The Icicle Thief*).[6] According to Lewis, both works exemplify the concept of retrospective time in narrative theory, where the time line is folded in on itself and the memory of the perceiver reconstructs the fragmented continuities.

The pacing of events in Ex. 10.1 relates to criticisms concerning length in Bruckner's symphonic writing. Note that on average, harmonies change once every one or two measures, with little variation until the pace is accelerated in bars 69 and 70 for the approach to the cadence. William Benjamin has remarked

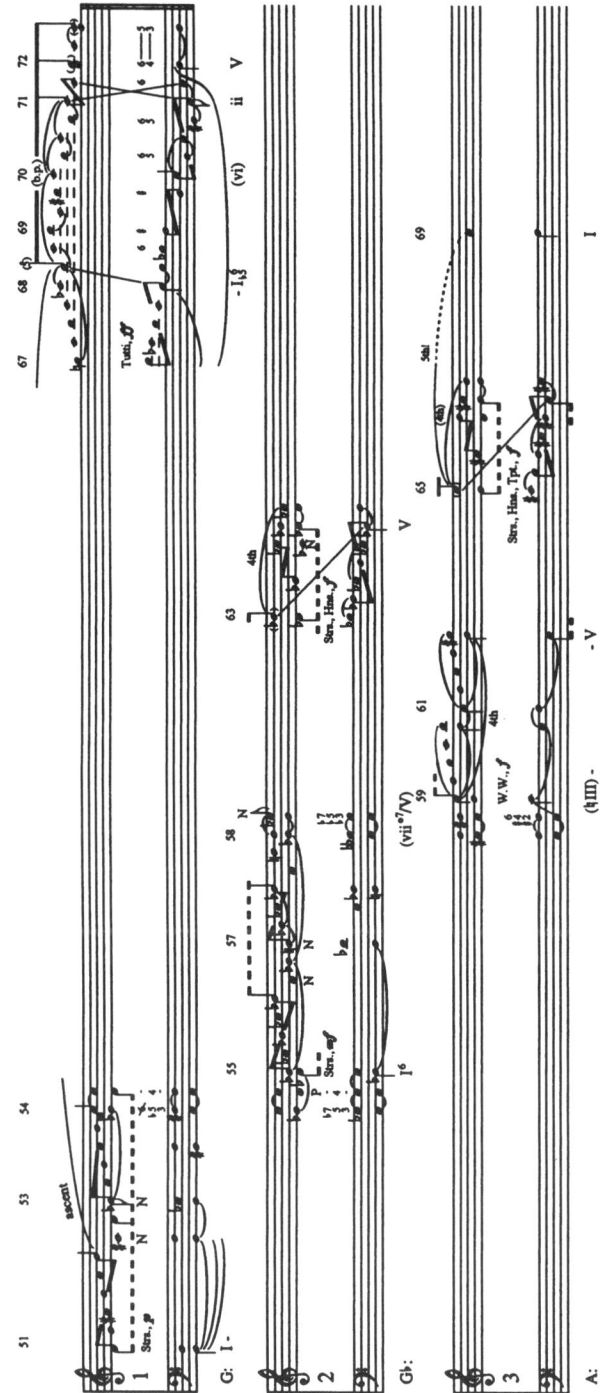

Ex. 10.1 Bruckner's Eighth Symphony – first movement, second theme

on the 'leisurely', steady pacing of tonal events in Bruckner as an absolute necessity, given the chromatic complexity of the music.[7] The harmonic rhythm may be more rapid or fluctuating in the music of, say, Mendelssohn, because the middleground structures supporting the detailed progressions are simpler and more easily comprehensible than the ambiguous structures of Bruckner; if such an approach were used for the discontinuous spans of Bruckner, incomprehensibility would be the result. The chromatic complexity of Bruckner's music also contributes to a sense of greater perceived length on the part of the listener, according to the 'storage size model' of cognitive psychologist Robert Ornstein.[8] In short, Ornstein's model suggests that the more information a passage contains, the longer its subjective duration (subject, of course, to other factors like ease of processing and the condition of the individual listener). Because the discontinuities of Ex. 10.1 contain high amounts of information which are difficult to process, its perceived time would be greater than its actual clock time. These observations help to explain the perception of length in this example, but are not intended as a negative criticism; indeed, its length is absolutely necessary, owing to the way in which it is written.

We now turn to the Scherzo from the second movement of the symphony, addressing its non-linear as well as linear aspects. This time we begin with a non-linear element – the relative proportions of its sections and subsections. Kramer believes strongly that proportions can be perceived, particularly after repeated hearings of a composition.[9] He claims that listening for proportions is a non-linear right-brain activity, since it involves a holistic perception of an entire piece or section all at once through memory, rather than a concentration on linear process from moment to moment. As such, progression and order are *not* involved in hearing proportions. For example, if sections of a movement are balanced, the order of those sections is immaterial; only their equal lengths relative to one another are important. Hence, proportions involve the state of 'being' rather than 'becoming'. Further, since this movement is a Scherzo with very strong rhythmic and metric markedness, I believe that a case can indeed be made here for the ability of the listener to recognize proportional relationships.

As shown in Ex. 10.2, the quasi-exposition of the Scherzo may be divided affectively into three Kurthian waves,[10] each with a climax more intense than the previous one. The dynamic markings which document the waves below the staff are reinforced by texture, orchestration and pitch as well. For example, the high point at bar 33 is defined by heavy brass scoring, *fortissimo*, its A major harmony serving as the point of furthest remove from both C minor (the opening key) and E♭ major (the closing key). The principal climax at bar 49 is marked by the only triple forte indication, the addition of an active tympani figure, and a sustained, highly dissonant B♭ pedal point in the soprano against the prevailing A♭ minor harmony. The three waves are perfectly symmetrical into the midpoint between bars 32 and 33, displaying the proportion 24:16:24, or 3:2:3. The bottom of Ex. 10.2 relates a different (though not necessarily contradictory) perspective: here the exposition is heard in two equal halves, supported by a

Ex. 10.2 Diagram showing Kurthian waves in the Scherzo

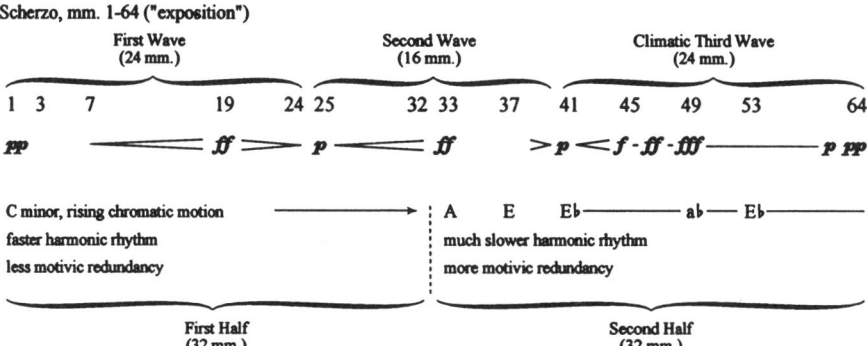

Scherzo, mm. 1-64 ("exposition")

change at bar 33 to a much slower harmonic rhythm and greater literal repetition of the basic motive. This interpretation responds to the sudden intrusion of A major at bar 33 as an irruptive edge separating what follows from what has come before. In both the tripartite and bipartite models, the bald repetition of the E♭ major chord in bars 53–64 is absolutely necessary to produce the balanced proportions – so much for the criticism that these grandiose bars constitute empty bombast! The redundancy of bars 53–64 also adds to the perceived length of the last unit as the listener anticipates the close at 64; this period of 'waiting for the end' counterbalances the reduction in perceived time for the second half of the piece brought on by the significant reduction in content – the slower harmonic rhythm and greater motivic redundancy.

Though both proportional models are viable, is one preferable to the other? In order to suggest an answer to this question, I will consider another factor: the time set up by the music's internal clock, its meter and hypermeter.[11] Example 10.3a provides a proportional reduction of the exposition, where each measure of the original music is represented by a quarter-note value. The combining of measures into four-bar hypermeasures is thus shown as quarter notes combining to form measures of 4/4 time; any irregularities appear as measures with an irregular number of beats. The four-bar hypermeasures combine in turn to form large hypermeasures, bracketed and numbered at the top of the example, and marked by thick bar lines in the music. The interaction of the hypermeter with the pitch structure of the piece is illustrated by the voice leading graph in Ex. 10.3b. By connecting this pitch structure to the hypermeter and examining its proportions, this model combines both linear and non-linear aspects into a single hearing of the passage.

Interestingly enough, the pattern of three large hypermeasures (bracketed at the top of the example) corresponds exactly to the three-part wave model from Ex. 10.2. The three large hypermeasures each prolong a single middleground soprano pitch: g^1 for the first large unit (bar 3), a^{b2} (bar 25) for the second large unit, and b^{b2} (bar 41) for the third large unit.[12] The broadly ascending melodic

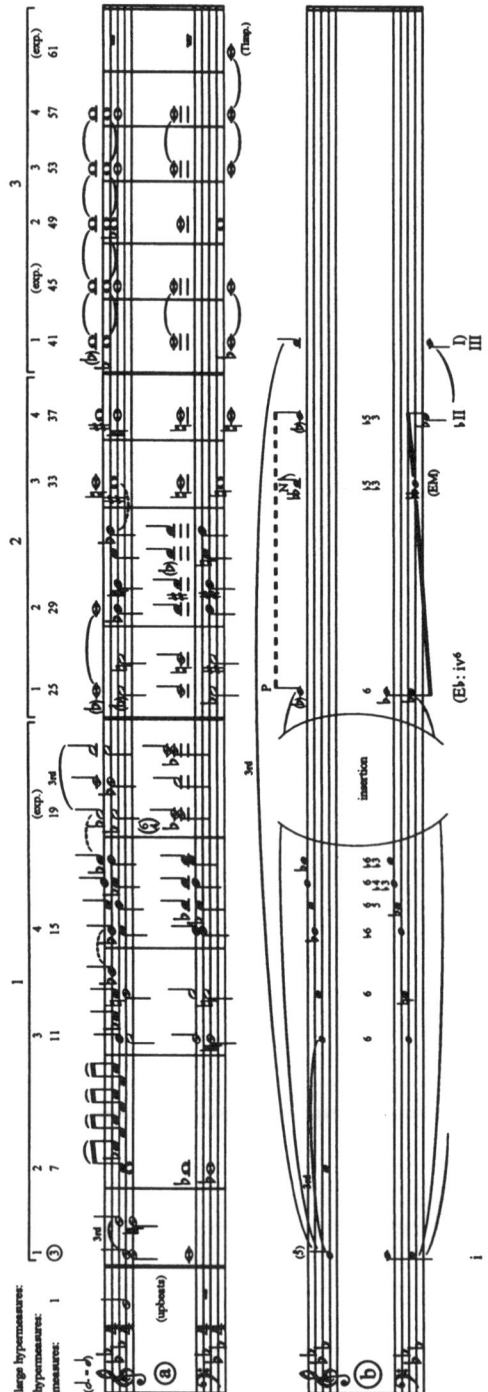

Ex. 10.3   Proportional reduction of the exposition of the Scherzo

264

third from G to B♭ is motivic, and may be heard over several different time spans, as labeled on sketches 'a' and 'b'; it may ultimately be traced to the second, third and fourth notes of the primary motive itself. The reason why waves 1 and 3 (the first and third large hypermeasures) are longer than the middle wave now becomes clear: each undergoes expansion. Large hypermeasure 1 begins with two introductory upbeat bars, and ends with an extra hypermeasure of six bars (19–24). As sketch 'b' shows, this irregular 6/4 hyperbar is a chromatic insertion (in the early nineteenth-century sense) which temporarily interrupts the ascending parallel sixths in the soprano-bass counterpoint; this discontinuity lends further support to hearing bar 25 as a new beginning. Along the same lines, the striking A major chord at the midpoint of the section (bar 33) does not fall on a hypermetric downbeat, weakening its possible perception as the beginning of a new unit. Instead, reference to the voice leading graph clarifies its true function (and spelling) as B♭♭ major, an embellishing chord providing consonant support for the neighbor note b♭♭^{2} in the soprano.[13] By combining aspects of linear as well as non-linear time in this passage, we have been able to arrive at a preferred model for hearing its relative proportions – the three-part Kurthian wave.

Example 10.4 documents the same approach applied to the quasi-development of the Scherzo. Its 70 bars constitute a single wave culminating at bars 91–4; the return to tonic at bar 95 and the subsequent falling motion divide

Ex. 10.4   Diagram of the quasi-development of the Scherzo

Scherzo, mm. 65-134 ("development")

the 70 bars into 30 + 40, as shown. The first 30-measure unit contains the harmonic move from III to the dominant, with a two-measure expansion in bars 89–90. The second half begins at bar 95 with a 12-measure unit featuring the inverted theme in the woodwinds, and a progression from tonic to dominant (actually through the diatonic circle of fifths – an interesting archaism by the time of this composition). The twelve-measure unit is repeated in sequence down a fifth in bars 107ff., now in the strings, with a massive 16-measure extension in bars 119–34. During the extension hemiola is followed by a dissolution of the theme through fragmentation, eventually to only two notes. This addition explains the longer clock-time length of the second half (bars 95–134), but its perceived length might be shorter. Though not shown on the example, each half of this section contains two large hypermetric downbeats: bars 65 and 81 for the first half, bars 95 and 107 for the second. As in the exposition of the Scherzo, if each subsection contains the same number of hypermetric downbeats, they might be perceived as roughly equal in proportion in non-linear time.

The final example of temporality in Bruckner's Eighth Symphony invokes Jonathan Kramer's most controversial concept, and may prove to be the most controversial point of this discussion. Kramer defines non-linear vertical time as a state of timelessness brought on by musical stasis.[14] Rather than eliminating time altogether, however, vertical time transforms ordinary time into an 'eternal now', a 'timeless temporal continuum, in which the linear interrelationships between past, present and future are suspended'.[15] This concept resonates with Sigmund Freud's view of dreams and the self-conscious: since the unconscious mind does not operate in a linear fashion, past, present and future all co-exist in an eternal state of 'being'. Though all of Kramer's examples of vertical time emanate from the avant-garde literature of the present century, I admit to being intrigued by the possibility that the Apotheosis at the close of the Finale of the Bruckner Eighth could communicate to the listener the essence of a vertical time experience. It is well known that this section (Ex. 10.5) combines elements of the principal themes of all four movements to achieve a glorious culmination. But apart from its obvious cyclical aspects, could it also be an example of vertical time? From an internal musical perspective, the combination of thematic material from all movements simultaneously would seem to suggest the fusion of at least past with present; since it was obviously the intent of the composer that this work have future performances, this thematic amalgam could also represent future time. Moreover, the passage certainly communicates a quality of stasis,

Ex. 10.5   End of the Finale

from motivic, textural and harmonic standpoints, though the time allotted to this stasis is much more brief than in Kramer's models. If the internal evidence is not entirely convincing, let us also consider the symphony's external perspective: the composer's program for the work and his deeply held religious beliefs, as they might pertain to the question at hand.

The details of Bruckner's own programmatic comments about the Eighth Symphony (whether actual or attributed) are well known: the death-clock or *Totenuhr* at the end of the first movement (most likely in reference to the revised, quiet ending); the German Michael as an Austrian character in the Scherzo and Finale; and the death march and transformation in the Finale.[16] Bryan Gilliam has aptly labelled these descriptions as 'ex post facto pictorial tags' which appeared after the revision of the work in 1890, casting doubt on the legitimacy of their connection to the original version completed in 1887.[17] Whether or not these descriptions point to the genesis of the work, they at least provide evidence that Bruckner was not violently opposed to the idea of death and transfiguration as a subtext for the symphony – ample permission, if you will, for a modern-day listener to ascribe this meaning to the composition. Given Bruckner's fervent Roman Catholicism, the nature of the transfiguration after death is quite clear – the attainment of salvation as the purified soul enters into heaven, an eternal state of bliss in the presence of the Almighty. Note the use of the word 'eternal', that is, *timeless*. If the Apotheosis were a metaphor for heaven, it would represent a timeless state, lending some support to my argument for the experience of vertical time in this passage.[18] Although I am still somewhat dubious myself about this interpretation, I must confess that I find it appealing. One might even take the argument one step further: if we accept a vertical time reading of the Apotheosis, the unison passage added at the end in the 1890 revision (see the bracket in Ex. 10.5) is completely out of place, since it destroys the beautiful vertical stasis of the previous bars.

In conclusion we might again return to the words of critic Lawrence B. Johnson. In reviewing several recent recordings of Bruckner symphonies, he disapproves of two conductors who attempt to make the music too 'aggressive' or 'brilliant', in part to answer 'the modernist need to make Bruckner relevant'. Johnson insists that 'Bruckner's symphonies work best in their own continuum of space, time and, implicitly, spirit'.[19] Perhaps the temporalities in these symphonic testaments are too rich and subtle to be explained in linear terms alone. Through the concepts of discontinuity, multiply-directed time, proportion and vertical time, I hope to have offered the reader some food for thought about the ways that non-linear as well as linear time might inform our hearing of the Eighth Symphony.

Notes

1. Lawrence B. Johnson, 'Symphonies That Unfold as if Outside the Boundaries of

Time', *The New York Times*, 29 March 1998, section 2, p. 42.

2. The objections raised by Eduard Hanslick and his circle of Brahms-partisans reverberate to the present day, particularly among those who favour an overtly formalist approach to the understanding and appreciation of music.

3. Jonathan D. Kramer, *The Time of Music: New Meanings, New Temporalities, New Listening Strategies* (New York and London: Schirmer, 1988). The following summary is derived from chs. 1 and 2.

4. William E. Benjamin recognizes the same phenomenon in the first theme groups of the first and last movements of the Eighth; he comments that secondary keys are often presented 'in discontinuous fragments, interrupting an equally discontinuous representation of the primary tonality'. See 'Tonal Dualism in Bruckner's Eighth Symphony', in *The Second Practice of Nineteenth-Century Tonality*, ed. William Kinderman and Harald Krebs (Lincoln and London: University of Nebraska Press, 1996), particularly pp. 239–49. Benjamin interprets these discontinuities in terms of 'dual or multiple prolongation', where a passage is controlled by 'two or more underlying harmonies, affiliated to different tonics by virtue of distinct webs of voice leading' (p. 239).

5. Kramer, *The Time of Music*, p. 46.

6. Christopher Lewis, 'The Mind's Chronology: Narrative Times and Harmonic Disruption in Postromantic Music', in *The Second Practice of Nineteenth-Century Tonality*, pp. 114–49.

7. Benjamin, 'Tonal Dualism in Bruckner's Eighth Symphony', pp. 253–4.

8. Robert E. Ornstein, *On The Experience of Time* (New York: Penguin, 1969). Jonathan Kramer provides a useful summary of Ornstein's theory in *The Time of Music*, pp. 333–45.

9. Kramer, *The Time of Music*, pp. 42–3.

10. Ernst Kurth, *Bruckner* (Berlin: Hesse, 1925), I/2, ch. 2. Most of this chapter appears in a very useful English translation in *Ernst Kurth: Selected Writings*, trans. and ed. Lee A. Rothfarb (Cambridge and New York: Cambridge University Press, 1991), pp. 151–207. In discussing Kurth's theory, Stephen Parkany describes the wave (*Welle*) as 'the distinctive dynamic essence that takes precedence over the standard concept of 'theme'; this dynamically conceived musical unit is set into motion by an intensification (*Steigerung*), comes to a climax (*Höhepunkt*), then ebbs to a low point (*Tiefepunkt*)'. Stephen Parkany, 'Bruckner and the Vocabulary of Symphonic Formal Process' (Ph.D. dissertation, Univ. of California, 1989), ch. 2, particularly pp. 98–100.

11. The following analysis draws heavily on techniques popularized by Carl Schachter and William Rothstein. See Schachter, 'Rhythm and Linear Analysis: Durational Reduction', in *The Music Forum*, 5 (1980), pp. 197–232; Rothstein, *Phrase Rhythm in Tonal Music* (New York and London: Schirmer, 1989).

12. Note that the soprano a♭[2] is first harmonized in m. 25 by A♭ minor $^6_3$, then by F♭ major (the Phrygian II of E♭) in m. 37.

13. A♭–B♭♭–A♭ becomes the principal pitch motive in the next movement of the symphony.

14. Kramer, *The Time of Music*, pp. 54–7 and 375–97.

15. Kramer, op. cit., p. 387.

16. The most comprehensive treatment appears in 'Das Programm der Achten Symphonie', in Constantin Floros, *Brahms und Bruckner: Studien zur musikalischen Exegetik* (Wiesbaden: Breitkopf und Härtel, 1980), pp. 182–229. See also Robert Simpson, *The Essence of Bruckner* (London: Camelot; Philadelphia: Chilton, 1968), pp. 165–6.

17. Bryan Gilliam, 'The Two Versions of Bruckner's Eighth Symphony', in *19th-Century Music*, 16 (1992), p. 65. Gilliam traces the history of the *Totenuhr* description

(supposedly offered by the composer himself) in early Bruckner biographies by Decsey and Göllerich-Auer.

18. Psychoanalyst Peter Hartocollis equates timelessness with the experience of ecstasy, where one is totally free from the cares of the outside world. 'On the Experience of Time and its Dynamic, with Special Reference to the Affects', in *Journal of the American Psychoanalytic Association*, 24 (1976), pp. 368–70; quoted in Kramer, *The Time of Music*, p. 377.

19. Johnson, 'Symphonies That Unfold', p. 42.

11   The facts behind a 'legend': the Ninth Symphony and the *Te Deum*

John A. Phillips

Bruckner's injunction that, should he not live to complete an instrumental Finale, his *Te Deum* should be used as, or in place of, a fourth movement to the Ninth Symphony has often been dismissed as fiction. How, it is asked, could Bruckner have intended to complete a D minor symphony in C major; why indeed should one concern oneself about a Finale at all, given the sublime ending of the Adagio? This article will not attempt to debate the aesthetic or analytical pros and cons of this question, but rather examine some of the references to a link between the Ninth Symphony and *Te Deum* and Bruckner's intention to use the *Te Deum* as a conclusion to the symphony should he be unable to finish the instrumental Finale. It will also consider the issue of whether and when Bruckner conceived of some sort of instrumental transition to the *Te Deum*, and what form that transition may have taken. As the following discussion reveals, these issues have important implications for our understanding of Bruckner the composer and for the performance of his last and most monumentally conceived symphony.[1]

The Ninth and the *Te Deum*

There is little question that the Ninth Symphony was planned by Bruckner from the outset as a four-movement, purely instrumental symphony. An undated anecdote recorded by the biographer August Göllerich quotes Bruckner as saying: 'I'll not try to compete with Beethoven. D minor's fine, it's such a good key, but with a chorus, like Beethoven – no, Bruckner's not that stupid'.[2] There are also indications that the composer had at least some idea of the thematic substance of all movements, including the Finale, at an early stage. For instance, the brief choral work *Das Deutsche Lied* (WAB 63), written in April 1892, anticipates several aspects of the Finale by over three years. The Finale was

270

also to make explicit the idea of a 'spiritual link' between the Ninth and the *Te Deum* by adopting the string figuration of the latter as a central symphonic motive, an idea that appears already in the earliest sketches for the movement.[3] According to one important source, the movement was also intended to end as a 'song of praise to the dear Lord', with a musical idea identified as an 'Allelujah'.[4]

It is also significant that Bruckner was often in quite serious ill health from 1892 onward, and that the composition of the entire Ninth Symphony, not just its Finale, was overshadowed by lengthy bouts of illness. It is therefore hardly surprising that he appears almost from the outset to have reckoned with the possibility he might not live to complete the symphony. Max Auer records that in early 1891 Bruckner played sketches to the Viennese conductor Hermann Haböck, asking his advice. Haböck relates that: 'Already back then he was explaining: "If I can't manage it, the *Te Deum* comes at the end" '.[5] At the beginning of March 1891 Bruckner played passages 'from all movements' of the Ninth to the visiting Dresden conductor and composer Jean Louis Nicodé (although at this stage neither Adagio nor Finale would have been very close to the form in which we recognize them today).[6] Again, Auer records Nicodé as adding: 'I wouldn't like to swear to it, but I even believe that he already made the comment to me then: in case he shouldn't live to see the completion of an independent 4th movement, his *Te Deum* was to be regarded as a concluding movement'.[7] Strikingly, there is no evidence that Bruckner ever expressed an opinion concerning the fact that appending the *Te Deum* would effectively conclude a D minor symphony in C major, a stumbling block to commentators ever since.

But the idea of using the *Te Deum* apparently constituted an important aspect of Bruckner's conception of the symphony. In Joseph Gruber's memoirs we read:

> Before his death he expressed the desire that, in performance [of the Ninth] one should use, in place of the final movement which he was no longer able to compose, his *Te Deum*. Of this powerful *Te Deum* he once said the following: 'When my dear Lord calls me before his judgement throne, I will point to my *Te Deum* which I dedicated to him, and I hope he will be a merciful judge!'[8]

Unfortunately the context of the passage gives no indication of a date on which these remarks may have been made. But similar remarks survive from Bruckner's doctor Joseph Kluger:

> The Master also spoke of his intentions concerning the Ninth Symphony to Dr Kluger, who reported: 'Bruckner characterized it as "Homage to Divine Majesty". Here too the last movement would have developed the leading idea in fullest clarity. But this intention of the righteous master came to pass in a manner different from that which Bruckner expected. Unable to write this fourth movement as a result of serious illness, the concept of the whole suggested to him the idea that he should, as the clearest expression of his homage to divine majesty, append his *Te Deum*, completed in 1884, to the three movements of the Ninth.'[9]

Although Auer situates Kluger's words within the context of 1896, both passages speak of Bruckner as unable to *compose* a fourth movement rather than unable to *finish* one, and hence probably derive from statements made prior to 24 May 1895, when work on the Finale actually began.[10] This accords with a statement made by the composer in the course of his final university lecture on 5 November 1894.[11] According to Ernst Schwanzara, who attended Bruckner's university lectures for three academic years running (1891–4) and took down the composer's words stenographically, Bruckner noted:

> The movements of my IXth Symphony are already finished, the first three completely; only in the 3rd movement I still have some nuances to add.
> With the Symphony I imposed a heavy burden of work upon myself. Considering my age and ill-health I shouldn't have done it. [...] Should I die before the completion of the symphony, my *Te Deum* should be played in place of the fourth movement. I have already decided so.[12]

The indications of connections between the Ninth and the *Te Deum*, and the directive that the *Te Deum* should conclude the symphony continue through Bruckner's return to composition in May 1895, and recur throughout the last two years, as in this anonymous newspaper report of mid-October 1895:

> [...] the master goes on composing tirelessly; he has completed his Ninth Symphony as far as the Finale and is thinking about appending to the composition his earlier *Te Deum* as a complete conclusion [vollständiger Schluß]. 'I dedicated the Eighth Symphony to my good Emperor and the Ninth Symphony to the dear Lord, in deep reverence; because of that it should end with a *Te Deum*, and then I'll lay down my pen for ever', said the great man a few days ago, speaking to a friend who had come to visit.[13]

Bruckner continued to work persistently on the Finale throughout the autumn and winter of 1895, advancing as far as the fugue, compositionally speaking the midpoint of the movement, by mid-December 1895.[14] Over the ensuing months he appears to have completed most of the remainder, probably at least as far as the beginning of the coda. A report in the *Steyrer Zeitung* of 10 May 1896, recounting Franz Bayer's visit to Bruckner, confirms: 'the concluding movement of his Ninth Symphony he has probably sketched in its entirety, but he himself no longer hopes to be able to complete its working-out'.

The Transition to the *Te Deum*

Although perhaps overemphasized by Auer, there is no question that Bruckner, confronting the possibility that he might indeed die before completion of the Finale, thought about using the instrumental torso of the movement as a transition ('Überleitung'), or kind of symphonic introduction, to the *Te Deum*.[15] Two surviving reports give some idea of Bruckner's intentions.

Firstly, Bruckner is said to have improvised a transition to the *Te Deum* at the piano, which Stradal allegedly transcribed from memory (although no such sketch has come to light):

> The Master's pupils August Stradal and Altwirth affirm that he played them a 'transition to the *Te Deum*' which Stradal noted down from memory. This transition was to have led from E major to C major, the tonality of the *Te Deum*. Surrounded by the string figuration of the *Te Deum*, a chorale was heard that is not to be found in the *Te Deum*. [...] According to the information given by the witnesses mentioned [...] the master appears not to have planned an independent musical transition from the Adagio to the *Te Deum*, but one from the reprise (of the Finale), where the coda should begin. As he recognized that the completion of a purely instrumental Finale was impossible, he attempted to create an organic link to the *Te Deum*, which had been suggested to him as a conclusion.[16]

The place apparently described appears at first sight to be from the reprise of the chorale, presumably by-passing the resumption of the triplet texture in the last six measures of the lost bifol. [30/'31'].[17] Most likely Stradal's description, as related by Auer, corresponds to a continuation of the quaver string figuration modulating into the opening of the *Te Deum*. However, the reprise of the chorale begins in D major, begging the question as to whether the E major starting point cited was not simply a misprint for D major. There are many such misprints in the biography,[18] while the only substantial passage in the Finale in E major is the chorale in the exposition, which is not accompanied by any *Te Deum* figuration in the strings (although the motive enters in the flute at the beginning of the development). There is, however, a hitherto unexplained pencil annotation, '*Te Deum*', on bifolio 11A/'12', 13 measures before the appearance of the motive itself in the flute.[19] Although the foregoing passage is fully and apparently definitively scored out, with rests in all otherwise unoccupied systems, a pencil sketch transposing the second statement of the chorale into C major can be found in the oboe and bassoon staves for 12 measures preceding the annotation. If the annotation '*Te Deum*' has anything to do with this sketch, it is not impossible that Bruckner may have conceived this transposition with the idea of joining up with the *Te Deum* at that point.

Mention should also be made of a curious continuity draft for the development section, bifolio '14'E, which according to the paper ruling used would appear to have been written post-May 1896, but which is curiously dated by Bruckner '14. Jänner'.[20] The draft shows a variant of the *Te Deum* motive in minims, but apparently modulating into C major, and is the only one of several late variants for this passage to do so. While there is not enough information to permit more than idle speculation, it is not impossible that this bifolio could represent a sketch for a transition to the *Te Deum* from the development section of the movement, the date written, perhaps, merely as a personal memorandum. For Bruckner heard his *Te Deum* for what was to be the last time at a Philharmonic concert under Richard Perger on 12 (not 14) January 1896.[21] In contradiction to the wording given in Stradal's testimony, on the other hand, the preceding passage of the score does not feature *Te Deum* figuration in the strings, and bifolio '14'E itself places a new dotted minim–crotchet motive in the first violin stave.

The second literary reference to a transition to the *Te Deum* derives from Anton Meißner, the composer's companion and amanuensis in his last years, who prepared his music paper for him and was also active as secretary and copyist.[22] In an article published in 1947 (Meißner died in 1945) we read:

> The transition to the fourth movement of his Ninth he conceived with motives from his *Te Deum*, which was, after all, intended to be the final movement of the symphony. And during this transition the choral singers were to walk onto the podium in solemn procession.[23]

It is striking that Meißner apparently refers to the *Te Deum* here as if it was a matter of course that it was to constitute the 'fourth movement' of the Ninth. Concerning the dating of the passage, the remarks appear within the context of Easter 1895, but Meißner may simply have been putting down ideas more or less as they occurred to him, or there may have been editorial interference from his editor Viktor Keldorfer. The version of Meißner's text published in Göllerich-Auer appears to have been taken from a common source but includes details not found in the 1947 publication, and comparison suggests the occurrence described more likely took place a year later, in April or May 1896. Max Auer explains that Bruckner's idea of using the Finale as a transition to the *Te Deum* was prompted by a suggestion made by the conductor Hans Richter. In Auer's shorter Bruckner biography (as published in 1923 and 1934) Richter is cited as first proposing the use of the *Te Deum* to Bruckner as a Finale; Auer meanwhile discovered, however, that Bruckner had thought of the idea himself much earlier, and in the 1941 edition the reference to Richter is eliminated altogether.[24] Auer then explains Bruckner subsequently taking up the idea of using the unfinished Finale as a transition to the *Te Deum*:

> He now appeared to think about a transition to the *Te Deum* and promised, as Meißner recounted, 'an overwhelming effect with the broad entry march of the principal theme, blasted out by the wind band, and the ensuing distantly reminiscent, familiar and original introductory measures of the *Te Deum*, as well as the entry of the singers. He wanted, as he explained to Meißner several times while playing, "to rattle at the gates of eternity"'.[25]

However, Bruckner appears to have subsequently discarded the idea quite emphatically. The final words of the passage in Meißner's memoirs were either not known to Auer, or omitted by him on purpose, for Meißner concludes: 'Yet none of his musical drafts satisfied him. He indignantly slammed the keyfall of the piano down in front of me and said: "They should simply hang the *Te Deum* onto the Symphony."'[26]

While apparently garbled – and one must recall not only that Meißner's memory may have been dimmed by the passage of time, but also that the text published in 1947 was edited by Keldorfer – it is possible that Meißner, like Stradal and Altwirth, was also speaking of a transition passage from the reprise of the chorale ('the broad entry march of the principal theme'), with figuration 'distantly reminiscent' of the *Te Deum* continuing to the entry of the singers at the beginning of the choral work itself. If one agrees that this is more likely to have occurred subsequent to Easter 1896 rather than Easter 1895, and if Bruckner soon revoked the idea of using the Finale as a transition, this readily accords with what we know about Bruckner's progress on the composition of the Finale. For by May 1896 Bruckner appears to have arrived at a crucial hurdle in the composition of the score; sketches dated 19–23 May reveal that Bruckner ceased forward composition on the score at this point in order to refine the form of a crescendo passage and extended 24-measure harmonic sequence concluding in a pedal point on D – probably the final cadence of the movement.[27] In the margin of this sketch stands 'Bogen 36', an apparent indication of the point at which the contents of this sketch were to be inserted in the score. As the last surviving orchestral bifolio we have (containing the end of the chorale reprise) was originally numbered 31, it is clear that Bruckner by this time must have extended the score well into the coda.[28] All ensuing dates concern revisions, so there is every likelihood that, in accord with his usual compositional methods, Bruckner may have completed the drafting out of the entire score in its essential continuity (complete string texture) around June, before returning to the beginning of the movement to systematically complete its orchestration.

Subsequent references to the *Te Deum* and the Finale in the Göllerich-Auer biography confirm both the ongoing status of the *Te Deum* as 'emergency conclusion' as well as continuing work on the Finale, despite Bruckner's gradual mental and physical deterioration. To Karl Almeroth and Adalbert von Goldschmidt, who visited Bruckner around the end of September 1896, Bruckner remarked how much he regretted the impossibility of completing the Finale and, making reference to the dedication of the work, again specified the *Te Deum* as the best conclusion.[29] To Franz Brunner, a pupil of Bruckner's who visited him at much the same time and noted the numerous pages of manuscript lying about the room, Bruckner is said to have noted with resignation, '"Well, if I don't finish they'll just have to use the *Te Deum*".'[30]

Bruckner's '*vi-de*' indications in the *Te Deum* and Finale

Leopold Nowak, in the Vorwort to the 1974 edition of the *Te Deum* mentions a cut indicated in the autograph of the *Te Deum* (ÖNB Mus. Hs. 19.486), namely from letter 'Q', the beginning of the 'Salvum fac', to letter 'V', the beginning of the double fugue on the words 'In Te, Domine, speravi'. According to the present writer's colleague Benjamin Gunnar Cohrs, who examined the autograph in September 1996, this cut is indicated in ink and in the spidery, trembling hand characteristic of Bruckner's old age; presumably then, it may have been made in 1895–6 and have something to do with Bruckner's plans to use the *Te Deum* in connection with the Ninth.[31] Nowak, however, claimed the cut 'must have been made at the instigation of Hellmesberger, whose enthusiasm for the *Te Deum* led him to consider performing it in the Hofkapelle on the occasion of the conferring of the biretta on Cardinal Ganglbauer on November 22 1884. In the event, however, Hellmesberger found the work too long [...]'.[32] Just what evidence may have led Nowak to this conclusion remains as yet unknown, but until both the handwriting of the cut and the circumstances surrounding Nowak's assertion of the connection with a possible performance in 1884 is investigated, there remains no clear proof that the cut was made in connection with the Finale of the Ninth.

It is also possible that several '*vi–de*' markings found in the Finale score may have been conceived with the use of the previously composed torso of the movement as a transition to the *Te Deum* in mind.[33] The cuts are distributed fairly evenly through the development, fugue (reprise of the principal theme), and reprise of the second subject, and actually emphasise the clear structural integrity at which the score, despite its mutilation subsequent to the composer's death, had obviously arrived.[34] They also demonstrate the loss of both earlier, that is, discarded and replaced, bifolios of the score, as well as lost later versions, and as their notation, on internal evidence, preceded the renumbering of score bifolios in May or June 1896, they could indeed have had some connection with the use of the torso of the Finale as a transition.[35] While several of the renumbered (and hence presumably definitive) bifolios of the exposition have apparently been lost, so that it is not possible to assess what, if any, corresponding cuts Bruckner might have indicated in the second subject in the exposition, the surviving cuts already involve over 120 measures in a score that, excluding the coda, was already well over 550 measures in length. In comparison – if indeed the cut indicated in the *Te Deum* has anything to do with the possibility of linking of the two works in performance – it may or may not be significant that the excision of 145 measures from the 513-measure score of the *Te Deum* is roughly analogous. If the *Te Deum* cut was proposed by Bruckner in connection with the symphony, there would seem to have been little point in such a radical truncation were it to have stood as an independent fourth movement (513 measures versus the 567 measures of the first movement); the most likely reason for Bruckner proposing a cut in the *Te Deum* would have been its use in conjunction with some or most of the Finale as a transition or introduction to it.

Yet there is no question that, rather than content himself with the using the *Te Deum* either alone or with the Finale, Bruckner subsequently proceeded with the composition of the instrumental movement with great determination. The score undoubtedly progressed well beyond the point in the reprise from which the transition appears to have been envisaged, and quite likely extended, in a minimum of continuous string texture, as far as the final measures of the work. In his last months Bruckner appears to have drafted a number of not always definitive revisions to the opening of the exposition and of the development; it may well be significant that the expansions he was willing to make to the latter suggest that he was clearly not at all concerned, by that point in time, about making the movement any shorter.

Summary and Implications

To summarize, the underlying sequence of events in relation to Bruckner's thinking about a link between the Ninth Symphony and the *Te Deum* would appear to have been:

1. The Ninth, although planned from the outset as a purely instrumental symphony, was dedicated to the 'dear Lord'; its Finale, intended to end with a 'song of praise', was motivically linked to the music of the *Te Deum*. Beset by recurrent ill-health throughout the composition of the symphony, Bruckner repeatedly and unequivocally specified the use of the *Te Deum* as an 'ersatz Finale' for the Ninth should he not live to complete a fourth movement.

2. With composition of the Finale well advanced, Bruckner appears to have turned to the idea of creating a transition to the *Te Deum* sometime in Spring 1896, considered using the torso of the Finale itself as a vast instrumental 'introduction', and probably an adaptation of the chorale in the reprise so as to lead into the *Te Deum*. Manuscript evidence also suggests he may have considered a transition from one or more points in the earlier part of the movement. It is conceivable that several cuts found throughout the extant fragments of the Finale score, as well as a massive cut marked in the score of the *Te Deum*, may have had some connection with the practical considerations imposed by such a huge, compound formal conception.

3. Not long after, Bruckner appears to have rejected this solution, and continued, in spite of failing mental and physical health, with the composition of the Finale, which undoubtedly progressed well beyond that point in the reprise from which the transition appears to have been envisaged. Nonetheless, there is no indication that Bruckner ever revoked his previous pronouncement that, should he not live to complete the Finale, the *Te Deum* should be used in its place. Indeed, he reiterated it on several occasions.

In conclusion, it should not be imagined that any of the literary sources cited in this article represented dissenting or little-known views at the time. Hardly any of the 21 reports published in various Vienna newspapers and journals on the occasion of the first performance of the Ninth (with the *Te Deum*) by Ferdinand Löwe in February 1903 refrain from mentioning Bruckner's directive that the *Te Deum* should follow the Adagio, and there are more references made to the existence of sketches for a transition to the choral work than to the existence of an independent Finale.[36] But of these critiques, many (significantly, not all) also endorse the views of both Ferdinand Löwe and his friend the critic Robert Hirschfeld, who wrote the programme notes for the first performance. The *Te Deum* conclusion, followed by Löwe in 1903 out of 'pious obligation to the wishes of the master', was discounted in both the Preface to the 1903 score and in the extensive programme notes for the first performance by Robert Hirschfeld as unnecessary, either on the grounds that the nature of the Adagio obviated the necessity of any fourth movement, or that a work in C major could not conclude a work in D minor. Among the few dissenting voices, Max Kalbeck noted quite rightly that it was no worse concluding a D minor symphony with a C major *Te Deum* than with an E major Adagio; another pointed out, referring to Hirschfeld's words: 'It can't be such a profane thought "to expect a fourth movement" when Bruckner himself regarded one as necessary and was only prevented from composing the intended Finale by his failing strength'.[37]

Such voices were, however, in the minority. Although the practice of occasionally pairing the two works continues to the present day, aesthetic preference gradually took precedence over what was widely acknowledged to have been Bruckner's explicit wishes. The huge mass of surviving material of the Finale fared even worse in this process of disinformation: it was most often dismissed as nothing more than fleeting or indecipherable sketches, or confused with the issue of a transition to the *Te Deum*. The idea that the Finale might hold some significance for a deeper understanding of the first three movements was soon lost from view. The *Te Deum*, too, gradually came to be understood as basically extrinsic to the musical character or 'programme' of the symphony. That Bruckner himself may have wanted the *Te Deum* performed 'as' or 'in place of' a fourth movement, should he not complete one, or what he may have wished to say in doing so, was simply disregarded.

What is perfectly clear is that ending a performance of the Ninth Symphony with the Adagio, as is common practice today, would have been anathema to its composer. His specification of the *Te Deum* as an apparently quite obligatory conclusion to the Ninth Symphony, as well as the idea of using a pre-composed D minor movement as a transition to it – despite the manifest stylistic and tonal dichotomy between symphony and choral work – indicates, firstly, that the 'quadratic character' of the whole symphony was extremely important to him, and in order to maintain it he appears to have been willing to compromise on issues of tonal, thematic and stylistic unity. The Adagio, despite the reading given by the majority of conductors and interpretations placed upon it by critics and audiences, in no wise represented any kind of conclusion or final artistic statement for the composer.

Moreover, and perhaps more importantly, both Bruckner's indication that the instrumental Finale was to conclude with a 'song of praise', as well as his specification of the *Te Deum* as a 'fall-back measure' should the instrumental movement remain unfinished, reveal that the dedication of the Ninth to the 'dear Lord', above any intrinsically musical considerations, constituted an integral part of Bruckner's conception of the Ninth Symphony from the outset and remained uppermost in his intentions concerning its conclusion. By performing the Ninth Symphony in three movements we are in effect violating Bruckner's conception of the entire work. In light of the evidence it is high time that musicologists and conductors seriously reconsider this issue.

Notes

1. This article is a much condensed summary of sections dealing with this issue in the author's doctoral dissertation 'Bruckner's Ninth Revisited; towards the re-evaluation of a four-movement symphony' (in progress). Warm thanks is due to Prof. Timothy Jackson (Dallas) for his many valuable editorial suggestions, and at whose urging this article was written, as well as to Dr Crawford Howie (Manchester) and Prof. Paul Hawkshaw (Yale) for their careful readings. Research has shown that the Finale of the Ninth survives in far more fragmentary form than Bruckner himself left it, and alters our perception of a movement which most commentators had until recently dismissed as disjointed sketches. See the author's article 'Neue Erkenntnisse zum Finale der Neunten Symphonie', in *Bruckner Jahrbuch 1989–90* (Vienna: Musikwissenschaftlicher Verlag, 1992), pp. 115ff. and his publications on the Finale in *Bruckner Sämtliche Werke B, Rekonstruktion der Autograph-Partitur* (Vienna, 1994, 1999), *Faksimile-Ausgabe* (1996) and '*Studienband*' (in preparation).
2. Göllerich-Auer, vol. IV/3, pp. 457f. Translations from the German, which in many cases attempt to reproduce colloquial language, are by the present writer; original wording has been omitted for reasons of space.
3. Cf. the sketch Wn Mus. Hs. 3194, fol. 6r; *Faksimile-Ausgabe* of the Finale, p. 11.
4. This derives from detailed information passed on by Bruckner's doctor Richard Heller, in an article entitled 'Anton Bruckners letzter behandelnder Arzt' edited by Auer (although reproducing Heller's words), in Karl Kobald, ed., *In Memoriam Anton Bruckner. Festschrift zum 100. Geburtstage Anton Bruckners* (Zurich–Leipzig–Vienna: Amalthea, 1924), p. 26. The passage concerned is quoted also in the present writer's *Rekonstruktion der Autograph Partitur* of the Finale, p. 142.
5. Göllerich-Auer, IV/3, p. 138.
6. Ibid., p. 146.
7. Ibid.
8. Joseph Gruber, *Meine Erinnerungen an Anton Bruckner: Ernste und heitere Episoden aus seinem Leben* (Einsiedeln: M. Ochsner, 1928), p. 37.
9. Göllerich-Auer, 4/3, p. 560.
10. See the entry in Bruckner's calendar for that year, '24. Mai 895. 1. mal Finale neue Scitze', quoted in Göllerich-Auer, IV/3, pp. 544 and 612. Bruckner had been seriously ill over the winter of 1894–5.
11. Auer (in both the one-volume biography *Anton Bruckner: Sein Leben und Werk* (Zurich–Leipzig–Vienna: Amalthea, 1923), p. 311, and in Göllerich-Auer, IV/3, p. 445) erroneously gives the date of Bruckner's last lecture as 12 November. The point is noted by Ernst Schwanzara, ed., Anton Bruckner: *Vorlesungen über Harmonie und Kontrapunkt an der Universität Wien* (Vienna: Österreichischen Bundesverlag, 1950), p. 98, which provides an explanation of Auer's error.
12. Schwanzara, ed., *Bruckner Vorlesungen*, pp. 97f. Auer quotes an almost identical version in the Göllerich-Auer biography (IV/3, p. 446), based on an account made by Theodor Altwirth (cf. IV/3, p. 432). This passage gives the final words as: 'I have already decided *and arranged* it (Ich habe es schon so bestimmt und *eingerichtet*)' (italics added). The words 'and arranged' were perhaps added by Auer in order to give weight to the biographer's contention that Bruckner had composed a *transition* to the *Te Deum* (see pp. 274ff).
13. Under the rubric 'Theater, Kunst, Musik und Literatur', in *Neuigkeitsweltblatt* (Vienna) 13 October 1895, p. 3.
14. See concerning the chronology of the movement the Foreword to the *Faksimile-Ausgabe* of the Finale.
15. Auer went as far as publishing a formal outline of the Finale with the *Te Deum* as

the intended and definitive conclusion of the movement: Göllerich-Auer, IV/3, p. 620. The idea of a transition was vigorously denied by such scholars as Alfred Orel (see his concluding remarks on the Finale in Alfred Orel, ed., *Bruckner Sämtliche Werke A, Entwürfe und Skizzen zur IX. Symphonie*, Vienna: MWV, 1934, p. 139); Hans Ferdinand Redlich (*Bruckner and Mahler*, London: Dent, 1955, pp. 104 and again 105) and Leopold Nowak (*Anton Bruckner. Musik und Leben* (Vienna–Munich: Österreichischer Bundesverlag, 1964), p. 86).

16. Ibid., pp. 613f.
17. Cf. the present writer's *Rekonstruktion der Autograph-Partitur* of the Finale, footnote p. 129; the passage in question begins on p. 124.
18. For instance in Auer's formal outline of the Finale (Göllerich-Auer, IV/3, p. 620) the second subject group is quoted as being in F, when in fact it is in G major.
19. See the *Autograph-Partitur* of the Finale, p. 50, and concerning the possible transition sketch the footnote on p. 47.
20. *Faksimile-Ausgabe*, pp. 229f. Full details of the subdivisions of paper rulings used in the score and their implications for the chronology of the movement will be found in the 'Studienband' on the Finale (forthcoming).
21. 'Bruckners letzter behandelnder Arzt', p. 29; similarly Göllerich-Auer, IV/3, pp. 548 and 550, and Auer, *Anton Bruckner: Sein Leben und Werk* (Vienna: MWV, 1934), p. 331.
22. Meißner prepared much of Bruckner's music paper for the Finale (that is ruled up measure lines and wrote the names of instruments in the margin); he also copied the entire first movement of the Ninth Symphony (Wn Mus. Hs. 29.305) and a few measures of the Finale (see *Faksimile-Ausgabe*, pp. 113f.).
23. Viktor Keldorfer, ed., 'Aus den Auszeichnungen Anton Meißners', *Die Furche: Jahrbuch 1947*, p. 84.
24. Cf. for instance the 1934 version (*Bruckner Sämtliche Werke A*), p. 348, and 1941 edition, (likewise *Bruckner Sämtliche Werke A*), p. 426.
25. Göllerich-Auer, IV/3, p. 559.
26. Keldorfer, ed., op. cit., p. 84.
27. See *Faksimile-Ausgabe*, pp. 45ff., *Autograph-Partitur*, pp. 139ff.
28. In the process of completing the orchestration, and subsequent to the composition of the surviving bifolios and sketches for the end of the score, Bruckner appears to have returned to the beginning of the movement, where he transferred the cramped, 36-measure contents of bifolio 2F onto two bifolios, '2'E and '3'E, and in consequence was obliged to renumber all ensuing, valid bifolios of the score by one higher.
29. Göllerich-Auer, IV/3, p. 572.
30. Ibid., pp. 572f.
31. The information was communicated in a fax to the present writer dated 4 October 1996.
32. Foreword to vol. 19 of *Bruckner Sämtliche Werke B* (translation Richard Rickett).
33. This suggestion was first made by Benjamin Gunnar Cohrs.
34. These cuts are as follows:
    Firstly, the annotation '*de + v[on] 13. Bogen*' in bifolio 15D/ '16' (*Autograph-Partitur* (hereinafter AP), p. 72; cf. also p. 61, note 1). As no surviving version of bifolio 13 contains any mention of a '*vi-de*', this must indicate the end of a cut that began on a lost version of bifol. 13. An examination of the musical texture of the passages in question suggests that, to have been musically practical, this cut must have been proposed prior to the renumbering; i.e. the bifolio referred to would have been a bifolio originally numbered 13, not a renumbered 12; the cut would accordingly have involved roughly 30 to 40 measures.
    Secondly, the annotation '*vi (unis) im 21. Bogen*' in bifolio 18D/'19' (AP, p. 84),

which ends at the beginning of the unison passage on p. 2 of bifolio 21D/'22' with the annotation '*Unis[on] / de C m.[oll]*' (AP, p. 84). As the '*vi*' annotation refers to bifolio 21, not 22, it is apparent that this cut was again specified prior to the renumbering; its implementation in performance would have eliminated fully 41 measures from the score, including the development and climax of the fugue, and beginning of the ensuing crescendo passage.

Thirdly, the annotations '*1. vi =*', crossed out, and immediately below it '*1. vi =*' again, in bifolio 23D/'24' (AP, p. 102).

The first of these indications, which Bruckner apparently found unsatisfactory, ended precisely eight pages later, on p. 3 of bifolio 25D/'26' (AP, p. 111) with the marking '*1. de (8 Seiten)*', likewise struck through; this cut, which would have deleted 34 measures from the course of the second subject group, was rejected in favour, apparently, of a shorter cut which (assuming a harmonically analogous endpoint) must have ended at the F♯ major 'Trio' section probably beginning on p. 3 of the lost bifolio (24/'25') (AP, p. 107).

Finally, the annotation '*2. vi =*' on p. 4 of bifolio 26F/'27' (AP, p. 116) which would most likely have ended with the resumption of D minor and of the triplet figuration on the fourth-to-last measure of lost bifolio (27/'28'), probably cutting the last 24 measures from the reprise of the second subject group.

35. See concerning the renumbering note 28. A more detailed explanation is found in both the *Autograph-Partitur* and *Faksimile-Ausgabe* of the Finale.
36. Cf. Löwe's Foreword to the 1903 score (Vienna: Doblinger): 'Sketches for an extensive transition have come down to us; what can be drawn from them permits only vague hints of the final intentions of the Master'. The critiques are published in full in Manfred Wagner, ed., *Geschichte der Österreichischen Musikkritik in Beispielen* (Tutzing: Schneider, 1979), pp. 235ff.
37. Quoted in Manfred Wagner, ed., op. cit., pp. 242ff. and 270ff. respectively.

Part Three
Man, Musician and Reception

12 On unity between Bruckner's personality and production

Constantin Floros

I see human significance in his work at the risk of underestimating his artistry
(Karl Amadeus Hartmann on Bruckner[1])

Questions and Views

The most basic questions in the psychology of creative artists encompass the secret of inspiration, the question of the source from which artists create their work – a topic which throughout history has been pursued and discussed from various points of view. Initial theories regard artistic inspiration as exalted suggestion, a gift of the muses or even divine revelation. This view, which permeates Europe's entire intellectual history, can be traced back to classical antiquity. To a certain extent it forms a bond connecting the religious beliefs of Hildegard von Bingen with Johannes Brahms's aesthetic precepts. It was transported into the twentieth century in a secular version – that an artist does not obey his own wishes, but is led by his creative instinct. This is why Arnold Schönberg felt himself to be a mouthpiece of heavenly power in his final years.[2] Karlheinz Stockhausen thinks of himself as a courier who transmits messages whose meaning he does not comprehend.[3] In a similar vein, Theodor W. Adorno asserted that composers such as Gustav Mahler and Alban Berg transformed themselves into 'instruments', to 'subordinate organs of execution', in order to produce meaningful works of art.[4]

According to a different concept, which by all appearances can be traced to Johann Wolfgang von Goethe, an artist's creation is based on 'internal experience'. Many leading composers (Richard Wagner, Gustav Mahler, Béla Bartók, Arnold Schönberg and Alban Berg, to name only a few) were utterly convinced that a close tie exists between life and art, that experience constitutes an indispensable prerequisite for artistic creation – a veritable *conditio sine qua non*. As a result, Mahler professed time and again in differing circumstances that his music was *gelebt* (lived) and that his symphonies had been conceived in an autobiographical light.[5] Strauss's autobiographical tone poems – *Ein Heldenleben*, op. 40 and *Sinfonia domestica*, op. 53 – stem from Richard Wagner.[6] Many personal problems, which deeply troubled Richard Wagner, also found an artistic outlet in his music dramas.[7]

The difficulties which Bruckner's peers experienced with both him and his music find their most basic explanation in the fact that Bruckner did not fit the popular artistic mould of his time. Many people perceived a crass discrepancy between his bizarrely striking personality and the splendour of his music. Already within his lifetime, his personal image developed the features of a fool and simpleton. According to Pfohl, Gustav Mahler, who loved and cherished Bruckner, once coined the phrase, 'Bruckner, a naive man – half genius, half imbecile'.[8] In 1924, Oskar Lang, who ranks Bruckner among the great 'metaphysicists' in German music, still spoke of the composer's 'curious dual character': hence his 'exceptional genius' was restricted solely to 'unconscious creative activity'; on the other hand, there was hardly any place for genius in the 'subjective-personal' (interpersonal) realm.[9]

For a long time it was disputed whether the romantically embellished tenet of unity in the life and work of great artists also holds true in Bruckner's case. Up to the present day the discussion of the important relationship between his personality and his work has been dominated by diametrically opposed views. Rudolf Louis asserted in the preface to the first edition of his monograph, published in 1905: 'In hardly any other musician of recent times is the artist so inseparably fused with the person, and the art-work regarded as a true and honest reflection of its creator's personality, as it is with Bruckner'.[10] The anthroposophist, Erich Schwebsch, in contrast, appears to be the first, outspoken advocate of the opinion that the interpretation of Bruckner's music does not require the composer's 'external biography' at all. His conclusion is that Bruckner's 'external life, for that very reason, actually plays no decisive part in the evolution of his works'.[11]

Which of these opinions most closely approaches the truth?

Erwin Ringel's 'Psychogramm' of Bruckner

In September 1977 the renowned psychiatrist, Erwin Ringel, gave a lecture in Linz, Austria, entitled *Psychogramm für Anton Bruckner* which caused an uproar.[12] Ringel shocked the public with his hypothesis that Bruckner had been mentally ill. He supposedly suffered from a neurosis without being aware of it. Ringel cited several symptoms which appeared to support his hypothesis. On the one hand, Bruckner was 'a terribly insecure person ... anything but confident'; on the other, his relationships with others were definitely 'disturbed'. This was to be seen in correlation with an insufficient sense of personal value on the one hand and a great respect for authority on the other. A further significant neurotic symptom was Bruckner's infantile nature. As a result of unresolved conflicts from his early childhood, Bruckner supposedly remained an 'infantile' person. For this reason, many of his associates felt the need 'to tend to him, to give him a helping hand, but also to restrict the freedom of choice'. Ringel was completely aware of the explosive nature of his comments. He attempted to put them into perspective by referring to an observation of the Swiss psychoanalyst, Wilhelm Stekel, whose considered opinion it was that 'every artist is a neurotic – yet not every neurotic an artist'.

The resulting questions which most urgently command our attention include: (1) What evidence is there to support Ringel's description of Bruckner's pathological state; and (2) How can the 'psychogramm' of a deceased artist be put together? In his instructive study of Leonardo da Vinci, Sigmund Freud demonstrated the boundaries which circumscribe the abilities of psychoanalysis in a purely biographical context. 'The material at the disposal of psycho-analytical examination' is, as Freud explains, 'data of a life history, on the one hand the chance meeting of circumstance with environmental influences, on the other the individual's reported response'.[13] Applied to Bruckner's case, this means that the psychiatrist can only undertake a description of his personality traits once the historian has completed his work – that is to say, once all data, which inform us about the composer's personality, has been gathered, reviewed, critically examined and evaluated. That implies not only the documents but also the transmitted anecdotes whose relevance despite legitimate reservations should not be underestimated.[14] In this connection it is gratifying that Renate Grasberger and Erich Wolfgang Partsch provided a portrait of Bruckner 'in selected reminiscences and anecdotes' in 1991.[15] It should be borne in mind that Erwin Ringel could not have had access to this, in part, extremely important material. All appearances indicate that he relied on Karl Grebe's narrow monograph, and so it is understandable that his proposed psychograph (personality description) is based at least in part on improper premises.[16] Two instances follow.

As mentioned, Ringel claimed to be able to diagnose 'a deeply reduced sense of self-worth' in Bruckner. Although he could not deny that Bruckner's life contained signs of self-confidence, he considered them to be very infrequent. In general, Bruckner's example appeared to Ringel to make an impressive case for Alfred Adler's hypothesis that 'lack of confidence sometimes leads its victim to overcompensate for his deficiency'.[17] It is noteworthy that reports by various students and close friends of Bruckner's do not match up with this portrayal in any respect. Everything indicates that Bruckner possessed great self-confidence, although he felt unrecognized nonetheless. He suffered from the fact that his works, which meant a great deal to him, for the most part were denied recognition. His student, Franz Marschner, reported: 'His manner appeared impressive to me at the time, embodying much self-confidence and a trait of greatness'.[18] 'The strong sense of self, which understandably filled him', he continues, 'often gave way to feelings of repression and profound doubt whether his enemies weren't indeed right on some accounts. "If I can't compare myself with Schubert and such masters, at least I know that I'm 'someone' and that my work is of importance", he would reassure himself'. Franz Schalk spoke of his former teacher in a similar vein:

> Consciousness of his own greatness could sometimes shine from within him in a split second and had a fascinating effect on young people. There were moments when he thought he had made a breakthrough, only to feel that much more bitterly the indifference, even disregard, he experienced at the hands of those in authority at the time.[19]

A further characteristic, for which we have Josef Kluger, abbot of Kloster-neuburg, to thank for bringing to our attention, is very informative.

> It always remained an unsolved puzzle of Bruckner's character: his deep humility (I choose this word intentionally) alongside his proud self-confidence. Yes, both sides of his character sometimes appeared so suddenly, so conspicuously, and in such close proximity to each other that they must have confused many people who consequently tended to consider the former to be simplicity and the latter vanity.[20]

It can no longer be doubted that Bruckner possessed not simply strong self-confidence, but also a pronounced sense of mission. The more one deals with his biography, the clearer it becomes that he organized his life around composition. Theodor W. Adorno spoke of his teacher, Alban Berg, that he subordinated his 'empirical existence' to the primacy of production;[21] the same can be said of Bruckner.

A second matter requires clarification. In the past fifteen years Bruckner's biographers have been successful in eradicating many prejudices against the great symphonist. They have managed above all to prove that the supposedly naive composer from Ansfelden was a pragmatic thinker, a 'social climber', who climbed the rungs of a steep career-ladder with amazing determination. Can findings like this be brought into accord with Bruckner's supposed 'infantility'?[22]

Bruckner's 'Bizarre' Aspects

Anton Bruckner was perhaps the only important composer of the nineteenth century who was perceived as a fool by many of his contemporaries. In many circles he was considered a simple, odd person, an eccentric, an original. Not only his appearance, but also his aura made a peculiar impression on many people. His unfashionable dress, his upper Austrian rural dialect, his unusual habits and his devout religious mannerisms must have been alienating in cosmopolitan Vienna. The manner in which the former country teacher, diocesan and cathedral organist behaved, impressed many people as bizarre.

Of more consequence than his conspicuous exterior was the strangeness of his aura. His personality was diametrically opposed to the conventions of the period. Franz Schalk was certainly correct when he spoke of the cleft between his revered teacher and that same teacher's environment.[23] Bruckner, with 'his great childlike soul', was supposedly a helpless and defenceless figure in an age 'in which there was increasing emphasis on speculative, reflective and material matters'. According to Schalk, even the general character of his era stood in total contrast to Bruckner's 'innermost nature':

> It was the age of moral and spiritual liberalism, in which intellectualism and calculation overrode all other human urges and threatened to seize hold of world power, but also in which he [Bruckner] unexpectedly intruded with his great symphonies and with his medieval, monasterial concept of humankind and life.

A few years ago Johannes-Leopold Mayer, arguing from a sociological point of view, arrived at a similar perspective, labelling Bruckner's music as a 'social nuisance' and the composer himself as an 'anti-citizen'.[24]

As indispensable as sociological considerations are in discussing the problems which concern us here, the greatest insight can be gained from an intensive study of Bruckner's personality. Rudolf Louis wrote of Bruckner that he lived in 'a world totally foreign to us' – a well-contemplated statement which one comes to appreciate as one deepens one's understanding of Bruckner's spiritual world, especially his religiosity.[25]

His student Friedrich Klose made important and equally credible observations. He wrote:

> Bruckner was a devout Catholic; it was not any sort of aesthetic or poetic leaning which tied him to the worship of his church, but rather his indomitable belief in it, in the omnipotence, wisdom and benevolence of his God and the promise of a better life after death.[26]

Klose justifiably questions whether Bruckner would have triumphantly traversed 'his existence's path of suffering,' as he describes it, 'if his veritably indomitable belief in divine providence and justice had not provided a firm support'.

His unquestioning belief, his religious steadfastness, which appears to have obliterated any doubt, and, last but not least, his devotional practices had an alienating effect on many people. The incessant prayer and spiritual 'exercises' which were part of his daily life during his time in Vienna seemed to many to be incompatible with their conception of an artist. Johannes Brahms's much-quoted remark, that Bruckner was a poor, deluded person whom the clerics of St Florian had on their conscience, is evidently a reference to Bruckner's apparently exaggerated religiosity.[27] Josef Schalk and Hugo Wolf provide concurring reports that Bruckner's religiousness intensified in the final years of his life.[28]

Bruckner was so well read in the Bible that he could hold his own against many theologians. He also showed a lively interest in Christian literature, such as David Friedrich Strauss's *Das Leben Jesu*, a very controversial book at the time.[29] In contrast to Hugo Wolf, Gustav Mahler, and many of his self-educated students, he had no interest in European literature and philosophy. Heated debates about Arthur Schopenhauer and Friedrich Nietzsche left him cold.[30] Some of his students drew the conclusion that he 'had hardly any intellectual needs' – a totally misleading and incorrect claim which was hopelessly confused with a 'lack of intelligence'.[31]

Dr Alexander Fränkel's detailed and comprehensive report is important in this connection. Dr Fränkel, a physician, frequented the Riedhof Restaurant in Josefstadt with Bruckner for many years. Fränkel certainly conceded that Bruckner had a very modest level of general education, but he pointed out his aptitude 'in all realms of knowledge', his ability to broaden his intellectual horizon and the adaptability of his intellect, as well as vouching for his above-average intelligence: 'Even if the sum of knowledge, which he carried with him, had no great weight, his intelligence vastly exceeded the average talent'.[32]

Study of the relationship between word and music in Bruckner's vocal works – an extremely important area of research which has been only preliminarily tapped as yet – enables one to draw conclusions regarding his great intelligence, his rich imagination, and his ability to transform poetic into musical images. Bruckner was able to interpret the text with the same degree of subtlety in his sacred and secular works, employing principally leitmotivic techniques for this purpose.[33]

Theodor W. Adorno couched his view of Mahler's relationship to Bruckner in the following way:

> No matter what apparent advantage Bruckner's dark and deep unaffected demeanour had over Mahler's disunity – it is still regarded as clumsiness on Bruckner's part, a somewhat unyielding structure which has no firmer foundation than that the influence of Nietzsche had not yet filtered through to St Florian.[34]

If one disregards the value judgements implicit in this sentence, reference is made to something very apt, namely to the fact that Bruckner remained oblivious to the repercussions of Friedrich Nietzsche's re-ordering of all values. The affirmative intention and apparently unbroken strength of his often exuberant music can be traced primarily to the steadfastness of his religious belief – a steadfastness to which Gustav Mahler sometimes remained aloof. And if Adorno's observation that Mahler found it difficult to submit to authority, should be correct, then the opposite can be said of Bruckner.[35]

Matters of Creativity

Like many other creative people, Bruckner firmly believed that he had a special mission to fulfil on earth. A feeling of responsibility for his work determined the course of his life. He regarded his composition as a duty imposed from above, as his frequently authenticated remarks about his God-given gift and talents indicate.[36] Time and again he proclaimed that he had God to thank for his music, that God was to be honoured for many of the ideas that had occurred to him, and even that the 'dear Lord' himself had inspired many themes.[37]

In a conversation with Richard Specht, Gustav Mahler once stated with regard to his Eighth Symphony that he had 'perhaps never worked under such compulsion'; it had been 'like a sudden vision' – the entire work had stood before his eyes, and he had only to write it down, as if it had been 'dictated' to him.[38] Bruckner related similar incidences when, he maintained, he received many of his revelations in his sleep. In one of these a violist had played the main theme of his Seventh Symphony to him in a dream.[39] His former composition teacher, Ignaz Dorn, supposedly dictated the main theme in the Finale of this symphony in a dream, and Ludwig Spohr requested in a dream that he write down the *Te Deum* which Spohr dictated to him.[40] Obviously Bruckner considered inspiration to be divine revelation; nevertheless, he attached no less importance to working out the details. He was in the habit of saying that he worked very slowly and gave everything that came to him due consideration.[41] He was, as Friedrich Klose once put it, 'a hard worker who had to wrest blessing from his God in fervent, heated prayer'.[42]

It can be shown that Bruckner, like many of his colleagues, was often stimulated by pictures, associations and extra-musical ideas during the compositional process, and this determined the musical structure of many of his scores. The frequently made and emphatically defended hypothesis that his entire symphonic work was conceived solely as autonomous music does not hold true. Only a prejudiced commentator would dispute that many plausible connections exist between his (admittedly clumsy) hermeneutic explanations of the Fourth and Eighth Symphonies and their musical realization.[43] Significant in this context are Bruckner's handwritten hermeneutical entries in the autographs and copies of his works, such as the meaningful words 'night', 'dreams' and 'confused dreams' in a copy of the first version of the 'Romantic' Symphony.[44]

Bruckner's Symphonies: 'Human' or 'Cosmic' Music?

Of basic importance to the way of hearing music in the Middle Ages was its classification into the harmony of the spheres, the music of humans and instrumental music.[45] It is odd how the ideas of *musica mundana* and *musica humana* persevere far beyond the Middle Ages into modern times. For instance, the concept of the harmony of the spheres dominated Johannes Kepler's thinking and experienced a late blossoming in the literature of the Romantic period.[46] From Claudio Monteverdi onwards, music is defined by many composers and theorists as the art of sentiment, emotion, and feeling, and it is in this way that many profess directly or indirectly a belief in 'human' music. The dualism between 'human' and 'cosmic' music plays a part in the history of Bruckner interpretation in so far as many scholars branded Anton Bruckner as a representative of 'cosmic' music. Anthroposophists, mystics, followers of Rudolf Steiner, and a number of musicologists favoured this point of view.

Above all, Erich Schwebsch, who initiated a new era in the interpretation of Bruckner with his book on the composer written in 1921, must be mentioned.[47] The ideal to which he subscribes is that music is a 'cosmic art'. Schwebsch sketched the development of recent music with the intention of showing how it continually receded from 'simple playful instinct' to become an 'expression of deepest human experience'. He was not content with this assessment alone, but went a step further and made the paradoxical claim that music was indeed returning 'along a path to cosmic art' due to its 'humanization', thus raising it from the narrow 'inter-personal, all-too-human' realm to the 'creative heights of the striving ego's experience at an extra-personal level'. Schwebsch was an advocate of the view that great musicians consciously or unconsciously 'created their total life-work out of an extra-personally guided inner disposition.' And so he coined the phrase: 'To be a musician in the highest sense, as Bruckner was, means becoming an instrument upon which the cosmos plays'.

With these captious insights, Schwebsch prepared the way for Oskar Lang and Fritz Grüninger.[48] They interpreted Bruckner as a great metaphysicist and, in turn, exerted a great influence on Ernst Kurth, who stylized Bruckner as a mystic, a view *en vogue* in the 1920s. Kurth's thinking is similar in many respects to that of Lang and Schwebsch. To stylize Bruckner as a mystic, it was necessary to 'cleanse' his image of human traits; hence Kurth was able to write that it was 'such a presumption, to desire constantly to approach a mind like Bruckner's at an all-too-human level'.[49] Bruckner supposedly endowed music with 'what it once was, before it was relegated to an all-too-human realm'. One is better able to appreciate this stance when one considers that Kurth criticized expressionism and reprimanded its followers as artists 'who expose themselves more than music'. Like Schwebsch, later interpreters such as Ernst Bloch and Peter Gülke also attempted to designate Bruckner a representative of 'cosmic' music.[50]

Against these opinions, one should consider the fact that the nineteenth century – seen as a whole – was oriented *anthropocentrically* and not *cosmocentrically*. In other words: not the cosmos, but man stood at the centre of thought and the art-theory of this period. Even the music of this eventful age can be said to be 'human' music in the most emphatic sense of the term; its subjective and confessional elements cannot be overlooked.

Music as Confession

Many prominent nineteenth-century composers believed that personal experience was an indispensable requirement for artistic creation. One should not be surprised, then, that autobiographical aspects also play an important role in Bruckner's works. Thus his F minor Mass is amongst his most personal creations. Its time of composition coincides with a period of crisis in Bruckner's life: in the spring of 1867 Bruckner had a nervous breakdown and required treatment at the sanatorium in Bad Kreuzen.[51] In his later years he told his close friend, Theodor Helm, the story of the genesis of the *Benedictus* which is related to his stay in the sanatorium.[52] On Christmas Eve 1867, after an hour of ardent prayer, the melody of the movement came to him, and it was with this that he, on the verge of becoming insane, found himself again. In gratitude for his deliverance from a 'spiritual death' he incorporated a passage from the *Benedictus* in the Adagio of his Second Symphony (mm. 179–83). But Bruckner was not satisfied with this single significant quotation, and inserted a passage from the *Kyrie eleison* into the Finale of the Symphony where it appears twice (mm. 200ff.)

One cannot help asking if a connection exists between the F minor Mass and the Second Symphony. Could his Second Symphony also have a religious connotation? To answer this question we have to take into consideration the fact that Bruckner finished the sketches for the Adagio on 19 July 1872. A few days before, on 16 June, he performed the F minor Mass with the *Hofopernorchester* (court opera orchestra) at the Augustinerkirche in Vienna. This information suggests that Bruckner had the Mass 'in his ears' as he composed the Second Symphony and helps us to understand better what motivated him to quote the *Benedictus* in his Adagio. Consequently the *Benedictus* quotations have an eminently personal meaning and need to be viewed in an autobiographical light; they are meant as a token of gratitude for Bruckner's convalescence and regained creativity.

More than one observation proves yet again that the Adagio of the Second Symphony has a particular religious connotation. It is the first movement of a symphony by Bruckner that bears the designation '*feierlich*' (solemn/festive), contains the so-called *Marienkadenz* (cadence of the Virgin Mary) and includes a *pizzicato*-accompanied chorale. It is also in A flat major, the same key as the *Benedictus* of the F minor Mass.[53]

The more one becomes immersed in Bruckner's symphonic style, the more obvious it becomes that its categorization as a classic example of 'absolute' music is highly problematic. This is particularly clear when one considers several passages in Bruckner's symphonies that have a precise non-musical meaning. For instance, the end of the exposition in the first movement of the Third Symphony is interspersed with elements possessing religious connotations. At the climax of the third theme complex, the trumpets play a chorale which proves to be a paraphrase of the *Crux fidelis* melody (second version, mm. 203–9). Later the flutes and trumpets quote the *miserere* phrase from the *Gloria* of the D minor Mass – the meaning of this passage as a plea for mercy comes to mind immediately. A solo flute is then assigned a melody designated '*misteriös*' and the exposition closes with modal chordal progressions which recall Palestrina.

The Adagio of the Third Symphony is one of those pieces by Bruckner whose inspiration is known: in his later years Bruckner told his friend Josef Kluger that he composed the *Andante* of the Adagio (the second theme-complex at letter B) on 15 October 1872 in memory of his mother, Theresia, whose name-day he always celebrated with a Mass. The next day, the theme of the *Misterioso* (the third theme-complex) occurred to him.[54] Numerous observations confirm these statements and help us to recognize that the Adagio of the Third Symphony must also be considered in its biographical context. Thus the *Andante* section is modelled on a kind of music that Bruckner liked to use in his sacred works for the portrayal of religious miracles and the setting of prayer. The third theme, described as *Misterioso* by the composer, has a distinctive chorale character; particularly conspicuous is the fact that the *Schlafmotiv* (sleep motif) from Wagner's *Die Walküre* is quoted towards the end of the movement (original version, mm. 263–9). There are several indications of a semantic nature, therefore, that Bruckner composed this passage in memory of his deceased mother.

In August 1884 Bruckner composed his Prelude in C major for Harmonium WAB 129, better known as the 'Perger Prelude', in St Florian. This 27-measure piece evolved from the *Schlafmotiv* (sleep motif) of *Die Walküre*, repeated many times in different transpositions. A more detailed comparison reveals that it is a note-for-note quotation presented in the form which it assumes in the third Act (third scene) of Wagner's opera. The exact allusion is to the music to Wotan's words: *In festen Schlaf verschließ' ich dich*. Here Bruckner quotes not only the descending chromatic melodic line but also includes some of the chord progressions, which he adapts in certain places (see Ex. 12.1).

What is the significance of the *Schlafmotiv* in this piece? In August 1884, Bruckner, whose tremendous admiration for Wagner is well known, travelled to the Bayreuth *Festspiele*. On the train journey to Bayreuth he met the Perger leather merchant, Josef Diernhofer (1844–1904). In remembrance of their mutual stay in Bayreuth, Diernhofer asked Bruckner to write a small composition for his harmonium.[55] The Prelude both commemorates the trip to Bayreuth and (through the quotation) pays homage to Wagner.

When speaking about the devotional character of Bruckner's music, one must also refer to the Fifth Symphony. When Bruckner began to sketch the Adagio, he was in a state of deep depression. 'My life has lost all of its joy and desire – in vain and to no avail' ('*Mein Leben hat alle Freude und Lust verloren – umsonst und um nichts*'), he wrote on January 12, 1875 to his patron, Moritz von Mayfeld.[56] Thus it may seem logical to conclude that the Adagio strikes a note of death and mourning. On the whole, though, the Fifth is conceived as a powerful work, a *Monumentalsymphonie* (monumental symphony), embodying an ideal of sublimity, strength and power. Typical of Bruckner is the following statement, made in 1874, one year after a great economic depression: 'Since the present situation of the world from an intellectual standpoint is one of weakness, I escaped to inner strength and am writing powerful music' ('*Weil die gegenwärtige Weltlage, geistig gesehen, Schwäche ist, flüchte ich zur Stärke und schreibe kraftvolle Musik*').[57]

Bruckner also spoke of his Fifth as the '*Phantastische*' ('Fantastic') – obviously an allusion to the famous *Symphonie fantastique* by Hector Berlioz, a composer whom he held in high regard.[58] Admittedly the Fifth became better known as the '*Glaubenssymphonie*' ('symphony of faith'), a name which can be better understood when one considers that chorale elements appear in abundance and that the Finale concludes with a magnificent (Bruckner called it 'grandios') four-part chorale.

Ex. 12.1   Bruckner: Prelude in C major for harmonium WAB 129

5. Präludium C-Dur

Finally the Ninth Symphony, which Bruckner is known to have wanted dedicated to the 'good Lord', must be mentioned as a convincing example of devotional symphonic music. What is quite remarkable about this seemingly expressionistic work is the wealth of quotations worked into the Adagio. They justify viewing the movement as an autobiographically inspired composition, which expresses premonitions of death by a devout man, his religious beliefs and his hope for God's mercy.[59]

Although he greatly respected tradition and took advantage of the knowledge provided by 'musical science', Bruckner sided with those who believed expression in music to be of primary importance.[60] He himself wrote in a letter to Franz Bayer, the choir director in Steyr, that 'Counterpoint is not genius, just the means to an end'.[61] In literary studies one is accustomed to differentiating the 'subjective' from the 'objective' author.[62] If one transfers these categories to the history of music, one could describe Bruckner as a 'subjective' composer who always created out of a deep need to express himself. Unlike many other composers he did not keep himself at a distance from his work, but rather identified with it. Therefore, one does his music an injustice when one classifies it as 'cosmic' or ignores or trivializes the significant amount of personal information incorporated in it. Johann Wolfgang von Goethe once said that all of his works are just 'fragments of a large confession'.[63] It would not be an exaggeration to maintain that this statement can also be applied unconditionally to the music of Anton Bruckner. [English translation by H. J. Raths and Michelle Pucci.]

Notes

1. Karl Amadeus Hartmann and Waldmar Wahren, 'Briefe über Bruckner', in *Neue Zeitschrift für Musik*, 126 (1965), pp. 272–6, 334–8 and 380–7; quote on p. 274.
2. H.H. Stuckenschmidt, *Schönberg–Leben–Umwelt–Werk* (Munich, 1989), p. 473.
3. Louise Duchesneau, 'The Voice of the Muse: A Study of the Role of Inspiration in Musical Composition' [*European University Studies, Series XXXVI, Musicology*], 19 (Frankfurt am Main, 1986), 68.
4. Theodor W. Adorno, *Mahler. Eine Musikalische Physiognomik* (Frankfurt am Main, 1960), p. 169; *idem*, 'Berg. Der Meister des kleinstes Übergangs', in *Österreichische Komponisten des XX. Jahrhunderts*, 15 (Vienna, 1968), 23. See also the present author's *Alban Berg. Musik als Autobiographie* (Wiesbaden, 1993).
5. See the present author's *Gustav Mahler, Band 1: Die geistige Welt Gustav Mahlers in systematischer Darstellung* (Wiesbaden, 2/1987), 136–42.
6. Constantin Floros, 'Psychodramen, tönende Autobiographie und illustrierende Programmmusik. Zu Richard Strauss' Tondichtungen', in *Kongreßbericht zum VI Internationalen Gewandhaus-Symposium Richard Strauss 1989* (Frankfurt/Leipzig, 1991), pp. 36–40, 39 in particular.
7. Paul Bekker, *Wagner. Das Leben im Werke* (Stuttgart, Berlin and Leipzig, 1924); Dieter Schickling, *Abschied von Walhall. Richard Wagners erotische Gesellschaft* (Stuttgart, 1983).
8. Ferdinand Pfohl, *Gustav Mahler. Eindrücke und Erinnerungen aus den Hamburger Jahren* (ed. Knud Martner, Hamburg 1973), p. 15. See also the present author's 'Von Mahlers Affinität zu Bruckner', in *Bruckner Symposion Linz 1986: Bruckner, Liszt, Mahler und die Moderne* (Linz, 1989), 109–17.
9. Oskar Lang, *Anton Bruckner. Wesen und Bedeutung* (1/1924; Munich, 2/1943), p. 21.
10. Rudolf Louis, *Anton Bruckner* (1/1905; Munich, 2/1918), pp. XIIIff.
11. Erich Schwebsch, *Anton Bruckner. Ein Beitrag zur Erkenntnis von Entwicklungen in der Musik* (Stuttgart, 1/1921; Augsburg, 2/n.d.), p. 82. See also Karl Grebe, *Anton Bruckner in Selbstzeugnissen und Bilddokumenten*, [*Rowohlts Mono-graphien*, 190], (Reinbek bei Hamburg, 1972), p. 7: 'The explanation of Anton Bruckner's work does not permit its integration into the story of his life. [...] His life makes no reference to his work, his work none to his life; this uncomfortable fact must form the starting point of inquiry'.
12. Erwin Ringel, 'Psychogramm für Anton Bruckner', in *Bruckner Symposion Linz 1977* (ed. Franz Grasberger, Linz 1978), pp. 19–26.
13. Sigmund Freud, 'Eine Kindheitserinnerung des Leonardo da Vinci (1910)', in

Studienausgabe X: Bildende Kunst und Literatur (Frankfurt am Main, 4/1969), pp. 87–159; in this case p. 156.

14. Manfred Wagner, 'Gefahr der Anekdote' in *Bruckner Symposion Linz 1977* (Linz, 1978), pp. 27–33.

15. Renate Grasberger/Erich Wolfgang Partsch, *Bruckner – skizziert. Ein Porträt in ausgewählten Erinnerungen und Anekdoten* [*Anton Bruckner. Dokumente und Studien*, VIII], (Vienna, 1991).

16. Karl Grebe, op. cit.

17. Ringel, loc. cit.

18. Göllerich-Auer, IV/2, 130 and 133, in *Bruckner – skizziert*, p. 12.

19. Franz Schalk (ed. Lili Schalk), *Briefe und Betrachtungen* (Vienna/Leipzig, 1935), p. 92.

20. Josef Kluger, 'Anton Bruckner und das Stift Klosterneuburg', in Karl Kobald, ed., *In memoriam Anton Bruckner* [*Festschrift zum 100. Geburtstag Anton Bruckners*], (Zurich/Vienna/Leipzig, 1924), pp. 121ff.

21. Theodor W. Adorno, *Berg* (1968), p. 41.

22. Manfred Wagner, 'Bruckner in Wien. Ein Beitrag zur Apperzeption und Rezeption des oberösterreichischen Komponisten in der Hauptstadt der k.k. Monarchie', in *Anton Bruckner in Wien. Eine kritische Studie zu seiner Persönlichkeit*, *Anton Bruckner. Dokumente und Studien*, II (Graz, 1980), pp. 9–74, in this case 16–20.

23. Franz Schalk, op. cit., pp. 76 and 87ff.

24. Johannes-Leopold Mayer, 'Musik als gesellschaftliches Ärgernis – oder: Anton Bruckner, der Anti-Bürger. Das Phänomen Bruckner als historisches Problem', in *Anton Bruckner. Dokumente und Studien*, II (Graz, 1980), pp. 75–160.

25. Rudolf Louis, op. cit. (1918), p. 25.

26. Friedrich Klose, *Meine Lehrjahre bei Bruckner. Erinnerungen und Betrachtungen* (Regensburg, 1927), p. 97.

27. Letter from Brahms to Elisabeth von Herzogenberg, 12 January 1885. See Max Kalbeck, *Johannes Brahms* III (Berlin, 2/1912), p. 408, footnote 1.

28. Josef Schalk to Franz Schalk, 24 September 1896: 'As regards Bruckner, I can only report sad events. His mind has deteriorated and collapsed and more and more the ghost of religious delusion takes him captive. It leaves an horrific impression, and a quick end seems to be the best, since there is no hope of any improvement'. Quoted from Lili Schalk (footnote 20), p. 65. Also Hugo Wolf to Hugo Faißt, 25 October 1896: 'For Bruckner, the immortal, a gentle death (he passed away during breakfast) was true redemption, since he suffered recently from bouts of religious delusion'. See Hugo Wolf's letters to Hugo Faißt (Stuttgart and Leipzig, 1904), p. 125.

29. Carl Hruby, *Meine Erinnerungen an Anton Bruckner* (Vienna, 1901), p. 38f.

30. Friedrich Eckstein, 'Die erste und die letzte Begegnung zwischen Hugo Wolf und Anton Bruckner', in *In memoriam Anton Bruckner* (1924), 44–59, in this case p. 57.

31. Klose, op. cit., 97f.

32. Göllerich-Auer IV/2, 14–24; printed in *Bruckner – skizziert*, 30–2.

33. See my discussion of Bruckner and Liszt in *Bruckner Symposion Linz 1986*, pp. 181–8.

34. Adorno, op. cit., p. 92f.

35. Ibid., p. 180f.

36. See *Bruckner – skizziert*, pp. 11 and 65, and Louis, *Anton Bruckner* (1918), p. 179.

37. *Bruckner – skizziert*, pp. 64–6.

38. Richard Specht, in *Tagespost* 150, 14 June 1914.

39. *Bruckner – skizziert*, p. 149.

40. The psychoanalyst, Waldemar Walden, wrote to Karl Amadeus Hartmann about Bruckner's dreams: 'The explanation of Bruckner's dream, in which Kitzler dictates

298 Perspectives on Anton Bruckner

the main theme of the Seventh to him, does not appear difficult to me. Bruckner was a very anxious person and had to adopt ingenious methods if he was to run a risk. From the time of his successful Third Symphony onwards, he had utilised motives of signal-like brevity as his main themes. Now it was a question of establishing the legitimacy of a wide-spun theme which was already in embryonic form within him. And so, without further ado, he allowed his own teacher, who assuredly would not offer him anything which broke the rules, to dictate it to him. It was an act of cunning with which he overcame his own reservations'. See also *Bruckner – skizziert*, p. 150.

41. Ibid., p. 100f.
42. Klose, op. cit., p. 94f.
43. See the present author's *Brahms und Bruckner. Studien zur musikalischen Exegetik* (Wiesbaden, 1980).
44. Leopold Nowak, 'Anton Bruckner, der Romantiker', in *Über Anton Bruckner. Gesammelte Aufsätze 1936–1984* (Vienna, 1985), pp. 153–9, in this case p. 157.
45. Hermann Abert, *Die Musikanschauung des Mittelalters und ihre Grundlage* (Halle, 1905; repr. Tutzing, 1964); Gerhard Pietzsch, *Die Klassifikation der Musik von Boetius bis Ugolino von Orvieto* (Halle an der Saale, 1929; repr. Darmstadt, 1968).
46. See the present author's *Gustav Mahler*, I, p. 161f.
47. Erich Schwebsch, op. cit., p. 77f.
48. Fritz Grüninger, *Anton Bruckner. Der metaphysische Kern seiner Persönlichkeit und seiner Werke* (1/1930; Augsburg, 2/1949).
49. Ernst Kurth, *Bruckner* (Berlin, 1925), p. 213.
50. See Ernst Bloch, *Zur Philosophie der Musik* (Frankfurt am Main, 1974), p. 50f., and Peter Gülke, *Brahms – Bruckner. Zwei Studien* (Kassel/Basel, 1989), p. 119.
51. Eva Marx, 'Bad Kreuzen – Spekulationen und kein Ende', in *Bruckner-Symposion Linz 1992*, pp. 31–9.
52. Göllerich-Auer, 3/1, p. 473.
53. For a more detailed discussion of this topic, see my essay, '*Die Zitate in Bruckners Symphonik*' in *Bruckner-Jahrbuch 1982–83*, pp. 7–18.
54. Göllerich-Auer, *Bruckner* IV/1, p. 260.
55. Erwin Horn, 'Präludium für Harmonium in C-dur' in Uwe Harten, ed., *Anton Bruckner. Ein Handbuch* (Salzburg and Vienna, 1996), 339–41.
56. Harrandt-Schneider, *Bruckner Briefe I*, pp. 153-4.
57. Quoted from Hans Sittner, 'Anton Bruckner und die Gegenwart', in Franz Grasberger, ed., *Bruckner Studien. Leopold Nowak zum 60. Geburtstag* (Vienna, 1964), pp. 99–104; in this case, p. 103.
58. For a more detailed discussion of this topic see my book *Brahms und Bruckner. Studien zur musikalischen Exegetik* (Wiesbaden, 1980), p. 162.
59. Floros, 'Zur Deutung der Symphonik Bruckners. Das Adagio der Neunten Symphonie', in *Bruckner-Jahrbuch 1981*, pp. 89–96.
60. Anton Bruckner, *Vorlesungen über Harmonielehre*, p. 78.
61. Auer, *Bruckner gesammelte Briefe*, p. 272.
62. René Wellek/Austin Warren, *Theorie der Literatur* (Fischer Athenäum Taschenbücher Literaturwissenschaft, Frankfurt am Main, 1972), p. 76.
63. Johann Wolfgang von Goethe, *Dichtung und Wahrheit* II, p. 7.

13   Bruckner – the travelling virtuoso

Crawford Howie

The title of this chapter is deliberately 'provocative'. 'Bruckner the virtuoso' – of that there is no doubt; there are several eyewitness accounts of his playing at St Florian from the 1840s onwards, at Kremsmünster, Klosterneuburg, Vöcklabruck, Linz Cathedral (he was clearly the most qualified applicant for the vacant position in 1855) and several churches in Vienna.[1] In addition, he was often asked to give his professional advice and assessment concerning the registration of new or restored organs. Until his later years when his technique began to falter, he impressed and often astonished those who were privileged to hear him. As he grew older Bruckner complained that arthritis affected his fingers, but it seems that his pedal technique remained very secure. It was invariably striking and occasionally spectacular, both in repertoire pieces and in improvisational playing. Pedal trills, figurations and double pedalling (not only in octaves, but also as obbligato two-part playing) aroused universal admiration. There were times when, in playing the organ part in performances of other composers' works and in accompanying the liturgy at church services, he was not so sensitive as he should have been, but these were minor blemishes and, indeed, were largely confined to the twilight of his career.[2] 'Bruckner – the travelling virtuoso', on the other hand, is not a title that readily springs to mind. Until the mid-1880s, when he began to make a reputation for himself as a composer outside the immediate confines of his native Austria, his only journeys abroad were his annual 'pilgrimages' to Bayreuth. But there are two or three notable exceptions, and it is these which will provide the substance of this chapter.

It is well known that Johann Herbeck was largely responsible for Bruckner's move from Linz to Vienna in 1868. Although the composer was racked with self-doubt for most of the early part of the year and had misgivings about his future financial security, Herbeck eventually prevailed upon him to follow his instincts and to take up the two posts offered him – a lectureship in Harmony and Counterpoint at the Conservatory and a post at the *Hofkapelle*. His duties at the *Hofkapelle* were initially no more than those of an unpaid supernumerary organist, in which he alternated with the other two organists, Rudolf Bibl and

Pius Richter, but he occasionally received fees for 'services rendered'. On 13 July 1869 he confided to his Linz friend, Moritz von Mayfeld, that Herbeck had promised he would 'probably receive some holiday money from the court [treasury]'.[3] He received official notification of the payment of sixty florins a fortnight later, on 27 July.[4] Over a year later, in November 1870, he was granted a sum of 100 florins. There were other *ex gratia* payments of this kind until the beginning of 1878 when, on Hellmesberger's recommendation, he was finally appointed a salaried member of the *Hofkapelle* with an annual income of 800 florins.[5]

The payment in July 1869 was possibly in recognition of Bruckner's success in representing Austria as an organist in Nancy and Paris at the end of April and beginning of May. A new Merklin organ had been installed in the church of St Epvre in Nancy and the Hapsburg court had been invited to send an organist to participate in a kind of organ festival. Rudolf Bibl was approached first but declined, and Bruckner was the next choice. Moritz von Mayfeld alluded to the 'Nancy opportunity' and the possibility of 'triumphs in foreign parts' in a letter to Bruckner in November 1868,[6] and Bruckner referred to his imminent departure for France in a letter to Dr Prohaska on 15 April 1869.[7] Bruckner left Vienna on 24 April and played the organ in Nancy on Wednesday 28 and Thursday 29 April. On the first day he played a Prelude and Fugue by Bach and a free improvisation. On the second day he improvised on the 'Emperor hymn', the theme of the slow movement from Haydn's String Quartet op. 76 no. 3.[8] Bruckner was pleased with his performances and reported to Herbeck that the audience reaction had been most favourable:

> The concerts are over. There was a lot of ceremony. In my first days here and even at the first concert a Parisian organist (Mr Vilbac) appeared to be the clear favourite. But I had the connoisseurs on my side already at the first concert. At the second (yesterday, 29 April) my playing was received in a manner which I cannot really describe except that it stirred me. Members of the nobility, the Parisians, the Germans and the Belgians vied with each other in paying me their respects which was all the more surprising after Vilbac (a very dear, fine French artist and friend of Thomas) played some very well prepared French pieces ... I have no idea what will be reported in the papers – unfortunately, I will not be able to understand it! I have only the verbal opinions of experts – modesty compels me to be silent about those – and the reception and applause of the public. Amiable young ladies from the highest nobility even came up to the organ to show their appreciation.[9]

None of the newspaper reports of the two concerts went into any detail about the individual performances. The reviewer for *L'Espérance*, however, had the following to say about Bruckner's contributions:

> M. Bruckner, organist of His Majesty the Emperor of Austria and Professor of Organ at the Conservatory of Music in Vienna, ended the concert [on 28 April] in an appropriate manner with an elegant and skilful improvisation in which the most serious qualities of the true artist were revealed. On the following day, 29 April, a large and well-disposed number of people re-gathered for another concert in the beautiful nave of St Epvre. The Viennese artist M. Bruckner developed the Austrian national hymn with an uncommon richness of harmony and vigour of execution.[10]

The reporter for the *Journal de la Meurthe et des Vosges* described Bruckner as 'one of the best organists we have ever heard, a man of the highest taste, of the most comprehensive and most prolific knowledge', and added that the Austrian court was fortunate to possess such an artist.[11]

In the letter to Herbeck mentioned earlier Bruckner also requested three days' extension to his leave as the 'gentlemen who paid for me' were insistent that he travel to Paris and try out a new organ there. The firm of Merklin-Schütze obviously wanted to make as much use of Bruckner as possible in the short time available! On Monday 3 May Bruckner gave a concert to an invited audience in Merklin-Schütze's own building. He improvised on a theme from his First Symphony. His most ambitious playing, however, was reserved for a concert on the magnificent five-manual organ in Notre Dame Cathedral. He improvised on a theme submitted by a Parisian organist, A. Chauvet, and evidently impressed some of the leading French composers who were present and congratulated him warmly after the concert. While in Paris he visited Auber, Gounod, and the firm of Cavaillé-Coll.[12] As his concerts in Paris were not advertised widely and were private rather than public affairs there were very few reviews, but a report of the first concert in the *Revue et Gazette musicale* drew attention to the high quality of his playing which combined 'enormous skill' with 'much taste' and 'great vigour'.[13]

Bruckner's French successes naturally aroused great interest in both Linz and Vienna and there were several newspaper reports. The reviewer for the *Linzer Zeitung* regarded these successes as an honour not only for Bruckner himself but also

> ... for the land and place where this affable and unassuming artist was born. The mayor of St Florian sent Herr Bruckner the following note to mark this occasion: 'With our heartiest congratulations on your most praiseworthy successes in Nancy and Paris which are an enduring credit not only to you and your German-Austrian fatherland but also to Upper Austria, where you were born, and St Florian in particular.'[14]

On 20 May there was a short report by Ludwig Speidel in the *Wiener Fremdenblatt* and on 13 June Hanslick's article 'Erfolge eines österreichischen Organisten in Frankreich' appeared in the *Neue freie Presse*. As it was Bruckner's intention at this time to pursue his organ-playing career both in Germany/Austria and further afield, he used the opportunity to send a copy of Hanslick's article, in which his organ playing was described as having 'made a huge impression, putting almost all the other performances in the shade',[15] to Barthold Senff, the editor of the *Signale für die musikalische Welt* in Leipzig. Senff duly obliged and Bruckner's successes were reported in the *Signale* on 24 June. There was a further report in J. E. Habert's *Zeitschrift für katholische Kirchenmusik*.[16]

The main event of 1871 for Bruckner was undoubtedly his visit to London. First, he had to take part in a competition to determine who would represent Austria in a series of demonstration concerts of the newly installed Willis organ in the Albert Hall. Although it was probably a foregone conclusion that he would win this competition, Bruckner had to abide by the rules. The competition took place on 18 April and he was informed on 24 April that he had been successful. A further official letter from the Chamber of Trade and Industry reminded Bruckner that, starting on 2 August, he would be required to perform 'two programmes each of at least one hour's duration daily between 10 in the morning and 6 in the evening at times specified by the committee'. The fee would be £50 which was inclusive of travel and accommodation costs and would be given to him at the end of his concerts.[17] Although Auer specifies that Bruckner 'received his travelling expenses from Herbeck who had given him advice about the journey', there is no record of this money coming from the *Hofkapelle*. The Lord Chamberlain granted him official leave from the middle of July until the end of September, however.[18] When Bruckner wrote to his former teacher, August Dürrnberger, to inform him that he was using his theory book, *Elementar-Lehrbuch der Harmonie-und Generalbaß-Lehre*, in his new teaching post at St Anna's Teacher Training Institute, he took it for granted that Dürrnberger would have heard that he was going to London.[19]

Bruckner could not speak a word of English but he knew that a prominent Linz businessman, Anton Reissleithner, was intending to travel to England and he wrote to him on 13 July, suggesting that they travel together. Bruckner planned to leave Vienna on Thursday 20 July, spend an overnight in Linz and travel from there at 9.00 on Friday 21 July:

> ... My organ playing in London is scheduled to begin on 2 August. I must be there a week before this of course, and so I intend to travel from here to Linz next week, Thursday at the latest, and to continue my journey from Linz the following day at 9 in the evening. Please be certain to come and travel with me. I can usually be found on Sundays at the organ in the *Musikverein*. We will be able to make a splendid return journey through Switzerland ...[20]

But Reissleithner did not accompany him to England. Bruckner changed his itinerary and travelled to Nuremberg to visit the Zimmermann family whose acquaintance he had made ten years earlier during the 1861 Choir Festival. One of the family, F. Zimmermann, became his travelling companion and they arrived in London on Saturday 29 July, booking in at Seyd's Hotel in Finsbury Square. The Austrian ambassador in London, Count Apponyi, was contacted about Bruckner's visit and asked to provide all the support necessary.[21]

On the evening of his arrival in London Bruckner went to the Royal Albert Hall to practise. Although work had finished for the day and the steam engines working the bellows could no longer be heated, the manager of the hall allowed Bruckner to play for as long as there was enough steam left. Apparently the manager was so impressed when he heard Bruckner playing and experimenting with the different stops that he gave orders for the engines to be heated again. A number of people gathered round the organ to listen to Bruckner who played on until late evening.

Henry Willis (1821–1901) was one of the leading English organ builders in the nineteenth century. As well as building the Royal Albert Hall organ (1871) he also supplied organs for the Alexandra Palace, St Paul's Cathedral (1872), Salisbury Cathedral (1877), Truro Cathedral (1887), Hereford Cathedral (1893) and Lincoln Cathedral (1898). He was a great admirer of the French organ builder Cavaillé-Coll whom he met in the late 1840s, and there is a certain amount of French influence in his organs, e.g. use of pneumatic levers (in spite of his preference for tracker action), ventils and a predominance of reeds in the full choruses. The specification of the organ was 111 stops and Willis made considerable use of imitative strings, orchestral reeds and harmonic flutes:

> The multi-ranked mixtures of Great, Swell and Pedal were reminiscent of Cavaillé-Coll's schemes, as was the limited use (for the Pedal Organ) of ventils.[22]

While tin and lead were used in almost equal amounts for the internal pipes of the organ, the front pipes were largely of tin, all burnished and polished to a high degree.

> ... it is interesting that Willis made a positive virtue of the fact that the only wooden pipes to be found in the manual divisions of that instrument were the basses to four flutes ...[23]

We have very little idea of what Bruckner thought of the organ, or how it compared, in his judgement, with the magnificent St Florian organ. On the other hand, the organ recitals at the Royal Albert Hall received a fair amount of coverage from the leading music journals. The following paragraph appeared in the 'Table Talk' column of *The Musical Standard* on 5 August:

> Herr Anton Bruckner, court organist at Vienna, and Professor in the Conservatorium of that city, has arrived in London to play on the great organ of the Royal Albert Hall. Herr Bruckner is celebrated for his classical improvisations on the works of Handel, Bach and Mendelssohn.[24]

The Choir included details of the concerts and programmes from the end of July to the end of September. In the edition of 19 August there is a full list of concerts and programmes from Monday 31 July to Wednesday 16 August, including Bruckner's recitals which contained a mixture of pieces by Bach, Handel and Mendelssohn and a number of improvisations as already intimated in *The Musical Standard*. The details are as follows:

First recital, Wednesday 2 August, 12.00

1 Bach: Toccata in F major
2 Improvisation upon the foregoing
3 Handel: Fugue in D minor
4 Improvisation (original)
5 Bach: Improvisation on Fugue in E major
6 Improvisation on English melodies

Second recital, Thursday 3 August, 3.00

1   Mendelssohn: Sonata no. 1
2   Improvisation upon the foregoing
3   Improvisation (original)
4   Bach: Fugue in C sharp minor
5   Improvisation upon the Austrian national anthem
6   Improvisation upon the 'Hallelujah Chorus'

Third recital, Friday 4 August, 3.00

1   Bach: Concerto in A minor
2   Improvisation
3   Improvisation on Weber's '*Freischütz*'
4   Bach: Fugue in G minor
5   Improvisation
6   Improvisation on the English national anthem

Fourth recital, Saturday 5 August, 12.00

1   Bach: Concerto in C major
2   Improvisation
3   Improvisation on the song 'Lorelei'
4   Bach: Fugue in G minor
5   Improvisation on Schubert's song '*Fremd bin ich eingezogen*'
6   Improvisation upon the 'Hallelujah Chorus'

Fifth Recital, Monday 7 August

1   Bach: Toccata
2   Improvisation
3   Improvisation on a theme of Mendelssohn
4   Improvisation on melodies of Schubert
5   Improvisation on Mendelssohn's 'Hunter's Farewell'

Sixth Recital, Tuesday 8 August

1   Bach: Fugue in E
2   Improvisation
3   Improvisation on a German melody
4   Improvisation on a theme of Schubert
5   Fugue, improvised
6   Improvisation on the 'Hallelujah Chorus'[25]

All six programmes have a similar shape – no more than two original organ pieces, and a preponderance of improvisation on well-known melodies. Significantly, Handel's 'Hallelujah Chorus' appears three times. This was typical of the English organ recital of the time, in which the emphasis was on both instruction and entertainment, and a wide range of transcriptions of orchestral, instrumental, vocal and choral music was juxtaposed with original organ music. It is revealing to compare such a programme with a modern organ recital! There is no doubt that Bruckner had a small and fairly limited repertoire, which, according to Horn, was a 'shocking limitation for an organist who was acknowledged as Austria's most important representative of his instrument'.[26] But this was a deliberate choice on Bruckner's part. Seven years earlier, when he was contemplating giving organ recitals in Dresden and Leipzig, he had made his position absolutely clear in a letter to his friend Rudolf Weinwurm in Vienna:

> In connection with the journey [to Dresden and Leipzig], I am sorry to have to write that I do not have any repertoire, although I have played Bach and Mendelssohn. I have little time and desire to go to any particular trouble in this connection, because it has no purpose – organists are always poorly paid. In my opinion, if concerts cannot be arranged to run at a profit, it's best to play for nothing and to perform only fantasias etc. without having to memorise anything. I believe that there is an abundance of very capable organists out there able to give high-quality performances of the works of other composers ...[27]

There is no reason to believe that Bruckner changed his attitude in the intervening years. On the other hand, it would be wrong to assume that Bruckner did not make the necessary technical preparation for his London concerts. Even for his improvisations Bruckner would not have relied completely on the inspiration of the moment. Several of the themes were chosen regularly and the improvisations would have adhered to a similar overall structure each time, although the details would have changed from performance to performance. The Fugue in D minor WAB 125, one of the contrapuntal exercises which Bruckner submitted to the *Gesellschaft der Musikfreunde* examiners in November 1861, gives us some idea, albeit in embryonic form, of what a Bruckner improvised fugue would have been like, containing as it does examples of 'false entries', diminutions, augmentation, inversion and organ points.

The only English organist to play during this recital series was William T. Best (1826–97) who, like Bruckner, was renowned for his improvisations and virtuoso playing and was greatly admired for his impressive pedal technique particularly in Bach's organ works. In fact, Best gave the inaugural recital on 18 July.[28] Other foreign organists included Heintze, Lohr, Mailly, Saint-Saëns, Lindemann, Lux, Tod and Henrici.[29] It is clear that Bruckner was misinformed when he was advised that he would have to play twice daily. Although there is no mention in the English press of an organ competition being held as part of this recital series, Bruckner's later report to Göllerich suggests that there must have been some kind of unofficial improvisation contest.[30] There is a high degree of chauvinism in the press reports of the recitals. The main criticism, understandably, concerned the lack of any British representative apart from Best. In his review of the first series of recitals, the reporter for *The Musical Standard* was extremely critical of the foreign organists, although Bruckner fared better than Heintze or Lohr:

Upon the completion of Mr Willis's organ at the Albert Hall we were promised a series of performances by professors of high standing, both British and foreign. To what extent this promise has been fulfilled we propose now to point out. In the first place, the inaugural performance was given nearly a month ago, yet the sole representative of our native professors has been Mr W.T. Best. It is hardly necessary to state that a better could not be found, nor that the most refined taste could take the least exception to any part of Mr Best's ten or twelve programmes. Nevertheless England can boast of other performers of deservedly high repute, men who have in some cases made a certain branch of the art their 'speciality'. Will the London amateurs and the foreign visitors to the Exhibition have no opportunity of hearing the renowned improvisations of one professor or the equally celebrated fugue playing of another before the season quite dies out and no auditors are left for any music but the dash of the waves on the shingle or the sound of the wind through the pine branches? To this extent the Council has failed to fulfil its organ programme. Another part of the scheme, however – the presentation of foreign organ-players – has been carried out to the letter if not in the spirit. Recitals have been given by Mr G.W. Heintze from the Conservatorium, Stockholm, by Herr Johann Löhr [sic] of Pesth and by Herr Anton Brückner [sic], court organist at Vienna. Of these performances it may be said that, if they failed to satisfy the critic, they must have gladdened the heart of the true born Briton. Unfortunately in England artistic sympathies cannot always blend with patriotic feelings, but we confess to have experienced emotions of thankfulness, not to say glorification, at hearing a performance by Mr Best at 3 o'clock, after attending a recital by one of his continental rivals at 12. Modest mediocrity may be briefly passed over – we advert therefore no more definitely to Mr Heintze or Herr Löhr [sic] – but the playing of Herr Anton Brückner [sic] deserves a word or two. We were advised by the official programme that Herr Brückner's [sic] 'strong points were classical improvisations on the works of Handel, Bach and Mendelssohn'. We were therefore not altogether unprepared to find that the playing of Mendelssohn's No. 1 Sonata was a 'weak point', and such indeed was the case. It is only charitable to suppose that Herr Brückner [sic] had not the advantage of a previous trial of the organ, expecially as he evinced rather more control over the instrument in his succeeding improvisations. But in the course of our struggles after musical experience we have been present at more than one competitive performance for a church organistship; to the exhibitions of certain of the candidates there may be likened more or less the recitals of the eminent foreign professors at the Albert Hall. We trust the authorities will not disregard these remarks – that they will bring forward some of our good English organists, and a more careful selection from those eminent in other countries.[31]

In the 'Table Talk' column in the same issue of *The Musical Standard* the following report appeared:

The foreign organists of note who have given performances on the Albert Hall instrument are Herr J. Lohr, from Pesth; Herr C.W. Heintze, from Stockholm; Herr A. Bruckner, from Vienna; and M. Mailly, from Belgium. Bach's preludes and fugues have formed an important item in all the programmes.[32]

In the following issue of *The Musical Standard* the reporter renewed his attack on the choice of foreign organists in the 'Table Talk' column:

It is stated that the selection of organists for the public performances on the organ at the Albert Hall is made by the Hon. Seymour Egerton, the well-known conductor of the Wandering Minstrels. Whether this gentleman possesses any aptitude for this special duty is a matter of serious doubt, when the *fiasco* of the foreign organists who have already played is taken into consideration. The so-called 'International Congress of Organists' will, we fear, be an entire failure.[33]

The reporter had been clearly misinformed, however. A letter in *The Orchestra* from Col. Henry Y.D. Scott, the secretary of the Royal Commissioners specially appointed by Queen Victoria to supervise the International Exhibition in London, was obviously intended to correct faulty information and to clear up misunderstandings:

Her Majesty's Commissioners did not, as you imagine, issue any advertisement inviting foreign organists to play. It was the wish of the Commissioners that the opening of the organ should be signalised by performances by artists representing the various musical schools of Europe. With this view they requested each foreign Government taking part in the International Exhibition to name an organist to represent his country on the occasion, and all the gentlemen with whom engagements have been made were nominated by their respective Governments in compliance with this request.[34]

In any case one has to put a question mark against the musical judgment of *The Musical Standard* reporter. While he had more positive things to say about Lux's recitals,[35] he failed to mention Saint-Saëns's recitals. The writer of a letter to the editor in the 'Correspondence' column of the September 30 issue of *The Choir* also suggested that a 'congress of *English organists* would ... have yielded more satisfactory results' but conceded that the foreign organists had not had the same opportunity as Best of becoming acquainted with the organ:

... it must be mentioned that their only chance of making themselves acquainted with the organ, or preparing for their performances has been during an hour or two after six o'clock in the evening.[36]

The reporter for *The Orchestra*, on the other hand, spoke of these recitals in glowing terms.[37] In an earlier article he provided a much more sympathetic account of the respective merits of Heintze, Lohr and Bruckner and showed that he had some knowledge of the organ:

The first who has played was Herr Heintze of Stockholm, a young man still *in statu pupillari*. He executed some of the masterpieces of Sebastian Bach, some of the sonatas by Mendelssohn, some fugues and fantasias by Topfer, Merkel, Hesse, Kohler, Kuhmstedt, Markul and others of the modern German school. His performances were marked by much truth and considerable precision; but he failed in that iron, *staccato* touch which is essential for clear part-playing in the Albert Hall... In Herr Johann Lohr, of Pesth, we meet with a good musician and a player of considerable power. He is a combination of the new and the old schools. He gave us extracts from the symphonies of Liszt, marches by Chopin, songs by Schubert, pieces by Gottschalk, Markul, Pitoch and many others, interspersed with compositions by Beethoven and Mozart, together with the more distinctive organ music of Handel and Bach. Herr Lohr had great executive capabilities, and his ambitious attacks on the sonatas of Beethoven, and more especially so on the monstrous vagaries of the Abbé Liszt, proved in the end more astonishing than pleasing. He suffered from the same disadvantages as Herr Heintze, and certainly did not meet the requirements of the Hall, nor those of the instrument. There was much good playing, but nothing perfect ... The Court Organist of Vienna, Anton Bruckner, was third at the organ, and announced specially as great in 'extemporaneous performances'. We were told that 'Herr Bruckner's strong points are classical improvisations on the works of Handel, Bach and Mendelssohn'. He has given us a grand extempore Fantasia, which although not very original in thought or design, was clever, remarkable for its canonic counterpoint, and for the surmounting of much difficulty in the pedal passages. There can be nothing said extemporaneously [Extract]upon the National Anthem of Austria, and still less upon the Hallelujah Chorus of Handel; nor do we think any improvisation with any effect can be given upon the toccatas of Bach or the sonatas of Mendelssohn. Great composers exhaust their themes. Nothing can be added to the Hallelujah Chorus, nothing to a toccata of Sebastian Bach ...[38]

According to Göllerich, a letter sent from the Austrian embassy in London to the Chamber of Commerce in Vienna after Bruckner's third concert spoke of the 'extraordinary successes of the court organist Professor Bruckner sent by you'.[39] Professor Paul Stöving, who carried out some research on Bruckner's organ recitals in London for another of Bruckner's biographers, Franz Gräflinger, made the point that 'none of the important newspapers – *Times, Standard, Daily News'* – mentioned the composer or even the recitals, but added that this was hardly surprising since 'August is the quietest month for music in London, and the newspapers and people were concerned with other more important matters – political controversies, the aftermath of the Franco-Prussian War'.[40] Bruckner seems to have been sufficiently concerned about the lack of a report in the leading newspaper, *The Times*, whose music critic was in Germany at the time, to make an approach through the vice-consul, Dr von Pinsio, to the exhibition committee with the purpose of rectifying this 'anomaly'. When Dr von Pinsio replied, inviting him to submit an article of his own, Bruckner obviously had second thoughts.

Bruckner's visit to London included some engagements at the Crystal Palace. He did some sightseeing in his 'free' week between the Albert Hall and Crystal Palace concerts and particularly enjoyed travelling on the large London buses.

The Crystal Palace had been erected by Joseph Paxton for the Great Exhibition in Hyde Park in 1851 and had then been removed to a new site at Sydenham, about ten miles away, and officially 're-opened' there by Queen Victoria on 10 June 1854. The fourteen organs which had been built specifically for the 1851 Great Exhibition had also been relocated elsewhere. The instrument played by Bruckner when he gave his recitals there in the second half of August 1871 had been built by Gray and Davison for the first of the annual Handel Festivals in 1857. Some new stops were added in 1871 and 1882. Like the Royal Albert Hall organ, the influence of Cavaillé-Coll was clearly discernible, e.g. the use of combination pedals, the introduction of modern French stops and the employment of several mixtures and reeds:

The purpose of the rebuilt Crystal Palace was to combine recreation with education in a manner which the late twentieth century might consider daunting. A vast concert hall with room for an audience of 4000, and almost as many performers, dominated by a huge organ ... occupied the central space at the intersection of nave and main transept. The concerts, and in particular the Handel festivals, held here on a scale previously impossible in England became world famous, and during the opening ceremony Clara Novello, singing the solo parts of the National Anthem, reached a high B flat of such electrifying power that all the policemen present raised their helmets in the air contrary to precedent and discipline. More importantly, Madam Novello's triumphant trumpeting was held to have proven the safety of the building for all time.[41]

In his description of the organ in 1857 George Macfarren commented that the aim of the organ builders 'has been to produce an instrument, the varied qualities of which should combine all desirable musical beauty with force and grandeur of tone sufficient to qualify it for the part it is specially designed to bear in this great commemoration'.[42]

Bruckner's recitals in the Crystal Palace on 19, 21, 22, 23 and 28 August were in the context of lengthy popular concerts. A report in *The Musical Standard* of the final concert (28 August) mentions a recital by 'Herr Anton Bruckner, Court Organist of Vienna, who has already played at the Albert Hall. One of Mendelssohn's sonatas opened the programme, which included Bach's Fugue in E major and an improvisation on Handel's "Hallelujah". ....'[43]

The second Crystal Palace concert, on 21 August, took the form of a 'Great National German Festival'. It began at 2 pm with Weber's *Oberon* overture, continued with songs by Abt, Meyerbeer, Handel, Speyer, Mozart and Schubert, after which Bruckner played an improvisation on Schubert's song *Leise flehen meine Lieder* and, by popular request, an improvisation on the popular German song *Nacht am Rhein* which, according to Bruckner's own account, resulted in a tumultuous reception and even a proposal of marriage from an admiring female member of the audience![44]

There was an estimated audience of 70,000 at his third recital on Tuesday 22 August. After his fourth recital, on Wednesday 23 August, Bruckner wrote to his friend Moritz von Mayfeld in Linz from Seyd's hotel:

> Just finished. Have given ten concerts, six in the Albert Hall, four in the Crystal Palace. Tremendous applause, always unending. Encores required, i.e. I often had to play two extra improvisations at the end ... Many compliments, congratulations, invitations. Manns, the conductor of the Crystal Palace concerts, told me that he was amazed and that I must come again soon and send him some of my compositions. Dr Spinsio [sic] sends his greetings. I will soon be returning by way of Brussels, but I will not be playing any more as I am too tired and overwrought. I will keep Germany, Berlin, also Holland and Switzerland for later ...

As a postscript he added:

> Yesterday I played to an audience of 70,000 and had to give an encore, at the Committee's request: I wanted to give due respect to such great applause. On Monday I played with similar success in the concert etc. etc.
> NB Unfortunately, the 'Times' critic is in Germany, with the result that hardly anything has been written about me yet. Please be so good as to inform the 'Linzer Zeitung', i.e. Dr Dutschek.[45]

Although Bruckner informed Mayfeld that he did not intend to give any more concerts, the report in *The Musical Standard* alluded to above makes it clear that he played for a fifth time at the Crystal Palace on Monday 28 August. A programme of this 'Popular Ballad Concert' which consisted of ballads and duets mainly by English composers includes the following:

At Three o'clock,
Performance on the Festival Organ
By Herr Anton Bruckner
(Court Organist of Vienna)

1. Sonata .... Mendelssohn
2. Improvisation .... Bruckner
3. Fugue, E major .... Bach
4. Improvisation, 'Halleluja' .... Handel
5. Improvisation .... Bruckner[46]

From Bruckner's own recollections as related to Göllerich it would appear that he might even have played a sixth time at the Crystal Palace although there is no reference to this in any programme. It was suggested that he undertake a concert tour throughout England either then or the following year. At that point, however – as his letter to Mayfeld makes clear – he was understandably exhausted and his only wish was to return to Vienna. During his time in London he made several English friends and obviously earned the respect of several English organists including W.T. Best, who gave him a copy of his *Collection of Organ Pieces composed for Church Use* as a gift, and James Coward, the resident Crystal Palace organist, who presented him with a copy of his *Ten Glees and a Madrigal* with the dedication 'Anton Bruckner from James Coward with best wishes. Organist of the Crystal Palace and Sacred Harmonic Society'. He was most impressed with the friendliness of his English hosts and showed a great interest in English organs with their concave pedal arrangement.

At the end of his series of English recitals there was an extremely complimentary review in *The Morning Advertiser*:

Professor Bruckner from Vienna.

When the International Exhibition and Royal Albert Hall were opened, the Council issued an invitation to artists of all nations to come over and test the excellence of the great organ. Amongst those who accepted this invitation was Herr Anton Bruckner, Court Organist and Professor at the Conservatoire. The executions by this disciple of art are truly excellent, and quite worthy of the fatherland of Haydn and Mozart. Herr Bruckner executes the classical compositions of Bach, Mendelssohn and others with great easiness which leaves the hearer nothing to desire, and which would certainly even satisfy the composers themselves in the highest degree. But where Herr Bruckner excels is in his improvisations, in which you will find a great easiness and abundance of idea, and the ingenious method by which such idea is carried out – grave or solemn, melodious or charming, brilliant or grand – is very remarkable. The London public has fully acknowledged Herr Bruckner's perfect execution, and many have expressed a hope that this first visit may not be the last. We join in. Bruckner may publish some of his most successful compositions for the benefit and enjoyment of the musical public who, we are sure, would be very pleased to become better acquainted with the works of this thorough artist.[47]

In its report of Bruckner's successful London visit the *Linzer Zeitung* reproduced *The Morning Advertiser* review as a typical example of the friendly reception of Bruckner on the part of the English press.[48]

Pursuing Manns's suggestion that he should send some of his own music to be performed in London, Bruckner wrote to the Committee of the International Exhibition on 3 January 1872 asking if he should forward one of his works. In a letter of reply, Major-General Scott, the secretary of the Committee, asked Bruckner to send the score and parts of his composition so that it could be considered for performance at the opening of the Exhibition.[49] On 30 April Bruckner informed the Committee that he had forwarded the score of his D minor Mass. The receipt was acknowledged by J.A. Wright, the secretary of the Executive Committee.[50] The Mass was not performed and there are no records of any preliminary rehearsals. Four (!) years after his London recitals Bruckner eventually received a medal from the Exhibition Committee in recognition of his efforts.[51] Reports that he had been awarded a prize by Queen Victoria were totally unfounded.

Bruckner maintained contact with his travelling companion, N. Zimmermann, for some time. Zimmermann wrote to him on 1 December, recalling their stay in London and mentioning that, on a recent business trip, he had happened to open a copy of the *Illustrierte Zeitung* and read an article on the Albert Hall organ in which Bruckner's name was mentioned.[52] In another letter to Bruckner the following year, Zimmermann thanked him for his kind invitation to stay in his apartment during the forthcoming Vienna World Exhibition and wished him every success with his plans to undertake a concert tour of England.[53] But this planned concert tour did not materialize. Teaching commitments and work on the Second and Third Symphonies occupied most of his time and left little time for regular organ practice. His visits to France and Britain were interesting diversions in a life which gradually took on a fairly predictable pattern. When he travelled out of Austria in later years it was normally either to make an annual 'pilgrimage' to Bayreuth or to attend performances of his works in cities like Berlin, Leipzig and Munich. Occasionally he took the opportunity of playing the organ in the towns or cities he visited. His technique was much less secure by now but the power of his playing could still astonish and move his listeners. During his summer vacation in 1880, for instance, he travelled to Oberammergau to see the Passion Play and then fulfilled a long-cherished desire to visit Switzerland. His first 'port of call' was Zurich where he played the organ in the cathedral on 28 August. His itinerary took him next to Geneva (29 August), Chamonix (30 August–4 September), back to Geneva where he played the organ in the cathedral (5 September), Lausanne (6 September), Freiburg where he played in the cathedral after a concert given by Vogt, the resident organist (7 September), Bern where he made a great impression on Dr Jakob Mendel, the cathedral organist (8 September) and Lucerne (8–10 September). More than four years later, when he was in Leipzig from 27 to 30 December 1884 to attend the final rehearsals and the world première of his Seventh Symphony, Bruckner was invited to give a guest recital on the recently installed Walcker organ in the new Gewandhaus building. The Walcker organ-building firm, based in Ludwigsburg (8 miles north of Stuttgart), had a worldwide reputation. It was responsible for the organs in Schwerin, Merseburg and Riga Cathedrals and the large organ in the Music Hall, Boston, USA and Bruckner would have been familiar with three of its organs in Vienna, viz. in the *Gesellschaft der Musikfreunde*, the *Votivkirche* and St Stephen's Cathedral. The inaugural recital was given on 11 December and, nearly three weeks later, Bruckner had the distinction of being the first foreigner to play the new organ. His recital, on 29 December, included improvisations on the slow movement of the Seventh and on a theme submitted by Alex Winterberger, the Leipzig music teacher and critic. Unlike the première of the Seventh on the following evening which was reported widely, there were no newspaper reviews of the recital.[54]

Two and a half years later, on 23 May 1887, Hans Richter conducted the first British performance of Bruckner's Seventh Symphony in St James's Hall, London. In an earlier article in the *Musical Times*, C.A. Barry provided a biographical sketch of the composer and an analysis of both the Seventh and the Te Deum and reminded his readers of Bruckner's visit to London in 1871:

> In England the name of Anton Bruckner, which is not to be found in any biographical musical dictionary, either English or foreign, that we have been able to consult, will probably only be familiar to a few from the fact that he was one of a number of foreign organists who, by invitation, repaired to this country with the view of exhibiting their skill upon the newly created organ of the Royal Albert Hall and that of the Crystal Palace ...[55]

One detects the same British chauvinism in the critical reception of the symphony in 1887 as had been demonstrated in some reviews of Bruckner's organ playing sixteen years earlier. The *Musical Times* reviewer was disappointed that the 'hopes not unnaturally raised by reports from abroad' had not been realised, particularly as 'every man with a heart in him must desire success for a composer of sixty-three, who has vainly struggled after fame all his life'. His criticism of the work reads like many a contemporary Austrian review. We notice the same praise for 'many fine passages in the slow movement' and an admission that 'every movement ... contains something for admiration'. But the symphony was found to be extremely long – 'a fault substantially aggravated by lack of proportionate interest', there was an 'extraordinary mixture of scholasticism with the freedom of the Wagnerian school' and a large amount of 'pretentious endeavour'. Whereas the audience reaction to Bruckner's organ playing had been positive and often acclamatory, however, the audience attending the performance of the symphony either listened 'with unmistakable coldness' or left.[56] Nine years later, in November 1896, the writer of the

'Bruckner' obituary notice in the *Musical Times* alluded to the composer's lack of recognition in this country:

> ... we are aware that to many amateurs ... the remarkable Austrian composer, if not heard of for the first time, will be little more than a name. And yet ... it is a name around which some fierce, if bloodless, battles have been fought on the Continent. Anton Bruckner has been glorified by some as the 'Wagner of the Symphony'... He has been suffered by his most zealous partisans to be placed, indeed, upon the same pedestal with Johannes Brahms, but on condition that he should be allowed to tower head and shoulders above him. Sufficient elements here for determined and bitter contention. On the other hand, he has been looked upon by the great majority of his critics as a mere learned musical pedagogue, devoid of the divine gift of imagination, whose compositions are so many intricate contrapuntal exercises on a vast scale.

And while this 'subject of such diametrically opposed opinions' had been living 'the quiet and uneventful life of an organist and teacher in the Austrian capital, a modest and unassuming man, adding symphony to symphony to the number of eight, together with other works of equal pretentions', it had only been in the past few years, thanks to the efforts of conductors like Hans Richter, that there had been a significant increase in the performances of his compositions in Austria and Germany.[57] British audiences, however, had to wait many years before a Bruckner symphony could be guaranteed a regular place in an orchestra's repertoire. At the end of the nineteenth century, probably only a small number of people would have recalled his visit to London as an organ virtuoso in 1871.

To sum up, Bruckner was by no stretch of the imagination the Paganini or the Liszt of the organ. His contact with the Czech organ virtuoso, Robert Führer, earlier in his career may very well have convinced him that the travelling life was not for him. He was certainly not suited temperamentally to a rootless musical career of this kind which lacked security. He needed stability and order in his life, particularly when he began to flex his compositional muscles. His almost obsessional concern with financial matters only underlines this. Unlike other organist composers (Bach and Liszt, to name but two) he wrote very little for the organ and what he did write gives us no more than an inkling of his prowess as an organist, and his stature as a composer.

Notes

1. The most thorough account of Bruckner's early years as an organist (up to 1855) and the kind of tuition he would have received is provided by Othmar Wessely in his 'Der junge Bruckner und sein Orgelspiel', in *Anton Bruckner Dokumente und Studien*, 10 (Vienna, 1994), pp. 59–96. For a penetrating discussion of Bruckner's interpretative and improvisational skills as an organist, see Erwin Horn, 'Zwischen Interpretation und Improvisation. Anton Bruckner als Organist', in *Bruckner-Symposion 1995* (Linz, 1997), pp. 111–39. Horn has also edited the recently published *Werke für Orgel* volume in *Bruckner Sämtliche Werke B*, XII/6 (Vienna, 1999).

314 Perspectives on Anton Bruckner

2. For instance, he incurred the displeasure of Franz Liszt when he took part in a performance of the first part of the oratorio *Christus* in the large *Musikverein* hall in Vienna on 31 December 1871. For some of his *Hofkapelle* colleague, Pius Richter's diary entries concerning Bruckner's tendency to over-elaborate accompaniments, see Otto Biba, 'Einiges über Anton Bruckner. Aus den Tagebüchern Pius Richters und nach persönlichen Erinnerungen zusammengestellt von Dr. Edmund Richter', in *IBG- Mitteilungsblatt*, 17 (May 1980), pp. 16–19.
3. Harrandt-Schneider, *Bruckner Briefe I*, p. 110.
4. *Anton Bruckner Dokumente und Studien*, I (Graz, 1979), pp. 52–4.
5. Ibid., pp. 90–5 for documentation of this appointment.
6. Letter dated Linz, 14 November 1868; see Harrandt-Schneider, *Bruckner Briefe I*, p. 99.
7. See Harrandt-Schneider, *Bruckner Briefe I*, pp. 102–3.
8. See Göllerich-Auer, IV/1, pp. 85–7 for the programme of the concert which included soprano solos and choral pieces.
9. From a letter to Herbeck, dated Nancy 30 April 1869; see Harrandt-Schneider, *Bruckner Briefe I*, p. 104.
10. From a report in the edition of 2 May; see Göllerich-Auer, IV/1, pp. 90–1.
11. From a report in the edition of 1 May; see Göllerich-Auer, IV/1, p.92.
12. See also Harrandt-Schneider, *Bruckner Briefe I*, p. 109 for the text of a letter (Paris, 23 June 1869) from August Neuberger, the managing director of the firm, offering Bruckner assistance in any future concert tours.
13. See Göllerich-Auer, IV/1, pp. 98–9 for an extract from this report in the *Revue et Gazette Musicale*, 36/9, May 1869, also ibid., p. 94 for a brief report in *Le Ménestrel*, May 1869. Also see Josef Burg, 'Anton Bruckners musikalische Begegnungen in Frankreich', in *IBG-Mitteilungsblatt*, 15 (June 1979), pp. 2ff. for further information about the Paris concerts, and Burg, 'Der Komponist Anton Bruckner im Spiegelbild der französischen Musikpresse seiner Zeit', in *Bruckner-Jahrbuch 1987/88* (Linz, 1990), pp. 95–112, for later French critical reaction to Bruckner as a composer.
14. From the report of Bruckner's visits to Nancy and Paris in the edition for 19 May. See Göllerich-Auer, IV/1, pp.99–102 for full report.
15. See Göllerich-Auer, IV/1, pp.104–5 for full report.
16. For general information about Bruckner's visits to Nancy and Paris in 1869 and London in 1871, see Mosco Carner, 'Anton Bruckner's Organ Recitals in France and England', in *Musical Times*, 78 (1937), pp.117–19, and Franz Grasberger, 'Anton Bruckners Auslandreisen', in *Österreichische Musikzeitschrift*, 24 (1969), pp. 630–5.
17. See Harrandt-Schneider, *Bruckner Briefe I*, pp. 122–4, for three letters from the Chamber of Trade and Industry (*Handels- und Gewerbekammer für Österreich unter der Enns*) to Bruckner, dated 28 March, 24 April and 10 July 1871.
18. See *Anton Bruckner Dokumente und Studien*, I, 57–9.
19. Letter dated Vienna, 16 May 1871 (and not 16 March 1871, as stated in earlier editions of the letters by Auer [1924] and Gräflinger [1924]); see Harrandt-Schneider, *Bruckner Briefe I*, p. 123.
20. See Harrandt-Schneider, *Bruckner Briefe I*, p. 125.
21. The rough draft of the letter from the Lord Chamberlain's office to Apponyi, dated Vienna 5 August 1871, is printed in *Anton Bruckner Dokumente und Studien* I, pp. 59–60.
22. Nicholas Thistlethwaite, *The Making of the Victorian Organ* (Cambridge, 2/1993), p. 434. There is a photograph of the console of this organ in ibid., p. 370.
23. Ibid., p. 437. For further information, see Hopkins, E.J. and Rimbault, E.F., *The Organ, its History and Construction*, 3/1877.

24. *The Musical Standard* 1, no. 366, New Series. London (Saturday 5 August 1871), p. 167. Similar preview in the *Musical World*, 49 / 22 (5 August 1871).
25. *The Choir*, 12, no. 247 (Saturday 19 August 1871), p. 116.
26. Erwin Horn, *Bruckner Symposion 1995*, 112.
27. From letter dated Linz, 1 March 1864. See Harrandt-Schneider, *Bruckner Briefe I*, 41–42.
28. The recital, which included Bach's Prelude and Fugue in E flat (St Anne's) BWV 552, Best's arrangement of Handel's Organ Concerto No. 1, Mendelssohn's Organ Sonata no. 1, and pieces by S.S. Wesley, Hopkins and Henry Smart, was reviewed in the *Musical Times*, 15 / no. 342 (August 1 1871), p. 171. The report of the same recital in *The Choir*, 12, no. 245 (Saturday 5 August 1871), p. 88 referred to a review in the *Guardian*: '... though it evidently afforded extreme pleasure to a tolerably numerous audience in the low-priced parts of the hall, from a musical point of view, it would have been far more satisfactory had Mr Best thought more of the music before him than upon the instrument upon which he was playing ...'
29. Details of their programmes can be found in *The Choir* nos 248, 249 and 251 and 254 (Saturday 26 August, Saturday 2 September, Saturday 16 September and Saturday 7 October).
30. See Göllerich-Auer, IV/1, pp.147–8.
31. Article 'Organ Recitals at the Albert Hall', in *The Musical Standard*, I, no 367, New Series. London (Saturday 12 August 1871), pp. 188–9. The reviewer for the *Musical World* (49/33, August 1871) was equally unfriendly. Michael Musgrave remarks that 'Bruckner was clearly a victim of anti-German feeling'; see his *The Musical Life of the Crystal Palace* (Cambridge, 1995), p. 256, footnote 19.
32. Ibid., p. 197.
33. 'Table Talk' column in *The Musical Standard*, 1, no. 368, New Series. London (Saturday 19 August 1871), p. 209.
34. *The Orchestra*, 16, no. 412 (Friday 18 August 1871), p. 315.
35. 'Reports' in *The Musical Standard*, 1, no. 371, New Series. London (Saturday 9 September 1871), p. 239.
36. The letter, dated 'London, Sept. 20th, 1871' and signed 'A Lover of Justice' was printed in *The Choir*, 12, no. 253, p. 214.
37. Article in *The Orchestra*, 16, no. 413 (Friday 25 August, 1871), pp. 329–30.
38. Article 'Concert-Organ Playing at the Royal Albert Hall', in *The Orchestra*, 16, no. 411 (Friday 11 August 1871), pp. 297–8.
39. See Göllerich-Auer, 4/1, p. 157.
40. See Franz Gräflinger, *Anton Bruckner. Bausteine zu seiner Lebensgeschichte* (Munich, 1911), p. 78.
41. Anthony Bird, *Paxton's Palace* (London, 1976), pp. 130–1. The specification of the large organ, first published in the *Musical World*, 35 (1857), pp. 391–3, is also printed in Thistlethwaite, op. cit., pp. 477–9 and Musgrave, op. cit., pp. 148–9. The specification of a second, smaller but still substantial, instrument installed by J.W. Walker and Sons in the Concert Room of the Crystal Palace in 1868 is given in Musgrave, op. cit., pp.156–8. It was evidently intended for participation in choral and orchestral music, also soloistically and in concertos.
42. G.A. Macfarren, *Programme of Arrangements for the Handel Festival*, 1857; quoted by Musgrave in op. cit., pp. 145–6.
43. 'Reports' in *The Musical Standard*, 1, no. 370, New Series. London (Saturday 2 September 1871), p. 229.
44. See Göllerich-Auer, IV/1, p. 162. See also Käthe Braun-Prager, 'Mei liabe Lady, dös ist nix!', in *Neues Österreich*, 4 August 1957, and 'Anton Bruckner in London', in *Wiener Zeitung*, 15 August 1958. Evidently the lady concerned asked Bruckner to return soon but to learn English in the meantime. Bruckner's retort was that he was

    too old to learn English and that if she wished to speak to him again she should learn German!

45. See Harrandt-Schneider, *Bruckner Briefe I*, p. 126. There is a facsimile of the letter between pages 160 and 161 in Göllerich-Auer, IV/1.

46. A copy of this programme as well as a copy of Mendelssohn's F minor Sonata with an indication of the registration in the Adagio and the additional note 'Kryst' were part of Bruckner's estate. See Göllerich-Auer, IV/1, pp.164–5.

47. *The Morning Advertiser,* 1 September 1871; reprinted in Göllerich-Auer, IV/1, pp. 168–9.

48. *Linzer Zeitung*, 16 September 1871. See Göllerich-Auer, IV/1, pp. 170–2.

49. Letter dated 12 March 1872; see Harrandt-Schneider, *Bruckner Briefe I*, p. 132.

50. Letter dated 10 June 1872; see Harrandt-Schneider, *Bruckner Briefe I* , p. 133.

51. See letter from the Austrian Chamber of Commerce enclosing the medal, Vienna 13 July 1875, in Harrandt-Schneider, *Bruckner-Briefe I*, p. 157.

52. See Göllerich-Auer, IV/1, pp.174–5.

53. Letter dated Nuremberg, 19 September 1872; see Harrandt-Schneider, *Bruckner Briefe I*, p. 136.

54. See Steffen Lieberwirth, *Die Gewandhausorgeln* (Leipzig-Dresden, 1986), pp. 7–38 and 'Das erste Organist eines Orgelkonzertes im Neuen Gewandhaus zu Leipzig – Anton Bruckner', in *Bruckner Jahrbuch 1987/88* (Linz, 1990), pp. 87–92, for further details including the specification of the *Gewandhaus* organ. There is a photograph of the organ in Lieberwirth, *Anton Bruckner und Leipzig* [*ABDS 6*] (Graz: Akademische Druck- und Verlagsanstalt, 1988), p. 35.

55. From Barry's article, 'Anton Bruckner', in *The Musical Times* 27 / 520 (1 June 1886), pp. 322–4. The original intention was to give the first British performance in one of the 1886 'Richter Concerts'.

56. From review in *The Musical Times* 28 / 532 (1 June 1887), pp. 342–3.

57. *The Musical Times* 37 / 645 (1 November 1896), p. 742.

14 Students and friends as 'prophets' and 'promoters': the reception of Bruckner's works in the *Wiener Akademische Wagner-Verein*

Andrea Harrandt

The *Wiener Akademische Wagner-Verein* was founded in 1872 to perform the works of Richard Wagner, Hugo Wolf and Anton Bruckner. Soon after its foundation a group of young pupils and friends of Bruckner joined forces to promote his works. According to Viktor Boller:

> Those men, who included Franz Zottmann, Josef Spur, Karl Bernard Oehn, Richard Hirsch and, later, Ferdinand Löwe ... had in common not only a holy appreciation of our Master, which bound us together, but also an unbounded enthusiasm for Anton Bruckner which, as his works became better known, was transferred to the Society as a whole'.[1]

In subsequent years Bruckner's symphonies were introduced to the *Wagner-Verein* in arrangements for piano (two hands, four hands) or two pianos at so-called '*Internen Abenden*' (internal evenings), at a time when the performance of the orchestral versions presented difficulties. In the first performance of these arrangements on 12 November 1879, Hans Paumgartner and Felix Mottl played the Adagio and Scherzo from the Third Symphony. Although it is no longer possible to ascertain all the dates of these piano performances of the symphonies, it is possible to trace their history in general.

The prime movers of these performances were Josef Schalk (who became Artistic Director of the society in 1887) and Ferdinand Löwe. As well as Josef, his brother Franz, and Löwe, many other interesting people were members of the Society; although most of them entered non-musical professions and were unsuccessful as composers, they were active in promoting Bruckner in different

317

ways – as performers, critics or editors of his works. They included Otto Böhler, Viktor Christ, Friedrich Eckstein, August Göllerich, Theodor Helm, Camillo Horn, Cyrill Hynais, Josef Kluger, Max von Oberleithner, Carl Bernhard Oehn, Theodor Reisch, and Franz Zottmann.[2]

Bruckner and the *Wiener Akademische Wagner-Verein* form an important chapter both in the reception of Bruckner's works in Vienna and in the composer's life: in the *Verein* he was understood, honoured, revered and admired. From a letter which Bruckner wrote to the *Verein* on 15 October 1873 we learn that he joined the Society soon after his stay in Bayreuth in September: 'I will be glad to be a member of a Society where intelligence and eagerness for the truly noble are represented so gloriously'.[3]

From its inception the *Wagner-Verein* performed Wagner's music. The location of these 'internal evenings' was Bösendorfer's concert hall in the Herrengasse (no. 6) which was opened in November 1872. Later the Society, together with all its events, moved to the small hall in the newly-built *Musikverein* building where its 'internal evenings' became of great importance for Viennese musical life. On 19 November 1879 *Die Presse* reported that 'the so-called internal evenings of the *Wagner-Verein* have reached a position which is growing stronger from year to year'. As one of the major aims of the Society was to direct attention not only to Wagner but also to other 'German' composers whose music could not be heard in the concert halls, 'we are indebted to the *Wagner-Verein* for the opportunity in recent years to hear rare works which were unknown to the musical public'. Leon Botstein considers that it was very important for new music such as Bruckner's to be performed in this way, as 'the anticipation of a work's actual sound before a live hearing made the live event that much more impressive'.[4]

Works by Bruckner such as the *Te Deum*, motets, the String Quartet and the String Quintet were performed by the *Wagner-Verein*; but in this article attention will be focused principally on the symphonies. One of the earliest piano reductions of a Bruckner symphony was arranged by Gustav Mahler and, probably, Rudolf Krzyzanowski soon after the first performance of the Third Symphony in December 1877; Mahler and Krzyzanowski played this reduction at the Vienna Conservatory in the presence of Karl Goldmark and Josef Schalk.[5]

Arrangements of symphonic works, which remained as close as possible to the original text, were very popular in the nineteenth century. Piano arrangements played an increasingly important role in concert life, and the arrangements of Bruckner's symphonies in particular have been described as 'well-known examples' of this genre.[6] They were an important means of disseminating and increasing understanding of Bruckner's music in late nineteenth-century Vienna.

The first known public performance of a Bruckner symphony arranged for piano took place on 12 November 1879 in the Bösendorfer hall. Hans Paumgartner and Felix Mottl played the second and third movements of the Third Symphony in Mahler's arrangement nearly two years after its first orchestral performance in the *Musikverein* hall. The critic for *Die Presse* reported: 'There is no more reliable indicator of the worth of a musical work than the effect it has when heard more often, and this work made a thrilling and electrifying impression'.[7] The next concert took place on 4 February 1880 in the Bösendorfer hall. Once again Hans Paumgartner and Felix Mottl played the piano parts in their own arrangement of the second and third movements of the Fourth Symphony in the composer's presence. This was the first performance of the work and its reception was one of well-deserved 'vociferous appreciation', but one critic expressed his desire to 'hear it in full orchestral sound' so that he would be able to say more about it.[8] The Scherzo provoked 'thunderous applause which increased when the composer appeared'.[9] In the same year the duo performed the first movement of the Fourth Symphony on 7 October. It was Felix Mottl's farewell appearance before he left Vienna for Karlsruhe to become director of the Court Theatre. On 10 December 1881, he conducted the Fourth Symphony in Karlsruhe, but without success.

Besides these internal evenings of the *Wagner-Verein* there were weekly meetings with lectures and recitals. The members were able to hear Bruckner's music on these occasions as well. The performance of movements from the Fourth Symphony at one such meeting on 12 January 1881, for instance, was perhaps by way of preparation for the orchestral concert on March 20 when Hans Richter conducted the symphony in the *Musikverein*.[10] On 24 March 1882, in a concert given by Josef and Franz Schalk, Josef performed his arrangement of the Scherzo from the Third Symphony. One reviewer praised both Schalk for his arrangement and Bruckner for the vitality of his composition, which was by no means 'only a series of phrases strung together'.[11] Max Kalbeck, one of the harshest critics of Bruckner's music, was forced to mention the 'well-earned recall' of the composer to which he responded 'in the most gracious manner'.[12] At the end of the year Josef Schalk planned to perform the Fifth Symphony in the presence of Carl von Stremayr,[13] the dedicatee of the work, but the performance had to be cancelled because Stremayr's daughter took ill. Schalk and Zottmann gave their first joint recital of a Bruckner arrangement on 10 February 1883, when they played the first and third movements of the Seventh Symphony, although Bruckner had still not finished the work![14] On 7 May 1883 they played the Third Symphony on two pianos.[15]

In the Schalk brothers' next recital, on 29 January 1884, Josef played the first and second movements of the Fourth Symphony. The reviewer remarked that the work had made a powerful impression, although performed on the piano rather than the orchestra.[16] A few days earlier Ferdinand Löwe gave his first recital, playing his own arrangement of the Adagio from the First Symphony. The same reviewer remarked on its 'surprisingly passionate upsurge after an over-long contemplative stasis'.[17] In his later recollection of this performance, Theodor Helm commented very favourably on both the piano arrangement (specifically its faithfulness to the original orchestral version) and Löwe's interpretative powers.[18]

Soon after, on 27 February 1884, Schalk and Löwe played the Seventh

Symphony.[19] On 16 January 1884 Bruckner had written to Josef Schalk: 'Do you really intend to play two movements with Löwe on two pianos? You must know only too well (as does Löwe) that a symphony like mine cannot produce its proper effect when played with two hands only ... I would be very grateful if I could hear it once, for the sake of the tempi'.[20] On 4 November 1884, Josef Schalk achieved great success in performing the Adagio of the Seventh and the Scherzo of the Fourth Symphony. In a review of the performance, he was described as one of the 'most brilliant and musically educated pianists in Vienna'. The Adagio of the Seventh was called the 'most interesting number of the evening'. The reviewer added, however, that it was difficult to 'gain a convincing impression of this extremely complicated piece of music on hearing it for the first time' and that it lost its full effect in being played on the piano. He also criticised a few insensitive and tactless people who had left the hall during the playing of the Adagio![21]

For the next recital, a so-called '*Bruckner-Abend*' which took place on 22 December 1884, Josef Schalk and his new partner Ferdinand Löwe, who had given his first recital in January, again joined forces. They played the whole of the First Symphony on two pianos in an arrangement by Löwe. This work had been performed in its entirety only once before – on 9 May 1868 in Linz – under the direction of Bruckner himself. Although the symphony was not yet known in Vienna, the two-piano performance was highly successful. According to Theodor Helm, the Scherzo made the greatest impact.[22] In addition Löwe played the first movement of the Fourth and Schalk the third movement of the Third, and their performances also received very favourable reviews: 'We know that these two young men are working with touching devotion and enthusiasm for the revered Bruckner. So they can be called artistic apostles'.[23] Bruckner was presented with a laurel wreath which bore the inscription 'to the German master'. In a letter to Josef Schalk he described the concert as the 'greatest success' he had ever experienced.[24] On December 24 Bruckner was able to write proudly to his sister Rosalie: 'On Monday in Vienna I received the greatest applause and a wonderful laurel wreath'.[25] Two days later he departed for Leipzig to witness the first performance of his Seventh Symphony.

A report in the *Deutsche Kunst- und Musikzeitung* reveals just how important these concerts of piano arrangements were for Bruckner. Schalk and Löwe, two young men 'endowed with singular artistic gifts', were commended for 'at least retrieving the honour of musical Vienna which has so terribly ignored its native composer, the most important among living composers for the future of the symphony, by providing superb, finely-conceived piano interpretations of a few of his orchestral works'.[26] Another young man – Hugo Wolf – also lent his support. In his article in the *Wiener Salonblatt*, which appeared just two days before the Leipzig première of the Seventh, he asked: 'Bruckner? Bruckner? Who is he? Where does he live? What can he do?' He continued:

> It would certainly be rewarding, then, to give this inspired evangelist more attention
> than he has been accorded up to now. It is a truly shocking sight to see this

extraordinary man barred from the concert hall. Among living composers (with the exception of Liszt, of course) he has the first and greatest claim to be performed and admired.[27]

As a result of Hermann Levi's efforts on the composer's behalf, Bruckner was elected an honorary member of the *Wagner-Verein* at the general assembly on 22 January 1885.[28]

On 23 April 1885, Löwe and Schalk again played the Adagio and Finale from the First Symphony in Löwe's arrangement and the first movement of the Third Symphony on two pianos. One critic wrote that

> Every sincere music lover was indebted to both artists for arranging some movements from Bruckner's symphonies for piano and presenting them to the public with youthful enthusiasm ... and with such astonishing technical assurance that they and the composer who was present were received with acclamation at the end of each movement ...[29]

On 30 December 1885, Löwe again partnered Schalk in a performance of the first and third movements of the Seventh Symphony in a two-piano arrangement – a performance that was greeted with enthusiasm although it 'cried out for an orchestral interpretation'.[30] Only a few days later Gutmann published the piano score (for four hands) of the symphony.[31] The first orchestral performance in Vienna took place on 21 March 1886 in a concert in the *Musikverein* sponsored by the *Wagner-Verein*. It was a great success and Bruckner was again presented with a laurel wreath. On 25 March he sent his 'warmest and most heartfelt thanks' to the *Verein*.[32]

On 18 March 1886, Löwe and Schalk played the Seventh Symphony in a weekly meeting of the *Wagner-Verein*. This evening was of great importance for Friedrich Klose (1862-1942), who had just arrived in Vienna and was accepted as a private student by Bruckner. Through Mottl he joined the *Wagner-Verein*. Klose had the opportunity to hear Bruckner's music for the first time at this 'internal evening' and, at the end of the performance, felt both 'unbounded admiration' for the composer and 'overflowing joy' in the knowledge that he was now a pupil of this great man.[33]

The first performance of the Fifth Symphony on 20 April 1887 – in a two-piano version played by Josef Schalk and Franz Zottmann – was an evening of great significance. There had been some trouble with Bruckner before the concert because he did not want the performance to go ahead.[34] But, as Theodor Helm pointed out, the Fifth Symphony was not known at all in Vienna: 'Schalk and Zottmann performed a noble and honourable task by giving us an insight into the creative mind of our genial Bruckner ... they acted as pioneers in their penetration of the intricate symphonic textures'.[35] Once again, however, there was a call for an orchestral performance to provide a clearer understanding of this 'extremely bold work'.[36] Löwe, Schalk and Zottmann were given honourable mention in the *Wagner-Verein* annual report for 1887: 'With untiring eagerness they made it their task to present rich, select musical delights to that intimate circle in the weekly meetings'.[37]

On 22 January 1888, Hans Richter conducted the Fourth Symphony in the *Musikverein*. Just a few days before (on 19 January) Josef Schalk played this work in a so-called 'Ladies' Evening' of the *Wagner-Verein*. In a weekly meeting on 17 February 1889, Löwe and Schalk played movements from different symphonies. Only three days before Hans Richter conducted the first performance of the third version of the Fourth Symphony (24 February 1889), Josef Schalk played this work in another 'Ladies' Evening'.

During the following year it was Löwe who took the lead in performing Bruckner on the piano. He played the Adagio and Scherzo from the Third Symphony on 5 March 1890 and was commended for 'achieving the best possible results in making the polyphony clear'.[38] On 30 December 1891, Löwe played the second and fourth movements of the First Symphony, less than three weeks after the first performance of the revised version of the work in a Philharmonic concert (13 December). Once again Löwe was praised as an 'unsurpassable interpreter of Bruckner's music' and the critic noted that he played the movements 'from memory with thrilling effect'.

In 1892 there were two performances of movements from the Eighth Symphony in the weekly meetings of the *Wagner-Verein*. On 22 November, Josef Schalk played the first movement in an 'internal evening' and one reviewer described his performance as a 'commendable preparation' for the forthcoming orchestral performance of 'this most remarkable work' which took place on 18 December.[39] Other reviewers were more critical, however. One remarked that difficult works of this nature demanded 'a four-hand performance at the very least' and even then were of interest only to those who already knew them. For those who were not acquainted with the work, a piano performance was 'of very little practical use'.[40] Another made the point that, even in the hands of accomplished pianists who were able to produce an orchestral sound on the piano, there was something 'extremely incomplete' about the piano arrangements of the 'most recent orchestral works written by German composers'.[41] A further performance of the first movement of the Eighth was announced for February 1893.

On 29 November 1894, Löwe played the first movement of the Sixth in an 'internal evening' – the first performance of this particular movement, as Wilhelm Jahn and the Vienna Philharmonic had performed only the second and third movements of this symphony on 11 February 1883. According to one critic:

> The hero of the evening was Professor Löwe who has still not received sufficient recognition as an excellent musician and specialist performer of Bruckner's music. His recital of the first movement of the Sixth, rendered with great accuracy and played with an orchestral sound, was unanimously admired. We also wish to put on record that Löwe played this very difficult movement from memory.[42]

The *Deutsche Zeitung* reported that Löwe's performance of an orchestral movement, which was 'one of the most interesting but also one of the most difficult to understand', was 'a highlight of the evening'.[43] The *Ostdeutsche*

Rundschau critic agreed that the performance was excellent but observed that the piano score just hinted at the beauty of the orchestral score and could only 'whet one's appetite for an orchestral performance'.[44] The Viennese public had to wait a few years before they were able to hear the whole symphony. In 1899 Gustav Mahler conducted an orchestral performance of an abbreviated version with instrumental modifications. Löwe played the fourth movement at a *Wagner-Verein* concert on 7 April 1900. It was not until March 1901 that an uncut orchestral performance of the work was given in Stuttgart.

On 28 November 1895, Löwe performed the first three movements of the Fifth Symphony; there was not enough time for the fourth movement. The reviewer mentioned that it was a 'risky business' to 'keep the public interested for a full hour in a difficult work which requires one's full attention'. Nevertheless, Löwe's playing (by memory) had gripped the audience throughout.[45] While according Löwe due praise for his exemplary performance, Camillo Horn maintained that Bruckner's music lost much of its attraction when not played by an orchestra.[46]

After Bruckner's death his friends and students, especially Ferdinand Löwe, continued to perform the piano scores of his symphonies. Löwe's performance of the first movement of the Sixth Symphony during a concert in 1897, for instance, elicited the typical response that he had the ability to 'give some idea of the instrumentation' of the work in his playing.[47] Ferdinand Foll frequently played the symphonies on Thursdays at the weekly meetings of the *Wagner-Verein*.[48] There was always a memorial concert on Bruckner's birthday and, in later years, after the turn of the century, the Society arranged cyclic performances of Bruckner's symphonies.

In 1889 some members left the 'Academic' *Wagner-Verein* for political and anti-Semitic reasons. In the following year a new ('Neuer') *Richard Wagner-Verein* was founded by a group of men including August Göllerich, Camillo Horn, Hans Puchstein and Josef Stolzing, all of them former members of the *Wiener Akademische Wagner-Verein* and all of them writers for anti-Semitic newspapers.[49] While the *Wiener Akademische Wagner-Verein* had the financial support of the Bayreuth Festival as its general aim, the 'new' Society, according to its statutes, existed to promote and propagate 'knowledge and appreciation of Wagner's reformatory efforts and his music dramas through lectures and discussions'.[50] This new society was more German and nationalistic and promoted an idealistic German ideology which was formulated 'in accordance with the German spirit ... Only the German spirit shall be our guide! This is our way!'.[51] It saw Wagner as an educator of the German people. Its general aim was to propagate German art to German people and to make a vital contribution to German life. The strict nationalistic and anti-Semitic basis of the *Neuer Richard Wagner-Verein* was in accordance with the views of Georg von Schönerer; one of its patrons was Houston Stewart Chamberlain.[52] Its motto was: '*German* guests are welcome every evening!'.

Like the 'Academic' *Wagner-Verein*, the new Society held weekly meetings and performed the music of Wagner, Liszt and Bruckner, but in a more intimate way. The first recital to include Bruckner's music took place on 8 October 1890, when two movements from the Seventh Symphony were played. One of the most important artists in the new *Wagner-Verein* was Cyrill Hynais.[53] Hynais made piano arrangements of the early Symphony in F minor as well as the Fourth and Seventh Symphonies. Though he was a member of the *Akademischer Wagner-Verein* he performed both his own and Bruckner's works in the *Neuer Wagner-Verein*.

The next recorded performance of Bruckner's music was on the evening of 20 January 1892, when Hynais and Max von Oberleithner played the Third Symphony with 'enthusiastic loving devotion'.[54] In a memorial evening for Richard Wagner a month later, on 17 February, Victor Bause was Cyrill Hynais' piano partner in a performance of the Adagio of the Seventh Symphony.[55] On 30 March 1892, Hynais and Bause played the first movement of the Eighth Symphony at a weekly meeting of the Society which also included a lecture on 'Richard Wagner abroad' by Houston Stewart Chamberlain. There were subsequent performances of the first movement of the Third Symphony (22 February 1893) and the first movement of the Fourth Symphony (May 1893) by Bause and G. Schnabel. Schnabel and Riedel played the second and third movements of the Third Symphony at a Wagner memorial concert on 20 February 1895. There are no records of any other Bruckner performances in the *Neuer Wagner-Verein*.

The *Akademischer Wagner-Verein* must be given due credit for its pioneering work on behalf of Bruckner and his music in Vienna. But there was also a 'downside' to his close association with the Society in that he came into contact with enthusiastic partisans who were responsible for the 'rift' with Brahms.

The significance of the piano performances is aptly summed up by Franz Grasberger:

> The four-hand arrangements of his symphonies by students and disciples in the *Wagner-Verein* corresponded neither in principle nor in detail with what he ultimately desired but they represented at least a form of tonal realisation at a time when it was initially very difficult for him to secure orchestral performances and when, later, he still had to struggle to have them played in their proper setting.[56]

Up to the present day these piano performances have attracted very little attention. But in a period when there is a more historically informed approach to performance practice it is now fashionable again to give piano performances not only of symphonies by Bruckner but also, for example, of those by Brahms and Mahler.[57] And so, at the beginning of the twenty-first century, we are able to experience the sound of the late nineteenth century either actively or passively.

Notes

1. Extract from Viktor Boller's memorial speech for Josef Schalk, 22.11.1900, *28. Jahresbericht des Wiener akademischen Richard Wagner-Vereins für 1900* (Vienna,

1901), p. 16. Viktor Boller (1853–1904) was a lawyer. He was chairman of the *Wagner-Verein* from 1884 to 1894 and appointed Josef Schalk as its Artistic Director.

2. Otto Böhler (1847–1913) was director of the Böhler steel-works. He was also an artist and made silhouettes of Viennese musical life. Viktor Christ (1869–1902) was one of Bruckner's students at the Conservatory of Music in Vienna and became a court musician later. He made a copy of Bruckner's Eighth Symphony. Friedrich Eckstein (1861–1939) was introduced to Bruckner as a private student by the Schalk brothers and Ferdinand Löwe. As a young man August Göllerich (1859–1923) got to know both Liszt and Bruckner. Theodor Helm (1843–1920) was a critic and one of Bruckner's advocates in Vienna. Camillo Horn (1860–1941) was one of Bruckner's private pupils. He later became a music teacher and a choral and orchestral conductor. Bruckner met Josef Kluger (1865–1937), an admirer of Wagner, at Klosterneuburg Abbey. Kluger later became abbot there. Max von Oberleitner (1868–1935) was a lawyer and one of Bruckner's private pupils from 1889 to 1894. As far as Oberleitner was concerned, Bruckner was the 'spiritual Richard Wagner'. Carl Bernhard Oehn (1858–1923) was an employee of the First Austrian Bank. He was Bruckner's student and an unsuccessful composer. He took an active part in the publication of Bruckner's music. Theodor Reisch was a lawyer and one of the executors of Bruckner's will.

3. Wst, I.N. 72.862; printed in Harrandt-Schneider, *Bruckner Briefe I*, p. 139.
4. Leon Botstein, 'Music and its Public: Habits of Listening and the Crisis of Musical Modernism in Vienna, 1850–1914'. Ph.D. dissertation (Harvard University, 1985), p. 452.
5. Göllerich-Auer IV/1, p. 482.
6. Helmut Loos, *Zur Klavierübertragung von Werken für und mit Orchester des 19. und 20. Jahrhunderts* [*Schriften zur Musik*, 25] (Munich-Salzburg, 1983), p. 26.
7. *Die Presse*, 19 November 1879. Felix Mottl (1856–1911) had a reputation not only as a pianist but also as a conductor in his later years. Hans Paumgartner (1844–1896) worked as a lawyer until 1880. After this concert he devoted himself to music, as a pianist and a critic for the *Wiener Zeitung*. Two years later he married the famous opera singer, Rosa Papier.
8. *Morgenpost*, 7 February 1880.
9. *Deutsche Kunst- und Musikzeitung*, 10 February 1880.
10. See *9. Jahresbericht des Wiener Akademischen Wagner-Vereins für das Jahr 1881* (Vienna, 1882), p. 4.
11. *Die Presse*, 31 March 1882.
12. *Allgemeine Wiener Zeitung*, 29 March 1882.
13. Carl Ritter von Stremayr (1823–1904) was Minister of Culture and Education and one of Bruckner's patrons.
14. Franz Zottmann, born in Hainburg in 1858, was a pianist and teacher at the Vienna Conservatory.
15. For the programme, see Göllerich-Auer 4/2, p. 82. In the same concert Julius Winkler and his quintet performed Bruckner's String Quintet.
16. *Deutsche Zeitung*, 7 February 1884.
17. Ibid.
18. See Göllerich-Auer, IV/1, p. 577.
19. See Göllerich-Auer, IV/2, p. 156.
20. Wn F18 Schalk 178a.
21. *Deutsche Zeitung*, 6 November 1884.
22. *Deutsche Zeitung*, 24 December 1884.
23. *Allgemeine Kunst-Chronik*, 17 January 1885.
24. Wn F18 Schalk 151/2/2/1.

25. The original of this letter is in the Museum für Geschichte der Stadt Leipzig; printed in Harrandt-Schneider, *Bruckner Briefe I*, p. 233.
26. *Deutsche Kunst- und Musikzeitung*, 1 January 1885.
27. *Wiener Salonblatt*, 28 December 1884.
28. See the letter from the *Wagner-Verein* to Levi, 26 February 1885, Wn Mus. Hs. 3197.
29. *Deutsche Kunst- und Musikzeitung*, 1 May 1885.
30. From the review in the *Morgenpost*, 31 December 1885.
31. Schalk and Löwe performed the symphony not only in the *Wagner-Verein* but also in the *Tonkünstler-Verein* on 11 January 1886.
32. The original of this letter is in Wst.
33. Friedrich Klose, *Meine Lehrjahre bei Bruckner. Erinnerungen und Betrachtungen* (Regensburg, 1927), p. 16.
34. For further information, see Thomas Leibnitz, *Die Brüder Schalk und Anton Bruckner [Publikationen des Instituts für Österreichische Musikdokumentation]*, 14 (Tutzing, 1988), pp. 111–17.
35. *Deutsche Zeitung*, 26 April 1887.
36. E.v. Hartmann, in *Musikalische Rundschau*, 1 May 1887.
37. *15. Jahresbericht des Wiener Akademischen Wagner-Vereins für das Jahr 1887* (Vienna, 1888), p. 12.
38. *Musikalische Rundschau*, 10 March 1890.
39. *Deutsche Zeitung*, 24 November 1892.
40. *Deutsches Volksblatt*, 7 December 1892.
41. *Ostdeutsche Rundschau*, 18 December 1892.
42. *Deutsches Volksblatt*, 2 December 1894.
43. *Deutsche Zeitung*, 4 December 1894.
44. *Ostdeutsche Rundschau*, 18 December 1894.
45. 'Hagen' in the *Ostdeutsche Rundschau*, 3 December 1895.
46. *Deutsches Volksblatt*, 7 December 1895. Horn (1860–1941), one of Bruckner's private students, became a composer and taught at the Vienna Academy of Music from 1918. He used his position as music critic of the *Deutsches Volksblatt* to support Bruckner and his music.
47. *Ostdeutsche Rundschau*, 24 March 1897.
48. Ferdinand Foll, the artistic director of the *Wagner-Verein*, was an important personality in the Society. Particular mention is made of his 'conscientious and discerning' playing on frequent occasions in the *Wagner-Verein* report for 1890. See the *18. Jahresbericht des Wiener Akademischen Wagner-Vereins für das Jahr 1890* (Vienna, 1891), p. 12.
49. For further information, see Margaret Notley, 'Bruckner and Viennese Wagnerism', in Timothy Jackson and Paul Hawkshaw, eds, *Bruckner Studies* (Cambridge, 1997), pp. 54–71.
50. Winfried Schüler, *Der Bayreuther Kreis von seiner Entstehung bis zum Ausgang der Wilhelminischen Ära. Der Wagnerkult und Kulturreform im Geiste völkischer Weltanschauung* (Münster, 1971), p. 58.
51. *Ostdeutsche Rundschau*, 28 September 1890, p. 8.
52. *Ostdeutsche Rundschau*, 2 November 1890.
53. Cyrill Hynais (1867–1913) was encouraged by Josef Schalk to study counterpoint with Bruckner at the Conservatory from 1883 to 1885. He became a primary school teacher, composer and music journalist and, later, chorus-master of the *Wagner-Verein*. In Bruckner's later years he performed an important role in the publication of the composer's works, supervising the publication of the Mass in D minor, Psalm 150 and *Helgoland*.
54. *Ostdeutsche Rundschau*, 2 November 1890.

55. Victor Bause (b. 1865) studied at the Vienna Conservatory with Epstein, Vockner, J.N. and Robert Fuchs and Bruckner (harmony, counterpoint and organ). He became a pianist, composer, music teacher and chorus-master and was artistic director of the *Neuer Wagner-Verein* for two years.

56. Franz Grasberger, 'Selbstkritik, Überzeugung und Beeinflußung. Zum Problem der Fassungen bei Anton Bruckner', in *Bruckner-Symposion Linz 1980: 'Die Fassungen'* (Linz, 1981), p. 37.

57. Some of these are already available on CD, for instance Bruckner's Third Symphony in Mahler's arrangement played by the piano duo Evelinde Trenkner and Sontraud Speidel, or the original versions of Brahms's First and Fourth Symphonies performed by the Crommelynck Duo.

15 Anton Bruckner and 'German music': Josef Schalk and the establishment of Bruckner as a national composer

Thomas Leibnitz

'What is German music?' In August 1934, Friedrich W. Herzog posed this question in *Die Musik*, a periodical at that time known as the 'official organ of the NS-Kulturgemeinde'.[1] Herzog provided a rather indistinct answer which included such ideas as 'longing and a sense of the infinite, an urge to fulfil constructive tasks, an overwhelming impulse to create, a manifest love of freedom'.[2] Later he argued in a more concrete way by giving examples of the 'idea of Germanness in music'. He mentioned four names that we constantly encounter in this context: Bach, Beethoven, Bruckner and Wagner.[3] It cannot be denied that Bruckner, along with Wagner, was a *persona gratissima* of National Socialistic cultural policy. Hitler himself ordered a Bruckner bust to be exhibited in the Valhalla near Regensburg, a 'Reichs-Bruckner-Orchester' was founded in Linz in 1942 and Bruckner was performed more frequently than ever before.[4] Do the personality and works of Anton Bruckner have any bearing on all this? Or can this Bruckner cult be explained simply by the leading National Socialists' individual preference for the composer? In this chapter we will try to address the question of the 'German' in Bruckner, especially as understood in the composer's own time.

It is easy to understand why we hear nothing about Bruckner as a 'German' composer after 1945: the Bruckner cult in the Third Reich had become an awkward and embarrassing topic. The Nazis' adulation was not a subject for research nor were questions asked about its historical roots. On the one hand, this was an understandable position: burdening Bruckner with the negative connotations of National Socialism could not be in the interests of Bruckner supporters who wanted to improve the composer's position in international musical life. They could state with good reason that Bruckner himself had no specific nationalistic attitude. On the other hand, it is impossible to deny that the 'German' idea played an important role in the older Bruckner literature, even during the composer's lifetime. We ought to examine the criteria by which music was considered typically 'German' in the late nineteenth century and ask whether Bruckner indeed fulfilled these conditions. A comprehensive investigation of this subject would, of course, be too extensive for this chapter. Only one aspect will be dealt with – and it will serve to illustrate the point in the manner of a *pars pro toto*: the public presentation of Bruckner by his pupil and friend Josef Schalk.

The group of friends and pupils who gathered round Bruckner during his lifetime boasted as its most important members the brothers Josef and Franz Schalk and Ferdinand Löwe, who undeniably played a crucial role in the dissemination of Bruckner's music in Austria and abroad. The composer's young friends played his works in piano versions to familiarize the public with his new and unusual musical style, and they promoted his cause in programme guides to his works and in periodicals. Bruckner, who was very inept at presenting himself verbally, greatly appreciated this type of help. Their enthusiastic service on the composer's behalf, however, soon developed a life of its own, the situation becoming most acute when a decision had to be reached about the final form of a score. Here, friendly interventions ranged from valuable consultation and suggestions to unauthorised revisions (such as the revision of the Fifth Symphony by Franz Schalk and the revision of the Ninth Symphony by Ferdinand Löwe, to name but two examples). Many of Bruckner's symphonies conquered the concert halls of the world not in the composer's versions but in revisions completed by his friends and pupils. The result was that, as the Critical Edition was being published and the original versions of these works came to light in the 1930s, Bruckner was to a certain extent 'rediscovered.' We will not deal with this question here, as it has already been widely discussed in the Bruckner literature, but rather focus on the image of Bruckner presented to his contemporaries by his pupils and friends. In spite of all the criticism with which we now dismiss the activities of the members of the Bruckner circle, it must be stated that this subjective manipulation was nevertheless motivated by the idealistic intention of promoting Bruckner's cause.

Although Josef Schalk's engagement on behalf of Bruckner and Hugo Wolf is of much greater interest than his own career as a performer, his biography deserves consideration. Born 24 March 1857 in Vienna, he became a pianist and piano teacher at the Conservatory of the *Gesellschaft der Musikfreunde* in Vienna. His life was overshadowed by a long battle with asthma, the disease that led to his untimely death on 7 November 1900. His parents intended him to pursue technical studies,[5] but the school reports preserved in his estate in the Music Collection of the Austrian National Library show very bad grades, especially in mathematics and scientific subjects. At the age of about ten he began to study the piano; in the years 1877 to 1880 he continued his musical education at the Vienna Conservatory where Julius Epstein became his teacher in piano and Anton Bruckner his teacher in theory and composition. He received excellent grades from both, and we can be certain that at this time he had already decided to become a musician. Even the musical partisanship which would remain characteristic for the rest of his life can be seen in these early years: in his estate we find a receipt for the payment of eight florins to the 'Patronatverein pro Bayreuth 1878'.[6] After the early death of his father, Schalk had to provide for his mother, his young brother Franz and his sisters by giving private lessons. In the light of the critical financial situation of the young musician and his family, this contribution to the Bayreuth Festival attests to the fervour of the young Wagnerian's idealism at this time.

In 1879 Schalk became a member of the *Wiener Akademische Wagner-Verein*. The *Wagner-Verein* was a haven for an elitist and uncompromising conception of art, and its central focus was Wagner and his theoretical writings. An almost religious aura typified the meetings of the society; even as late as 1904 Ernst Decsey wrote in his biography of Hugo Wolf: 'Typical of this group was a cultivation of art which had a kind of religious character to it; it was only with reluctance that they decided to reveal this to the public'.[7] Even in this group, Schalk and his friends formed the 'extreme left' (in the words of Decsey).[8] The circle which would do so much in the following years to disseminate and popularize Bruckner's works included Ferdinand Löwe (a *Wunderkind* at the piano and, later, a well-known conductor of Bruckner's works), Franz Zottmann, Richard Hirsch, Bernhard Oehn and others. Being well-read and possessing a certain intellectual flair, Josef Schalk was soon regarded as a leading light among the members; from October 1887 onwards he was the artistic leader of the *Wagner-Verein*.

As Schalk's practical musical activities are not germane to our discussion, it need only be mentioned here that he arranged for the first performance of Bruckner's String Quintet in F major to take place in the *Wagner-Verein* on 17 November 1881. Together with Ferdinand Löwe and Franz Zottmann, he gave the first performances of Bruckner's First, Third, Fifth and Seventh Symphonies in versions for two pianos, and he succeeded in persuading Arthur Nikisch, the conductor of the Leipzig *Stadttheater*, to give the first orchestral performance of the Seventh Symphony in Leipzig in December 1884. This event, which was followed by a very successful performance of the same symphony by Hermann Levi in Munich, is rightly considered Bruckner's breakthrough to international fame.

Schalk regarded the composer's good standing in the contemporary press as being as important as the successful performance of his works in the concert hall. Besides contributing to musical discussions and writing articles in various newspapers, he published a laudatory account of Bruckner in the *Bayreuther Blätter* in October 1884. This article introduced Bruckner for the first time to the public beyond the borders of Austria. In it we already find in an embryonic form the *topoi* typical of Bruckner reception in the years to come, *topoi* that would persist well into the twentieth century: the close connection between Bruckner and Wagner, the labelling of Bruckner as a specifically 'German' composer (who is associated with 'nature' in opposition to 'decadent society') and, finally, the conception of his music as inhabiting a sublime sphere opposed to common musical taste and censorious music criticism.

Bruckner–Wagner

Schalk refers in dramatic terms to the neglect Bruckner has experienced at the hands of contemporary musical authorities and continues:

> Simply out of consideration to the artist, nobody could really offer him effective help. Far from recognizing the real reasons for this in his pure and innocent mind, Bruckner – confused, dismayed, even overcome by self-doubt – finally saw only one salvation: the way to <u>Him</u> [Wagner]. Only He, whose greatness had long filled his soul with glowing enthusiasm, could calm him; he wanted to rush to Him and to cast his work before the penetrating eye of the Sublime. ... Only the One always remained true to him and, at a time when hopes for the planned *Stylbildungsschule* [Performance School] in Bayreuth had not yet been completely abandoned, it was He who spoke to Bruckner the friendly words of consolation in his singularly benevolent manner: 'Trust me, I myself will perform your works'.[9]

Thus Bruckner was clearly and unreservedly assigned to the Wagnerian camp. It is important to point this out, as the cultural world at that time was divided strictly into pro- and anti-Wagnerians. For Bruckner this proved more of a liability than an asset. Eduard Hanslick, for instance, could claim with some plausibility that Bruckner was being promoted by the Wagnerian party for purely tactical reasons. After the first Viennese performance of the Seventh Symphony on 21 March 1886, he wrote:

> Bruckner is the latest idol of the Wagnerians. It cannot be said that he has come into fashion, because the public does not want to follow this fashion at all; nevertheless, Bruckner has become a military rallying-cry, and the 'second Beethoven' a tenet of faith for the Wagner community.[10]

In fact, Schalk distorted the real nature of the relationship between Bruckner and Wagner and indulged in wishful thinking. Bruckner undoubtedly adored Wagner in an almost submissive manner, but his adulation was directed at Wagner the musician, not Wagner the thinker or the ideologist. For Wagner, on the other hand, Bruckner played only a minimal role, if any. He relegated to his wife the task of writing the letter thanking Bruckner for the dedication of his Third Symphony. In Cosima's diaries, which note Wagner's words and acts down to the most trivial details of everyday life, Bruckner is mentioned only in passing and not in a flattering manner. On 8 February 1875, Cosima notes: 'We are having a look at the symphony by the poor organist Bruckner from Vienna'.[11] These words reveal much about the way Bruckner was thought of and talked about in Bayreuth during Wagner's lifetime.

The 'German' composer

Schalk begins his Bruckner article with a quotation from the final scene of Wagner's *Die Meistersinger*: '*Was deutsch und echt wüsst' keiner mehr, lebt's nicht in deutscher Meister Ehr'!*' ('No one would know what is German and genuine if it did not reside in the glory of German masters!') and, at the outset of the article, acquaints us with the reasons for the specific quality of 'Germanness' in Bruckner: it lies in the 'earnestness' and 'purity' of his artistic aims. These, in turn, stem from his origins and his education. Bruckner, after all, 'had grown up in rural tranquillity, shaped only by the revelations of wonderful nature, not by the influences of a miseducated society'.[12] In this stylized idealization, Schalk purposely ignores the reality of Bruckner's youth which was in no way formed merely by 'rural peace' and 'wonderful nature', but far more by the principles of Metternich's authoritarian rule and by the restrictions of clerical life to which Bruckner was subjected at St Florian. For Schalk, the devout Wagnerian, it was imperative to sketch a portrait of Bruckner in the context of Wagnerian thinking, to depict the composer in the form of the ideal 'German artist'.

In Wagner's terms the word 'German' combined nationalistic tendencies with an abundance of such ethical creeds as idealism, rejection of practical rationality, and renunciation of commercial thinking. As Wagner himself once put it, being German means doing a thing for its own sake.[13] Wagner's approach articulated the uneasiness caused by the estrangement between life, work and art emerging at this time, a growing problem in the dawning industrial age in which the strict division of labour, the growth of commerce and banking, and the commercialization of all products, even artistic ones, assumed ever vaster dimensions in daily life. The thinly disguised enemy in all this – again as a result of interrelated national, racial and ethical questions – was the 'Jew', a word that in time became associated with a conglomerate of 'negative' ideas such as liberalism, rationality, philosophical and religious scepticism, internationalism and commercial thinking. Thus, in Wagner's dialectic view of the world, Jewry represented the general antithesis to the Germanness he was propagating – an opposition which could be described in a series of antithetical pairs: idealism–rationalism, nature–civilisation, unselfishness–profiteering, inspiration–calculation, in short 'German' v. 'un-German'.

Josef Schalk studied his Wagner carefully, a fact he proved a year later with his article '*Anton Bruckner und die moderne Musikwelt*' ('Anton Bruckner and the Modern Music World') published in the periodical *Deutsche Worte*.[14] The title alone contains a clear allusion to Wagner's article 'Modern' published in 1878, an aggressive and anti-Semitic settling of accounts with the contemporary musical world. Though Schalk avoids explicitly anti-Semitic wording, he clearly presumes that Wagner's negative use of the term 'modern music world' was well known to insiders. As if to underscore the point, the introduction to this article also strongly recommends reading Wagner's artistic and political writings, in particular his report to King Ludwig of Bavaria about the proposal to build a German music school in Munich. In Schalk's opinion, these writings had not had the impact they deserved, but their dissemination and influence had been confined largely to the opera house.[15] In this essay, Schalk's description of the 'German Bruckner' is even more radical than in the *Bayreuther Blätter* article:

> It may very well have been an obstacle in the way of Bruckner's recognition that his music is more German than anything we have hitherto encountered in purely instrumental music. Certainly not more German than Bach and Beethoven in the basic elements of their character or their works, but more German in the form of expression. That foreign influence, which for centuries had suppressed the unpretentiousness and the universality of the German spirit in all areas and in all respects, has for the first time been broken completely in instrumental music.[16]

Here a view of Bruckner is established that a few years later would inspire August Göllerich, Bruckner's 'anointed biographer' to write the following lines:

> In the sphere of that most German activity – in the realm of music – he has struggled and won through, a consolidator of uniquely German feeling, a preacher of the truest German faith, who eternally proclaims to the world that the noble and beautiful is not given to us for the sake of fame and gain, but that it is German to do something for its own sake and out of the joy of doing it. This faith has infused, strengthened and preserved our Master, Anton Bruckner, throughout his life![17]

This substantial appropriation of Bruckner's personality and works for the cause of 'Germanness' seems all the more strange as we do not have a single spoken or written utterance by the composer that would legitimize such a position. It is true that Bruckner was anxious not to provoke any of the authorities of his time. Promoting an explicitly nationalistic German position in Austria during the second half of the nineteenth century smacked of opposition. After all, Austria's identity as a state was founded on dynastic principles and the idea of supra-nationality. Nothing would have been more foreign to Bruckner than to become a dissident. Why, then, did he not protest against the nationalistic pronouncements of his apologists? The answer is rather simple: he did not want to do anything that would antagonize the few champions of his cause. Furthermore, we can presume that he was unaware of the polemical and aggressive aspects of nationalistic German rhetoric.

The mystical sphere of Bruckner's music – 'a new and earnest language'[18]

When Josef Schalk defines Bruckner's musical language in his 'pure instrumental music' as 'more German than anything hitherto', he uses the word 'German' not in the chauvinistic or militaristic sense, but rather as the essence of an aesthetic or even moral standard. According to his understanding, 'German music' makes heavy demands not only on the work itself but on the listener as well. Recurring throughout his writing like a virtual refrain is the counter-example which does not attain this level of quality – a type of music which he disparagingly calls 'amusement'.

> The work of a man like Bruckner, who abandoned the tired ways of the post-Mendelssohnian age and in whose works one instinctively felt a kind of dangerous affinity to the achievements of the greatest and most hated of the innovators, was completely rejected. And why not? Was one expected to comprehend also in the field of pure instrumental music a new and earnest language that had nothing whatsoever in common with the usual fashion of pure amusement?![19]

Essentially Schalk is laying claim to Bruckner's music and its appropriate manner of reception. In short, the way should be paved for an elevating and purifying kind of art in opposition to the light, consumer-oriented demands of the musical public. A year earlier, in October 1884, Schalk also gave a speech to the members of the *Wagner-Verein*. The speech had very much the character of a manifesto and was published. According to Schalk, the type of 'high and earnest musical art' which he supported, was largely neglected in Vienna, whereas the 'genre of un-German, sentimental salon music … modern trivialities, a kind of confectioner's music'[20] was successful.

> The efforts of the author have nothing to do with such art. For him it is a matter of promoting the unostentatious presentation of the neglected masterpieces of our sublime musical art represented by the three central figures: Bach, Beethoven and Wagner. By its very nature this excludes any concessions to the entertainment of uneducated or miseducated listeners.[21]

Schalk was often accused of misunderstanding the absolute musical character of the symphonies and bestowing upon them programmatic interpretations which, in turn, created the false notion of Bruckner as a 'programmatic musician.' This reproach is not quite correct, at least as far as Schalk's aims are concerned, since he stated: 'I am convinced of the impossibility of explaining purely symphonic works by means of poetic ideas'.[22] It was Schalk's intention to offer a kind of verbal assistance to help the audience understand the compositional structure of a Bruckner symphony upon first hearing. Emphatic poetic metaphors were meant to transport the members of the public to a sphere of sacred and devoted meditation. It is important to note in this context that we do not find a 'programme' here in the sense of a musically illustrated plot. If we take as an example Schalk's description of the Adagio from the Seventh Symphony, we will notice that he avoids even a concrete programmatic allusion to the death of Richard Wagner, although such a claim would have been demonstrable in view of Bruckner's own remarks:

> Second movement. An overwhelming experience – the loss of the noblest of God's warriors – awakens the feelings that are proclaimed in these tones, feelings of truly sublime grief springing from a great and manly heart, a hero's lamentation sung for the champion of the spirit with whose parting we are deprived of all the loftiest ideals. Every memory comes to life under the pain of suffering: long-suppressed feelings of childhood and of youthful desire. All that has been lost gathers itself in our spirit once more and points to an eternity lying out there beyond us. Thus the land of promise and of Elysian fields, separated from us by chasms and guarded by

the flaming swords of the cherubs, opens itself to our awakened senses. But now the picture becomes hazier, the paroxysm of joy is dissipated and the power of our sorrow re-asserts itself. Untimely solace, profound grief and, finally, despairing self-accusation which gradually fades away to a dying whimper. In response to this suffering, the clouds open themselves up and heavenly brilliance shines forth. The sinner bows his head in deepest ardour, falls to his knees and beats his breast. And, as he sighs and acknowledges that he is unworthy of the paradise which he has beheld, a ladder to heaven grows ever upward from the foundation of his pain. The most solemn tones radiate outward, penetrating and purifying, and raise him up to catch a glimpse of eternal majesty, their echo now resounding from every corner of heaven. Hovering gently over all this is the spirit of eternal love, who looks down in the noblest grief upon the purified suffering of the son of earth and, transfiguring him, takes him in.[23]

There are contradictory accounts of the manner in which Bruckner himself reacted to such poetic interpretations. Bruckner once referred to an article published under the name of Franz Schalk in the *Deutsche Kunst- und Musikzeitung* on 9 January 1885 as the 'most wonderful article ever written about me'.[24] The article, which described the first performance of the Seventh Symphony, was in fact written by Josef Schalk and contains many parallels to the paragraph quoted above. On the other hand, Carl Hruby writes in his memoirs that Bruckner was very angry about Schalk's descriptions and had commented on them with the words:

Why on earth did he have to choose my symphony to write poetry? The fellow certainly knows exactly what was in my mind when I wrote it – at best the thought of a couple of hundred florins which I could get for it from a publisher.[25]

Bruckner's irritation in the case of the Eighth Symphony, for instance, was due to the fact that Hanslick limited his review of the work mainly to derisive comments about the 'childish hymn-like tone' of Schalk's description of the work.[26] Bruckner was obviously angered by the negative public reaction rather than the text itself whose literary qualities he was probably not capable of judging. In fact, Bruckner was uninterested in literature of any kind, as we know from authentic reports by his contemporaries.

To sum up, we can state that Bruckner himself did not create a self-image as a specifically 'German' composer; this image was the work of his propagandists who were themselves motivated by German nationalist ideology. Josef Schalk was the first among them but by no means the last. So, was the 'German Bruckner' merely a big misunderstanding? This was how the problem was addressed in Bruckner research after 1945. From this point on Bruckner again became the 'musician of God' (Max Auer, Leopold Nowak); later on a new picture emerged in contrast to the idealised image in Göllerich-Auer's monumental biography, a new and anti-Romantic image in which Bruckner's 'Germanness' was no longer a topic. But can we totally separate a work from its reception history? Or, to put the question another way, can we find any immanent qualities in Bruckner's works that might legitimize such interpretations by his contemporaries, even if Bruckner himself would not acknowledge them? Let us, in closing, at least consider this complex question.

The Bruckner literature traditionally takes a rather defensive stance with regard to the relationship of Bruckner as composer to Wagner as composer. Here the emphasis lies on highlighting Bruckner's independence, on drawing attention to the differences in orchestration in both composers, and on contrasting Bruckner's origins as an organist with Wagner's orientation towards music drama. It seems that the suspicion that Bruckner could be regarded as a Wagner epigone has to be constantly avoided.[27] Although we have to acknowledge all these arguments, we must also ask why, despite such clear differences, so many contemporary critics, friends and enemies unanimously associated Bruckner with Wagner. Was this association created solely by the external appearance of the works, by their monumentality, by the special use of brass instruments, by Bruckner's employment of Wagner's orchestral colours (e.g. the Wagner tubas)? Did they hear similarities in harmonic tendencies, for example in the use of mediant progressions typical of both composers? All this certainly played a role, but we learn from contemporary statements that friends and enemies alike were also sensitised to the spiritual aspect of Wagner's and Bruckner's music: a quality stemming from the music that demanded total devotion from the listener. In both cases they were confronted with a kind of music that did not require rational, critical listening, but rather aroused a state of overwhelming feeling that brought listening into the vicinity of a mystical and cultic experience.

Important as it was in Bruckner's lifetime, this manner of reception played an even greater role between the First and Second World Wars and during the period of National Socialism. The antithesis between Bruckner's mystical world and the 'modern world' (meant in a negative sense), as it was defined for the first time by Josef Schalk, became the central idea of Bruckner interpretation, or rather of Bruckner worship, for such music was not subjected to rational analysis, but rather adored as an inexplicable phenomenon. The 'modern world', which, after the collapse of the old political and social order, seemed to be more dangerous and menacing than ever before, served as a foil for the many Bruckner societies which sprang up at this time to revere the composer in an almost religious manner. Like the Bayreuth Festivals of this period, the Bruckner societies became places of refuge for an obstinate, anti-modern and anti-rational way of thinking.

Emil Petschnig, an adversary of Schoenberg, saw Bruckner as a bulwark against modernism, a rallying-point against the 'confused and unpopular musical tendencies of our time' and against the 'materialistic aims of artistic life'.[28] In 1929 Fritz Grüninger, chairman of the *Badischer Brucknerbund*, prepared the audience at the first Baden Bruckner festival for the coming musical event with the following words:

> Before entering the cathedral of Bruckner's art it is necessary to gather one's inner strength in order to be able to forget all evil, to cast off everything small and narrow-minded from one's own personality, and to save oneself from the haste, pressure and noise of the world. A new morning must dawn in the soul. A festival

mood must prevail. Only then will the grand outer Bruckner festival become an inextinguishable inner festival for each one of us; for Bruckner festival is synonymous with Bruckner devotion, a divine experience.[29]

Erich Schwebsch warned in 1924 of the 'rapacious blood-sucking intellect'[30] which could not comprehend the phenomenon of Bruckner and recommended 'meditative preparation' instead of rational analysis so that the music could unfold its 'influence on the forces of the soul'. Peter Raabe, president of the *Reichsmusikkammer*, prefaced his Bruckner monography of 1944 with a quotation from Goethe's *Faust*: 'Here is a miracle, just believe in it!'[31] In the foreword, he invites us to learn the 'earthiness of art' from Bruckner:

> Within the German culture of the nineteenth century he appears to us like a great admonition: do not think that all the redemptive quality of art lies in refinement, in over-stylizing and etherealizing; but remember that art grows out of nature and remains great only as long as we continue to sense its presence.[32]

It would be a separate and interesting subject of investigation to try to isolate the compositional aspects of Bruckner's scores that may have inspired such interpretations. One thing is certain: though the elevation of Bruckner's symphonies to a metaphysical phenomenon did not stem from the composer, the manner in which his music was understood and described by his adherents relates to qualities immanent in his scores. It cannot be denied that the 'German' frame of mind associated with his art, the uncompromising dedication and irrationality that it demanded, caused it to be fatally linked to the psychological profile of Fascism and National Socialism and helps explain the high esteem in which Bruckner was held by the Third Reich. A statement of this kind is not meant as a 'character assassination' of Bruckner but rather as an attempt to deal honestly with the darker aspects of his music in a complex reception history.

Notes

1. Friedrich W. Herzog, 'Was ist deutsche Musik? Erkenntnisse und Folgerungen', in *Die Musik*, 26:11 (1934), pp. 801–6.
2. '*Sehnsucht und Unendlichkeitsempfindung, Drängen nach aufbauenden Taten, überzeugender Schaffensdrang, selbstverständliche Freiheitsliebe*', Ibid, p. 801.
3. Ibid, p. 802.
4. Hanns Kreczi, *Das Bruckner-Stift St. Florian und das Linzer Reichs-Bruckner-Orchester (1942–1945)* [*Anton Bruckner Dokumente und Studien*], 5 (Graz: Akademische Druck- u. Verlagsanstalt, 1986).
5. Ernst Decsey, *Hugo Wolf. Bd. III: Der Künstler und die Welt. 1892–1895* (Leipzig and Berlin, 1904), p. 4.
6. Estate of the brothers Josef and Franz Schalk in the Music Collection of the Austrian National Library, F18 Schalk 13.
7. '*Es war dieser Gruppe eine Kunstpflege eigentümlich, die den Charakter des Religiösen an sich trug, und sich nur zaghaft entschloss, an die Öffentlichkeit damit zu gehen*', Decsey, *Wolf*, p. 4.
8. Ibid, p. 4.

9.   '*Thatkräftige Förderung konnte nun, schon aus Vorsicht, Niemand mehr dem Künstler zu Theil werden lassen. Weit entfernt davon, in seinem reinen, kindlichen Gemüthe die wahren Ursachen hiervon zu erkennen, verwirrt, bestürzt, ja in Zweifeln über sich selbst befangen, ersah Bruckner endlich nur eine Rettung noch: den Weg zu Ihm. Er allein konnte ihn beruhigen, Er, dessen Grösse seit langen seine Seele mit glühender Begeisterung erfüllte; zu Ihm wollte er eilen und sein Schaffen dem durchdringenden Auge des Erhabenen unterbreiten. […] Nur der Eine blieb ihm immer treugeneigt, und zur Zeit, als die Aussichten auf Errichtung jener geplanten Stylbildungsschule in Bayreuth noch nicht ganz geschwunden waren, war er es, der in seiner eigenartig liebreichen Weise zu Bruckner die freundlichen Trostworte sprache: 'Verlassen sie sich auf mich; ich selbst werde Ihre Werke noch aufführen".'* Josef Schalk, 'Anton Bruckner', in *Bayreuther Blätter* (October 1884), pp. 3–5.

10. '*Bruckner ist der neueste Abgott der Wagnerianer. Man kann gerade nicht sagen, daß er Mode geworden ist, denn das Publikum will diese Mode nirgends mitmachen; aber Bruckner ist Armeebefehl geworden und der 'zweite Beethoven' ein Glaubensartikel der Wagner-Gemeinde.*' Neue Freie Presse, 30 March 1886.

11. '*Wir nehmen die Symphonie von dem armen Organisten Bruckner aus Wien vor*', Martin Gregor-Dellin and Dietrich Mack, eds, *Cosima Wagner. Die Tagebücher I* (Munich, 1976/77), p. 894.

12. '*… in ländlichen Frieden aufgewachsen, nur den Offenbarungen einer herrlichen Natur, nicht den Einflüssen einer verbildeten Gesellschaft zugänglich*', Schalk, op. cit., p. 1.

13. Richard Wagner, '*Deutsche Kunst und Deutsche Politik*' in *Gesammelte Schriften und Dichtungen*, 8 (Leipzig, 1873), p. 124.

14. Josef Schalk, 'Anton Bruckner und die moderne Musikwelt. Vortrag, gehalten in Wiener Akademischen Wagner-Verein', in *Deutsche Worte* (December, 1885), pp. 1–8.

15. '*Da indeß gerade die diesbezüglichen Schriften Wagner's wie vor allem der Bericht an Se. Majestät den König Ludwig von Baiern über eine in München zu errichtende deutsche Musikschule wenig gelesen zu werden pflegen, ja leider auch bisher ohne alle Einfluss auf das musikalische Leben, außerhalb der Opernbühnen, geblieben sind, so möchte ich mit meinem heutigen Versuche wenigstens ein erneutes Interesse für jene Schriften hervorrufen. Ich verweise hier umsomehr auf dieselben als sie mir stets die kostbarsten, ja einzigen Beweise der Richtigkeit meiner persönlichen Anschauungen und Erfahrungen geliefert haben.*' Ibid, p. 1.

16. '*Es mag immerhin auch mit ein Hindernis für die Anerkennung Bruckners gewesen sein, daß seine Musik deutscher ist als alles was wir bisher in der reinen Instrumentalmusik besitzen. Gewiß nicht deutscher freilich als Bach oder Beethoven, was den Grundcharakter ihres Wesens und ihrer Werke betrifft, aber deutscher in der Form des Ausdruckes. Jener fremde Zwang, welchen sich die Bescheidenheit sowohl als die Universalität des deutschen Geistes auf allen Gebieten jahrhundertelang auferlegt hatte, erscheint hier in der Instrumentalmusik zum ersten Male vollständig gebrochen.*' Ibid., p. 6.

17. '*Auf dem Felde deutschester Bethätigung, im Reiche der Musik, hat er gerungen und erreicht, ein Befestiger eigenst deutschen Fühlens, ein Prediger echtest deutschen Glaubens, der immerdar der Welt verkündet, daß das Edle, Schöne nicht um des Ruhmes und Vortheiles wegen in die Welt tritt, daß es deutsch sei, eine Sache, die man treibt um ihrer selbst willen und aus Freude an ihr zu treiben. Dieser Glaube hat unseren Meister Anton Bruckner zeitlebens durchglüht, gestählt und erhalten!*' August Göllerich, 'Anton Bruckner. Die beim Bruckner-Commers nicht gehaltene Festrede', in *Deutsches Volksblatt* (13 and 15 December, 1891).

18. '*eine neue und ernste Sprache*', Josef Schalk, 'Anton Bruckner', in *Bayreuther*

Blätter, p. 3.
19. '*Das Schaffen eines Mannes, wie Bruckner, der die ausgefahrenen Geleise der Nach-Mendelssohn'schen Zeit verliess, aus dessen Werken man instinktiv eine Art gefährlicher Verwandtschaft mit den Errungenschaften des grössten und bestgehassten Neuerers herausfühlte, war unbedingt verworfen. Was? Sollte man etwa auch auf dem Gebiete der reinen Instrumentalmusik eine neue und ernste Sprache vernehmen müssen, die mit dem gewohnten Tone eines gediegenen Amüsements durchaus nicht übereinstimmen wollte?!*' Ibid., p. 3

20. '*Genre undeutscher, sentimentaler Salonmusik*'; '*moderne Nichtigkeiten, eine Art Zuckerbäckermusik*', Wn F 18 Schalk 436.

21. '*Mit solcher Kunst haben die Bestrebungen des Gefertigten nichts gemein. Für ihn handelt es sich um die prunklose Wiedergabe der so gänzlich vernachlässigten Meisterwerke unserer erhabenen Tonkunst wie sie durch die drei Hauptnamen Bach, Beethoven und Wagner gekennzeichnet ist. Von vornherein schließt dies jede Concession an das Vergnügen ungebildeter oder verbildeter Hörer aus.*' Ibid.

22. '*Das Bemühen, durch poetische Ideen den Inhalt rein symphonischer Werke zu erläutern, gestehe ich mir unumwunden als vergeblich ein*', Josef Schalk, 'Anton Bruckner', in *Bayreuther Blätter*, p. 6.

23. '*2. Satz. Ein ungeheures Erlebniss, der Verlust des Edelsten der Gottesstreiter, ruft die Empfindungen auf, welche sich in diesen Tönen künden. Empfindungen einer wahrhaft erhabener Trauer, eines männlich großen Herzens. Eine Heldenklage des Geistesheros nachgesungen, mit dessen Hingang alle heiligsten Ideale uns umflort, ja entrissen schienen. Unter dem Druck des Schmerzes wird jede Erinnerung wach: längst verstummte Gefühle der Kindheit, der jugendlichen Sehnsucht. Alles Verlorene sammelt sich im Geiste wieder und deutet hinaus auf ein ausser uns liegendes Unvergängliches. So enthüllt sich dem verklärten Blick durch Abgründe geschieden und von flammenden Schwertern der Cherubim bewacht, das Land der Verheißung, paradiesische Gefilde. Doch das Bild wird trüber, der Krampf der Verzückung löst sich, das Recht des Schmerzes macht sich wieder geltend. Vorzeitiger Trost, gesteigertes Weh, endlich verzweifelnde Selbstanklage, die nach und nach bis zum Stöhnen ermattet. Dem Leide öffnen sich die Wolken, Himmelsglanz bricht hervor. In tiefer Inbrunst, das Haupt gesenkt, kniet der Sünder und schlägt an seine Brust. Und als er seufzend unwürdig sich bekennt des erschauten Paradieses, da baut sich allmählig auf der Grundlage seines Schmerzes eine Himmelsleiter höher und höher hinan. Die feierlichsten Klänge wallen auf ihr einher, durchdringend, reinigend heben sie ihn empor des Anblicks ewiger Majestät selbst theilhaftig zu werden, deren Echo jetzt widerbraust von allen Himmelswänden. Darüber leise schwebend der Geist ewiger Liebe. Er blickt herab in erhabensten Schmerze auf das geläuterte Weh des Erdensohnes und nimmt ihn verklärend in seine Obhut.*' Josef Schalk, '*Erläuterung zu Bruckners 7. Symphonie*' [printed programme note, not dated], Wn F 18 Schalk 334.

24. '*... allerherrlichsten Aufsatz, der je über mich geschrieben worden ist*', Anton Bruckner, letter to Franz Schalk, 23 January 1885, Wn F 18 Schalk 54/2.

25. '*Warum er si g'rad mei Sinfonie ausg'sucht hat zum Dichten, dös Locherl woas g'wiss, was i mir dabei denkt hab – höchstens an a paar hundert Gulden, die mir a Verleger dafür zahlen könnt.*' Carl Hruby, *Meine Erinnerungen an Anton Bruckner* (Vienna, 1901), p. 17.

26. '*kindlichen Hymnenton*', *Neue Freie Presse*, 23 December 1892.

27. See *Bruckner, Wagner und die Neudeutschen in Österreich. Bericht des Bruckner-Symposions im Rahmen des Internationalen Brucknerfestes Linz 1984* (Linz, 1986).

28. '*zerfahrene, unpopuläre Kunsttreiben unserer Tage ... materialistische Bestrebungen des Kunstlebens*'. Quotation from Christa Brüstle, 'Musik für Verehrer. Ein Beitrag zur Geschichte der frühen Bruckner-Rezeption', in

Österreichische Musikzeitschrift, 51/1 (1996).

29. '*Vor dem Eintritt in den Dom Brucknerscher Kunst ist es nötig, Innenkräfte zu sammeln, die stark machen, alles Böse zu vergessen, alles Kleine, Enge von der eigenen Persönlichkeit abzustreifen, sich zu retten vor dem Hasten und Drängen und Lärmen der Welt. Es muß Morgen werden in der Seele. Festtagsstimmung muß Einzug halten. Nur dann wird das große Brucknerfest zu einem unauslöschlichen, inneren Brucknerfest, denn Brucknerfest bedeutet Brucknerandacht, Erleben der Gottheit.*' *I. Bädisches Brucknerfest 6. bis 10. November 1929*, special edition of the *Karlsruher Wochenschau* (1929), p. 14.

30. '*gierigen Vampyr Intellekt*'. Erich Schwebsch, 'Zu Anton Bruckners 100. Geburtstag', in *Neue Musikzeitung*, 45 (1924), pp. 261–6.

31. '*Hier ist ein Wunder, glaubet nur!*' Peter Raabe, *Wege zu Bruckner* [*Deutsche Musikbücherei* 19], (Regensburg 1944).

32. '*Seine Erscheinung steht in dem Gesamtbilde der deutschen Kultur des 19. Jahrhunderts wirklich da wie eine Riesenmahnung: glaubt nicht, daß alles Heil der Kunst im Verfeinern liegt, im Überspitzen und Vergeistigen, denkt daran, daß sie herauswächst aus der Natur und nur groß bleibt, solange man diese in ihr spürt ...*' Ibid., 11.

16 Siegmund von Hausegger: a Bruckner authority from the 1930s

Christa Brüstle

The Austrian composer and conductor Siegmund von Hausegger was one of the best-known figures of the 'Bruckner Movement' of the 1930s and 1940s. He is still considered a pioneer with respect to the so-called '*Originalfassungen*' of Bruckner's symphonies, since he conducted the first performance of the original version of the Ninth Symphony in Munich on 2 April 1932.

But it was not only as a conductor that Hausegger supported Bruckner. From 1927 he was also an active member of the newly-formed Bruckner Society and he became a central figure in the International Bruckner Society which developed from it. His service as a Bruckner apostle was carried out predominantly in Germany, and his importance as a Brucknerian in Germany increased when Hitler came to power in 1933. During the period of National Socialist supremacy Hausegger remained a Bruckner authority, particularly as a conductor of the 'original versions' of his works. Consequently he played an important role in the practical dissemination of the scores of the first *Bruckner Complete Edition* (edited by Robert Haas and Alfred Orel) during the 1930s and 1940s. It is well known that this was a time when these scores began to supersede the first printed versions which were no longer regarded as original or authentic.

In the following study some facets of Hausegger's career as a Bruckner conductor and admirer as well as an active member of the Bruckner Society will be illuminated. It will be shown that his personal, moral and cultural convictions shaped the course of his career and that they particularly influenced his activities in Germany during the years 1933–45. The light that can be thrown on the Bruckner conductor as a practical musician will also draw attention to one important fact which has been scarcely registered up to now, namely that although Hausegger publicly was a prominent advocate of the 'original versions', privately he had reservations. Not least, any thorough discussion of this discrepancy between the conductor's public disclosures and airing of privately held views will ultimately lead to the question (and that applies to this chapter as well) of how original the 'original versions' were at the time.

Despite having been viewed as a great authority by Bruckner devotees, no detailed investigation of Hausegger's role as a Bruckner conductor has ever been undertaken. Apart from some old, mostly short and apologetic sketches of his life and work, there is very little literature on him.[1] Recently Hausegger's former pupil Rolf Agop published some brief reminiscences,[2] and in 1994, on the 100th anniversary of the Munich Philharmonic, Dietmar Holland considered Hausegger in a most valuable study of the Munich Philharmonic's Bruckner tradition. A less detailed study of the same subject had appeared in 1985.[3] Between 1920 and 1938 Hausegger was the chief conductor of the orchestra, which first received the name 'Münchner Philharmoniker' in 1928; since 1908 it had been known as the 'Konzertvereins-Orchester'. Neither the *Bayerische Staatsbibliothek* in Munich, *Musikabteilung* (D: Mbs) which has the Hausegger Nachlass, nor the Munich *Hochschule für Musik* (the former *Akademie der Tonkunst*, of which Hausegger was President from 1920 onwards) has documents which shed light on his role as a Bruckner authority. More revealing is a series of letters to the Bruckner biographer Max Auer in the *Nationalbibliothek* in Vienna, *Musiksammlung* (Wn Fond 31 Auer 318).

Before considering Hausegger's significance for the 'Bruckner movement' in the 1930s and 1940s, I will discuss his views on music and Bruckner – attitudes which were formed around the end of the nineteenth century and which revealed themselves in the years before and after the First World War, the period of his activities as a conductor. On the twenty-fifth anniversary of Anton Bruckner's death, in 1921, the Berlin *Allgemeine Musikzeitung* conducted a 'Bruckner survey'. The journal canvassed prominent personalities on the contemporary German music scene to find out how they regarded the current public appreciation of Bruckner and what was their own position with regard to Bruckner.[4] At that time already well known as a Bruckner conductor, Siegmund von Hausegger was the first to respond. His judgement of Bruckner's position in current musical life, like that of many of his conservative-minded musical colleagues, reflected a moralizing and pessimistic attitude towards contemporary culture: in his opinion, public musical life was threatened by the 'superficiality, untruthfulness and inadequacy of a musical culture directed solely by commercial motives'. This trend was to be resisted. In fact the 'pure spirit of Bruckner' and his music could strengthen and assist one in combatting these 'low' aspects of contemporary musical life.[5]

Behind Hausegger's statement lies the 'classical' notion of the ethical powers of music. Performing and listening to a special repertoire – in this case the music of Bruckner – can bring about moral discipline and help forge an inner resistance to the 'decadent' aspects of civilization. Hausegger felt that it was advisable to be wary of the ever expanding wave of Bruckner's popularity, since his music, by virtue of its higher meaning, must at all costs avoid falling victim to passing fashions. These would diminish and, indeed, jeopardize the 'synthetic–creative capacity of conductor and listener'; without this, Bruckner could be neither properly performed nor absorbed by the listener.[6] Hausegger's opinions were shared by other contemporaries, among them the conductors Wilhelm Furtwängler and Hermann Abendroth and the writers on music Ernst Decsey and Karl Grunsky. It may be recalled here that, before the First World War, August Halm had also pointed an accusing, moralizing finger at German musical life and proposed redemptive education of the young through Bruckner's music.[7]

Although Siegmund von Hausegger acquired a reputation for himself as a teacher at the *Akademie der Tonkunst*, he was known first and foremost as a conductor and composer and, to a lesser extent, as a writer on music. His collection of essays *Betrachtungen zur Kunst*, published in 1921, contains general as well as polemical discussions of the themes of music and musical life in art and society. In these essays Hausegger sets forth his fears and exhortations concerning the 'Decline or Ascent' ('*Niedergang oder Aufstieg*') of the art of music – the central theme around which his contribution to the Bruckner survey of the *Allgemeine Musikzeitung* also revolved.[8] In his more or less polemical discussions of the term 'modern' and his defence of the 'classical' – i.e. the 'eternally fresh imperishable values' (a reference to the fact that contemporary composers also claimed the description 'classical' for themselves) – we can detect the influence of Oswald Spengler's philosophical–historical book *Der Untergang des Abendlandes*, first published in Vienna in 1918.[9] In a table in which Spengler compares different cultures, we find the following description of art in the nineteenth and twentieth centuries: 'Being without any inner form; metropolitan art as the norm, titillation, rapidly changing fashions, lacking in any symbolic substance'.[10] Hausegger also complained that music was reduced to the state of being a 'luxury article', an 'empty thrill, window-dressing' and 'pure sensation'.[11] His views, like those of many other Wagnerians of his time, combined cultural criticism, a belief in progress and extreme conservatism. He believed, for example, that 'it is reserved for us Germans to be able to view music as a spiritual force called on to help restore our nationhood to health. And this hope must arise logically from a consideration of the nature and *Weltanschauung* of our nation'.[12]

Through the Austrian conductor speaks the voice of the pan-German patriot whose entirely contemporary national pathos simply excludes the possibility of the existence of music, of whatever quality, in other countries. For Wagnerians, the pre-eminence of German music as something 'genuinely German' was not just self-evident (however it was explained or justified); equally self-evident was the notion that a belief in this viewpoint guaranteed a better future. Hand in hand with such thinking went a similarly 'accepted' anti-Semitic attitude. Concerning Bruno Walter's participation in a Bruckner performance, Hausegger wrote in a letter of 27 October 1931 to Max Auer:

> Walter's name has programmatic significance. He is seen by the Jews as their leader, as the successor, as it were, to Gustav Mahler. Our Society [i.e. the International

Bruckner Society, Vienna], like all cultural institutions in Germany, runs the risk of being taken over by power-hungry Jews who would attempt, consciously or unconsciously, to alter the nature of an association dedicated to a pure German master.[13]

From his youth Siegmund von Hausegger was at home in the Bayreuth circle. As Rudolf Flotzinger has observed, the zeal for Wagner of his father, Friedrich von Hausegger, author of the treatise *Musik als Ausdruck* (1885), certainly left its mark on him.[14] From 1895 to 1896 he organized introductory evenings at Bayreuth for the Graz Richard Wagner Society (a concert performance of the *Ring* being one such event) and, according to his own testimony, he helped out musically in Bayreuth itself in 1898.[15] As a conductor and composer he remained a follower of the *Neudeutsche Schule*.[16]

Hausegger states that his first acquaintance with Bruckner's music occurred in 1886 at a performance in Graz of the Seventh Symphony, conducted by Carl Muck. A second, lasting impression was left on Hausegger by the first performance on 9 April 1894 of the Fifth Symphony (also in Graz), conducted by Franz Schalk. In addition, he must have come into contact with Bruckner, even if indirectly, through his father who reported on Bruckner concerts and published an obituary on the composer in the *Grazer Tagblatt*.[17]

Hausegger's own active involvement with Bruckner's music began with a performance of the Seventh Symphony which he conducted in Munich on 10 February 1899.[18] In 1899 he had taken over the direction of the newly established '*Volkssymphoniekonzerte*', which were intended to afford all levels of society the opportunity of hearing demanding classical music. On 17 December 1900 Hausegger gave a performance of Bruckner's Eighth Symphony for the first time in Munich.[19] The Munich orchestra had been trained as a Bruckner ensemble in the 1897–8 season by its chief conductor Ferdinand Löwe, who returned to the post between 1908 and 1914. Siegmund von Hausegger was acquainted with both Bruckner pupils Löwe and Franz Schalk at the beginning of his conducting career.[20] They were both active into the 1920s and 1930s – Löwe died in 1925 and Franz Schalk in 1931 – before the *Bruckner Gesamtausgabe* edited by Robert Haas and Alfred Orel was under way.

At the end of the 1920s and beginning of the 1930s, Hausegger's missionary zeal for his Austrian compatriot Bruckner received a powerful new stimulus. In the summer of 1929 Hausegger founded a Munich branch of the International Bruckner Society, and he took over the organization of the Society's first two Bruckner festivals in October 1930 and October 1933. On both occasions – that is, before and after Hitler came to power – the conductor received support from representatives of the city and the state.[21] After 1933 Hausegger became unofficial President of the German branch of the International Bruckner Society at a time when, in many areas, political relations between Austria and Germany were somewhat strained (the Nazi party, it should be recalled, had been forbidden in Austria since 19 June 1933).[22] But the self-evident function of music as a 'cultural bridge' enabled the Austrian-based International Bruckner Society, with Hausegger's help, to carry out its propagandist work on behalf of its musical hero in Hitler's German Reich.[23]

Hausegger's role as intermediary between the Nazi state and the International Bruckner Society can be seen in the preparations for the installation of the Bruckner bust in Valhalla near Regensburg on 6 June 1937. Hausegger co-ordinated the musical aspects of the event and gave a concert with the so-called original version of the Fifth Symphony after the ceremony in Valhalla, which was attended by the Führer. This staged consecration of Bruckner's bust by Hitler and Goebbels signified the symbolic return of the composer to the German Reich – one year before the '*Anschluß*'.[24]

According to Rolf Agop's recollections, Hausegger suffered some indignity in March 1933 at the hands of the Nazis: he was removed from the conductor's desk for not playing the *Horst Wessel-Lied* (the official 'anthem' of the Nazi party). This episode seems not to have had any damaging consequences for him nor caused him to distance himself from the regime. Hausegger bore witness to his embracing of National Socialism – even though he was not a Party member – for example, by signing the Prussian Academy of Art's loyalty address to Hitler; by taking part in the protest against Thomas Mann's 1933 Wagner essay '*Leiden und Größe Richard Wagners*' and, last but not least, by appearing at SS-concerts and Reich Party Rallies. In November 1934 he performed Bruckner at a concert in Munich intended as the SS's art manifesto, and on 7 September 1937 he conducted the Finale of the Fifth Symphony (in the 'original version') at the Reich Party Rally in Nuremberg.[25]

In a note to Max Auer dated 9 September 1937, Hausegger wrote: 'I was deeply affected by the Führer's speech and by the honour afterwards of being able to conduct the glorious music of our great master. I was also extremely pleased that my orchestra participated in this honour'.[26] It is, moreover, by no means certain that the Nazis relieved Hausegger of the presidency of the *Akademie der Tonkunst*, as his pupil Agop claims. It is more likely that he retired in the 'normal' way (he was 62 years old) after submitting a formal request to the Reichsstatthalter of Bavaria, Franz Xaver Ritter von Epp. The records relating to this appear to be lost with the exception of the cover of the relevant file surviving in the Berlin Document Centre (BDC); it is clear from this, however, that the pertinent file contained details of a petition from Hausegger to Epp. After retiring from the Academy, Hausegger was able to dedicate himself more fully to conducting the Munich Philharmonic and to composing which, as his letters reveal, was his express desire.[27] When, in 1938, he retired as conductor of the orchestra, this too was as a result of his own free will. In a letter to Max Auer of 5 February 1938 he wrote: 'I am very pleased that Kabasta will succeed me. I see in him a very like-minded colleague and, besides that, an artist and a man of gratifying distinction'.[28]

In view of all this, Agop's recollections should be treated perhaps with a little circumspection. One should also mention that the political assessments contained in the surviving Hausegger files in the Berlin Document Centre (BDC) are of an entirely positive nature. In 1939 his application for admission to the *Reichsschrifttumskammer* was processed (this had become necessary because Hausegger planned to publish his father's writings) and, in 1942, political assessments were sought as Hausegger was to be honoured with the Goethe Medal, a Nazi culture prize.[29]

Something of a 'hiccup' occurred in November 1939, as Hausegger's second wife Helene (Bronsart von Schellendorf) had not been able to prove that she was of pure German descent, but this 'problem' seems to have been 'solved'. The conferral of the Goethe-Prize on Hausegger on his 70th birthday (16 August) might have been a recompense for the 'hiccup'.[30] The recommendation of the conferral of the Goethe Medal on Hausegger was made by the Bavarian Ministry of State for Education and Culture on 22 April 1942. It was supported by the Music Section of the Third Reich's Propaganda Ministry, the Ministry of State for Scholarship Learning and National Education (*Reichsministerium für Wissenschaft, Erziehung und Volksbildung*) and the President of the Reichsmusikkammer. However, in July 1942, it was still not certain whether Hitler would endorse the recommendation.[31] A political report of the NSDAP Regional Committee in Munich on 25 July 1942, delivered by Otto Meissner, the chief of the Führer's and Chancellor's Presidential Chancellery (*Präsidialkanzlei des Führers und Reichskanzlers*), appears to have finally secured the endorsement of the recommendation. In this report we read, *inter alia*:

> Dr von Hausegger, whose activities as an artist deserve the highest recognition, has also, as a man, won the party's esteem by his commendable attitude as a representative of national-socialist views. He has taken the keenest interest in all the party's endeavours. The intended award of the Goethe Medal on the occasion of his 70th birthday is an honour which will give pleasure to all representatives of the party and the people.[32]

Of course, Hausegger also received the prize in recognition of his services as a Bruckner conductor and as an activist on behalf of the International Bruckner Society, renamed, after 1938, the German Bruckner Society.

By 1942, the year of the Goethe Prize, a younger generation of conductors was already on the rise, among them Karl Böhm, Herbert von Karajan and Eugen Jochum (one of Hausegger's pupils). Through broadcasts and recordings they were already reaching a wider audience during the war and, of course, reached an even wider public after 1945. Hausegger was increasingly overshadowed by Wilhelm Furtwängler who, though not an unreserved supporter of the original versions, was considered by the Nazi leaders as Germany's leading conductor; on this account he was given the reins of the German Bruckner Society in 1938.[33]

To conclude, some of the 'highlights' in Hausegger's career as a Bruckner conductor can be 'recalled'. One should mention first of all, perhaps, his endorsement of the so-called '*Originalfassung*' of the Ninth Symphony which, as stated earlier, he performed for the first time on 2 April 1932 in Munich. On that occasion the published version of the score by Ferdinand Löwe (from 1903) and the '*Originalfassung*' edited by Robert Haas and Alfred Orel were both played in front of an invited audience. It was decided that the version of the philologists was indeed performable and that the Löwe edition should be considered only as an 'arrangement', an 'inauthentic version' of the Ninth Symphony. Hausegger, who had clearly considered the results of Haas's and Orel's work very deeply and who was a practical advisor to the *Gesamtausgabe* until 1937, wrote in the International Bruckner Society's publicity booklet: 'The original editions establish once and for all the authentic character of Bruckner's symphonies, and this must claim our unswerving loyalty'.[34] As a practical musician and conductor, however, Hausegger – like many other conductors at that time – was obliged to accommodate himself, as it were, to the results of Haas's and Orel's work. He did this by supporting the '*Originalfassung*' in public, while personally considering, for example, Löwe's arrangement of the Ninth musically far superior to the 'original', as is clear from a letter of 4 February 1930 to Max Auer:

> All in all, a comparison of the two scores reveals that Löwe's alterations to the instrumentation almost always signify a considerable improvement on, and lead to a clearer exposition of, the musical idea. Löwe's sensitivity, his erudition and his fidelity to Bruckner's intentions are remarkable. Nevertheless, one should not overlook the fact that the 'original score' [i.e. Haas' edition] shows us a quite different Bruckner to the one we find in Löwe's edition.[35]

Just how Hausegger reconciled theory and practice or the positions of philology and practical performance in his own interpretations of the '*Originalfassungen*' could only be demonstrated if one were able to compare his performances (by means, for example, of performance-related material or through recordings) with the printed scores. The only known recording by Hausegger was that of the Ninth Symphony, made on 26 April 1938 in Berlin for Electrola; it has recently been issued as a CD on the Preiser Records label.[36] A similar, apparently contradictory, state of affairs can be seen in Hausegger's attitude to the '*Originalfassung*' of the Fifth Symphony which he performed for the first time on 28 October 1935 in Munich. Hausegger had always advocated, when the performance situation required it, a reinforcement, so to speak, of the closing chorale in the Finale – an alteration Franz Schalk had made, with Bruckner's approval, at the Graz première, a performance, as mentioned earlier, that was attended by Hausegger. Thus, for instance, a performance of the '*Originalfassung*' of the Fifth Symphony on the occasion of the 1939 *Großdeutsches Brucknerfest* in Linz, St Florian and Vienna was given by Hausegger with a separately positioned brass section. 'Overwhelmed by the effect of the separate brass section (cleverly positioned in the gallery)', reported the *Volksstimme*, the official Nazi Party newspaper of the '*Oberdonau Gau*' (Upper Danube district), 'the audience applauded conductor and orchestra most enthusiastically'.[37]

It was, of course, exactly this emphasizing of the closing chorale that had been condemned as an undesirable 'effect' in the first (1896) printed edition. From

Hausegger's comments in the above-mentioned publicity booklet, it is clear that he considered many passages in the first edition of the Fifth Symphony as being well-suited to the performance situation – just like, moreover, his colleagues Peter Raabe, President of the *Reichsmusikkammer* (Reich Music Division), and Hermann Abendroth, long-time conductor at the Gewandhaus in Leipzig.[38] We need to be mindful, therefore, when considering this and other aspects of the 'Bruckner movement' in the 1930s and 1940s that we are, among other problems, dealing with a great contradiction between theory and practice.

Already before 1933, Siegmund von Hausegger saw in the Nazis a means of realizing his conception of a new relationship between society and music. He believed in the deep significance of societal change: music was to be discovered anew and its spiritual significance properly recognized; concerts were no longer to be luxury entertainments but occasions where one could come together for the contemplation and veneration of the 'holy art of music'. Bruckner's music seemed to demand as well as to embody to the full such veneration. Under the Nazis, however, this 'art-and-music-religion' was exploited as a propaganda instrument of the totalitarian state, although many musicians seem not to have been aware of this perversion.

In his 1933 essay '*Leiden und Größe Richard Wagners*', Thomas Mann had characterized Wagner as 'that mighty and ambiguous phenomenon of German and Western life'.[39] One could say in conclusion here that those, like Hausegger, who failed to understand Thomas Mann and protested against him, those who could not or would not see the fractured and ambiguous nature of Wagner's art as recognized by Mann and Nietzsche before him, were clearly unable to comprehend anything of the infinitely more dangerous ambiguity of Hitler and his politics.

Acknowledgement

For their kind help in the translation and editing of the text I should like to express my sincere thanks to John Arthur, Crawford Howie and Timothy Jackson.

Notes

1. Hausegger was born in Graz in 1872 and died in Munich in 1948. Cf. Paul Ehlers, 'Siegmund von Hausegger als Bruckner-Dirigent. Zum 60. Geburtstag Siegmund von Hauseggers', in *Zeitschrift für Musikwissenschaft*, 99 (1932), pp. 867–70; and Wilhelm Zentner, 'Siegmund von Hausegger' in *Jahrbuch der deutschen Musik*, 1 (1943), pp. 110–21.
2. Rolf Agop, 'Siegmund von Hausegger (1872–1948), Erinnerungen eines 36 Jahre jüngeren Schülers', in *Bruckner-Jahrbuch 1989/90* (Linz: Anton Bruckner Institut Linz, 1992), pp. 303–8.

3. See Dietmar Holland, 'Aus der Bruckner-Tradition der Münchner Philharmoniker. Der Weg zu den "Originalfassungen"', in Regina Schmoll gen. Eisenwerth, ed., *Die Münchner Philharmoniker von der Gründung bis heute* (Munich: Universitätsdruckerei und Verlag C. Wolf und Sohn, 1985), pp. 171–82; see also Friedrich von Hausegger, 'Mein Vater: Siegmund von Hausegger', ibid., pp. 299–304; and Dietmar Holland, '"... und gilt nur späteren Zeiten": Der Weg zu den Original- und Frühfassungen der Symphonien Anton Bruckners', in Gabriele E. Meyer, ed., *100 Jahre Münchner Philharmoniker* (Munich: Alois Knürr Verlag, 1994), pp. 247–83.
4. See Paul Schwers, 'Eine Bruckner-Rundfrage', in *Berliner Allgemeine Musikzeitung*, 48 (1921), pp. 671–91.
5. Ibid., p. 672: '*Was im Musikleben unserer Zeit aller echten Kunst schädlich und feindlich ist, erweist sich als solches auch unserem Meister gegenüber: die Äußerlichkeit, Unwahrheit und Unzulänglichkeit einer lediglich durch geschäftsmäßige Beweggründe geleiteten Musikpflege. Sie zu bekämpfen wird uns gerade der lautere Geist Bruckners stark machen.*'
6. Ibid., p. 673: '*An die synthetisch-mitschöpferische Fähigkeit des Dirigenten wie des Hörers werden [bei Bruckner] ... besonders hohe Ansprüche gestellt.*'
7. August Halm, *Die Symphonie Anton Bruckners* (Munich: Georg Müller, 1914, 2/1923) and *Von zwei Kulturen der Musik* (Munich: Georg Müller, 1913, 2/1920); see also his article 'Melodie, Harmonie und Themenbildung bei Anton Bruckner', in *Neue Musik-Zeitung*, 23 (1902), pp. 170–4, 196–8, 211–14 and 227f. For more on Halm see Rudolf Stephan, 'August Halm', in MGG 5, cols. 1376–80, 'Über August Halm', in *August-Halm-Preis 1989 für Ernest Bour. Festschrift* (Trossingen: im Auftrag der Staatlichen Hochschule für Musik, 1989), pp. 6–13, and in Albrecht Riethmüller, ed., *Musiker der Moderne. Porträts und Skizzen* [*Spektrum der Musik 3*], (Laaber: Laaber, 1996), pp. 9–20.
8. See *Siegmund von Hausegger, Gesammelte Aufsätze. Betrachtungen zur Kunst* (Leipzig: Kistner & Siegel, 1921), particularly his essays 'Modern' (1906), p. 41f., 'Sind Klassisch und Modern Gegensätze?' (1908), pp. 42–60, 'Niedergang oder Aufstieg? Musikalische Betrachtungen vor Beethovens 150. Geburtstag' (1920), pp. 220–9.
9. Spengler's was a popular book whose title served almost as a motto of the times. Cf. H. Stuart Hughes, *Oswald Spengler. A Critical Estimate* (New York and London: Charles Scribner's Sons, 1952).
10. Oswald Spengler, *Der Untergang des Abendlandes* (Munich: C.H. Beck, 1923, Deutscher Taschenbuch Verlag, 11/1993), between pp. 70 and 71; *Kultur der 'Zivilisation'*: '*Das Dasein ohne innere Form. Weltstadtkunst als Gewohnheit, Luxus, Sport, Nervenreiz. Schnellwechselnde Stilmoden ... ohne symbolischen Gehalt.*'
11. 'Niedergang oder Aufstieg? Musikalische Betrachtungen vor Beethovens 150. Geburtstag', in *Gesammelte Aufsätze*, p. 223 ('*... an die Stelle des inneren Wertes tritt der leere Reiz, an die Stelle des Gehaltes die Aufmachung, an die Stelle des Ereignisses die Sensation*'), Hausegger saw the roots of a 'moral breakdown' in this development.
12. Ibid., p. 221: '*Uns Deutschen ist es vorbehalten geblieben, die Musik als eine geistige Macht anzusehen, die berufen ist, mit zu wirken an der Gesundung unseres Volkstums. Und diese Hoffnung muß sich folgerichtig aus Beanlagung und Weltanschauung unseres Volkes ergeben.*'
13. Wn Fond 31 Auer 318: '*Walters Name hat programmatische Bedeutung. Er wird vom Judentum als ihr Führer, sozusagen als der Nachfolger Gustav Mahlers angesehen. Unserer Gesellschaft [der Internationalen Bruckner-Gesellschaft, Wien] droht wie allen kulturellen Unternehmungen in Deutschland, die große Gefahr, daß*

sich das stets machtbereite Judentum auch ihrer bemächtig und versucht, bewußt oder unbewußt seinen Geist in unsere, einem rein deutschen Meister geweihte Vereinigung zu bringen.'
I am most grateful to the Nationalbibliothek, Vienna, and Hofrat Dr Günter Brosche, for kindly allowing me to examine the sources.

14. Rudolf Flotzinger, 'Bruckner – Hausegger – Wagner' in Othmar Wessely, ed., *Symposium Bericht: Bruckner, Wagner und die Neudeutschen in Österreich* (Linz: Anton Bruckner Institut Linz, 1986), pp. 201–10.

15. A curriculum vitae and other documents can be found in the Berlin Document Centre (BDC [Bundesarchiv, Berlin-Lichterfelde]).

16. Hausegger's largely forgotten compositions include orchestral works (e.g. the symphonic poems *Barbarossa* of 1900 and *Wieland der Schmid* of 1903), vocal works (songs and choral works) as well as early stage works (e.g. the 'humorous-fantasy in three acts' *Zinnober*, after E.T.A. Hoffmann, 1895).

17. *Grazer Tagblatt*, 13 October 1896; cf. Rudolf Flotzinger, 'Bruckner – Hausegger – Wagner', pp. 207f., 210.

18. 'Konzertbericht', *Münchner Neueste Nachrichten*, 12 February 1899, p. 2.

19. 'Konzertbericht', *Münchner Neueste Nachrichten*, 19 December 1900, p. 2 (a 'Moderner Abend' of the Kaim Orchestra).

20. See Reinhard Rauner, *Ferdinand Löwe. Leben und Wirken: I. Teil 1863–1900* [*Studien zur Musikgeschichte Österreichs* 3], (Frankfurt am Main: Peter Lang, 1995); and Thomas Leibnitz, *Die Brüder Schalk und Anton Bruckner. Dargestellt an den Nachlaßbeständen der Musiksammlung der Österreichischen Nationalbibliothek* (Tutzing: Schneider, 1988).

21. This is demonstrated in the letters in Wn Fond 31 Auer.

22. The NSDAP, as well as other parties, was banned in Austria after Engelbert Dollfuß came to power (he was Chancellor from 1932 to 1934). In establishing his authoritarian Austrian state, Dollfuß sought the assistance not of Hitler but of Mussolini primarily. See Lucian O. Meysels, *Der Austrofaschismus. Das Ende der ersten Republik und ihr letzter Kanzler* (Vienna and Munich: Amalthea, 1992).

23. 'Propaganda' here means 'promotion' and 'missionary publicity work'; for more on this not unproblematic term, cf. Wolfgang Schieder and Christof Dipper, 'Propaganda' in Otto Brunner, Werner Conze and Reinhart Koselleck, eds., *Geschichtliche Grundbegriffe. Historisches Lexikon zur politisch-sozialen Sprache in Deutschland*, 5 (Stuttgart: Klett-Cotta, 1984), pp. 69–112.

24. Hausegger took responsibility for the correspondence with the Bavarian minister, Ludwig Siebert. The chief organizers of the event besides Hausegger were the conductor and president of the *Reichsmusikkammer*, Peter Raabe (honorary member of the IBG) and the Regensburg publisher of the *Zeitschrift für Musik*, Gustav Bosse. This is described in detail in the author's dissertation entitled '*Anton Bruckner und die Nachwelt. Zur Rezeptionsgeschichte des Komponisten in der ersten Hälfte des 20. Jahrhunderts*' (Freie Universität Berlin, 1996) which has been published by J.B. Metzler: Stuttgart, 1998. Cf. Bryan Gilliam, 'The Annexation of Anton Bruckner. Nazi Revisionism and the Politics of Appropriation', in *The Musical Quarterly*, 78 (1994), pp. 584–609; and Albrecht Riethmüller, *Die Walhalla und ihre Musiker* (Laaber: Laaber, 1993).

25. See Joseph Wulf, *Musik im Dritten Reich. Eine Dokumentation* [*Kultur im Dritten Reich. Eine Dokumentation*, 5]. (Frankfurt am Main and Berlin: Ullstein, 1989), pp. 56f., 147–9 and 314–16; Fred K. Prieberg, *Musik im NS-Staat* (Frankfurt am Main: Fischer Taschenbuch Verlag, 1982); and Erik Levi, *Music in the Third Reich* (New York: St Martin's Press, 1994).

26. Wn Fond 31 Auer 318: '*Die Rede des Führers war mir ein großes Erlebnis, nicht minder, im Anschluß daran die herrliche Musik unseres großen Meisters haben*

dirigieren zu können. Über die auch meinem Orchester zuteilgewordene Auszeichnung habe ich mich außerordentlich gefreut.'

27. The following compositions from the late 1930s are listed as part of Hausegger's bequest to the Music Section of the Bavarian State Library (D:Mbs): six Lieder for voice and piano (autogr. 1938–41, Mus. mss. 6492), three choruses for mixed voices a cappella to poems by Josef Weinheber (autogr. 1938, Mus. mss. 6493, printed by Schott, Mainz) and music for a fairy-tale play *Die goldene Kette* (autogr. 1935–9, Mus. mss. 6487).

28. Wn Fond 31 Auer 318: '*Ich freue mich sehr, daß Kabasta mein Nachfolger wird. In ihm erblicke ich den engeren Gesinnungsgenossen und dazu einen Künstler und Menschen von erfreulichem Range.*' Oswald Kabasta (1896–1946) had been musical director of the *Wiener Rundfunk* from 1931 and from 1935 permanent conductor of the *Gesellschaft der Musikfreunde* and the *Wiener Symphoniker*. He was a member of the Nazi party. Cf. Engelbert M. Exl and Michael Nagy, eds., '*...mögen sie still meiner gedenken.*' *Die Beiträge zum Oswald Kabasta Symposion in Mistelbach vom 23. bis 25. September 1994* (Vienna: Vom Pasqualatihaus, 1995).

29. BDC: documents in connection with the inquiry into the preparation of the application for admission to the *Reichsschrifttumskammer*. 30 May 1939 (file: II D 021391); e.g. political assessment of the NSDAP committee for the Munich–Upper Bavaria region, 22 May 1939.

30. The general directions for the conferral of the Goethe Prize included, *inter alia*, the following instruction: 'the Goethe medal will be awarded for particularly outstanding achievements in the areas of art and science ... The distinction is to be not so much the recognition of a single achievement as the culmination of the life-work of an artist or scientist' (copies of the general directions were sent to the presidents of the *Reichskulturkammern* on 8 March 1941; source R 55/96 (Bundesarchiv, Berlin-Lichterfelde).

31. These details are found in documents of the *Reichspropagandaministerium* R 55/97 (Bundesarchiv, Berlin-Lichterfelde).

32. Berlin Document Centre.

33. Max Auer, who until then had occupied the position of president of the International Bruckner Society (IBG), was dismissed for political reasons. The society was 'brought into line'. However, very little changed as far as its structure and objectives were concerned. The provisional director and general secretary of the German Bruckner Society was the lawyer Friedrich Werner, who had represented the interests of the IBG and the Musikwissenschaftlicher Verlag, Vienna, for a long time. He undertook this task again when the IBG was re-established after 1945.

34. Anton Bruckner. *Wissenschaftliche und künstlerische Betrachtungen zu den Originalfassungen* (Vienna: IBG, 1937), p. 46: '*Die Original-Ausgaben stellen ein für allemal den authentischen Grundcharakter der Symphonien Bruckners fest, dem unbedingt Treue bewahrt werden muß*'. In a letter to Max Auer, 26 November 1937 (Wn Fond 31 Auer 318), Hausegger explicitly refused to continue to be specifically named as an advisor in the volumes of the Gesamtausgabe, as he 'would have to be in the position to check the text much more intensively than is actually the case.'

35. Wn Fond 31 Auer 318: '*Alles in allem ergibt ein Vergleich der beiden Partituren, daß L's [Löwe's] instrumentale Änderungen fast durchwegs eine wesentliche Verbesserung und klarere Herausarbeitung der musikalischen Idee bedeuten. Die Feinsinnigkeit, Sachkenntnis und Treue, mit der L. [Löwe] vorging, sind bewundernswert. Immerhin darf nicht übersehen werden, daß wir aus der Original-partitur einen etwas anderen Br. [Bruckner] kennenlernen wie aus der L.'schen [Löweschen]*'.

36. Cf. Dietmar Holland, ' *"... und gilt nur späteren Zeiten"*' in Gabriele E. Meyer, *100*

352 Perspectives on Anton Bruckner

Jahre Münchner Philharmoniker, pp. 247–83. I wish to record my thanks here to Dr Meyer for her assistance. On 13 November 1996 she wrote to me about the Hausegger material in the Munich Philharmonic library: 'There is no collection of Hausegger documents. There are … only a series of Hausegger programmes and a few photos. There is also the original shellac recording of the original version of Bruckner's Ninth Symphony …; it dates from the year 1938 and, in fact, is the first recording ever made by the orchestra. There are no miniature or conducting scores available.'

37.   *Volksstimme*, 2 July 1939.

38.   For instance, Peter Raabe wrote about the '*Original-* or *Ur-fassung*' of the Fifth Symphony (ed. Robert Haas in *Bruckner Sämtliche Werke A*) in a letter to Max Auer, 14 February 1937: 'In fact this symphony is not well scored in its original version. It is quite clear from this score that Bruckner had good reason to get assistance from experienced orchestral experts. Much of it is very clumsy, and some of it – for instance, the clarinet which enters alone over and over again in the introduction to the final movement – verges on the ridiculous.' ('*Diese Symphonie ist wirklich nicht in der Urfassung gut instrumentiert. Man merkt an dieser Partitur grade deutlich, daß Bruckner Grund hatte, sich von erfahrenen Orchesterkennern helfen zu lassen. Vieles ist ganz unbeholfen, manches – wie z.B. die immer wieder allein kommende Klarinette in der Einleitung zum letzten Satz – ist an der Grenze der Lächerlichkeit.*'). See Wn Fond 31 Auer 448.

39.   See Thomas Mann's Wagner essay (April 1933) in Erika Mann, ed., *Thomas Mann: Wagner und unsere Zeit. Aufsätze, Betrachtungen, Briefe* (Frankfurt am Main: Fischer Taschenbuch Verlag, 1963, 1983, 1990), pp. 63–121.

17 Ludwig Wittgenstein's remarks on Bruckner

Peter Palmer

Ludwig Wittgenstein was born in Vienna in 1889, when Bruckner had begun sketching his Ninth Symphony and was in the process of revising his Eighth. The young Ludwig grew up in a musical family.[1] His mother Leopoldine had studied with Goldmark, while his aunts received piano lessons from Clara Schumann. His father Karl, a successful industrialist, played the violin. Ludwig's eldest brother Hans, who died young by his own hand, was regarded by the great teacher Julius Epstein as a musical genius. Another brother, Paul, was to become a celebrated concert pianist; after losing an arm in the First World War he commissioned works for the left hand from Richard Strauss, Ravel, Prokofiev, Britten and others. The Joachim and Rosé Quartets played in the Wittgenstein home on the Alleegasse, as did the violinist Marie Soldat and the cellist Pablo Casals. In 1892 Karl Wittgenstein arranged a private performance of Brahms's Clarinet Quintet which was attended by the composer. The blind Viennese composer Joseph Labor performed on the Wittgenstein chamber organ. Other visitors to the family's music room included Mahler and the conductor Bruno Walter.

Ludwig's piano studies were unproductive, but he later taught himself the clarinet. He could whistle a melody with accuracy and sensitivity: there are stories of his whistling Bach fugues with a friend. In his musical tastes Wittgenstein always remained a conservative. His passion was for the Austro-German masters from Haydn to Brahms. Whereas he did not care for Wagner's *Tristan* or *Parsifal*, he admired *Meistersinger* and claimed to have heard up to thirty performances of that opera while studying in Berlin. Since he never took to Mahler as a composer, it is hardly surprising that he came to regard Alban Berg's music as outrageous.

In 1908 Wittgenstein left Berlin in order to study engineering in Manchester. There, Hans Richter – a name familiar to him from Vienna – had just conducted a programme comprising Beethoven's Ninth Symphony and Bruckner's *Te Deum*. Ludwig Wittgenstein's three years in the north of England coincided with the last years of Richter's engagement as principal conductor of the Hallé

Orchestra. The student went to a number of Hallé concerts. He may have heard Richter conduct Bruckner in Manchester; it is also possible that he attended the première of Elgar's First Symphony.[2]

In 1912 Wittgenstein heard a Birmingham Festival performance of Brahms's *German Requiem* under Henry Wood. The same concert featured two extracts from Strauss's *Salome*, which he described in his diary as 'rot, but very clever and amusing in consequence'.[3] By that time he had moved from Manchester to Cambridge, where spare moments were devoted to making music with G.E. Moore and David Pinsent. The latter died in World War I, but Moore was to be a life-long friend.[4] During his first stay in Cambridge Wittgenstein interested himself in the psychology of music and contributed to a paper on the subject of rhythm. His particular admiration for Beethoven as man and musician was noted by Bertrand Russell, to whom Wittgenstein sent volumes of Beethoven's letters. The experience of hearing Beethoven's Ninth with Russell (on 10 June 1913) was, he said, a red-letter day in his life. Russell voiced his scepticism about music's ability to civilize people, considering it too apart, too passionate, and too remote from words. There is an entry in Wittgenstein's *Notebooks* which may be read partly as a rejoinder to Russell: 'Musical themes are in a certain sense propositions. And so the recognition of the essence of logic will lead to the recognition of the essence of music'.[5]

The above statement dates from 1915. Sixteen years later Wittgenstein made the following observation about Western classical music:

> To some people music seems to be a primitive art, with its few notes and rhythms. But it is only the surface which is simple, whereas the substance which makes possible the interpretation of this manifest content has all that infinite complexity which we find adumbrated in the externals of the other arts, and which music tacitly conceals [*verschweigt*]. It is in a certain sense the most sophisticated [*die raffinierteste*] of the arts.

This remark appears among Wittgenstein's *Vermischte Bemerkungen*, a post-humously published selection of jottings.[6] They range over a variety of topics: for instance they take a somewhat iconoclastic view of Shakespeare. The musical remarks concern individual composers and more general matters. In 1941 Wittgenstein was reflecting on counterpoint with regard to the lessons that Schubert intended taking with Simon Sechter. It could, he muses, be extremely difficult for a composer to resolve the question of the specific relationship that '*I*, with *my* proclivities, should enter into with counterpoint'.

In 1948 Wittgenstein pondered at length on the understanding of music:

> The understanding of music has a certain *expression*, both during the hearing and playing of it and at other times. Sometimes physical movements are part of this expression, but it may be only a matter of how a person possessing musical understanding plays or hums a piece, and occasionally of the comparisons he draws, and of ideas which as it were illustrate the music.

Wittgenstein's concern with the 'musical phrase' suggests that he may have been acquainted with Hugo Riemann's ideas. The understanding of music is, he maintained, eine *Lebensäusserung des Menschen*: 'a vital expression of Man'.

Bruckner's name occurs in seven different entries in *Vermischte Bemerkungen*. The earliest dates from 1929, the year Wittgenstein returned to Cambridge. It touches on a supposed national characteristic: 'I think the "good old Austrian" is an especially difficult concept to grasp. It is, in a certain sense, *subtler* than anything else, and its truth is never on the side of probability'.[7] Artists whom Wittgenstein sees as exemplifying this quality are the writers Grillparzer and Lenau, and the musicians Bruckner and Labor. Two years later he tentatively ascribed a racial characteristic to Bruckner's music. No longer, he wrote, did it share the long and narrow, possibly Nordic features of Nestroy, Grillparzer, Haydn and others. Instead it was altogether round and full and possibly Alpine in aspect, even more so than Schubert's music.[8]

Also in 1931, Wittgenstein made the first of two comparisons between Bruckner and Brahms:

> Compositions which are written at the piano, upon the piano, compositions which are written thinking with one's pen, and compositions written solely with the inner ear are bound to be *totally* different in character from one another and to make a totally different impression. I feel sure that Bruckner composed solely with his inner ear and with an idea of the orchestral sound, Brahms with his pen. Of course, the reality is not that simple.[9]

The second comparison dates from 1934 or 1937:

> In the era of the silent films all the classical composers would be played to accompany a film, but not Brahms and Wagner. Brahms was not used because he is too abstract. I can visualize an exciting scene in a film with a musical accompaniment by Beethoven or Schubert, where I might glean from the film a kind of understanding of the music. But not an understanding of Brahms's music. Bruckner, on the other hand, goes with a film.[10]

Unfortunately none of the jottings can be dated precisely, or it would be easier to hazard a guess at an external stimulus. In the case of the latter remark it is possible that Wittgenstein knew of Schoenberg's *Begleitungsmusik zu einer Lichtspielszene* (1930). At all events his contention has been accepted implicitly by the modern film director Luchino Visconti, for in Visconti's *Senso* the soundtrack combines extracts from Verdi's *Il Trovatore* with the Adagio of Bruckner's Seventh Symphony. Whether the film can assist an understanding of the Adagio is a moot point. But certainly its coda has underlying associations – the death of Wagner – that chime with the Venetian setting of *Senso*. The claim that Bruckner is less abstract than Brahms deserves consideration (even if the mind still boggles at the notion of Bruckner as movie composer). It could be argued that Brahms led to the largely non-scenic musical vistas of Reger, whereas Bruckner leads to the Adagietto of Mahler's Fifth Symphony and to its role in the film version of Thomas Mann's novella, *Death in Venice*.

In 1938 Wittgenstein made two further jottings about Bruckner that have been published in *Vermischte Bemerkungen*. By that time, thanks to Siegmund von Hausegger and like-minded conductors, concertgoers were just starting to become aware of the original versions of Bruckner's symphonies. Karl Böhm conducted Robert Haas's edition of the Fourth in London and recorded the Fourth and Fifth Symphonies for the Electrola company, on eight and nine '78s' respectively.[11] Wittgenstein wrote: 'It can be said of a Bruckner symphony that it has *two* beginnings: the beginning of the first and the beginning of the second idea. These two ideas are related to each other not like blood relatives but like a husband and wife'.[12] This resembles an orthodox restatement of the dramatic principle behind Classical sonata form. The apparently surprising thing is that Wittgenstein ignores Bruckner's *third* subjects. Various terms have been used to characterize the three subjects in a Brucknerian first movement. Max Auer saw them as forming a psychological unity: the first subject stood for *Geist* (mind, spirit), the second for *Gemüt* (heart), the third for *Wille* (will).[13] But such a constellation could escape anyone who was familiar with Bruckner's symphonies in their mutilated versions, and that is how Wittgenstein must have got to know them. When Mahler, for example, conducted the Vienna Philharmonic in the Sixth Symphony, his cuts included the third subject-group.[14]

Following straight on from the above remark on Bruckner's symphonies, Wittgenstein offers his only published comment on a particular work. It is so rich in its connotations as to be worth examining in detail:

> Bruckner's Ninth is, as it were, a *protest* against Beethoven's, and that is what makes it tolerable, which it would not be if it were some kind of imitation. Its relationship to Beethoven's Ninth is very similar to that between Lenau's Faust and Goethe's, that is to say, between the Catholic and the Enlightenment Faust, etc. etc.[15]

Goethe's *Faust* drama is a central text in modern European literature. Lenau's *Faust*, by comparison, has not received anything like the same attention, although many musicians will be acquainted with the two 'scenes' Liszt based on the work: *Der nächtliche Zug* and *Der Tanz in der Dorfschenke*, known in its piano version as *Mephisto Waltz* no. 1. (Incidentally, Lenau's poetic evocations of a village dance whipped up by a fiddler are often recalled by Bruckner's Scherzi.) Lenau's *Faust* first appeared in 1836, four years after Goethe's death and the long-awaited advent of Goethe's *Faust*, Part Two. Lenau called his text a 'poem' and a 'rhapsody'. It comprises twenty-three scenes, some of them made up wholly of narrative. The Romantic progenitor of this particular Faust is Byron's Manfred, and the 'poem' deals not with the hero's salvation but with the Berliozian topic of his damnation. Lenau's poetry in general has been criticized for its lack of objective correlatives, but precisely that 'lack' is his deepest theme. Lenau's Faust contemplates a life without absolute values. In the scene which replaces Goethe's 'Prologue in Heaven' at the beginning of the 'poem', Faust is saved by Mephistopheles from falling off the edge of a precipice. From then onwards he is forever courting danger. Mephisto persuades him to renounce Christ; he also isolates him from Nature and plunges him into a whirlpool of lust. The result is a total disorientation foreshadowing that experienced by

Lenau's Don Juan (skilfully captured in the tone poem by Strauss). Faust begins to hallucinate and stabs himself in the heart.

In 1946 Wittgenstein wrote of his fear of madness. He wondered if 'the abyss' did not exist solely in his imagination. The one indication to the contrary, he wrote, was the experience of Lenau before him: 'For in his *Faust* there are ideas of a type with which I too am conversant. Lenau puts them into Faust's mouth, but they are certainly his thoughts about himself. The important thing is what Faust says about his *loneliness*, or *isolation*'.[16] Lenau's drama, Wittgenstein adds, is remarkable in that Man only has dealings with the Devil. '*Gott rührt sich nicht*' – 'God does not stir.'

Indeed, the poetic drama makes little mention of God. And yet it was greeted in some quarters as a Christian response to Goethe's allegedly pagan *Faust*. Hans Martensen, a young Danish theologian, published a monograph arguing that Lenau's drama glorified theism. This prompted the poet to bring out a revised version intended to clarify Faust's attitude towards the Christian religion. His Faust now became anti-clerical. Later, Lenau regretted having written his drama 'too soon'; he would rather, he said, have written a Gnostic poem with Lucifer as the main character. He also discussed with his Viennese friend Joseph Fischhof the idea of an oratorio entitled *Judas Iscarioth*.[17]

Wittgenstein's remark on Bruckner's Ninth Symphony does not necessarily impute any Faustian features to Bruckner. But Ernst Kurth did go so far as to employ the adjective '*faustisch*' in the first volume of his study of the composer.[18] He drew attention to Bruckner's thirst for knowledge of both a theoretical and a practical kind. Bruckner showed a lasting interest in the natural sciences, becoming downright notorious for his fascination with human corpses. In that respect his activities are reminiscent of the second scene of Lenau's *Faust*, where the hero and his famulus inspect a body in the 'anatomical theatre'. Did Bruckner, like Faust, perhaps see in the human nervous system a symbol of the Biblical tree of knowledge? In 1835, just before the first version of Lenau's *Faust* appeared, the Hegelian thinker David Friedrich Strauss published his de-mythologizing *Life of Jesus*. It would be idle to suggest that Bruckner was ever a great reader, but he is said to have surprised others with his knowledge of this book.

Kurth ascribes the various manifestations of Bruckner's eagerness to learn – in the field of music theory but also elsewhere – to a desire to reach the mystical ground of things. At least once in Bruckner's life, the desire carried him to the brink of madness. Yet meaning and method may be discerned even behind the composer's manias: thus Wassily Kandinsky finds his obsession with dots perfectly explicable in *Point and Line to Plane*.[19]

Eventually, doubtless after intense soul-searching, Bruckner perceived that he was cut out to be an artist rather than a servant of the Church. It is true that Fritz von Uhde painted *The Last Supper* with the composer as one of the Apostles, but Bruckner had virtually rejected that path. In Kierkegaard's terms, he conformed to the type of the 'genius' rather than the type of the 'apostle'. The three completed movements of his Ninth Symphony contain associations both sacred and secular, and so do the sketches for the Finale. If Bruckner refers back to his D minor Mass, he also refers back to *Germanenzug*. Such reminiscences of his Linz years amount to a very human *De Profundis*.[20]

To sum up: only in a limited sense does Lenau's *Faust* present a Catholic reaction to Goethe's *Faust*. Nor can Bruckner's Ninth be seen entirely as a Catholic reaction to the philosophy of the Enlightenment, as transmitted through Beethoven's Ninth. Lenau himself dismissed the idea that his *Faust* drama constituted a challenge to Goethe's. Goethe, he said, had no monopoly of the subject; there were many possible versions. Similarly, Bruckner never set out to counter the import of Beethoven's Ninth, to write a *contrafactum*. He explained his choice of the same key to Göllerich by saying simply that he was especially fond of D minor, and that his principal theme seemed to work best in that tonality. If he had lived to complete his Finale, it is clear that its expressions of triumph would have taken an utterly different form from Beethoven's. But both composers, each in his own way and – partly – for his own age, preached the '*ideal* revolution' that Wittgenstein recognized in Beethoven's Ninth.[21] It was characteristic of the mystic in Bruckner that he should want to dedicate his Ninth Symphony to God. *Vis-à-vis* Beethoven, he does not adopt the role of either protester or imitator.

Although his central thesis may not altogether hold water, Wittgenstein's remark is illuminating in two respects. First, there is the validity and force of the parallel between Lenau and Bruckner, for all the outward differences between an Upper Austrian schoolmaster's son and an Austro-Hungarian aristocrat. Lenau embodied the main preoccupations of the European nineteenth-century Romantics: the reaction against rationalism, Nature-worship, nostalgia for a childhood faith, metaphysical ecstasy. Are there not elements of all these in Bruckner? Even the lure of nothingness is something which he may well have experienced in his darkest hours in Linz. The one Romantic characteristic singularly lacking in Bruckner is egoism; as an artist he never became bogged down in subjectivity. But the vividly demonic component in Lenau's poetry may be said to correspond to the high dissonance level in Bruckner's Ninth Symphony. Lenau's euphonious dissonances have their purely musical equivalent in late Bruckner, not to mention such early twentieth-century composers as Schreker.

Wittgenstein's second illumination arises from the way he anticipates a famous phrase of Thomas Mann's: the 'taking back' of Beethoven's Ninth Symphony. The phrase occurs in Mann's *Doctor Faustus* novel, and it refers to the last masterpiece of the fictional German composer, Adrian Leverkühn.[22] Like the Fausts of Goethe and Lenau, Leverkühn has had dealings with the Devil. Now the Scherzo of Bruckner's Ninth Symphony lends itself to more than one reading: dark indeed on paper, it sounds more sheerly devilish in some interpretations than in others. But the link between D minor and diabolism has a longish history, from Mozart's opera *Don Giovanni* to Reger's 'Inferno'

Fantasy and Fugue for organ, opus 57.[23] As it stands, in its magnificent incompleteness, Bruckner's Ninth may be felt to throw Beethoven's and Schiller's hopes for humanity into question before ending in radiant quiescence. Surely there is no misreading the Adagio's heart-rending ninth-chord. Like Adrian Leverkühn's orchestral cantata, the movement begins as a lament; only in its closing stages does it attain to a hope beyond hopelessness, the transcendence of despair. Bruckner's Ninth was conceived in the same spiritual climate as Nietzsche's *Also sprach Zarathustra*, a climate of which the Wagner tuba seems the musical incarnation.[24]

To revert, briefly, to Beethoven's Ninth Symphony: Wittgenstein remarked on the irony pervading the first movement's fugato section. Nicholas Cook has gone further by detecting a basic ambivalence in Beethoven's setting of the *Ode to Joy*.[25] Here the 'Turkish' music is viewed as a deconstruction of Schiller's text. Are the multitudes embracing before an absent deity? As Cook points out, it may take a modern listener to hear the Finale this way. And the modern listener is equally apt to read his own uncertainties – the uncertainties of Wittgenstein's *Philosophical Investigations* – into Bruckner's Ninth. If so, then Wittgenstein as musical commentator provides an important corrective. It is contained in a remark on Bruckner (1931) that has not yet been quoted:

> The most accurate picture of a whole apple-tree bears, in a sense, infinitely less resemblance to it than the smallest daisy does. And in this sense a symphony by Bruckner is related to a symphony of the heroic age infinitely more closely than a Mahler symphony is. If the latter is a work of art, then one of a *totally* different kind.[26]

By 'heroic age', it may be safely assumed, Wittgenstein meant the age of Beethoven rather than the age of Liszt.

As noted earlier, Wittgenstein was a conservative in musical matters. Another comment on Mahler in *Vermischte Bemerkungen* denies him any artistic merit as a composer whatever. Many people of Wittgenstein's generation shared Max Reger's view that Mahler had overstepped certain limits observed by Bruckner and had thereby become a caricature of Bruckner.[27] This conservatism in no way detracts from Wittgenstein's reception of the heroic Bruckner, the Alpine Bruckner or the Bruckner who matched Grillparzer and Lenau in subtlety. And his reference to a 'truth' that is 'never on the side of probability' sounds a cautionary note in the face of continuing efforts to complete Bruckner's Ninth.[28]

In conclusion, there is one feature of Bruckner's style upon which Wittgenstein did not remark but which must have influenced his thinking. Cultural historians have proposed a link between the homage to silence at the end of the *Tractatus Logico-Philosophicus* and the importance of silence to Schoenberg and Webern. In the light of Wittgenstein's musical preferences, however, that homage can be seen as a tribute to the Brucknerian pause and to Bruckner's profound logic. As Wittgenstein put it to Paul Engelmann (1917): '*Nothing* is lost if one does not seek to say the unsayable. Instead, that which cannot be spoken is – unspeakably – *contained* in that which is said!'

Acknowledgement

I am grateful to David Blake and Robert Pascall for encouraging me in the writing of this article.

Notes

1. See Brian McGuinness, *Wittgenstein: A Life – Young Ludwig (1889–1921)* (London, 1988).
2. An observation made by my wife.
3. Diary entry for 4 October 1912.
4. On 5 August 1945 G.E. Moore wrote to Wittgenstein: 'I am afraid we must put off playing Bruckner's VIIth to you till after you come back'. See *Wittgenstein: Cambridge Letters*, edited by Brian McGuinness and G.H. von Wright (Oxford/ Cambridge Mass., 1995). An editorial footnote states: 'From a letter to his [LW's] sister Helene it seems that the Bruckner was played for him in March 1946'.
5. See Ludwig Wittgenstein, *Notebooks 1914–1916*, edited by G.H. von Wright and G.E.M. Anscombe (Oxford, 2/1979). This recurring idea in Wittgenstein's writings is discussed by P.B. Lewis, 'Wittgenstein on Words and Music', in: *Ludwig Wittgenstein: Critical Assessments*, 4, edited by Stuart Shanker (London/Sydney/ Dover N.H., 1986).
6. Ludwig Wittgenstein, *Vermischte Bemerkungen*, edited by Georg Henrik von Wright in cooperation with Heikki Nyman (Frankfurt am Main, 1977). English version: *Culture and Value*, translated by Peter Winch (Oxford, 1980). The present translations are my own.
7. '*Ich glaube, das gute Österreichische (Grillparzer, Lenau, Bruckner, Labor) ist besonders schwer zu verstehen. Es ist in gewissem Sinne subtiler als alles andere, und seine Wahrheit ist nie auf Seiten der Wahrscheinlichkeit*'.
8. '*Die Musik Bruckners hat nichts mehr von dem langen und schmalen (nordischen?) Gesicht Nestroys, Grillparzers, Haydns etc., sondern hat ganz und gar ein rundes, volles (alpenländisches?) Gesicht, von noch ungemischterem Typus als das Schuberts war*'.
9. '*Kompositionen, die am Klavier, auf dem Klavier, komponiert sind, solche, die mit der Feder denkend und solche, die mit dem inneren Ohr allein komponiert sind, müssen einen ganz verschiedenen Charakter tragen und einen Eindruck ganz verschiedener Art machen.*
   Ich glaube bestimmt, daß Bruckner nur mit dem inneren Ohr und einer Vorstellung vom spielenden Orchester, Brahms mit der Feder, komponiert hat. Das ist natürlich einfacher dargestellt, als es ist. Eine Charakteristik aber ist damit getroffen'.
10. '*In den Zeiten der stummen Filme hat man alle Klassiker zu den Filmen gespielt, aber nicht Brahms und Wagner.*
    Brahms nicht, weil er zu abstrakt ist. Ich kann mir eine aufregende Stelle in einem Film mit Beethovenscher oder Schubertscher Musik begleitet denken und könnte eine Art Verständnis für die Musik durch den Film bekommen. Aber nicht ein Verständnis Brahmsscher Musik. Dagegen geht Bruckner zu einem Film'.
11. See Karl Böhm, *Ich erinnere mich ganz genau: Autobiographie*, edited by Hans Weigel (Munich, 4/1975), p. 46. English version: *A Life Remembered: Memoirs*, translated by J. Kehoe (London, 1992).
12. '*Von einer Brucknerschen Symphonie kann man sagen, sie habe zwei Anfänge: den

Anfang des ersten und den Anfang des zweiten Gedankens. Diese beiden Gedanken verhalten sich nicht wie Blutsverwandte zu einander, sondern wie Mann und Weib.'

13. Max Auer, *Anton Bruckner: Sein Leben und Werk* (Zurich/Leipzig/Vienna, 5/1947), p. 181.
14. See Ernst Hilmar, ' "Schade, aber es muß(te) sein": Zu Gustav Mahlers Strichen und Retuschen insbesondere am Beispiel der V. Symphonie Anton Bruckners', and especially pp. 192–4, in *Bruckner-Studien*, edited by Othmar Wessely (Vienna, 1975).
15. '*Die Brucknersche Neunte ist gleichsam ein* Protest *gegen die Beethovensche und dadurch wird sie erträglich, was sie als eine Art Nachahmung nicht wäre. Sie verhält sich zur Beethovenschen sehr ähnlich, wie der Lenausche Faust zum Goetheschen, nämlich der katholische Faust zum aufgeklärten, etc. etc.*'
16. *Vermischte Bemerkungen*, pp. 102–3.
17. Lenau conceived the idea after hearing part of Mendelssohn's *Paulus* oratorio. See my article 'Some Musical Echoes of Lenau: An Article in Honour of Othmar Schoeck' in *German Life and Letters*, 40/4, July 1987.
18. Ernst Kurth, *Anton Bruckner*, I (Berlin, 1925), p. 201. For the sake of balance it should be noted that Walter Niemann wrote a few years earlier: 'Bruckner was no Faust-nature like Beethoven or Wagner' (Niemann, *Die Musik der Gegenwart*, Stuttgart/Berlin, 1922, p. 138). At the same time, Niemann argues, the spiritual content of Bruckner's music is far from naive; the pain and the doubt render it thoroughly 'modern'.
19. Wassily Kandinsky, *Point and Line to Plane*, translated by Howard Dearstyne and Hilla Rebay (Dover Edition: New York, 1979), p. 43, n. 1.
20. Hence it was only too easy for the Nazi regime to dissociate Bruckner from the Roman Catholic Church – see Bryan Gilliam's article 'The Annexation of Anton Bruckner: Nazi Revisionism and the Politics of Appropriation', in *The Musical Quarterly*, 78/3, Fall 1994. Not even Bruckner's *Psalm 150* can be described as an expressly 'churchy' work: both internal evidence (the style) and its commissioning for a secular occasion speak against this.
21. As recalled by Theodore Redpath, *Ludwig Wittgenstein: A Student's Memoir* (London, 1990).
22. Curiously, for Erich Heller 'it is always the person Wittgenstein who appears before my eyes whenever I try to imagine what Adrian Leverkühn may have looked like'. See Heller, *In the age of prose: Literary and philosophical essays* (Cambridge, 1984), pp. 134–5.
23. According to Reger, his opus 57 was inspired by the 'Inferno' section of Dante's *Divine Comedy*. A Catholic upbringing does seem relevant to the way that both *Don Giovanni* and the Reger organ piece close in D major. Bruckner surely intended his Ninth Symphony to end in that key; it is noteworthy, however, that he never began a symphony in the 'angelic' key of C major.
24. Bruckner's symphonies with Wagner tubas might be regarded as a musical triptych, with the Eighth – to which Walter Abendroth and the conductor Eugen Jochum gave the sobriquet 'Apocalyptic' – as the central panel. For some provocative reflections on 'the heteronomy of compositional praxis', see Norbert Nagler, 'Bruckners gründerzeitliche Monumentalsymphonie', in *Musik-Konzepte*, 23/24 (edited by Heinz-Klaus Metzger and Rainer Riehn), January 1982, especially pp. 109–13.
25. Nicholas Cook, *Beethoven: Symphony No. 9* (Cambridge, 1993), pp. 103–4.
26. '*Das genaueste Bild eines ganzen Apfelbaumes hat in gewissem Sinne unendlich viel weniger Ähnlichkeit mit ihm, als das kleinste Masliebchen mit dem Baum hat. Und in diesem Sinne ist eine Brucknersche Symphonie mit einer Symphonie der heroischen Zeit unendlich näher verwandt, als eine Mahlerische. Wenn diese ein*

Kunstwerk ist, dann eines gänzlich *andrer Art. (Diese Betrachtung aber selbst ist eigentlich Spenglerisch.)'*

27.   As related by Reger's pupil Hermann Unger. See *Max Reger-Brevier*, edited by Adolf Spemann (Stuttgart, 1923), p. 39. That it does not take a conservative cast of mind to set Bruckner above Mahler is indicated by Stravinsky's comment: 'I think that the Adagio of the Ninth Symphony [of Bruckner] must be accounted one of the most truly inspired of all works in symphonic form. Indeed, Mahler seems much less original than Bruckner, when one knows this music, and no composer of that period is so personal a harmonist as Bruckner'. See Igor Stravinsky and Robert Craft, *Expositions and Developments* (London, 2/1981), p. 61, n. 1.

28.   Nonetheless I gladly accede to William Carragan's plea not to dismiss the idea of completing Bruckner's Ninth. 'All of the completers have done their best to present Bruckner's material in a congenial context'. ('The Bruckner Versions Once More' in *American Record Guide*, March/April 1995).

18   Richard Wetz (1875–1935): a Brucknerian composer

Erik Levi

An obvious starting point for assessing the extent to which Anton Bruckner's music influenced succeeding generations of composers would be to examine the compositional output of those musicians who enjoyed the benefit of the master's teaching at the University of Vienna and the Vienna Conservatoire during the latter part of the nineteenth century. However, any comprehensive investigation of this nature is bound to be problematic since a great deal of the music written by Bruckner's pupils and disciples has fallen into almost complete oblivion. Yet even if one's line of enquiry was simply confined to analysing the work of those of greater importance, it would be equally doubtful as to whether any decisive conclusions could be drawn. Take Hugo Wolf, for example. Although there is little doubt that the younger composer was a devoted admirer of Bruckner, attempts to delineate a clear musical lineage between the two composers seem artificial and unconvincing. Similarly, despite writing eloquently about his studies with Bruckner, Friedrich Klose appears to have been relatively uninfluenced by his teacher's music, having drawn greater inspiration from Berlioz and Liszt.[1]

A better case could be made for both Gustav Mahler and Franz Schmidt. In both harmonic and structural terms Mahler clearly assimilated certain aspects of Bruckner's language.[2] Nonetheless for the most part, his orchestration sounds radically different, and his emotional horizons seem far removed from that of his teacher.[3] Perhaps the only significant Bruckner pupil to whose music the term Brucknerian can be confidently applied remains Franz Schmidt, and this arguably is only pertinent to his first two Symphonies. Indeed, what emerges from this brief summary is the strong possibility that despite the enormous admiration that both his teaching and compositions generated amongst his most devoted students, Bruckner's influence was more limited than one might have expected. Certainly, any suggestion that Bruckner was the founding father of a distinctive school of composition, as in the case of his almost exact contemporary, César Franck (1822-90), is open to debate.[4]

A parallel situation with regard to Bruckner can be gleaned from surveying musical developments in Germany during the same period. Although Bruckner's music found considerable favour, thanks largely to the efforts of the conductors Hermann Levi and Artur Nikisch, it would be misleading to argue that the music of the leading members of the younger generation of German composers reflected his influence. Indeed, the leading issue of the day remained the aesthetic arguments that separated adherents of Brahms from those of the New German School of Wagner and Liszt. Notwithstanding contemporary propaganda that regarded him as a Wagnerian symphonist, Bruckner's adherence to abstract musical concepts must have seemed anomalous particularly to those composers committed to the cause of programme music and music-drama. During the first 20 years of the twentieth century, this situation gradually changed, and in reading some contemporary histories of the period, one can find reference to a few musical figures who appear to have taken Bruckner as a model and ideal. Amongst those most frequently cited were the symphonists Hermann Bischoff (1868–1938), Paul Büttner (1870–1945), Wilhelm Petersen (1890–1968), Fritz Brun (1878–1959) and Richard Wetz (1875–1935) from the German-speaking world[5] and in Scandinavia, Wilhelm Stenhammar (1871–1927), Paul von Klenau (1883–1946) and Jean Sibelius (1865–1957). Of the German composers, only Wetz managed to attain anything more than local prominence. Although his work is hardly known nowadays, he was an interesting and much-respected figure who aroused enthusiasm especially from German musicians of a conservative outlook. While hardly a composer of the front rank, his music certainly deserves reappraisal, particularly in the light of his fascinating assimilation of Bruckner's musical style.

Before discussing the exact nature of Bruckner's influence upon Richard Wetz, it is necessary, however, to fill in some biographical information on the composer. Born in Gleiwitz in Upper Silesia, the son of a businessman, Wetz began to compose at an early age, but his development was necessarily hindered by the fact that he was living in an extremely provincial musical environment. Determined to advance his career and achieve a more sophisticated compositional technique, he enrolled at the Leipzig Conservatoire in 1897, where his teachers were Salamon Jadassohn and Carl Reinecke. Yet Wetz quickly became disillusioned with the reactionary academicism of these teachers, and withdrew from the Conservatoire after only six weeks. He then undertook private lessons with Richard Hoffman, director of the Leipzig *Singakademie*, but these lasted only six months. Three years later, Wetz moved to Munich where he became a pupil of Ludwig Thuille. Once again, he soon became disaffected by academic study, particularly Thuille's demands that he master the rigours of fugal writing before finding his own individual style. Wetz's next port of call was Stralsund where, thanks to the help of the conductor Felix Weingartner, he was appointed music director in 1901. But Wetz's career as a theatre conductor was short-lived. He left Stralsund after three months and barely survived the same amount of time in Barmen the following year, before deciding to return to Leipzig in 1903 where he lived in almost complete isolation for the next three years.

In 1906 Wetz was appointed director of the *Musikverein* and *Musikakademie* in Erfurt, a position he held until 1925. During this period, he began to attract more attention as a composer. For example, in 1908 Artur Nikisch conducted the first performance of Wetz's *Kleist Ouverture* in Berlin and Leipzig with some success, and a number of his *Lieder* began to feature regularly in recital programmes of the time. However, Wetz's attempts to establish a reputation as an opera composer ended in failure. Of his two completed works in this genre only *Das ewige Feuer* (1906) reached the stage in Düsseldorf in 1907, but it enjoyed little favour there or at any other German theatres.[6] After this Wetz abandoned opera composition altogether, concentrating his energies on choral and orchestral music, chamber music and song. In 1916, he was appointed to teach composition at the Music Conservatory in Weimar where he became Professor in 1920. He began work on his First Symphony in 1915, composing two more works in this genre in 1920 and 1923. In the following years, Wetz completed two large-scale choral works, a *Requiem* and a *Christmas Oratorio*. A further oratorio based on poems by Goethe was left unfinished at his death.

At the height of his career Wetz attained some recognition of his talents by being elected to membership of the Prussian Academy of Arts in Berlin in 1928 – an honour which he shared concurrently with Igor Stravinsky. Yet despite achieving this distinction, Wetz remained a rather peripheral figure in German musical life. To a certain extent, he was personally responsible for this neglect, having been reluctant to promote his own work more widely. Geographically, he was isolated from the major centres of German musical life, having refused all offers of prestigious teaching appointments outside his native Thuringia. It is also significant that although his compositions attracted the interest of some influential musicians, most notably the conductors Peter Raabe (later President of the *Reichsmusikkammer* from 1935 to 1944) and Georg Schumann, he was overlooked by others of higher profile such as Wilhelm Furtwängler, Bruno Walter and Erich Kleiber.

There are other reasons for the neglect of Wetz's music. The composer openly recognized that he had reached his stylistic maturity at the very time when late Romanticism was being superseded by other musical styles in Germany. Although a conservative reactionary who remained alienated from the cultural milieu of the Weimar Republic,[7] Wetz failed to engage in musical polemics in the very public manner of his contemporary Hans Pfitzner. Despite earning the enthusiastic approbation of scholars such as Alfred Heuss, the influential editor of the *Zeitschrift für Musik,* the tide only seemed to turn in his favour in the late 1920s and early 1930s, and particularly after the Nazis came to power. Doubtless, Wetz's musical outlook, as well as his commitment to Alfred Rosenberg's *Kampfbund für deutsche Kultur,* which he joined in 1933, should have endeared him to the Nazi cultural hierarchy.[8] Furthermore, interest in his work would have been enhanced through the publication in 1935 of the first detailed monograph on the composer by Hans Polack.[9]

Yet the Wetz revival was short-lived. Six years after his death, he was virtually a forgotten figure – a point that was painfully emphasized when his work was featured in the March 1941 issue of *Zeitschrift für Musik* as part of a special edition entitled '*Zu Unrecht vergessene Komponisten*'.[10] Perhaps the establishment of a Richard Wetz *Gesellschaft* in Gleiwitz on the 27th June 1943 might have helped to restore the composer's diminished reputation.[11] But the *Gesellschaft*'s ability to generate interest in Wetz was severely limited, given that cultural life within the Reich virtually ceased to exist by the middle of 1944. Inevitably, any attempts to revive Wetz's music in the aftermath of the Second World War were doomed to failure, since German musical life embraced modernism with even greater fanaticism than during the Weimar Republic.

In the propaganda campaign to promote Wetz's name more widely, much of the writing produced on the composer during and immediately after his life stressed his kinship with Bruckner.[12] But Wetz himself was similarly responsible for emphasizing his indebtedness, producing both a book and several articles on the composer.[13] We can follow the extent of his personal response to Bruckner's music from reading his correspondence with his childhood friend Martha Grabowski, published in the 1975 documentary study edited by Erich Peter and Alfons Perlick. What emerges from this is that Wetz discovered Bruckner's music only on his return to Leipzig in 1903 and much later than other favoured nineteenth-century composers, including Liszt, Wagner and Brahms. It seems that the experience of hearing Artur Nikisch conduct the Seventh Symphony proved cathartic. Thus when Wetz assumed his position at Erfurt three years later, he did everything possible to make Bruckner's music more widely known. This unbounded enthusiasm for Bruckner's music was already communicated in a letter from Erfurt dated 24 September 1906:

> Yesterday I performed Bruckner's Second Symphony. I was given the score to look through the day before yesterday ... and never before had I felt the breath of genius at first glance as strongly as I did with this work.[14]

One year later Wetz conducted Bruckner's Third Mass in F minor in Erfurt – a courageous piece of programming since this was only the third such performance of the work in the German Reich. We know from his correspondence with Martha Grabowski that he revived the Mass in 1913 at a concert in Leipzig, describing the work as 'a miracle' and commending in particular the Benedictus as containing some of Bruckner's 'most profound' music.[15]

Wetz's admiration for '*den lieben Anton*' knew no bounds.[16] His letters to Martha Grabowski are littered with panegyrics to the composer whose art encompassed everything that he believed was missing from the so-called 'New Music'.[17] For instance in a letter dated 18 September 1909, he claimed that 'only in Beethoven and even then very rarely', had he encountered such 'deeply felt spirituality' as in the Adagio of the Seventh Symphony.[18]

For Wetz, the Seventh Symphony was:

> the purest form of heavenly bliss ... I often long to merge into its immense purity

and float in this music like an island full of blossom in a clear deep lake. If eternity could move and speak, you would hear such sounds.[19]

Wetz's most public declaration of devotion to Bruckner's music appeared in an autobiographical programme note published in the booklet of the Erfurt Wetz Music Festival in June 1923:

I consider getting to know the works of Bruckner to be my last great experience. Bruckner was to be of crucial importance in my development as a composer. It took me almost ten years to absorb and digest fully his works.[20]

In the same essay Wetz went on to claim that it was only through Bruckner's art that he came to understand Bach and Schubert, and that these three masters provided the 'basis for his entire creative outlook'.[21]

A year before this autobiographical sketch appeared, Wetz completed his extended monograph on Bruckner. The book formed part of a series of musical biographies that were published by the Leipzig firm of Philipp Reclam, and was in fact one of a significant number of Bruckner studies that appeared in German during the period immediately after the First World War.[22] That such interest in Bruckner should have occurred at this precise moment in time is no mere historical coincidence. In the turbulent post-war cultural climate in both Germany and Austria, Bruckner was regarded, particularly in musically conservative circles, as a beacon of national purity – a composer whose loftiness of expression represented the very antithesis of the subversive internationalist modernism which had become the order of the day. Not surprisingly, the majority of those writing about Bruckner saw themselves as being in the vanguard of this reactionary trend.

In terms of its scholarship, Wetz's book hardly breaks new ground. For much of the biographical material, Wetz relies upon information provided by Rudolf Louis and Franz Gräflinger – a debt that is openly acknowledged in the preface. More interesting, however, are Wetz's forthright views, often expressed in highly ornate prose and supported by quotations from numerous German poets. As a devoted Brucknerian, one would expect to find a staunch defence of the composer and a refutation of any charges of naiveté and a lack of structural control. But Wetz takes frequent opportunity to digress from his main area of enquiry. Scattered through the book, for example, are hostile comments not only against the music produced by Germany's enemies during the First World War, but also with regard to contemporary musical developments. As one might expect, Wetz could not resist the temptation to contrast the spiritual profundity of Bruckner with what he saw as the shallowness of new music:

The lack of inner substance in this new music (only virile creative power can bring forth such substance) was replaced by a brilliant technique which was intended to dazzle and distract the listener from this lack of artistic essence. With harmony, technique, rhythm and instrumentation becoming more and more finicky and over-refined, a situation had to arise sooner or later where the new so-called progressive works would simply resemble each other, just as two peas in a pod. It comes as no surprise therefore that in order to create something original, composers eventually began to attack and even dispute the basic components of music: harmony, metre and tonality were declared to be a hindrance, and in order to turn their own consumptive poverty into lusty virtue, composers invented the concept of superfluous melody. This is the point at which the idea of progress has arrived today.[23]

In the final paragraphs of the first chapter which deals with Bruckner's life, Wetz once again strays from the subject at hand. Allowing himself the opportunity to comment further on Germany's current artistic climate, he presents a utopian vision of future national regeneration. In appealing directly to such sentiments, Wetz's remarks represent an ominous foretaste of the kind of writing that would become all too familiar during the Third Reich:

> When German artists will finally reach the conviction that it is their moral duty to give to the German people above all such works which are expressions of the German soul in all its wonderful beauty and moving intensity, then the unhappy disunity and distractedness in our spiritual and artistic life will disappear and a holy bond will unite all hearts; where spirit and soul are united, there will be only one purpose: a people can have no higher ambition than wanting to be itself.[24]

Although the writing of musical biographies must have been an exceptionally burdensome task for someone whose major concern was with composition, this clearly was not the case for Wetz. Examination of Wetz's correspondence with Martha Grabowski certainly confirms his enthusiasm for the project. Indeed, once the task had been completed, Wetz was prepared to confess that writing the Bruckner book had brought him ' a much greater clarity about myself and about my whole creative achievement'.[25]

It is instructive to place Wetz's 'greater self-awareness' in the context of his own compositional development. From 1903 to 1913, the ten years referred to in his 1923 autobiographical sketch, Wetz began the long process of promoting, studying and absorbing Bruckner's music. Yet at that particular time Wetz's own composing interests were orientated primarily towards *Lieder* and opera – musical genres that were largely outside Bruckner's orbit. But between 1914 and the publication of his monograph on Bruckner, Wetz had abandoned opera and embarked upon writing in abstract forms. The major fruits of this change of outlook were the three Symphonies, and it is these works in particular that best demonstrate Wetz's credentials as a successor to Bruckner.

The First Symphony, composed in the key of C minor, occupied Wetz for over two years in the middle of the First World War. In a letter to Martha Grabowski, the composer openly acknowledged that the time of its composition in his life, and its key signature openly invited the critics to draw parallels with Bruckner. 'Is it not curious', he wrote, 'that I am just as old as the dear Bruckner, and that he also wrote his First Symphony in C minor?'[26]

But the work's relationship to Bruckner's symphonic oeuvre extended far beyond a mere matter of date and tonality – a point Wetz acknowledged when playing through the Symphony to Peter Raabe in 1916.[27] This Brucknerian influence is evident in a number of areas – orchestral forces and orchestration, structural features, melodic and harmonic sequences – and sometimes even extends to almost literal quotation.

Probably the first striking connection with Bruckner lies in Wetz's orchestra. In effect the forces Wetz utilizes (double woodwind including cor anglais and bass clarinet, four horns, three trumpets, three trombones, tuba, timpani, harp and strings) are no larger than those employed in Wagner's *Tristan und Isolde*. With the exception of the cor anglais and bass clarinet the ensemble also hardly differs in nature from that of the majority of Bruckner's Symphonies, and can be regarded as more typical of the mid- to late-nineteenth century rather than the twentieth century. Without doubt, Wetz's adherence to such an ensemble, not to mention his functional rather than colouristic conception of the orchestra, demonstrated a rejection of the contemporary trend in German music for writing for huge numbers of players as manifested in such works as Mahler's final symphonies or Richard Strauss's *Alpine Symphony*. It is also significant that having nailed his colours to the mast of tradition, Wetz, like Bruckner, retained more or less the same size of orchestra for his other two Symphonies.

In terms of orchestration, there are a number of interesting connections between Bruckner and Wetz. Perhaps at first glance, Wetz's often blended and thickly scored textures, especially in orchestral tuttis, appear to be more indebted to Wagner. However, this may be deceptive since Wetz would only have been familiar with Bruckner's symphonies as published in the rearranged Wagnerian editions by Löwe and Schalk. But even allowing for the fact that Wetz could not have heard or studied Bruckner's orchestration in its original guise, there are still numerous passages in the First Symphony that are unmistakably Brucknerian in their sound-world. A good example occurs at letter K (*sehr ruhig*) in the development section of the first movement where Wetz unequivocally imitates Bruckner's penchant for presenting strings, wind and/or brass as separate and contrasting instrumental groups (Ex. 18.1).

At the opposite end of the dynamic spectrum, many orchestral climaxes in this movement and the Finale are conceived in terms of Brucknerian pedal points. Again, it is noticeable that Wetz eagerly absorbs Bruckner's layered technique of superimposed ostinato patterns (Ex. 18.2).

There is a good deal of evidence to suggest that the overall plan of Wetz's First Symphony is conceived along Brucknerian lines. The first movement (*Ruhig bewegt*) in orthodox sonata form has both the emotional weight and broad structural conception that one might associate with Bruckner. Likewise, Wetz's rumbustious and peasant-like Scherzo recalls the Austrian master, as does the slower Trio in duple time whose lyrical character can be compared to the equivalent section in Bruckner's Eighth Symphony. Although conceived on a smaller scale, Wetz's slow movement has similar hymn-like expressive qualities to the third movement of the Eighth. Only the fast-flowing Finale departs noticeably from its model, for despite recourse to widely fluctuating tempi (a feature that is certainly evident in the Finales of Bruckner's Third, Fourth and

Ex. 18.1   Wetz: Symphony No. 1: first movement development section

Reprinted by permission of **SIMROCK/RICHARD SCHAUER** Music Publishers London-Hamburg

Ex. 18.2   Wetz: Symphony No. 1: early orchestral climax in the first movement

Ex. 18.3   Similarities in orchestration between Wetz and Bruckner

(a) Wetz: Symphony No. 1 – coda to the Finale

(b) Bruckner: Symphony No. 4 – coda to the Finale

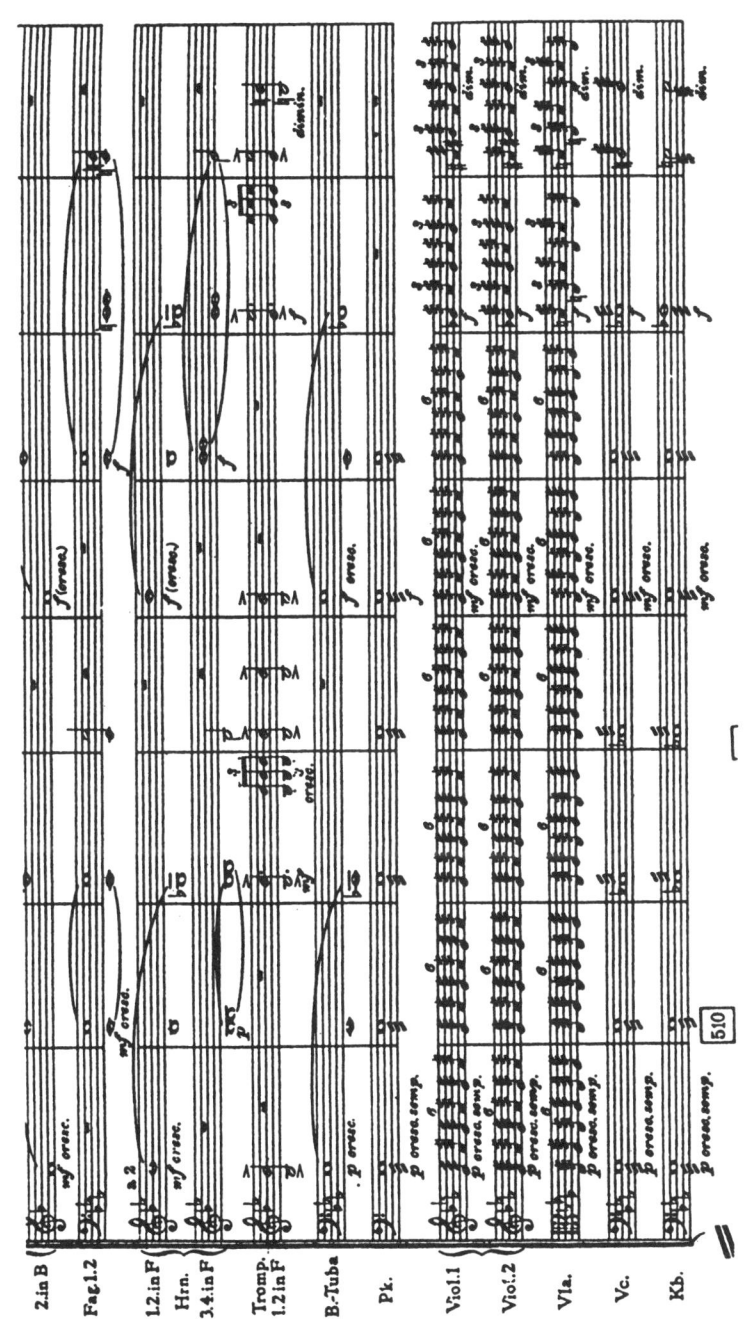

Ex. 18.3 concluded

373

Eighth Symphonies), the emotional character seems less obviously related to Bruckner. But even in this movement, Wetz cannot escape paying homage to Bruckner. A brass chorale, 19 bars after letter V, foreshadows a change of pace and metre (*Ruhig bewegt*) and a monumental coda which begins with tremolando murmurings in the upper strings that are similar in nature to those in the coda of Bruckner's Fourth Symphony (Ex. 18.3).

As the music rises to an awesome climax, Wetz reintroduces the opening idea of the Symphony (Letter X *Kraftvoll und gemessen*) played in augmentation in the brass accompanied by swirling ostinato patterns in the rest of the orchestra – a passage of 23 bars that is evidently derived from the closing bars of the 1889 version of Bruckner's Third Symphony. It should be noted, however, that in Wetz's resolution, there is no transformation of the *Urmotif* into the major key.

Ex. 18.4   Wetz: First Symphony: first movement *Urmotif*

In terms of internal structural detail, Wetz adopts certain features that are intrinsically Brucknerian. The Symphony's *Urmotif* stationed on a C minor pedal point and accompanied by an insistent string ostinato (Ex. 18.4) is an obvious starting point, although the passage is far more protracted in length than the opening of many of Bruckner's symphonies and Wetz's subsequent development of the material moves at a less broad pace.

A far better example of an extended section that is characteristically Brucknerian in outline is the codetta to the exposition in the first movement. As is often the case in Bruckner, Wetz signals its appearance with a dramatic interruption that halts the triumphant resolution of the second subject – a procedure that would have been familiar to Wetz from the closing passage to the Adagio of the Ninth Symphony. There follows a sustained pedal point (at letter F) of 15 bars on E flat with tremolando lower strings (violas and cellos) and a characteristic juxtaposition of major and minor tonality generated by a horn call of a falling sixth (Ex. 18.5). A similarly conceived passage (also on an E flat pedal) with repeated horn calls also appears at letter G in the Finale.

Perhaps of all the movements, the third (marked *Sehr langsam und ausdrucksvoll*) best demonstrates Wetz's strong indebtedness to Bruckner. Both the opening material, a simple clarinet melody in A flat, preceded by a characteristically Brucknerian Neapolitan sixth progression, juxtaposes major and minor tonalities over a syncopated string accompaniment (Ex. 18.6), and the valedictory horn chords in parallel sixths in the coda (5 bars after Letter L) echo similar passages in the Adagio of Bruckner's Eighth Symphony (Ex. 18.7). Moreover as in some of Bruckner's symphonies (e.g. Nos 1, 3 and 7), Wetz composes a contrasting idea in 3/4 time that appears both in the exposition and recapitulation. It is also noteworthy that Wetz punctuates this idea with its inversion in the flute, yet another Brucknerian device (Ex. 18.8).

Other Brucknerian features in this movement include the use of chorales in the strings (letters E and L), brass (9 bars after D) and wind (letter H), an orchestral tutti passage (6 bars before letter F) which with its insistent funereal dotted quaver and semiquaver patterns in the strings recalls a similarly conceived passage in the slow movement of Bruckner's Fourth, rising tremolando passages in the violins (5 bars after letter D), and the use of an elaborately decorative first violin line that accompanies the return of the first idea (letter G) – a compositional device Bruckner occasionally employed at the beginning of the recapitulations in his own slow movements (e.g. the Adagio of No. 1).

In terms of tonality Wetz follows Bruckner's propensity for sustaining the home key for both the opening movement and the Scherzo. Yet throughout the First Symphony Wetz appears to be far less exploratory than Bruckner in his tonal modulations which tend towards classical conventions. Probably the most daring tonal juxtaposition can be found in the middle section of the Scherzo which is in the distant key of B major. But although this section is punctuated by some extremely chromatic harmony, it is noticeable that Wetz preserves the classical principles of modulating towards the dominant and back to the home key.

Ex. 18.5 Wetz: First Symphony – codetta to the exposition of the first movement

Ex. 18.5   concluded

Reference has already been made to Wetz's penchant for Brucknerian pedal points, for example in the opening and closing bars of the first movement. In terms of chromatic harmony, Wetz's use of sequential progressions frequently follows a pattern made familiar in Bruckner's Ninth Symphony (Ex. 18.9). When employing diatonic harmony, there are occasions such as in the second and third movements where Wetz quotes almost verbatim a chordal progression that Bruckner employed so memorably in the slow movement of the Eighth Symphony (Ex. 18.10).

As demonstrated by the *Urmotif*, the melodic ideas in Wetz's First Symphony are generally more four-square in design than those used by Bruckner, and the frequent recourse to sequences tends to inhibit natural symphonic development.[28] It is noticeable too that at moments where Wetz seems to lose his way (such as in the development of the first movement), he resorts to somewhat aimless reiteration of Bruckner's favoured quintuplet patterns. A more convincing absorption of Brucknerian principles is the lyrical second subject of the first movement which in melodic, harmonic and contrapuntal design (especially the use of diminution of the melody as an inner part) reminds one of the second group in the slow movement of the Sixth Symphony (Ex. 18.11).

While emphasizing the degree to which Wetz's First Symphony is influenced by Bruckner, it would be misleading to claim the work as mere pastiche. For example, with regard to scoring Wetz rarely employs unison passages of the kind that frequently occur in Bruckner, nor does he imitate the older composer's fondness for pizzicato string writing. Apart from these aspects of the orchestration, there are several passages in the work which strike a more individual note, the most notable being the rather unexpected bursts of aggression near the end of the first movement, and the turbulent, even melodramatic mood swings that characterize the exposition and development of the Finale. A number of commentators on the work have suggested that these gestures of defiance are of an autobiographical nature, reflecting the composer's disillusionment with the progress of the First World War. Elsewhere, the enigmatic recurrence of the *Urmotif* in the Scherzo and the first movement's second idea in the Finale seem

Ex. 18.6   Opening of the slow movements of Wetz's First Symphony and Bruckner's Eighth Symphony

(a) Wetz

(b) Bruckner

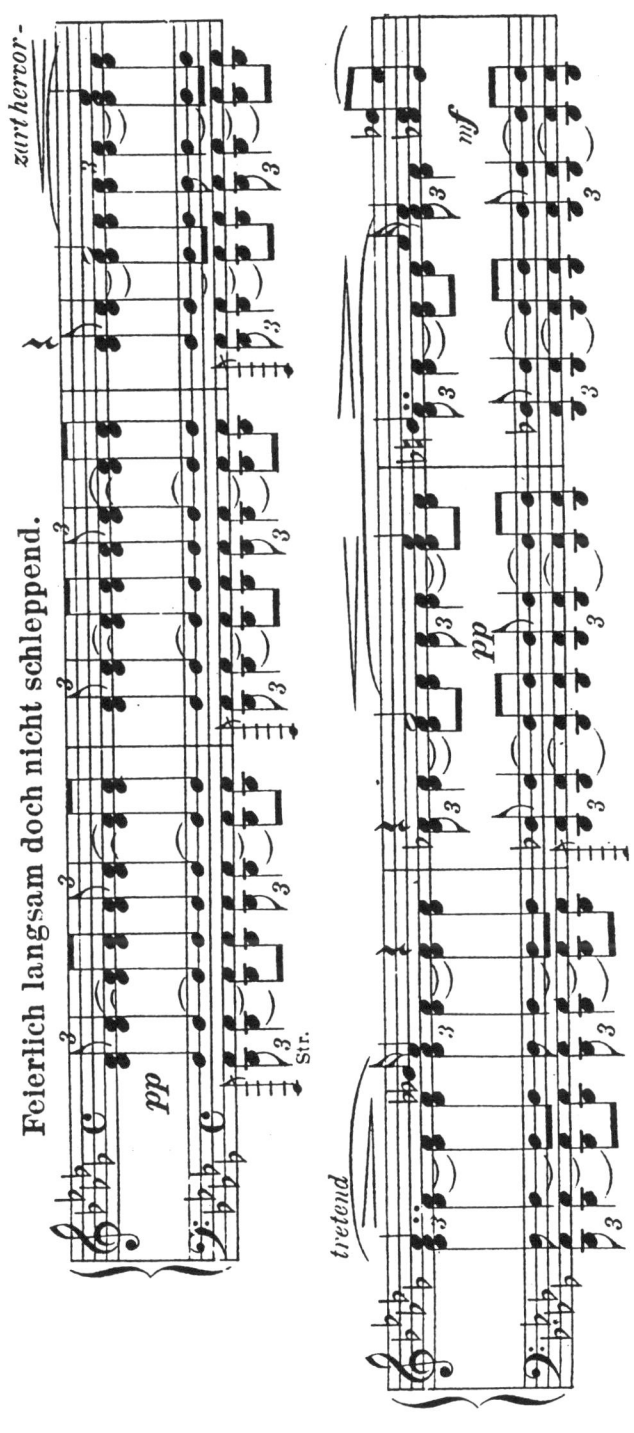

379

Ex. 18.6   concluded

(a) Wetz

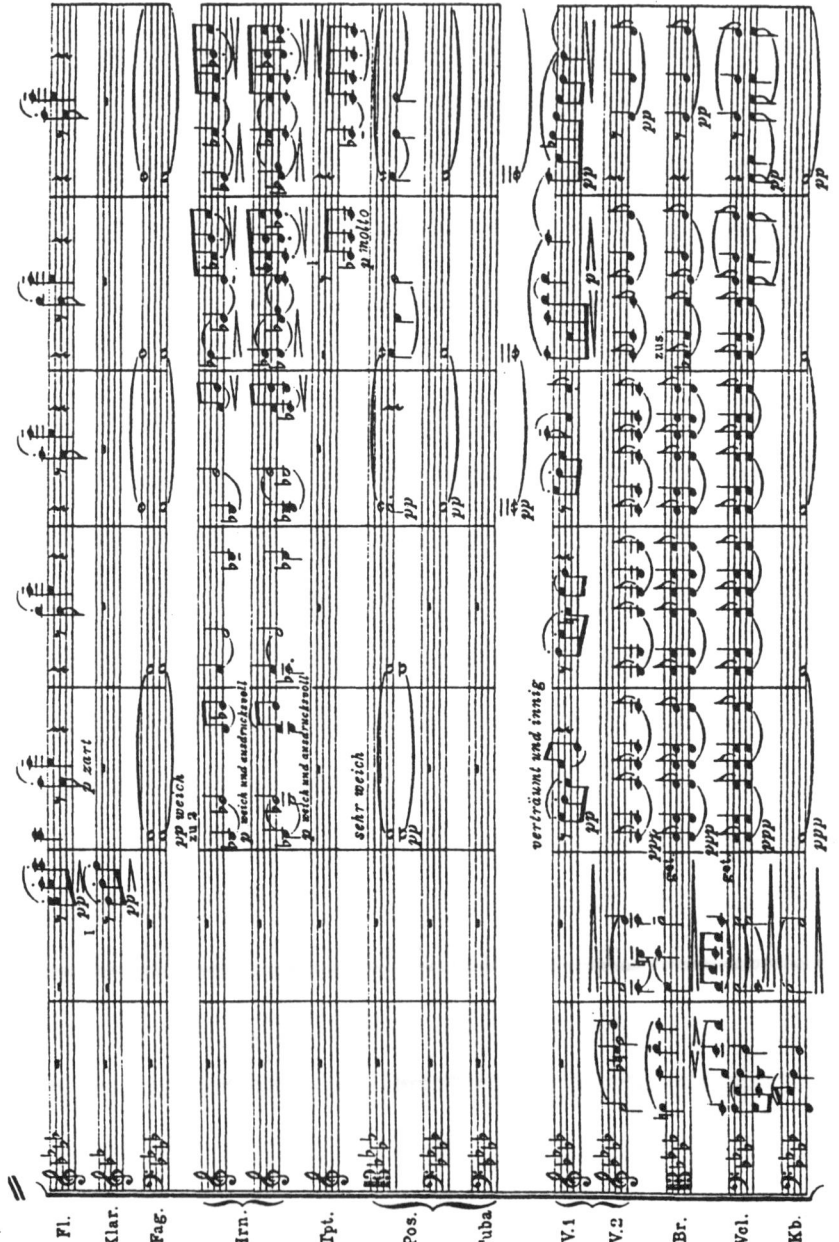

Ex. 18.7   Coda of the slow movements of Wetz's First Symphony and Bruckner's Eighth Symphony

380

(b) Bruckner

Ex. 18.7   concluded

far removed from the kind of unifying principles employed by Bruckner,
reminding one more of Tchaikovsky, Liszt or César Franck. In addition, some
elements of Wetz's musical language (passages in consecutive sixths, simple folk-
like melodies and a tendency to thicken the middle registers) appear close to
Brahms.

Ex. 18.8   Second ideas in the slow movements of Wetz's First Symphony and Bruckner's
Third Symphony

(a) Wetz

(b) Bruckner

Ex. 18.8   concluded

Peter Raabe conducted the first performance of the First Symphony in Weimar on the 23 January 1917. Although initial reaction to the work was positive and resulted in further performances throughout Germany, the score was only published seven years later in 1924 by Simrock. This time delay, coupled with the lack of interest shown in the score by some of Germany's more prominent conductors, did not help to further Wetz's cause. Nonetheless, the experience of writing the Symphony proved liberating, for in the following years Wetz completed two further works in the same genre, both of which were first championed by Peter Raabe.

Of the two symphonies, the Third in B flat seems closer to Bruckner than its predecessor, though any Brucknerian features appear to have been more absorbed into Wetz's own style than in the First Symphony. The work has four movements with the da capo Scherzo placed third. Like the First Symphony, the opening movement (*Langsam-Kräftig, bewegt*) is conceived on a large scale. It begins with an extended slow introduction in which the horns intone a motto theme (Ex. 18.12) that pervades the entire symphony. Significantly, although Bruckner only began one of his symphonies (No. 5) with a slow introduction, the groping and uncertain character of the music, as well as the almost constant use of string tremolandi, clearly inhabit a similar sound world to that of the older composer.

Ex. 18.9   Sequential progressions in the first movement of Wetz's First Symphony and the Trio from the second movement of Bruckner's Ninth Symphony

(a) Wetz

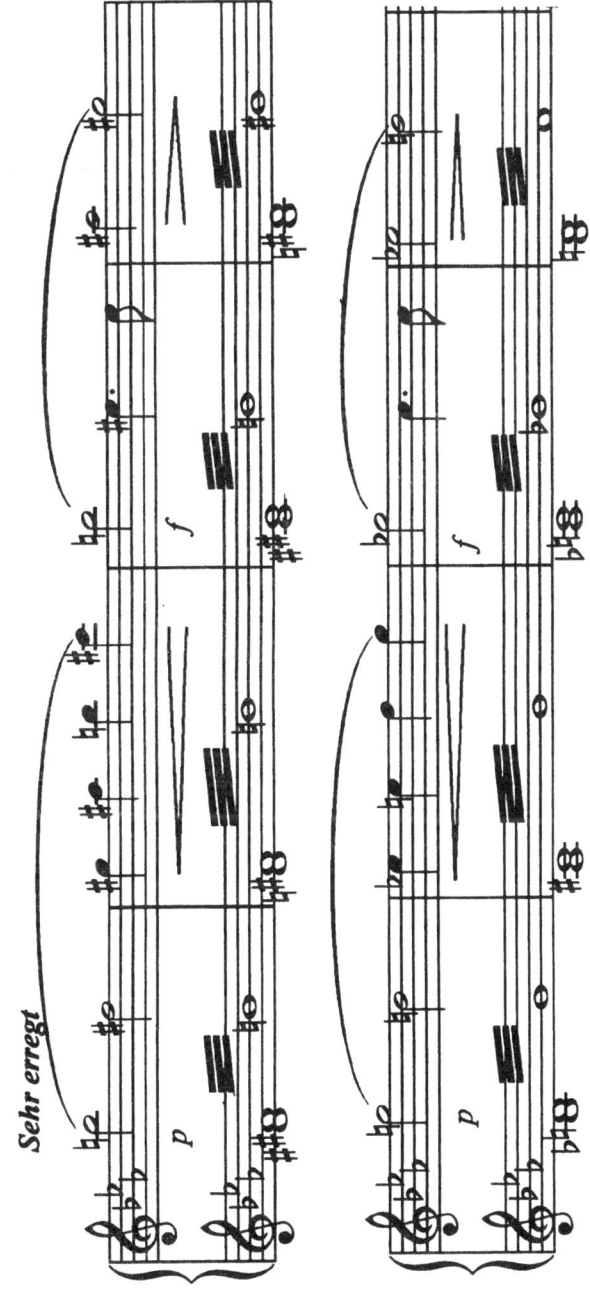

(b) Bruckner

Ex. 18.9 continued

(b) Ex. 18.9 concluded

When Wetz eventually arrives at the main Allegro of the first movement, the underlying martial character of the violin motif has the kind of resolute quality familiar from the first movement of Bruckner's First Symphony (Ex. 18.13a). Even more Brucknerian, however, is Wetz's ingenious Lisztian transformation of this idea into a brass chorale near the close of the movement (Ex. 18.13b).

Structurally, this Allegro follows a similar pattern to that of the First Symphony in conforming to orthodox sonata form, with the lyrical, almost Schumannesque, second idea (its quaver figuration clearly deriving from the second subject of the first movement of Bruckner's Ninth) being subjected to brass augmentation at the close of the exposition (Ex. 18.14).

There are some definitive Brucknerian features in the slow movement, a funeral march marked *Sehr langsam, mit klagendem Ausdruck* whose world-weariness, dark scoring and central tonality of C sharp minor appear distantly related to the Adagio from Bruckner's Seventh Symphony. Wetz maintains the feeling of conflict that was so prevalent during the opening movement with frequent intensification of texture and restless modulations. Even the calmer second idea is punctuated by the chromatically descending four-part harmonies familiar from the slow movement of Bruckner's Ninth (Ex. 18.15).

The connection with Bruckner's Ninth Symphony is further reinforced at the dissonant opening chord of the Scherzo (*Nicht zu schnell und mit Humor*) (Ex. 18.16) – a movement whose po-faced humour sounds somewhat forced in the context of this emotionally turbulent work. There is also an element of contrivance about the Finale. As in the First Symphony, this is the movement in which Bruckner's influence is less pervasive. Again, the intention is to compose a cyclic movement in which themes from the earlier part of the symphony are interwoven into the structural plan. But the conception lacks a sure sense of direction, and the final restatement of the opening Allegro theme of the first movement, now in a triumphant major mode, seems hollow and unconvincing. Yet despite the flawed Finale, the Third marks a considerable advance on the First. The first three movements demonstrate a much more subtle attempt at thematic integration and Wetz's contrapuntal skills draw effective interconnections between all the contrasting ideas. In addition, there are far fewer passages where Wetz seems to be marking time.

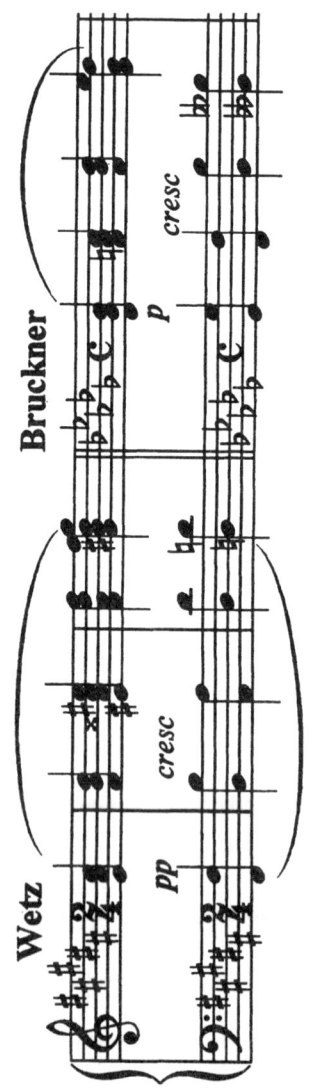

Ex. 18.10   Choral progressions in the second movement of Wetz's First Symphony and the third movement of Bruckner's Eighth Symphony

Ex. 18.11   Canonic imitation in lyrical passages in Wetz and Bruckner

(a) Wetz: First Symphony: first movement

Ex. 18.11 concluded

(b) Bruckner: Sixth Symphony second subject second movement

Ex. 18.12   Wetz: Third Symphony: motto theme from the introduction to the first movement

Ex. 18.13   Wetz: Third Symphony. Thematic transformation of the violin motif in the main Allegro of the first movement (a) into a brass chorale near the close (b)

(a)

(b)

Ex. 18.14   Quaver figuration linking the second subject of the first movement of Wetz's Third Symphony with the second subject of the first movement of Bruckner's Ninth Symphony

(a)

Ex. 18.14 concluded

(b)

Ex. 18.15   Wetz Third Symphony – chromatically descending four-part harmonies of the second idea in the slow movement

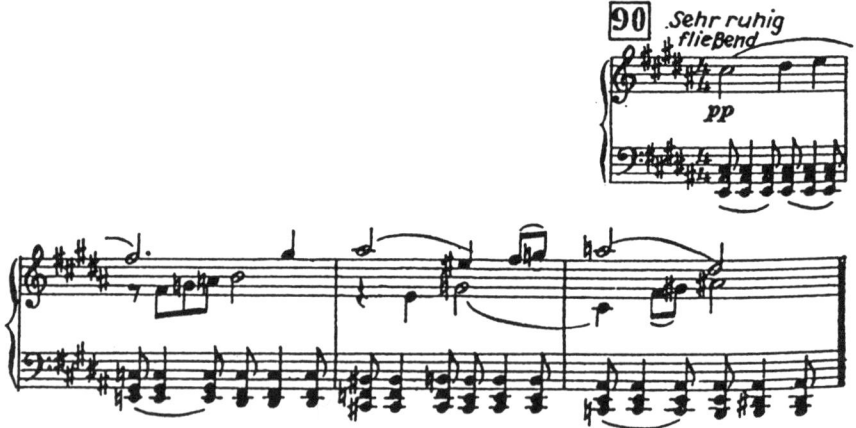

Ex. 18.16   Wetz: Third Symphony – tonally ambiguous harmonies at opening of the Scherzo compared with the opening of the Scherzo of Bruckner's Ninth Symphony

(a) Wetz

Ex. 18.16 concluded

(b) Bruckner

Although the Third Symphony enjoyed 17 performances throughout Germany during its first few years of existence, it was destined to remain unpublished and still awaits serious reappraisal.[29] The same can be said for its predecessor which is the most original of Wetz's Symphonies. In this three-movement work in A major, Wetz dispenses with the Scherzo and composes a fantasia-like Finale that for once moves inexorably from the opening *Urmotif* and seems a natural outcome of all that had appeared before. The structurally

Ex. 18.17   Wetz: Second Symphony

(a) String figurations accompanying the first motif in the opening movement

(b) Dramatic string chorale interjections in the first movement

concise slow movement, another funeral march with a prominent cor anglais solo, is equally impressive and emotionally affecting.

In both these movements, it is far more difficult to pinpoint passages which clearly derive from Bruckner, though certain features of the harmony and orchestration that have been discussed in relation to the First Symphony are still perceptible. Similarly, the opening sonata form movement contains some Bruckner reminiscences, most notably the string ostinato figurations that accompany the *Urmotif* (Ex. 18.17a) and a dramatic string chorale interjection (Ex. 18.17b) which recalls a similar passage in Bruckner's Ninth. But the music as a whole resists the kind of detailed stylistic comparisons with Bruckner that were deemed appropriate for the First Symphony.[30]

It is somewhat surprising that while the Symphonies remain the most convincing works for demonstrating Wetz's strong indebtedness to Bruckner, other compositions written around the same period seem comparatively unaffected by this influence. Both of the two String Quartets (1916, 1923), for example, are defiantly classical in structure with only the slow movement of the earlier work reflecting a similar emotional kinship to the slow movement of the First Symphony. Nonetheless, Wetz's decision to devote his final years to the composition of large-scale choral works (a *Requiem, Weihnachts-Oratorium* and an incomplete oratorio based upon texts by Goethe) can be regarded as a Brucknerian gesture. Disillusioned by the neglect of his symphonies and chamber works and by the general trends in musical development during the Weimar Republic, Wetz retreated into a mystical-religious world which could effectively accommodate a conservative, even archaic, musical language. The obvious sincerity and conviction with which Wetz embraced this style made a deep impression on the German public, resulting in a level of recognition that had been denied to him earlier in his life. In some respects this triumph late in his career appears analogous with Bruckner's own belated successes in the 1890s, the crucial difference being that the older composer's last works follow a much more daring path, foreshadowing the changes in musical language that were to take place during the first years of the twentieth century, whereas those by Wetz cling defiantly to a German tradition that had effectively run out of steam by the 1920s.

Notes

1. See Friedrich Klose, *Meine Lehrjahre bei Bruckner* (Regensburg, 1927).
2. See Timothy L. Jackson's paper, 'The Wagnerian "Embrace" Metaphor in Bruckner and Mahler', read at *Das Bruckner-Problem* conference, Freie Universität, Berlin, October 1996 and due to be published in a *Beiheft* of the *Archiv für Musikwissenschaft*, ed. Albrecht Riethmüller. Also Jackson's 'Bruckner and tragic reversed sonata form' in *Bruckner Studies* (Cambridge: Cambridge University Press, 1997), pp. 199–201.
3. It is interesting to note that the stylistic connections between Bruckner and Mahler

have been more thoroughly explored in Bruckner literature in English than in German. (See for example, Dika Newlin's *Bruckner, Mahler, Schoenberg* [London, 1947 rev. 1978] and Hans F. Redlich's *Bruckner and Mahler* [London, 1955 rev. 1963]). This may be explained by a tendency earlier in the century to regard Bruckner and Mahler as very similar composers, particularly in the English-speaking world.

4. It is interesting to compare Bruckner's position with that of Brahms. While Brahms never pursued a career as a pedagogue (his sole composition pupil was Gustav Jenner), countless composers from many countries imitated his musical style.

5. See, for example, Alfred Einstein's article 'German Orchestral Music from 1880', in Alfred Eaglefield-Hull, ed., *A Dictionary of Modern Music and Musicians* (London, 1924), p. 181. Einstein's opinion is substantiated by various other dictionary entries in the relevant editions of *Riemanns Musiklexikon*. Significantly Wilhelm Furtwängler's name does not appear in the context of such articles, although there is little doubt that the great conductor's Three Symphonies (1903, 1947, 1954) follow in the tradition of Bruckner. See also the *Grosse Brockhaus Lexikon* (Leipzig, 1942): 'In his symphonies, Wetz remains very close to Bruckner'. (p. 121).

6. In Hamburg, for example, *Das ewige Feuer* was staged only once on 26 February 1908; see Joachim E. Wenzel, *Geschichte der Hamburger Oper 1678–1978* (Hamburg, 1978), p. 84.

7. Wetz's bitterness at cultural developments in Germany during the 1920s can be illustrated by reading his extensive correspondence with Martha Grabowski which is published in Erich Peter and Alfons Perlick, eds, *Richard Wetz (1875–1935) als Mensch und Künstler in seiner Zeit. Eine Dokumentation mit zeitgenössischen Darstellungen und Selbstszeugnissen* (Dortmund, 1975). See, for example, the letter dated 22 October 1927 where Wetz refers to Krenek's *Jonny spielt auf!* as the 'epitome of vulgarity' (p. 346).

8. Wetz's name came briefly to the forefront in Nazi cultural politics after the publishers Kistner and Siegel sent a copy of the composer's recently completed Violin Concerto to the violinist Adolf Busch together with a note that concluded with the greeting 'Heil Hitler'. As a staunch anti-Nazi, Busch objected to such a gesture and pointedly returned the score to the publishers. Predictably, the Nazi musical press relished the opportunity to denounce Busch's unpatriotic behaviour. See Joseph Wulff, *Musik im dritten Reich* (Gütersloh, 1963/1966), p. 148.

9. Hans Polack, *Richard Wetz. Sein Werk und die geistigen Grundlagen seines Schaffens* (Leipzig, 1935).

10. George Armin, 'Richard Wetz und kein Anfang', in *Zeitschrift für Musik*, 108 (March 1941), p. 160–5. Wetz's neglect at this time is substantiated if one consults Wilhelm Altmann's article 'Statistischer Überblick über die im Winter 1941/42 Stattfindenden Reihekonzerte' which lists the performance of only two works (the *Kleist Ouvertüre* and *Weihnachts-Oratorium*) during the season. See *Zeitschrift für Musik*, 109 (March 1942), p. 108.

11. Nazi support of the *Richard Wetz Gesellschaft* was guaranteed through the appointment of Peter Raabe as its President and Albert Dreetz from the Ministry of Propaganda as one of its council members. It should be noted too that Dreetz wrote an article on Wetz in the *Jahrbuch der deutschen Musik 1944* (Leipzig, 1944) published under the sponsorship of the Ministry.

12. See in particular Walter Hapke's article 'Der Sinfoniker Richard Wetz', in *Zeitschrift für Musik*, 102 (1935), pp. 14–17.

13. Wetz's two major writings on Bruckner are: *Anton Bruckner, sein Leben und Schaffen* (Leipzig, 1922) and 'Die Instrumentation Anton Bruckners', in *Das Orchester* (May–July 1932).

14. Peter and Perlick, eds, op. cit., p. 166.

15. Ibid., p. 238.
16. Ibid., p. 236.
17. Ibid., p. 327.
18. Ibid., p. 208. This opinion was reiterated several times throughout these letters, as for example, after conducting the Fourth Symphony in Leipzig in 1913: i.e. '*Bruckner ist als Sinfoniker der einzigste, nach Beethoven noch in Frage kommt Tiefer, inniger hat man nach Beethoven niemand empfunden*'. Ibid., pp. 244–5.
19. Ibid., p. 248.
20. Reprinted in Polack, *Richard Wetz* (Leipzig, 1935), p. 115.
21. Polack, p. 115.
22. Other books on Bruckner that were published at this time included studies by Ernst Decsey (1919), Franz Gräflinger (1921), Hans Tessmer (1922), Max Auer (1923), Georg Gräner (1924), Oskar Lang (1924), Alfred Orel (1925) and Ernst Kurth (1925). In addition, the major study by August Göllerich and Max Auer was begun in 1922.
23. Richard Wetz, *Anton Bruckner, Sein Leben und Schaffen* (Leipzig, 1922), p. 27.
24. Ibid., pp. 65–6. In view of the particular sentiments expressed, it is significant that this quote is reproduced at the end of Polack's 1935 monograph on p. 114 – an overt attempt to emphasize Wetz's ideological respectability in the context of the Third Reich.
25. Peter/Perlick, op. cit., p. 310.
26. Peter/Perlick, op. cit., p. 262.
27. Peter/Perlick, op. cit., p. 273.
28. Despite pursuing a ten-year analysis of his output, it is highly unlikely that Wetz would have consulted Bruckner's original manuscripts and therefore become aware of his propensity in his early years for numbering the bars in individual sections, or his later practice (post 1875–6) of numbering bars in phrases.
29. A commercial long-playing record of the work was issued in 1984 on the *Deutsche Harmonia Mundi* label (HM/IOM 692) under the auspices of the *Anthologie Ostdeutscher Musik*.
30. A CD of Wetz's Symphony no. 2 is now available (CPO 999 695–2) [1999].

Index